OXFORD PAPERB

Pocket Fowler's
Modern English Usage

Robert Allen, the editor of this Pocket edition, is
an experienced lexicographer and writer on a
wide range of language issues. A former Senior
Editor of the *Oxford English Dictionary*, Chief Editor
of the *Concise Oxford Dictionary* (1990), and an
Associate Editor of the *Oxford Companion to the
English Language* (1992), he has written widely on
the use of English in modern times. He now
works as a freelance writer and editor, and is the
author of two titles in Oxford's 'One Step Ahead'
series, *Punctuation* and *Spelling* (2002).

Oxford Paperback Reference

The most authoritative and up-to-date reference books for both students and the general reader.

Pocket Fowler's

Modern English Usage

Edited by

ROBERT ALLEN

OXFORD
UNIVERSITY PRESS

OXFORD

UNIVERSITY PRESS

Great Clarendon Street, Oxford OX2 6DP

Oxford University Press is a department of the University of Oxford.
It furthers the University's objective of excellence in research, scholarship,
and education by publishing worldwide in

Oxford New York

Auckland Bangkok Buenos Aires Cape Town Chennai
Dar es Salaam Delhi Hong Kong Istanbul Karachi Kolkata
Kuala Lumpur Madrid Melbourne Mexico City Mumbai Nairobi
São Paulo Shanghai Singapore Taipei Tokyo Toronto

Oxford is a registered trade mark of Oxford University Press
in the UK and in certain other countries

Published in the United States
by Oxford University Press Inc., New York

British Library Cataloguing in Publication Data

Data available

Library of Congress Cataloging in Publication Data

Data available

ISBN-13: 978-0-19-860947-6

4

Typeset in Swift and Meta
by Interactive Sciences Ltd
Printed in Great Britain by
Clays Ltd, St Ives plc

Preface

H. W. Fowler's *Modern English Usage*, first published in 1926, is known and consulted wherever English is spoken. It has twice been revised, by Sir Ernest Gowers in 1965 and by R. W. Burchfield in 1996. These three writers represent different approaches to the study and use of English. Fowler, a former schoolmaster and (with his brother) first compiler of the *Concise Oxford Dictionary*, led an austere and isolated life on Guernsey and later in Somerset and wrote in a linguistic tradition which regarded grammar as primarily prescriptive, i.e. as essentially a system of laying down rules; yet he had a genuine concern for the ordinary user coping with the difficulties of writing and speaking good English, and rarely abandoned good sense for pedantry. Gowers was a senior Whitehall civil servant whose view of English was deeply affected by what he regarded as the excesses of bureaucratic language; his guidance on speaking and (more particularly) on writing English, published in *Plain Words* (1948; in later editions called *The Complete Plain Words*), was aimed chiefly at the world of officialdom. Burchfield, formerly Chief Editor of the *Oxford English Dictionary*, is an Oxford lexicographer whose knowledge of language is rooted in the historical tradition of collecting and assessing evidence of the ways in which language is used and the ways in which it changes.

This *Pocket* edition, the first attempt to fit Fowler's work in a smaller compass, is based mainly on Burchfield's 1996 edition (with revisions published in 1998). Reducing its size to about 40% has been achieved partly by reducing the number of entries (a little over 4,000 instead of nearly 8,000) and partly by shortening those that have been retained. The aim has been to present the arguments and recommendations in a more accessible form for quicker consultation, usually by writing more concise entries but also by reorganizing material and in some cases by expanding it. About 150 completely new entries have been added, both topic entries (e.g. *American English, gender-neutrality, new words*) and entries on individual items (e.g. *anorak, deceptively* as in *deceptively spacious*, the intransitive use of *obsess, proactive*), and information presented in the parent work in the form of lists has been reorganized as tables (e.g. *confusable words, Latin plurals, sobriquets*). Some conventions have been simplified; for example, in the guidance on pronunciation the International Phonetic Alphabet has been replaced by a system that most users will find more straightforward.

The publication in 1998 of *The New Oxford Dictionary of English* has enabled me to review the recommendations on spelling and other features.

The publishers and I hope that the authority evoked by the names Fowler, Gowers, Burchfield, and Oxford will, in this edition, be tempered by an accessibility that will bring their work to an even wider readership.

Acknowledgements

I have been fortunate in being able to consult the British National Corpus, a language database consisting of 100 million words of modern English assembled by a consortium of academic and industrial partners with government funding and launched in 1994. This material affords rich insights into the uses of ordinary English words, and has provided over 800 attributed examples out of a total of about 1600 examples that are new to this edition.

I should like to thank Sarah Barrett and Anne Seaton, both of whom read the entire text and made many important suggestions, as a result of which the text has been considerably improved.

REA

Edinburgh 1999

Abbreviations

Abbreviations, other than the standard ones, have been restricted to a handful of frequently occurring items:

AmE	American English
BrE	British English
c	century (19c = 19th century, and so on)
ME	Middle English (from 1150 to 1500)
OB	Old English (up to 1150)

The following bibliographical references are used:

Fowler (1926)	H.W. Fowler, *A Dictionary of Modern English Usage* (1926)
Fowlers (1906)	H.W. and F.G. Fowler, *The King's English* (1906; a second edition was published in 1907 and a third in 1931)
Gowers (1965)	Sir Ernest Gowers, *A Dictionary of Modern English Usage* (second edition, 1965)
OED	*Oxford English Dictionary*
OED2	*Oxford English Dictionary*, second edition (1989)

The symbol ⊠ is used to show uses that are regarded as incorrect or unacceptable.

Phonetic transcriptions

The letters used to indicate pronunciations are those of the ordinary English alphabet with their normal values. The following special cases should be mentioned:

e	the indeterminate sound as in *garden* and *porter*
ah	as in *dark*
aw	as in *awful* and *born*
dh	as in *this*
iy	as in *ice*
oh	as in *bone*
oo	as in *boot*
oo-e	as in *sure*
ow	as in *cow*
uh	as in *book*
zh	as in *measure*

Primary stress is indicated by bold type, e.g. the noun *project* is given as **proj**-ekt, and the verb as pre-**jekt**.

Cross-references

Text references to other entries are indicated by small capital letters, e.g.:

esthete, esthetic are American spellings of AESTHETE, AESTHETIC.

Glossary

The principal grammatical terms used in this book are as follows. Further information on some of them, and on other terms, can be found in the main text:

active voice   the form of a verb in which the subject performs the action and the object (if there is one) is affected by the action (*The house **stands** on a corner* / *France **beat** Brazil in the final*). See also PASSIVE VOICE below.

adjective   a word that describes another word, usually a noun or pronoun (*the **green** door* / *The weather was **pleasant*** / *She is **French***)

adverb   a word that qualifies a verb (*She speaks **softly***), an adjective (***rather** nice*), or another adverb (***very** quickly*)

attributive   denoting an adjective or noun that is put before another word, normally a noun, to qualify or describe it in some way (***brown** shoes* / ***table** lamp*)

clause   a group of words normally containing a verb and its subject. A main clause makes sense by itself and can constitute an entire sentence, e.g. *The train arrives at 6 o'clock*. A subordinate clause is one that qualifies a main clause, e.g. *The train arrives at 6 o'clock **if it is running on time***.

conjunction   a word used to join words, phrases, and sentences, such as *and*, *but*, and *if*

countable nouns   nouns that form plurals, e.g. *ship*, *crisis*, *fellow-traveller*, *kindness* (= a kind act). See also MASS NOUNS and UNCOUNTABLE NOUNS below.

determiner   a word that goes before a noun and determines its status in some way, such as *a*, *the*, *this*, *all*, and *such*.

diphthong   a vowel in which the sound changes within a syllable, as in *coin*, *day*, *deer*, *loud*, *pain*, *wear*, etc.

infinitive   the simplest uninflected form of a verb (*come*, *make*, *try*, etc.), and the form that appears as the headword in dictionaries.
A *to*-infinitive is this form preceded by *to*: *I want **to go** to the library.*

inflection   the change in the form of a word to indicate a change in its grammatical role, e.g. from singular to plural in nouns (*book* / *books*, *church* / *churches*) and from present tense to past tense in verbs (*want* / *wanted*, *make* / *made*)

interjection   an exclamation such as *ah*, *gosh*, and *whoops* (often printed with an exclamation mark)

intransitive   denoting a verb that does not take an object (*We **arrived** at noon*)

main clause   see CLAUSE above

Glossary

mass nouns   nouns which form plurals with the meaning 'a type of . . .' or 'a quantity of . . .', e.g. *bread*, *medicine*, *wine*. See also COUNTABLE NOUNS above and UNCOUNTABLE NOUNS below.

modifier   a word that modifies or qualifies the meaning of another word. Modifiers are usually attributive nouns (***table*** *lamp* / ***expiry*** *date*) and adjectives (*a **large** cake* / *the **English** language*), or adverbs (*We're **almost** ready*).

noun   a word that names a person or thing, including common nouns (*bridge*, *girl*, *sugar*, *unhappiness*) and proper nouns (which name specific persons or things, e.g. *Asia*, *Concorde*, *Dickens*)

passive voice   the form of a verb in which the object of the active verb (see ACTIVE VOICE above) becomes the subject and the subject of the active verb is optionally expressed as an agent introduced by the preposition *by*. The passive voice is illustrated by the sentences *Brazil **were beaten** in the final* and *Brazil **were beaten** by France in the final.*

predicative   denoting a word, especially an adjective, that is used after a linking verb (*The food was **terrible*** / *They are becoming **angry***)

preposition   a word that stands before a noun or pronoun (or later in a sentence, referring back to a noun or pronoun) and establishes its relation to what goes before, such as *after*, *on*, *for*, and *with* (*They came **after** dinner* / *the man **on** the platform* / *What did you do it **for**?*)

pronoun   a word used instead of a noun or noun phrase that has already been mentioned or is known, including the personal pronouns *I*, *you*, *she*, *us*, etc., the relative pronouns *that*, *which*, *who*, etc., the interrogative pronouns, *who*, *what*, etc., and the demonstrative pronouns *this*, *that*, *those*, etc.

subordinate clause   see CLAUSE above

tense   the form of a verb in relation to time, e.g. present tense (*makes*), past tense (*made* / *has made*) and future tense (*will make* / *is going to make*)

that*-clause**   a subordinate clause introduced by the conjunction *that* (*I know **that it is true)

***to*-infinitive**   see INFINITIVE above

transitive   denoting a verb that takes an object, i.e. has a following word or phrase which the action of the verb affects (*They **lit** a fire*)

uncountable nouns   nouns which do not form plurals, e.g. *adolescence*, *heating*, *richness*, *warfare*. See also MASS NOUNS and COUNTABLE NOUNS above.

verb   a word that describes an action or state and is normally an essential element in a clause or sentence: *She **locked** the door* / *We **were** lucky*

Aa

a, an, called the indefinite article (or, by some grammarians, determiner). In origin, *a* and its by-form *an* are versions of the Old English *an* meaning 'one'.

1 Before all normal words or diphthongs *an* is required (*an actor, an eagle, an illness, an Old Master, an uncle*). Before a syllable beginning in its written form with a vowel but pronounced with a consonantal sound, *a* is used (*a eulogy, a unit, a use; a one, a once-only*). Before all consonants except silent *h*, *a* is usual: *a book, a history, a home, a household name, a memorial service, a puddle, a young man*; but, with silent *h*, *an hour, an honour*.

2 In most circumstances *a* is pronounced with an unstressed indeterminate sound ə or ən, but it is sometimes emphasized as ay or an in slow diction or to emphasize singleness (*I said a piece, not several*). Practice differs with *h*-words in which the first syllable is unstressed: *a* (or *an*) *habitual criminal*; *a* (or *an*) *hotel*. There is evidence, especially in written English, for the continued use of *an* before *habitual, historian, historic(al), horrific,* and *horrendous,* but the choice of form remains open. However, *an hotel* now sounds dated (1930s) and *a hotel* is more usual.

3 With single letters and groups of letters that are pronounced as individual letters, be guided by the pronunciation: *a B road, a TUC leader*; but *an A road, an FA Cup match, an SAS unit* (assuming the abbreviations are not mentally expanded to their full forms, which would alter the choice).

4 *A* and *an* normally precede the word or words they determine (*a popular person, an ugly building*), but it follows the adjectives *many, such,* and *what* (*many a year, such a family, what an awful nuisance!*). It also follows any adjective preceded by *as* or *how* (*Iris Murdoch is as good a writer as Virginia Woolf | He did not realize how tiresome a person he could be*) and often an adjective preceded by *so* (*So bold a move deserved success*), although *such* is now more usual (*Such a bold move deserved success*). In some circumstances the positioning is optional: either before or after an adjective preceded by *too* (*too strict a regime* or *a too strict regime*) and before or after the adverbs *quite* and *rather* (*at quite an early hour* or *at a quite early hour*; *it's rather a hard puzzle* or *it's a rather hard puzzle*). With *few* and *lot,* however, the only possible order is *quite a few* and *quite a lot. A good few* is now commonly used.

5 *A* and *an* are also used to distinguish a particular person or artistic or literary creation: *Do you know a Lucy Smith? | They own a Van Gogh | She plays a Broadwood* [piano]; and to denote a standard quantity of something that is normally uncountable: *Do you want a beer? | I've been trying a new cheese.* Note also the following uses in time measurement: *once a fortnight, £20,000 a year, half an hour, 50 miles an hour.*

6 The indefinite article has been used with nouns of multitude (*a dozen eggs, a million pounds*) for centuries. A fairly recent extension of this use is with an adjective (usually the present or past participle of a verb) between article and noun: *The police found themselves confronted by an estimated two hundred youths | The dyke was an astonishing 30 feet wide*.

abacus. The normal plural is *abacuses*.

abbreviations. There are several kinds of abbreviations: shortenings, contractions, initialisms, and acronyms.

1 *Shortenings* of words, though formerly condemned by literary figures such as Addison and Pope (18c), are now a common convention, with varying degrees of formality (*ad* = advertisement, *bike* = bicycle, *pub* = public house, *rhino* = rhinoceros, *telly* = television). Some are the usual forms, with the original forms now regarded as formal or technical (*bus* = omnibus, *fridge* = refrigerator, *gym* = gymnasium, *turps* = turpentine, *zoo* = zoological garden).

2 *Contractions* are a type of shortening in which letters from the middle of the word are omitted (*Dr* = doctor, *St* = saint) and are sometimes marked as omitted by use of an apostrophe (*can't* = cannot, *we've* = we have).

3 *Initialisms* are abbreviations consisting of a sequence of the initial letters of words that are pronounced as separate letters: *a.m., BBC, DoE, MP, UN*. Practice varies as to including full points between the letters; the style recommended here is not to include them when all the initials are capitals and in some other

cases. When the form has a plural, this is formed by adding an *-s*, now normally without an apostrophe (e.g. *MPs* rather than *MP's*). Possessives are formed in the usual way (e.g. *MP's* singular, *MPs'* plural).

4 *Acronyms* are initialisms that have gone one stage further and acquired the status of words, being pronounced and treated grammatically as such (*Aids, Nato, radar*). In some cases the original expansions have become irrelevant, as with *laser* and *radar*. (See more fully at ACRONYM.)

abdomen. Stress is normally on the first syllable.

abduction (18c) is the forcible leading away of a minor (with or without the minor's consent) for marriage or seduction or the breaking of a legal custodial arrangement for the children of divorced parents. Although there is some overlap in meaning with *kidnap* (late 17c), kidnapping is not restricted to minors and is usually done for the purpose of demanding a ransom from the victim's family or employers. The more recent *hijacking* (20c, of unknown origin) applies specifically to vehicles, especially aircraft. All three words were applied to the seizure and detention of political hostages in the Middle East in the 1980s. *Carjacking* is a very recent (1990s) urban development.

abductor is spelt *-or*, not *-er*.

abetter is spelt *-er*, but *-or* in legal terminology.

abide is now limited to two main meanings, and has lost many others over seven centuries of use along with several redundant inflections, including *abode*. The principal meaning 'to bear, tolerate' is now only used in negative contexts, usually with a modal auxiliary verb (*Those ordinary Aryan Australian girls whose coarse complexions and lumpy features he could not abide*—H. Jacobsen, 1986). Its other main meaning in current use is with *by*, meaning 'to stand firm by' (*We must abide by our decision*). In its other meanings, it tends to be used mostly in the present tense, most famously as an imperative in a hymn (*Abide with me; fast falls the eventide*—H. F. Lyte, 19c), or as a participial adjective (*I accept this award with an abiding faith in America*—Martin Luther King, 1964, accepting the Nobel Peace Prize).

abjure, adjure. *Abjure* means 'to renounce on oath' (*He had abjured, he thought, all superstitions*—Iris Murdoch, 1985) and to abjure one's country (or realm) is to swear to abandon it for ever. By contrast, *adjure* means 'to request earnestly' with or (now) more frequently without an oath (*They were all talking at once, adjuring each other to have fresh cups of tea*). Neither word is in everyday use, but they are found in literature and can cause confusion when wrongly used.

-able, -ible.
See box overleaf

abled, meaning 'able-bodied, not disabled', is a revival of an obsolete 16c word, and is first recorded in print in the US in the 1980s. It is rapidly spreading, in various combinations, to denote a particular ability: *Deaf dogs should have the same right to compete against their hearing-abled peers*— *Dog World*, 1993. More significantly, in the form *differently abled* (or *otherly abled*) it has been adopted as a term of political cor-

rectness as a more positive alternative to *disabled* and *handicapped*: *They were gentle . . . kids, who took endless pains to guard against what they referred to as 'the exploitation of the differently abled'*—A. Maupin, 1992.

ableism, meaning 'discrimination in favour of the abled' (i.e. against the disabled), is one of the newest *-ism* words, first recorded in the US in the early 1980s. There is a corresponding adjective and noun *ableist*: *The cover design appears to be rather male-dominated, white, ableist*— *Rouge*, 1990 So far both words seem settled in form, with little sign of variants *ablism* and *ablist*, although these may yet come. See -ISM.

able to. The construction *to be able to* (do something), with an active *to*-infinitive, is a natural part of the language, extending to inanimate as well as animate subjects (*By his proceeding to the beach . . . the next phase of the attack was able to proceed*—New Yorker, 1986). It plays a useful role in compensating for the deficiencies of *can* in the future and perfect tenses (*will be able to | have not been able to*), with modal verbs such as *might* (*I might be able to*), and with verbs such as *become, appear*, and *seem* (*They don't seem to be able to do it*). When the infinitive is passive, however, it is better to use *can* or *could*, and to avoid *able to*, which sounds too forced (*No evidence that an air rifle was able to be fired*—Times (heading of Law Report), 1988).

abode. In the meaning 'a dwelling-place', *abode* is falling into disuse except in two fixed expressions: (*of*) *no fixed abode*, used

-able, -ible

1 GENERAL. These two suffixes are derived from Latin endings
-abilis and *-ibilis*, either directly or through Old French. Of the two,
-able is an active suffix that can be freely added to the stems of
transitive verbs, whereas the set of *-ible* words is a closed one with
meanings that are less susceptible to analysis. A few words exist in
both forms (e.g. *collectable* and *collectible*); others appear to but differ in meaning (e.g. *passable, passible*). Most words are formed from
verbs, but some are formed from nouns (e.g. *comfortable, peaceable*).

2 MEANING. The primary meaning these suffixes convey is 'able
to be -ed' or 'capable of being -ed', e.g. *bearable, curable, manageable*.
Some meanings, however, are active rather than passive, e.g. *agreeable* = willing to agree, *changeable* = apt to change, *comfortable* =
able to give comfort, *viable* = able to live. Others, such as *reliable*,
are formed somewhat in defiance of syntax (here, *on* is suppressed). Many words acquire special meanings, e.g. *actionable, appreciable, biddable, creditable, disposable, forgettable, incredible, noticeable,
passable, remarkable, reprehensible, tolerable, unspeakable*.

3 SPELLING PROBLEMS. Some formations require alteration of the
stem, since both suffixes begin with a vowel. The most important
are:
  ▶**a** Words in *-y* (preceded by a consonant) change *y* to *i*: *dutiable,
rectifiable, undeniable*. But note *employable, enjoyable*.
  ▶**b** With some exceptions, words in silent *-e* lose the *e* when *-able*
is added: *adorable, excusable, lovable, losable, removable, usable*. But
note the preferred forms *giveable, hireable, likeable, nameable, rateable,
saleable*.
  ▶**c** Words in *-ce* and *-ge* normally retain the *e*: *bridgeable, changeable, chargeable, noticeable, peaceable*.
  ▶**d** Words of more than two syllables ending in *-ate* lose this ending when *-able* is added: *alienable* (not *alienatable*), *appreciable* (has
special meaning), *calculable, demonstrable, estimable* (has special
meaning), *inestimable* (has special meaning), *penetrable, tolerable*.
However, words of two syllables would not be viable without the
ending and therefore retain it: *creatable, debatable, dictatable, locat-
able, translatable*.
  ▶**e** A final consonant is normally doubled when it is doubled in
ordinary inflection: *biddable, forgettable, regrettable*.
  ▶**f** Words of more than one syllable ending in *-fer* double the *r*
when the stress is on the final syllable, but do not when the stress
is earlier in the word: *conferrable, deferrable, offerable, preferable, prof-
ferable, sufferable* (but in *transferable* the stress is variable on the first
two syllables). *Infer* makes *inferable* and *inferrable*, and *refer* makes
referable and *referrable*.

▶

► -able, -ible
continued

The following table shows the principal forms in *-able* and *-ible*, and also shows forms that are liable to be confused (e.g. *impassable* and *impassible*)

WORDS ENDING IN -ABLE

abominable
actionable
adaptable
administrable
admittable
also admissible)
adorable
advisable
agreeable
alienable
amenable
amiable
analysable
appreciable
arguable
ascribable
assessable
atonable
available
bearable
believable
blameable
bribable
bridgeable
calculable
capable
changeable
chargeable
clubbable
collectable
comfortable
conceivable
conferrable
confinable
confusable
consolable
contractable
(*of a disease;
see also*
contractible)

copiable
creatable
creditable
curable
datable
debatable
declinable
defendable
(*in literal meanings; see also*
defensible)
deferable
definable
delineable
demonstrable
demurrable
deniable
desirable
despicable
developable
dilatable
dispensable
disposable
dissolvable
drivable
durable
dutiable
eatable
educable (= *able to be
educated*; *see also* educible)
endorsable
equable
equitable
evadable
excisable
excitable
excusable
expandable (*also* expansible)
expendable
expiable

extendable
(*also* extendible,
extensible)
feeable
finable
foreseeable
forgettable
forgivable
framable
gettable
giveable
hireable
illimitable
immovable
immutable
impalpable
impassable
(= *unable to be
crossed; see also*
impassible)
impeccable
imperturbable
implacable
impressionable
improvable
indefatigable
indescribable
indispensable
indubitable
inflatable
inimitable
insufferable
irreconcilable
irreplaceable
justifiable
knowledgeable
laughable
leviable
likeable
liveable

►

▶ -able, -ible
continued

WORDS ENDING IN -ABLE CONTINUED

losable
lovable
machinable
malleable
manageable
manoeuvrable
marriageable
measurable
mistakable
movable
mutable
nameable
noticeable
objectionable
obtainable
operable
palatable
payable
peaceable
penetrable
perishable

permeable
persuadable
(*also* persuasible)
pleasurable
preferable
prescribable
preventable
pronounceable
provable
rateable
readable
receivable
reconcilable
rectifiable
registrable
regrettable
reliable
removable
reputable
retractable
saleable
scalable

serviceable
sizeable
solvable
statutable
storable
suitable
superannuable
timeable
tolerable
traceable
tradable
transferable
tuneable
unconscionable
undeniable
unexceptionable
unget-at-able
unknowable
unmistakable
unscalable
unshakeable
usable

WORDS ENDING IN -IBLE

accessible
adducible
admissible
(*also* admittable)
audible
avertible
collapsible
comprehensible
contemptible
contractible
(= *able to be
shrunk*; see also
contractable)
convertible
credible
deducible
deductible

defensible
(*of an argument etc.*; see
also defendable)
destructible
diffusible
digestible
dirigible
discernible
discussible
dismissible
divisible
educible (= *able to be
educed*; see also educable)
eligible
exhaustible
expansible
expressible

extendible
(*also* extendable,
extensible)
feasible
flexible
gullible
impassible
(= *unfeeling*; see
also impassable)
inaudible
incorrigible
incredible
indelible
indigestible
indivisible
infallible
inflexible

▶

► -able, -ible
continued

WORDS ENDING IN -IBLE *CONTINUED*

intangible	negligible	reproducible
invincible	ostensible	resistible
invisible	perceptible	responsible
irascible	perfectible	reversible
irreducible	permissible	risible
irrepressible	persuasible	suggestible
irresponsible	(*also* persuadable)	suppressible
irresistible	plausible	susceptible
irreversible	reducible	
legible	reprehensible	

of someone without a permanent address, and *right of abode*, especially as applied to citizens of Hong Kong who sought the right to settle in Britain after 1997. It has not entirely gone from literature in its ordinary use (*The house, standing at the edge of a fair-sized tract of woodland and once, perhaps, the abode of gamekeepers* —Kingsley Amis, 1974).

abolishment, abolition. Both words date from the 16c and have been used principally with reference to concepts and institutions such as authority, laws, beliefs, feelings, and sins. In the 18c and 19c, *abolition* took on special meanings relating to the slave trade and capital punishment, which caused *abolishment* to be restricted to more neutral and ad hoc uses emphasizing the process rather than the result (*The deregulation of financial markets and abolishment of fixed commission rates*—Institutional Investor (NEXIS), 1989 | *It's a negation of him, an abolishment of him, like ripping a medal off his chest*—Margaret Atwood in New Yorker, 1990).

aborigines. This Latinate word, specifically applied since the 16c to the inhabitants of a country *ab origine* (from the beginning) has largely given way to *aboriginals* in the plural. For the singular, the etymologically indefensible form *Aborigine* has become firmly established in Australia (early 19c); for the plural, use *Aboriginals* (with a capital initial letter, in Australian contexts, in both cases). The adjective is always *Aboriginal*. The abbreviated form *Abo*, used with varying degrees of affection and hostility, is common in Australia, both as a noun and as an adjective.

abortive, aborted. The central meaning of *abortive* since the time of Shakespeare has been 'coming to nought, fruitless, useless, unsuccessful'. It can be applied to attempts, efforts, missions, coups, proposals, etc., and to any action that proves to be unsuccessful, even the most trivial (*An abortive attempt to do the Times crossword*—A. N. Wilson, 1982). *Aborted* is not, despite the protestations of the American writer

William Safire, a better alternative, since it denotes actual failure whereas *abortive* can be used of failure that is potential.

abound can have as its subject things that are plentiful or (followed by *in* or *with*) the place where things are plentiful: *Mulberry trees abound in Oxford* [note that *in* goes with *Oxford*, not *abound!*]—Jan Morris, 1978 | *A few years since this country abounded in wild animals*—A. Moorehead, 1963 | *The text, written in Yinglish and American, abounds in euphemisms*—*Observer*, 1974. The word is also common intransitively with no complementation: *When the idea of a university of the air was first floated, sceptics abounded.*—*Listener*, 1984.

about. 1 AS A PREPOSITION. In the meaning 'roughly, approximately' (eg. *It took about ten minutes*, *about* is the usual BrE word; *around* is also used, and is much more common in AmE. *Round about* is more informal, and is largely confined to BrE.

2 MEANING 'CONCERNING'. In this meaning, *about* is either a preposition or a conjunction (followed by *which, how,* etc.): (preposition) *The quarrels were about money* | (conjunction) *There was a great deal of discussion about which versions should be used.* Since the 1930s, the phrase *to be about* (something) has developed a special meaning 'to be primarily concerned with' and even 'to have as its aim', as in *Love and war were about winning, not fair play*—A. Price, 1982. When precision is important, it is better to use a less ambiguous phrase, e.g. *Love and war had winning as their purpose, and did not involve fair play.*

The phrase *what it's all about* is a cliché, and should be restricted to less formal contexts: *They like the feeling that they have had to fight other men for possession. That is what it is all about, really.*—Anita Brookner, 1984

3 USED INSTEAD OF OF. *About* is tending to replace *of* in uses such as *We're more aware about it* | *The Vietnamese are disdainful about Chinese cooking* | *The issue about how such things are monitored.*

4 BE ABOUT TO. In affirmative contexts, *to be about to* denotes intention: *I am about to go shopping.* A more idiomatic negative use, *not about to* (do something), should only be used informally: *I'm not about to foist something on the general public just for the sake of releasing something*—*Record Mirror*, 1982. In more formal usage, it is better to use one of several alternatives such as *do not intend to* (or, more emphatically, *have no intention of*), *am not likely to*, etc.

abridgement is the better spelling, rather than *abridgment*.

abrogate, arrogate. *Abrogate* means 'to repel, annul, or cancel' and is used with reference to laws, rules, treaties, and other formal agreements (*The Cabinet clung stubbornly to the belief that the mere signing of the agreement itself abrogated imperial preferential tariffs*—D. Aitchison, 1969 | *He abrogated at once the Penal Code*—W. H. Auden, 1969); *arrogate* means 'to lay claim to without justification' (*That sort of writing which has arrogated to itself the epithet 'creative'*—D. J. Enright, 1966 | *The illegal but effective authority which the Assembly of the United Nations seemed now to have arrogated to itself*—H. Macmillan, 1971).

absolutely. This word has a string of important meanings in the broad area 'in an absolute position, manner, or degree', and can be applied to many domains of physical and conceptual activity including language and politics. It has also come to be used as a mere intensive (*absolutely awful, absolutely essential, absolutely out of the question*). In conversation, *absolutely* is used 'absolutely' (i.e. without a grammatical complement) as a strong affirmative reply: *'Is he nice?' I asked . . . 'Absolutely,' she said and glowed*—source in British National Corpus, 1978 | *'Communism was a form of Antichrist.' 'Ooh, absolutely, absolutely.'*—spoken material in British National Corpus, 1993. With *not*, it is often used in speech as an emphatic refusal or denial: *Because your mother insisted. 'Absolutely not.'*—B. Neil, 1993.

absolve. 1 Pronunciation is now normally with -z-, not -s-.

2 The usual construction is with a direct object, or in the passive, followed by *of* or *from*: *It absolved him of all responsibility*—L. A. G. Strong, 1948 | *Dollar was absolved of personal liability for the line's debts*—*Time*, 1950 | *Absolve me from all spot of sin*—James Agee, 1950.

abstract nouns. The Fowlers (1906) and Gowers (1965) warned against the excessive use of abstract nouns, Gowers coining the term 'abstractitis' as a label for his disapproval. The principal area of offence is in official documents and formal writing. The Fowler brothers attacked 'the far-fetched, the abstract, the periphrastic, the long', and gave the following as an example: *The signs of the times point to the necessity of the modification of the system of administration* [rewrite as *It is becoming clear that the administrative system must be modified*]. Gowers

gave another example: *Participation by the men in the control of the industry is non-existent* [rewrite as *The men have no part in the control of the industry*].

abuse has in the 20c developed a sinister violent meaning, 'maltreatment or (especially sexual) assault of a person', and is now widely familiar in the specific context of *child abuse*, of which various aspects include *physical abuse, ritual abuse, sexual abuse*, and even *satanic abuse*. At the same time its older meaning, 'misuse or improper use', has been greatly extended in explicit combinations such as *alcohol abuse, drug abuse, heroin abuse, solvent abuse, steroid abuse*, etc., all associated with harmful or narcotic substances. Few semantic developments have such appalling social implications as these.

abysmal, abyssal. The currency of these two words is in inverse proportion to that of the parent words: *abysmal*, with its figurative meaning 'very bad' and a literal meaning relating to gorges, outer space, etc., is common, whereas *abyssal* is limited to technical usage in oceanography, 'belonging to one of the deepest levels of the ocean' (e.g. in the term *abyssal floor*). By contrast, *abyss* is still used (usually in figurative use, e.g. *They are staring into the abyss*), whereas *abysm* is not. Examples of *abysmal*: (figurative) *Some doctors have an abysmal lack of knowledge about the range of social services available* —*British Medical Journal*, 1975 | *The day was hot, the organisation . . . excellent, and the cricket of generally abysmal quality*—*Wisden Cricket Monthly*, 1992 | (literal) *Far, far beneath in the abysmal sea*—P. Allardice, 1990.

academic. The central meanings of this word ('of or belonging to an academy or institution for higher learning') survive, but a little more than a century ago it developed a depreciatory range of meanings 'merely theoretical, having no practical applications': *All the discussion, Sirs, is—academic. The war has begun already*—H. G. Wells, 1929 | *The strike . . . was dismissed as 'largely academic' by Merseyside Health Authority—Times*, 1990.

accent. 1 The noun is stressed on the first syllable and the verb (meaning 'to lay stress on, to emphasize' in various senses) on the second.

2 In general use, an accent is 'individual, local, or national mode of pronunciation', as in *a Scottish accent, a slight accent*, etc.: *She had . . . the accent of a good finishing school*—John Braine, 1957 | *'Crème de framboises,' she read in her governessy accent*—S. Hill, 1969 | *She resembled Jackie Kennedy, but—surprisingly—had a strong Scottish accent*—J. Bow, 1991. It is also used to mean the position of the stress in a word, and a sign put on a word in writing to mark a feature of its pronunciation: *You must pronounce this all as one word with the accent on the first syllable*—C. S. Lewis, 1955. There are other special meanings in art and music. The meaning relating to pronunciation is the earliest one, and has given rise to extended uses, in which accent means 'a distinctive feature or emphasis': *After 1926 the accent was to lie on the development of technical education*—R. Pethybridge, 1990 | *The early autumn of 1992 produced no less than four major auctions with an accent on matters aeronautical*—*FlyPast*, 1992. This use is common in advertising and marketing: *Accent is on*

comfort when you step in for a relaxing drink—promotional material in British National Corpus, 1990s.

3 As a verb, *accent* means 'to place an accent on (a word or syllable)'. In figurative meanings, *accentuate* is invariably used: *I observed a severe grey skirt, the waist accentuated by a leather belt*—William Golding, 1967 | *Collingwood also has a rather learned look, accentuated by steel spectacles*—R. Cobb, 1985.

accept, except. There is little danger of confusion in spoken contexts, since all they have in common is their similar pronunciation in running discourse, but their spelling is open to confusion. David Crystal reports in his book *Who Cares About English Usage?* (1984) that several of 20 English undergraduates asked to choose between *Shall we accept | except his invitation to dinner* chose *except*.

access, accession. 1 AS NOUNS. The two words are hardly at all interchangeable: *accession* means arrival or admission, whereas *access* means the opportunity of arriving or of admission. Accordingly, *accession* to the throne means becoming sovereign, whereas *access* to the throne means the right or opportunity to petition the sovereign. An *access* of a physical or emotional feeling such as fever, fury, joy, despair, is a sudden attack of it regardless of the physical or emotional state beforehand; an *accession* of strength, or an *accession* to a library, is something added to an existing stock.

2 AS VERBS. Since the 1890s, *to accession* has meant 'to enter as a new book in a library' (*The new books have been promptly accessioned*—G. M. Jones, 1892).

More recently, *access* has taken on a verbal meaning 'to gain access to (data held in a computer)', e.g. *Design engineers can now access the computer directly through terminals in their offices—Scientific American*, 1977. A possible metaphorical application of the computing model of human behaviour may be seen in a new meaning in psychology: 'to experience (deep feelings)', as in *Deciding all of a sudden that he's got to do some grieving, learn to access his rage—New Republic*, 1992. Use of the verb in more generalized contexts, such as *The kitchen may be accessed from the dining room*, should be avoided (use *reach, approach, enter*, etc., or rephrase).

accessary, accessory. These two words come by different routes from the same Latin source of our word *accede*. In AmE, *accessory* is dominant both as a noun and as an adjective, and it has fast become so now in BrE, although *accessary* is still used occasionally (where before it was used invariably) as a term in law in both varieties. But *-ory* is preferable in all meanings: *As the one person who knew of their illegalities I felt I was becoming an accessory after the fact—S. Unwin, 1960 | If he buried the captain, as he says, he's an accessory—R. Macdonald, 1971 | Accessory ideas associated with the principal idea—M. Cohen, 1977.*

As a noun, *accessory* has become widely used in the 20c to refer to smaller articles of dress (gloves, handbag, etc.) or the extras in a motor vehicle (fog-lights, radio, etc.). Example: *Accessories . . . may be considered essential to an outfit.—Alison Lurie, 1981.*

accommodate, accommodation. These are among the most commonly misspelt words in English: there are two *c*s and two *m*s. The verb *accommodate* is followed by *to* when it means 'adapt' and by *with* when (less usually) it means 'to equip, supply, oblige': e.g. *His eyes quickly accommodated to the gloom | Major Kent was accommodated with a hammock chair—G. A. Birmingham, 1908.*

accompanist is now the standard form of the word for 'a person who plays a musical accompaniment'. The by-form *accompanyist*, used by Dickens, is now occasionally encountered in AmE.

accomplice, accomplish. The standard pronunciation of both words is now -kum-, not -kom-.

according. 1 *ACCORDING AS.* This is now well established as a subordinating conjunction meaning 'depending on whether, to the extent to which', despite Fowler's long warning (1926) against its use: e.g. *Llanaba Castle presents two quite different aspects, according as you approach it from the Bangor or the coast road—Evelyn Waugh, 1928.*

2 *ACCORDING TO.* This is used as a complex preposition, and means (a) in a manner that is consistent with (something), e.g. *Everything went according to plan*, (b) as stated by (a person or authority), e.g. *According to our records, the account is in credit | I have acted according to my conscience—*Anthony Blunt, 1979 | (with an element of uncertainty or disbelief) *According to them, we're supposed to stay at home*, (c) in a manner or degree that is in proportion to (something), e.g. *Arrange the blocks according to size and colour | My price varied from twenty to fifty pounds according to* *the neighbourhood and the customer*—Graham Greene, 1966.

account. The phrase *on account of* is a slightly formal preposition meaning 'because of' (*He remained miserable and ashamed, largely on account of his appetite which continued to torment him*—Anita Brookner, 1988). Its use (with or without *of*) as a conjunction is nonstandard: e.g. *Take your three days off, Mr. Barlow, only don't expect to be paid for them on account you're thinking up some fancy ideas*—E. Waugh, 1948 | *Account of you think you're tough you're going up to State Prison where you'll have to prove it*—E. Leonard, 1994 (US).

accountable is mostly used in the construction to be accountable to someone for something: e.g. *Labour MPs . . . would at least have the authority to keep a Labour government accountable to them for what they say and do*—Tony Benn, 1979. Its old use as an opposite of unaccountable (*By George—it was a very accountable obstinacy*—George Eliot, 1876) is now rarely found.

accumulative see CUMULATIVE.

accusative is a grammatical term denoting a noun or pronoun that is governed by a verb or preposition, e.g. *house* in *Then we saw the house* and *They stood in front of the house*. In English it is only certain pronouns that change their form in the accusative (e.g. *him, them, us*): see CASES.

accuse is now always used in the construction to accuse someone *of* something: e.g. *He accused the sound technicians of sabotaging the record*—M. Puzo, 1969 | *People jumped up and accused her of making common cause with the Nazis*—D. May, 1988. Other constructions (e.g *The Romanists accuse the Prot-*

estants for their indifference—Southey, 1809) have fallen out of use.

accused. *The accused*, meaning a person who has been accused in law, is an everyday use. *The* or *an accused man, person, banker*, etc., in which the individuals are only generically identified, are also routinely acceptable. It is inadvisable, however, to use expressions such as *the accused thief* or *the accused rapist*, which specify the type of criminal, since identification with the crime is in question by the very use of the term *accused* (*alleged* might be a better word here).

Achilles' heel, Achilles' tendon. Use an apostrophe in both expressions for consistency, even though the connection with Achilles is remote in the second.

acid. Since the 1960s, when *acid* was first used to mean the hallucinogenic drug LSD, the word has developed all the connotations of a sub-culture. Those taking drugs came to be called *acid heads* or *acid freaks*; and their way of life came to depend on going on *acid trips* at *acid parties* to the sound of *acid rock* or *acid jazz*. More recently (1988), the (apparently unrelated) term *Acid House* (or just *House*) has been applied to a style of music and dancing imported to Britain from Chicago, and associated with widespread use of hallucinogenic drugs. These uses are striking examples of the transformation of the primary sense of a basic term in a technical subject, in this case chemistry.

acid rain. Many people are surprised to learn that *acid rain*, i.e. rain with significantly increased acidity as a result of atmospheric pollution, is first recorded (with slightly different connotations) as early as 1859. Its wide currency in English across the world is recent, and especially since the problem was brought to the attention of the UN in 1972; it appeared first in technical writing and then passed rapidly into everyday use.

acid test. When Fowler was preparing the first edition of *Modern English Usage*, he remarked that *acid test* was undoubtedly the popularized technical term 'most in vogue at the moment of writing (1920)'. In scientific use it meant the use of nitric acid to test for gold; in transferred use it had acquired the broad sense 'a severe or conclusive test', a use that was popularized by Woodrow Wilson two years before Fowler was writing (*The treatment accorded Russia by her sister nations in the months to come will be the acid test of their good will—Times*, 1918). For other extensions of technical terms see the table at POPULARIZED TECHNICALITIES.

acknowledgement. This spelling is preferred in BrE, although *acknowledgment* is more usual in AmE.

acoustic. 1 PRONUNCIATION. Earlier in the 20c two pronunciations were competing with each other: one with -ow- and the other with -oo-. The second has prevailed, despite Fowler's prediction that 'if the word came into popular use, it would probably be with -ow-', based on traditional assumptions about the English pronunciation of Greek.

2 The noun *acoustics* is construed as singular when used to mean 'the science of sound' (e.g. *Acoustics is a branch of physics*), and

as plural when used to mean 'the acoustic properties of a building' (e.g. *The acoustics of the cathedral are magnificent*).

acronym. 1 This term, which was first used in the 1940s, denotes a type of abbreviation made up of a set of initials that are pronounced as a single word, as *Nato* is (as distinct from *BBC*). An *acronym* is generally treated as a word in its own right in other ways, for example in the formation of plurals when appropriate. Examples of familiar acronyms include: *Aids* (acquired immune deficiency syndrome), *Anzac* (Australian and New Zealand Army Corps), *ASH* (Action on Smoking and Health), *SALT* (Strategic Arms Limitation Talks), *Unesco* (United Nations Educational, Scientific, and Cultural Organization), and *WASP* (White Anglo-Saxon Protestant). Some of these, especially the names of organizations, start off as ordinary abbreviations (often with full stops) and develop into acronyms; others (e.g. *ASH*) are deliberately contrived so as to lend themselves to pronunciation as words and hence acquire acronym status artificially.

2 Examples of acronyms that form ordinary nouns are *laser* (light amplification by stimulated emission of radiation), *radar* (radio detection and ranging), and *SWOT* (strengths, weaknesses, opportunities, strengths: used in business assessments). Some general acronyms are highly forced, notably *POSSLQ* (person of the opposite sex sharing living quarters, often pronounced **poss**-əlk).

3 In everyday use, *acronym* is sometimes applied to abbreviations that are properly initialisms, since they are pronounced

as separate letters (e.g. *EU* = European Union, *VCR* = video cassette recorder).

act, action. 1 The distinction between the two words in their general meanings is not always clear: we are judged by our acts or by our actions. In general, however, *action* has more of the notion of performance, and extends to inanimate things (we can speak only of the *action*, not of the *act*, of a machine), whereas *act* connotes more strongly the fact of something done and also implies responsibility rather more necessarily than *action* does (hence the *Acts of the Apostles*, not the *Actions*, which Fowler (1926) suggested as the logical preference). *Action* is also used attributively in expressions such as *action committee, painting, replay,* etc., whereas *act* is not. The *actions* of a person are usually viewed as occupying some time, and (in the plural) denote the habitual or ordinary deeds of a person, the sum of which make up his or her conduct. *Act*, by contrast, normally means something brought about rapidly or over a short period, especially in phrases with *of* (*an act of God, an act of madness*).

2 Both words have special meanings which are exclusive to each (an *act* of a play, an *act* in a variety show, military *action*, etc.), and in fixed expressions (*to put on an act, caught in the act, to clean up one's act, to take action, where the action is, a piece of the action,* etc.).

3 *Action*, in its modern use as a transitive verb meaning 'to take action on (a decision or request, etc.)' is best left to the evasive language of business managers (*Dismissal will be actioned when the balance of probabilities suggests that an employee has committed a criminal act—Daily Telegraph,* 1981).

activate, actuate. *Activate* (17c) originally meant 'to make active' (as in *activate the lungs*). It fell out of use for a time at the end of the 19c, and was marked as obsolete in the first *OED*. New uses in physics, chemistry, and other branches of science have brought it back into prominence and *actuate* (also 17c in current meanings), once dominant, is now in decline. *Activate* is the normal word in mechanical contexts such as burglar alarms, traffic lights, flight plans, and also occasionally in the context of human behaviour, where the choice is perhaps influenced by *motivate* (e.g. *Are they activated by concern for public morality?*). *Actuate* is less common in physical and mechanical contexts, and is generally restricted to less appealing abstract qualities such as anger, greed, jealousy, malice, etc. (*His opposition was actuated by a different and more compelling motive than that of her other relatives*—David Cecil, 1948 | *Peirce was actuated by the analogy with science, not by a vision*—J. Barzun, 1983).

active. The active voice of verbs is illustrated by the sentence *France beat Brazil in the final,* in which the subject of the verb (*France*) performs the action and the object (*Brazil*) is affected by the action. The passive equivalent is *Brazil were beaten by France in the final,* in which the grammatical roles of the two participants in the action are reversed. See PASSIVE.

actual is often used redundantly in ways that add nothing to the meaning: *Mr Healey said the press did not print Labour's actual policies. 'Not a sausage.'—Times*, 1981. Examples of legitimate use are: *He gathered there were few actual artists in the room* [as distinct from would-be artists]—Beryl Bainbridge, 1980 | *The actual total* [as distinct from the provisional total] *was surely higher—Scientific American*, 1980.

actuality has driven out *actualness*, which was recorded by Johnson and was used as a synonym meaning 'the state of being actual' up to the end of the 19c. *Actualities* are 'actual existing conditions or circumstances'; in addition, *actuality* has acquired a special concrete meaning, 'a film record or radio or television broadcast of an event as it actually occurs' (*The films began with 'actualities', the record of more or less formal current events*—H. G. Wells).

actually is one of a number of words, like *definitely, really, surely*, etc., which are used freely as emphasizers, either in relation to words or phrases (*Often it wasn't actually a railway station but a special stopping place in the middle of nowhere—New Yorker*, 1987) or as sentence adverbs qualifying a complete statement (*I'd like to see those scrap books again, actually—* Lee Smith, 1983 | *'I told you, I've got problems at work.' 'Actually, you didn't.'*) Such uses are more common in speech, where they help with continuity and sentence balance. It is clearly a useful if somewhat overused word.

actuate see ACTIVATE.

acumen. The 19c pronunciation as recorded in the *OED* was with the stress on the second syllable. This is still the dominant pronun-

ciation in AmE, but in BrE stress on the first syllable is now standard.

ad, advert are frequent colloquial shortened forms of *advertisement*, both dating from the middle of the 19c and now widespread in informal use (*If you examine the adverts for personal computers . . . you'll find that almost nowhere do the ads promise you any kind of concrete benefit—Your Computer*, 1984).

AD should always be placed—in recognition of what it stands for (*anno Domini*, in the year of Our Lord)—before the numerals it relates to, i.e. AD 44 (not 44 AD). It is customary for convenience, however, to write 'the third century AD' to correspond to 'the third century BC'. In print, AD is often put in small capitals. Note that the alternative CE (for 'Common Era') is often used as a culturally neutral alternative, along with BCE ('before Common Era').

adamant. Its use an as adjective meaning 'stubbornly unshakeable or inflexible' is surprisingly recent (1930s); as a noun meaning a hard rock or mineral it goes back to the time of King Alfred, originally as a vague term often imbued with fabulous associations, and later as a synonym for 'diamond'. In modern use the noun is 'only a poetical or rhetorical name for the embodiment of surpassing hardness', and the adjective is the principal use (*His appointment had met with the adamant opposition of almost all the Fellows—Tom Sharpe*, 1974), also giving rise to an adverb *adamantly* (*When she mentions him at all in her diary, it is in adamantly negative terms—S. Quinn*, 1988).

adapter, -or. In one's own writing it is good to reserve *adaptor* to the device and *adapter* to the meaning 'a person who adapts (something or to something)', but any hard-and-fast rule-stating will not be matched by the evidence, so be prepared for either form in either meaning.

addenda is a plural form meaning 'a list of additional items'; if there is only one, *addendum* is the word to use. *Addenda* should be treated as plural, not (except informally, like *agenda*) as singular (as in *a new edition with an invaluable addenda*).

addle, addled. The usual word now is *addled*, and is applied (a) to eggs, and (b) figuratively, to brains (i.e. the mind). Originally, *addle* was a noun meaning 'stinking urine or other liquid filth', although its associations have usually been with eggs and heads, both seen as capable of 'addling', hence *addle-brain(ed), addle-head(ed)*, etc.

addresses. It is now customary to use as little punctuation as possible in addresses, omitting commas at the ends of lines and before street names, e.g.:
Mr J Smith
44 High Street
Newtown
(A postal code can be put on the same line as the town or below it.)

-ade. Nearly all words of two or more syllables ending in *-ade* are derived from French, although some are originally from other Romance languages. Most of these are now pronounced -ayd, not -ahd: *accolade, arcade, balustrade, brigade, brocade, cascade, cavalcade, crusade, lemonade,* *marmalade, masquerade, palisade, parade, serenade, tirade*. A small group vary between the two pronunciations, including: *esplanade, fanfaronnade, fusilade, glissade, pomade, promenade, rodomontade*; and a few are always pronounced -ahd: *aubade, ballade, façade*.

adequate. **1** In its meaning 'proportionate to the requirements', sufficient, *adequate* is most commonly used without a complement (*There is an adequate supply of food in the flooded area*). When it has one, this is either *for* or *to* (*Their earnings are adequate for/to their needs*). It is also used idiomatically to mean 'barely sufficient': *The standard rapidly sinks to a level which is, at best, adequate but at worst incompetent.*

2 Arguments that *adequate* is an absolute are as invalid and contrary to usage as similar arguments for *unique*. Language is rarely as absolute as purists would like, and it is natural to find *adequacy* graded by adverbs and in terms of comparatives and superlatives (*We are seeking a more adequate return on our investments | The work done is fairly adequate | The most adequate description yet released of the horror of the hijacking*).

adherence, adhesion. Both words were adopted from French in the 17c, and come from the Latin verb which also gives us our verb *adhere*. *Adherence* is now mostly used in figurative senses relating to beliefs, loyalties, etc., whereas *adhesion* has tended more and more to imply physical contact between surfaces, e.g. the grip of wheels on road or rail, the sticking or gluing together of two surfaces, etc. Contrary uses are also found, especially of *adhesion* in figurative meanings, but these no longer sound natural (*He is in fact more rigid in his adhesion to his old doctrines*—Beatrice Webb, 1952 | *Others . . . fell under his control through the adhesion to France of their ruler, the Prince-Bishop of Liège*—Winston Churchill, 1957).

ad hoc (Latin, 'to this') has been recorded in English since the 17c, principally as an a quasi-adjective meaning 'designated for a specific purpose' as in an *ad hoc committee* or an *ad hoc appointment*. It should normally be printed in italic. Although strictly speaking it should not be qualified by reducing or intensifying adverbs such as *fairly* or *very*, this is common in less formal English (*The arrangement seems extremely ad hoc to them*), and in the 20c *ad hoc* has generated an array of startlingly un-Latinate derivatives such as *ad-hoc-ery* and *ad-hoc-ism* (sometimes with medial hyphen, sometimes without).

adieu is pronounced əd**yoo**. The plural is preferably *adieux* (pronounced with final -ooz, not *adieus*).

adjacent, adjoining. An *adjacent property* is normally one that is nearby without necessarily touching the one being considered in relation to it. Similarly, *adjacent angles* in a triangle are separated by the length of one side of the triangle, an *adjacent room* can be across a corridor, and *adjacent tables* are next to each other, but with a space between. *Adjoining* invariably denotes contact, and is therefore preferable when this meaning is unambiguously required; as a participle it can also govern a following noun rather like a preposition (e.g. *She and Susan had rooms adjoining, so*

she had none of the creepy feelings one often gets in a strange house—M. Gervaise, 1983 | *There were a lot of policemen in surrounding streets and in the park adjoining the embassy*—*Independent*, 1989).

adjective. 1 GENERAL. The term *adjective* was itself an adjective for a hundred years before it became used as a noun for one of the parts of speech. Joseph Priestley, in *The Rudiments of English Grammar* (1761), was perhaps the first English grammarian to recognize the adjective as a separate part of speech, although some earlier writers had used the term in this way. An alternative term, first used in the mid-19c, is *modifier*, which also covers the grey area of attributive nouns and nouns 'passing into adj.' (as the OED called them), for example *city* in *city council* and *table* in *table lamp*. For a more detailed analysis of types of adjective, the reader is referred to a standard grammar such as Greenbaum's *Oxford English Grammar* (1996), 134–41.

An adjective has three forms, traditionally called a positive (or absolute), e.g. *hot, splendid*, a comparative, e.g. *hotter, more splendid*, and a superlative, e.g. *hottest, most splendid*.

2 ATTRIBUTIVE AND PREDICATIVE. Most adjectives can be used in two positions: either before the noun (attributively, as in *a black cat, a gloomy outlook*) or after it, normally separated by a verb of state (predicatively, as in *the cat is black, the outlook seemed gloomy*). A few adjectives, usually denoting status, exceptionally stand immediately after the noun (postpositive, as in *the body politic, the president elect*).

Some adjectives are normally restricted to predicative position (e.g. *afraid, aware*), and others are restricted to attributive position, either always (e.g. *main* as in *the main reason* | ✖ *this reason is main*) or in certain meanings (e.g. *big* as in *He is a big eater* | ✖ *As an eater he is big*, *mere* as in *This is mere repetition* | ✖ *The repetition is mere*, and *whole* as in *Have you told the whole truth* | ✖ *The truth I have told is whole*). In these examples, predicative status has to be achieved by repetition of the noun or by the use of *one* (*The truth I have told is the whole truth* | *This reason is the main one*).

Other adjectives that have been restricted in the past are now becoming more mobile; for example, *aware* and *ill* are increasingly heard (often modified by an adverb) in attributive position, as in *a highly aware person* and *an ill woman*.

3 COMPARISON. Adjectives of one or two syllables normally form their comparative and superlative forms by adding *-er* and *-est*, sometimes with modification of the stem (*soft, softer, softest; happy, happier, happiest*). Adjectives of more than two syllables are normally preceded by *more* or *most* instead of inflecting (*more frightening; most remarkable*). For special effect, however, a polysyllabic adjective will sometimes be inflected (*'Curiouser and curiouser!' cried Alice*—L. Carroll, 1865 | *One of the generousest creatures alive*—Thackeray, 1847/8 | *The winningest coach in Southwest Conference basketball history*—Chicago Tribune, 1990). See also -ER AND -EST FORMS OF ADJECTIVES. Conversely, *more* and *most* are sometimes used, for emphasis or special effect, when inflected forms are available: *This was never more true than at present* | *That was the most cruel thing you could have said*.

4 'ABSOLUTE' ADJECTIVES. Some adjectives, because of their meaning and function, are called *absolute* or *non-gradable*, and are not normally used in comparative or superlative forms and cannot be qualified by adverbs that intensify or moderate along a notional range such as *fairly, largely, more, rather,* or *very*: these are classifying adjectives such as *dead, rectangular, scientific,* or descriptive adjectives with a meaning that does not permit gradability, such as *equal, impossible, supreme, total, unique*. There are exceptions to this rule, but these are normally obvious special cases: *All animals are equal but some animals are more equal than others*—George Orwell, 1945 | *His profile is . . . most utterly perfect*—Jane Gardam, 1985. Absolute adjectives can be regularly qualified by adverbs that denote an extreme or completeness, such as *absolutely, completely,* and *utterly,* since these are consistent with the non-gradable function of the adjectives concerned: *The . . . ghosts . . . made the place absolutely impossible*—Harper's Magazine, 1884. In this sentence, *absolutely impossible* is acceptable, and so is *completely* or *utterly impossible*, but *fairly* or *rather impossible* would not be.

5 POSITION OF ADJECTIVES. In numerous fixed expressions denoting status, an adjective is placed immediately after the noun it governs: e.g. *attorney-general, body politic, court martial, fee simple, heir apparent, notary public, poet laureate, postmaster-general, president elect, situations vacant, vice-chancellor designate, the village proper*. In other cases, an adjective can follow a noun for syntactic reasons, i.e. as a matter of sentence structure rather than peculiarity of expression (*The waiter . . . picked up* *our dirty glasses in his fingertips, his eyes impassive*—Encounter, 1987), or for rhetorical effect (*Before the loving hands of the Almighty cradled him in bliss eternal*—Nigel Williams, 1992).

6 HYPHENATION. There is no need to insert a hyphen between a combination of adverb in *-ly* and adjective qualified by it, even when it stands in attributive position: *a highly competitive market | abundant recently published material | lawfully elected prime ministers | fully qualified lawyers.* When the adverb does not end in *-ly*, however, a hyphen is normally required to reinforce its status: *a well-known woman | an ill-defined topic.*

7 COMPOUND ADJECTIVES. These have proliferated in the 20c, and are formed from combinations of noun + adjective (*accident-prone, acid-free, child-proof, computer-literate, machine-readable, user-friendly, water-insoluble*) noun + past participle (*computer-aided, custom-built, hand-operated*), noun + *-ing* participle (*data-handling, pressure-reducing, stress-relieving*). Some formations are based on longer phrases (*back-to-basics, in-your-face*) and some of the more informal compounds give rise to adverbial derivatives (*balls-achingly, mind-blowingly*).

A new kind of compound adjective emerging in technical and scientific work is the type *landscape ecological principles* (= the principles of landscape ecology), in which the second element of the name of the subject (*landscape ecology*) has been turned into an adjective. Another example is *physical geographical studies*, where it would be better to say studies in physical geography.

8 ADJECTIVES USED AS ADVERBS. Some adjectives have corresponding adverbs that are identical,

e.g. *fast, late, straight*, and the type *monthly, weekly*, etc. So you can say *He left in the late afternoon* or *He left late in the afternoon*. Adverbs without *-ly* and those in *-ly* often occur in close proximity ('*I play straight, I choose wisely, Harry,*' he assured me—John Le Carré, 1989). In other cases, adjectives are used as adverbs only informally, often in fixed expressions such as *come clean* and *hold tight*. To these may be added *real* and *sure*, which in the UK are often taken to be tokens of informal North American speech (*That was real nice | I sure liked seeing you*).

9 ADJECTIVES USED AS NOUNS. A typical extension in the use of some descriptive adjectives is with the, forming plural (or occasionally singular) nouns meaning 'those who are . . . ', e.g. *the beautiful, the deaf, the poor, the sublime, the unemployed, the unusual.*

Other adjectives stand as countable nouns: *the ancients, the classics, collectables, explosives, submersibles.*

10 TRANSFERRED EPITHETS. A curiosity of English is the ways in which an adjective can be made to operate obliquely, qualifying a person or thing other than the word it relates to grammatically. This is a further extension of the standard use of adjectives to classify things in relation to their human associations; a *female toilet* means a toilet for women and a *gay bar* means a bar frequented by homosexuals: '*It's not your stupid place,*' she says. '*It's anyone's place.*'—Penelope Lively, 1987 [the person addressed, not the place, is stupid] | *I will be sitting quietly at the kitchen table stirring an absent-minded cup of coffee*—Chicago Tribune, 1989 [the person, not the coffee, is absent-minded]. The

traditional name for this phenomenon is *transferred epithet* or
hypallage.

adjudicator is spelt *-or*.

adjure see ABJURE.

adjust. Three new uses of this
verb have entered the language
in the 20c: **1** Intransitive, with or
without to: to adapt oneself to
something (*She seemed to have adjusted to her new status with little
difficulty*—L. Niven, 1983 | *She needs
time to adjust*—S. King, 1979).

2 Intransitive, standing for passive: to be capable of being adjusted (*The barrel . . . can adjust
right up to the neck of the lamp*—
Habitat Catalogue, 1982).

3 Transitive, with *for*, in the
presentation of statistical information (*Lenders vary as to when
they adjust your repayments for tax
relief*—What Mortgage, 1986).

administer, administrate. For
many centuries, the normal word
corresponding to *administration*
and meaning 'to manage (affairs)'
has been *administer* (*The Rezzoris
were minor Austrian gentry adminis-
tering the outposts of empire*—
London Review of Books, 1990). In
recent years, however, the longer
form *administrate* (first recorded
in the 17c) has increasingly been
used as a kind of newly invented
back-formation, and is now awkwardly challenging *administer* in
its traditional meanings: *The machinery of such aid is still primed by
administrators eager to go out and
administrate*—Times, 1981 | *The
Sports Council has begun a major investigation into discovering new ways
to administrate a drug-detecting
system*—Times, 1988.

Administer is, on the other hand,
routinely used to mean 'to give
(medicine) to a patient' (*I was

brimming with alcohol—administered
to loosen my tongue—A. Price, 1982)
and is also being increasingly
used in two other meanings:

1 to inflict (punishment, blows,
etc.) on someone (*Two others held
her feet while the headmaster administered the cane*—B. Emecheta, 1974).

2 in medical contexts *administer*
is used instead of *minister* to (an
injured person, etc.): *The fact that
Ranjit is still alive today is a tribute
to the ambulance attendants who administered to him at the scene*—
Oxford Times, 1977 | *American doc-
tors, being vastly rich, have better
things to do with their leisure time
than administer to patients at
weekends*—Times, 1994.

admission, admittance. Like
many doublets, these two words
have competed with each other
for several centuries (*admission*
first recorded in Middle English,
admittance in 1589) without ever
establishing totally separate roles.
In the meaning corresponding to
admit = 'to acknowledge or accept
as true', *admission* is the word to
use, not *admittance*. Where they
get in each other's way is in
meanings related to 'the action
of admitting, letting in, to a
place'. *Admission* is the dominant
word of the two: it alone has a
countable use (*There are more admissions in the sciences this year*),
and it is the only one to have developed attributive uses (*admission
fee, money, officer, ticket*). *Admittance*
hangs on determinedly, especially
as the word used on notices on
entrances (e.g. *No admittance except on official business*) but also as
an erroneous alternative in meanings where *admission* is required
(*The DTI's lack of admittance of neg-
ligence in this affair is a travesty of
justice*—Times, 1988).

admit. **1** *Admit of* is now only used in the meaning 'to allow as possible, leave room for' (always with an abstract object: *The circumstances will not admit of delay | It seems to admit of so many interpretations*), and even here the construction seems old-fashioned. In its other meanings, *admit* is transitive (*He admitted the injustice of it*, not ✗ *He admitted of the injustice of it*), and takes a *that*-clause as a common construction (*He admitted that it was unjust*).

2 The phrase *admit to*, meaning 'to confess to, to acknowledge', is a relatively recent addition to the language (*Senior Ministry officials yesterday admitted to a catalogue of errors*—*Times*, 1989).

adopted, adoptive. The correct use of each word is as follows: a child is *adopted* and its parents are *adoptive*. The distinction has become eroded in recent usage, especially in extended uses with reference to countries, homes, etc.

adult. **1** It is usually pronounced with stress on the first syllable in BrE and on the second syllable in AmE, but the distribution is uneven among educated speakers throughout the English-speaking world.

2 Since the 1950s, changing social attitudes have caused the word *adult* to be used euphemistically with the meaning 'sexually explicit', applied to certain categories of films, magazines, etc.

advance. **1** *ADVANCE, ADVANCED.* The meanings are different, *advance* being a noun used attributively or as a modifier to mean 'placed in advance; going before', as in *advance copy, advance guard, advance payment*, etc., whereas *advanced* means 'far on in development' as in *an advanced degree, an advanced age, an advanced young woman*, etc.

2 *ADVANCE, ADVANCEMENT.* *Advance* is much the commoner word of the two in the general sense of 'progress, going before' (*the advance of knowledge | an advance of £100 | the advance of old age | seats booked in advance*, etc.). *Advancement* is far from extinct (*1985|6 was another year of great advancement for Glaxo Inc. | The structure of the department allows for speedy advancement*) but has a different meaning, 'raising to a higher position; promotion' and should not be used in the general sense that *advance* has. *The advance of new ideas* means their increasing effect, whereas the *advancement of new ideas* means encouraging and supporting them.

adverb. **1** GENERAL. The term *adverb* covers a wide variety of words, and is the least satisfactory of the conventional word categories applied to English. The principal adverb uses answer the question 'how?' or 'in what manner?', many of these being formed by the addition of the suffix *-ly* to adjectives (e.g. *carefully, quickly, steadily, well*), 'when?' or 'how often?' (e.g. *soon, regularly, yesterday*), 'where?' (e.g. *downstairs, here, outside*), and 'to what extent?' (e.g. *extremely, hardly, somewhat*). For a more detailed analysis of types of adverb, and for further terminology, the reader is referred to a standard grammar such as Greenbaum's *Oxford English Grammar* (1996), 141–52.

2 FORMATION OF ADVERBS. The most common formation is

achieved by adding -ly to adjectives, as in *regularly, steadily,* and *quickly.* Other adverbs are identical with adjectives (*fast, well*), and members of a third type are formed by adding other elements such as *-ward(s), -ways* and *-wise* to nouns, as in *edgeways, homewards,* and *clockwise* (some of these are also adjectives). In the 20c the range of adverbs ending in *-wise* has increased enormously, with many new ad-hoc (and often criticized) formations, such as *anthemwise* and *hind-foot-wise.* Use of these should be confined to occasions when a jocular or other special effect is called for.

3 POSITION OF ADVERBS. ▸ a Adverbs that qualify single words such as adjectives, nouns, and other adverbs generally precede them as closely as possible (*often late | very large | quite a while | too modestly.*

▸ b The position of adverbs in phrases and clauses follows fairly clear rules, i.e. between an auxiliary verb and a main verb (e.g. *Roosevelt's financial policy was roundly criticized in 1933 | He had inadvertently joined a lonely-hearts club*), except for emphasis or when the adverb belongs closely to what follows the main verb (*There is little chance that the student will function effectively after he returns to China*), between one auxiliary verb and the next when there is more than one (e.g. *A car dealer who could certainly have afforded to hire someone*), and not between a verb and its object (*Gradually the Chinese communists abandoned the Soviet methods | He dutifully observes all its quaint rules | They aim to set each subject briefly into context | Did he hear her correctly?*. See also ONLY, SPLIT INFINITIVE.

4 SENTENCE ADVERBS. Some adverbs (such as *clearly, happily, hopefully, thankfully, unhappily*) refer to a whole statement, and form a comment associated more closely with the speaker or writer than with what is said. This can be seen by comparing the use of *unhappily* as an ordinary adverb of manner (*She went unhappily to bed*) with its use as a sentence adverb (*She was, unhappily, too ill to leave the house*). In this use, the adverb often stands at the beginning of the sentence: *Clearly, we will have to think again.*

Use of sentence adverbs is well established in English, and the only one that has given rise to controversy is *hopefully,* which has developed this role in the mid-20c (see HOPEFULLY).

5 ADVERBIAL USE OF NOUNS OF TIME. The adverbial use of days of the week (singular and plural) and similar words, familiar in AmE and some other varieties, is not common in current BrE: *From now on gentlemen, Tuesdays and Thursdays you're going to learn to think like white men*—V. O'Sullivan, 1985 (New Zealand) | *Tuesday night, the board approved the addition of a new subsection*—Chicago Tribune, 1987 | *I was to be offered an option of taking her with me summers*—Saul Bellow, 1987 (US).

6 COMPARISON OF ADVERBS. See -ER AND -EST.

adversary is stressed on the first syllable.

adverse, averse. These two words both come from the Latin word *vertere* 'to turn', but *averse* (= turning away) is used of people and means 'opposed to', whereas *adverse* (= turning towards, hostilely) is used of things and means 'opposing one's interests; unfavourable' (*adverse circumstan-*

ces, adverse weather conditions) or even 'harmful' (*the adverse effects of drugs*): *Surprisingly, the adverse effects appeared to be worse for younger drivers and worse for men than women*—*Today*, 1992 | *This proud, but humiliated, most complicated of politicians was not averse to flattery*—M. Almond, 1992.

advert see AD.

advertise is spelt -*ise*, not -*ize*.

advertisement is pronounced with the main stress on the second syllable in RP, but often on the third syllable (ad-və-**tiyz**-mənt) in many regional varieties of English.

advertising, language of. In a study of the use of language to influence and persuade people, the American scholar Dwight Bolinger (*Language, the Loaded Weapon*, 1980) describes several techniques which advertisers share with other persuaders in manipulating language to their own ends. These may be summarized as (1) literalism, in which an assertion is made that is literally true but will normally be understood in special ways that the advertiser intends (e.g. *Dentists recommend Colgate* suggests that all dentists recommend it whereas only two need be found to justify the statement made), (2) euphemism, in which less favourable aspects are made to sound more appealing (e.g. something that is *average* may be described as *standard* and a small quantity of a product may be described as *handy version* or *fun size*), and uninteresting concepts are made to sound more interesting (e.g. *crafted* instead of *made, ultra-pure* instead of *clean* or *fresh*), (3) use of jaunty vocabulary and slogans (e.g. *Drinka pinta milka day, Every*

picture tells a story), and (4) the use of special syntax to associate the customer with a product (e.g. *Aren't you glad you use Dial?* and *Put a tiger in your tank*, both of which make an assumption to flatter and reassure the customer). See also EUPHEMISM, SLOGAN.

advice, advise. 1 *Advice* is a noun ('an opinion given about future action') and advise a verb ('to give advice to'), in both BrE and AmE: *The hardest thing is knowing where to go to get help, to get the advice and information you need*—*The Face*, 1990 | *It may make sense to take professional advice on the wording of an appropriate letter*—M. Edwards, 1991 | *We're advising all our clients to sit tight, at the moment, and neither to buy nor to sell*—A. Davidson, 1989 | *'I would advise against it, sir,' said George Thomas*—P. Junor, 1991.

2 Both words are used in a special sense in commercial and related uses: *advice* here is countable and is used to mean 'piece of information' (usually in the plural) or 'a document giving information' (*Now we're looking to encourage our customers to send remittance advices electronically*— *Accountancy*, 1993), and *advise* means 'to notify, to give information to' (*The student will be advised of the name and address of the tutor*—*Tutors' Handbook* 1990/91).

advisedly. 1 It should be pronounced as four syllables.

2 The only surviving meaning of four given in the *OED* is 'after considerable thought; as a result of deliberation' (*It was advisedly that the terms of reference excluded the public sector.* —D. Lawrence, 1988 | *I used the words 'an abuse of his powers' advisedly*—*Weekly Law Reports*, 1992).

adviser, advisor. The OED makes it plain that both forms occur with equal frequency throughout the English-speaking world, despite impressions that -er is predominantly BrE and -or AmE. Advisor is probably influenced by the existence of advisory; but adviser is preferable: *The Service would never forgive me a mucky divorce, dear—not its legal adviser—*John Le Carré, 1989 | *The goose . . . shuffled off to see if she could find some advisors*—Jeanette Winterson, 1985.

advocate verb. **1** In a letter written in 1798 Benjamin Franklin asked Noah Webster, the lexicographer of American English, to use his authority to 'reprobate' this word, which was then new in the meaning 'to recommend or plead in favour of', although the verb had been in use for at least a century and a half with the meaning 'to act as advocate'.

2 Fowler's view (1926) that 'unlike *recommend, propose, urge,* and other verbs, *advocate* is not idiomatically followed by a *that*-clause, but only by an ordinary noun or a verbal noun' has proved to be unsound. All three constructions are found and are acceptable: (noun) *He had been expelled by the National Executive for continuing to advocate a political alliance with Communists*—George Brown, 1971 | (verbal noun) *I would advocate the keeping of animals at school*—A. S. Neill, 1915 | (that-clause) *The UN envoy advocated that sanctions be imposed in South Africa.*

-ae, -as, as plurals of nouns in -a. Most English nouns in -a are from Latin (or Latinized Greek) feminine singular nouns, which have in Latin the plural ending -ae. But some have a different Latin origin: e.g. *subpoena* is not nominative, *comma* and *drama* are neuter forms, and *addenda, data,* and *stamina* are plurals, and so with these words plural in -ae is not possible. Other words are not from Latin at all: e.g. *sofa* is from Arabic and *swastika* is from Sanskrit.

Of those words that are genuinely able to have plurals in -ae, some more technical ones do so (*algae, larvae*), whereas those in general use form English plurals in -as (*areas, ideas, villas*) and those in both technical and general use have both forms depending on the domain of use (*antennae* or *antennas, formulae* or *formulas, nebulae* or *nebulas*).

ae-, e-. There is a tendency to simplify spellings with *ae-* in BrE to *e-* in AmE, e.g. *esthetic* for *aesthetic* and *anemic* for *anaemic*, but both types are used.

aeon, meaning 'a long period of time', is spelt with initial *ae-* in BrE and as *eon* or *aeon* in AmE. The pronunciation in both spellings is **ee**-on. See also EPOCH.

aerie, aery (nest of a bird of prey) see EYRIE.

aesthete, aesthetic are spelt with initial *ae-* in BrE and pronounced **ees**-theet and ees-**thet**-ik. In AmE they are often spelt *esthete* and *esthetic*, and are pronounced **es**-theet and es-**thet**-ik.

affect, effect. 1 These two words are often confused. It should be remembered that *effect* is most common as a noun meaning 'a result or consequence' (*In England, at any rate, education produces no effect whatsoever*—Oscar Wilde), and that *affect* is most common as a verb meaning 'to have an effect on' (*Bodily exercise indirectly affects all the organs of the* *body | These measures chiefly affect* [i.e. are directed at] *drug-pushers | It will not affect* [i.e. have a bearing on] *his chances of promotion).* As a noun, affect survives only as a technical term in psychology. As a verb, effect means 'to bring about, cause, have as a result'.

2 *Affect* also means 'to assume (a character); to pretend to have or feel or do something, etc.' (*As he reached the pick-up point, he should affect to slow down as if hunting for a car*—John Le Carré, 1989). This is a different word although it is ultimately related to the one above.

affinity. When *affinity* implies a mutual relationship or attraction, it is normally followed by *between* or *with* (*The affinity between Britain and most of her former colonies | Beckett . . . stresses that he wrote the little book on order, not out of any deep affinity with Proust*—M. Esslin, 1980). If the feeling is one-sided, it is necessary to use other words, such as *sympathy, affection, feeling*, etc., and these are followed by *for*. *Affinity* also has technical meanings, e.g. in metallurgy.

affix is a grammatical term for word elements added at the beginnings or ends of words (e.g. *anti-, post-, re-, -able, -ness, -tion*). It is also used for elements put in the middle of words (infixes) such as Eliza Doolittle's *abso-blooming-lutely.*

afflict see INFLICT.

aftermath. The original sense in agriculture (a second or later mowing or the crop of grass which springs up after the first mowing) is 16c (along with *after-crop* and *aftergrass*) and the figura-

tive sense is 17c. In its figurative meaning, aftermath usually denotes something unpleasant or unwelcome in itself or something that follows on an unpleasant or unwelcome event (such as war or disease), but these unfavourable connotations are not present in the literal meaning. Examples: *Depression is sometimes an immediate aftermath of completing a piece of work*—A. Stoor, 1979 | *In the immediate aftermath of Wolsey's fall from power, his advisers offered him a range of options on how to obtain the annulment*—C. Durston, 1991 | *The Gulf War and its aftermath have shown the crucial need for stronger and more effective world institutions capable of upholding international law*—Liberal Democrat Publications, 1992).

afterward, afterwards. *Afterward* is restricted to North America (*Afterward, he had a long and satisfying career with the city Welfare Department*—New Yorker, 1987 | *Afterward they were enormously and finally sick of each other*—Alice Munro, 1987 (Canada)), whereas *afterwards* is the customary form in the UK, Australia, New Zealand, and South Africa, and is an optional by-form in North America.

age. There are two idiomatic uses that differ between BrE and AmE: (1) BrE has *for ages*, and AmE has *in ages* (*I haven't seen her in ages*—Jay McInerny, 1988), (2) BrE has *at the age of* . . . , and AmE has *at age* . . . (*It all started when he got diphtheria, at age eighteen*—New Yorker, 1991).

aged is pronounced as one syllable in (e.g.) *The house has aged well,* and as two syllables in (e.g.) *an aged man.*

ageing is preferable as a spelling to *aging*, although both are in use.

agenda. 1 The essential plurality of this word (= things to be done) has been worn to extinction by usage. Its dominant sense now is 'a list of items of business to be considered at a meeting, etc.' and it is often used in extended or figurative meanings (*Mrs Walton said she hadn't a spare moment. She had a busy agenda*—Beryl Bainbridge, 1975 | *There is a feeling that we have got to draw up a new agenda now*—Marxism Today, 1986). It has even produced a plural in *-as* (*Our students' ideas and agendas*—Daedalus, 1988). The singular *agendum* is purely notional, although it is occasionally used, e.g. in the context of academic bodies (*The Estates Bursar was called on to introduce Agenda Item 3. They mean Agendum 3, thought Jake*—Kingsley Amis, 1978).

2 The phrase *hidden agenda* (first recorded in 1971) has powerful and sometimes sinister connotations (*Sex was the hidden agenda at these discussions*—Margaret Atwood, 1987 | *The hidden agenda could easily appear to be that 'our drama is the least important thing in the school'*—B. Woolland, 1993).

aggravate. The meaning 'to annoy or exasperate' has existed in good sources since the early 17c; despite this, Fowler (1926) recommended that it 'should be left to the uneducated'. The dominance of the current sense has not put paid to the original meaning, 'to increase the gravity of', and the two meanings now stand side by side in a relatively unthreatening manner. Examples: (older sense) *These misfortunes were greatly aggravated by the policies of the English Government*—Winston Churchill, 1958 | (later sense) *Do not aggravate them, be quiet, smile nicely*—Peter Carey, 1982 | *Jane Fairfax aggravates her in all sorts of ways*—T. Tanner, 1986. The later meaning has given rise to a common participial adjective *aggravating* (like *annoying*): e.g. *It was aggravating that he had to do so many little jobs himself*—Mary Wesley, 1983.

aggravation. 1 The 20c has seen an increase in the harassment of appointed or elected officials and of other people in positions of authority, e.g. schoolteachers. The words most commonly used in this context is *aggravation* (first recorded in this meaning in 1939), and its colloquial equivalent is *aggro* (1969). In more recent use they have come to signify trouble or difficulty in general: *Members of the public are quite able to make their own claims assisted and guided by department officials without having these people coming in and causing aggravation*—Times, 1978 | *A certain amount of agricultural aggro is a regular part of the French way of public life*—Times, 1984 | *I am acutely conscious that I have been a source of aggravation to Pa recently over my stupid allergy to vegetables*—I. Maitland, 1993.

2 *Aggravation* is still used to mean 'making more serious or grave': e.g. *It would have been a very unnecessary aggravation of his difficulties to have two different popes in lands which he intended to unite once more*—R. W. Southern, 1990.

aggression. Note that it has two gs.

aggressive. 1 Note that it has two gs.

2 The commercial world of the 20c has added the meanings 'self-assertive; energetic, enterprising' to the word when it is applied to the techniques of marketing and salesmanship or to selling goods or services: *We are seeking an aggressive senior level manager with excellent business acumen* — advertisement in *The Times*, 1985.

aggressor. Note that it has two gs and is spelt -*or* not -*er*.

agitator is spelt -*or*, not -*er*.

ago, since. *Ago* is followed by *that*, not *since*, in constructions of the type *It is 10 years ago that* [not *since*] *he died*. *Since* is used without *ago*: e.g. *It is 10 years since he died*.

agree is used intransitively (without an object) with *about, on, to, upon*, and *with*, or with a *that*-clause, and transitively (with an object) to mean 'to arrange or settle (a thing in which various interests are concerned)'; there are examples of this transitive use in the *OED* from the 16c. In the 20c, another transitive use, equivalent to 'agree to; approve' has become common in BrE. This use is sometimes disapproved of but without any good reason, since the only difference is that one party rather than several is involved in the decision. Examples: *The tax inspector has agreed your allowances | The Russians have agreed a wide list of categories* — *Bookseller*, 1959 | *The European Commission yesterday agreed a supplementary budget for this year which would use up every single European currency unit (ECU) available to the EEC budget* — *Times*, 1983.

agreement. **1** Grammatical agreement (also called *concord*) is the correct relation to each other of different parts of a sentence, so that (for example) the form of the verb corresponds to its subject (*The house was small, and its walls were painted white*), and the gender and number (singular or plural) of a pronoun conforms to that of the person or thing it refers to (*He had never been close enough to a girl to consider making her his wife*). As English has lost many inflections over centuries of use, agreement is more closely restricted to particular aspects of sentence structure than it is in some other languages (e.g. German).

2 Lengthy sentences in which the verb is separated from its singular subject by intervening words in the plural can cause the speaker or writer to put the verb in the plural, but this is incorrect: *The consequence of long periods of inactivity or situations in which patients cannot look after themselves* ☒ *are often quite severe and long-lasting*. Here there are three options: change *consequence* to *consequences*, change *are* to *is*, or (probably best) recast the sentence more simply, e.g. *Long periods of inactivity . . . can often have quite severe and long-lasting consequences*.

In shorter sentences, the verb is also often forced out of agreement with its subject when a significant plural noun intervenes (note the mischief played by the word *of* here as elsewhere): ☒ *Copyright of Vivienne's papers are in the keeping of the Haigh-Wood family* — *Literary Review*, 1985 | ☒ *The spread of nuclear weapons and technology are likely to make the true picture very different* — *Daedalus*, 1991 | ☒ *At least one in two churches are likely to be burgled next year* — *Times*, 1992. Care should be taken to ensure proper agreement in such cases.

3 Difficulties also occur when the form of the subject is not so obviously singular or plural, for example when it is a phrase (e.g. *fish and chips* | *more than one*), when it includes an indefinite such as *each, every, any,* or *none,* when it has a parenthetic addition whose grammatical status is unclear (e.g. *My brother, together with a whole lot of his friends, . . .*), when it is a single word of doubtful number (e.g. *agenda* or *data*), or when it is a collective noun (e.g. *the government, a group of people*).

TWO NOUNS JOINED BY *AND*. These normally form a plural subject and require a plural verb: *Speed and accuracy are what is needed* | *Fish and chips are served in the evening.* But when the noun phrase is regarded as a singular unit, it can take a singular verb: *Fish and chips is my favourite meal* | *Romeo and Juliet is showing at the local cinema.* This can extend to concepts that are distinct in themselves but are regarded as a single item in a particular sentence: *A certain cynicism and resignation comes along with the poverty of Italian comedy.* The convention is very old, with evidence dating back to Old and Middle English. Clearly there will be borderline cases, and then it is what sounds natural that matters: *The hurt and disbelief of parents' friends and families is/are already quite real* | *The extent and severity of drug use in the United States has/have been a shock to the medical director.*

INDEFINITE PRONOUNS. In many cases, these (*each, either, every, everybody, neither, none, no one,* etc.) govern a singular verb, but sometimes the context calls for a plural, especially when the sense is of collectiveness rather than individuality: (singular) *Neither of these figures illuminates the case*

against Trident—David Steel, 1985 | *None of her features is particularly striking*—David Lodge, 1962 | (plural) *Neither the government nor the tribunal, surely, want to bear responsibility*—Daily Telegraph, 1987 | *None of our fundamental problems have been solved*—London Review of Books, 1987. See also EACH, EITHER, EVERY, NEITHER, NONE.

In the case of *one of those who,* the verb can be either singular or plural depending on whether *one* or *those* is regarded as the antecedent of *who:* (singular) *Perhaps you were one of those fellows who sees tricks everywhere*—Peter Carey, 1985 | *I am one of those people who wants others to do what I think they should*—Joan Bakewell, 1988 | (plural) *Lily had . . . been one of those numerous people who are simply famous for being famous* [note that *numerous* plays a part in emphasizing plurality]—Iris Murdoch, 1987 | *That's one of those propositions that become harder to sustain the further they're explored*—Kingsley Amis, 1988.

SUBJECTS WITH PARENTHETIC ADDITION. Nouns joined by other linking words or quasi-coordinators (e.g. *accompanied by, as well as, not to mention, together with,* etc.) are followed by a singular verb if the first noun or noun phrase is singular, because the addition is not regarded as part of the grammatical subject: *A very profitable company such as British Telecom, along with many other companies in the UK, is not prepared to pay a reasonable amount* | *Daddy had on the hairy tweed jacket with leather elbow patches which, together with his pipe, was his trade mark.*

WORDS LIKE *AGENDA* AND *DATA*. These are plural in form but are usually singular in sense and govern a singular verb: in *The agenda* *is on the table*, the reference is to a single item. The process can be discerned more clearly in the older word *news*, which has long been construed as a singular noun despite its plural form: *Is there any news?*. See AGENDA, DATA.

COLLECTIVE NOUNS. These are, by contrast, words such as *committee, government, group*, which are singular in form but often plural in sense. In BrE, the practice is well established of construing such words either with a singular verb (when unity or collectivity is being emphasized) or with a plural verb (when individuality or corporateness is being emphasized). Examples: (singular) *Each succeeding generation of gallery visitors finds it easier to recognize Cubist subject-matter | A group of four young men, in denim overalls, was standing close to him |* (plural) *The jury retired at five minutes past five o'clock to consider their verdict | Let us hope that the Ministry of Defence are on your side this time.* It is important to avoid a mixed style, as in � *The government has decided to postpone their decision.*

In AmE it is customary for a singular verb to be used with collective nouns: *The government routinely imposes differential taxes on hotels, bars . . . and the like—Bulletin of the American Academy,* 1987. But collective nouns of the type *a + noun + of + plural noun* can govern a singular or plural verb: *A fleet of helicopters was flying low—New Yorker,* 1986 | *A handful of bathers were bobbing about in the waves—*Philip Roth, 1987 | *A rich and detailed picture of a world in which a multitude of elements were intertwined—New York Review of Books,* 1989.

OTHER PLURAL FORMS TREATED AS SINGULAR. (1) Titles of books, plays, films, etc. (because the words 'the book etc. known as . . . ' are implicit): *Great Expectations is an account of development of identity | Star Wars has diverted some six billion dollars from the federal treasury.* (2) Names of illnesses (because the words 'the illness known as . . . ' are implicit): *Mumps often occurs in adults | Measles is normally a childhood disease.*

4 CLASH OF AGREEMENT. Sometimes there is a clash of agreement within a sentence, for example when the speaker or writer wants to express neutrality of gender, where recourse to the plural is an old device: *Everyone was in their shirt-sleeves—*F. Tuohy, 1984 | *No one in their senses wants to create instability—*Denis Healey, 1985 | *I really resent it when I call somebody who's not home and they don't have an answering machine—*Chicago Tribune, 1988 | *Each parent has a duty to do the best for their own child—*Independent, 1996.

5 SUBJECT–COMPLEMENT AGREEMENT. When a subject and a complement of different number are separated by the verb *to be* (or verbs such as *become, seem,* etc.), the verb should agree with the number of the subject: (singular) *The only traffic is ox-carts and bicycles | The problem is the windows | The view it obscured was pipes, fire escapes, a sooty-walled well |* (plural) *The socials were a big deal to her | The house and garden were a powerful cauldron of heat and light | The March events in Poland were a natural stage in the evolution of communism.* There are some exceptions, depending on the sense in particular cases: *More nurses* [i.e. the subject of more nurses] *is the next item on the agenda.*

See also COLLECTIVE NOUN, EITHER, GENDER-NEUTRALITY, MANY, NEITHER, THERE IS.

-aholic. This suffix derived from *alcoholic*, meaning 'someone addicted to alcohol' (late 19c), forms words that mean kinds of addiction, and has moved into common use in the last three or four decades, principally in *workaholic* (1968), and also in words such as *sugarholic* (1965), *golfaholic* (1971), *newsaholic* (1975), and *bookaholic* (1982), and in more fanciful and ad hoc uses such as *footballaholic* (1974) and *spend-a-holic* (1982). It has proved to a useful and productive word element, whose progress in the language is to some extent a reflection of social preoccupations.

aid. The noun dates from 1940 in its meanings 'material help given by one country to another' (*Christian aid, foreign aid, Marshall aid*, etc.), and took on a further use as the second element in the names of occasions organized to raise money for charitable causes (*Band Aid, Fashion Aid, School Aid, Live Aid*, etc.). The use was triggered by Band Aid, the name of a rock group formed by Bob Geldof in 1984 to raise money for the relief of famine in Ethiopia.

aid, aide. An *aid* is someone who helps (in various ways), whereas an *aide* denotes either of two more specific functions: (1) short for *aide-de-camp*, a high-ranking officer in the armed services (*Brigadier Monson summoned his five closest aides for a working lunch*—N. Barber, 1984), (2) a person employed as an assistant or ancillary worker, especially in a hospital or as a visitor to the home of an ill or elderly person (*Just before he died a nurse's aide brought his dinner tray into the room*—E. L. Doctorow, 1989).

Aids, the virus condition, is the most memorable acronym of the

20c; it is made from *acquired immune deficiency syndrome*. It is now normally spelt as a word, usually with a capital initial, and rarely as *AIDS*. This spelling preference has been intensified by the occurrence of several combinations such as *Aids-related* (*complex*), *Aids-free, Aids vaccine, Aids awareness*, and *pre-Aids*.

aim. The verb has two principal constructions in its abstract meaning: you can *aim at* something (analogous with aiming at a target in the physical meaning) or *at doing* something, or you can *aim to do* something (*The directive aims at ensuring open passage through the borders—Financial Times*, 1984 | *Much imagination has gone into the project, which aims to attract half a million visitors a year—Times*, 1983). The construction with *to*, for long the more common option in AmE, has excellent credentials, and is modelled on the analogy of similar verbs such as *intend, mean, plan*, etc. In the passive, however, only the *at* construction is possible (*We should aim to re-cycle half our household waste within 10 years.—Independent*, 1989 | *The summit also agreed to aim at completing an ambitious co-operation agreement with the new government —Guardian*, 1989 | *The technology in question is aimed at improving the quality of life of the inhabitants—N. Woodall, c.1991*).

ain't. 1 *Ain't* is one of the most controversial words in current English, arousing passions that one would never have dreamt of from such a seemingly inoffensive word. 'Do you hear? Don't say "ain't" or "dang" or "son of a buck" . . . You're not a pair of hicks!' scolds a mother in a *New Yorker* short story. In 1942 Eric Partridge could hardly bear to include it ('I blush to record it') in *Usage and Abusage*, and *Webster's Third New International Dictionary* of 1961 included it solely on grounds of currency, earning widespread condemnation for not castigating it more strongly. Because social disapproval is so strong, no dictionary of current English will admit it to the ranks of standard English. The reasons for this lie in the word's history.

2 *Ain't* is an undisputed element in Cockney speech, whether in Dickens (*'You seems to have a good sister.' 'She ain't half bad.'*— *Our Mutual Friend*, 1865) or in the outrageous rantings of the television character Alf Garnet. It also features widely in the language of comic strips. The *OED* notes that 'the contraction is also found as a (somewhat outmoded) upper-class colloquialism. It has also been espoused in intellectual circles as an affectation, which tends to confuse the issue (*I've not the spirit to pack up and go without him. Ain't I a craven*—Virginia Woolf, 1938 | *Still working the Cape Cod and Florida cycle. And it ain't too bad*— *Yale Alumni Magazine*).

3 The formation of *ain't* is irregular, which in part accounts for the stigma attached to it. It is an 18c word, attested earlier in the form *an't* (e.g. in Fielding). Unlike other contractions, such as *isn't*, *aren't*, and *haven't*, *ain't* is not a reduced form of any logical ancestor. Note, by the way, that *aren't* also is exceptional in being used in tag questions for *am I not* as well as *are they not*, *are you not*, and so on (*I'm coming too, aren't I?*). The logical contraction *amn't*, is not in use, presumably because it would be too awkward to articulate (and might be shortened to *an't* or *ain't?*).

4 It is unlikely that *ain't* will be admitted to standard English in the foreseeable future, if ever. For now, it stands at the door, out on the pavement, not yet part of the language household except as an affectation or in catchphrases, at best handled with tweezers and at worst regarded as the clearest single token of illiteracy.

air *verb*. In the meaning 'to broadcast', this modern use (first recorded in 1943) is frequent in AmE (*It aired a heartwarming TV commercial on the importance of savings institutions*—Wall Street Journal, 1989) but it is not often encountered in BrE (*The obligation to keep records of all programmes aired*— Economist, 1981 | *Aired over eight consecutive nights, Roots came up roses for ABC*—Time, 1977).

ait (pronounced to rhyme with *hate*), an originally Old English word for an islet on a river (especially the Thames in London), is best spelt *ait*, rather than the alternative *eyot*.

aitch see H.

à la is used in English without regard to gender, despite being feminine in French (the corresponding masculine form au is not used in this way in English). Apart from its use in phrases borrowed whole from French (e.g. *à la carte*, and cookery terms such as *à la meunière*, where *au* can of course also occur, as in *au gratin*), it is used as a semi-naturalized preposition, grammatically free though often appearing in print in Italics (*There were giant landscape photocollages à la David Hockney | The BBC should give serious consideration to an autumn shuffle à la 10 Downing Street*).

albeit (15c) is not an archaism, despite its sound and its formation on a subjunctive verb (*all be it that*); the shorter form *albe*, attested from about the same date, is now obsolete. Use with a *that*-clause was early suppressed (Chaucer) and is now largely redundant, although it is sometimes found in print. Hence it often behaves more like an adverb than a conjunction. It has an archaic ring and is often used as a quasi-archaism: *It is an unwelcome, albeit necessary, restraint*—A. Storr, 1972 | *A great line of poetry, albeit by a mendacious fascist, will outlast . . . the most sanctified of good deeds*—Times Literary Supplement, 1988.

albino has the plural form *albinos*.

alga is normally used in its plural form *algae*, pronounced **al**-jee.

alibi is properly a legal term meaning 'a plea that when an alleged act took place one was elsewhere'. The earliest use of *alibi* (18c) corresponded to that of the Latin adverb meaning 'elsewhere': those under suspicion had to prove that they were *alibi* (elsewhere). From this use it rapidly hardened into a noun: an *alibi* was 'an instance of being alibi' (*Since you think I murdered him, I had better produce my alibi*—S. Brett, 1979). In the 20c it has developed a colloquial weakened meaning 'an excuse; a plea of innocence' (*I have an alibi because I'm going to have a baby*—L. P. Hartley, 1951 | *The power-loom provided both the State and the employers with a cast iron alibi*—E. P. Thompson, 1980). This colloquial use is first recorded in American sports writing and then in detective fiction (naturally, or surprisingly, enough). The corresponding sense of 'a person providing an alibi' has followed suit (*Tom and Maureen are my alibis*—C. Hare, 1949) and there is even a verb, although its inflection is too awkward for widespread use (*She's alibi-ed by Mrs. Fitch*—J. Cannan, 1958 | *There's got to be someone to alibi us*—L. Duncan, 1978).

alien. From the 14c to the 19c inclusive, *alien* as an adjective meaning 'of nature or character different from' was followed by *from* (*This uncouth style, so alien from genuine English*—H. Reed, 1855). About the turn of the century, this construction gave way to one with *to*, by analogy with words like *adverse, repugnant,* and *opposed*, rather than *different*. The construction with *to* is now routine (*Thinking, and certainly brooding, were quite alien to his character*—J. C. Oates, 1980 | *The implied snobbery of the remark was quite alien to the whole way in which she had been brought up*—A. N. Wilson, 1982). The construction with *from* still occurs from time to time (*A reflection upon how far man has come to feel himself alien from the animal kingdom of which he is a member*—A. Storr, 1968).

all. 1 ALL OR ALL OF. *All* can be used before singular or plural nouns, and *of* is not needed except before pronouns standing alone (*all human life | all the time | all children | all tickets | all of them | all you people*). The construction with *of* is comparatively recent (first recorded c.1800) and is probably due to association with *none of, some of, little of, much of,* etc. (*He will have to be all of these things*—Anita Brookner, 1986 | *All of the company's profits had been used to salary him*—B. Ripley, 1987 | *At each stop, all of us visitors were greeted by a hail of celebratory statistics*—

New Yorker, 1989). There is also a common idiomatic use with quantities (*It must have been all of fifteen minutes of . . . dull, homesick silence*—Mark Twain, 1883 | *He was all of thirty-three, solitary and unsure of himself*—G. Graham, 1944).

2 When *all* is the subject of the verb *to be* followed by a plural complement, the linking verb is expressed in the singular: *All I saw was fields*—Nigel Williams, 1985 | *In some sense, all we have is the scores—incomplete and corrupted as they often are*—New Yorker, 1989.

3 See also ALL RIGHT, ALL THAT, ALL TOGETHER, ALL TOLD, ALREADY; for *all but* see BUT 7.

all-around is an optional AmE variant to *all-round* (*The best all-around American school | A good all-around player*).

allay has inflections *allays, allayed, allaying*.

allegedly is pronounced as four syllables.

allegory, fable, parable. 1 All three words denote a narrative or story that symbolizes other persons and events. *Allegory* flourished in medieval literature and later (Spenser's *Faerie Queene*, 1590–6; Bunyan's *Pilgrim's Progress*, 1678–84, in which the journey of the hero Christian stands for the life of the human soul; Dryden's *Absalom and Achitophel*, 1681), and allegorical elements are present in much modern writing, e.g. Virginia Woolf's *Between the Acts* (1941), which by means of a village pageant presents 'a communal image of rural England, past and present'.

2 A *parable* is a special kind of allegory, especially in the New Testament, in which a moral point is made from an everyday

story. A *fable* also makes a moral point, but is couched in terms of fictional characters who are often made to do impossible things (e.g. animals speak).

allergy dated from the early 20c in its pathological meaning 'sensitiveness to pollen, certain foods, antibiotics, etc.' It is attested earlier in German (*Allergie*) and is derived from Greek words *allos* 'other, different' and *ergon* 'work'. Its extended meaning, involving antipathy to all sorts of things, dates from the 1940s; an early instance is a famous one in Auden: *Before the Diet of Sugar he was using razor blades And excited soon after with an allergy to maidenheads*—For Time Being, 1944. *Allergic* dates in its original meaning from about the same time as *allergy*, and its extended use is recorded slightly earlier (1937 in the *OED*). In recent use, allergies and being allergic have extended to things like change, the number 13, opera on television, negotiating with terrorists, colonels (1942), scissors, and other things ranging from the sinister to the apparently harmless.

alley has the plural form *alleys*.

allot *verb* has inflected forms *allots, allotted, allotting*, but note *allotment* (one *t*).

allow. 1 This verb matches *admit* in having a wide range of common uses, transitive and intransitive, with *that*-clauses, and with an infinitive complement. For several centuries it has alternated in many meanings with the phrasal verb *allow of*; some of these meanings are now obsolete, but one has survived, presumably to avoid ambiguity with *allow* = 'permit, authorize', although it sounds old-fashioned (e.g. *Jortin is willing* *to allow of* [= accept as valid] *other miracles*—J. R. Lowell, 1849).

2 In the meanings 'to acknow-ledge, concede', *allow* followed by a clause has been in continuous use since the 17c (e.g. *I suppose it will be allowed us that marriage is a human society*—Milton, 1643 | *'You know best, Captain,' Hugh Macroon allowed with grave courtesy*—Compton Mackenzie, 1947).

3 The construction *allow as how*, meaning 'to state as an opinion, have to admit that' is restricted to AmE and dialect uses (*She allowed as how my old friend J. J. was flying on Monday morning*—N. Thornburg, 1976 | *He allowed as how she was faithful*—T. Morrison, 1981).

allowedly is pronounced as four syllables.

all right is still the preferred way of writing this common expression. The alternative form *alright*, though often found in private writing and in popular journalism and magazines, is not fully accepted, despite various arguments in its favour, especially: (1) the need to distinguish it from the use in which *all* is a pronoun and not an adverb, as in *He finished the crossword and got it all right*, (2) the analogy of *altogether, already*, etc., which similarly need to be distinguished from two-word forms having other meanings, and (3) its pronunciation as a single word. None the less, *all right* should be used for the time being, not *alright*. Examples: (all right) *One advantage of the permissive society is that it's all right to live together before marriage*—Woman's Own, 1971 | *It's all right for you . . . You won't have to do the post-mortem with these guys*—Len Deighton, 1974 | *'Oh, all right', she said, 'go and be*

damned.'—Graham Greene, 1980 | (alright) *They've been bloody inscrutable alright*—P. Cave, 1979 | *You'll be alright, love*—Chinua Achebe, 1987 | *If you've got the ears to know what sounds good you're going to be pretty much alright*—Guitarist, 1992.

all-round SEE ALL-AROUND.

all that, as in *not all that good*, is common as a colloquial intensi-fier (*I looked around the stock. It wasn't all that brilliant, I must admit*—J. Leasor, 1969). Gowers (1965) judged that the use was 'now well on its way to literary status', and it is indeed now a standard construction, though still having a whiff of the conversational about it.

all together, altogether. These are often confused, because their meanings encroach on one another. *All together* means 'everyone together', and the word *all* is usually removable without damaging the syntax or affecting the meaning: e.g. *One victim and five suspects, all together in a sealed room*—A. Morice, 1971. *Altogether* is adverbial and means 'entirely; in every way': e.g. *The idea of counselling in schools is not altogether new*—Times, 1970 | *Martinez was not altogether unknown. But the antagonism of people in Chicago is insignificant. He has another ball game in mind altogether*—Saul Bellow, 1982 | *Like Ruskin, he can at times write sentences which I would call 'woozy'; that is to say, too dependent upon some private symbolism of his own to be altogether comprehensible to others.*—W. H. Auden, 1970.

all told. This phrase, meaning 'when all are counted to included', is first recorded in 1850. Originally used in contexts that included numbers (e.g. *There are 12 all told*), it has now spread to unquantified contexts (e.g. *All told, I enjoyed life in the army*), although this is best avoided except in casual conversation.

allude, allusion. 1 To *allude* to someone or something is to mention them 'indirectly or covertly', i.e. without mentioning their name, unlike *refer*, which means to mention them directly, i.e. by name. So if you *refer* to Julius Caesar you name him, whereas if you *allude* to him you identify him without naming him, e.g. 'the Roman dictator assassinated in 44 BC'. In practice, *allude* is often used to mean 'refer' (e.g. *In his surviving works, Aristotle never mentions Alexander by name nor alludes directly to his stay in Macedonia*—R. L. Fox, 1972 | *He had star quality, an element often alluded to in Arlene's circle of show-biz friends*—Gore Vidal, 1978).

2 *Allusion* and *reference* should follow the same principle, *allusion* involving indirect mention and *reference* involving direct mention by name, but again in practice the distinction blurs at the edges (*She came across allusions to her family in the papers*—Vita Sackville-West, 1931 | *Midway in the questioning . . . he'd begun to notice the number of allusions to a particular November weekend*—Truman Capote, 1966 | *There were hints and allusions about his troubles to his friends*—D. Halberstam, 1979 | *She was . . . annoyed that he could make her feel so uncomfortable by his veiled allusion to last night*—A. Murray, 1993.

3 Beware of confusion between *allusion* and *illusion*, which means 'a deception or misapprehension about the true state of affairs'.

ally. 1 This is now normally stressed on the first syllable, both as a noun and as a verb.

2 The verb has four typical constructions: (1) transitive, (2) intransitive, (3) reflexive (*Since Siegfried alone has the strength to win the Valkyrie for Gunther, they must ally themselves with him*—A. Huth, 1985), (4) passive (*We hear she's currently allied with a very flakey anarchist guy*—John Le Carré, 1983).

3 *Allied* is used as a general adjective meaning 'relating to or belonging to allies (or Allies, usually particular ones)' (*The man . . . made his astonishing parachute jump into allied territory*—*Times*, 1970 | *The Vice President also wants to know just what allied or U.S. initiatives Europeans would welcome to get the stalemated talks . . . going once again*—*Times*, 1977).

almanac is now spelt *-ac* except in traditional titles including *The Oxford Almanack* and *Whitaker's Almanack*.

alongside. *Alongside* has been used as a preposition with or without *of* for some two centuries and both constructions are still available, although use with *of* is now often restricted to constructions with a verbal noun (*The transport Stamboul . . . was alongside the harbour wall*—D. A. Thomas, 1988 | *Alongside of preaching the Gospel . . . there are other ways in which we have to change the lives of these savages*—Christopher Hampton, 1974).

already. 1 As an adverb (*I have already paid*), *already* is spelt as one word, and is not to be confused with the two separate words *all ready* (*We are all ready to start now*).

2 *Already* is sometimes used in AmE and other varieties, and informally in BrE too, to mean 'yet, still' or even (in its weakened use) 'now', as in the following examples: *If I were a man and your ma was fifty-five already I should still be mad for her*—R.Y. Stormberg, 1920 (South Africa) | *Give me the watermelon already*—D. Greenburg, 1964, US | *I called you up but you weren't there already*—J. Platt, 1984 (South Africa)). This use is non-standard, and should be avoided except in informal contexts.

alright see ALL RIGHT.

also. 1 *Also* should be used as an adverb (*Besides being an astronomer and mathematician, Grassi was also an architect*), and not a conjunction equivalent to *and* or *as well as* (*Remember your passport and money; also the tickets* | *He has made a good impression. He writes well and keeps to deadlines. Also, he's an agreeable person*).

2 The normal position is with the verb (*It was also held to be the cause of the milder form of the illness known as AIDS-related complex*—New York Review of Books, 1986 | *Both wines also come in sweeter demi-sec version*—Which?, 1984 | *The equipment needed can be used quite legitimately . . . But it can also be used to hack into other people's computers*—Times, 1985). It is pedantic and against natural usage to insist on positioning *also* to clarify the part of the sentence it is chiefly referring to, as in *My brother also is coming* [i.e. as well as my sister], to distinguish from *My brother is also coming* [i.e. as well as telephoning]. *Too* is a far more mobile word and serves this purpose much better.

alternate, alternative. 1 Both words are adjectives and nouns and come from Latin *alternus* meaning 'every second' and have had closely related meanings over several centuries of usage. Now however, there is a clear distinction which needs to be observed. *Alternate* as an adjective means '(of two things) each following and followed by the other', as in alternate days. *Alternative* means 'available or usable instead of another', as in *an alternative solution to the problem*. In other words, *an alternative thing* replaces something else, whereas *an alternate thing* exists as well as something else. In 20c AmE, *alternate*, with stress on the first syllable, has usurped the territory of *alternative* in its ordinary meaning (*An alternate way to make these rellenos is to stuff the meat mixture into whole green chiles*—San Diego Union, 1987).

2 Since the late 1960s the adjective has increasingly been used to mean 'purporting or claiming to represent an acceptable or preferable alternative to that in traditional use', as in *alternative medicine* (mainly homoeopathic or holistic), *alternative energy* (non-nuclear and not using fossil fuels), *alternative fuel* (and *alternative-fuel vehicles*, AFVs), *alternative birthing* (avoiding artificial methods), *alternative society* (rejecting traditional values), *alternative technology* (conserving resources), *alternative theatre* (using non-traditional techniques).

3 *Alternative* as a noun means something that is available or usable instead of something else. The traditional view that an *alternative* must be one of two possibilities, because the source word, Latin *alter*, means 'other of two' is not sustainable, and alternative has been regularly used since the mid-19c with reference to any number of possibilities (*Mr. George Bush, the U.S. Vice-President, last night confirmed Washington's willingness to consider alternatives to its zero option proposals for banning intermediate range nuclear missiles from Europe—Financial Times*, 1983 | *The aim of counselling is to open up the personal world of experience in which the person feels 'stuck' so that he or she may find alternative ways of coping with the world of events which confronts him or her—Counselling*, 1983). The traditional use is still found, and lies at the heart of the word, most often as *the alternative* (*The alternative of 'public limited company' is the abbreviation 'p.l.c.'—Companies Act*, 1980).

4 *Alternate* as a noun is much less common. In AmE it is often used with the meaning 'an alternative', a reserve (player), a variant (*I was fourth alternate in the Miss Teenage South Carolina pageant*—William Boyd, 1984 | *The twelve jurors and six alternates in Room 318 of the United States Courthouse—New Yorker*, 1986). In BrE this meaning is not found, although it is related to one that was in use in the 18c.

5 *Alternate* is also a verb (pronounced -neit in the final syllable), meaning '(of two or more things) to succeed one another in turns': *In a democratic system political parties expect to alternate in office*—P. Richards, 1988.

although, though.
Though can always be used instead of *although*, but the same is not true the other way round.

1 Both words can be used as a conjunction introducing a subordinate clause (*He did well, although he did not win an outright majority—Economist*, 1981 | *Though there was a tendency for students to factionalize, there were always students good

about diplomacy—Christian Science Monitor*, 1982 | *Although the defendant had undoubtedly committed an offence of failing to give full particulars, that was not an arrestable offence—Times*, 1984). Where they are interchangeable, however, *although* generally has a stronger concessive force, and is somewhat more usual in initial position in a sentence.

2 In the following uses, *though* alone is possible: (1) as an adverb in medial or final position (*It is true though that one misses out on one's husband's early years of struggle—Times*, 1985), (2) in inverted constructions (*Young though he is, he doesn't look it*), (3) in the fixed expressions *as though* and *even though* (*Anderson is a borderline New Waver who looks as though she has been out in the rain upside down—Washington Post*, 1982 | *He was by no means a dry, boring theoretician even though he wrote extraordinarily advanced books on dance*—Margot Fonteyn, 1980).

alto
has the plural form *altos*.

altogether
see ALL TOGETHER.

aluminium.
The BrE spelling accords well with other element names such as magnesium, potassium, sodium, etc., whereas the AmE spelling *aluminum* (stressed on the second syllable) is the one adopted by its discoverer, Sir H. Davy, in about 1812.

alumnus
(stressed on the second syllable) means a former student or pupil, and comes from a Latin word meaning 'nursling'. It is more common in AmE than in BrE. The plural form is *alumni* (pronounced -niy) and the female form is *alumna* (plural *alumnae*, pronounced -nee). Rival views on

the pronunciation of Latin words in English mean that the masculine and feminine pronunciations are sometimes reversed.

a.m. As an abbreviation of Latin *ante meridiem* 'before noon', *a.m.* is pronounced as two letters and written in the form *8.15 a.m.* (or *am*; in AmE *8:15 a.m.*). Note that *12.00 a.m.* is midnight and *12 p.m.* is midday; because of the uncertainty these designations cause, the explicit forms *12.00 midnight* or *12.00 midday* are often to be preferred. The abbreviation is sometimes used informally as a noun: *I arrived here this a.m.*

amateur. The standard pronunciation is now **am**-ə-tə.

ambidextrous. Note the spelling *-trous*, not *-terous*.

ambience, meaning 'surroundings, atmosphere', is derived from French *ambiance* (a form which is also occasionally used in English). It is firmly established in the language after a century or so of use. Both spellings are in use, although *ambiance* differs in having a non-naturalized nasal pronunciation of the final syllable. The corresponding adjective *ambient* has developed a special meaning relating to instrumental electronic 'New Age' music: *Ambient music looks to have a future in this country as the official artform of the cyberpunks—Face*, 1995.

ambiguity. 1 *Ambiguity* in language denotes the possibility of more than one meaning being understood from what is heard or read. Intentional ambiguity can be effective, for example as a literary device or in advertising. Our concern here is with unintentional and misleading ambiguity that occurs in ordinary speech

and writing, most often as a result of poor word order. The Fowlers (1906) devoted several pages to ambiguities of this kind, but their (mostly literary) examples now seem contrived and unreal, as do many of the examples given in grammar books.

2 Typical ambiguities in everyday language usually involve the association of a word or phrase with the wrong part of the sentence (*The council plans to notify parents whose children are affected by post*, where *by post* should be placed after *parents*), or the unclear application of a negative (*They did not go out to water the plants*, which can mean either they did not go out at all, or they did go out but not to water the plants; similarly with the type *We did not go to the shops because we were expecting visitors*: see BECAUSE 2).

3 Ambiguity also arises from words that have more than one meaning or function, as in *Visiting friends can be tiresome* | the famous line *The peasants are revolting* | *The Minister appealed to her supporters*, and from false or unclear reference, as in *If the children don't like their toys, get rid of them* | *We only have two first editions* (and no other books?).

In speech, ambiguity is nearly always eliminated by intonation; in writing, attention to these relatively few problem areas will be enough to avoid the ambiguities that matter.

ambivalent, ambiguous. The terms *ambivalent* and *ambivalence* are first recorded in about 1916 in the context of psychology, and in particular the Jungian notion of 'the coexistence in one person of contradictory emotions or attitudes towards a person or thing'

(*OED*). C. S. Lewis distanced himself somewhat from using *ambivalent* when he said that 'Death is . . . what some modern people would call "ambivalent". It is Satan's great weapon and God's great weapon'. *Ambivalent* applies to feelings and attitudes, whereas *ambiguous* refers to more concrete things such as statements and events and their meanings: (ambivalent) *This sad state of affairs may be attributed to feckless parents or to a society which projects its standards and values in such an ambivalent way*—H. Pluckrose, 1987 | *Women can be extremely ambivalent about their own ambition and aggression at work*—She, 1989 | *Examination of what is entailed and what is expected have produced ambivalent conclusions*—State of Prisons, 1991.

Ambivalently is also found, often where *ambiguously* would be more suitable: e.g. *The people who inhabit Gormenghast, ambivalently described as 'figures' and 'shapes', are poised between the two meanings*—M. H. Short et al., 1987.

amen is pronounced both **ah**-men and **ay**-men.

amend, emend. **1** *Amend* is the more common word, used of making adjustments to a document or formal proposal (such as a parliamentary act), and also as a special word for 'to change' or 'to alter' in the context of personal behaviour. Its etymological meaning is 'free from fault' (from Latin *mendum* or *menda* 'fault, blemish'), and there is always a notion of correction or improvement in its meaning.

2 *Emend* and *emendation* are used mainly to refer to the activity of textual scholars in proposing changes in the reading of texts and manuscripts so as to make them more intelligible or remove errors.

America. To English speakers outside North America, the term *America* means first and foremost the USA, and *North America* is used to denote a larger geographical area including also Canada and Mexico. The terms *American* and *North American* are used correspondingly as adjectives and nouns. *Central America* refers to the countries in the narrow strip of land to the south of Mexico (including Guatemala, Nicaragua, and Panama), and *South America* to the region to the south of the Panama Canal, including Argentina, Brazil, Chile, Colombia, etc.

American English.
See box overleaf

American Indian, as a term for an aboriginal inhabitant of North America and parts of the Caribbean, is less offensive than *Red Indian*, but *Native American* (see NATIVE) is even more acceptable. *Indian* is an ethnically erroneous name which is due to a mistaken identification of the area by European explorers in the 15c and 16c.

amid, amidst. *Amid*, recorded as a preposition and adverb before the Norman Conquest, developed two by-forms, *amides* (cf. *always*) and *amidst* (cf. *against, amongst*). *Amides* has dropped out of use, and *amid* and *amidst* have survived only as prepositions. In the 1880s the *OED* noted that 'there is a tendency to use *amidst* more distributively than *amid*, e.g. of things scattered about, or a thing moving, in the midst of others'. It is difficult to discern this distinction maintained in current use. Both words have an air of formality, especially *amidst*, which

American English

1 GENERAL. Fowler in *Modern English Usage* (1926) did not include an entry on American English and said little on the subject, although he cast occasional aspersions on so-called 'undesirable aliens' (such as *belittle*). Since then attitudes to American English have hardened, and the prevailing view among some who seek (or claim) to preserve standards in English is often hostile. However, it is linguistically misconceived and historically unjustified to regard the American influence on English as necessarily harmful; both varieties have been enriched by contact with each other and with other varieties, including Australian English and South African English. It should also be remembered that Canadian English (influenced by French) is a valid variety, and the boundaries between the Englishes of Canada and the USA are becoming much harder to draw precisely.

American English differs from British English in several important ways, in matters of vocabulary, spelling and inflection, idiom, grammar, pronunciation, and punctuation. Some of the more significant differences are due to uses that disappeared in BrE but survived in AmE (such as the use of *gotten* as a past participle of *get*, and the use of *theater* and other spellings in *-er*), and others are due to developments in AmE after it went its own way.

2 VOCABULARY. AmE has long been a copious source of new vocabulary in BrE, and many items are now used with little or no awareness of their origin (e.g. *belittle, commuter, OK, to snoop, to fly off the handle*). Recently imported Americanisms tend to cause the most disapproval (e.g. the sentence adverb *hopefully*, verbal forms of nouns such as *hospitalize*, cultural 'media' terms such as *gameshow*, phrase-based words such as *downsizing* and *ongoing*, and slang vocabulary such as *cop-out* and *hacking*), and whole areas of vocabulary development such as the political correctness movement (which has given us *intellectually challenged, vertically challenged*, and other euphemisms in which a 'positive' word *challenged* has replaced a 'negative' word *handicapped*). There are significant loans in the other direction: *central heating, gay* (meaning homosexual), *miniskirt*, and *kiss of life* are all British in origin and are now widely used in North America. Some terms are known only on one side of the Atlantic because the institutions they denote are confined to one side, e.g. *duplex* (in the US) and *giro* (in the UK). The table shows some of the more important differences of core vocabulary between the two varieties.

BRITISH	AMERICAN
aeroplane	airplane
aluminium	aluminum
aubergine	eggplant

▶

▶ American English

continued

BRITISH *CONTINUED*	AMERICAN *CONTINUED*
autumn	fall
banknote	bill
biscuit (dry)	cracker
biscuit (sweet)	cookie
bonnet (of car)	hood
braces	suspenders
brooch	pin
bumper (of car)	fender
chemist's	drugstore
chips (food)	French fries
cinema	movie theater
coffin	casket
courgettes	zucchini
crisps	potato chips
curtains	drapes
drawing pin	thumbtack
driving licence	driver's license
dustbin	garbage can
estate agent	realtor
first floor	second floor
flat	apartment
frying pan	skillet
ground floor	first floor
handbag	purse
icing	frosting
kerb	curb
lavatory	washroom
lift	elevator
lorry	truck
main road	highway
motorway	expressway
nappy	diaper
pavement	sidewalk
petrol	gasoline or gas
potato chips	French fries
pram	baby carriage
queue	line
railway	railroad
rise (in salary)	raise
roundabout (in road system)	rotary
rowing-boat	rowboat
rubbish (domestic)	trash
shoelace	shoestring

▶

▶ American English
continued

BRITISH *CONTINUED*   AMERICAN *CONTINUED*

BRITISH *CONTINUED*	AMERICAN *CONTINUED*
sweets	candy
tap (for water)	faucet
tart	pie
traffic jam	gridlock
tram	streetcar
trolley (at supermarket or airport)	cart
trousers	pants
underground	subway
undertaker	mortician
veranda	porch
vest	undershirt
waistcoat	vest
wallet	billfold
windscreen	windshield
zip	zipper

3 SPELLING AND INFLECTION. Some spelling differences concern particular words and are not applied systematically (e.g. AmE *aluminum, maneuver, pajamas*); these need to be verified in a dictionary that records both spellings (such as the *Concise Oxford Dictionary*). The principal systematic differences in BrE and AmE spelling are:
▶ **a** Simplification of the digraph vowels *-ae-* and *-oe-* to *-e-* (as in *ameba* and *estrogen*; but initial *ae-*, as in *aesthetic*, still tends to dominate in AmE as well as BrE). This is beginning to make an impact on British spelling, for example *encyclopedia* (much deprecated largely on grounds of intellectual snobbery). See also FOETUS.
▶ **b** Use of *-ense* instead of *-ence* as a noun ending (as in *defense* and *pretense*; see also LICENCE).
▶ **c** Use of *-er* instead of *-re* as a noun ending in many words (as in *center* and *theater*); but note *acre, massacre, mediocre,* and *ogre* in both varieties.
▶ **d** Use of *-or* instead of *-our* as a noun ending (as in *color* and *harbor*).
▶ **e** Reduction of *-ou-* to *-o-* (as in *mold*).
▶ **f** Use of *-l-* instead of *-ll-* in verbal inflection (as in *instal, rivaled, traveler*) and converse use of *-ll-* instead of *-l-* (as in *installment, skillful*).
▶ **g** Suppression of a final mute *-e* in inflection (as in *milage* and *salable*), but not after a soft *c* or *g* (as in *changeable*).
▶ **h** Reduction of final *-ogue* to *-og* (as in *analog* and *catalog*).
▶ **i** Exclusive use of *-ize* instead of *-ise* in verbs that allow both spellings in BrE, and variant use of *-ize* in verbs that are only spelt *-ise* in BrE (as in *civilize, privatize,* and *advertize*).

▶

▶ **American English**
continued

▶ **j** Use of *-z-* occasionally instead of *-s-* (as in *analyze* and *cozy*).

4 IDIOM. There are occasional differences in shared idioms. Examples are: BrE *man on the street* | AmE *man in the street* | BrE *a new lease of life* | AmE *a new lease on life* | BrE *leave well alone* | AmE *leave well enough alone*.

5 GRAMMAR. Most of the more important grammatical differences concern use of auxiliary and modal verbs (*do, have, shall, will*, and others such as *dare*):

▶ **a** AmE favours the type *Did you go?* rather than *Have you been?*, *I don't have* rather than *I haven't got*, *They just left* rather than *They've just left*, *I didn't use* (or *used*) *to* rather than *I used not to*, and *Let's not* rather than *Don't let's* (as in *Let's not argue*). These preferences are also found to a lesser degree in BrE.

▶ **b** Some BrE constructions are not available in AmE, e.g. BrE *We weren't to know* (BrE/AmE *We couldn't know* or *couldn't have known*), BrE *meant to* (= BrE/AmE *supposed to*) as in *The food here is meant to be very good*.

▶ **c** There are differences in the way prepositions are used. For example, AmE has *out the window* and *off of the floor* where BrE has *out of the window* and *off the floor*.

▶ **d** AmE has retained *gotten*, an older form of the past participle of *get* which has fallen out of use in BrE. It is used in AmE as well as got. See GOTTEN.

▶ **e** AmE differs in the use of *shall* and *should*: see SHALL AND WILL, SHOULD AND WOULD.

▶ **f** For differences in the use of *dare* and *need*, see DARE, NEED.

▶ **g** See also MAY, MIGHT; OUGHT.

6 PRONUNCIATION. As with spelling, there are particular differences and systematic differences. Examples of the first are *schedule* (sk- in AmE, sh- in BrE) and *tomato* (tə-**may**-toh in AmE, tə-**mah**-toh in BrE). It is beyond the scope of this book to explore the pronunciation systems of both varieties in detail, but a few special differences might be mentioned:

▶ **a** The letter *r* is pronounced or partly pronounced when it occurs in the middle of a word whether or not it is followed by a vowel, whereas typically it is not in BrE received pronunciation, as in *hard* and *rare*.

▶ **b** The vowel *a* is pronounced a as in *had*, not ah as in *hard* in words such as *after, can't, dance*, and *path*.

▶ **c** Pronunciation of short o as in *box* is closer to ah as in *barks*.

▶ **d** Pronunciation of yoo as in *tube* is closer to oo as in *boob*.

▶

▶ American English
continued

▶**e** Pronunciation of *er* in words such as *clerk* rhymes with *murk*, not with *mark* as in BrE.

▶**f** Pronunciation of final syllables in *-ile* (as in *fertile* and *hostile*) is -əl, not -iyl as in BrE.

▶**g** Pronunciation of *t* following *n* and followed by an unstressed syllable is much less marked in AmE than in BrE (as in *mental* and *twenty*).

7 PUNCTUATION. American practice differs in the use of quotation marks and associated punctuation (see QUOTATION MARKS) and uses a different style in dates (see DATES). Other points are noted in individual entries on punctuation marks.

is much less common (496 examples in the 100m-word British National Corpus as opposed to 1,096 of *amid*). Typical examples: (amid) *I . . . have often stood by the Frome at Woolbridge, enjoying the mellow manor house amid its water-meadows*—Times, 1987 | *'We shall enjoy strong, sustained growth and prosperity into the 1980s,' he said amid Conservative cheers*—Daily Telegraph, 1989 | (amidst) *He returned here for more tests amidst rumours that he had Parkinson's disease*—Washington Post, 1984 | *This woman, sitting with such modest dignity amidst my students and colleagues*—Michael Frayn, 1989. In general use, *amid* and *amidst* have tended to be replaced by *among* or *in the midst of*.

amoeba is the customary UK spelling (US *ameba*). The plural is *amoebas* (US *amebas*); *amoebae* is only used in technical contexts.

amok, amuck. The word is normally used in the phrase *to run amok/amuck*, meaning 'to run about wildly in a violent rage', and is an extension of a particu-

lar meaning in Malay anthropology (*Edward now wore the manic look of some animal transferred into the wrong environment, as though he might run amok, or bite*—Penelope Lively, 1990). It also has figurative uses not involving physical action (*With Thatcher running amok through the welfare state, lobby groups are preoccupied defending what was once thought unassailable*—New Scientist, 1991 | *It wasn't his fault that her feelings seemed to be running amok*—E. Rees, 1992). The spelling *amok*, which is closer to the original Malay *amoq* meaning 'attacking in frenzy', is more common and preferable.

among, amongst. 1 *Among* is now much more common (22,864 in the 100m-word British National corpus as opposed to 4,552 of *amongst*). It is the oldest form, which gave rise to the by-forms *amonges* (14c, no longer in use) and *among(e)st* (16c). There is no demonstrable difference of meaning between the two forms, and the distribution is unclear except that *amongst* seems to be less common in AmE than in BrE. An older view, which Fowler (1926) followed, that *amongst* is commoner before a word beginning with a vowel, is not borne out by the evidence. Examples: (among) *The giants war among themselves*—J. M. Coetzee, 1977 | *There were a lot of young people among the temporary staff*—Penelope Fitzgerald, 1980 | *Britain also has the lowest level of welfare expenditure among the countries of the European Community*—*Times*, 1985 | (amongst) *They fight amongst themselves*—W. Wharton, 1978 | *He was grateful to the Kabbels . . . for taking account of her amongst their berserk schemes*—Thomas Keneally, 1985 | *They stood on the edges of the lamplight amongst the wattles by the creek*—Peter Carey, 1988.

   2 *Among* is much more often used than *amongst* in the expression *among other things*. This expression is strictly illogical, since *among* is inclusive and *other* is exclusive, but it is well established and usually causes no adverse comment. Perhaps it gets by on the coat-tails of the Latin equivalent *inter alia*, also self-contradictory but which few would venture to challenge.

   3 For choice of *among* and *between*, see BETWEEN 2.

amoral see IMMORAL.

amount, number. *Amount* is normally used with uncountable nouns (i.e. nouns which have no plural) to mean 'quantity' (e.g. a *reasonable amount* of *forgiveness, glue, resistance, straw*, etc.), and *number* with plural nouns (e.g. a *certain number of boys, houses, jobs*, etc.). *Amount*, however, is fast breaking into the territory of *number*, especially when the following plural noun is regarded as an aggregate or collection. Ex-

amples: *Fame had magnified the amount of the forces*—1849 in *OED* | *I have any amount of letters for you*—George Bernard Shaw, 1893 | *I expect you get a fair amount of road accidents on these winding roads*—Rachel Billington, 1988 | *Billy's had a tremendous amount of problems*—T. McGuane, 1989 (US) | *Booksellers have less and less space for the amount of books that are being published*—*The Author*, 1990 | *The amount of bulbs she would find between the stones next spring*—A. Huth, 1991. Note that *quantity* can be used with all types of nouns (*a large quantity of parcels* | *a small quantity of sugar*).

ampersand is the name of the symbol & used as a short form of 'and'. It was used extensively by H. W. Fowler, both in print and in writing, and is most common in handwritten work, although the more cursive plus sign + is tending to oust it. It also occurs frequently, often for stylistic purposes, in company names, as in *Marks & Spencer*. The word itself is a contraction of '& per se (= by itself) and', which was the way that printers once referred to the character; the form of the symbol is perhaps a stylized version of Latin et 'and'.

ample. Fowler (1926) wrote that *ample* was 'legitimate only with nouns denoting immaterial or abstract things' such as *opportunity, praise, provision*, and *time*. He did not accept that it could be properly used in attributive position before nouns like *butter, coal, oil*, and *water* that denote substances of indefinite quantity, although it was acceptable to place it predicatively with such words, as in *The coal is ample*. The logic was uncharacteristically opaque, and the argument untenable. Although *ample* is still most often used with words such as *evidence, opportunity, provision, scope, time, warning,* etc., there is ample evidence of its use with material substances: *It was also to be a station for the motor-car age, situated on ample land with large car-parks*—J. Richards et al., 1988 | *The River Lea forming the eastern boundary of the metropolis provided good communication, ample supplies of water, and motive power for the mills*—J. Marriott, 1991 | *For anyone else this might have seemed ample funds for an expedition*—I. Tree, 1991.

amuck see AMOK.

an (indefinite article) see A, AN.

anaemia, anaemic are spelt *-ae-* in BrE and *-e-* or *-ae-* in AmE.

anaesthetic is spelt *-ae-* in BrE and *-e-* in AmE.

analogous is pronounced with a hard *g*. It should not be used as a general synonym of *similar*, but of comparisons involving analogy, i.e. identifiable characteristics or procedures in common. In practice it is most often used in technical contexts: *The transmission electron microscope is analogous to a conventional light microscope*—*Scientific American*, 1971.

analogy. 1 In language *analogy* is the process by which the use of words follows precedents set by other words without going through all the stages that produced those precedents. This is a fundamental aspect of the way languages develop, and applies to all aspects of usage, including word-formation, spelling, inflection, meaning, collocation, and pronunciation. For example, the noun *starvation* (18c) was formed on the analogy of other words

such as *vexation* (15c); the dialect and AmE past form *dove* (from *dive*) was formed on the analogy of *strove* (from *strive*); the pronunciation of *controversy* on the first or second syllable is by analogy with types represented respectively by *matrimony* and *monotony*. The formation *seascape* (and later *skyscape* and *waterscape*) was modelled on *landscape*, *workaholic* on *alcoholic*, and *sexist* (and later *ageist* and others) on *racist*; and the use of the phrase *annus horribilis* ('dreadful year') by Queen Elizabeth II with reference to 1992 was a powerful extension of the existing phrase *annus mirabilis* ('wonderful year').

2 Sometimes false analogies come into play, leading to uses that either appear erroneous (as sometimes in the speech of children) or prevail despite the falseness of the analogy (as with *alright*, modelled on *altogether*). More often, the role of analogy is overlooked by those who criticize aspects of usage (such as the sentence adverb *hopefully*) in isolation.

analyse is spelt *-yse* in BrE and *-yze* in AmE.

analysis has the plural form *analyses* (pronounced *-seez*).

anathema. 1 The meaning has changed over several centuries of use. Originally a Greek word meaning 'a thing dedicated' it then came to mean 'a thing dedicated to evil; an accursed thing' and then, in the context of the Christian Church, 'the act or formula of consigning to damnation', in which use it is still found with historical reference; the plural is anathemas (e.g. *The pope had ended the Council with two final anathemas which were intim-*

ately connected with Anselm's situation—R. W. Southern, 1990).

2 Its use as a quasi-adjective meaning 'accursed' and in weakened senses 'intolerable', often followed by to, dates from the 18c: *The policy they embraced was however anathema to many Conservatives, who rightly saw in it the beginning of the end of British rule in India*—Roy Jenkins, 1988 | *This leads very quickly to the 'hoping something turns up' syndrome which is anathema to most managers*—J. Harvey-Jones, 1988 | *One proposal by itself was anathema; the two together were poison*—A. Goodman, 1993.

and. 1 The simplest-looking words are often among the most complicated in use, and *and* is no exception. The normal function of *and* is to join words, phrases, and sentences: *John and Mary are brother and sister* | *They dealt with the matter quickly and efficiently* | *an acute and wary sense of the ordinary.* In some cases it links parallel words that form a fixed expression that cannot normally be reversed (*fish and chips,* ⊠ *chips and fish; first and foremost,* ⊠ *foremost and first; Romeo and Juliet,* ⊠ *Juliet and Romeo*).

2 For guidance on grammatical agreement in sentences with subjects containing and (e.g. *Fish and chips is/are my favourite meal*), see AGREEMENT.

3 *And* is often omitted for contextual effects of various kinds, especially between sequences of descriptive adjectives which can be separated by commas or simply by spaces (*The teeming jerry-built dun-coloured traffic-ridden deafening city*—Penelope Lively, 1987).

4 There is a persistent belief that it is wrong to begin a sentence with And, but the practice will be found in literature from Anglo-Saxon times onwards, especially as an aid to continuity in narrative and dialogue. The *OED* provides examples from the 9c to the 19c, including one from Shakespeare's *King John: Arthur. Must you with hot Irons, burne out both mine eyes? Hubert. Young boy, I must. Arthur. And will you? Hubert. And I will.* It is also used for other rhetorical purposes, especially to denote surprise (*O John! and you have seen him! And are you really going?*—1884 in *OED*) and sometimes just to introduce an improvised afterthought (*I'm going to swim. And don't you dare watch*—G. Butler, 1983). It is however poor style to separate short statements into separate sentences when no special effect is needed: *I opened the door and I looked into the room* | ⊠ *I opened the door. And I looked into the room.*

5 *And all* is a well-established tag added to the end of a statement, as in *Isn't it amazing? He has a Ph.D. and all*—J. Shute, 1992. With the nominal meaning 'also, besides, in addition', the use has origins in dialect, as can be seen from the material from many regions given in the *English Dialect Dictionary* (often written in special ways, e.g. *ano', an'-all, an' a'*). In many of the examples it seems to lack any perceptible lexical meaning and to be just a rhythmical device to eke out a sentence.

6 *And also* has special uses, to show progression (*faster and faster*), cause and effect (*do that and I'll send you to bed*), duration (*they ran and ran*), a large number or quantity (*miles and miles*), and addition (*four and four are eight*), purpose (where *and* replaces *to: Try and come tomorrow*). See also TRY AND.

7 Another special use, recorded in the *OED* from the 16c, is to express 'a difference of quality between things of the same name or class', as in W. S. Gilbert's lines from the Gondoliers (1889): *Well, as to that, of course there are kings and kings. When I say I detest kings I mean I detest bad kings.* To this we may add some modern examples: *There are ways to steal and there are ways to steal—New Yorker*, 1988 | *There is homelessness and homelessness. The word has become a shibboleth for opposition politicians and the 'caring' media . . . The sort of homelessness which means despair is quite different from the sort that means adventure—Times*, 1991.

and/or is a formula indicating that the items connected by it can be taken either together or as alternatives. Its principal uses are in legal and other formal documents, but in general use it is often inelegant: *The Press has rather plumped for the scholar as writer, and/or as bibliophile—Cambridge Review*, 1959. A more comfortable way of expressing the same idea is to use 'X or Y or both', and in some cases 'or' by itself will do.

anemone. Note that the sequence of consonants is *n-m-n*, not (as is sometimes heard) *n-n-m*. The words comes from Greek *anemos* 'wind' and is therefore akin to the English word *animated* and related words.

angle *noun.* This word had been used since the 1870s in the meaning 'the aspect from which a matter is considered' (*The old stagers . . . the men who knew all the angles, who had great experience—Nevil Shute*, 1944), often with a defining word: the *OED* gives examples of statistical angles, selling angles,

and propaganda angles. Examples: *For US television . . . competition for the same audience within the same time-slot drives producers and planners to look for the new exploitation angle which will differentiate their product within the market—Screen*, 1991 | *He is always on the alert for a new angle, always individual in expression—Art Newspaper*, 1992. In more formal English, *standpoint* is a better word to use.

angle *verb.* **1** This is a more specific word for 'to fish' and means 'fish with a hook and line'. In ordinary use *fish* is the normal word: you would say *I am going fishing tomorrow* even if *angling* were technically correct.

2 The verb in its meaning 'seek an objective by devious or calculated means' (*She . . . did angle for mee, Madding my eagernesse with her restraint—Shakespeare, All's Well* v.iii.212) is a figurative use of this word, and has no connection with the word described in the preceding entry, apart from occasional contextual overlaps. It is usually followed by *for*: *Ralph had begun to angle for an invitation by reminiscing about the joys of the traditional family Christmas—A. Taylor*, 1992.

Anglo-. People in Scotland and Wales understandably view this combining form (as in *Anglo-French, Anglo-Irish*, etc.) with some distaste, but it continues to be used as the standard term. The alternative term *Brito-* has not acquired any general currency, and is restricted to certain special cases, e.g. *Brito-Arctic* (relating to British territory in the Arctic) and *Britocentric* and related words.

annex, annexe. In BrE the verb is *annex* and the noun *annexe*; in

AmE the noun is usually also spelt *annex*.

anniversaries. The normal practice is to refer to the 10th, 20th, 30th, etc. anniversary of an event, but special names have come to be associated with the more significant anniversaries. The principal names for wedding anniversaries are *silver* (25 years), *ruby* (40), *golden* (50), and *diamond* (60, sometimes 75). For public events the following terms are used: *centenary* or (AmE) *centennial* (100), *sesquicentenary* (150 years), *bicentenary* (200), *tercentenary* (300), *quatercentenary* (400: NB not *quarter*-), *quincentenary* (500), *sexcentenary* (600), *septcentenary* (700), *octocentenary* (800), *millenary* (1,000). In AmE, the compounds end in -*centennial* rather than -*centenary*. See CENTENARY.

announcer is first recorded in 1922 to mean a broadcaster who announces programmes or reads the news. The term has given way to some more specific terms: *anchorman* (1958), *anchorperson* (1973), *host*, *newscaster* (1930) or *newsreader* (1925), and *presenter* (1967).

annual see PERENNIAL.

annul is spelt with one *l*, and has inflected forms *annulled*, *annulling*. The corresponding noun is *annulment*.

anorak, a word of Greenland Eskimo origin, has taken on a new meaning from its association with people waiting around in cold weather (in anoraks, supposedly) to watch trains and aeroplanes or do other things the rest of the world can sneer at. Hence an *anorak* is 'a boring, studious, or socially inept person with unfashionable and solitary inter-

ests'. Its most common application is in the field of computing, as one might expect: *'Cyberspace' is no longer the preserve of techno-nerds and anoraks— Guardian*, 1994. Derivatives like *anorakish* and *anoraksia* are on the way.

anorexic, anorectic. Both words, adjectives derived from *anorexia* meaning 'obsessive loss of appetite', are in use. In general use, *anorexic* is now more common, and is used absolutely as a quasi-noun. Examples: *He became listless, anorexic, and increasingly sleepy, refusing to eat or crawl— Lancet*, 1961 | *Contrary to the popular image of the disturbed teenager, the anorexic is not typically a product of a 'broken home'*—S. Macleod, 1989 | *Do they think I'm anorexic, or just plain thin?*—J. Dawson, 1990.

another. For *one another* see EACH 3.

antagonize. 1 -*ize* is the preferred spelling, although -*ise* is common.

2 The dominant sense now is 'to evoke hostility or opposition or enmity in': *Not wishing to antagonise the Colonel or his Officers, I suggested a compromise*—B. Millim, 1991. Its earlier meaning 'to contend with, oppose' is not recorded in the *Concise Oxford Dictionary* (1995), although its technical meaning '(of one force etc.) to counteract or tend to neutralize (another)' is recorded. When the letter A of the *OED* was being written, the current meaning was new, and it gave only a single quotation of 1882. The technical meaning is still used, although it is hardly familiar: *Our first object must be to antagonize the poison and at the same time uphold his powers*—J. G. Farrell, 1973.

ante-, anti-. **1** These two prefixes need to be distinguished, if
only to ensure correct spelling.
The first means 'before, preceding' and forms words such as
antenatal ('before birth') and
antechamber ('a room leading to
another'). The second, which is
much more common, means 'opposite, opposed to, against', and
forms words such as anti-aircraft,
anti-American, and anti-hero ('the
opposite of a hero').

2 The *OED* points out that the
model for all these words is *Anti-
christ* and its derivative *antichris-
tian*, which along with antipope
were the only examples in use before 1600. There are no *anti-* combinations in Shakespeare.

antenna has the plural form *antennae* (relating to the sensory organs of insects) and *antennas*
(relating to radio aerials).

anterior, meaning 'before (in
time or place)', is followed by *to*,
not *than* (*There is a certain paradoxical logic to thinking of writing as anterior to speech*—Paragraph, 1986).

anticipate. **1** Here lies another
of the great usage battlegrounds,
where the conflict is all the more
fraught for overlapping meanings
that confuse the issue. The two
primary and undisputed meanings are (1) to be aware of (a
thing) in advance and act accordingly (e.g. *Lecky has anticipated
what the animal liberationists are
now saying*—Listener, 1983) and (2)
to forestall (a person) and take action before they do (e.g. *I'm
sorry—do go on, I did not mean to
anticipate you*—John Le Carré).

2 Fowler scornfully rejected a
third meaning, to expect or fore-
see (e.g. *Wing mirrors were selling
better than they had ever
anticipated*—Margaret Drabble, 1987 |

*They have every right to be there,
and we do not anticipate any change
in that status*—USA Today, 1988 | *One
would not expect Cleopatra to have
suffered such a fate, nor did she herself anticipate it*—A. Fraser, 1988).
This meaning is classed as 'disputed' in the *Concise Oxford Dictionary* (1995) and is placed
second, although it might now
reasonably be placed first on currency grounds, because it is comfortably the dominant sense.

3 Both *expect* and *anticipate* (in
this meaning) can be constructed
with a *that*-clause, but only *expect*
can be constructed with *to* (*I ex-
pect to arrive tomorrow* | ☒ *I antici-
pate to arrive tomorrow*).

antisocial see UNSOCIABLE, UN-
SOCIAL.

anxious. *Anxiety*, 'uneasiness or
trouble of mind' (first recorded in
a work of *c.*1525 by Sir Thomas
More) underlies the traditional
meaning of *anxious*, and in the
20c the development of psychiatric concepts such as *anxiety
neurosis* have strengthened the belief that a morbid state of mind
is involved in the terms. In the
18c, *anxious* came to mean 'full of
desire and endeavour' and was
constructed with *to*; the phrase
anxious to please appeared in Robert Blair's poem *The Grave* (1743),
and Lord Nelson declared in 1794
that 'The General seems as anxious as any of us to expedite the
fall of the place'. Examples: *No
one seemed very anxious to come up
with the spondulicks*—Private Eye,
1980 | *She's very anxious that you
should like her*—A. N. Wilson, 1982 |
*We are desperately anxious to see
the Advanced Passenger Train
succeed*—Railway Magazine, 1982 |
*There are a number of men only too
anxious to buy themselves a knighthood who might be most attracted to*

a project that catches the public sympathy—Claire Rayner, 1991.

any. **1 USE WITH SINGULAR OR PLURAL NOUNS.** *Any* can be used with a singular or plural noun, or with an uncountable noun such as *homework* and *happiness*, to denote choice from three or more people or things (for choice from two, *either* is used): *The most basic of data security precautions for any individual or company employing microcomputers is the making of back-ups*—*Times*, 1985 | *This letter is addressed to you and is not being copied to any other party*—*Daily Telegraph*, 1986 | *At any moment a change in voltage can wipe out what one has written*—*Listener*, 1985 | *Any food found in passengers' luggage will be confiscated* | *Neither government was behind it, nor were there any sponsors, angels, captains of commerce or industry*—*Los Angeles Times*, 1986. When used with a singular countable noun (i.e. one that has a plural, such as *book* or *person*) it is always assertive in meaning: *I did not want any book* (= I wanted a particular book) as distinct from *I did not want any books* (normally = I wanted none) and *I did not want any sugar* (normally = I wanted no sugar).

2 AS A PRONOUN. *Any* functions as a pronoun as well as a determiner: *By dialling 1, 0, a three-digit access code and the area code and number, a caller can use any of eight different long distance companies*—*New York Times*, 1985 | *If you keep ferrets don't let any escape* | *It's as good an excuse as any to buy a new car.*

3 WITH COMPARATIVE AND SUPERLATIVES. It is better to use a comparative with *any other* than a superlative with *any*: not ☒ *the most brutal piece of legislation of any passed by this government* but *a*

more brutal piece of legislation than any other passed by this government. An alternative is to use *all* instead of *any*: *the most brutal piece of legislation of all those passed by this government.*

4 *ANY ONE* AND *ANYONE*. As one word, *anyone* means the same as *anybody* and is interchangeable with it (*Anyone could do that* | *Anybody could do that*). As two words, it means 'any single person or thing', as in *You can have any one you like* (*any you like* would include the possibility of more than one). Examples: *The virtual photon rematerializes into any one of a very large number of possible combinations of new particles*—*Scientific American*, 1978 | *Any one of half a dozen umbrella titles would equally well match the variety of the contents of this military miscellany*—*Times Literary Supplement*, 1977.

5 OTHER ONE-WORD AND TWO-WORD FORMS. *Any more* is used chiefly after a negative and is usually written as two words in BrE (*He is not lying there any more*—Penelope Lively, 1987), although it is found more often as one word in other varieties and occasionally also in BrE (*He wasn't a schoolkid anymore*—M. du Plessis, 1983 (South Africa) | *You don't feel so blasé anymore going out on your [firefighting] calls*—*New York Times*, 1984 | *Britain is not that sort of country anymore*—*Sunday Times*, 1988).

Anyhow is only written as one word and is a (usually more informal) alternative for *anyway* (*Anyhow I'm carving out a career there teaching the boss's daughter to read novels*—Thomas Keneally, 1985 | *Home is not the place for charm anyway*—*London Review of Books*, 1987). Note that *any way* is spelt as two words to retain their separate meaning, as in *Is there any way I can help?* and *Do it any way you like.*

Any place and *any time* are also often spelt as single words in AmE: *She said she would vote for him anytime*—New Yorker, 1987 | *I wouldn't have wanted to know her as a child, but once a man, anytime*—M. Doane, 1988 | *Why didn't we ever get to go anyplace?*—New Yorker, 1988.

The archaic adverbial form *any ways* survives in the Book of Common Prayer (*All those who are any ways afflicted . . . in mind, body, or estate*) and in the Authorized Version of the Bible (*And if the people of the land doe any wayes hide their eyes from the men*). Otherwise it is restricted to informal AmE: *So who promised this guy anything anyways?*

6 AS AN ADVERB. *Any* is correctly used as an adverb to emphasize a comparative adjective or adverb (*They are not treated like schoolgirls any longer* | *He can't play any better* | *She refuses to go any further*). In informal AmE, and occasionally in BrE, it can stand alone with the meaning 'at all': *We're used to responsibility. Doesn't worry us any*—Agatha Christie, 1937 | *It's not going to help any with my exams*—New Yorker, 1988.

apart from, aside from. *Apart from* has been standard in BrE from the early 17c (e.g. *There are few exciting and visitable relics of [Mesolithic] human life apart from caves*—R. Muir, 1983 | *The raven, who apart from anything else was much stronger in the air than the dove*—Julian Barnes, 1989); *aside from*, an equivalent expression used alongside *apart from* in AmE since the early 19c (*Aside from that, the church leadership had trouble figuring out exactly what to do about him*—New Yorker, 1986) is now found from time to time in BrE contexts (*Aside from abolition of exchange controls by the other major economies, the Government insists that Britain's inflation rate be brought more in line with that of her trading partners*—Guardian, 1989 | *Aside from the eclipses, January, February and March are key months for professional matters and your personal aspirations*—Today, 1992).

apartheid is correctly pronounced -tayt in standard English, not -tiyt.

apex. The standard plural form is *apexes*, although *apices* is sometimes found in more technical contexts.

apiece, meaning 'for each one', is normally placed immediately after a direct object (*After buying his brothers a pint apiece [he] had to be content with a half for himself*—Melvyn Bragg, 1969 | *The actresses have one beautiful costume apiece*—New Yorker, 1987).

a posteriori, a Latin term meaning 'from what comes after', is pronounced with the initial *a* as in *hate* and the final *-i* as in *eye*. It is used to characterize reasoning or arguing from known facts to probable causes, as in the proposition 'The prisoners have weals on their backs, so they must have been whipped'. The opposite concept is A PRIORI.

apostrophe. Fowler (1926) gave no information on this punctuation mark at the letter A except a cross-reference to an entry called 'possessive puzzles', which sounds rather more entertaining. He concentrated on a number of difficulties arising from use of the apostrophe, and the same tactic is adopted here in a place where the user will be more likely to look. Each problem is headed by a typical example that illustrates it.

In general, it should be borne in mind that the apostrophe denotes either (1) a possessive, or (2) omitted letters.

1 GIRL'S, GIRLS' AS POSSESSIVE. The first is singular (one girl), and the second is plural (two or more girls).

2 WOMEN'S AND CHILDREN'S AS POSSESSIVE. When the plural ends in a letter other than *s*, the possessive is formed by adding *'s*: *the children's games*, *the men's boots*, *the oxen's hoofs*, *the women's cars*, etc.

3 VIDEO'S FOR RENT. This is the so-called 'grocers' apostrophe', an apostrophe misapplied to an ordinary plural, particularly in words ending in *-o* but also in quite harmless words such as *apple's* and *pear's* (e.g. *pear's 30p a pound*). It is, needless to say, illiterate in ordinary usage.

4 WHO'S AND WHOSE. These are sometimes confused (e.g. *Who's turn is it ?*): see WHO'S.

5 POSSESSIVE OF NAMES ENDING IN -S. Add *'s* to names that end in *s* when you would pronounce them with an extra *s* in speech (e.g. *Charles's, Dickens's, Thomas's, The Times's, Zacharias's*); but omit *'s* when the name is normally pronounced without the extra *s* (e.g. *Bridges', Connors', Mars', Herodotus', Xerxes'*). With French names ending in (silent) *-s* or *-x*, add *'s* (e.g. *Dumas's, le Roux's*) and pronounce the modified word with a final *-z*.

6 HERS, ITS, OURS, ETC. An apostrophe should not be used in pronouns of this type (e.g. *a book of hers*). Note that *its* is normally used in attributive position, i.e. before a noun (*Give the cat its dinner*) and should be distinguished from *it's* = 'it is': see ITS, IT'S.

7 MPS, THE 1990S, ETC. The apostrophe is no longer normally used in the plural of abbreviated forms (e.g. *Several MPs were standing around*), although it is of course used in the possessive (e.g. *The BBC's decision to go ahead with the broadcast*). It is used in plurals when clarity calls for it, e.g. *Dot your i's and cross your t's*.

8 I'LL, THEY'VE, YOU'RE, ETC. The apostrophe is used to form these regular contractions with pronouns, and occasionally with nouns (e.g. *The joke's on them*): see ABBREVIATIONS 2.

9 CELLO, FLU, ETC. The apostrophe is no longer needed in words that are originally contractions but are now treated as words in their own right, e.g. *cello, flu, phone, plane*. Other words retain them in their spelling, usually in medial rather than initial position, e.g. *fo'c'sle, ne'er-do-well, o'er, rock 'n' roll*.

10 BARCLAYS BANK, ETC. The apostrophe is rapidly disappearing in company names and other commercial uses, e.g. *Barclays Bank, Citizens Advice Bureau*. Though occasionally disapproved of, the practice can be justified as an attributive rather than possessive use of the noun (i.e. *Barclays Bank* is attributive, implying association with *Barclays*, whereas *Barclays' Bank* is possessive, implying ownership by people called *Barclay*).

appal is the correct BrE spelling (AmE *appall*), with inflections *appalled, appalling*.

apparatus is normally pronounced with *-rat-* as in *rate* (not as in *part*). The plural is *apparatuses*.

apparent is normally pronounced with short *a* (as in *bat*);

pronunciation as in *parent*, though once dominant, is only occasionally heard.

appeal. The transitive use as a legal term is AmE (e.g. *Curtis had announced that it will appeal the verdict—Publisher's Weekly*, 1963). The equivalent in BrE is *appeal against* (e.g. *The mother appealed against the court's decision—International Journal of Law & Family*).

appear, appeared. For the type *She appeared to have encouraged him*, see PERFECT INFINITIVE.

appeasement, meaning 'the process of satisfying a potential aggressor', has had unfavourable overtones since its use in the 1930s with reference to Nazi Germany, and now always carries the implication of making shameful or inadvisable concessions. As late as the 1920s, it was used more neutrally, as in Winston Churchill's statement in relation to Turkey, *Here again I counsel prudence and appeasement*.

appendix has the plural form *appendices* (with reference to parts of books and documents) and *appendixes* (in surgery and zoology).

apposition. 1 *Apposition* is the placing of a noun or noun phrase beside another noun and noun phrase, where it shares the same grammatical function, as in *A portrait of Benjamin Disraeli, the famous statesman*, in which *the famous statesman* is in apposition to *Benjamin Disraeli*. Words in apposition are called *appositives*. In this example, the appositive gives additional information, and is called *non-restrictive*; in other cases, the appositive is an essential part of the expression and is called *restrictive*, e.g. *William the Conqueror, the author Penelope Lively*.

2 Note that the appositive element can stand first when it is a descriptive title or identifier preceding a name, e.g. *Chancellor Kohl of Germany, civil rights campaigner Martin Luther King*. Originating in AmE, this practice is rapidly spreading to BrE, especially in newspapers.

3 For a more detailed treatment of apposition, see Greenbaum, *Oxford English Grammar* (1996), 230–33.

appraisal has now nearly ousted *appraisement* in non-technical language, although *appraisement* was dominant in the 19c. The derivative *reappraisal* is a 20c formation.

appraise, apprise. Like many near-sounding words with some relation of meaning, these are often confused. Appraise means 'to assess the value of (something or someone)' (e.g. *When a man is stripped of all worldly insignia, one can appraise him for what he is truly worth*—Charles Chaplin, 1964 | *It was an interval at least long enough for him to appraise the situation*—Antonia Fraser, 1988). Apprise means 'to inform, to give notice to' and is normally constructed with a personal object followed by *of* (e.g. *He was annoyed that I had not bothered to apprise him of the upsetting news sooner*—P. Bailey, 1986).

appreciate. Its normal meaning 'to acknowledge with gratitude', especially in business correspondence (e.g. *I appreciate everything that you have done to help us*) and to form polite requests (e.g. *It would be appreciated if you would reply by return of post*) is unexceptionable. More controversial is its use with *how* or a *that* clause (e.g.

*I appreciate that you are disap-
pointed by the outcome*). Gowers
(1965) discouraged this use, proposing *realize* instead, which is
sometimes the better word although in some contexts the notion of *sympathize* is also needed.

apprehend, comprehend. In
the meanings in which they overlap, these two words denote
slightly different aspects of
understanding. *Apprehend* means
to grasp or perceive a general
idea or concept, whereas *comprehend* means to understand an argument or statement. Both can
be followed by a simple object or
by a *that*-clause. Examples (apprehend) *Neither could apprehend the
nature of their relationship, and each
was flattered by it*—Patrick White,
1957 | *She drew a breath, long
enough to apprehend that he was
about to step from one world into
another*—Iris Murdoch, 1962 | *Their
use of the word 'consciousness' refers
to the system of meaning through
which we apprehend the world*—S.
Bloch, 1984 | *We are slow to appre-
hend danger; would much rather ig-
nore some threat to our way of life,
hoping it will go away*—Daily Tele-
graph, 1992 | (comprehend) *Speak
more slowly so that we can comprehend everything you say*—Bernard
Malamud, 1966 | *To comprehend lan-
guage fully, to assemble it correctly
and to express it properly is a task
that has no equal in human
capability*—A. Smith, 1984.

apprise is spelt *-ise* not *-ize*. For
its meaning, see APPRAISE.

a priori, a Latin term meaning
'from what is before', is pronounced with *a* as in *hate* and
with both *i*s as in *eye*. It is used
to characterize reasoning or arguing from causes to effects, as in
the proposition 'Because they

were wearing handcuffs it was
obvious that they had been taken
into custody'. The opposite concept is A POSTERIORI.

apropos is pronounced with
stress on the first syllable and the
last syllable as in so. In English it
is always written, despite its
French origin (17c), as one word
without accent. Its main uses are
as a preposition, with or without
a linking of (e.g. *Her voice, as has
been mentioned apropos that of Bou-
dicca, was not harsh*—Antonia Fraser,
1988 | *Apropos of nothing she de-
clared that love must be
wonderful*—G. Clare, 1981). Although
sometimes used with *to*, under
the influence of *appropriate*, this
is not recommended.

apt, liable, prone. 1 *Apt to* and
liable to, followed by an infinitive,
are virtually interchangeable, except that *liable* carries a greater
notion of responsibility for the
result, which is generally implied
to be undesirable. Examples: *Pick
up any 'documentation' . . . and you
are apt to be . . . bombarded by
gibberish*—New York Times, 1982 |
*Your cylinder-lock (what people are
apt to call a 'Yale')*—Oxford Consumer, 1983. In this use, *apt to* is
tending to force out the alternative *prone to*, although this is still
used in relation to habits and
continual actions: *The one unquestionable advantage of the multiflora
stock is the fact that it is less prone
to throw up suckers than any of the
others*—N. Young, 1971.

2 *Liable to* and *prone to*, unlike
apt to, can be followed by a simple object, and in this use *liable to*
also has the meaning 'subject to
(a penalty)': *Many of these children
are chesty, prone to colds*—Guardian,
1967 | *The affected children them-
selves are liable to behavioural problems such as temper tantrums*—

Journal of the Royal Society of Medicine, 1980 | *Anyone convicted of giving away examination papers to candidates will be liable to two years in jail—Daily Telegraph*, 1982.

3 *Likely to*, followed by an infinitive, is an alternative when referring to a particular or immediate possibility rather than a generalized probability, and can refer to favourable or neutral circumstances as well as unfavourable ones: *A plan to help young home-buyers is likely to be announced within the next week—Times*, 1973 | *Teachers who refuse to cover for absent colleagues or attend staff meetings are likely to have pay deducted from now on—Times Educational Supplement*, 1985.

aquarium has plurals *aquariums* (general use) or *aquaria* (technical use).

Arab, Arabian, Arabic. 1 These three terms refer to different aspects of Arabia and its people: *Arab* means a member of the Semitic people now inhabiting large parts of the Middle East and North Africa, and is also used as a quasi-adjective before a noun (*the Arab people* | *Arab hopes* | *Arab philosophy*); *Arabian* is an adjective having geographical reference to Arabia (*the Arabian peninsula* | *an Arabian camel* | *Arabian fauna*); and *Arabic* is a noun and adjective denoting a language (*Do you speak Arabic?* | *Arabic literature*).

2 *Arabic* is written with a capital initial in the expression Arabic numerals (the numbers 1, 2, 3, etc., as distinct from the Roman numerals I, II, III, etc.). It is written with a small initial in *gum arabic*, a type of gum exuded by African acacia trees.

3 The expression *street Arab*, first recorded in 1859, and for about a century commonly applied to a homeless child or other vagrant living on the streets, is now regarded as offensive and is rarely used.

arbiter, arbitrator. *Arbiter*, a more literary word (16c), is now restricted to the meaning 'a judge or authority' as in an arbiter of taste. For the meaning 'a person appointed to settle a dispute', the slightly older form *arbitrator* (15c) is now the correct word to use, although the meanings overlap and arbiter is still often found in this meaning. Examples: (arbiter) *She was not so much an arbiter of fashion as she was fashion itself—D.* Halberstam, 1979 | *The great nineteenth-century critic and arbiter of taste, John Ruskin—L.* Hudson, 1985 | *Reith was the true successor of the Victorian headmaster, rapidly establishing a range of sporting events which the BBC in its capacity as the sole arbiter of airways deemed to be of national significance—R.* Holt, 1989 | *Harley then insisted that the tournament director, who is the ultimate arbiter at professional tournaments, be summoned—M.* Hamer, 1991 | (arbitrator) *Either party may apply to have the dispute referred to arbitration by the judge or by an outside arbitrator—R. C. A.* White, 1985 | *If the award of the arbitrator proves unreliable the court does have the power to set aside such an award—L.* Brown, 1987 | *The arbitrator may decide that The Post Office is not legally liable but that there are special circumstances in your favour that mean you were not really at fault—* Royal Mail Information Leaflet, 1991.

arc *verb*, meaning 'to produce a luminous electrical discharge' is inflected arced, arcing, with the c hard despite being followed by an *e* and *i* respectively.

archaeology is the BrE spelling; *archeology* is AmE.

archaism. **1** Archaisms are words and phrases that have fallen out of general use but are used for special effect, normally in literature. These vary in effect from the gently old-fashioned or jocular (e.g. *erstwhile, gentlewoman, goodly, hence, lest, methinks, perchance, quoth*) to the unnatural or even unusable (e.g. *peradventure, whilom*).

2 Archaisms are most commonly found in allusive use in literature, e.g. *If Mimi's cup runneth over, it runneth over with decency rather than with anything more vital*—Anita Brookner, 1985 (an Old Testament allusion to *Psalms* 23:5) | *The whole creation groaneth and travaileth in pain together*—Iris Murdoch, 1987 (a New Testament allusion to *Romans* 8:22). Archaic word forms also occur in titles, as in *The Compleat Girl* (by Mary McCarthy, 1963, in allusion to Isaak Walton's *The Compleat Angler*), *Whitaker's Almanack* (which preserves an older spelling of *almanac*), and in fixed expressions such as *olde worlde* and many new formations modelled on *a-changing*, e.g. *a-basking, a-brewing, a-wasting.*

3 See also the separate entries for ALBEIT, NAY, UNBEKNOWN.

ardour is spelt *-our* in BrE and as *ardor* in AmE.

are, is see AGREEMENT.

aren't I see BE 4.

argot is a term for the jargon of a special group or class of people. See JARGON.

arguably is first recorded only in 1890, and did not appear in the original *OED*; now it seems indispensable. It is used as an ordinary adverb and as a sentence adverb (qualifying a whole statement). Examples: *Arguably, this is another kind of corruption, but it was in general a very long-range bribery, and it was invariably offered in the guise of friendship*—R. M. Sunter, 1986 | *Fibich was arguably worse off even than Hartmann, for he knew no one*—Anita Brookner, 1988 | *Meet the man with the surname everyone knows, Giorgio Armani, who arguably adorns more bodies worldwide than any other living designer*—Clothes Show, 1991.

arise. Note that *arise* and *rise* are intransitive verbs (i.e. they cannot take an object and cannot be used in the passive), whereas *arouse* and *rouse* are generally transitive. Its meaning 'to get out of bed' has now given way to *rise*, except in literary use, and its principal current meaning in ordinary speech and writing is 'to come into existence or be noticed'; usually with reference to abstract concepts such as questions, difficulties, doubts, thoughts, results, etc. See also AROUSE.

armadillo has the plural form *armadillos*.

armour is spelt *-our* in BrE and as *armor* in AmE.

aroma. **1** *Aroma* now denotes any pleasant smell, as befits a word that originally meant 'spice' (13c to 18c), and has given rise to aromatherapy, 'massage or other treatment using extracts and essential oils', which likewise befits the special meaning of aroma 'the distinctive fragrance exhaled by a spice, plant, etc.'.

2 The plural is *aromas*.

around, round. 1 In general, BrE prefers *round* and AmE prefers *around*, both as an adverb and as a preposition, except in certain more or less fixed expressions or restricted collocations. In BrE it is usual to say *all the year round*, *Winter comes round*, *The wheels go round*, *Send the book round*, *Show me round*, whereas in all these cases AmE would normally use *around*.

2 *Around* is obligatory in fixed expressions such as *fool around, mess around, sit around*, etc, *all around* (as in *All around there are signs of decay*), and *to have been around*. In some of these, *about* is also possible, but not *round*.

3 BrE still tends to prefer *about* as a preposition meaning 'approximately', although *around* is also used (e.g. *There are about/ around 100 in all | Come about/ around 4 o'clock*), whereas AmE generally prefers *around*. See ABOUT.

4 However, the distribution of *around* and *round* is subject to considerable variation in practice, as the following examples show: (*around* as preposition) *Jesse . . . moped around the house all day*— Lee Smith, 1983 (US) | *The area around Waterloo*—R. Elms, 1988 (UK) | *They stood grouped around their luggage*—M. Bracewell, 1989 (UK) | (*round* as preposition) *It stood just round the corner from his father's house*—Van Wyck Brooks, ante 1961 | *A map rolled up round a broom handle*—Jeanette Winterson, 1985 (UK) | *He looked round the table as if daring anyone to smile*—David Lodge, 1988 (UK) | (*around* as adverb) *Stay around till she gets back*—New Yorker, 1989 | *Hartmann's sunny . . . attitude was marvellous to have around*—Anita Brookner, 1988 (UK) | *The devices have been around a while*—USA Today, 1988 | *I went*

around to the front door—New Yorker, 1989 | (*round* as adverb) *In the end she talked me round*—Nina Bawden, 1987 (UK) | *The news had gotten round pretty fast*—New Yorker, 1998.

arouse. The relation of *arouse* to *rouse* is much like that of *arise* to *rise*, i.e. *rouse* is almost always preferred in the literal sense with a person or animal as object. *Arouse* is chiefly used to mean 'to call into being' with reference to feelings and emotions. Generally, if you *rouse* someone you wake them or stir them into activity; if you *arouse* them, you excite them or make them angry or suspicious: *The word 'theory' has always aroused suspicion amongst the English, who see themselves as practical people and sound empiricists*—B. Bergonzi, 1990 | *About five o'clock we were roused by the distant thudding of an engine*—S. Stewart, 1991.

arrogate see ABROGATE.

artefact, 'a product of human art or workmanship', is the more common spelling in BrE; in AmE *artifact*, corresponding to pronunciation rather than etymology (Latin *arte factum*, 'made by [human] art'), is dominant.

artiste, rhyming with *feast* and meaning 'a professional performer, especially a singer or dancer', is a separate borrowing from French and not a feminine form of *artist*, which has the distinct meaning of someone who works in one of the fine arts. *Artiste*, which carries no notion of artistry, is now regarded as at best an affectation and at worst an insult; usually a word such as *performer* would do just as well. Examples: *Peruvian singers, Cuban ballerinas and Swiss circus artistes are among 80 troupes and cultural* *delegations—Daily Telegraph*, 1992 | *Distinguished people make a practice of visiting the opera, and pull rank so as to meet the artistes, especially attractive females—*R. Butters, 1991.

as. 1 PROBLEMS WITH AS . . . AS . . . In this common construction, the first *as* is an adverb, and the second is either a preposition or a conjunction.

▸**a** When no verb follows, e.g. *as good as we* | *as good as us*, there is no problem with nouns after *as* because nouns do not inflect, but some pronouns do. The two patterns are *as . . . as I/we/he/she/they* and *as . . . as me/us/him/her/them*. (It and you are of course invariable.) In normal conversational English the second pattern is more usual, and the first is only used in more formal contexts or in an effort to avoid censure from purists. It should be added that both patterns are grammatically sound, since *as* can function as a preposition (as it does in *as good as us*) and as a conjunction (as it does in *as good as we* | *as good as we are*). In these cases, the first *as* is classified as an adverb (**as** *good as . . .*)

▸**b** Note that choice of case can determine meaning when there might be ambiguity, as in *I don't like George as much as them* [= I don't like George as much as I like them] | *I don't like George as much as they* [= I don't like George as much as they like him]. This facility is not available with nouns (e.g. *I don't like George as much as Henry*), and ambiguity must then be clarified either by intonation (in speech) or by rephrasing (in writing, e.g. *I don't like George as much as I like Henry*, or better, *I prefer Henry to George*).

▸**c** Note also that in negative constructions the first (adverbial) *as* can be replaced by *so*: *not so good as us*. With so, it is unusual to use the I/we/he/she/they option.

2 AS = 'IN THE CAPACITY OF'. In this use, *as* is a preposition, and it is used to show the role or function of a person or thing: *I hear you are employed as a teacher* | *It is as a cellist that she is best known*. Care must be taken to avoid false links with the *as* clause, as in the following examples, which at best show poor style and at worst are downright ambiguous: *As a medical student his call-up was deferred—*Penelope Fitzgerald, 1986 | *As a 32-year-old law enforcement professional, you know that I do not like being forced to release prisoners from jail—Chicago Tribune*, 1988 [Who then is the professional?].

3 OMISSION OF AS. The preposition *as* is usually omitted after certain verbs which designate or classify people or things in certain ways, including *appoint, certify, choose, consider, count, deem, elect, nominate, proclaim, pronounce, rate, reckon*. With other verbs, the *as* must be included; these are: *accept, acknowledge, characterize, class, define, describe, intend, regard, see, take, treat, use*. Note that *consider* and *regard*, although having much the same meaning, differ in the matter of *as*: *We regard you as a model pupil* | *We consider you a model pupil*.

The adverb *as* is sometimes casually omitted in spoken English in comparisons: *She used to come regular as clockwork* | *It was soft as butter* | *They were good as gold*. This is not good practice in more formal or written English.

4 AS = 'BECAUSE'. Fowler (1926) rejected the use of *as* = 'because' when it followed the main clause, as in *I gave it up, as he only laughed at my arguments*; but he permitted it when the *as* clause came first, as in *As he only laughed at my arguments, I gave it up*. This objection now sounds as dated as the examples chosen, and the position of the clause is determined not by spurious principles of syntax but by the degree of emphasis needed for each part of the sentence.

5 *AS*, RELATIVE PRONOUN. Its use as a relative pronoun is now largely confined to the constructions *same as* or *such as*: *We can expect the same number to turn up as came last year* | *Such repairs as have been made to the house are most acceptable*. These constructions are less common in everyday spoken English. Other constructions with *as* as a relative pronoun occur only in non-standard or regional English, both in BrE and AmE: *It's only baronets as cares about farthings*—Thackeray, 1847/8 | *This is him as had a nasty cut over the eye*—Dickens, 1865 | *I don't know as I expected to take part in this debate*—Harper's Magazine, 1888 | *There's plenty as would like this nice little flat, Mr. E*—Anthony Burgess, 1963.

6 *AS AND WHEN*. This now common phrase meaning 'whensoever' is surprisingly recent, not being recorded in the *OED* before 1945. It is also used elliptically in informal (especially spoken) language to mean 'when possible, in due course'. Examples: *He would . . . snatch pub meals as and when he could*—P. McCutchan, 1975 | *All bream . . . will devour a small fish as and when the opportunity arises and they have the inclination to do so*—G. Marsden, 1987 | *(elliptical) They confirmed the existing main roads as future traffic arteries to be widened 'as and when'*—Listener, 1965 | *She can redo them and we just microwave them as and when*—

spoken material in British National Corpus, 1992.

7 *AS FROM*, *AS OF*. The formula *as from* is used in contracts and agreements to indicate the date from which certain items or clauses are to take effect. This use is reasonable when the date is retrospective: *The rate of payment is increased as from the 1st September last*. For present and future dates the *as* is superfluous: *Your redundancy takes effect from today* [not *as from today*].

Phrases of the type *as of now, as of today*, etc., first recorded in the work of Mark Twain in 1900, are now well established in standard English in the UK and elsewhere. Examples: *I'm resigning from the committee as of now*—D. Karp, 1957 | *As of today, I do not believe Tebbit has enough votes to win*—J. Critchley, 1990.

8 *AS IF*, *AS THOUGH*. ▶ **a** These two conjunctions are virtually interchangeable, except that *as if* is somewhat more natural in exclamations (*As if I would!*).
▶ **b** When the conjunction introduces a possibility or likelihood (often after a verb like *appear, look, seem*, or *sound*) the normal tense is used: *He speaks as though even the rules which we freely invent are somehow suggested to us in virtue of their being right*—M. Warnock, 1965 | *When the left wing of the Labour Party looks as if it is going to lose, it is described as bananas*—Times, 1980 | *It is as if he has given up on America and in so doing he has given up on grappling with the complexity of his position and allegiances*—Times Literary Supplement, 1986.
▶ **c** When the conjunction introduces a comparison based on a hypothetical or impossible proposition, either the past tense or the subjunctive is used, which co-

incide in form except that the third person singular subjunctive of *to be* is *were*, not *was*. It is impossible to draw a meaningful distinction in current usage between these two alternatives, which only exist in this case, except that the subjunctive *were* theoretically denotes a stronger element of hypothesis or supposition than does the past tense *was*: *Most of them had been out of touch with him for many years, but he spoke to them as if it was only yesterday*—David Lodge, 1980 | *As if India were not already finding batting hard enough, the crowd started . . . performing what is apparently called the 'human wave'*—*Times*, 1986 | *His body felt as though he were trembling, but he was not*—B. Moore, 1987 | *He devoured all, exhausted, as though his life was in danger*—A. S. Byatt, 1987. An elliptical construction, with the verb *to be* omitted, is also possible: *The* tanpura *player . . . strummed the strings as if in a mesmerised state*—Anita Desai, 1980.

9 AS PER. This preposition, meaning 'in accordance with', is more or less restricted to business correspondence and to such publications as DIY manuals (e.g. *as per specification*). In general use it occurs most frequently in the colloquialism *as per usual* and humorous variants of it: *So I took her up a cup of tea . . . as per usual on her headache days*—Katherine Mansfield, 1923 | *I'll stay in a pub . . . As per usual*—J. Bingham, 1970 | *Same old jolly camp-fire life went on as per usual*—Julian Barnes, 1989 | *She knew better, didn't she. As per always*—P. Bailey, 1986.

10 AS SUCH. *As such*, meaning 'in this capacity' or 'accordingly', is an established and valid expression, but it tends to be over-used in contexts where it adds little meaning: (useful) *Euro-MPs are not against the Euro-quango as such*—*English Today*, 1985 | (redundant) *Today, computers do little computing as such outside of specific areas. They are more concerned with manipulative tasks such as word processing*—*New Scientist*, 1987. In many cases, an expression such as *in principle* would serve better: instead of *There is no objection to the sale of houses as such*, write *There is no objection in principle to the sale of houses*.

11 AS TO, AS FOR. These are called complex prepositions, and they have a useful role to play when a simple preposition like *of* or *about* is not available or has another meaning. (1) *As to* means 'concerning' or 'with regard to': *It is correct as to colour and shape* | *The rates of postage vary both as to distance and weight*.

When a simple preposition is available, as it often is after a noun, it is better to use it: ⊠ *'Vladimir telephoned the Circus at lunch-time today, sir,' Mostyn began, leaving some unclarity as to* [use *about* or *regarding*] *which 'sir' he was addressing*—John Le Carré, 1980 | *The setting and languages leave no doubt as to* [use *about* or *concerning*] *its Africanness*—*English World-wide*, 1980 | *Western newspapers have been full of speculation as to whether China was playing a 'Soviet card' against the United States*—*Christian Science Monitor*, 1982

12 For *such as*, see SUCH.

as bad or worse than . . . | as good or better than . . . are examples of mixed constructions in which an element, in this case the second *as* (*as bad as, as good as*) has been omitted. It is common, especially in spoken English, but it is incorrect and should be avoided. The sentence *We're sure they can judge a novel* *just as well if not better than us* (*London Review of Books*, 1987) should be corrected to *just as well as, if not better than, us* (note also the punctuation).

ascendancy, ascendant. **1** The preferred spellings are *-ancy, -ant*, although *ascendency* and *ascendent* are still sometimes found in print.

2 *Have ascendancy over* and *be in the ascendant* are the normal phrases, and refer to a position of power achieved, not of power being gained. *Ascendant* here means 'supreme' or 'dominant', not 'ascending'.

Asian, Asiatic. **1** Both words are pronounced with *-s-* as in *measure* or as *-sh-*. In AmE the first is far more common.

2 In the second half of the 20c *Asian* (a slightly older word) has replaced *Asiatic*, as noun and adjective, when the reference is ethnic, because *Asiatic* is thought to have depreciatory overtones. In BrE *Asian* is also used with reference to people from Asia, especially the Indian subcontinent, or their descendants, living in Britain.

aside, a side. Written as one word, *aside* is an adverb meaning 'to or on one side', as in *to put aside, to take aside*, etc., or a noun meaning words in a play spoken to the audience out of hearing of the other characters. In the meaning 'on each side' it must be written as two words, as in *They are playing five a side* and *a five-a-side team*.

aside from see APART FROM.

as per see AS 9.

assassinate, assassination. **1** The traditional meaning of *as-*

sassinate is 'to kill an important person for political reasons' has been extended in recent times to include any person regarded by his or her killers as a political or sectarian target, for example in Northern Ireland or the Middle East. The corresponding noun *assassination* has followed this tendency. Examples: *Palestinian guerrillas sought for a second time in three months to assassinate King Hussein*—Henry Kissinger, 1979 | *A boy who, during the vicious war in Liberia, has seen first his mother and then his father, his two elder brothers and his two elder sisters, savagely assassinated in front of his eyes by the guerrilla troops*—spoken material in British National Corpus, 1993 | *Assassinations of individual foreigners later escalated into massive bombings*—Bulletin of the American Academy, 1994.

2 In the 20c an older figurative meaning of assassinate, meaning 'to destroy (someone's reputation)' has also been revived: *Helping the Prime Minister in his political battle to assassinate Mr. George Brown*—Guardian, 1962. The noun is especially common in the expression character assassination: *So that was Minter's true objective: character assassination of a popular politician—the modern journalist's stock-in-trade.*—R. Goddard, 1990.

asset. Fowler (1926) called this a 'false form', meaning that the true form was *assets*, derived from a late Anglo-French word which came in turn from Latin *ad satis* meaning 'to sufficiency', while *asset* was the lazy writer's alternative when unwilling to choose between words such as *possession, gain, advantage, resource*, and other synonyms. *Assets* was originally construed as singular but after about 1800 was construed as plural, giving rise to the singular form *asset*, which is now standard in a range of physical and non-physical meanings: *The Mini's greatest asset is probably its road-holding*—*Times*, 1975 | *Mays Cottage was a period piece, completely unrestored, which in these days seemed to be an asset*—Margaret Drabble, 1975 | *His greatest asset was his enthusiasm*—*Today*, 1992. It is also the basis of combinations such as *asset card* and *asset-stripping*.

assignment, assignation. An *assignment* is an allocation, and in law a legal transfer of a right or property, or the document that effects the transfer. It is also a task or piece of work allotted to a person, in this meaning originating in AmE. The dominant meaning of *assignation*, which is pronounced with a hard g, is now 'an appointment to meet, especially between lovers'. Its original meaning of 'apportionment' is not often used now.

assimilation is the process by which the formation of words is influenced by existing words, and the spelling and pronunciation of word-elements are affected by the elements that follow or come before. The word *cockroach*, from Spanish *cucaracha*, achieved its modern spelling by being assimilated in the 18c to the English words *cock* and *roach*. In spelling, *in-* is assimilated to *il-* in words such as *illumination* and to *im-* in words such as *impossible*. In phonetics, an initial *s* can be assimilated to *sh-* when preceded by a word ending in *sh* or *ch*, as for example in *lunch score*.

assist has the same meaning as *help*, and shares the same grammatical constructions. In many contexts the two words are interchangeable, but *help* is usually preferable, *assist* being, in Fowler's term (1926), a 'genteelism' to be avoided. However, *assist* has connotations of formality that are sometimes needed, as in *A young man who assisted him with the management of the farm*—Truman Capote, 1966: *who helped him* would have seemed too casual.

assume, presume. 1 Both words can mean 'suppose' and are often interchangeable in this meaning. Fowler (1926) maintained that there is a stronger element of postulation or hypothesis in *assume* and of a belief held on the basis of external evidence in *presume*, but in practice the uses are not always that distinct. Both words can be followed by a *that*-clause (or one with *that* omitted), by an object followed by a *to*-infinitive, or by a simple object: (assume) *Throughout the book . . . the authors assume the validity of neo-classical economics as taught in the United States*—*Times Literary Supplement*, 1974 | *When you're young you assume everybody old knows what they're doing*—Martin Amis, 1987 | *This is assumed to refer to some sort of demonstration similar to April's Peking riot*—*Daily Telegraph*, 1976 | (presume) *I often hear the ungrammatical term 'one pence'. I presume this is because the occurrence of a single penny is becoming a thing of the past*—*Daily Telegraph*, 1974 | *The Able Criminal . . . may be presumed . . . to be emotionally stable and 'well-adjusted'*—Eric Ambler, 1977.

2 *Assume* and *presume* also coincide in a range of meaning that may be summarized as 'to take on oneself', although you generally assume roles and identities but presume attitudes and bearings. The intransitive use with a *to* infinitive is available only with

presume. Examples: *He was writing 'Gerontion', a dramatic monologue in which he assumes the persona of the 'little old man'*—Peter Ackroyd, 1984 | *He looked surprised—almost annoyed—as if a servant had presumed too great a familiarity*—P. P. Read, 1981 | *It is a reckless ambassador who would presume to preempt his chiefs*—Henry Kissinger, 1979.

assuming is used to mean 'on the assumption that', and being participial is open to the often tiresome objection that the subject of the sentence has to be capable of assuming things, whereas of course the conceptual subject of the phrase is the people involved: *Assuming that the museum is open on Monday, the car will pick us up at 10 a.m.* There is no doubt at all about the meaning here.

assure, assurance. These are terms used principally in the context of life insurance, although even here the verb is no longer common. You *insure* your life and take out *life assurance* (or *insurance*). Both words are rapidly becoming redundant except in conservative business circles.

assure, ensure, insure. These three words overlap in meaning, and all have to do with aspects of certainty or security. *Assure* means 'to make (a person) sure, to convince', and can be followed by *of* or a *that*-clause (*I assure you of my love* | *I assured him that he had not been overlooked*. It also has special uses in *to rest assured* ('to be comfortably certain') and as an adjective *assured,* meaning 'self-confident'. *Ensure* means to 'make certain, guarantee', and is followed either by a simple object or (more commonly) by a *that*-clause (*These measures will ensure success* | *Security checks at airports will ensure that no firearms are carried by passengers*). *Insure* is restricted to the meaning 'protect by insurance' (*Are you insured?* | *We had better insure the new paintings*).

assuredly is pronounced as four syllables.

asterisk (*). This has many special uses, the most common of which is as a marker in a text to draw attention to a footnote, or in a handwritten document to signal an addition. It is also used, especially in older writing, to stand for letters omitted from coarse slang words, e.g. *c**t, f**k.* In linguistic usage, it denotes (1) a postulated (unrecorded) form of a word, and (2) an incorrect or deprecated usage, e.g. **They promised us to go.*

asthma is pronounced **ass**-mə in BrE, and **az**-mə in AmE. The *-th-* is not normally pronounced in either variety.

astronaut is first recorded, with hypothetical reference, in 1929. It is now the standard term for a person trained to travel in a spacecraft. A Russian space traveller, however, is called a *cosmonaut.*

as well as. 1 This is used both as a conjunction, in which case a following pronoun agrees with a preceding noun or pronoun (*It was obvious that he had been consulted as well as I*—Graham Greene, 1965), or, more commonly, as a preposition (in which case the last example would read . . . *as well as me*). It may also be followed by a verbal noun, especially when it is put at the beginning of a sentence: *As well as being highly collectable . . . they make surprisingly roomy containers for all sorts of items*—Daily Tele-

graph, 1980. Here usage has over-
taken Fowler's preference (in
many cases) for a form of the
verb that matches the verb used
earlier in the sentence (e.g. *His
death leaves a gap as well as creates
a by-election*). This construction is
only possible with transitive
verbs; though favoured by some,
it no longer sounds natural.

2 A verb following a subject
that includes *as well as* should
agree with the noun or pronoun
that precedes *as well as*: *He be-
lieves that tutor as well as pupil benefits from the arrangement—Oxford
Today,* 1990. This is because the
addition (here, the phrase *as well
as pupil*) is regarded as a parenthesis and not as part of the
main sentence (as it would be if
as well as were replaced by *and*).
See also AGREEMENT 3.

asylum. **1** The word is no longer
used, except with historical reference, of a psychiatric hospital,
which is now typically called
clinic, psychiatric unit, or simply
hospital or by its name. The principal use of *asylum* now is to denote the status (in full, *political
asylum*) sought by political refu-
gees.

2 The plural *asylums* is only
used in the older meaning.

at. **1** *AT ABOUT.* The *OED* illustrates this use (e.g. *at about seven
o'clock in the evening*) with examples from 1843 onward, and
occasional objections must now
be set aside.

2 *AT ALL.* In Standard BrE, this
prepositional phrase meaning 'in
every way, in any way' is restricted to negative constructions,
questions, and conditional state-
ments: *I did not speak at all | Did
you speak at all? | If you spoke at all.*
Its earlier use meaning 'of all, al-

together' survives in Ireland and
in some BrE and AmE dialects
(e.g. *John Cusack is the finest dancer
at all*—P. W. Joyce, 1910).

3 *AT OR IN.* It is more usual to
use *in* when permanent location
or continued habitation is involved, and is required when the
place is a country or region rather than a place such as a town
or city: *Timbuktu is in Mali | He lives
in Helsinki | The festival takes place
in Salzburg in August | She grew up
in Switzerland. At* is more usual
with reference to more transitory
association, and is much more
common with specific places: *The
plane landed at Nadi in Fiji | There is
a railway station at Leuchars.* A further distinction is demonstrated
by the sentences *They are at St Andrews* [= a member of the University]
and *They are in St Andrews* [living in
or visiting St Andrews].

4 *WHERE IT'S AT.* This colloquial
expression, meaning 'the fashionable scene or area of activity',
swept into AmE in the 1960s and
is now common in BrE and other
varieties. It should be avoided in
more formal English.

ate is normally pronounced to
rhyme with *bet*, although pronunciation to rhyme with *bait* is also
common.

attitude. One might say that
this is now a word with attitude,
in its 20c meaning 'aggressive or
uncooperative behaviour', which
represents a special application
of one kind of characteristic attitude (in the established meaning
'a person's settled opinion or behaviour'): *If I'm out there for months
with everybody yelling at me, I'm
going to cop an attitude—New York
Times,* 1985. The word is still moving on, and now has a positive
connotation, 'assertiveness, style,
panache': *In this job, you've gotta*

have attitude, hang loose, ready for anything—*Police Review*, 1990. It should only be used in this way informally; more formally the word needs explicit clarification: for the first meaning use *uncooperative attitude* or even simply *poor* (or *bad*) *attitude*, and for the second meaning *strong* (or *positive*) *attitude*.

attributive. 1 In grammar, *attributive* denotes a word, normally an adjective or noun, that is put before another word, normally a noun, to qualify or describe it in some way (eg. *brown* in *brown shoes* and *table* in *table lamp*). See further at ADJECTIVE 2.

2 English allows several nouns to be placed in succession, as in a museum conservation department, and this practice is especially common in newspaper headlines, which aim at concision: *sex cinema blaze man pleads guilty—Independent*, 1995 and *expenses row councillor forced out—Evening News* (Edinburgh), 1995.

audit *verb*. British readers of American books and newspapers might be puzzled by the use of *audit* to mean 'to attend (a class) informally' without working for a particular qualification: *She audited his undergraduate lectures; she waylaid him in the department office*—Alison Lurie, 1974.

auger, augur. *Auger* is an Old English word for a tool for boring holes. *Augur*, from the Latin word for soothsayer, is used occasionally to mean a prophet, but is more usual as a verb in the expressions *augur well* and *augur ill*, meaning 'to portend, to suggest a specific outcome'. Examples: *Everything augured badly—they weren't meant to be together*—E. J. Howard, 1965 | *The novel augured*

well for a successful career in fiction-writing—J. Pope Hennessy.

aught is an Old English word that survives only in the fixed expressions *for aught I know* and *for aught I care*, and as such is restricted to literary or archaic use.

augur see AUGER.

aural, oral. *Aural* means 'to do with the ear' (from Latin *auris* ear) and *oral* means 'to do with the mouth' (from Latin *os, oris* mouth). An *oral examination* is one done by speaking rather than by writing; an *aural examination* is a medical examination of the ear. Both words are pronounced the same way, with the first syllable as in *or*, adding to the confusion. See also VERBAL.

Australian English. 1 Most of the distinctive features of Australian English concern pronunciation, vocabulary, and idiom; there are few differences in the written or literary language.

2 PRONUNCIATION. The sound of Australian English is characterized principally by its vowels, which differ from those of BrE in several ways: the vowels of *fleece, face, price, goose, goat, mouth* all begin with rather open, slack sounds not unlike those used in Cockney speech; the vowels of *dress, strut, start, dance, nurse* have a much closer and tighter sound than in BrE. In unstressed syllables, Australian -*es* and -*ed* (as in *boxes* and *studded*) have a sound like *e* in *garden*, so that *boxes* sounds much the same as *boxers*, whereas BrE has the sound of *i* as in *pin*; Australian final -*y* and -*ie* (as in *study* and *studied*) has a longer sound more like *beat* than *bit*. Australian English is closer to AmE in its lighter pronunciation of *t* and *l* when occurring between vowels (as in *butter* and *hollow*).

3 VOCABULARY AND IDIOM. The main differences arise from the local landscape, natural history, and way of life, and can be seen in geographical names (e.g. *bush, creek, paddock, scrub*; conversely BrE *brook, dale, field, forest* are rare in Australian), in names of plants and animals, some of Aboriginal origin and borrowed further in BrE (e.g. *budgerigar, wallaby*). Word formations peculiar to Australian English include a productive colloquial suffix *-o* in word such as *commo* = communist and *smoko* = tea-break. Relatively few items of general vocabulary, whether neutral or informal in register, have come into BrE (e.g. *barrack, crook* = 'ill, unwell', *dinkum, ropeable* = 'angry', *walkabout*), and still fewer idioms (the best known probably being *she'll be right* = 'all will be well').

authentic, genuine. **1** Fowler (1926) tried to establish a distinction in meaning between these two words, reserving *authentic* for the truthfulness of (for example) a book's contents or a picture's subject and *genuine* for the status of its alleged creator. In the sentence *The Holbein Henry VIII is both authentic and genuine*, the implication is that the portrait really is of Henry VIII (and therefore *authentic*) and is really by Holbein (and therefore *genuine*). This distinction is difficult to maintain in practice, and items such as documents, antique furniture, signatures, and many others are regularly described as *authentic* or *genuine* without any identifiable distinction in meaning.
2 An especially important domain in which *authentic* has been used in recent years is that of

'early' music (i.e. before about 1700), where *authentic instruments* are those made and played according to the principles of the period in which the music was written; and so a violin (for example) can be an *authentic* Baroque one, although it may be of modern manufacture and therefore not *genuine* or *original*.

author. **1** *noun.* An *author* is a male or a female writer; *authoress* is now not only largely extinct, but regarded as depreciatory or even offensive.

2 *verb.* The verb is 16c, some two centuries later than the noun, and has been used both transitively and intransitively, although predominantly in the passive: *Whenever the students thought they were evaluating the work of a man, they assessed it as far more impressive than when they thought it was authored by a woman*—M. Ross, 1989. In the 20c this use of *author* has been greatly extended in AmE and BrE with reference to areas of activity outside the arts, such as sport and the cinema. *Co-author*, meaning to share authorship, is now common.

3 *Authoring* is a recent addition to the language of computing, and means 'the process of creating multimedia documents for electronic publishing': *In order to profit from the possibilities of hypertext, teachers have to be provided with powerful authoring environments which allow them to create complex hypertexts.*—*Literary and Linguistic Computing*, 1992.

authoritarian, authoritative. These two words should be carefully distinguished as their implications are quite different. *Authoritarian* is generally used of people or their actions and has the unfavourable meaning 'favouring or encouraging strict obedience to authority' (with overtones of excess); *authoritative* is generally used of things that people say or write, and has the favourable meaning 'recognized as true or dependable'. Examples: (authoritarian) *In industry we have had continuing trench warfare deriving from low pay, and authoritarian and remote management.—Times*, 1973 | (authoritative) *The most authoritative and comprehensive reference book published on the world's rare, endangered and threatened birds.—Birds*, 1979.

automaton has the plural form *automata* when understood collectively and *automatons* when understood individually. See LATIN PLURALS.

automobile. This word, together with *car*, is the standard term in AmE, but in BrE it is used little apart from in the name *Automobile Association*. In BrE *limousine* has connotations of ostentation, whereas in AmE it is a normal word for a large chauffeur-driven car or small bus such as regularly carry people to and from airports.

autumn see FALL.

auxiliary verbs. An auxiliary verb is one that is used with another verb to form a particular tense or mood, for example *be* in *We were pleased*, *have* in *They have gone*, and *do* in *Do you mind?* Sometimes more than one auxiliary verb is used to form a tense, as in *We will be going* and *You have been warned*. Some verbs, such as *can, may*, and *would*, are called modal (or modal auxiliary) verbs, and others (notably *dare* and *need*), though less obviously auxiliary in function, are called semi-

modal verbs because they behave in similar ways (for example, you can say *dare not* and *need not*, which is characteristic of auxiliary verbs). See also BE; CAN; DO; HAVE; MAY, MIGHT; MODAL VERB; OUGHT; SHALL AND WILL.

avail. 1 The noun is used frequently in the somewhat literary phrases *of no avail* and *to little/no avail*, meaning 'having little or no use or effective result', and poses no problems.

2 There are also straightforward verb uses that are also slightly formal or literary in flavour, as in *Words avail very little with him* and *His good works availed him nothing*, and the reflexive use *avail oneself of* as in *to avail oneself of opportunities*. The reflexive construction is also found in the passive, especially in AmE: *Individual contracts may not be availed of to defeat or delay the procedure—Legal Times*, 1982 (US). In BrE this use should be avoided in favour of words such as *use, exploit, employ*, and *utilize*.

avant-garde is a 15c word originally meaning 'the front part of an army' (now expressed by *vanguard*). It has been revived in the 20c to mean 'pioneers or innovators', especially in the arts; its main uses are in the expression *the avant-garde*, in attributive uses such as *the avant-garde cinema* and *avant-garde design*, and with a qualifying word such as *the Berlin avant-garde*. It retains a French pronunciation with a nasalized second syllable in *avant*.

avenge, revenge. The principal differences to bear in mind are (1) that you *avenge* a person (including *yourself*) or an act but *revenge* only an act or *yourself* (usually *on* someone), and (2) that *avenge* is only a verb but *revenge* is a noun as well (in fact more commonly so). Differences in meaning, though proposed from time to time, are too subtle to have any practical use as guidance. Examples: (avenge) *The ferocity and guile with which Absalom had avenged the rape of his sister*—D. Jacobson, 1970 | *That brave god will leap down from his steed when he has to avenge his father's death*—K. Crossley-Holland, 1980 | *Through characterization the novelist has the means to avenge himself on his enemies*—P. D. James, 1993 | (revenge) *It wasn't just that I could never revenge myself upon him*—S. Mason, 1990 | *If I were to revenge myself upon you . . . that would be an act of despair*—Iris Murdoch, 1993.

averse. 1 *AVERSE, AVERSION.* Both words are followed by *to*, despite arguments (notably by Dr Johnson, challenged at some length in the *OED*) that *from* should be used. Examples: *Nor was he averse to being reminded of Calcutta*—Anita Desai, 1988 | *Vic wasn't averse to keeping Everthorpe guessing whether he and Robyn Penrose were having an affair*—David Lodge, 1988 | *He had a lifelong aversion to British officialdom*—John Le Carré, 1989 | *Dr Mainwaring's prescription had not cured her aversion from the prospect of becoming hopelessly senile in the company of people who knew her*—Kingsley Amis, 1974

2 *AVERSE, ADVERSE.* See ADVERSE.

avid, meaning 'eager or greedy', is used either attributively (before a noun, commonly an agent noun such as *collector* or *reader*) or predicatively followed by *for* (or, now rarely, *of*): *Since getting the equipment two years ago, I've become an avid collector of compact discs*—*CD Review*, 1992 | *He was avid for news of how it was all going, and regretting that he couldn't be part of it*—J. Spottiswoode, 1991.

avoid, avert, evade. *Avoid* and *evade* overlap in meaning, but *evade* has a stronger sense of guile or trickery in escaping from an obligation (such as paying income tax). *Avert* means 'to turn aside' (which is its literal meaning in *averting one's gaze*, etc.), and so 'to take action to prevent (something unwelcome, such as danger)'. Examples: *Measles vaccine should be avoided by children who are receiving steroids*—D. J. Rapp, 1970 | *These rules could be evaded, but their evasion was preferable to a reign of snoopery and an encouragement of informers*—A. Paton, 1981 | *In striving to avert a danger he thinks he sees lying ahead he may take the very measures which are necessary to bring it about*—P. H. Kocher, 1972. There is a corresponding difference in meaning between the nouns *avoidance* and *evasion*.

avouch, avow, vouch. *Avouch*, meaning 'to assure, guarantee, acknowledge' and overlapping with *avow*, can be found in the Bible (AV), Spenser, Marlowe, Milton, Byron, and Thackeray, but despite these fine credentials is no longer in general use. *Avow* is still in use and means 'to declare (a belief, one's faith, an intention, etc.)'. *Vouch* is restricted to the phrase *to vouch for* (somebody or something), as in *I can vouch for him* and *I can vouch for his honesty*.

await, wait. *Await* is a transitive verb meaning 'to wait for', and cannot be used without an object: *We will await the outcome* is equivalent to *We will wait for the* *outcome* (but has a stronger element of suspenseful expectation); *We will await and see* is ungrammatical. *Wait* is generally intransitive (and transitivized by *for*), but has a limited number of collocates in transitive use, as in *Wait your turn* and *Don't wait tea*.

awake, awaken, wake, waken.

1 FORMS. Although the history of these words, and in particular of the various forms of past tense and past participle, is highly complex (see the *OED* entry), in current use *awake* and *wake* can be paired as strong verbs having a change of vowel, and *awaken* and *waken* can be paired as weak verbs. For the first pair, the past forms are *awoke* and *woke*, and the participial forms are *awoken* and *woken*. The second pair are regular, with past and participial forms *awakened* and *wakened*.

2 MEANINGS. All four verbs can be used transitively or intransitively, but *wake, awaken*, and *waken* are more formal or literary in effect. *Wake* is the only one to be followed optionally by *up*. Examples will clarify all these points: (awake) *I awoke from a deep sleep | She awoke to the sound of driving rain | She awoke her sleeping child | The accident awoke old fears |* (awaken) *They awakened at dawn | There was enough noise to awaken the dead | There is a need to awaken motorists to the dangers of speeding in foggy conditions | The episode awakened her interest in impressionist painting |* (wake) *When do you usually wake in the morning? | I usually wake up at seven | Will you wake me up when it's time to go? | We woke up early this morning | I woke her up when it became light | I was woken by the wind in night |* (waken) *They wakened at dawn | We were wakened by the storm | When*

she fell asleep nothing would waken her.

aware. 1 *Aware* is generally predicative in use, i.e. it stands after a noun or as a complement after a verb such as *be, become, grow, seem,* etc. It can be followed by *of* or a *that*-clause: *I had to be aware of . . . the balance between committed pro-marketeers and committed anti-marketeers*—Harold Wilson, 1976 | *The young people are well aware that they are being ripped off by these parasites*—*Frendz*, 1971.

2 In the 20c, uses of *aware* either alone or attributively (before a noun) have become more common in the generalized meanings 'well-informed' and 'alert to circumstances' which do not refer to particular items of knowledge: *Revolutionarily aware people can't be fooled by these kinds of people*—*Frendz*, 1971 | *The painfully aware state that seems to have succeeded her earlier calm*—Anita Brookner, 1985 | *The people concerned are caring, concerned and aware—and you haven't the faintest idea what they're talking about.*—*Times*, 1986. Use with a qualifying adverb, as in *environmentally aware*, is also well attested, both attributively and predicatively.

3 The noun *awareness* has developed a corresponding generalized meaning: *Lord Scarman recognises that the awareness campaign needs forcefully to target the government*—*City Limits*, 1986.

awesome has followed the route of *awful*, and other words like *fantastic, dreadful, tremendous*, etc., in acquiring, especially in AmE, a favourable meaning 'very good or impressive', and this meaning is spreading into BrE alongside its traditional meaning 'inspiring awe'. Examples: *The roadside drinkers stare open-mouthed at the sight*

*of the awesome Ford GT40—Today,
1992 | If the English performances in
Paris and Edinburgh had been exe-
cuted by New Zealand they would be
proclaimed as awesome and
unstoppable—Rugby World and Post,
1992.*

awful. 1 There are two main
stages in the development of this
word from its primary meaning
(which goes back to the time of
King Alfred) of 'inspiring awe'.
First, from about 1800 it came to
mean 'very bad' (as in *awful weather, an awful time*); then gradually
it was reduced further in force to
take on the role of a catch-all intensifier deriving its sense from
the context (as in *an awful lot of
money*). It has also served as an
adverb meaning the same as *awfully*, i.e. little more than 'very'
(*it's awful cold*), but this use is
non-standard.

2 The corresponding adverb *awfully* has followed the same route,
and now means little more than
'very' (as in *awfully kind of you*). All
these uses are best restricted to
spoken or casual written English
and should be avoided in more
formal contexts.

awhile, a while. Both expressions have the same origin in the
word *while*, but it should be
noted that *awhile* is strictly adverbial whereas *a while* is a noun
phrase (very often preceded by

for): *When he reached the street-sign
he stopped awhile and stood beneath
it*—Colin Dexter, 1983 | *I'm going
away for a while*—B. Neil, 1993. Confusion is aggravated by the fact
that *a while*, although a noun
phrase, can also have a semi-
adverbial function: *We had to wait
a long while* [= for a long while].

axe is the standard spelling in
BrE and other varieties apart
from AmE, which favours *ax*. In
BrE the verb has inflected forms
axes, axed, axing.

axis has the plural form *axes*,
pronounced **ak**-seez.

aye. 1 The *OED* notes that the
word meaning 'yes' appears suddenly about 1575 and is common
about 1600, but its origin is unknown. Its principal uses now are
in some northern British varieties
(especially Scottish), as a parliamentary term (*The ayes have it*),
and in nautical language (*Aye aye,
sir*) It is pronounced as in *eye*.

2 The word meaning 'ever', as
in *for aye*, is a different word first
recorded about 1200. It is pronounced as in *hay*.

3 Both words are also spelt *ay*.

azure is a horrid word to pronounce and is best avoided altogether, but if needs must then
a first (stressed) syllable as in *bat*
and a second as in *pure* is the
best option.

Bb

babe, baby. *Babe* is now either a
literary word, being regularly
used in the Bible (*Authorized Version*, but *baby* in the *New English
Bible*), or a colloquial and affectionate form of address to a
young woman (originally AmE
but increasingly found in BrE: *He
looked me up and down. 'Who you,
babe?'*—A. Billson, 1993). In a recent development, *babe* also
means (with third-person reference) a sexually attractive
woman: *The smartly dressed hooker
swept in surrounded by a bevy of
near naked film babes.*—*Daily Mirror*,
1995. *Baby* is also used as a term
of affection (e.g. *my poor baby*)
and has a special use implying
feebleness or lack of courage (*He's
a real baby when it comes to having
injections*). In this meaning *baby*
has many recent and colourful
synonyms such as *chicken*, *funk*,
and (most recently) *wimp*.

bacillus is pronounced with a
soft *c*. The plural is *bacilli*, with
the final -*i* pronounced like *eye*.

back. A use that is chiefly AmE
but familiar in the UK and likely
to become BrE eventually is *back
of*, meaning 'behind, in the back
of' (*His computer . . . locates a spare
space back of the plane*—*Keyboard
Player*, 1986). But *in back* and *in
back of* are unlikely to make the
transition, being markedly AmE
and un-British (*'What luck,' she
muses, sliding back in [the car].* 'Get
in back, Herman.'*—B. Ripley, 1987 |
*Should I or should I not go out to the
swimming pool in back of my sister's
condominium?*—A. Beattie, 1980).

back-formation. 1 A *back-
formation* is a word (often a verb)
formed from a longer word (often
a noun) which appears to be a derivative of the newer word; for example, *burgle* (19c) is a
back-formation from *burglar*
(which is six centuries older) and
sculpt (19c) from *sculptor* (17c).
Some words are revived as back-
formations, such as *conject* (which
occurs in Chaucer and Shakespeare); see also ADMINISTER, AD-
MINISTRATE.

2 Many established back-
formations cause little comment;
examples are *diagnose* (from *diagnosis*), *donate* (from *donation*), *laze*
(from *lazy*), *legislate* (from *legislation*), and *televise* (from *television*),
whereas others are regarded as
tasteless or inappropriate; the
chief targets are *enthuse* (from *enthusiasm*) and *liaise* (from *liaison*),
which should be avoided by those
anxious to impress, even though
the alternatives are usually
phrases such as *be enthusiastic* and
form a liaison (although *interact*
will often do).

backlog. The current figurative
meaning 'arrears of uncompleted
work' is a fairly recent Americanism (1930s) which rapidly passed
into British use. The original
physical meaning 'a log placed at
the back of a fire' is 17c; in between is an earlier meaning 'a reserve supply', which extended in
use to abstract things (for example, goodwill) and gave rise to
the current meaning. In this
meaning it is often used with a
preceding noun, e.g. *capacity back-*

log, orders backlog: *They find a backlog of work building up, in which important but less urgent planning and
discussing never get to the top of the
pile*—G. Claxton, 1989 | *Jordan tem-
porarily closes its border with Iraq to
ease the refugee backlog*—Keesings,
1990 | *Extra staff brought in to clear
the backlog should be kept on until a
thorough review is made*—J. King et
al., 1993.

backslang is a type of slang in
which words are pronounced
backwards and take on a special
(often derogatory) meaning, such
as *yob* for 'boy'.

back to basics is a 1990s political slogan invoking a return to
fundamental principles of honesty and decency, which is likely
to recur from time to time. When
used adjectivally, it should be hyphened (*a back-to-basics campaign*).

backward, backwards. 1 For
the adverb, both forms are in
use, although *backward* is somewhat more common in AmE and
backwards in BrE: *Talk ran backward
from the events of the morning*—A.
Munro, 1987 (Canada) | *I walked
backward to look at her in the
sun*—E. L. Doctorow, 1989 (US) | *Not
knowing where he was, and trying to
work his way backwards*—R. Cobb,
1985 (UK). In the fixed expressions
bend (or *lean*) *over backwards*, *backwards and forwards*, and *to know
backwards*, *backward* is only found
occasionally outside AmE: *He'll
bend over backwards to please a
client*—M. Bail, 1975 (Australia) | *An
eclectic collector . . . , he knows the
showrooms backwards.*—Financial
Times, 1983 | *The door kept swinging
backwards and forwards*—Anita
Brookner, 1984 | *From the study
above them . . . came the sound of
footsteps moving backwards and for-*

wards across the floor—R. Border,
1991 | *They move backward and for-
ward between denial and anger and
depression, unable to break out of
the circle of despair*—G. Carmichael,
1991.

2 For the adjective, the correct
form in standard English is *backward*: *He watched her walking away
without a backward glance.*—R. Sut-
cliff, 1954 | *Getting involved with the
blind in any way seemed like a backward step*—Ved Mehta, 1987. In addition to the directional meanings,
backward has the meaning 'mentally retarded, slow to learn', although this is now disfavoured by
many as being depreciatory.

bacterium is a singular noun
and its plural is *bacteria*. Erroneous uses of bacteria as a singular
noun are regrettably common in
newspapers: *A common gut bacteria
may be a major cause of rheumatoid
arthritis*—Independent, 1991.

bad, badly. 1 After the verb *feel*,
bad is an adjective complement
(meaning either 'guilty, ashamed'
or 'unwell') rather than an adverb: *To be absolutely honest, what I
feel really bad about is that I don't
feel worse*—Michael Frayn, 1965.
After *to be* and most other verbs,
badly is required: *He is behaving
badly* | *They badly wanted to see the
game* | *My brother was badly
wounded in Tunisia* | *The Smiths are
not badly off*. In these cases, *bad* is
used only informally or in dialect: *I only came cause she's so bad
off*—L. Hellman, 1934.

2 In a slang (principally youth
slang) use originating in US Black
English, *bad* means the very opposite of its traditional meaning,
i.e. 'excellent, very good', and in
this meaning even has special degrees of comparison *badder, bad-
dest*: *She said that part of the*

problem was that they often wanted to distinguish themselves by being badder than their rivals. Badder? Surely the comparative of bad is worse? But then worse has connotations of being less good at doing something. — *Spectator*, 1993. This is a good example of how one of the most basic words can be twisted and pulled in all directions, rather as *wicked* and *mean* have been in the past.

bade, the past tense of *bid*, is pronounced bad.

bafflegab, a term for abstruse technical terminology, was coined by Milton A. Smith, assistant general counsel for the American Chamber of Commerce, who defined it as 'multiloquence characterized by a consummate interfusion of circumlocution . . . and other familiar manifestations of abstruse expatiation commonly utilised for promulgations implementing procrustean determinations by governmental bodies.'

baggage. 1 *Baggage* and *luggage* overlap in use, although *baggage* generally connotes something heavier and bulkier and less easily transportable by hand. Some collocations are more or less fixed, e.g. *excess baggage, baggage claim, baggage handler*; and a few British railway stations still have *left-luggage* offices (rarely, though occasionally, *left-baggage*). In the US a person who looks after the baggage of passengers on a train or at a hotel is called a *baggage-man*. At air terminals *hand baggage* and *hand luggage* seem to be freely used in both BrE and AmE.

2 In figurative uses, baggage is always used: *It's the emotional baggage I'm hauling around that's caus-*

ing all the trouble — *She*, 1989 | *She was not an intellectual; her philosophical baggage was comparatively light.* — K. O. Morgan, 1990 | *They dispatched their excess female baggage at the Strand Gate where the Sheriff was closing in on them, and then headed across the quicksands to Rye* — R. Long, 1990.

bail, bale. 1 The spelling *bail* (ultimately from Old French *bailler* 'to take charge of') is always used with reference to securing the release of a person with a guarantee of his or her reappearance in court on an appointed day. Figuratively, too, a person or organization may be *bailed out*, or released, from a debt or other difficulty.

2 In the meaning 'to scoop water out of a boat', or 'to make an emergency parachute jump from an aircraft' the spelling *bale* (*out*) is now usual, as if the action were that of letting a *bale* (i.e. bundle, as in *bale of hay*) through a trapdoor, even though the word is of different origin from the noun *bale* (from Old French *baille*, 'bucket').

balance. 1 The noun is about four centuries older than the verb, and has derived several figurative uses from its primary meaning of 'an apparatus for weighing', as for example in accounting (where the notion of balancing the books is ever-present) and in more abstract uses such as *the fragile balance between peace and war*. Two centuries ago, the word branched out from the accounting sense in the US and came to mean 'something (other than money) left over' (*I'll bring the balance of our things* | *The balance of the penalty still has to be paid*). This use is not good style in unquantified contexts when a simpler word such as *rest* is available.

2 The word occurs figuratively in a number of fixed or semifixed expressions such as *balance of nature, balance of power, balance of probabilities, in the balance, on balance, to redress the balance, to strike a balance*. These are all established and acceptable uses.

baleful, baneful. These two rather literary words overlap in meaning, giving rise to confusion. *Baleful* (from *bale*, 'misery') means 'having an evil influence' or 'menacing', and is used in particular of people's presence or appearance, whereas *baneful* (from *bane*, poison) developed from its earlier meaning 'poisonous' to 'causing harm or ruin'. Examples: (baleful) *The baleful presence of his father in the house was like a constant reproach*—R. Hayman, 1981 | *Foghorns boom in still longer and lower choruses of baleful warning*—Iain Banks, 1986 | (baneful) *The baneful memory of that night haunted her, sometimes tormented her*—Iris Murdoch, 1987. *Baleful* is the more likely to be needed in spoken English, especially with reference to looks and glances.

bale out see BAIL.

balk see BAULK.

ball game, ballpark. 1 *Ball game*, an American name for baseball, has formed the core of several colloquial idioms in which it means 'a state of affairs', as in *a whole new ball game*. Because of its wide scope of alternative reference, it seems to fit naturally into BrE and to be understood perfectly well in other countries where baseball is hardly known:

It was a different ball-game in those days and you bloody well know it—W. J. Burley, 1991.

2 *Ballpark*, though even more remote culturally, has also entered BrE in the idiom *in the right ballpark*, meaning 'approximately correct'. Colourful though it is in casual conversation, it is certainly to be avoided in more formal contexts.

balm is pronounced bahm, and is most commonly used in its figurative meaning 'a healing or soothing influence or consolation' (e.g. *a balm to the senses*). Originally it meant a fragrant medicinal liquid exuded from certain trees.

balmy, barmy. These two words come from two roots, although the lines of descent have become intertwined: *balmy* (meaning 'deliciously fragrant') comes from *balm* (see that entry above) and *barmy* (as now used colloquially, meaning 'stupid') comes from *barm*, meaning 'froth'. However, *barmy* is an altered form of *balmy*, which also had the colloquial meaning in the 19c and early 20c. Consequently they may be regarded as spelling variants; but current usage favours the distinction given above.

baluster, banister. The *OED* describes *banister* as a corruption of the slightly earlier word *baluster*; both are 17c. A *baluster*, though once having the meaning that *banisters* (plural) now has, means a single curved or ornamental post supporting a *balustrade* round a gallery or terrace. A *banister* is a single post supporting a handrail at the side of a staircase, and is generally used, in the singular or more usually in the plural *banisters*, to mean the entire structure including the rail.

ban is a common journalistic word, ideally short for headlines, for 'prohibit' or 'make illegal'; as such, and because of its staccato effect in speech, it permeates everyday language. In earlier periods it meant 'to summon' and 'to curse'. In modern times, the slogan *ban the bomb* (i.e. the nuclear bomb) gave it a special currency in the 1960s. Other things that have been banned or been under threat of banning include trade unions (Solidarity in Poland until 1984, workers at the UK's GCHQ in Cheltenham), English football teams playing in European competitions (for several years from 1985), the publication of certain books and articles (e.g. *Spycatcher* in the UK in 1987), and the selling of various products such as unpasteurized milk in the EU and beef on the bone in the UK (1998).

banal, pronounced bə-**nahl** and meaning 'trite, feeble, commonplace', is a loanword that has survived, despite the fulmination of Fowler in 1926 ('imported from France by a class of writers whose jaded taste relishes novel or imposing jargon'), because no other word in English enjoys the same touch of venom: *Books are filled with pictures rather than text, and with trivial content and banal style, to make them 'easier to read'.—New Scientist,* 1991. The alternatives listed by Fowler, including *commonplace* and *trite,* simply won't do, and nowadays we relish Gallicisms rather more than he did. For other words of this type, see LOANWORD.

baneful see BALEFUL.

banister see BALUSTER.

banjo. The recommended plural is *banjos,* although *banjoes* is also found.

Bantu (plural the same or *Bantus*), referring to a large group of Negroid peoples of Central and northern Africa, is now offensive both as a noun and an adjective, because of its irredeemable associations with the apartheid era in South Africa.

bar, barring. 1 *Bar*, used as a slightly formal preposition meaning 'except', has been in use since the 18c. In current use it is often followed by a number (or *none*): *My sister-in-law for whom I probably care more than I care for anyone in the world bar one other*—Penelope Lively, 1983 | *The best detection expert I know, bar none*—Ruth Rendell, 1983. It is also used in the idiom *all over bar the shouting,* when an outcome is all but assured; and in giving the odds in racing (e.g. *33-1 bar the rest*).

2 *Barring,* which is attested much earlier (15c) is also still used in the general meanings, and collocates regularly with words expressing misfortune or reversal: *Barring accidents, we should win another Grand Slam—Rugby World and Post,* 1991 | *The young working-class man in industrial employment could expect his income to reach its peak in early manhood and stay constant thereafter, barring disasters such as unemployment.* —J. Weeks, 1992.

barbarian, barbaric, barbarous. 1 These words had their origins in people's ideas about foreign languages. The Greek word *barbaros,* 'barbarian', which is the ultimate source of all these words, meant someone who spoke words sounding like *ba ba.* To the Greeks, the *barbarians* were foreigners, and principally the Persians, but the word carried no depreciatory overtones in itself. Over the centuries the non-Hellenic, non-Roman, or non-Christian peoples became regarded as enemies who violated and plundered the civilized world, and this gave rise to the unfavourable connotations of the term *barbarian* and associated words. By an understandable process of sense-development, in the 16c to 17c the word came to be applied to any person or group regarded as uncivilized or uncultivated, and in current use has many extended meanings, although a major area of use is still historical: *Enlightenment man has undoubtedly been a man of power, but he has also been a barbarian*—A. Walker, 1988 | *Many survived the depredation of the barbarian incursion of the late third century from which Britain was spared*—G. Webster, 1991 | *She would not have minded if he had hired the Albert Hall to denounce her as a barbarian and certainly cared nothing for his kitchen sulks and drawing-room sarcasm*—A. T. Ellis, 1993.

2 Since the 15c, *barbaric* has been applied to foreign customs, language, and culture that are regarded as backward or uncivilized: *The noble savage . . . turns out to be a barbaric creature with a club and a scalping knife*—H. J. Laski, 1920 | *In this country we can kill people on the roads and walk free, and rape women and get away with around four years in prison—yet we have the cheek to call the Saudis barbaric*—Today, 1992 | *Some of the subsidiary practices [in fox-hunting] such as the 'blooding' of children are little short of barbaric*—Independent, 1998. Another (17c) use of the word, to describe exotic objects brought from abroad, has been

confined to literary contexts such as Lawrence of Arabia's description of Arab costume as *splendid and barbaric*. In modern use, it is applied to brutal or wicked physical treatment of people, and is somewhat stronger and more specific than *barbarous*, which has a more general reference and is softened by its use in aesthetic as well as physical contexts: *Formulating his phrases carefully in the barbarous French prose these people used*—D. Bagley, 1966 | *No doubt they are also the victims of a gross and barbarous fallacy*—Enoch Powell, 1991.

barbarism, barbarity. *Barbarism* has the widest scope of reference, being applied to matters of taste a well as human behaviour, and it has a special meaning in relation to language (see BARBARISMS). *Barbarity* (and occasionally *barbarousness*, although this is not normally needed) always refer to savage cruelty or extremely uncivilized behaviour. Examples: *It has taken a woman to remind us all that there are people out there who are determined that Northern Ireland will not be dragged down to the level of barbarity displayed by the terrorists*—Ulster Newsletter, 1991 | *He took up a new job in Berlin on the very day in 1930 when the Reichstag election heralded unprecedented barbarism in Europe*—New Scientist, 1991 | *I do not believe urban barbarism is about to engulf us*—East Anglian Daily Times, 1993.

barbarisms are words that are judged to be ill-formed for various reasons, usually because they are derived from a mixture of Latin and Greek roots (e.g. *television*) or a mixture of Latin/Greek and English roots (e.g. *breathalyser*). The objection is pedantic and irrational and is largely disregarded in the blizzard of present-day word-creation. See also LOST CAUSES.

barbecue is a noun and a verb (and has inflected forms *barbecues, barbecued, barbecuing*). It is sometimes written in facetious respellings such as *Bar-B-Q* (and hence *barbeque*), which are not standard.

barely, like *hardly* (see HARD 2) and SCARCELY, should normally be followed by *when*, not *than*, if a clause follows: *Chance had barely begun to sip his drink when dinner was announced*—J. Kosinski, 1983.

barman, barmaid are the BrE names for a man and woman respectively who serve drinks at a bar. The AmE equivalents are *barkeeper* (or *barkeep*) and *bartender*, although the gender distinction is less clear-cut.

barmy see BALMY.

baronage, barony. *The baronage* is the body of barons collectively, and *a baronage* is a listing of them. *Barony* is the rank or domain of a baron.

baroque is a term applied to certain forms of European art, architecture, and music of the late Renaissance and 18c. It is normally spelt with a small initial, as is *rococo*, which refers to a slightly later period of art and music (e.g. Watteau and Mozart rather than Rubens and Handel), although the two terms tend to overlap in some uses.

barring see BAR.

basal see BASIC.

basalt is pronounced **bas**-awlt.

base, basis. The two words overlap in meaning, but broadly *base* is physical (the *base of a column*, a poison with an *arsenic base*), while *basis* is figurative with a primary meaning 'that on which something depends', as in a *basis for action*, the *basis of an argument*, or doing things on a *friendly basis*. Expressions such as *on a regular basis* and *on a daily basis* are sometimes frowned on when simpler adverbs (*regularly, daily*) are available, but the longer forms often make the point more effectively and are well established. *Base* is occasionally found in figurative meanings too, especially in semi-fixed collocations such as *customer* (or *client*) *base* and *base of support*. In language, it has the special meaning of a philological root (*The word* cairn *is derived from a Celtic base*).

based. 1 BASED ON. To base one thing on another is to use the second as the basis for the first, and it is frequently used in the passive, as in *arguments based on statistics*. Avoid using *based on* as an unattached conjunction, especially in initial position as in *Based on statistics, we argue that . . . .*

2 -BASED. In the 20c, the participle *based* is commonly used in combination with a noun, meaning 'based on . . . ', as in *land-based, rule-based, science-based, technology-based*, etc.

basic, basal. Both are 19c words. *Basic* is the normal word in general contexts, and has usurped the role of other words such as *essential* and *fundamental*. *Basal* is used only in technical contexts and has a physical meaning more clearly connected with *base*: e.g. a *basal ganglion* is one situated at the base of the cerebrum.

basically has developed in the 20c from a specific meaning 'essentially, fundamentally', to a more or less meaningless sentence-filler comparable to *actually* and *really*: *Basically, I feel great, except for fatigue*—M. Ali, 1987 | *Basically I see myself as a frank individual*—Saul Bellow, 1988 | *Basically, decay is just a process*—K. Russell, 1988. This should be avoided in written English that aims to be precise and succinct.

basis see BASE. The plural form is *bases*.

bath, bathe (*verbs*). In BrE *to bath* is to have a bath (i.e. wash oneself immersed in a domestic bath), and *to bathe* is to go into the sea or a river to swim. In AmE, *bathe* is used much more commonly in the washing sense. In both varieties, *take a bath* is a common alternative.

bathroom in BrE means a place for washing and taking a bath, and may or may not include a lavatory; in AmE it is first and foremost a lavatory: *The man . . . grew up . . . in a town where he was unable to use the same bathroom as white residents*—*Chicago Tribune*, 1987.

baulk, balk. 1 PRONUNCIATION. It should be pronounced bawlk (with *l*).

2 SPELLING. The usual BrE spelling is *baulk*, although *balk* is more common in AmE. The primary use is as a verb meaning (1) followed by *at*: 'to hesitate, refuse to go on', as in *For one thing, the government may baulk at giving the financial guarantee*—*New Scientist*, 1991, (2) followed by *of*: 'to thwart', as in *I gave her the number and hung up feeling baulked of my escape*—L. R. Banks, 1987 | *Fenella*

had the feeling that they were simply mustering their strength again; they had been baulked of their prey and they had retired—B. Wood, 1993. There are a few technical noun meanings, including a line in billiards and snooker and a length of sawn timber; the same spelling rules apply.

BC should be placed after the numerals to which it relates, as in 55 BC. When a range of dates is given, the second date should be put in full, as in 55–53 BC (since 55–3 BC has another meaning). In printing style, BC is normally put in small capitals. The culturally neutral BCE ('before Common Era') is also used.

be. 1 LINKING SINGULAR AND PLURAL. Very often the subject of the verb *be* is singular and the complement plural, or vice versa, and in these cases the verb should agree with the subject: *Gustave is other animals as well*—Julian Barnes, 1984 | *These huge biographies are usually a mistake nowadays*—N. Stone, 1985. But when the subject is a collective noun, the verb may be in the plural, following the usual pattern with such nouns: *Its prey are other small animals*—David Attenborough, 1987. When the subject is the relative pronoun *what*, the verb is singular: *What I'm really interested in . . . is the objects in this house*—*New Yorker*, 1986.

2 SUBJUNCTIVE FORMS. The verb *be* has two residual subjunctive forms, *be* and *were*. Their use is rapidly disappearing, but there are one or two uses still left:

▸ **a** in an inverted construction replacing *if* or *whether*: *We would much prefer to support specific projects, be they in management schools or in university laboratories*—*Journal of the Royal Society of Arts*, 1986 |

Were this done, we would retain a separate Barwith skill—Times, 1986.

▶**b** after *if* in hypothetical conditions: *If the truth be told, I never wanted to fly away with the sky-gods*—J. M. Coetzee, 1977 | *If I were obliged to rough out a blueprint of the Church of the future, I would start with the need for good popular theology*—Gerald Priestland, 1982. However, the past indicative form *was* is often used instead of *were*, especially in conversational style: *I'd get out if I was you*—Maurice Gee, 1983.

▶**c** in dependent clauses after verbs of advising and instructing such as *demand, insist, suggest*, etc: *The Admiralty insisted that the case be clarified*—P. Wright, 1987 | *In order to broaden the 'target audience' of your newsletter . . . I might suggest that such material be written at a lower level of readability.—Underground Grammarian*, 1982; also after nouns and phrases of equivalent meaning: *It is important in today's vote that the principle itself be accepted—Times*, 1985.

▶**d** in certain fixed expressions such as *be that as it may, far be it from me, the powers that be*, etc.

3 THE CASE OF THE COMPLEMENT AFTER BE. The monks of Rheims, as quoted by the grammarian Dean Alford in 1864, cried out when they saw the anathematised jackdaw: 'That's him!' and not 'That's he!'. In both speech and writing, the type *it's me/him/her/us/them* is now virtually universal, except when a relative pronoun follows, as in *It was he who would be waiting on the tow-path*—P. D. James, 1986. See further at CASES 2.

4 REDUCED FORMS. *Am, is*, and *were* are reduced to *'m, 's*, and *'re* respectively after pronouns and nouns (*I'm over here* | *She's just coming* |*We're late, are we?*), except

when the noun ends in a sibilant sound (🗵 *The church's just up the road*). *Aren't*, used for *am not* in the question form *aren't I* as well as *are you/they not*, is irregular; *ain't* is irregular and widely deplored (see AIN'T).

5 ELLIPSIS OF BE. *Be* is often omitted, especially in informal contexts, in cases such as *They are sorry for what they did and anxious to make amends* | *We're leaving now and catching the 9.00 train*. When *be* is used as an auxiliary verb and as a linking verb in the same sentence, it must be repeated because its role is different: *The bill was overtaken by the 1964 election and its postponement was welcome*.

beat is largely defunct as a participial form, except in the phrase *dead-beat*. Otherwise it is confined to (especially AmE) dialect and non-standard uses: *You hear on television nowadays about little children getting beat up or treated nasty—New Yorker*, 1988.

beauteous is a literary and chiefly poetical word for *beautiful*, used memorably by Wordsworth (*It is a beauteous evening, calm and free*) and madly by Ophelia in *Hamlet*: *Where is the beauteous majesty of Denmark?*.

because. 1 BECAUSE, AS, SINCE, FOR. *Because* is a conjunction that normally introduces a dependent clause and answers the question 'why?' (or, sometimes, 'how?'). It can relate directly to the statement made, as in *I came because I wanted to see you*, which answers the (real or notional) question 'Why did you come?', or (like *for*) it can relate to the status of the proposition, as in *I know he committed suicide, because his wife told me*, which effectively answers the question 'How do you know he committed suicide?' and not the question 'Why did he commit suicide?'; in this sentence, the comma has an important structural function.

Because can also stand first in the sentence, as in *Because we missed the train, we had to wait a long time.* It is also in order to use *because* after an introductory *it is, it's, that's, this is,* etc.: *It is because these Christian values are apparently being cast off by the present leadership of the Conservative Party . . . that many Christians are turning to the Alliance.—Church Times,* 1985.

As and *since* are often used at the beginning of a sentence, and (unlike *because*) tend to emphasize the main statement rather than the reason. *For* can only follow the main statement, and is a coordinating conjunction, whereas *because* is a subordinating conjunction.

2 AFTER NEGATIVES. Using *because* after a negative statement (e.g. *I do not play cards because I enjoy good company,* i.e. one containing a word such as *not* or *never* or including a word in *un-* etc.) can technically cause ambiguity because it is not clear whether the reason given is an invalid one for a positive statement (i.e. *I do play cards, but not because . . .*), or a valid one for a negative statement (i.e. *I do not play cards, and the reason is . . .*). However, the context will often make the meaning clear: *Very many people . . . do not attend church because they are bored by ritualistic services—Lancashire Life,* 1977 | *Her twin was told she was unlikely to have children because of her husband's low sperm count.—Daily Telegraph,* 1979. When necessary, a comma will usually remove any ambiguity: *The graphic equalizer is not for every hi-fi customer, because*

it does require some skill, time and patience in usage—Gramophone, 1976.

3 *THE REASON IS . . . BECAUSE* *. . . . The reason for this was because I was the only one who could sign it, because the account was in my name—*Ben Elton, 1991. This construction is often rejected on grounds of style in favour of *the reason is . . . that . . . ,* since *because* is logically redundant after *reason.* But redundancy is a regular component of idiom, and given that both constructions are common it is becoming harder to insist on the point. In the following example, it would weaken the statement considerably to replace *because* with *that: The minipill was developed for one reason alone: because it was believed to provide safe contraception—New Scientist,* 1970. However, *because of* should be avoided in this kind of construction: ☒ *The reason we have no light is because of a broken fuse* should read *The reason we have no light is that the fuse is broken.*

4 *BECAUSE OF.* With the reservation given in the last paragraph, *because of* is a legitimate use in many positions in a sentence: *Because of the deterioration of the sugar in the blood it was decided, after consultation, to carry out an exchange blood transfusion—Glasgow Herald,* 1970 | *He'd have to watch his step . . . not to make a hash of things, because of over-anxiety—*J. Wainwright, 1976.

5 AT THE HEAD OF A DEPENDENT CLAUSE GOVERNING A MAIN CLAUSE, as in *Because we don't explicitly ask these questions doesn't mean they aren't answered—New Yorker,* 1986.This kind of construction, though common in speech, is awkward in written English because the main clause is uncomfortably delayed, and the

sentence should be recast, e.g.
*These questions are still answered
even though we don't explicitly ask
them.*

been and (gone and) —
appears in popular speech in
Dickens (*Pickwick Papers*, 1836),
and is still common in casual
and jocular contexts, although it
now sounds somewhat dated (*And
what's more, he's been and gone and
got it printed*—P. Bailey, 1986).

begin see COMMENCE.

begrudge, grudge. These two
words overlap in meaning, but
not completely. To *begrudge someone something* (such as success) is
to envy them for having it,
whereas to *grudge something* is to
resent the giving (by yourself or
someone else) of something that
you think you have a right to. Examples best clarify the distinction, although the meanings
overlap in practice: *Few people begrudge the aid we send to the starv-
ing or merely under-developed
regions of the earth*—Guardian, 1984
| *I imagine you won't grudge me a
glass of brandy first*—Penelope
Fitzgerald, 1988.

beg the question means,
strictly speaking, to question an
unproved assumption that is used
as the basis for an argument. For
example, to say that 'capital punishment is necessary because
without it murders would increase' begs the question because
an increase in murders is postulated rather than proved. In general use, *beg the question* has come
to mean (1) 'bring a question to
mind' (e.g. *John Major's vision of
Europe . . . begs the question: 'why
did the prime minister all but sacrifice
his office ratifying the Maastricht
Treaty . . . ?'*—Economist, 1993 and
(2) 'avoid a straightforward an-

swer' (e.g. *He simply begged the
question by saying that the decisions
he disapproved invented new rights*—
New York Review of Books, 1987).
These weakened meanings should
be avoided in precise English;
available alternatives are, for (1)
raise (or *suggest* or *invite*) *the question*, and for (2) *evade* (or *avoid*) *the
question.*

behalf is now used in BrE only
in the phrase *on behalf of* (AmE *in
behalf of*), which means (1) 'in the
interests of', and (2) 'as a representative of' (*He used to make pay-
ments and pick up money on behalf
of Mafia mobsters*—Times, 1982). It
should not be used to mean 'on
the part of', as in *The detail may
be trivial but it betrays an astounding
lack of appreciation on behalf of the
author*—Times, 1994.

being as should only be used in
casual conversation: *Being as how
you can't be married, you'd better
have him christened*—G. V. Higgins,
1979.

belittle is, to the surprise of
many, an Americanism, disapproved of by Fowler (1926) as an
'undesirable alien', at least in its
meaning 'decry, depreciate'. This
objection is a lost cause (see LOST
CAUSES); the verb is now standard
in BrE and has produced a quasi-
adjective, *belittling*. The physical
meaning 'to dwarf by contrast',
which Fowler accepted, is no
longer used.

belly is a standard word for the
front part of the human body
below the breast, despite marked
fluctuations in acceptability over
many centuries of use; alternatives are *abdomen* (more technical
and formal), *stomach* (more specific) and *tummy* (more colloquial,
especially in children's use).
There are many transferred uses,

e.g. the underside of an animal, the underside of an aeroplane, the front part of a cello, etc.

below, beneath, under. These three words appear to be synonymous, but many contexts call for one in preference to another. *Beneath* is somewhat more literary in use. *Under* in its physical sense is rather more literal than the other two: *under the bridge* means directly underneath it, whereas *beneath the bridge* suggests a wider area, and *below the bridge* can also mean downstream from it. It is customary to say *below par, below the belt, to go below* (in a ship), *the information below, the temperature is below 20 degrees*; conversely *a man under 40, under one's breath, incomes under £10,000, under the sun, under the circumstances, under one's thumb, under sentence of death*, and *beneath contempt, be beneath one.*

benchmark. This is a busy word with an interesting history and some recent developments. In its original physical meaning it referred to a wedge-shaped incision made by surveyors in a vertical surface so that a bracket could be inserted to form a *bench* or support for surveying equipment at a fixed and reproducible height. By the 1880s it had developed a figurative meaning, 'a point of reference, a standard'; more recently, the rapid growth in the use of personal computers has led to the development of *benchmark* software designed to perform comparative tests on different models. This meaning has also spawned a verb: to *benchmark* a system is to apply a benchmark test to it: *We haven't had a chance to completely benchmark the new low-cost Mac models—MacWorld, 1993.*

benefit has inflected forms *benefited, benefiting*, with one *t* not two.

benign is principally used in medicine to mean 'not life-threatening'; its opposite is *malignant*. The word *benignant*, meaning 'kindly' or 'beneficial', has largely fallen out of use.

bereaved, bereft. The verb *bereave*, meaning 'to deprive (someone)', is normally used in the passive. When the meaning refers in general ways to possessions, feelings, etc., the past participle is *bereft: Without her, he felt bereft as a child at a boarding school*—A. N. Wilson, 1982. Strictly, there should be a sense of being deprived; *bereft of* should not be used as a synonym for *lacking* or *without* (as in *bereft of manners*). In the context of death the form is *bereaved* (*If it is your own mother who is bereaved, the fact that you are grieving too will probably help you both a good deal*—E. Deeping, 1979), and this is frequently used adjectivally (*It needs to be remembered that bereaved people stay at home*—J. Pardoe, 1991 | *The bereaved have always wished to 'remember' their dead, in the literal sense of reconstituting form and feature*—R. Cecil, 1991).

berk is a BrE slang term for a fool. It is not usually regarded as strongly offensive, despite its association, via rhyming slang *Berkshire Hunt* (pronounced as in AmE), with *cunt.*

berserk, meaning 'wild, frenzied, is now mostly confined to the expression *to go berserk*. It is in origin a Norse word for a warrior who fought with wild fury. *Berserk* may be pronounced either bǝ-**zerk** or bǝ-**serk**, although the first is now more common.

beside, besides. *Beside* is only used as a preposition meaning 'next to' (*He heard Lee come up beside him*—A. Hassall, 1989), whereas *besides* is both an adverb meaning 'also, moreover' (*Besides, it was not the first disappointment*—S. Studd, 1981) and a preposition meaning 'as well as' (*Besides newsstands and supermarket checkouts, books are pumped out through mail-order clubs*—*Economist*, 1993). *Beside* also occurs in fixed expressions, e.g. *to be beside oneself, beside the point*, but it should not be used in a general way, as in ⊠ *Beside their homework, they have letters to write*, when *besides* is needed.

besiege like *siege*, is spelt -*ie*-.

bet has past and past participle forms *bet* and *betted*; both are correct although *bet* is preferable, and is more common in BrE and (even more) in AmE. But *betted* is also found (*I'd have betted you wouldn't be much good at taking somebody out*—Kingsley Amis, 1988). When a sum of money is specified, only *bet* is possible (*He bet me £50 he would win*).

bête noire is always written with the final *e*. The plural is *bêtes noires*, with both *s*'s silent.

better. 1 *HAD BETTER*. This common idiom is used in the form *We had better go home* or *We'd better go home*; the negative form is *We'd better not go home* and the interrogative *Hadn't we better go home?*. Informally (but not in more formal contexts), the word *had* is sometimes omitted: *We better go home*; and in some cases the preceding pronoun too: *When you're feeling censorious, better ask yourself which you'd choose*—P. D. James, 1986.

2 *BETTER, BETTOR*. In the meaning 'one who bets', *bettor* is more common in AmE, and *better* in BrE. *Bettor* has the advantage of being distinct from the comparative of *good*, although their distinct uses keep them out of each other's way.

between. 1 GENERAL. *Between* is an adverb (*houses with spaces between*) and a preposition (*houses with spaces between them*). We are concerned here with *between* as a preposition.

2 *BETWEEN* AND *AMONG*. Many people, and usage guides, cling to the idea (probably influenced by the use of *between* in relation to physical distance between points), that *between* is used when two people or things are involved and *among* must be invoked when more than two are involved. But this line is supported neither by the explanations of the *OED* nor by usage, which constantly refer to two or more parties: *Does he sigh between the chimes of the clock?*—J. M. Coetzee, 1977 | *Things that had happened a long time since—between Isaac and myself*—Nigel Williams, 1985 | *The death of his sister had changed things between Marcus, Ruth and Jacqueline*—A. S. Byatt, 1985 | *Museums have become an uneasy cross between theatre and boutique*—*New Yorker*, 1987.

There are, however, cases where *among* is the better word to use, normally when the underlying notion is of collectivity rather than separation: *There were a lot of very young people among the temporary staff*—Penelope Fitzgerald, 1980 | *The UN . . . does have machinery designed to . . . keep the peace among nations*—*Christian Science Monitor*, 1987. Conversely, *between* and not *among* is used when there only two people or things (as in the first 1985 example in the preceding paragraph), and when the people or things (of whatever number) are specified (as in the second 1985 example). Before reflexive pronouns (*ourselves, themselves*, etc) *among* and *between* are used interchangeably.

3 BETWEEN . . . AND . . . . *Between* should be followed by *and*, not other words such as *or*, as in the following examples: ⊠ [*This*] *leaves Britain with the choice between being ruined by runaway inflation or by a series of disastrous strikes—Daily Telegraph*, 1970 ⊠ *My feet got so sensitive I could sense the difference between tarvia, gravel, or concrete immediately—Islander* (Victoria, BC), 1972. Similarly, it is important to say *between 1914 and 1918*, or *from 1914 to 1918* (also expressed as *1914–18*), not *between 1914–18*. See also FROM.

4 BETWEEN EACH, BETWEEN EVERY. Constructions such as *22 yards between each telegraph pole* and *pause between every mouthful* are often deplored on the grounds that logical grammar calls for the addition of *and the next* to each group of words. Informally, however, this construction is typical and unexceptionable, although it is best avoided in more formal contexts. Examples: *The 30-minute headway between each bus reduced to a 50-minute headway—Courier-Mail* (Brisbane), 1970. The construction *between every two* is ambiguous as to 'between two' and 'between two pairs', and is best avoided.

5 BETWEEN YOU AND I, though found in Shakespeare (but so is *between you and him*, not *he*), is an example of hypercorrection, influenced perhaps by the purist insistence on sentences of the type *'Who's going?' 'Anne and I.'* (in which *Anne and me* is also possible). Since *between* governs both pronouns, the correct construction is *between you and me, between you and us*, etc.: *Tiny bit boring, between you and me*—Penelope Mortimer, 1962.

6 REPEATED BETWEEN. In long sentences, there is always a temptation to insert a second *between* as a *reminder* of what the statement is about: *You need to decide between voting for a party which, against all advice, introduced the poll tax, a form of tax first used in the 14th century, and one that dislikes the rates system but has no alternative to offer.* Putting a second *between* before *one that dislikes* is tempting because of the length of the sentence but it would be ungrammatical, and the sentence would be better recast.

beware is of Old English origin, and except for a period from about 1600 to the late 19c has lacked inflected forms, being used chiefly in the imperative (*Beware of the dog!*) or after a modal auxiliary such as *do* and *must* (*Do beware of the dog | We must beware of impostors*). Use with a direct object is found in Shakespeare (*Since I am a dog, beware my phangs—The Merchant of Venice* III.iii.7 | *Beware the Ides of March—Julius Caesar* I.ii.20) and other poetic writing, but is not a feature of ordinary speech or writing, except allusively.

bi-. This prefix causes much confusion in words such as *biweekly, bimonthly*, etc., because it is used to mean (for example) 'twice a week' as well as 'every two weeks'. Rules do not help because they are not universally followed; it is best to avoid the problem by using terms such as *twice a week* and *twice-weekly* on the one hand,

and *every two weeks* and *fortnightly* on the other.

biannual (19c) normally means 'twice a year', as distinct from *biennial* (17c), which means 'every two years' or 'lasting two years'. Since usage is not consistent on this point, it is sometimes better to use alternatives such as *half-yearly* or *twice-yearly* instead of *biannual* and *two-yearly* for *biennial*.

bias. The verb has inflected forms *biased, biasing*, although *-ss-* is also found. The plural of the noun is *biases*.

Bible. Use a capital initial when it refers to the scriptures collectively (*Read your Bible*), but a small initial when it refers to a copy of the book (*three bibles*) or is allusive (*Wisden is the cricketer's bible*).

bicentenary, a noun meaning 'two-hundredth anniversary' and also a corresponding adjective, is pronounced *-teen-* more usually than *-ten-*. It is the usual term in BrE, whereas *bicentennial* is more usual in AmE and elsewhere.

biceps is spelt the same in the plural.

bid has past tenses *bade* (in general meanings : *We bade them farewell*) and *bid* (in card games and the auction room: *We bid successfully for the portrait*). The corresponding past participle forms are *bidden* and *bid*.

biennial see BIANNUAL.

billion in BrE has since the 1950s come increasingly to mean 'a thousand million' as it always has in AmE, rather than its old BrE meaning of 'a million million'. In more idiomatic uses (as in *I've told you a billion times*) there is no precise meaning. When pre-

ceded by a numeral, the plural is *billion* (unchanged: *three billion people*), but *billions* is used when it is followed by *of* (*billions of people*).

bimonthly see BI-.

bin, short for *waste-bin*, has given rise in BrE to a transitive verb *to bin*, meaning 'to throw away' or (figuratively) 'to reject': *Who remembers the kind of middle-class good behaviour, thrift and modesty that have been binned along with Bromo, the Church Times and meals for one?—Independent on Sunday*, 1990. The inflections are *binned, binning*.

bivouac *verb* has inflected forms *bivouacked, bivouacking*.

biweekly see BI-.

black. In the 1920s this word began to replace *Negro, Negress*, and, more particularly, *Nigger*, as a term for a person of African descent. In Britain, *black* can mean people of South Asian as well as African origin (although it is preferable to use specific terms such as *Indian, Malay, Pakistani*, etc.); in AmE the term *African-American* is also used. For a time it was thought appropriate to spell *black* with a capital initial as a racial term, but the normal preference now is for a small initial.

black, blacken *verbs*. *Black* is used when the meaning is to deliberately make something black, as in blacking one's face, one's shoes, a person's eye, etc., in the meaning to declare something 'black' (i.e. to boycott it), and in the phrasal verb *to black out*. *Blacken* is more often used to imply an unintentional or fortuitous process (*the ceiling blackened with smoke*); unlike *black*, it can be used intransitively (*The sky blackened*), and is more common as a participial adjective: *Then you notice the blackened buildings, boarded up houses and the painted slogans in the housing estates—Woman's Own*, 1977. *Blacken* also has a special figurative use, 'to besmirch or tarnish', with reference to people's character, reputation, etc.

Black English is the form of English spoken by many blacks, especially as an urban dialect of the United States. The name (apart from a chance occurrence recorded in 1734), and the recognition of Black English as a distinctive and describable form of AmE, date from the time of the civil-rights movement in the 1960s. It has many distinct grammatical features (e.g. uninflected plurals and double negatives) and items of vocabulary, which are not imperfections but are characteristic of a creolized form of English.

blame *verb*. **1** Two constructions are now standard: *to blame someone for something* and *to blame something on someone*. Gowers (1965) described the second as a needless variant, but such strictures are futile in the face of incontrovertible evidence of usage.

2 The derivative in *-able* retains the final *e*: *blameable*.

blanch, blench. *Blanch* means first and foremost 'to make (something) white' (especially vegetables by dipping them in boiling water) and (intransitively) 'to become pale' (from fear, shock, embarrassment, etc.); a by-form *blench* is also used in this sense. Confusingly, there is another (Old English) word *blench*, which overlaps slightly with *blanch/blench* in its meaning 'to quail, flinch', as in *Strong men blenched and broke into a sweat of embarrassment when made to dance 'Ring-a-ring o' roses' in public outside Guildhall—Times*, 1974.

blatant, flagrant. *Blatant*, a word invented by Spenser, now means 'glaringly conspicuous', and overlaps in meaning with *flagrant* but has rather less of *flagrant*'s implications of offensiveness: *It was a blatant lie* means that the lie was obvious; *It was a flagrant lie* means that (when discovered) it was outrageous. The adverbial form *blatantly* (unlike *flagrantly*) has developed a weakened meaning, especially in youth slang, as a stock form of intensifier like *absolutely* and *extremely*.

blessed, blest. As an attributive adjective (i.e. used before a noun), *blessed* is pronounced as two syllables: *The Blessed Sacrament | every blessed night*. When used as the past tense and past participle of the verb *to bless*, it is pronounced blest (one syllable): *The bishop (had) blessed his wife and children before he died | I'm blessed if I know*. The spelling *blest* is now mostly confined to use in poetry and hymns.

bloc is a 20c loanword from French, meaning 'a combination of parties, governments, groups, etc. sharing a common purpose'. The phrase *bloc vote* is now being increasingly used instead of the traditional *block vote*. See also EN BLOC.

blond, blonde. These two forms retain a trace of the grammatical gender they have in French, since *blonde* is normally used (as a noun and an adjective) of a woman. With *blond*, however, the distinction is less clear-cut: a *blond*, or a *blond* person, can be a woman or a man, and *blond* hair can belong to either sex. Examples (BrE unless otherwise specified): *Crews of tall, blond men who hardly ever spoke*—T. Findley, 1984 (Canadian) |*His blond eye-lashes gave him a bemused look*—Penelope Fitzgerald, 1988 | *Her blonde plaits reaching half-way down her bony back*—Colin Dexter, 1989 | *The little girls whispered to each other, their blond heads shining in the rather dark room*—New Yorker, 1990 (US) | *Lugging that doll of hers, a thing with blonde shiny hair*—A. Duff, 1990 (NZ).

bloody. **1** *Bloody* developed its meaning in BrE as 'a vague epithet expressing anger, resentment, etc.' in the 18c, and rapidly became a mere intensive, especially in negative contexts (*not a bloody one*). The OED called it 'foul language', and as recently as 1995 the *Concise Oxford Dictionary* called it 'coarse slang'; but now, at the end of a millennium, it seems comparatively tame, and other words have taken on its former mantle of offensiveness: *You want to use your bloody loaf, Stubbs, or we'll never win this war the way you're carrying on*—Brian Aldiss, 1971.

2 As an adverb *bloody* has been used as an intensive since the later 17c in combinations such as *bloody drunk, bloody angry*, and *bloody ill*. G. B. Shaw was entitled to expect a sharp reaction from the audience when in 1914 he caused Eliza Doolittle to exclaim 'Walk! Not bloody likely.' As with the adjective, however, this use has weakened considerably in ef-

fect, especially in the period after the second World War, and television characters regularly use expressions such as *serves you bloody right* and *you bloody well do it or else*. Even so, the word belongs in the realm of strong language and can still cause disapproval or offence if used too freely.

3 These uses are recorded in American dictionaries, but are not properly part of AmE. It is a pleasing myth that Australians use them more freely and vigorously than in other parts of the English-speaking world, and the colourful entry in the *Australian National Dictionary* (1988) appears to support it, with examples of use steeped in the language of pioneering adversity and 'ranging in force from mildly irritating to execrable': *You must think yourself a damned clever bushman, talking about tracking a bloody dingo over bloody ground where a bloody regiment of newly-shod horses would scarcely leave a bloody track*—M. J. O'Reilly, 1944.

bloom, blossom. Cherry trees are said to be in *blossom*, roses in *bloom*. The difference corresponds largely to that between trees whose blossom is a sign of fruit to come and plants whose flowers are a culmination in themselves. In figurative uses the distinction is maintained; people and things *blossom* (or are in *blossom*) when they are full of promise and *bloom* (or are in *bloom*) when they are in their prime (as in *the bloom of perfect manhood*).

blow *verb*. The regular past and past participle are *blew* and *blown*. An older form, *blowed*, survives in the fixed expression *I'll be blowed*, as in *Well I'm* [or *I'll be*] *blowed* and *I'm blowed if I will*.

bluish is preferred, not *blueish*.

boat. A *boat* is a 'small vessel propelled on water' by various means, and includes vessels used for fishing, for cargo, or to carry passengers. A *ship* is a large sea-going vessel, especially when part of a navy. A submarine, however, despite its designation HMS, is referred to as a *boat* rather than a *ship* (if the choice has to be made between these two).

boatswain is now generally pronounced **boh**-sən regardless of whether it is spelt this way or as *bosun*.

bogey, bogie, bogy. The latest editions of the Oxford dictionaries prefer *bogey* for the golfing term and the mischievous spirit, and *bogie* for the railway term. *Bogy* is classed as a variant of *bogey* in the second meaning.

bog-standard is one of those highly informal but likeable expressions that seem older than the dictionaries would suggest. It does not appear in the *OED*, but finds a place in the *Oxford Dictionary of New Words* (1997) and the *Concise Oxford Dictionary* (1999). It is a graphic word of obscure origin (altered from *box-standard*?) meaning 'basic, standard', as in *The rest of the furniture is bog standard café tables and chairs—Time Out*, 1995.

boggle, boggling *verb. Boggle*, originally used of frightened horses, is used with and without an object: the mind can *boggle* at something and something can *boggle* the mind (or the imagination etc.). The expression *mind-boggling*, first recorded in *Punch* in 1964, pre-dates the regular transitive use, and has been joined since the 1970s by the more col-

loquial reduced form *boggling*: *Serious damage can mean even more boggling bills—Which?*, 1990.

bona fide, bona fides. 1 *Bona fide* is an adjectival and (now rarely) adverbial phrase meaning 'in good faith' and hence 'genuine(ly)' (*a bona fide tourist*); *bona fides* is a noun phrase meaning 'good faith' and hence 'honest intention'. *Bona fides* is singular in Latin, and is correctly treated as singular in English, despite its plural-looking form: *His bona fides has been questioned* not (notwithstanding euphony) *His bona fides have been questioned*.

2 The pronunciation is **boh**-nə **fiy**-deez.

bonne bouche in English means 'a dainty mouthful or morsel', referring to the food rather than (as in French) its taste. Fowler (1926) conceded that it was 'definitely established' and even tolerated the difference in meaning; but it is still regarded as non-naturalized and should be printed in italics.

bored is normally construed with *by* or *with*: *How bored she was with that face!*—D. Devine, 1970 | *He got bored with working in the scout hut*—L. Henderson, 1976 | *Very many people . . . do not attend church because they are bored by ritualistic services*—Lancashire Life, 1977. Use with *of*, sometimes heard conversationally, is non-standard: *I was conscious of all the problems . . . of getting bored of something the minute you get it*—N. Fairburn, 1992 (Scottish).

born, borne. It is sometimes forgotten that *born*, relating to birth, is a past participle of the verb *to bear*, and that *I was born on a Friday* means 'My mother bore me on a Friday'. *Born* is also used in figurative expressions such as *an indifference born of long familiarity*. In all other meanings, the past participle of *bear* is *borne* (*I have borne with this too long | He was borne along by the wind*), and this form is used with reference to birth when the construction is active, or when it is passive followed by *by* (the mother): *She has borne no children | Of all the children borne by her only one survived.*

Borstal is a former name for British institutions for reforming young offenders. It is still found in print in allusive use, but the correct terms to use now are *detention centre* and *youth custody centre*.

botanic, botanical. Both forms have been in use since the 17c. *Botanical* is more common in general use, although *botanic* occurs in traditional names such as the *Botanic Garden* in Oxford and the *Botanic Gardens* in Edinburgh.

both. 1 GENERAL. *Both*, when modifying a single item, refers to two things or persons (*both houses | both women*); when, as *both . . . and . . .* , it couples two items, each of these may be singular (*both the woman and the man*) or plural (*both the women and the men*), although care must be taken to avoid misunderstanding if the first item is plural, as in the example just given.

2 POSITION. *Both* is a mobile word and can be linked to particular pairs of sentence elements: *They work both by day and by night | He both loves and hates his brother | The work is both rewarding and enjoyable | I hope to be both a writer and a musician*. When there are more than two items involved, the word *both* should be omitted: *I want to be a writer, a musician, and a painter.*

3 AS PRONOUN. *Both* can also function as a pronoun, optionally followed by *of*: *I will try to see both | I will try to see both of the candidates | I will try to see both of you*; when used with a personal pronoun *both* must follow it: *I will try to see you both | You both look worried.*

4 AWKWARD CONSTRUCTIONS. Because *both* is so flexible in use, its intended meaning can be unclear in some uses:

▶ **a** *We both won a prize* can mean either (1) 'we both won one prize between us', or (2) 'we won a prize each'. It is better to use *each* or to rephrase with a word such as *joint*, as appropriate: *We each won a prize | We won a joint prize.*

▶ **b** *You will see a tree at both ends of the road* is not so much ambiguous as counter-intuitive, since the tree can only be in one place. Rephrase as *You will see a tree [or trees] at each end of the road.*

▶ **c** *Books are useful both for pleasure as well as for learning* is a sequence to be avoided: *both* should always be paired with *and*: *Books are useful both for pleasure and for learning*. Note also the repetition of *for*: see the next item.

▶ **d** *Her speech was both detrimental to understanding and to peace* needs to be rephrased so that the two elements governed by *both* match each other: *Her speech was detrimental to both understanding and peace* or *Her speech was detrimental both to understanding and to peace*; compare *Her speech was both detrimental to understanding and damaging to peace*. This applies especially to use of the definite or indefinite article: *Both the man and woman should be corrected to Both the man and the woman.*

▶ **e** *He was acting on both our be-halfs* is better expressed as *He was acting on behalf of us both.*

▶ **f** *We find them both equally responsible* is a common construction in speech, but *both* is strictly redundant, and should be omitted in more formal writing: *We find them equally responsible.*

bottleneck, meaning a holdup or constriction in traffic, dates from the late 19c, and is now used more widely of obstructions in processes of various kinds. Care should be taken to avoid unsuitable elaboration of the image, as in *curing* or *ironing out a bottleneck*, and strictly speaking a *bottleneck* cannot be *big* or *extensive* or even *major.*

bottom line is a term in accounting for the line in a profit-and-loss account that shows the final figure. It has developed a figurative meaning 'the decisive factor or objective', which should only be used informally: *The bottom line is that we all love music and want to play it*—New Musical Express, 1992. When the term is used in financial contexts it can be unclear whether the meaning is literal or not: *The bottom line could eventually mean demands for higher council tax bills*—television broadcast, 1993. In such cases it is better to use alternatives such as *consequence, crux, issue, upshot.*

bounden survives only in the somewhat dated and affected phrase *bounden duty.*

bowsprit is pronounced with *bow-* as in *low.*

brackets. The term is used generally of the punctuation marks (), [], { }, <>, although the first set is properly called *parentheses*, the second *square brackets*, the third *curly brackets* or *hooked brackets*,

and the fourth *angle brackets*. The mark resembling a curly bracket, used to link items on more than one line, is called a *brace.*

brand-new is the correct spelling, not *bran-new*. The term originally meant 'fresh like a *brand* [= burning torch] from a furnace'.

bravery, bravado, bravura. *Bravery* is a general word for 'being brave' or 'brave action' (as a virtue), whereas *bravado* means 'ostentatious courage or boldness', often concealing fear or reluctance: *It was a gesture of bravado rather than a serious business proposition*—Richard Branson, 1989. *Bravura* is a florid or showy style of playing in music, and does not have a general meaning.

breach, breech. The spelling of these two words is often confused. *Breach* is a noun and verb meaning 'a break' or 'to break' (as in *a breach of contract*, *to breach the enemy's defences*), whereas *breech* means 'the back or lower part of something', and is applied principally to part of a rifle, the buttocks (now only in *breech birth*, when a baby is born bottom first), and (in the plural *breeches*, pronounced **brich**-iz), to a type of trousers.

breakdown can mean, in addition to its meaning in relation to machines, human health, and aspects of human behaviour, 'an analysis of statistics or information': *The breakdown of expenses . . . is relatively detailed in some cases but not in others*—J. Greenwood et al., 1989. Care should be taken to avoid possible confusion when the word might be understood in more than one way: *Management should first examine the data produced to ascertain whether any variance from the breakdown is* *due to site conditions or mismanagement*—A. Upson, 1987.

breakthrough, originally a military word and formerly a vogue word in its figurative use, is now commonplace. It is spelt as one word, is commonly qualified (especially in journalism) by words such as *new* and *major*, and is regularly followed by *in*, as in *a breakthrough in cancer research*.

breech see BREACH.

brier, briar. Both spellings are used of two distinct words, meaning respectively a prickly bush and a type of wood (or a pipe made from it). The preferred spelling for both words is *brier*.

bring, take. The essential difference between these two words corresponds to that between *come* and *go*, and is intuitive to a native speaker: *bring* implies movement towards, and *take* movement away from, the person speaking: *Take your bike and bring me a newspaper.* When the standpoint of the speaker is unstable, there is a choice: *Shall I bring the camera?* is spoken in terms of the destination and *Shall I take the camera?* in terms of the starting point. In other varieties of English, and in some dialects, the pattern differs.

Brit is a colloquial term (early 20c) for a British person, especially when abroad. It varies in offensiveness from the (more usually) affectionate (*Lots of Brits around this year*) to the hostile (*Brits out!*).

Britain, Great Britain, the British Isles, England, etc. 1 Use of these terms causes confusion. *Great Britain* refers to the largest island in the group, which is divided between England, Scotland, and Wales. Politically, it means these three countries (since the Act of Union of 1707), and excludes Northern Ireland, the Isle of Man, and the Channel Islands. *Britain* is an informal term with no official status; it often means the same as *Great Britain* but can also include Northern Island.

2 *The British Isles* is a geographical term for the group of islands including Great Britain and Ireland and also the smaller islands around them, such as the Isle of Man and the Scottish islands. *The United Kingdom* is a political term, in full *the United Kingdom of Great Britain and Northern Ireland*, and includes these countries but not usually the Isle of Man or the Channel Islands.

3 *England* strictly refers to a single political division of Great Britain, but it is commonly substituted for (*Great*) *Britain*, especially in AmE. This causes some offence in Scotland and Wales, and should be avoided in BrE. The same is true of the corresponding ethnic designation *English* used instead of *British*.

4 There is, surprisingly, no convenient general term for a citizen of the United Kingdom: *Briton* is normally confined to historical (or jocular) reference, and *Britisher* is AmE.

Briticism is the term for a language feature that is peculiar to BrE, not *Britishism*.

Brito- see ANGLO-.

Britpop is a colourful and useful informal term for the British pop music scene, but should be used with care as its scope of reference has become more specific in the 1990s.

broadcast *verb*, by analogy with *cast*, is unchanged in its past form and past participle: *The programme will be broadcast on Saturdays*.

broccoli is spelt with two *c*s and, despite its plural origin in Italian, is treated as a singular mass noun in English: *The broccoli is in the green dish*.

brochure, pamphlet. The two words used to be more or less synonymous, but have gone separate ways: a *brochure* is a glossy leaflet used in advertising, whereas a *pamphlet* is a small unbound printed booklet, normally meant to be informative rather than promotional. *Brochure* is stressed on the first syllable in BrE and on the second in AmE.

broker, as a Stock Exchange term, was replaced in the UK in 1986 by *broker-dealer* (which reflects increased responsibilities), although *broker* will still be found in informal use.

brother-in-law means (1) one's wife's or husband's brother, (2) one's sister's husband, (3) one's sister-in-law's husband. The plural is *brothers-in-law*.

browse. Grazing animals, rather than people browsing in books, provide the grammatical analogy for the new transitive meaning in computing, 'to read or survey (data files)': *The handy viewer lets the user browse the disc reading documents, viewing images, and unzipping program files—CD-ROM World*, 1994.

brunette is the standard form in BrE, and is invariably used of a woman. In AmE *brunet* is occasionally found, with the same restriction in use.

buffalo has the plural form *buffaloes*.

buffet, meaning refreshments, is pronounced **buh**-fay or (especially in *buffet car*) **buf**-ay. In AmE the stress is on the second syllable, pronounced the same way.

bugger is more acceptable as a swear-word than it used to be, at least in BrE. Uses such as *bugger me, bugger-all*, and *I'll be buggered* (*if*), are all commonly heard on radio and television, although they remain highly informal and should not normally be used outside the domain of casual conversation. The word remains somewhat more offensive in AmE.

bulk, as a noun preceded by *the* and denoting magnitude or size, is correctly used with *of* and a singular noun, as in *the bulk of the book | the bulk of his land | the bulk of the clergy*. It should not be used in this way with ordinary plural nouns: ⌧ *The great bulk of Guyanese Indians are Hindus or Moslems—Guardian*, 1972, although collective plurals are more acceptable: *In 1940 the bulk of the people were subliterate or illiterate—R. A. Crampsey*, 1973.

bunch as a collective noun in abstract senses (*a bunch of people | a bunch of questions*) varies widely in its degree of informality from simple metaphor (*A bunch of weary runners crossed the line at last*) to near-slang, often affected by the word it collocates with (*The government is behaving like a bunch of bandits*).

bur, burr. *Bur* is recommended for 'a clinging seed-vessel or catkin' and *burr* for 'a rough edge' and associated meanings.

bureau has the plural form *bureaux* (pronounced -z) in BrE, although *bureaus* is more common in AmE.

burgle, burglarize. *Burgle* is a BrE back-formation from *burglar*; *burglarize*, although the regular word in AmE, is treated with the same disapproval on this side of the Atlantic as *burgle* once was.

burnt, burned. These two forms for the past tense and past participle of burn are largely interchangeable, but *burned* is more common as the active past (*She burned her hand on the kettle | She has burned her hand*); in the passive, *burnt* is more adjectival (emphasizing the result), and *burned* more verbal (emphasizing the action): *The cottage was burnt down last week | The cottage was burned down by vandals*.

bus is now spelt without an apostrophe. As a noun it has the plural form *buses*, and as a verb it has inflected forms *buses, bused, busing*.

business, busyness. *Business* means 'one's affairs or concern' and associated meanings. For a noun meaning 'the state of being busy', use *busyness*.

but. 1 GENERAL. *But* is a preposition and conjunction, and is used contrastively: (preposition) *Everyone seems to know but me* | (conjunction) *Everyone seems to know but I don't*. In more modern usage, as the OED and Fowler (1926) have both recognized, the roles of *but* as a conjunction and preposition have become inextricably confused, and this fact gives rise to some vexed problems of usage. These are described in the following paragraphs, each headed by a typical example of the problem.

2 *Everyone but she* [*or her?*] *can see the answer.* Fowler explored this problem in some depth, and concluded that *but* in this meaning is more a conjunction than a preposition, and therefore the case of a following pronoun is variable. When the phrase introduced by *but* is associated with the subject of the sentence, the pronoun should be treated as subjective (i.e. *No one saw him but I*) and when the phrase is associated with the object, the pronoun should be treated as objective (i.e. *I saw no one but him*). When the association is not as clear-cut as this, the case of the pronoun is determined by the position of the *but*-phrase in the sentence: when the *but*-phrase is in the subject area, the pronoun should be treated as subjective (i.e. *Everyone but she can see the answer*) and when the *but*-phrase is in the object area it should be treated as objective (i.e. *Everyone can see the answer but her*). Usage is unstable when the verb is intransitive: *Everyone knows but her* is somewhat more natural than *Everyone knows but she*).

3 *I disagree. But what do you think?* The widespread public belief that *but* should not begin a sentence seems to be unshakeable. But it has no foundation in grammar or idiom, and examples are frequent in good literature: *All animals have sense. But a dog is an animal.*—Locke, 1690 | *But this rough magic I here abjure*—Shakespeare, *Tempest*, 1610 | *Of course they loved her, the two remaining ones, they hugged her, they had mingled their tears. But they could not converse with her*—Iris Murdoch, 1993. The initial position of *but*, as with *and*, is a matter not of grammar but of style.

4 *Who knows but that the whole course of history might* [*or might not?*] *have been different?* When this construction is used with a negative or (especially) in a question, there is always a temptation to make the second part of the sentence negative. It is usually better to rephrase: *Who knows: the whole course of history might have been different?*

5 *But your answer, moreover, is unacceptable.* A further contrasting word, such as *however, nonetheless, moreover,* etc., should not be used in a clause introduced by *but.* If the second word is needed (i.e. if *moreover* is the right word to use), omit *but: Your answer, moreover, is unacceptable.* Note, however, that *but still* is a standard idiom, especially informally: *It's late but still you did want me to stay.*

6 *He is not upset but he is relieved.* The repetition of *he is,* when this is the same person as at the first mention, is normally redundant: *He is not upset but relieved.* However, it is often added in conversation, with rhetorical emphasis on the second *is.*

7 IDIOMS. *But* is used in a number of fixed idioms:

▸**a** *ALL BUT. By the end of the war this attitude had all but disappeared*—P. Wright, 1987.

▸**b** *CANNOT (HELP) BUT.* The insertion of *help* is not attested before the late 19c but is now common: *The frailty of man without thee cannot but fall*—Book of Common Prayer, 1549 | *She could not help but plague the lad*—H. Caine, 1894 | *She could not help but follow him into the big department store*—B. Rubens, 1987.

▸**c** *BUT WHAT. It's no telling but what I might have gone on to school like my own children have*—Lee Smith, 1983 (US). This use is now old-fashioned, and limited to informal and non-standard uses.

▸**d** RHETORICAL USE. *Ah, but who built it, that we tiny creatures can walk in its arcades?*—Margaret Drabble, 1987. This use is not normally found in everyday English.

buzz word see JARGON, VOGUE WORDS.

by *prep. By* has so many functions that care should be taken to avoid ambiguity of the kind typified by the sentence, more hilarious than truly ambiguous, *He was knocked down by the town hall.* It is better to use another preposition such as *close to* or *in front of.* Fowler warned against the use of too many *bys* (in different senses) in one sentence, as in (not his example): *Send stories by reporters by fax by the end of Friday.* Such sequences are more likely to occur in more hurried forms of spoken English.

by, by-, bye. These three forms have different functions. *By* is a preposition or adverb (*Come by | By the river*); *by-* is a prefix meaning 'secondary, subordinate' (forming words such as *byroad* and *bylaw,* now often spelt as one word; in some cases, a variant spelling *bye-* is also found (e.g. *byelaw*), but this is best avoided); and *bye* is a noun meaning 'something additional or left aside' (e.g. in cricket and golf). The idiom *by the by* (in which the second *by* is a variant of *bye*) means 'by the way, incidentally'.

Byzantine is spelt with a capital initial when the reference is historical or cultural (*the Byzantine Empire*) and with a small initial when the meaning is 'intricate, complicated' (*byzantine intrigues*). There are several pronunciations in use; those recommended are **biz**-ən-tiyn and biz-**an**-tiyn.

Cc

cable has until recently been a mainly countable noun (*a cable* | *this cable*) meaning a length of thick rope or wire, or a telegram. With the arrival of *cable television*, its use as an uncountable noun (AmE, now also BrE) has been reinforced: *I'm watching a movie on cable*—L. Block, 1982.

cacao is a seed pod (or its tree) from which cocoa and chocolate are made, and should not be confused with the word *cocoa* itself. *Cacao* comes from a Nahuatl (Native Central American) word.

cachet is pronounced **kash**-ay and means (1) a distinguishing mark or seal, (2) prestige, (3) a capsule of medicine. Fowler wrote that it 'should be expelled' from the language, and it therefore joins the band of his LOST CAUSES.

cachou is a lozenge for sweetening the breath, and should be distinguished from the nut (and tree) *cashew*, especially as they are both pronounced **kash**-oo.

cactus. In general use the plural is *cactuses*, in botany it is often (but not always) *cacti*.

caddie, caddy. *Caddie* (originally Scottish) is a golf-attendant; *caddy* is a container for tea.

cadre means (1) a group of servicemen (pronounced **kah**-də), (2) a group of political activists (often pronounced **kay**-də).

Caesarian, Caesarean. The first spelling is now more usual, and the initial *c* is sometimes written small.

caesura, meaning 'a cut or division', is a term in prosody, both Classical and Old English, and refers to the division of a metrical foot between two words. In Old English (e.g. *Beowulf*) it is marked in print by an extra space between the words. In later English verse it is chiefly noticeable in long metres such as that of Tennyson's *Locksley Hall*: *Till the war-drum throbb'd no longer, || and the battle-flags were furl'd.*

café is occasionally spelt without an accent but should be spelt with one. It should be pronounced **kaf**-ay, not (except as a joke) kaff or kayf.

cagey is more recent than people realize (first recorded 1909) and is an Americanism. This is a better spelling than *cagy*, which is also found.

calculate. 1 The meaning 'to suppose or reckon', without any reference to working something out, is regional American in origin (19c, eg. *I calculate it's pretty difficult to git edication down at Charleston*) and is not standard in any variety of English. None the less it does occur: *Many executives . . . calculate that their best interests lie in not conforming to factory regulations*—S. Box, 1992. See also RECKON.

2 The corresponding adjective is *calculable*.

calendar, meaning a list of days and months, is spelt this way. *Calender* (with -*er*) is a press for paper or cloth, and COLANDER is a strainer.

calends, the first month of the ancient Roman calendar, is spelt with a *c-* not a *k-*.

calf. Both words (the animal and the part of the leg) have the plural form *calves*.

calibre is pronounced **kal**-i-bə. The American spelling is *caliber*.

caliph is pronounced **kay**-lif and is spelt with a *c-*. Other spellings have fallen out of use.

callus means 'a hard thick area of skin or tissue', and should be distinguished from *callous*, which is related to it but now much more often means 'unfeeling, insensitive'.

calorie, originally a unit of heat (from Latin *calor*, 'heat'), in the 20c has stepped out of the physics laboratory into general use as a measure of the energy value of food. The general public have adopted what physicists call the *large calorie* (i.e. the amount needed to raise the temperature of 1 kilogram of water through 1°C).

cambric, meaning a fine white linen, is pronounced **kam**-brik, or sometimes **kaym**-brik.

camellia is spelt with two *l*'s, despite its pronunciation kə-**mee**-li-ə.

cameo has a plural *cameos*. In its meaning 'a small character part in a play or film', it is used mainly attributively, as in *cameo part, cameo role*, etc.: *Rather than play these zonking great parts . . . I will try to find some dazzling little cameo roles—Times*, 1976.

campanile, a bell-tower, is Italian, and is pronounced kam-pə-**nee**-li.

can *noun. Can* is the word generally used in BrE for the container when the contents are liquid (*a can of beer | a can of soup*). When the contents are solid, *tin* is more usual (*a tin of beans | a tin of peaches*) but *can* is used for this too in AmE.

can *verb.* The verb *can* is classed among the MODAL VERBS, and has a wide range of uses, expressing (1) possibility, (2) ability, (3) permission (where it overlaps with *may*). Examples: (1) POSSIBILITY *Anyone can make a mistake | Manned spacecraft can now link up with other spacecraft in outer space | He can be very trying.*

(2) ABILITY *His four-year-old son can already ride a bicycle | Murray could read more than forty languages.*

(3) PERMISSION *No one can play the organ without the consent of the vicar | Can I speak to your supervisor, please?* In more formal or polite contexts, *may* is preferable and more usual, e.g. *May I have another sandwich, please?*. However, in the past tense, *could* has replaced *might*, e.g. *At that time only rectors could* [= were entitled to] *receive tithes.* In some cases, *can* is not interchangeable with *may*, e.g. *I'll drop in tomorrow, if I can.*

canard means 'an unfounded rumour or story' and is pronounced either kan-**ahd** or **kan**-ahd.

candelabrum, because of its Latin origin, has the plural form *candelabra*, but *candelabra* has taken on a new life as the more common singular form for the word meaning 'a large branched candlestick or lamp-holder', and has its own plural *candelabras*:

four silver candelabras—Walter Scott, *Ivanhoe*.

cannon. 1 This word for a large gun is now confined, apart from its historical reference, to a shell-firing gun in aircraft (a use first recorded in 1919). Historically the word is used both as an ordinary noun (with plural *cannons*), and as a collective (as in Tennyson's *Cannon to the right of them, Cannon to the left of them,* etc.).

2 *Cannon* should be carefully distinguished in spelling from *canon,* meaning (1) 'a rule' and (2) 'a member of a cathedral chapter'; confusion can be unfortunate.

cannot is usually written as one word, although *can not* occurs from time to time in letters, examination scripts, etc. The contraction *can't* is fairly recent (around 1800) and does not occur (for example) in Shakespeare. *Can't* is often articulated even when *cannot* is written.

canoe *verb* has inflected forms *canoes, canoed, canoeing.*

canon see CANNON.

cant now usually means 'insincere pious or moral talk': *shameful surrender to the prevalent cant and humbug of the age*—Daily Telegraph, 1992. Its older (18c–19c) and often derogatory meaning, 'the secret language or jargon used by certain classes or professions', is confined to historical novels and scholarly discussion of language.

can't see CANNOT.

canto, a division of a long poem, has the plural form *cantos* (recommended) or *cantoes.*

canvas, canvass. 1 *Canvas* with one *s* means 'coarse cloth'. The plural is *canvases* and as a verb ('to cover or line with canvas') it has inflected forms *canvasses, canvassed, canvassing.*

2 *Canvass* with two *s*'s is a verb meaning 'to solicit votes' and a noun meaning 'the soliciting of votes'. Its inflections retain the double *s* (*canvasses, canvassed,* etc.).

capercaillie is a Scottish Gaelic word for a wood-grouse. This is now the normal spelling (formerly also *capercailzie,* the *z* representing *y* in older Scots orthography), and the pronunciation is cap-ə-**kay**-li.

capita, caput see PER CAPITA.

capital, capitol. *Capital,* the most important town or city of a country or region, is to be distinguished from *Capitol,* which is (1) the hill in Rome where the geese saved the day, and (2) the American legislative building in Washington DC (and other similar buildings in the USA).

capitalist is now normally stressed on the first syllable, although you still occasionally hear it stressed on the second.

capitals. Capital letters are used to signal special uses of words, either (1) to mark a significant point in written or printed matter (especially the beginning of a sentence), or (2) to distinguish names that identify particular people or things from those that describe any number of them. Practice varies when people and things do not always fit neatly into one or other of these two categories. This article deals with the elementary uses first, and then with the less straightforward ones.

1 BASIC USES. Capital letters are used almost invariably (1) to begin a new sentence (or a quotation within a sentence), (2) as the first letters of proper names and personal names (*New York | John Smith*), (3) in certain special cases by convention, e.g. the personal pronoun *I*. These elementary rules cause little difficulty, but beyond them practice and usage become unstable, and different publishing houses have varying sets of rules about them.

2 OTHER USES.

▸ **a** Prefixes and titles forming part of names referring to one person: *the Duke of Wellington, Sir Bob Geldof, Her Majesty the Queen, Queen Elizabeth the Queen Mother, His Excellency the American Ambassador.* When the reference is general, i.e. to many such people, a capital is not used: *every king of England from William I to Richard II* (where *king* is a common noun like *monarch* or *sovereign*).

▸ **b** Titles of office-holders when these refer to a particular holder: *I have an appointment with the Mayor | He was appointed Bishop of Durham*; but not when the reference is general or descriptive: *He wanted to be a dean | When I become king.*

▸ **c** Recognized and official place-names: *Northern Ireland* (but *northern England*, which is simply descriptive), *Western Australia, South Africa, New England, the Straits of Gibraltar, Plymouth Sound, London Road* (when it is an address; but *Take the London road*, i.e. the road to London, which is descriptive).

▸ **d** Names of events and periods of time: *the Bronze Age* (and, e.g., *Bronze-Age Crete*), *the Middle Ages, the Renaissance, the First World War* (but *the 1914–18 war* is generally regarded as descriptive). Archaeological and geological eras are now generally often written with

a small initial: *chalcolithic, palaeolithic.*

▸ **e** Names of institutions, when these are regarded as identifying rather than describing: *Christianity, Buddhism, Islam, Marxism, the (Roman) Catholic Church, the House of Lords.* The word *State* has a capital initial when it is meant to refer to the institution as a whole, so as to distinguish it from the ordinary use of the word; similarly *Church* is an institution (*disestablishment of the Church*) whereas *church* is a building or local body (*go to church | the church down the road*).

▸ **f** Abbreviations and initialisms are usually spelt with capitals, whether they refer to institutions or are more generic (*BBC, MPs*); but acronyms, which are pronounced like words and tend to behave like words, often become wholly or partly lower-case (*Nato, radar, Aids*).

▸ **g** Names of ships and vehicles: *The Cutty Sark*, *HMS Dreadnought*, | *the US bomber Enola Gay.* Note also *a Boeing*, *a Renault | a Spitfire*, which are trademarks: see next section.

▸ **h** Proprietary names (trademarks): *Anadin*, *Cow & Gate*, *Kleenex*, *Persil*. A capital initial should strictly also be used when the reference is generic (e.g. *can you lend me a Biro*), but in practice this is more common in the regulated world of published print than in general writing.

▸ **i** Words derived from proper names: *Christian* (noun and adjective), *Macchiavellian*, *Shakespearian*. But a small initial is used when the reference is remote or conventional, or merely allusive: *arabic letters, french windows, mackintosh, wellington boot*; and when the sense is an attribute or quality suggested by the proper name: *chauvinistic, herculean, titanic*. Verbs follow the same rule: *bowdlerize*, *galvanize*, *pasteurize*. The guide in this area is the extent to which the name on which the word is based is present in the meaning used, as it clearly is with *Shakespearian* but not with *titanic* (which is undoubtedly used by many who are unaware of the mythological Titans).

▶ **j** Medial capitals. The uses we have discussed so far all concern the first letters of words. Use of capitals within words is confined exclusively to commercial usage, and has no other purpose or effect than to highlight or distinguish the name: *CinemaScope*, *InterLink*.

capping, as in *rate-capping*, is a modern UK political term of some potency, increased with the replacement of local rates by the notorious community charge (poll-tax) in 1989–90, and no less so with its further replacement by the council tax in 1993. A more welcome development is its use with reference to fixed mortgage rates. As a result of all these changes, *capping* is now often used as a word in its own right: *How can capping lead to accountability?—Hansard*, 1992.

caption. Fowler called this 'rare in British use, and might well be rarer'. Despite this disapproval (see LOST CAUSES), it is now a common word on both sides of the Atlantic, meaning (1) a title below an illustration and (2) a heading to a newspaper article or book chapter. Despite this meaning, it comes from Latin *capio* 'to take', and has no direct connection with Latin *caput*, 'head'.

carafe was once the normal Scottish term for a crystal jug for serving water. Fowler classed the Victorian English use (a water-bottle with a tumbler placed over it) as a genteelism, but its 20c meaning, an open-necked container for serving wine, is unexceptionable.

carat, caret. *Carat* (AmE *karat*) is a measure of the purity of gold; *caret* is a mark ($\wedge$) for showing an insertion in printing or writing.

caravanserai is pronounced with stress on -van- and the final syllable rhyming with *eye*. It means an inn for travelling merchants or pilgrims in the Middle East (first noted by the geographer Hakluyt in 1599), and is of Persian origin. Several other spellings are now thankfully extinct.

carburettor. This is the standard spelling in BrE, as distinct from AmE *carburetor* (with one *t*).

carcass, the dead body of an animal, is the preferred form (rather than *carcase*) and has the plural form *carcasses*.

care. The modern colloquial expression *I couldn't care less* dates from the 1940s (*OED*: the first example is of a book title). More recent is the AmE expression *I could care less*, which has more or less the same meaning. The stress pattern is different: normally on *couldn't* in the first and on the pronoun *I* in the second, which suggests an awareness of the switch and in some measure accounts for the synonymy of two apparently opposite constructions.

careen is originally a nautical word (recorded by the geographer Hakluyt in 1600) referring to the tilting or turning over of a ship, either at sea or in dock for repairs. In AmE *careen* has developed the meaning 'hurtle or rush headlong': *A lot of Russians* *careening along the road on liberated bicycles*—H. Roosenburg, 1957 | *The van careened across the road, almost running into the ditch*—B. Moore, 1987. In this use it has been influenced by the similar-sounding but unrelated word *career*, which is the standard word for this meaning in BrE.

caret see CARAT.

cargo has the plural form *cargoes*.

Caribbean is spelt with one *r* and two *b*'s. In BrE the main stress is on the third syllable; in AmE and in the Caribbean itself, it falls either on the second or the third syllable.

caries is pronounced **kair**-eez (two syllables).

carillon, meaning a set of bells, has various pronunciations in the *OED* and its derivative dictionaries. The dominant one is probably kə-**ril**-yən, although **kar**-il-yən is also given. A French pronunciation, more common in the 19c, is now hardly heard.

caring, in its meaning 'compassionate' as in *caring society* and *the caring professions*, has come to acquire strong political overtones since the Thatcher years of spending cuts in the social services, and it is now difficult to regard or use it neutrally. The *Sunday Telegraph* reported in 1985 that 'the word *caring* in the context of the Tory Party meant that Mrs Thatcher intended to lower her voice another octave'.

carousal, carousel. 1 *Carousal* is pronounced kə-**rou**-zəl and means a good time with drinking.

2 *Carousel* is pronounced ka-rə-**sel**, and means (1) a tournament, (2) a merry-go-round, and (3) a

moving (and usually circular) conveyor-belt system for delivering passengers' luggage at airports.

carrel is a private cubicle for study in a library (20c) and is a revival of a much earlier use denoting a small enclosure or study in a monastery in medieval England, a meaning which died out with the dissolution of the monasteries in the 16c.

cartel in its modern use referring to a price-fixing business arrangement is pronounced kah-**tel**, influenced by the German word *Kartell*. In its earlier use referring to the exchange of prisoners, its stress was on the first syllable.

Carver, carver. These are two words meaning types of chair. A *Carver* (with capital *C*) is in AmE a chair with arms, a rush seat, and a back having horizontal and vertical spindles. It is named after J. Carver, the 17c governor of Plymouth Colony. A *carver* (small *c*) is in BrE the principal chair of a set of dining chairs, intended for the person who carves.

case. 1 There are two distinct nouns:
  ▸ **a** The one meaning 'an example of an occurrence': *In this case they are wrong*. From this use there have developed several idiomatic phrases (*in case, in any case, in some cases, in the case of*) as well as several more concrete meanings, notably in law (*the case for the prosecution*) and medicine (*seven cases of cholera*). There is also the grammatical meaning, which seems to have little to do with the others but is connected etymologically. The word dates from the 13c in English and is derived ultimately from Latin *casus*, 'falling', hence 'occurrence'.

▶ **b** The one meaning 'receptacle or container etc.': *Put the cases in the car*. The origin of this word is Latin *capsa* (with the same meaning), and it also dates from the 13c in English. Although this word has given rise to several technical meanings, e.g. in masonry and printing, it has been far less productive of idioms.

2 Most people use these words without difficulty and probably without any awareness that there are two separate words. Usually they do not get in each other's way, but beware of using a phrase with *case*, especially *in the case of*, when it is not needed: *In every case except that of France the increase has been more rapid than in the case of the U.K.* [where *In every country except France the increase has been more rapid than in the U.K.* is preferable]. Fowler gave many examples as evidence of what he called 'flabby writing', but such a strong reaction is less justified today when the idiom seems dated and in decline.

3 The idiom *in case* is also a conjunction: *Take your umbrella in case it rains*. In AmE, it can also mean 'if' (i.e. it is a shortening of the phrase *in the case that*): *In case it rains I can't go* [= If it rains I can't go]. Coming at the beginning of a sentence, this use can cause initial confusion to speakers of BrE.

cases. 1 Cases are the functions of nouns, pronouns, and adjectives in sentences, as reflected in their endings or some other aspect of their form. The chief cases we are concerned with are:
SUBJECTIVE (or nominative): the function of subject of a verb or sentence (e.g. *house* in *The house was on fire*).

OBJECTIVE (or accusative): the function of object, after a transitive verb or preposition (e.g. *book* in *Give me the book* and *Look in the book*).
Of less concern in English are
GENITIVE (or possessive): the function of possession or ownership (e.g. *Jane's* and *my* in *Jane's umbrella is in my car*).

DATIVE: the function of reference or relation (e.g. *me* in *Give me the book*).

Most English speakers now think of cases chiefly in connection with other, more inflected, languages such as Latin and German. In English, case-endings and case-forms, which were once a feature of nouns (*stan, stanes, stane* meaning 'stone'), have become restricted over many centuries to plurals and possessives of nouns (*books, children, boy's, girls'*, etc.) and to the pronouns (*me, whom, ours*, etc.). One consequence of this disappearance of cases is that English speakers may have partially lost an instinctive power to recognize case distinctions. Another way of looking at it is that the reduction process is continuing.

2 The concept of case helps to clarify certain problems of English usage:
▶ **a** What happens after the verb *be*. Since the subject and the complement of *be* are historically in the same case (i.e. *be* does not take an object), *it is I* and *it is he* (or *she*) are grammatically sounder than *it is me* and *it is him* (or *her*). However, usage is changing and it is becoming more and more difficult to sustain *It is I* (and still worse, *It is only we*) in speech without risking affectation.
In writing, greater care is often needed. Many writers tend to pre-

fer the subjective forms, especially when the pronoun is followed by a relative clause beginning with *who* or *that*: *If I were he, I should keep an eye on that young man*—C. P. Snow, 1979 | *This time it was I who took the initiative*—R. Cobb, 1985 | *That might very well be he at this moment, causing the doorbell to chime*—Kingsley Amis, 1988. But notice the difference in reported, especially informal, speech: *Too much of a bloody infidel, that's me*—Thomas Keneally, 1980 | *'So . . . ' says Jasper. 'That's him, the old fraud.'*—Penelope Lively, 1987 | *Can this be me? Driving a car?*—*New Yorker*, 1988.

VERDICT: In less formal English the objective (*It is me*) is acceptable and often preferable (*Can this be I?* offends euphony and even common sense). In more formal English the subjective is preferable except where this produces awkwardness.

▶ **b WHAT HAPPENS AFTER *AS* AND *THAN*.** A problem arises because these function partly as prepositions and partly as conjunctions, and their roles are not clear-cut. In broad terms when *as* or *than* are felt to be prepositions the objective case is used (*as lucky as me*), and when they are felt to be conjunctions the subjective case is used (*as lucky as I*, with *am* understood). Examples: *He was as apprehensive as I about our meeting*—J. Frame, 1985 | *I hope you have a more cheerful Christmas than we*—Evelyn Waugh, 1955 | *He was eight years older than I*—Lord Hailsham, 1990 | *He seems to be as lonely as me, and to mind it more*—David Lodge, 1991 | *I wanted you to be wiser than me, better than me*—P. Hillmore, 1987.

VERDICT: There is a marked tendency towards using the objective case in more recent writing, with the subjective sounding more formal and often decidedly old-fashioned (as in the Waugh and Hailsham examples). See also AS 1, THAN 1.

▶ **c WHAT HAPPENS AFTER *BUT*.** The objective form is preferable, though in practice both types occur: (subjective) *No one understands it, no one but I*—J.M. Coetzee, 1977 | (objective) *'Who knows about this?' 'Nobody but me and a couple of guys here on the platform know for sure.'*—M. Machlin, 1976. See also BUT 2.

▶ **d WHAT HAPPENS AFTER *NOT*.** Since this is more common in speech, the objective case is common: *'Who did this thing?' 'Not me.'* In writing, the subjective occurs more frequently: *It must be he who is made of india-rubber, not I*—Angela Carter, 1984. (This is an extended example of the use after *be* discussed in 2a above.)

▶ **e *WHO* AND *WHOM*.** This is one of the most contentious pronoun issues of our age. *Whom* seems to be on the decline; but it is incorrectly used as much as *who* (hyper-correction again): *Do you know whom it was that came last night?* (where *whom* is the complement of *be* and not the object of *know*). The issue is more fully discussed in the article WHO AND WHOM.

▶ **f CASE-SWITCHING.** Change of case in pronouns within the same sentence is a common feature of English, and often goes unnoticed. Examples: *Me, I don't trust cats*—Garrison Keillor, 1989 | *Me thinking I'd probably got some filthy fever in spite of the jabs*—Julian Barnes, 1989 | *We sat down on either side of the radiogram, she with her tea, me with a pad and pencil*—Jeanette Winterson, 1985 | *It's not you who should be asking for pardon, but me who should be down on my knees*—M. Dobbs, 1989.

cashew see CACHOU.

casino has the plural form *casinos*.

casket. In America and some other English-speaking countries outside Britain, *casket* is used as an alternative for *coffin*. The exchangeability of the two words is illustrated by newspaper reports of the funeral of the Philippine ex-president, Ferdinand Marcos, in October 1989: (caption) *Imelda Marcos kisses the casket containing the body of her late husband;* (text) *Mr. Marcos' coffin . . . was borne by 10 pallbearers—Chicago Tribune.* In BrE, a *casket* is a container for funerary ashes.

cast *verb.* This Old Norse word has competed for centuries with Anglo-Saxon *throw*, and its credentials include an array of 83 meanings in the *OED*. In current usage, however, it often sounds archaic or rhetorical, influenced by the New Testament *He that is without sin among you, let him first cast a stone*—John 8:7, and is largely restricted to a range of familiar phrases and idioms, such as *cast an eye over, cast lots,* and *cast aside*. In ordinary contexts, *throw* is the more natural word.

cast *noun,* **caste. 1** *Cast* is derived from the verb and has a number of special meanings, including the actors of a play or film, an object made in metal, and its use as in *a person of a moral cast*, plus a host of curious technical meanings (e.g. in hawking).

2 *Caste*, referring to class divisions in India, is now the established spelling, although *cast* is much more common before 1800. It is derived from Spanish and Portuguese *casta*, 'race, lineage', and is related to *chaste*.

caster, castor. The two forms represent several words and overlap in usage: *caster* is the only spelling for a few technical meanings; *castor* (a different word) is the only spelling for the oil; and both are used for the sugar (which is named after the type of pot it was put in) and for the small swivelling wheel on the feet of furniture. Although you are never wrong if you use *castor* for the principal meanings, *caster* is recommended for the sugar, and *castor* for the small wheel.

casualty. The main current meaning is now 'a person killed or injured in a war or accident'. The historically earlier meaning of the mishap itself is less common, although the two are sometimes hard to distinguish, e.g. *There were many casualties in this war.*

catachresis means 'against usage' and is a grammatical term referring to the improper use of words. Typical examples in everyday language are the use of *infer* to mean *imply* (but see INFER, IMPLY) and the use of *refute* to mean *repudiate*. Examples of literary (and therefore acceptable) catachresis include Dylan Thomas's phrase *once below a time*.

catacomb. Now pronounced **kat**-ə-koom; but **kat**-ə-kohm is heard in AmE.

catch *verb. Catch you later*, now also shortened to *catch you*, stands alongside *see you (later)* as a phrase of farewell: *'Yeah, catch you, mate,' said Stephen, and slid out the door*—F. Kidman, 1988.

catchphrase is a term (mid-19c) for a phrase that catches on quickly and that is often used without direct allusion to its first occurrence (when this is known). Examples are: *Not tonight, Josephine* (associated with Napoleon but more likely a Victorian music hall invention), *for my next trick* (from magicians' patter), and more recently *nice one, Cyril* (from a 1972 TV advertisement) and *have a nice day* (1970s, originally AmE, exact origin disputed). Many more examples are given in Eric Partridge's *Dictionary of Catch Phrases* (1977). More recent catchphrases include *economical with the truth* (1986, used by the Cabinet Secretary, Sir Richard Armstrong), *get a life* (early 1990s), *level playing field* (1980s, originally AmE), and *move the goalposts* (1980s). See also CLI-CHÉS.

catch-22, from the title of a novel by Joseph Heller (1961), is used mainly in the phrase *a catch-22 situation*, which strictly does not mean any dilemma or difficulty but one 'from which there is no escape because of mutually conflicting or dependent conditions'.

category. Fowler (1926) insisted tersely that category 'should be used by no one who is not prepared to state (1) that he does not mean *class*, and (2) that he knows the difference between the two'. It seems that the word may belong in the category of Fowler's lost causes, since it is doubtful if the distinction is maintained in general (as opposed to philosophical) usage. Examples: *She placed them in two categories: the honest imbeciles and the intelligent imbeciles*—Olivia Manning, 1960 | *Certain men at Vauxhall's were . . . placed in a special category to preserve their higher rate of pay*—Spare Rib, 1977 | *Generally speaking there are two categories of small boy . . . the studious, eyes-down-in-a-book*

type and the outdoor scuffed shoes clothes-in-a-mess variety—Morecambe Guardian, 1978.

cater *verb.* There are two typical constructions, with *for* (which is more usual), and with *to* (perhaps influenced by *pander*, and more common in AmE). There is no real distinction in meaning between the two, except that use of *to* with a personal object seems less natural, at least in BrE: *The following suggested items can be obtained from shops which cater for local Chinese communities*—China Now, 1978 | *Gingerbread caters for all categories of single parents*—Times, 1980 | *He feels cheated because society does not cater to his irrational wishes*—Bruno Bettelheim, 1960 | *Unlike other corporate hospitals, ours is just a diagnostic centre which caters to everybody*—Business India, 1986.

catholic is a word of Greek origin meaning 'universal' and 'of universal human interest', and retains this meaning in English when spelt with a small initial (as in *science is truly catholic*). When spelt with a capital initial it refers to the Roman Catholic Church, although historically its range of reference is wider than this, embracing all Churches claiming to be descended from the ancient Christian Church. Although the meaning is clear in (for example) *Catholics and Protestants*, use Roman Catholic when there is any room for uncertainty.

cavalcade is derived from Latin *caballus* 'horse', and was brought into English via French with meanings associated with marches or processions on horseback. The association with horses was rapidly discarded, and in the 17c any procession came to be called a cavalcade. Noel Coward used the word as the title of a play in 1931, and claimed to have revived it in the process. The final element -*cade* forms the (irregular) basis of the word *motorcade*, used for a procession in motor vehicles and first recorded in AmE in 1913.

caveat is pronounced **kav**-i-at, and means 'a warning or reservation': *Any discussion of legal action must be preceded by a caveat on costs*—M. Binney et al., 1991 | *Bearing in mind some caveats below, it is possible to predict the relative difficulty of a writing task*—National Curriculum, 1989. In more formal and technical writing, *caveats* are *entered, issued, put in*, etc.: *Catherine Destivelle issued a similar caveat from the floor about the situation in the Alps*—Climber and Hill Walker, 1991.

cease. This 14c loanword from French is slowly yielding to *stop* (as *cast* has to *throw*) except in a few set phrases (notably *cease-fire* and *without cease*) and where 'we substitute it for *stop* when we want our language to be dignified' (Fowler, 1926). Fowler thought that *cease* ought to be allowed to go into honourable retirement, but it appears to have plenty of active life left for special uses. It is also capable of being followed by a *to*-infinitive, often producing a better effect, whereas *stop to* do something has its own special meaning ('pause to' or 'make a special effort to'). We could not, for example, substitute *stop* for *cease* in the following sentence without virtually reversing the sense: *Turner in a long and awesomely prolific career never ceased to observe and comment on nature*—Daily Telegraph, 1973.

ceiling has been used by government departments and adminis-

trators since the 1930s to mean 'an upper limit' (as in *a ceiling on prices*), and is sometimes contrasted with *floor*, which is a lower limit. As with *target*, care needs to taken not to couch it in contexts that are incongruous: a ceiling can be reached, for example, or raised or lowered or adjusted, or can be high or low or unrealistic, but it cannot (without absurd effect) be extended or exceeded or increased. It is also unwise to associate it with words that are also associated with it in its literal use, such as *suspend*.

cello is the normal word for *violoncello*, and it is spelt without an initial apostrophe. The plural is *cellos*. If the full form has to be used, note the (Italian) spelling *violon-*.

Celsius is a particular scale of temperature based on a hundred degrees from freezing to boiling, and is named (like *Fahrenheit*) after an 18c scientist. Note that *centigrade* is a generic term for any such scale, and has been displaced by the more exact *Celsius* in weather reports and general usage.

Celt, Celtic are pronounced with initial k-, except for the name of the Glasgow football club, which is pronounced s-.

censer, censor, censure. 1 A *censer* (from an Anglo-French root related to *incense*) is a vessel for burning incense; a *censor* (from a Latin word meaning 'to assess') is an official who decides on the suitability of films, plays, etc. for public performance.

2 As a verb, *censor* 'to act as censor of', should be distinguished from *censure* 'to criticize harshly'.

centenary is pronounced sen-**teen**-ǝ-ri. It is the usual term in BrE (as both noun and adjective) to denote a hundredth anniversary. In AmE and elsewhere, *centennial* is more usual. For forms based on *centenary* denoting longer periods (*bicentenary, sesquicentenary,* etc.) see ANNIVERSARIES.

centigrade see CELSIUS.

centre around, centre round, influenced by verbs of motion such as *gather* and *move,* is now a common construction for the meaning 'to have (something) as a centre; to be mainly concerned with', criticism on the grounds of illogicality notwithstanding. Examples: *That strange figure around whom this account properly centres*—W. Sansom, 1950 | *There is the added enticement of a plot centred around a real historical event*—Listener, 1983. To be completely safe, use *centre on, base on,* or *revolve (a)round.*

centrifugal, centripetal are stressed on the third and second syllables respectively. Their meanings are complementary: *centrifugal* relates to movement away from a centre and *centripetal* to movement towards a centre. *Centrifugal* occurs more often, and this may account for the change in stress, which was formerly also (somewhat awkwardly) on the second syllable.

century. 1 The end of a millennium makes everyone aware of the difficulty of reckoning when a century (let alone a millennium) truly begins and ends. In arithmetical terms, the 21st century should be reckoned as beginning on 1 January 2001, since 2000 is strictly the last year of the 20th century (and 2nd millennium). But who is going to wait until the end of the year 2000 before celebrating the millennium? In popular usage, a new century begins on 1 Jan. of the year ending in -00, and this is unlikely to change however loudly purists may protest.

2 Nonetheless, in formal reckoning each century (*the 5th, the 16th,* etc.) contains one year beginning with the number that names it, and this is the last (or, in the case of BC dates, the first), and 99 years beginning with a number that is lower by one, so that 763, 1111, 1300, and 1990, belong to the 8th, 12th, 13th, and 20th centuries respectively.

ceremonial, ceremonious. *Ceremonial,* meaning 'with or concerning ritual or ceremony', is a neutral descriptive adjective (as in *ceremonial occasions* | *ceremonial dress* | *for ceremonial reasons*). *Ceremonious,* meaning 'having or showing a fondness for ceremony', is a more evaluative and judgemental word. The difference can be seen by contrasting *ceremonial entry* with *ceremonious entry*: the first is an entry marked by normal ceremony, whereas the second is an affectedly elaborate or grand entry. Examples: *Lord Mackan has had a busy programme of special ceremonial events on top of his normal Household chores*—Sunday Express, 1981 | *On the far side of the hearth the headman was sitting with his legs crossed, his back very straight, ceremoniously smoking a hookah*—M. Connell, 1991. *Ceremonial* is also used as a noun, meaning 'proper formalities': *He had had to fight for everything he had done, fight the people who wanted to wrap him up safely and wheel him out for a bit of ribbon-cutting and ceremonial*—P. Junor, 1991.

certainty, certitude. Leaving aside special meanings in philosophy, both words imply the absence of doubt about the truth of something, but *certitude* is a more subjective feeling whereas *certainty* is, strictly speaking, verifiable. In practice, however, *certitude* is falling out of use, and *certainty* is taking over its functions. Examples: (certainty) *He was filled with certainty, a deep, sure, clean conviction that engulfed him like a flood*—R. P. Warren, 1939 | *He never had the absolute certainty that one day he'd get the boat*—R. Ingalis, 1987 | (certitude) *An obsession with statistics as the sole ground of certitude in a changing world*—Encounter, 1964 | *We craved certitude and order, and Oxford gave us both*—Ved Mehta, 1993.

cervical means 'relating to the neck' (as in *cervical vertebrae*) or 'relating to the cervix (or neck of the womb)'. The term has emerged from the domain of laboratories with the advent of nationwide cervical screening and cervical smears. Its pronunciation in general use, **serv**-i-kəl, is being influenced by the preference in medical circles for sə-**viy**-kəl.

chagrin. The dominant standard pronunciation of the noun in BrE is **shag**-rin, and in AmE shə-**grin**. The adjective derived from it is spelt *chagrined*, pronounced the same way with the addition of a final -d.

chairman, chairwoman, chairperson, chair. The term *chairman*, which combines connotations of power with grammatical gender bias, is a keyword in feminist sensitivities about language. *Chairwoman* dates from the 17c, but (as the OED notes) it was hardly a recognized name until the 19c, and even then it did not

solve the problem of how to refer neutrally to a chairman/chairwoman when the gender was unknown or irrelevant. Two gender-neutral alternatives have emerged in the 20c: *chairperson* and *chair*, both first attested in the 1970s, although *chair* was already in use to mean 'the authority invested in a chairman': *I was recently challenged for using 'chairman' to describe my position. My accuser went on to assert that I was being insensitive to the work of the Equal Opportunities Commission by not using 'chairwoman', 'chairperson', or 'chair'.*—Ann Scully, *Times*, 1988. *Chair* seems to be more popular than *chairperson*, partly because it seems less contrived and partly because it is more malleable in meaning, whereas *chairperson* requires the impossibly cumbersome derivative *chairpersonship*. *Chairperson* tends still to be used as an alternative for *chairwoman* rather than for *chairman or chairwoman*. See also -PERSON.

challenged has established itself in the 1980s and 1990s as a combining element forming politically correct alternatives to potentially sensitive or offensive descriptions of people, as in *cerebrally challenged* (= stupid), *intellectually challenged* (= backward), *physically challenged* (= disabled), and *vertically challenged* (= shorter than average). Most of these, however, are not used outside the more extreme realms of the PC movement, especially when alternatives are available that are less depleted of semantic relevance (e.g. *children with special needs* for *educationally subnormal* and *backward*).

chamois is pronounced **sham**-wah, with plural spelt the same and pronounced **sham**-wahz.

When it means *chamois leather*, it is normally pronounced **sham**-i and **sham**-iz.

champagne should strictly speaking be used only of a sparkling white wine from the Champagne area of France, although it is loosely used of other similar wines.

changeable is spelt with an *e* in the middle to preserve the soft sound of the *g*.

chap, meaning 'man, boy', is a 16c shortening of *chapman* meaning 'pedlar'. It originally meant 'a buyer, customer', and only acquired its present-day colloquial meaning in the 19c.

chaperone, meaning 'someone who accompanies a young unmarried woman', is the recommended spelling, not *chaperon*. It is pronounced **shap**-ə-rohn.

char is short for *charlady* and *charwoman*, and as a verb has inflected forms *charred, charring*. Other terms such as *cleaner* (in offices) and *daily help* (in private houses) are now more usual, and *char* has a decidedly period flavour about it.

character. Fowler (1926) argued that *character* should not be used (1) as an alternative to forming abstract nouns in *-ness*, *-ity*, etc., e.g. *Every housing site has its own unique character—Country Life*, 1972 [instead of *uniqueness*], and (2) in the construction *of a . . . character* (with an adjective before *character*), e.g. *Of completely different character was the imported . . . Moorish furniture which first made Liberty's reputation—*E. Joy, 1972 [instead of *Completely different was . . .*]. These economies should be kept in mind in more formal written contexts, although *character* is

well established in more general usage as an alternative for *quality* or *nature*.

charge *noun. In charge of* has two constructions: A can be *in charge of* B, and B can be *in the charge of* A (with an inserted *the* now usual) or in A's charge (in which case *the* is implicit). In all cases, A is given authority over B. Examples: *She didn't think it unreasonable to put Sebastian in Rex's charge on the journey—*Evelyn Waugh, 1945 | *Until they are 12 months old, the hound puppies are in the charge of the walkers who keep them at their homes—*Leicester Mercury, 1984 | *I was recently . . . put in charge of six other copywriters, two of them men—*New York Times, 1980. However, the construction *in charge of* will be found with the meaning 'in the charge of' (as distinguished above) in writing of the earlier part of the 20c, and in these cases only the context can prevent ambiguity: *The young prince was doing lessons at Ludlow in charge of the Queen's brother, Lord Rivers—*Josephine Tey, 1951.

charisma. 1 This is originally a Greek word meaning 'gift of grace'. It acquired its current meaning 'a gift or power of leadership or authority' when the sociologist Max Weber used it in this way (in German) in 1922. It has been used widely in association with major political figures, including J. F. Kennedy, Mikhail Gorbachev, and Nelson Mandela, and is now used as a synonym for 'influence' or 'authority' or even 'attraction' or 'charm' in various contexts, impersonal as well as personal: *Spacecraft sent there in recent years have dispelled legends and added reams of sound, ordered data, yet the charisma of Mars remains—San Francisco Examiner,*

1976 | *She presents well, has charm, charisma and vitality, but comes across as severely intellectual—Business*, 1991 | *Despite promo pics that make them look like 12-year-olds, their 'charisma' is more David Cassidy style—New Musical Express*, 1976.

2 The adjective *charismatic*, in addition to its religious meanings (as in *the charismatic movement*), has developed in line with *charisma*, and there is also an adverb *charismatically*: *He had a charismatic quality about him that had long made him one of Europe's most eligible bachelors*—A. MacNeill, 1989 | *She blossomed from a precocious teenager . . . into a charismatically attractive woman with towering talent.*—S. Stone, 1989.

charlatan, meaning 'a person falsely claiming special knowledge', is pronounced **shah**-lə-tən.

chastise is spelt *-ise*, not *-ize*.

château should be spelt with a circumflex on the *a*, although many newspapers print it without because they lack this character in their font sets. The plural is *châteaux*, pronounced with a final -z.

chauvinism is still used in its original meaning, associated with the eponymous Napoleonic veteran Nicolas Chauvin, of 'exaggerated or aggressive patriotism'. In English (though not in French) it has developed a range of extended uses signifying other kinds of excessive loyalty or prejudice, including *economic chauvinism, white chauvinism, female chauvinism*, and, most famously, *male chauvinism* (first recorded in 1970). *Male chauvinism* and *male chauvinist* are so well established now that they are often used in the simple forms *chauvinism* and

chauvinist, usually without any danger of ambiguity because the context is all.

cheap, cheaply *adverbs. Cheap* has one meaning, 'at a low price', and regularly follows the verb as closely as possible: *Picture-books seem to end up by being sold off cheap as remaindered volumes—Country Life*, 1981. *Cheaply* has this meaning and also means 'in low esteem': *The small Renault is underpowered and rather cheaply built*—M. Harris, 1980. A regular idiom is *to come cheap* (or occasionally *cheaply*): *A gondolier doesn't come cheap—but punting down the canals is the very best way to explore—Best*, 1991 | *The brothers enjoyed the hedonistic pleasures of the big city's pleasures that did not come cheaply*—R. Long, 1990.

check, cheque are the AmE and BrE spellings respectively for an order written on a bank account. In AmE, *check* is also the word for BrE *bill* (in a restaurant).

checkers is the AmE name for the game in BrE called *draughts*.

cheerful, cheery. For the ordinary meanings 'full of cheer, cheering, gladdening', *cheerful* is the usual word, and can be applied to a person or a person's appearance or disposition, as well as to utterances and activities (e.g. *a cheerful conversation* | *cheerful cries* | *a cheerful time*) and occasionally places (*a cheerful room*). It also occurs in the informal fixed expression *cheap and cheerful*, meaning 'simple but practical', and is used more generally with the notion of tolerant good humour (e.g *a cheerful acceptance of the inevitable*). *Cheery*, which Dr Johnson called 'a ludicrous word', is more colloquial, is suggestive of high spirits, and is used to describe a person, mood, voice, etc.

cheers, long established as a salutation used before drinking, has developed a meaning in BrE noted by the *Times* columnist Philip Howard: *By a remarkable transition from the pub to the sober world at large* cheers *has become the colloquial synonym in British English for 'thanks'*—*Times*, 1978. In a sense halfway between these two, *cheers* also means 'goodbye'.

cheque is the standard BrE spelling for the word in its banking sense. See also CHECK, CHEQUE.

chequered is the standard BrE spelling for the word in its literal meaning 'having a pattern of alternately coloured squares' and in its figurative meaning 'uneven, of varied fortune', as in *a chequered career*.

cherub has a plural *cherubim*, pronounced **cher**-ə-bim when referring to angelic beings, and *cherubs* when referring to adorable children. The adjective *cherubic* is pronounced chi-**roo**-bik.

chide, meaning 'scold', in current usage has a past tense and past participle *chided*, although these forms have been unstable (with *chid*, *chode*, and *chidden* also recorded) over the word's thousand years of history.

childish, childlike. Both words tend now to be used to describe the behaviour of adolescents and adults rather than children. *Childish* has developed a generally depreciatory meaning 'having the immature characteristics of a child', whereas *childlike* has the favourable meaning 'having the good qualities associated with a child'. Examples: *His childlike curiosity about life was held in check by*

childish timidity—M. Holroyd, 1974 | *John observing his daughter, saw her now as more grown-up, less childish*—Iris Murdoch, 1976 | *She habitually wore an expression of childlike wonder*—R. West, 1977.

chimera, a word for a mythological being and with figurative meanings, is the recommended spelling, not *chimaera*. It is pronounced kiy-**mee**-rə.

Chinese, Chinaman. *Chinese* is the standard word, both as a noun (with plural the same) and an adjective, for people and things relating to China. *Chinaman*, the form recommended by Fowler (1926), has developed unfavourable overtones and is no longer in ordinary use.

chiropodist, meaning 'someone qualified to treat the feet', was regarded by the *OED* as a factitious (i.e. artificial) formation, since the significance of the element *chir-* (not certainly from the Greek word for 'hand') was unclear. Time has healed the etymological wounds and the term is now in ordinary use, as is the corresponding noun *chiropody*.

chock-full is now the dominant form, having triumphed over variants such as choke-full and chuck-full. These spelling difficulties have been aggravated by uncertainty as to the origin of the element *chock*, which also occurs in *chock-a-block* (with the same meaning).

chop, cutlet. A chop (17c) is a slice of meat (usually pork or lamb) cut from the loin, usually including a rib. A cutlet (early 18c) is a neck-chop of mutton or lamb, or a small piece of boneless veal for frying. A nut cutlet is a portion of meat substitute, often made from nuts and shaped like a cutlet, for vegetarian use.

chorale is derived from German *Choral(gesang)* and means a stately hymn tune. In AmE it also means a choir or choral society. The final e was added to reinforce the pronunciation with stress on the second syllable (kə-**rahl**); compare *locale* and *morale*.

chord, cord. 1 Although we are dealing here with three English words, their histories are very much intertwined, and their ultimate origin is in the Latin word *chorda* which has several meanings. To begin with, there are two distinct words spelt *chord*: (1) in music, a group of notes sounded together to form the basis of harmony (this is a shortening of *accord* respelt with an initial *ch-*), and (2) a technical word in mathematics and engineering, meaning a straight line joining the ends of an arc, the wings of an aeroplane, etc. (this is a 16c refashioning of *cord* after the initial *ch* of the Latin source). The idiom *to strike a chord* relates, somewhat surprisingly, to the second of these meanings.

2 The word *cord* = string, rope, etc., and in *spinal cord, umbilical cord, vocal cord*, etc., is descended, via Middle English and Old French *corde*, from Latin *chorda* in its meaning 'a string of a musical instrument'. The anatomical sense is sometimes spelt chord, but this spelling is not recommended.

Christian name. In a multicultural society such as Britain and the USA have become, this term should be avoided in favour of the culturally neutral *first name* or *forename*. In AmE *given name* is also used.

chronic is used of a disease that is long-lasting (as opposed to *acute*), and has the same implication of continuing severity when used of other circumstances. An *acute* problem is intense but brief, whereas a *chronic* problem is severe and likely to persist: *Richard Wallace . . . bought no furniture, not wishing, perhaps, to add to the already acute problems of storage space*—D. Mallett, 1979 | *Traffic congestion has become so chronic in Britain's cities that vehicles travel at an average speed of just 8 mph*— Back Street Heroes, 1988. The word is also used colloquially as a term of mild disapproval, especially in the phrase *something chronic*.

chrysalis has a plural *chrysalises* in general use or *chrysalides* (four syllables with stress on the second) in technical usage.

chuffed has the general colloquial meaning 'pleased, delighted': *You were pleased at the time. Chuffed in fact.*—Paul Scott, 1977. In some local uses in the UK the word also means the exact opposite, 'displeased, disgruntled': *Don't let on they're after you, see, or she'll be dead chuffed, see?*—C. Dale, 1964. The explanation seems to be that the two meanings reflect different uses of the dialect word *chuff*, which means 'proud, conceited' in some parts of the country and 'ill-tempered, surly' in others.

chute is the standard spelling in the meanings (1) a sloping channel or slide, and (2) a parachute.

cicada is pronounced si-**kah**-də, although si-**kay**-də is also heard.

cigarette is normally stressed on the third syllable in BrE and on the first syllable in AmE. Even in BrE, however, the stress can fall on the first syllable when the rhythm of the sentence seems to prefer this (as in *Cigarettes are dear*).

cinema has prevailed over *kinema*, which was still an option when Fowler wrote (1926); he also defended the shortening against the claims of the full form *cinematograph*. Today, in BrE one goes to the *cinema* to see a *film*; in AmE one goes to *the movies* or to a *theater* to see a *movie*. In Australia and New Zealand, one goes to *the pictures* or a *picture theatre* to see a *film*. However, *movie* is spreading fast into BrE and other varieties, and will undoubtedly take over in the end (*In many ways this movie heralded a new dawn in gritty British film-making—Radio Times*, 1998). *Motion pictures*, or the *motion-picture industry*, is used of the business world of film-making in all varieties of English.

cipher is the recommended spelling, not *cypher*.

circumcise is spelt -*ise*, not -*ize*.

circumstance. The debate about the merits of *in the circumstances* and *under the circumstances* has continued for most of the 20c. The pedantic view is that since circumstances are, etymologically speaking, around (*circum*) us, we must be *in* them and not *under* them; but Fowler rightly rejected this argument as puerile and observed that *under the circumstances* 'is neither illogical nor of recent invention (1665 in OED)'. The OED further noted that 'mere situation is expressed by *in the circumstances*, action affected is performed *under the circumstances*', a subtle distinction that is useful as a general guide: *Never, under any circumstances, solder connections to the tags with them already on the*

cartridge—Hi-Fi Sound, 1971 | *As a writer, and collector of unusual information, I would be interested to hear from people who have seen the 'little people' or any strange, apparently non-human beings, under any circumstances whatever—Stornoway Gazette*, 1973 | *In very special circumstances, you might be pressured into parenthood—Proceedings of the Classical Association*, 1977 | *As from today, M[inimum] L[ending] R[ate] will cease to be posted except in very unusual circumstances—Daily Telegraph*, 1981. Choice is also affected by the presence of an adjective or other qualifier for *circumstances*: *in present circumstances, in straitened circumstances, under these circumstances, under no circumstances*, etc., are all idiomatic constructions.

city is applied in many English-speaking countries to any large town, and the official use of the term varies from country to country. In Britain it is properly used of a town that is declared to be a city by royal charter and has a cathedral. As a result cities vary greatly in size and population: Edinburgh (population 400,000), Oxford (population 100,000) and Wells (population 8,000) are all cities, as is the City of London, which is the business centre of the capital although no more than one square mile in area and having a resident population of less than 6,000.

clad see CLOTHE.

claim *verb*. There are several areas of difficulty with this word. The first concerns *claim + that*, and the second *claim + to*. The third concerns the expression *to claim responsibility*.

  1 *CLAIM + THAT*. In this construction, *claim* should not be used as a mere synonym for *allege, assert, declare, maintain, say*, etc., but should contain an element of argued contention: *He claimed that adding VAT to domestic fuel and power would help create a greener and cleaner world by stimulating the use of more energy efficiency measures—Environment Digest*, 1990 | ⊠ *The Sun claims that the Stonebridge council estate in north London 'is Britain's tinderbox where Los Angeles-style riots could explode at any time'—New Statesman*, 1992.

2 CLAIM + TO. Fowler objected to the use of this construction when the subject of *claim* is not the same as the subject of the infinitive; so *I claim to be honest* is acceptable but ⊠ *I claim this to be honest* is not. Passive constructions such as ⊠ *Their oyster farm is claimed to be the only one of its kind in Europe—Times*, 1975 would also be rejected on the same principle. The weight of current usage, however, has all but overturned this rule, and it is principally on grounds of style that alternative constructions using *assert, contend, maintain*, etc., might be preferred.

3 CLAIM RESPONSIBILITY FOR. In news reports, it is often said that a particular group *claimed responsibility* for (an attack, bombing, etc.). The objection is that the use of *claim* implies something laudable or desirable, whereas a terrorist attack is neither. To avoid these sensitivities, it is advisable to use an alternative expression such as *admit responsibility* or *declare that* (they were responsible).

classic, classical. 1 *Classical* is the customary word when reference is to the arts and literature of ancient Greece and Rome (*a classical scholar | classical Greek |*

architecture of classical proportions), and also to serious or conventional music, i.e. that of Bach, Mozart, Beethoven, Brahms, etc. (although it applies more strictly to the 18th century, after the Baroque period and before the onset of Romanticism). *Classical* has come to be widely used in marketing circles to denote anything of traditional design: *Classical desk lamp with swivelling green metal reflector cowl on a brass stem—Habitat Catalogue*, 1982

2 *Classic* means 'of acknowledged excellence' (*the classic textbook on the subject*) or 'remarkably typical' (*a classic case of cerebral palsy*). In general use, it has come to mean little more than 'significant, noteworthy': *Most home workers are women . . . a classic case of powerless employees—Guardian*, 1973 | *The Nixon–Gandhi conversation thus turned into a classic dialogue of the deaf—*Henry Kissinger, 1979. The *Classic races* in Britain are the five main flat races, namely the Two Thousand and the One Thousand Guineas, the Derby, the Oaks, and the St Leger.

clauses. 1 A clause is a group of words normally containing a verb and its subject. A main clause makes sense by itself and can constitute an entire sentence, e.g. *The train arrived at 6 o'clock*. Alternatively, a sentence can be made up of more than one main clause linked by a conjunction, e.g. *The train arrived at 6 o'clock and the passengers got out*. A subordinate clause is one that qualifies a main clause, e.g. *The train arrived at 6 o'clock **when it was already dark*** or *The train arrived at 6 o'clock **in order to let the passengers out***. A clause can have the status of another part of speech; for example it can be an adverb (as in the sentence just given), an adjective (*The*

train **which left London this morning**
arrived at 6 o'clock), or a noun The
train arrived at **what we thought was
6 o'clock**. A relative clause is one
beginning with who, which, or that
that gives extra information, as
in the second example above.
Relative clauses can be restrictive
(or defining), as in the same example ('Which train? The one
from London') or non-restrictive,
as in The train, **which left London
this morning**, arrived at 6 o'clock (in
which the fact of leaving London
is incidental information and not
essential to the meaning).

2 There are various ways of
analysing clauses and sentences.
The most important abbreviations
used are S (subject), V (verb), O
(object), C (complement), and A
(adverbial), as in My son [S] con-
siders [V] the price [O] quite reasonable [C] in the circumstances [A]. For
a fuller description, and more
complex examples of notations,
see Greenbaum, Oxford English
Grammar, 311-55.

clean, cleanly. Clean has been
an adverb meaning 'completely,
outright' since Old English and is
still used as one, as in The bullet
went clean through his shoulder-
blade. Cleanly is an adverb of manner, and is often used
figuratively: His ability, when he is
wrong-footed, to extricate himself
cleanly from the resulting mess—
Observer, 1978. Note also the adjective cleanly (pronounced **klen**-li),
which means 'habitually clean':
The athlete's dancing vector, the spirit's need, And muscle's cleanly
diction—A. Hecht, 1977. This meaning will probably be more familiar in its derivative form
cleanliness, which is proverbially
next to godliness.

clear, clearly. The grammatical
situation is similar to that in the

preceding entry, with clear available as an adverb in two principal meanings, (1) 'completely'
(They got clear away), (2) 'in a clear
manner, with clear effect' (They
spoke out loud and clear). In this
last use, it should be pointed out
that clear, like loud, is used as a
semi-adjective; but it is usually
reckoned to be an adverb, as it is
in a number of fixed expressions
such as keep clear, stand clear, stay
clear, and steer clear. Clearly is an
adverb of manner, and can sometimes be used instead of clear in
meaning (2): They spoke out loudly
and clearly | The author writes clearly
and concisely. It is also used figuratively, often as a sentence adverb:
It clearly has the advantage of keeping all the lines from getting crossed
and establishing the priorities of
policy—Times, 1973 | Clearly a more
sensible definition of randomness is
required—Scientific American, 1975.

cleave. There are two words,
both from Old English, with this
spelling. One is a mostly literary
word for 'cut', and has inflected
forms (past) cleaved, clove, or cleft,
and (past participle) cleaved or cloven. The adjective is cloven in
cloven-footed and cloven hoof, and
cleft in cleft palate and in a cleft
stick. It is chiefly in these fixed expressions that the word is generally known. The other word
means 'to stick, adhere', and inflects more regularly (past)
cleaved, (past participle) cleaved. It
occurs chiefly in the Authorized
Version of the Bible (where a past
form clave is also found): The
Nobles held their peace, and their
tongue cleaued to the roofe of their
mouth—Job 29:10.

cleft see CLEAVE.

clench, clinch. Clinch is a 16c
variant spelling of clench, and has
since been regarded as a separate

word. We *clench* our teeth, fingers, and fists; and we *clinch* an argument, bargain, or deal. Lovers *clinch* when they embrace closely, and so do boxers and wrestlers when they embrace too closely. A remark or statement that decides an argument is (informally) a *clincher*. Usually nails are *clinched* (not *clenched*) to make a *clinker-built* (or *clincher-built*) boat.

clever see LOST CAUSES.

clew see CLUE.

clichés. 1 A cliché is a phrase that has become meaningless with overuse; for example, it is now meaningless to wish someone *a nice day* because a once sincere intention has become an empty cliché. The French word *cliché* means a stereotype printing block, which produced the same page over and over again.

2 Fowler's entry in this topic (1926) was less than six lines long, and quoted only two examples: *a minus quantity* (as in *Clothing among them was a minus quantity*) and *the order of the day* (as in *Engine troubles were the order of the day*). Since then, the list of fixed expressions that are commonly regarded as clichés has grown, and everyone has their own favourites from those they condemn in the usage of other people. Anthony Burgess mocked clichés in *Inside Mr Enderby* (1963): *He was, however, on the whole, taking all things into consideration, by and large, not to put too fine a point on it, reasonably self-sufficient.* The list can be extended with the following, among others: *at the end of the day, at this moment in time, conspicuous by one's absence, explore every avenue, in this day and age, keep a low profile, leave no stone unturned, on the back burner, over the moon, put your money where your mouth is, sick as a parrot, situation* (as in *crisis situation*), *level playing-field, not my cup of tea, take on board, until such time as, you name it.*

3 Despite a vigorous defence by Nicholas Bagnall (*A Defence of Clichés*, 1985), they are normally condemned or ridiculed on grounds of style. Christopher Ricks wisely observed (1980) that 'the only way to speak of a cliché is with a cliché'.

client has extended its range of use dramatically in recent years. It means, essentially, 'someone who buys the services of a professional person', such as a lawyer or accountant; and a prostitute traditionally has *clients*. Someone who buys something from a shop is a *customer*, doctors have *patients*, and hotels and restaurants have *patrons* (but takeaways are regarded as shops and have *customers*). In the more competitive world of privatized public transport, *passengers* are often referred to as *customers* or sometimes *clients*; this usage is entirely contrived. There is some shift of usage in the social services, in the interests of neutral description: a social worker, for example, will now claim to have *clients* rather than the more judgemental *cases* or *patients*.

climactic, climatic, climacteric. *Climactic* means 'forming a climax' (*For the climactic battle sequence . . . Lucas gathered all the old war movies he could find and spliced together their aerial-combat footage—Time*, 1977); *climatic* means 'relating to climate' (*The Tamworth* [*pig*] *. . . can adapt itself to a wide range of climatic conditions—Journal of the Royal Society of Arts*, 1977); and *climacteric* is a noun meaning 'the period of life when fertility and sexual activity are in decline'.

climate developed its figurative meaning 'the prevailing trend of opinion or public feeling' as early as the 17c, despite its modern ring. Examples: *The whole climate of thought will be different*—George Orwell, 1949 | *We must . . . take account of the intellectual climate of the time*—David Crystal, 1971 | *The social security structure of individual countries depends heavily on their political climate*—Accountant, 1972.

cling, after a period of instability, has now rejected the past form *clang*, and has settled for *clung* as both the past tense and past participle.

clone is derived from Greek *klōn* 'twig, slip', and came into use at the beginning of the 20c as a technical term in botany and biology. In addition to its now generally familiar original use, it has developed figurative meanings relating to close resemblances of various kinds between people and things: *Isn't he rather too much of a Benn clone?*—Observer, 1983 | *Amstrad [is] leading the cut price clones attacking IBM personal computers on price*—Marketing, 1986.

close, shut *verbs. Close* has a greater implication of formality and politeness than does *shut*, which often sounds merely peremptory. *Close the door* suggests an invitation, whereas *Shut the door* is a more straightforward command. *Closed* is also used in a number of fixed expressions: *a closed book, a closed shop, behind closed doors, a closed society.*

close, closely. The adjective *close* merges into an adverb in uses such as *come close, lie close, run close, stick close,* etc., especially in figurative uses: *No other car comes close for combining brilliant responsiveness with precise control*—advertisement in *Scientific American*, 1973 | *Opera and large gatherings ran each other close for first place among her dislikes*—J. Aiken, 1977. The adverb *closely* dates from the 16c and is used as an adverb of manner or degree, often in non-physical contexts: *Any programme of cuts . . . would have to be closely vetted*—Times, 1975 | *The only language closely related to Sinhalese is Maldivian*—Language, 1972.

clothe has two past and participial forms: *clothed* (the normal word) and *clad. Clothed* is suitable for most contexts (except when the less formal word *dressed* is called for), whereas *clad* is reserved for special uses: (1) as a literary word, and (2) with a qualifying word as in *ill-clad, insufficiently clad,* etc., and in figurative uses such as *ice-clad, ivy-clad,* etc. These uses also have a strong literary flavour.

clue is the normal spelling in the group of meanings to do with signs or evidence. *Clew*, which is a variant of the same word, is now principally used as a nautical term meaning 'the lower or after corner of a sail'.

co-.
See box overleaf

coastal see LOST CAUSES.

coccyx, meaning a bone at the base of the spine, is pronounced **kok**-siks. The plural is *coccyxes* or (more rarely) *coccyges* (**kok**-si-jeez).

cocoa see CACAO.

coffin see CASKET.

co-

is a prefix of Latin origin, and is used to form words that include the meaning 'together, in common'. Spelling practice varies with regard to use of a hyphen: some words (especially when the second element begins with a vowel) include it, whereas others are written as one word. The diaeresis (ö) that formerly punctuated words as in coöperate, is now largely disused. Recommended spellings are as follows:

coagulate	coextensive	co-opt
coalition	cohabit	coordinate
co-author (noun and	cohere	copartner
verb)	coincide	co-pilot
coaxial	coition	co-respondent (in divorce
co-determination	co-latitude	case)
co-driver	co-occur	co-signatory (to an
co-education	co-occurrence	agreement etc.)
coefficient	co-op	co-star
co-equal	cooperate	co-worker
coeval	cooperation	uncooperative
coexist	cooperative	uncoordinated
coexistent		

cogent. To be *cogent*, an argument has to persuade or convince; to be *coherent* (see next entry) it only has to make sense.

coherent, cohesive. Both words come from a Latin root related to our word *cohere*, but their meanings are different. *Coherent* means 'logical and consistent' and is applied to speakers and their arguments. See also COGENT. *Cohesive* means 'tending to stick together' and is generally used either physically (as with liquid mixtures, for example) or in abstract contexts: *Tephra . . . serves as an insulating material, and constitutes an important component of cement—National Geographic, 1972 | The demand for socially cohesive categories of Nature and Reason—T. Eagleton, 1976.*

cohort. A *cohort* (*cohors*) of the Roman army was an infantry unit equivalent to one-tenth of a legion, and typically consisted of about 500 soldiers. In the plural it has often been used as a literary word for 'army', as in Byron's reference to Sennacherib (1815): *And his cohorts were gleaming in purple and gold.* As well as a technical meaning in demography, the word has in the 20c developed a meaning (originally AmE) 'an assistant, colleague, accomplice', probably influenced by the coincidence of the first element with the prefix *co-*: *Mr Stratton consented . . . to partake together with his cohort of a sandwich and a glass of milk*—A. Cross, 1967 | *The impending trial of Bobby Seale, chairman of the Black Panther movement, and his eight cohorts in New Haven*—Sunday Times, 1970 | *Brock and Emma had one wall, Bob, Johnny and their cohorts the other wall and centre aisle*—John Le Carré, 1979. The incongruity of this use is masked by its frequent appearance in the plural, and the singular even appears to be a kind of back-formation. Language becomes vulnerable when the specific historical significance of words is so easily forgotten.

coinages are words and meanings used for the first time. Words created for the physical sciences (such as *gas* and *radar*) are often publicly coined (for example, in a journal), so that the moment and sources of their creation are recorded; but this is rarely the case with more general vocabulary unless this too is invented for a special purpose (as with *charisma* and *robot*) and still less so with slang and colloquial English, even when these are phrase-based. Coinages tend to be based on analogy (e.g. *software* from *hardware*), on compounding (e.g. *lunatic fringe, smart card*), on blending words (e.g. *motel* from *motor* and *hotel, edutainment* from *education* and *entertainment*), on use of prefixes and suffixes (e.g. *reflagging, privatization*), and on phrases, real or notional (e.g. *gobsmacked*). See also NEW WORDS.

colander, meaning 'a kitchen strainer', is spelt this way, although *cullender* will be found in older writing. See also CALENDAR.

Cold War, for the years of suppressed hostility between the USSR and the West after 1945, is spelt with capital initials. The concept disappeared with the collapse of communism in Eastern Europe from about 1989, but it is still referred to historically.

coleslaw is spelt *cole-*, not *cold-*. This element is from Dutch *kool* 'cabbage'.

colic has a derivative adjective *colicky* (with *k* to harden the sound).

coliseum, colosseum. Both are variants of the same word, derived from the ancient name (*colosseum*) of the Flavian amphitheatre in Rome, which in turn was named after a large statue (or *colossus*) of Nero which stood nearby. The form *Coliseum* is used of theatres and music halls and, especially in America, of theatres and large buildings used for sport or exhibitions.

collaborate, collaborator. The primary meaning of the verb, 'to work in conjunction with someone else', can still be used despite the sinister overtones it acquired when used of cooperation with the enemy during the second World War. This is true also of the agent noun *collaborator: Prof R G Mason and his collaborators at Imperial College used a new electromagnetic distance-measuring instrument*—Physics Bulletin, 1970.

collapsible is spelt *-ible*, not *-able*. See -ABLE, -IBLE.

collectable, collectible. Fowler (1926) said that the first is better, and this is still true. See -ABLE, -IBLE.

collective noun. 1 A collective noun is one that is singular in form and denotes a number of individuals, for example *audience, choir, committee, flock, multitude*. Apart from the names of individual animals, birds, etc. (*deer, grouse, sheep, trout*) and names for groups of them (*a pride of lions, a gaggle of geese*, etc.), and names of institutions, firms, and teams

(*BBC, Marks & Spencer, Tottenham Hotspur*, etc.), there are some 200 collective nouns in common use in English.

2 The principal question of usage with collective nouns is whether they should be treated as singular or plural. In BrE, the practice is well established of construing them either with a singular verb to emphasize unity or with a plural verb to emphasize individuality. The point is more fully discussed at AGREE-MENT 3. It is particularly important to maintain consistency within a statement, avoiding, for example, a singular verb with a plural pronoun following, as in ✖ *When the jury retires to consider their verdict.*

3 When a collective noun is followed by *of* + plural noun or pronoun (as in *a number of people*), there is a general preference for a plural construction: *A large number of conductors want to hear the great artists*—*Dædalus*, 1986 | *A handful of their members have been agents of Moscow*—*London Review of Books*, 1987; but again a singular is used when collectivity rather than individuality is the main point: *A decade ago there was only a handful of bioethicists in the country*—*British Medical Journal*, 1978.

4 Names of institutions and political entities, e.g. *the United States, the United Nations, the Vatican, the Commons, Congress*, are always treated as singular whether the form of the name is singular or plural (e.g. *The United States has demanded a more open Japan*—*Dædalus*, 1987 | *The CEGB finds it 25 per cent cheaper to buy in French electricity*—*Daily Telegraph*, 1987).

5 Names of animals, birds, and fish that are the same in the sin-gular and plural are treated as singular or plural (or as a singular mass noun) accordingly: *Five bison were grazing in a shaded part of the valley* | *Trout will for some time still be a premium fish, selling at about £1 each.*

6 For collective nouns of the type *a pride of lions* etc., see proper terms.

college has many long-established meanings: (1) a body of officials, membership of which is a privilege or honour, e.g. *College of Cardinals, College of Arms, College of Physicians*, etc., (2) an establishment for further education, normally part of a university as at Oxford, Cambridge, London, and elsewhere. In wider educational circles, *college* has been traditionally used in the names of some of the ancient public schools (notably Eton and Winchester). In more recent times, its has come to be applied to a broad group of educational and professional institutions: *business colleges, teacher-training colleges, sixth-form colleges, secretarial colleges, military* and *naval colleges, colleges of agriculture*, etc. One consequence of this is that general phrases such as being *at college* now need further elaboration.

collide, collision. There is no basis for the assertion sometimes made that these two words should be restricted to circumstances involving an impact between two *moving* objects. A vehicle can be said to *collide* with a tree, a bollard, or any other fixed object as well as with another vehicle, whether moving or not. In factual reporting, however, *hit* is often a more straightforward choice: [*They*] *died when their car hit a tree between Penzance* *and Land's End yesterday—Times*, 1990.

collocation is a term in descriptive linguistics for the customary association of words with other words. A *bystander* is usually said to be *innocent*, *consequences* are often *far-reaching*, and *politicians* are *cautiously optimistic*. Other aspects of collocation include the function words needed to complete the sense of other words (e.g *agree + with* or *to*) and the typical order of words, as in *fish and chips* and *spick and span*, neither of which can normally be reversed.

colloquial is a term used in dictionaries and books on language to describe the less formal vocabulary and grammar of everyday speech. In some dictionaries, *informal* is used instead (as being less judgemental), although the implications for usage are the same. *Slang* denotes a greater degree of informality, and typically involves a stronger element of metaphor or imagery. See SLANG.

collude, collusion. Both words involve a notion of fraud or dishonesty. It is correct to speak of dealers *colluding*, or acting *in collusion*, in insider dealing on the stock exchange; but it would not be correct to refer to authors *colluding* to write a book (the correct word would be *collaborating*).

colon. 1 The colon is the punctuation mark that is least used and least well understood in ordinary writing (as distinct from printing). The principal difference between it and the semicolon lies in the relation of what precedes and follows each in the sentence. A semicolon links two balanced or complementary statements, whereas a colon leads from the

first statement to the second, typically from general or introductory statement to example, from cause to effect, or from premiss to conclusion.

2 The respective roles of semicolon and colon are shown by the following example punctuated in two ways: *It was a beautiful day; we played cricket on the green.* | *It was a beautiful day: we played cricket on the green*. In the first version, the two statements about the weather and playing cricket are equally balanced and might alternatively be separated by *and* or written as two distinct sentences separated by a full stop. In the second version, the colon makes the second statement much more explicitly a consequence of the first.

3 A colon is also used to introduce a list: *The following will be needed: a pen, pencil, rubber, and ruler*. Note that the colon should not be followed by a dash, although this practice is more common in older printing.

4 In AmE, a colon follows the initial greeting in a letter (*Dear Ms Jones:*), where in BrE a comma is customary. A colon also separates hours and minutes in notation of time in AmE (*10:30 a.m.*).

colossal. In its physical sense 'of immense size', *colossal* dates from the early 18c, and was not listed by Dr Johnson (1755). The first use in its figurative meaning 'remarkable, splendid' is attributed to Mark Twain: *I do not suppose that any other statesman ever had such a colossal sense of humour, combined with the ability to totally conceal it—American Claimant*, 1892. This use, which verges on the colloquial, should be used sparingly: *Spending has been held back in part because of a colossal blooper by the*

House Ways and Means Committee—
Time, 1972.

colosseum see COLISEUM.

colour. In BrE the customary
spellings of words related to
colour are *colourable* (= specious,
counterfeit), *colourant* (= colouring
substance), *colourful*, *colourist* (= a
painter in colour), and *colourless*,
but *coloration* (= a colour scheme),
colorific (= producing colour), *color-
imeter* (= a measuring instrument), and *decolorize* (= remove
the colour from). In AmE all have
-or-, not *-our-*.

coloured, written with a capital
C, in South Africa denotes a person of mixed descent, and in the
plural denotes a racial group as
officially defined under the former apartheid laws. Its use by
white people in Britain and elsewhere meaning 'non-white' is
now rare.

columnist, meaning a writer of
a newspaper column, is pronounced with the n expressed.

combat is normally pronounced
with stress on the first syllable as
both noun and verb. The same
applies to the derivatives *combat-
ant* and *combative*. The verbal inflections are *combated, combating*.

combining forms. This term,
which may well have been used
first by the *OED* editors, denotes a
word form that is only used in
combination with other elements. The normal linking vowel is
-o (e.g. *Anglo-*, *electro-*) or *-i* (*alti-*,
horti-). Combining forms can also
occur at the ends of words (e.g.
-imeter, -ology).

come is one of several verbs
(others include *go* and *try*) which
can be followed by *and* instead of
to (*Come and see*). It can also be
followed by a participle in *-ing*
(*Will you come swimming tomorrow?*).
Occasionally, and usually for rhetorical effect, it is followed by an
infinitive without *to*: *We can sell
this house, you can come live with
us*—Lee Smith, 1983 (US) | *Come let
us say a prayer together*—Jane Gar-
dam, 1985 (UK).

come-at-able, meaning 'accessible', is recorded from the 17c,
but is less common than GET-
AT-ABLE. Also found are *come-
at-ability and uncome-at-able*.

comedian. In Shakespeare's
Twelfth Night (1601), Olivia asks
the disguised Viola, come to woo
her on behalf of Orsino with a
lover's speech ready to deliver,
'Are you a comedian?', meaning
'Are you a comic actor?'. At a
slightly earlier date (1581), the
word is recorded in the meaning
'writer of comic plays'; together
these constitute the earliest records of the word. Its current
meaning, applied both to men
and women, is 'a humorous en-
tertainer on stage, television, etc.'
A feminine form, *comédienne*, is
recorded from about 1860, but is
not much favoured now except
with historical reference. In the
meaning 'writer of comedies',
comedian is mostly used of the ancient writers Aristophanes, Me-
nander, Plautus, and Terence, to
distinguish them from the tra-
gedians Aeschylus, Sophocles, and
Euripides.

comic, comical. These two
words overlap in meaning, but
comic is the more common of the
two and is the only one with the
purely descriptive meaning 'relating to or in the nature of com-
edy', as in *comic actor* and *comic
opera*. *Comical* is a more evaluative
word, meaning 'funny, causing
laughter', as in *comical appearance*

and *a comical situation*; *comic* can also have this meaning but is often taken to imply intention rather than effect. The following examples demonstrate the different perspectives of these words in this meaning: *Both brothers laughed out loud at the deliberately comic delivery of his English phrases as they shook hands*—A. Grey, 1983 | *In reality, the relationship was a strained and sometimes comical mismatch, a 50-year-long saga of crossed purposes*—*Daily Telegraph*, 1992 | *He wiped his head, looking almost comical in his shorts and sandals*—N. Barber, 1992 | *Olson suggested that the truly comic element in the tale is an ironic one*—J. Hines, 1993.

comity, pronounced **kom**-i-ti, means 'considerate behaviour towards others': *Those participating in conversational encounters have to have a care for the preservation of good relations by promoting the other's positive self-image, by avoiding offence, encouraging comity, and so on*—H. G. Widdowson, 1990. It has a special meaning in international law, occurring often in the semi-fixed expression *comity of nations* (or *peoples*, etc.), of 'the mutual recognition by nations of the laws and customs of others': *The court accepted the need to pay healthy respect to the principles of comity*—D. McClean, 1992 | *It is important when considering applications under the Convention that it should be borne in mind that these are matters which affect the comity of nations*—*Weekly Law Reports*, 1992. It should not be used in the weaker meaning 'a group of nations that are well disposed to one another', although this is often found in print, e.g. *There were voices which spoke for Russia in the comity of civilised people other than those of ministers and Tsars*—Peter Ustinov, 1983.

comma. There is much variation in the use of the comma in print and in everyday writing. Essentially, its role is to give detail to the structure of sentences, especially longer ones, and to make their meaning clear by marking off words that either do or do not belong together. It usually represents the natural breaks and pauses that occur in speech. The principal uses are as follows:

1 To separate adjectives coming before a noun: *a cold, damp, badly heated room* | *a ruthless, manipulative person*. The comma can be replaced by *and* between a pair of adjectives to make a stronger effect: *a ruthless and manipulative person*. The comma is omitted when the last adjective has a closer relation to the noun: *a distinguished foreign politician* | *a dear little baby*.

2 To separate the main clauses of a compound sentence when they are not sufficiently close in meaning or content to form a continuous unpunctuated sentence, and are not distinct enough to warrant a semicolon. A conjunction such as *and, but, yet*, etc., is normally used: *The road runs close to the coast, and the railway line follows it closely*. It is incorrect to join the clauses of a compound sentence without a conjunction (the so-called 'comma splice'): ✖ *I like swimming very much, I go to the pool every day*. (In this sentence, the comma should either be replaced by a semicolon, or retained and followed by *and*.) It is also incorrect to separate a subject from its verb with a comma: ✖ *Those with the lowest incomes and no other means, should get the most support*. (Remove the comma.)

3 A comma also separates complementary parts of a sentence, and can introduce direct speech: *Parliament is not dissolved, only prorogued | The question is, can this be done? | He then asked, 'Do you want to come?'.*

4 An important function of the comma is to prevent ambiguity or (momentary) misunderstanding: *In the valley below, the houses look very small* (The valley is not below the houses) | *Mr Douglas Hogg said that he had shot, himself, as a small boy* (Mr Hogg shot things other than himself).

5 Commas are used in pairs to separate elements in a sentence that are not part of the main statement: *There is no sense, as far as I can see, in this suggestion | It appears, however, that we were wrong | There were, to be sure, at least four pubs in the village.* They are also used to separate a relative clause from its antecedent when the clause is not a restrictive or identifying one (see CLAUSES): *The book, which was on the table, was a gift.* (Without the comma, the relative clause would serve to identify the book in question rather than give extra information about it: *The book which/that was on the table was a gift*). A single comma usually follows adverbs (such as *already, however, moreover*) in initial position in a sentence: *Already, the sun was shining | Moreover, you were late home from school.*

6 Commas are used to separate items in a list or sequence. Usage varies as to the inclusion of a comma before and in the last item; the style recommended here is to include it (the so-called 'Oxford comma'): *We ordered tea, scones, and cake.* Other practice is to include it only to avoid ambiguity: *We ordered tea, bread and butter, and cake.*

7 Omit the comma between nouns in apposition (e.g.*my friend judge Leonard | her daughter Mary*), but retain it when the noun is a parenthesis (e.g. *His father, Humphrey V. Roe, was not so fortunate*)

8 Commas are used in numbers of four or more figures, to separate each group of three consecutive figures starting from the right (e.g. *14,236,681*). Omit the comma when giving house numbers in addresses (*44 High Street*), and in dates (*27 July 2001*).

commando has the plural form *commandos.*

commence, begin, start.

1 *Commence* is a more formal Latinate word for *begin* or *start.* Fowler's advice (1926) was to use *begin* and its derivatives except when these seem incongruous (which is in fact rare); occasions when *commence* is more appropriate include official announcements, statements of historical importance, and suchlike. It is therefore a sound rule to use *begin* in all ordinary contexts unless *start* is customary (e.g. *The engine started at once | They usually start work at 9.30 | The game started on time*), and to reserve *commence* for more formal occasions, such as the law (*to commence an action*), warfare (*Hostilities commenced on 4 August*), and the domain of ceremonial (*The procession will commence at 2 p.m.*)

2 Constructions available to *commence* are more limited than to *begin*; in particular *begin* can more readily be followed by a *to*-infinitive, whereas a verbal noun is now more natural after *commence*: *They began to eat* or *They began eating* but *They commenced eating.* However, *commence* + *to* will be found in older writing. Definitely to be avoided is a mixed style of *to* + verbal noun: ☒ *Then he commenced to coming by our place*—M. Golden, 1989.

commentate is an unsurprising back-formation from the noun *commentator*. It is first recorded as a rare word from the late 18c in the general sense 'to comment', and was revived in its current use in sports broadcasting in the 1950s.

commercialese is the special language of business correspondence. Sir Ernest Gowers, in his 1965 revision of Fowler's *Modern English Usage*, regarded commercialese as 'an artificial jargon', and quoted in his support a committee report on the teaching of English from as early as 1921. Gowers would be pleased to know that most of the more arcane terminology, such as *ult.* (= *ultimo*, last month), *prox.* (= *proximo*, next month), and *duly to hand* (= received) has since largely disappeared, although one or two phrases still linger in the correspondence of more conservative business people.

commercial traveller, first recorded in 1807, has now given way to *sales representative* (informally *sales rep*) as a term for an agent who sells a company's goods or services in an area.

commiserate was a transitive verb for about three centuries: *She did not exult in her rival's fall, but, on the contrary, commiserated her*—H. Ainsworth, 1871; but under the influence of *condole with* and *sympathize with*, it is now construed with *with* (despite the disapproval of Fowler, modified somewhat by Gowers): *We commiserated with one another on our various hurts*—K. Hulme, 1984.

commissionaire, meaning a uniformed door-attendant, is spelt with two *m*s and one *n*.

committee can take a singular or plural construction, depending on the sense. If the emphasis is on collectivity or unity, it is treated as singular; if the emphasis is on the individuality of its members, it is treated as plural. Examples: *The committee proposes an Official Information Act to cover leakage of information*—Times, 1972 | *The local party's General Management Committee will vote for their choice next Monday evening*—Wandsworth Borough News, 1977 | *An international committee on viral names has been looking into the problem*—Capital Gay, 1986. The status of singular or plural is unclear when the verb is in the past or constructed with an auxiliary verb such as *will* or *may*, and plural number is often clarified by resorting to an expression such as *the members of the committee: Key members of the . . . Committee concluded that only the existence of a 'mole' or 'sleeper' . . . could explain the many leaks and failures of the 1950s and 1960s*—Observer, 1981. See AGREEMENT 3.

common see MUTUAL.

communal is pronounced with stress on the first syllable.

commune is stressed on the first syllable as a noun, and on the second as a verb.

compact is stressed on the second syllable as a verb and predicative adjective. As a noun (meaning 'an agreement' or 'a case for face-powder') and as an attributive adjective, the stress is normally on the first syllable, except that it is variable in *compact disc*.

comparable is pronounced with main stress on the first syllable. Its uses with *to* and *with* correspond to the meanings given at COMPARE, with a marked preference in current usage for *to*: *This heroin is comparable in quality to that being sniffed by U.S. troops in Vietnam*—R. Parkes, 1973.

comparatively, like *relatively*, has been used since at least the early 19c as an intensifying (or 'downtoning') adverb, even where actual comparison is not involved: *He had had comparatively little to do with women*—P. Newton, 1972 | *It was a comparatively shabby office . . . Euram Marketing gave a distinct impression of watching the pennies*—G. Markstein, 1981. These uses are justified on the ground that there is usually implicit comparison of some kind, even if it is as vague as 'compared with others'. Fowler (1926) restricted his comment to the use of *a comparatively few* (with indefinite article), but Gowers (1965) extended the disapproval to the type *Casualties were comparatively few*, arguing that no comparison, not even an implicit one, is made. This distinction, however, is impossible to sustain, since *few* behaves like an ordinary descriptive adjective in being gradeable: if one allows *very few* the objection to *comparatively few* falls.

comparatives see ADJECTIVE 3, -ER AND -EST FORMS.

compare with, compare to.

1 In general usage, these two constructions tend to be used interchangeably; AmE generally prefers *to* when there is a choice, whereas in BrE the choice is more evenly divided. A broad distinction in principle should be kept in mind, namely that *compare to* is used to liken two things whereas *compare with* is used to weigh or balance one thing against another. When Shakespeare in his famous line asks *Shall I compare thee to a Summers day?*, he is likening, even though in the end he shows his beloved to be *more lovely* than a summer's day.

2 This broad distinction can be seen in the following modern examples, although the use of *to* in the 1976 example violates it: *American Opinion . . . compared the familiar peace symbol to an anti-Christian 'broken cross'*—*Time*, 1970 (likening) | *He did not individually compare other women with her, but because she was the first, she was equal in his memory to the sum of all the others*—J. Berger, 1972 (balancing) | *Compared to war-reporting of the Spanish war . . . Journey to a War is superficial and uninformative*—S. Hynes, 1976 (balancing) | *Salim's flight to London can be compared . . . to the Romeward journey in Virgil*—*London Review of Books*, 1979 (likening) | *The company produced a creditable performance, particularly when compared with the results of many of its competitors*—*Daily Telegraph*, 1992 (balancing).

3 When a subordinate clause or phrase is introduced by the participial form *compared*, the preposition is either *to* or *with*, although here usage is moving in favour of *to*: *The church looked dimly mysterious compared with the glare of the passage*—P. D. James, 1986 | *Compared to Ward's witch-hunters, Profumo is an almost blameless character in the story*—*London Review of Books*, 1987 | *This was a modest sum compared to what other people spent*—Tom Wolfe, 1987.

4 In BrE, though not in AmE, *with* is obligatory when *compare* is used intransitively, because the balancing rather than the likening notion predominates: *His achievements do not compare with those of A. J. Ayer—Sunday Times*, 1988 (UK) | *Ham and bamboo shoots do not compare to those made at Ying's—New York Times*, 1977 | *This compares with an average life expectancy in 1975 of 69.1 years for males and 75.2 years for females*—C. Ungerson, 1991. See also COMPARABLE, COMPARISON 2.

comparison. 1 For *comparison of adjectives*, see ADJECTIVE 3.

2 *Comparison* as the noun equivalent of *compare* is normally followed by *with*, not *to*, and this applies also to the expression *by* or *in comparison*: *By comparison with some of the 20 million tons a year North Sea finds it is a drop in the ocean—Daily Telegraph*, 1974 | *It doesn't bear comparison with the contact you can get with a live theatre audience*—S. Brett, 1977.

compass points. Use capital initials for *north, south, east,* and *west* when these are part of recognized names, e.g. *North London | South America | the East End*. The same applies to *northern, southern,* etc., when these have specific geographical reference, as in *Western Australia* and *Northern mythology*. In general reference, use small initials: *an easterly wind | southern parts of the country*. See CAPITALS 2C.

compendium has plurals *compendiums* (preferred) and *compendia*.

competence, competency.
1 Fowler (1926) remarked that 'neither has any sense in which the other cannot be used', and noted that the first form is gaining ground. This assertion remains generally valid, and in the meantime *competence* has won out in the currency battle over *competency*.

2 *Competence* was given a special meaning in language learning by Noam Chomsky in 1962: *competence* for him means what a speaker of a language knows implicitly, as distinct from *performance*, which is what the same person actually uses in language production.

complacent, complaisant have the same pronunciation apart from -s- in the first and -z- in the second. Both are derived from the Latin word *complacere* 'to please'. *Complacent* means 'calmly confident' and normally has unfavourable connotations, i.e. 'too easily satisfied; smugly self-confident': *A quarter of a century later, the conventional wisdom of British mandarins looks complacent, self-serving, ill-informed, and outmoded—Independent*, 1989. *Complaisant* means 'politely deferential' or 'too willing to please': *He went north to join his apparently complaisant wife for Christmas and Liza went to Cornwall*—P. Street, 1990. It is no longer much used in ordinary speech and writing (*obliging* and *acquiescent* are more common alternatives).

complement is a term in grammar for a word or phrase added to a verb to complete the predicate of a sentence. (In the examples that follow, the complement is in bold type.) The most common form of complement is the type that follows a verb of state such as *be, look, seem,* etc.: *I am **his brother** | She looked **lovely** | You seem **to be unhappy** | They remained **out of reach***. A complement can also relate to the object of a sentence rather than its subject (*He called his mother **a fool***), and the term is sometimes extended to include words and phrases that complete the sense of other words, e.g. adjectives (*fond **of chocolate***) and prepositions (*over **the moon***).

complement, compliment, complementary, complimentary.

1 *Complement* and *compliment* each function as noun and verb; in pronunciation they are largely indistinguishable except that in the verbal function *compliment* has a fuller -i- sound in its second syllable and both words have a more distinct -ment sound in the third syllable. Both words are derived from Latin *complere* 'to fill up'; *complement* means 'something that completes' and should be distinguished from *supplement* which means 'something that adds to'. A *compliment* is 'a spoken or written expression of praise'.

2 The derivative adjectives have corresponding meanings. *Complimentary* means 'expressing a compliment' and has the additional meaning 'given free of charge' (e.g. *complimentary tickets*). *Complementary* means 'completing' or 'forming a complement' (*Each of these regions is characterized by a broad range of complementary products*—M. Hudson, 1977), and has a number of special uses, e.g. in the expression *complementary medicine*, recorded from the 1980s.

complex is a term in psychology ('a group of repressed feelings or thoughts which cause abnormal behaviour or mental states'), usually with some qualifying word, e.g. *inferiority complex, Oedipus complex*, that has permeated everyday language in non-technical meanings. Examples: *Both of them had a complex about economy and living within a budget*—Mary McCarthy, 1954 | *The roadmen went and got into a muddle with their flags . . . One of them . . . apparently gets a power complex every time anyone puts a red flag into his hand*—C. Aird, 1973.

complexion is spelt -*xion*, not -*ction*.

complex prepositions. *Complex* (or *compound*) *prepositions* consist of two or more words together having the function of a preposition, e.g. *according to, apart from, in accordance with, with regard to.* Fowler (1926) objected to their overuse in journalism, 'stuffing up the newspaper columns with a compost of nouny abstractions'. He had a point, but they cause little trouble today and should only be avoided, as a matter of clear style, when something more simple is available: e.g. *about* or *concerning* will often do in place of *with regard to.* Others, such as *away from* and *out of*, are straightforward and necessary, since *away* and *out* (unlike *in*) do not function as prepositions by themselves.

compliment, complimentary see COMPLEMENT.

compose see COMPRISE.

composite is now pronounced **kom**-pǝ-zit, not -ziyt.

compound is pronounced with stress on the first syllable as a noun and on the second as a verb. To *compound a felony* in law is to condone it in exchange for some consideration, and does not mean 'to make (it) worse'. Note also that *compound* meaning 'a large enclosure' is an entirely distinct word derived via Portuguese and Dutch from Malay *kampong*.

compound prepositions see COMPLEX PREPOSITIONS.

comprehend see APPREHEND.

comprise. 1 *Comprise* is often confused with *compose, consist,* and *constitute*. All four words are used to describe how parts make up a whole, but they start from different ends of the equation. *Comprise* has the whole as its subject and its parts as the object, e.g. *The top floor comprises three bedrooms and a bathroom. Consist of* takes the same perspective, and one could equally say *The top floor consists of three bedrooms and a bathroom,* although it is more usual to use *consist of* with reference to ideas and concepts rather than physical things. It would be incorrect to reverse the construction with *comprise* in the form ☒ *Three bedrooms and a bathroom comprise the top floor.* The correct words to use here are *compose, constitute,* or (more informally) *make up.* See also INCLUDE.

2 It is even less correct to confuse *comprise* with *consist* and adopt a hybrid construction *comprise of* or *be comprised of.* Examples of correct uses: *The main installation at Dartford comprises three IBM central processors supporting some 350 terminals located throughout the UK*—Computers in Personnel, 1982 | *Love comprises among other things a desire for the well-being and spiritual freedom of the one who is loved*—Muriel Spark, 1984 | *A good society is a means to a good life for those who compose it*—Bertrand Russell, 1993. Examples of incorrect uses: *Internally, the chloroplast is comprised of a system of flattened membrane sacs*—Nature, 1970 | *Seven boys comprised the choir*—Garrison Keillor, 1985 | *The Saxe-Coburg inheritance is comprised of the ducal palace and three castles*—

Daily Telegraph, 1991 | *Rivers in this area are mainly comprised of domestic and industrial effluent, and many have been fishless in living memory*—K. Hawkins, 1993.

computerese. 1 The language of computer terminology has become familiar to the English-speaking world in the last twenty years or so as the technological revolution has impinged on the lives of most people both at work and in their homes. Since much of the development in this field has been led by the USA (IBM, Microsoft, etc.), English has become the electronic lingua franca much as it has been the international medium of communication in air travel and other domains. Most recently, the rapid expansion in use of the *Internet* (or *World Wide Web*) has produced a vocabulary of its own, both at technical level and in everyday slang. Much of the technical jargon is based on initialisms of three or more letters, such as *http* (= *hypertext transfer protocol*), *isp* (= *internet service provider*), and *www* (= *World Wide Web,* used in website *addresses*).

2 Other terminology is based on or adapted from words that belong to the basic core of English: one buys *hardware* and installs *software* on it, and occasionally *freeware*; one's desk becomes a *workstation*; many computer programs are manipulated by using a *mouse* to make choices from a *menu*; computer symbols are *icons*; and a location on the *Internet* is a *site,* which is *accessed* by means of a *home page,* and the data is explored by *browsing* or *surfing* (usually with a *browser*). One communicates by *e-mail* (= *electronic mail*) as distinct from *snail mail* (= the ordinary postal service), sends aggressive messages by *flaming* (a revival of an old meaning), and breaks into other people's systems by *hacking*. Medical analogy is invoked to alert users to the dangers of computer *bugs* and *viruses*, some of which may be *macro-borne* (= communicated by copying an infected macro program). What is most interesting from the point of view of language is how little of this vocabulary has developed extended meanings in other contexts, leaving the world of computer jargon a closed environment, borrowing words from everyday language and signally failing to return them.

concave means 'having an outline or surface like the *interior* of a circle or sphere', whereas *convex* means 'having an outline or surface like the *exterior* of a circle or sphere'.

concensus is incorrect; the correct spelling is CONSENSUS.

concern *noun*. In the meaning 'anxiety, worry', *concern* is normally followed by *about*, *at*, or *over*, or by a *that*-clause: *Concern has been expressed at the manner in which the whole operation has been put together and actioned—Rescue News*, 1985 | *'Big-band' Mozart; smooth, rich, warm, mellow and played with love and fastidious concern over the tiniest detail—CD Review*, 1992 | *He . . . expressed concern that someone had somehow managed to circumvent the safeguards—New York Times*, 1986. When purpose is involved, a *to*-infinitive is usual (*The . . . concern to analyse 'real' data in 'real' situations is revealing in this respect—Language & Communication*, 1984), and when the meaning is 'personal interest or involvement', it is more often followed

by *for*: (*It is only a shame that this outcome will have been brought about by market forces and legislation rather than by any innate concern for dog welfare—She*, 1989).

concerned. The idiomatic expression as *far as . . . is/are concerned* is well established and normally unexceptionable, but Gowers (1965) indicated where economy of style suggested alternatives; for example, *The punishment does not seem to have any effect so far as the prisoners are concerned* would be better expressed as *The punishment does not seem to have any effect on the prisoners*. Such economies are worth bearing in mind.

concessive. A concessive clause or phrase is one that is typically introduced by a conjunction such as *although*, *but*, or *though*, or by a preposition such as *despite* or *in spite of*, and expresses a sense that is contrary to what is expected in the rest of the statement: *Two letters in Portuguese were sent me to translate, although I knew no Portuguese—Graham Greene*, 1980 | *He . . . did well, although he did not win an outright majority—Economist*, 1981 | *His poems . . . though self-absorbed . . . are not self-admiring—*J. Carey, 1981 | *Gomba clinched the deal . . . despite a last-minute attempt by a trade union consortium . . . to make a counter-bid—Financial Times*, 1983.

concord see AGREEMENT.

concur, meaning 'to express agreement', has inflected forms *concurred*, *concurring*. It is normally used absolutely, or followed by *with* (a person, idea, etc.) and/or *in* (a matter), or followed by a *that*-clause: *If the doctor desires to treat the patient, he is often in a strong position to persuade such a* *relative to concur*—I. Kennedy, 1988 | *A later internal annual review of Birmingham's Partnership concurred with some of these findings*—P. Lawless, 1989 | *Modern biblical scholars concur that the letter ascribed to Jude is of too late a date to have been written by any contemporary of Jesus*—R. Leigh, 1992 | *I hope you will feel able to concur in my view that this is not an issue which can be postponed*—*Responses in Crime* (Windlesham), 1992.

condemn has a silent final -*n*, but this is pronounced in its derivatives *condemnable, condemnation*, and *condemnatory*.

condole see CONSOLE.

conduct is pronounced with stress on the first syllable as a noun and on the second syllable as a verb.

confederacy, confederation see FEDERATION.

confer has inflected forms *conferred, conferring*. In the meaning 'consult' it is normally followed by *with* (a person) and/or *about* or *over* (a matter). The derivative adjective is spelt *conferrable*.

confidant, confidante, stressed on the first syllable or (in the case of *confidante*) on the first or last syllable, mean 'a close friend in whom one confides', and refer respectively to a male or female and a female. They are alterations of an earlier form *confident* (stressed on the first syllable), and were probably attempts to imitate the French pronunciation of the final syllable -*ent*, -*ente*.

confine is pronounced with stress on the first syllable as a noun and on the second as a verb.

conflict is pronounced with stress on the first syllable as a noun and on the second as a verb.

confusable words.
See box overleaf

congeries pronounced kon-**jeer**-iz, is a collective name for 'a disorderly collection', and is singular despite its plural-looking form: *Whitehall, that congeries of government offices that takes in, for example, the Liverpool regional office of the Department of the Environment*—*Times*, 1985. The plural is also *congeries*.

conjugal is pronounced with stress on the first syllable.

conjunction. A conjunction is a word such as *and, because, but, for, if, or*, and *when* which is used to connect words, phrases, clauses, and sentences. Coordinating conjunctions join like with like: *The room is large **and** bright | She would have to go back **and** look for it | You can come in **but** you cannot stay long | Would you like tea **or** coffee?*. Subordinating conjunctions join a subordinate clause to a main clause: *I shan't go **if** you won't come with me | **As** we're early let's have a drink | I was late **because** I missed the train*. Pairs of conjunctions such as *either . . . or . . . and neither . . . nor . . .* are called correlative conjunctions: *He must be **either** drunk **or** mad | I **neither** know **nor** care*. Some conjunctions are used in BrE but not in AmE; these are *whilst* (*I would like to thank many friends and colleagues for their encouragement whilst I was writing this book*—R. Jackson, 1981), *now* (*Now the tourist season's starting it's better to have someone there, like a caretaker*—Iris Murdoch, 1980),

confusable words

1 Words are most often confused because they are alike in form (or spelling) and in some aspect of meaning, as with *fortunate* and *fortuitous*, or *prevaricate* and *procrastinate*. Some sets are confused simply in spelling, although the meanings and even the parts of speech differ (e.g. the verb *forbear* and the noun *forebear*). In some cases, the confusion is in one direction only: *infer* is used controversially to mean *imply* but the same is not true the other way round. In some cases, the overlap is so marked that distinction in actual usage is virtually impossible, as with *sensual* and *sensuous*. Some word sets have a long history of interaction and meaning overlap (e.g. *admission* and *admittance*), whereas in other cases a later word encroaches on an earlier word that, despite being originally distinct, is close to it in form and meaning (e.g. *biennial* on *biannual*; *childlike* on *childish*). Some sets consist of words that originally had the same meaning but diverged with time (e.g. *continual* and *continuous*; *ensure* and *insure*), whereas others consist of words whose relation in meaning has been unstable (e.g. *disinterested* and *uninterested*).

2 Confusability is a matter of language production and language understanding, since in some cases the writer/speaker will be unsure of which word to use, causing ambiguity or doubt from the outset, and in others the uncertainty will begin with the reader/hearer, either because of ignorance or because the context allows more than one interpretation. The following table shows sets of words that are commonly confused or used in place of each other, with date of entry of each word (in the part of speech, though not necessarily in the precise meaning, at issue) into English (or ME in the case of Middle English, i.e. before about 1470; and OE in the case of Old English, i.e. before 1150) and a brief summary of the primary meaning. The selection is representative but by no means exhaustive, and other sets will be found in this book.

For further information on the words given, see the individual entries.

WORD	DATE	MEANING	WORD 2	DATE	MEANING
adherence	ME	(to belief etc.)	adhesion	15c	sticking
admission	ME	(general meanings)	admittance	16c	right to be admitted
adverse	ME	unfavourable	averse	16c	opposed
affect	ME	cause change in	effect	16c	bring about
allusion	16c	indirect reference	illusion	ME	deceptive appearance

▶

► confusable words
continued

WORD	DATE	MEANING	WORD 2	DATE	MEANING
alternate	16c	one after another	alternative	16c	available instead
altogether	OE	entirely	all together	ME	everyone together
ambiguous	16c	(statements etc.)	ambivalent	20c	(feelings etc.)
amend	ME	change	emend	ME	alter (text etc.)
appraise	ME	assess value of	apprise	17c	inform
avoid	ME	keep away from	evade	15c	avoid by guile
baleful	OE	menacing	baneful	16c	causing harm
baluster	17c	(in balustrade)	banister	17c	(in staircase)
biannual	19c	twice a year	biennial	17c	every two years
censor	16c	act as censor of	censure	16c	criticize harshly
childish	OE	(immature qualities)	childlike	16c	(good qualities)
coherent	16c	logical and clear	cohesive	18c	sticking
complacent	17c	too confident	complaisant	17c	too willing to please
condole	16c	express sympathy	console	17c	give comfort to
continual	ME	repeated	continuous	17c	going on without a break
council	OE	administrative body	counsel	ME	advice etc.
credible	ME	believable	credulous	16c	too ready to believe
decided	18c	unquestionable	decisive	17c	conclusive
decry	17c	belittle	descry	ME	catch sight of
definite	16c	clear and distinct	definitive	ME	decisive, authoritative
deprecate	17c	disapprove of	depreciate	ME	lower in value
discomfit	ME	disconcert	discomfort	ME	make uneasy
discreet	ME	circumspect	discrete	ME	distinct
disinterested	17c	impartial	uninterested	17c	not interested
draft	16c	preliminary sketch etc.	draught	ME	air current etc.
elusive	18c	difficult to find	illusory	16c	deceptive in appearance etc.

►

▶ confusable words
continued

WORD	DATE	MEANING	WORD 2	DATE	MEANING
enormity	ME	(act of) wickedness	enormousness	17c	large size
ensure	ME	make sure	insure	ME	take out insurance on
euphemism	16c	milder term	euphuism	16c	affected style of writing
evince	16c	make evident	evoke	17c	draw forth (feelings)
exceptionable	17c	open to objection	exceptional	19c	unusually good
flaunt	16c	display ostentatiously	flout	16c	disregard (rules etc.)
forbear (verb)	OE	desist from	forebear (noun)	15c	ancestor
forego	OE	go before	forgo	OE	go without
forever	18c	continually	for ever	ME	eternally
gourmand	ME	glutton	gourmet	19c	food connoisseur
homogeneous	17c	of the same kind, uniform	homogenous	19c	of common descent
illegal	17c	against the law	illicit	16c	not allowed
imply	ME	strongly suggest	infer	15c	deduce, conclude
impracticable	17c	not able to be done	impractical	19c	not practical
inapt	17c	not suitable	inept	16c	clumsy, unskilful
incredible	ME	not believable	incredulous	16c	unwilling to believe
ingenious	ME	well thought out	ingenuous	16c	innocent, honest
interment	ME	burial	internment	19c	being interned
its	16c	(possessive pronoun)	it's	17c	= it is
luxuriant	16c	lush	luxurious	ME	comfortable and rich
masterful	ME	domineering	masterly	16c	highly skilful
militate	16c	have force (against)	mitigate	ME	make less severe
observance	ME	keeping a law or custom etc.	observation	ME	perception, remark
occupant	16c	person in a vehicle etc.	occupier	ME	person living in a property
official	ME	having authorized status etc.	officious	15c	aggressive in performing duty

▶

▶ confusable words
continued

WORD	DATE	MEANING	WORD 2	DATE	MEANING
perquisite	ME	extra privilege etc.	prerequisite	17c	something needed in advance
perspicacious	17c	having insight, perceptive	perspicuous	15c	clearly expressed
pitiable	ME	deserving pity	pitiful	ME	causing pity, contemptible
precipitate	17c	headlong	precipitous	17c	abruptly steep
prevaricate	16c	act evasively	procrastinate	16c	defer action
purposely	15c	intentionally	purposefully	19c	resolutely
refute	16c	prove to be false	repudiate	ME	reject, disown
regrettable	17c	causing regret, undesirable	regretful	17c	feeling regret
sensual	ME	gratifying the body	sensuous	17c	gratifying the senses
titillate	17c	excite pleasantly	titivate	19c	adorn, smarten
tortuous	ME	twisting, devious	torturous	15c	causing torture, tormenting

and nor (*His septic tank did not work, and nor did most others in the village—Eastern Evening News* (Norwich), 1976), *but nor* (*I am not a trained architect but nor was Sir Edwin Lutyens—Sunday Times*, 1985). The more important conjunctions are treated in separate articles: see AND, BECAUSE, BUT, FOR, etc.

conjure is pronounced **kun**-jə in the meaning 'to perform magical tricks' and kən-**jooə** in the meaning 'to beseech'.

conjuror is the recommended spelling, not *conjurer*.

connection is now the dominant spelling, although *connexion* (preferred by Fowler) will be found in older printing styles. Fowler also

wrote at length against what he regarded as the excessive use of *in connection with*, which he castigated as 'a formula that every one who prefers vigorous to flabby English will have as little to do with as he can'. Certainly, when a simple preposition such as *by* or *about* or *into* will do instead, it should be used: *Inquiries in connection with the vandalizing of a local school—U. Curtiss, 1979* (use *into* instead).

connote, denote. Both words mean broadly 'to signify' but that is where the correspondence ends. A word *denotes* its primary meaning; it *connotes* attributes associated with the broad primary meaning. So the word *spring* denotes the first season of the year, but connotes fresh growth, renewal, young love, and so on.

consensus. Note the spelling, not *concensus*. It means 'general agreement', and is often used (1) in collocations with *of*: *consensus of authority, evidence, opinion*, etc. (although *consensus of opinion* is strictly tautological), and (2) in more recent usage, in attributive uses such as *consensus view, consensus politics*, etc.

conscientious is spelt *-tious*, not *-scious*.

consequent, consequential. *Consequent* is used either attributively or with *on* or *upon* and means 'resulting, following in time', with an element of causation that is not present in the purely temporal word *subsequent*: *He does not mention the decline in . . . control consequent upon self-employment—Times*, 1973 | *Australian ratings terms have been revised to incorporate the introduction of colour TV and consequent multi-set use in many homes—TV Times* (Brisbane), 1977. *Consequential* has two principal meanings: (1) 'of the nature of a consequence or sequel' (*Conservative MPs are hoping that she will take the opportunity of the consequential changes in the junior ranks to bring in some new faces—Times*, 1986) and (2, despite Fowler's objections) 'of consequence, significant' (*He considered his notebooks far more consequential than his published prose—Times Literary Supplement*, 1989).

conservative, in the meaning 'moderate, cautious, low', as in *a conservative estimate*, is one of Fowler's LOST CAUSES. He regarded it as a ridiculous 'slipshod extension' and rejected it outright. But it is now well established in the language and is unexceptionable.

consider, in the meaning 'to regard as being', occurs in three typical constructions, two that are accepted and a third that is disputed: (1) with a noun or adjective complement in apposition to the object: *I consider her a friend | I consider her friendly*, (2) with *to be* inserted between the object and its complement: *I consider her to be a friend | I consider her to be friendly*, and (3) more controversially, influenced by words such as *regard* and *treat*, with *consider* followed by *as*: *I consider her as a friend | I consider her as friendly*. See further at AS 3. Construction (2) is especially common in reflexive use (*consider oneself to be . . .*), and (3) is the least common. Examples: *The patient improved considerably but could not be considered as cured*—M. Balint, 1968 | *The baby was considered to be at high risk*—*Lancet*, 1977 | *The village boys considered it a privilege to enjoy a stroll with him in the evenings*—M. Das, 1987. Note, however, that *as* can have a different syntactic function, associated with the object and not with *consider*, and these uses are acceptable: *Cologne Opera and San Francisco Ballet have both inspected the theatre and are considering it as* [= in its capacity of] *a venue—Times*, 1980. See also CONSIDERING.

considerable, meaning 'much; a lot of' is used in BrE only of abstract things, such as *attention, concern, difficulty, discussion, doubt, evidence, experience, improvement, interest, pain, pleasure, range, similarity, sums of money, thought, time, work*. In AmE it is used in this meaning of concrete things as well, especially mass nouns such as *grain, salt*, etc. BrE achieves this by using a formula such as *a considerable amount* (or *quantity*) *of*: *Rodney Lad . . . carried off a consid-*

erable amount of Kittitian property, leaving the local whites in an unpatriotic mood—Country Life, 1973.

considering has been used for centuries as a preposition and conjunction meaning 'taking into account (that)'. Like GIVEN and GRANTED, it is grammatically independent of the subject: *It's odd that one boasts considering that no one is ever taken in by it*—Virginia Woolf, 1921 | *He looks round his palace of a house with sniffly and quite unfair resentment, considering its comfort*—New Yorker, 1974. There is also an absolute use, which should only be used informally: *These were years of disappointment . . . for Nash, in what was, considering, a remarkably successful career in writing*—New York Times Book Review, 1990. See also PARTICIPLES 3,4.

consist is followed by *of* or *in*. *Consist of* means 'to have as its parts or elements' (in physical and abstract contexts): *Testing consists of checking that the students can carry out the task by the criteria detailed in the objectives*—Teaching Clinical Nursing, 1986 | *Otherwise her wardrobe consisted only of three or four shabby black skirts and four or five shapeless black sweaters*—Angela Carter, 1993; see further at COMPRISE. *Consist in* means 'to have as its essential features': *This defence consists in establishing . . . that the derogatory words—or at least their sting—were true*—Journal of the Royal Society of Arts, 1977. The two meanings can easily overlap, as can the notion of a thing's constituents and its characteristics: *Kim's Game consists in enumerating as many as possible of a miscellaneous assemblage of objects briefly glimpsed shortly before*—Michael Innes, 1972.

console. 1 *Console* is pronounced with stress on the first syllable as a noun (= panel, cabinet, etc.), and on the second syllable as a verb (= 'to comfort'). The words have different origins: the noun from Latin *solidus* 'solid' (cf. *consolidate*) and the verb from Latin *solari* 'to soothe'.

2 The verb *console* means 'to comfort' and takes an object: *David has us to console him*—A. Price, 1976. It should not be confused with the less common word *condole*, which means 'to express sympathy', and is followed by *with*: *The priest came to condole with Madeleine*—Michele Roberts, 1993.

consort is pronounced with stress on the first syllable as a noun, and on the second as a verb.

consortium has a plural *consortiums* or (occasionally) *consortia*.

conspicuous. The phrase *conspicuous by its* (or *one's*) *absence* is a cliché. See CLICHÉS.

constable should be pronounced kun-, not kon-.

construct, construe are related words (from Latin *struere* 'to build') which are both used to denote grammatical function. A word is *construed* or *constructed* with (e.g.) *on* when *on* is its regular complement, e.g. *insist on* and *rely on* (the *OED* abbreviates this to 'const. on'). You can also *construe* (but not *construct*) a sentence when you analyse its grammar in order to determine its meaning; this sense also has a more general application equivalent to 'interpret': *He asked his interrogators to specify anything he had written or said which could be construed as anti-Soviet*—R. Owen, 1985.

constructive in general use means 'helpful, positive', as in *constructive criticism*. In this meaning it is the opposite of *destructive*. In legal language it is often applied to 'what in the eye of the law amounts to the act or condition specified' (*OED*), and is current in the phrase *constructive dismissal*, whereby an employer so alters an employee's conditions as to make continued employment impossible.

construe see CONSTRUCT.

consummate is pronounced **kon**-syuh-mayt, with the stress on the first syllable, as a verb and kən-**sum**-ət, with the stress on the second syllable as an adjective (meaning 'complete, perfect').

consumption, in the meaning 'a disease causing wasting of the tissues', has been replaced in the 20c by more specific clinical names, especially by *tuberculosis* or *TB*.

contact *verb*. The meaning 'get in touch with' originated in the US in the early 1920s and was greeted with open hostility by purists for several decades. It is now established in AmE and BrE, although some older people who remember the controversy continue to avoid it. The stress pattern is unstable; most often the stress is on the first syllable, but the normal pattern of stress on the second syllable for the verb (and first for the noun) is beginning to establish itself.

contagious. A contagious disease is one transmitted by physical contact, as distinct from an infectious disease, which is transmitted by micro-organisms in the air or in water. In figurative use, *contagious* is used of welcome and unwelcome things (e.g. *corruption, folly, guilt, panic,* and *suffering,* as well as *laughter, shyness,* and *vigour*), whereas *infectious* is restricted to things that are welcome or pleasant (e.g. *enthusiasm, good humour, laughter, sense of fun, simple delight, virtue, zeal*).

contemporary, contemporaneous. **1** *Contemporary* has two main meanings: (1) 'living or occurring at the same time', both as an adjective (often followed by *with*) and as a noun (often followed by *of*): *Austen Layard, a contemporary of Wallace who had discovered the ancient city of Nineveh*—L. Blair, 1988 | *The finest novelists contemporary with him, particularly George Eliot and Hardy, are drawn to describe similar interiors for related, although slightly different, reasons*—P. Tristam, 1989, and (2) 'existing or done at the present time' (as in *contemporary literature*) and more 'up-to-date, modern' (as in *contemporary ideas* | *contemporary furnishings*). The risk of ambiguity is largely theoretical, although it might occur in a sentence such as *music performed on contemporary instruments*, where it is not clear whether *contemporary* refers to the time of the music or the time of the performance.

2 *Contemporaneous* (17c) is an adjective restricted to the first meaning, and is available when all risk of misunderstanding needs to be eliminated. It is found surprisingly often, especially in historical contexts: *Built in the thirteenth and fourteenth centuries, they are contemporaneous with many of the great Gothic cathedrals of Europe*—S. Stewart, 1991 | *Workers . . . experienced an absence of light and air that made conditions even in contemporaneous London and Paris seem favourable*—S. Lash, 1990.

contemptible, contemptuous.
Contemptible in current use means
'deserving contempt': *And above
all there is Harold Wilson, 'piggy-
eyed', deceitful and contemptible—
Independent*, 1989, whereas *contemptuous* means 'showing contempt': *He has a fine independence
of outlook and a contemptuous disregard for whatever is smart or fashionable among opinion-formers—Private
Eye*, 1977.

content. 1 *Content* is pronounced
with stress on the second syllable
as a verb (see 2), adjective, and
noun (meaning 'a contented
state': see 3), and on the first syllable as a noun (meaning 'what is
contained': see 4).

2 *Content oneself with* (not *by*) is
the right form of the phrase that
means 'not go beyond (some
course of action)', when followed
by a verbal noun: *Supporters of
this option claim it reinstates the
spectacle of democracy, while critics
content themselves with pointing out
that it is currently used in Iceland,
Bosnia, and parts of Turkey—New
Statesman*, 1992.

3 *Content* and *contentment* both
mean 'a contented state', but *contentment* is the more usual word,
with *content* found chiefly as a
poetical variant in the expression
to one's heart's content.

4 *Content* and *contents* both
mean 'what is contained' in physical and abstract senses. There is
little difference in meaning; *content* is more usual when the thing
in question is a mass noun (and
obligatory when preceded by a
defining word, e.g. *protein content*),
and *contents* is more usual when a
number of countable items is involved, but exceptions are not
hard to find: *Questions like the protein content of bacon butties . . . and
the vitamin rating of corned beef*

sarnies—Times, 1980 | *The whisky
bottle was still in play, though its
contents . . . had not shrunk
catastrophically—*M. Hatfield, 1981 |
*She took out the sink-tidy, with the
rubbish from breakfast, and slapped
the contents into the dust-bin—*R.
Barnard, 1981.

contest is pronounced with
stress on the first syllable as a
noun and on the second syllable
as a verb.

Continent. In the UK *the Continent* (capital *C*) still invariably
means 'the mainland of Europe'
as distinct from the British Isles,
as a geographical and cultural
designation not affected by Britain's membership of the European Union. A *continental breakfast*
(small *c*) is a light breakfast of
bread, rolls, coffee, etc., and a
Continental Sunday (capital *C*) is
one observed more as a day of
public entertainment (as held to
be customary on the continent of
Europe) than as a day of religious
observance (as held to be customary in Britain).

continual, continuous. 1 *Continual* is the older word (14c), and
once had all the meanings it now
(since the mid-19c) shares with
continuous (17c). Fowler (1926) expressed the current distinction
somewhat cryptically as follows:
'That is *-al* which either is always
going on or occurs at short intervals and never comes (or is regarded as never coming) to an
end. That is *-ous* in which no
break occurs between the beginning and the (not necessarily or
even presumably long-deferred)
end.'

2 *Continuous* is used in physical
contexts (such as lines, roads,
etc.) and is preferred in technical

contexts (e.g. *continuous assess-ment | continuous stationery | continuous wave*). The other principal use is with reference to time: *continuous* here means 'going on uninterrupted' whereas *continual* means 'constantly or frequently recurring'. The following examples show how difficult it is to keep the two meanings apart: *The correspondence between the two men was continuous throughout the next few months*—V. Brome, 1978 | *The continual underfunding of the Royal Shakespeare Company . . . was endangering its ability to . . . retain its talented staff*—Daily Telegraph, 1981 | *The 1840s were years of continuous self-education for Philip Henry Gosse*—A. Thwaite, 1984 | *The house and garden had seen their best days, and the decline was now continual, from season to season*—R. Frame, 1986 | *His son was a continual source of amusement and delight to him*—E. Blair, 1990. Note that other words are sometimes preferable, e.g. (in place of *continual*) *constant, habitual, intermittent, recurrent, repeated*, and (in place of *continuous*) *ceaseless, constant, incessant, unbroken, uninterrupted*. Note also that *constant* can be used to mean both *continual* and *continuous*.

3 Of the corresponding adverbs, *continually* (14c) is older by far than *continuously* (17c). Here, for some reason, the current distinction is clearer to see; *continually* can be defined as 'repeatedly; again and again' and *continuously* as 'without interruption': *This lost energy must be continuously supplied by the engines*—C. E. Dole, 1971 | *He said that the business of the court . . . was being continually held up by irrelevancies*—J. B. Morton, 1974 | *The black coat had lost its warmth and he shivered continually*—J. M. Coetzee, 1983 | *The synchronization was continuously monitored during*

the flight by checking the on-board clock—Nature, 1972. In the following example, *continuously* seems to be wrongly used for *continually*: *The Chinese officials also continuously stated that they could put a stop to inflation at any time*—P. Lowe, 1989.

continuance, continuation, continuity.

1 *Continuance* (14c) is much less common than *continuation* (also 14c). It is used when the context requires the meaning 'a state of continuing in existence or operation' (i.e. a fact) rather than 'the act or an instance of continuing' (i.e. a process), which calls for *continuation*. Examples: *The step-up in the air war might even jeopardize the continuation of the talks themselves*—Newsweek, 1972 | *It is absurd for continuance of non-returnable bottle production still to be allowed*—Times, 1973 | *Tiering [of dresses] is a continuation of the peasant theme that has been with us for what seems like a long, long time*—Detroit Free Press, 1978 | *Confusion has arisen about their desperate continuance of the struggle which was manifestly lost*—Antonia Fraser, 1988.

2 *Continuity* means 'the state of being continuous' or (more concretely) 'an unbroken succession (of a set of events)': *Each shipment of wood parts will have a continuity of quality*—House and Garden, 1972 | *A group of three large house mounds . . . was chosen for excavation to examine the sequence and continuity of occupation*—Times, 1973. It has a special meaning in the cinema and broadcasting, denoting the process whereby separate shots or recordings are linked together to form a continuous sequence with consistent details.

continue should not be followed by *on* (adverb), although this is sometimes found in informal writing: *I continued on down the street*—A. Bergman, 1975. Use either *continue* (without *on*) or a verb of motion (such as *go, move,* etc.) with on. This use of the adverb should be distinguished from the preposition *on*, which has a linking role and is quite acceptable: *The sensible thing to do would have been to continue on my way*—R. Perry, 1973.

continuous, continuously see CONTINUAL, CONTINUOUS.

continuous tenses are tenses (or more strictly, aspects of tense) of the types *I am staying, they were going,* etc., as contrasted with the simple tenses *I stay, they went,* etc. They are also known as *progressive tenses.*

contract is pronounced with the stress on the first syllable as a noun and on the second syllable as a verb, except that in the phrasal verb *contract in* (or *out*) the stress is more variable.

contractable, contractible see -ABLE, -IBLE.

contractions see ABBREVIATIONS 2.

contractual is the correct form, not (on the analogy of *procedural, structural,* etc.) *contractural.*

contralto has a plural *contraltos,* not (as in Italian) *contralti.*

contrary. 1 The position of the main stress has fluctuated over the centuries, and the *OED* notes that poets from Chaucer to Spenser and Shakespeare placed it on both the first and the second syllable according to need. In current English, the stress is now placed on the first syllable for the adjective and the noun, except in

the meaning 'perverse, obstinately self-willed', in which the stress is on the second syllable, probably under the influence of the nursery rhyme beginning *Mary, Mary, quite contrary.*

2 The phrase *on the contrary* is properly used only in a statement intensifying a denial of what has just been stated or implied: *You say that war is inevitable; on the contrary I think the outstanding differences between the two countries can be settled by negotiation. On the other hand* denotes a differing (not necessarily opposite) point of view, and is often paired with *on the one hand.*

3 The phrase *to the contrary* is used in AmE in the meaning of *on the contrary* (see 2), but in BrE is used only as a mid-sentence or end-of-sentence adverbial as in *There is plenty of evidence to the contrary.*

contrast. 1 *Contrast* is pronounced with stress on the first syllable as a noun and on the second syllable as a verb.

2 In current use, the verb is normally constructed with *with* or *and,* and is used transitively and intransitively: *Her sudden energy contrasted with Henry's sudden exhaustion*—J. Frame, 1970 | *Data is sometimes contrasted with information, which is said to result from the processing of data*—J. Chandor, 1970 | *Some anthropologists have sought to contrast the 'guilt cultures' of Western Europe with 'shame cultures'*—A. Giddens, 1977.

3 The noun can be followed by *to, with,* or *between,* and is also used in the fixed expressions *by contrast* and *in contrast* (*to* or *with*): *In contrast with ordinary grasshoppers, most of which live on the*

*ground, the long-horned grasshop-
pers do more climbing*—L. E. Chad-
wick, 1972 | *Gloria would have been
able to detect few noteworthy points
of contrast between sexual arousal
and rabies*—Martin Amis, 1973 | *In
contrast, the heaviest elements of the
same groups . . . are metallic or
semimetallic*—D. M. Adams, 1974 |
*Marx, by contrast, has a single-cause
theory: all the evils of society arise
from private property*—P. Johnson,
1977 | *The presence of scientists will
also allow 'hands-on' experiments to
be tried out, in contrast to previous
life-science experiments in space
which were fully automated*—Nature,
1978.

contribute. The standard pronunciation is with the main
stress on the second syllable, although pronunciation with stress
on the first syllable is increasingly heard.

controversy. The stress is always
placed on the first syllable in
AmE and normally in BrE too, although a variant with stress on
the second syllable is becoming
increasingly common, despite the
strictures of purists. Early stress
on words of more than three syllables is unusual in English (*excellency, matrimony*, and *presidency* are
others), and so the shift is not
surprising. The argument sometimes heard that a link vowel
should not be stressed is con-
founded by words such as *archaeology* and *helicopter*.

conundrum is a 16c word of unknown origin, perhaps a facetious
invention. It has a plural *conun-
drums.*

converse is pronounced with
stress on the first syllable as an
adjective and noun (= the opposite), and on the second syllable as
a verb (= to have a conversation).

convert is pronounced with
stress on the first syllable as a
noun and on the second syllable
as a verb.

convertible is spelt -*ible*, not
-*able*. See -ABLE, -IBLE.

convex. See CONCAVE.

convict is pronounced with
stress on the first syllable as a
noun and on the second syllable
as a verb.

convince. The use followed by a
to-infinitive with the meaning 'to
persuade' is recorded from the
1950s and is still disapproved of
by many, although it is now common, especially informally: *The
miners tried to convince their colleagues to join them*—broadcast on
BBC World Service, 1991.

cookie, not *cooky*, is the established spelling in its various
meanings: in AmE 'a biscuit' and
(slang) a person (as in *tough
cookie*), in Scottish 'a plain bun'.

coomb is the usual form (rather
than *combe*) in Britain for a valley
or hollow on the side of a hill or
a short valley running up from
the coast. In place-names, however, -*combe* is more usual, as in *Il-
fracombe, Winchcombe*, etc.

cooperate is now the preferred
spelling, without a hyphen and
without a diaeresis on the second
o. See CO-.

cope. The traditional construction followed by *with* has been in
common use since the 16c: *Like
many religious professionals, I cope
with festivals, but I can't really enjoy
them*—L. Blue, 1985. Absolute uses
without *with* have been recorded
since the 1930s: *It wasn't as if Mar-
cia was an invalid or unable to cope,
even if she was a bit eccentric*—
Barbara Pym, 1977.

copula in grammar is a verb, such as *be, become, feel, get*, etc., that links the subject and complement of a sentence, as in *He is a pilot | She felt annoyed | They look hungry | Will it turn cold?*. Such a verb is also called a *copular verb*.

cord see CHORD.

co-respondent, meaning 'a person named in a divorce case', should be distinguished from *correspondent*. See CO-.

corn means 'wheat or oats' in BrE, and 'maize' in AmE.

corporal, corporeal. Both words are now largely restricted to particular uses. Corporal means 're-lating to the human body' and is found chiefly in the expression *corporal punishment* (beating, spanking, etc., now effectively banned in schools in the European Union). In other uses, *bodily* or *personal* is more usual. *Corporeal* means 'bodily, physical, material, as distinct from spiritual': *Apart . . . from his existence as a corporeal omnipotent first cause, all else about God was a matter of faith*—R. S. Woodhouse, 1988.

corps, corpse. *Corps*, meaning 'body of people', is pronounced like *core* in the singular and like *cores* in the plural. It should be distinguished from *corpse*, meaning 'dead body', which is pronounced kawps.

corpus, meaning 'a collection of writings', has a plural *corpora*, although *corpuses* is increasingly found. In the domain of language and linguistics it is used to refer to a collection of texts of all kinds, written and spoken, which are read and analysed by a computer program designed to produce statistics and sort the material into accessible forms,

usually as a screen concordance of consecutive lines with the word being studied (the *keyword*) in the centre of each line. The best known corpora in current use are the British National Corpus, the Cobuild Corpus (Collins–Birmingham University International Language Database), and the Survey of English Usage (at University College London).

corpus delicti means literally 'the body of a crime', and refers to all the facts and circumstances that together constitute a breach of the law. In lay use, it means the concrete evidence of a crime, especially the body of a murdered person.

corrector, meaning 'a person who points out faults', is spelt *-or*, not *-er*.

correlative is each of a pair of words used to link corresponding parts of a sentence, e.g. *both . . . and . . .* , *either . . . or . . .* . Correlatives that involve a subordinate clause include *hardly . . . when . . .* and *if . . . then . . .* .

correspond. If one thing is similar or analogous to another, or related closely to it, it is said to correspond *to* it: *Gandhi's concept of Religion corresponds to his concept of Truth*—G. Richards, 1991. If one thing is in harmony or agreement with another, it is said to correspond *with* or *to* it: *There were two bedrooms to correspond with the rooms downstairs*—D. H. Lawrence, 1921 | *The broadcasting service should be conducted by a public corporation . . . and its status and duties should correspond with those of a public service*—R. Negrine, 1992. If two people exchange letters, they are said to correspond *with* one another: *Though it is not known how the two friends met, they* *were corresponding with each other by 1945*—F. Spalding, 1991. In all these meanings, *correspond* can also be used absolutely, without *to* or *with*: *My brother Michael . . . and I corresponded about socialism and religion*—Tony Benn, 1979. It is also common as a participial adjective *corresponding*: *For the corresponding period in the previous year 818 men had been accommodated, plus 22 women and one child*—B. Cashman, 1988.

corrigendum, meaning 'something that should be corrected', is normally used in its plural form *corrigenda*.

corrupter, meaning 'a person or thing that corrupts', is spelt *-er*, not *-or*.

corset, in its meaning 'a closely-fitting undergarment worn by women', should be used in the singular, although Somerset Maugham is not the only writer to have used it in the plural: *She did not put on her corsets again, but rolled them up*—Cakes and Ale, 1931. The derivative forms are spelt *corseted* and *corseting* (one *t*).

cortège, meaning 'a funeral procession', is printed in roman type with a grave accent on the *e*. It is pronounced kaw-**tayzh**.

cortex, meaning 'the outer part of a bodily organ' (as in *cerebral cortex*, referring to the brain), has the plural form *cortices*.

'cos is a reduced form of *because*, first recorded in 1828 and only used to represent informal speech: *'They'll be good if I tell them, Mister.' 'Then why aren't they?' ''Cos I tell 'em to be bad.'*—Evelyn Waugh, 1942 | *They wouldn't take me 'cos I'd had a touch of TB*—M. Butterworth, 1974.

cosmonaut see ASTRONAUT.

cosset, meaning 'to pamper', has inflected forms *cosseted, cosseting*.

cosy, as an adjective meaning 'comfortable' and a noun meaning 'a cover for a teapot', is spelt *cosy* in BrE and in other varieties except AmE, which prefers *cozy*. To *cosy up to* someone is a new phrasal verb, originally AmE, meaning 'to ingratiate oneself (with)', and is informal.

cot. There are two words with this spelling. The word meaning 'a small bed for a child' is Anglo-Indian; *cot death* is a recent formation (1970) for the unexplained death of a baby while asleep (the AmE form is usually *crib death*). The (mainly literary) word meaning 'a small shelter; a cottage' is Old English, and is used in combinations such as *sheep-cot*.

cote, pronounced like *coat*, is another form of the Old English word *cot* given in the preceding entry. It is most commonly used in *dovecote*, meaning 'a shelter for doves', and also occurs occasionally in other forms such as *sheep-cote* and *swine-cote* (these being hyphened).

couch, meaning 'an upholstered piece of furniture' differs from a *sofa* in having only one raised end and in being designed for lying on as well as sitting on. It also has special (and often evocative) uses as in *psychiatrist's couch*, on which the recumbent patient tells all. It is also a poetic word for a bed, but in ordinary use is essentially different from a bed: *I've made a bed up for you on the couch*—Martin Amis, 1973.

couch, a type of grass, is pronounced kooch.

could *modal auxiliary.* **1** See CAN. It functions as (1) the past tense of *can*, as in *We could see for miles*, (2) as a conditional equivalent to *would be able to*, as in *I could take you in the car if you like*, and (3) as a more tentative form of *can* in questions seeking permission: *Could I have another cake?.* The negative form is *could not*.

2 *COULD OF.* This is an illiterate alteration of *could've* = could have, and occurs in the writing of children and some adults.

council, counsel. 1 These are now distinct words and only distantly related. A *council* is an administrative body or meeting, and its members are *councillors. Counsel* is advice given formally and often professionally; *counsel* or *a counsel* is a barrister or other legal adviser. A *counsellor* is someone who gives professional advice, especially on personal and social matters; in AmE *counselor* is also a courtroom lawyer.

2 Note that in Britain a member of the *Privy Council*, the body of advisers appointed by the Queen, is a *Privy Counsellor*.

3 Only *counsel* can be used as a verb, meaning 'to give advice to'; it has inflected forms *counselled, counselling.*

countable nouns, also called *count nouns*, are nouns that form plurals, e.g. *ship, crisis, fellow-traveller, kindness* (= a kind act). They differ from *uncountable* (or *non-count* or *uncount*) nouns, which do not form plurals, e.g. *adolescence, heating, richness, warfare*; and from *mass* nouns, which form plurals only in the sense of 'a type of . . . ' or 'a quantity of . . . ', e.g. *bread, medicine, wine.*

Some words are countable in one meaning and uncountable in another, e.g. *ice, iron, paper.*

counterpart means 'the equivalent of a person or thing in another place or system'. It can refer to many aspects of similarity but principally has to do with function and behaviour, and is always preceded by a possessive word: *Southern schools are now more integrated than their northern counterparts—Times,* 1974 | *With the same power at his elbow as his Continental counterpart the British car assembly worker produces only half as much output per shift*—M. Edwardes, 1983.

counter-productive should be spelt with a hyphen. It is a modern word (first recorded in 1959) which has mushroomed in use to describe any action or series of actions having the opposite of the desired effect: *This sort of 'reds under the bed' scare . . . could only be counter-productive—Times,* 1972.

count nouns see COUNTABLE NOUNS.

countrified, countrify, meaning 'rural' and 'to make rural', should be spelt this way, not *countryfied, countryfy.*

coup, meaning 'a sudden and successful move', or 'an illegal seizure of power' (in full *coup d'état*), is pronounced koo. The plural is *coups*, pronounced kooz.

couple. 1 *Couple*, as in '*a couple of . . .* ', needs to be used and understood with care, as it retains its original meaning of 'two' alongside its more informal meaning 'a few'. *A couple of girls* will usually mean two girls, no more or less, whereas *a couple of hours* may mean two hours or three hours or an indeterminate period of time.

2 *Couple* is a singular noun that can be used with a singular or plural verb. A plural construction is usual when *couple* means 'two married people or partners' or when it is followed by *of* and a plural noun (see COLLECTIVE NOUN): *Palimony, the term for sharing money after an unmarried couple have split up*—*Time*, 1980 | *A couple of expressions have only come my way in the last month or so*—*Guardian Weekly*, 1981.

3 *Couple* has developed attributive uses in the constructions (1) *a couple more* (+ plural noun): *'How's your work?' 'Nearly done. A couple more days.'*—Maurice Gee, 1992 (NZ), and (2) more controversially, and principally in AmE, *couple* (+ plural noun): *In the next couple months we got to know each other like real buddies*—Garrison Keillor, 1989. This last use sounds decidedly alien to British ears, at least for now.

coupon should be pronounced **koo**-pon, not with a quasi-French nasalized second syllable.

course see OF COURSE.

courteous, courtesy are pronounced with initial **kert-**.

courtesan is pronounced kor-tə-**zan**, with stress on the last syllable.

courtier is pronounced with initial **kort-**.

court martial is spelt as two words as a noun (plural *courts martial*). As a verb it is spelt with a hyphen, and it has inflected forms *court-martialled, court-martialling*.

covert, meaning 'secret, disguised', is pronounced like *cover*, although the AmE pronunciation like *over* is gaining ground in BrE and elsewhere.

cowardly. Fowler (1926) criticized the use of *cowardly* to describe people and their actions in cases where 'advantage has [merely] been taken of superior strength or position', and where a word such as *cruel* or *unchivalrous* might be more appropriate. The increase of international terrorism in the last few decades has tended to bring the word into more frequent use in exactly the way Fowler described, with reference to acts that are reprehensible and brutal, but not cowardly, which implies a lack of courage. But perhaps cowardice in this usage lies in attacking those who are defenceless from a position of safety instead of fighting on equal terms, in which case the extension in meaning is justified.

cozy see COSY.

crabbed, meaning 'irritable' or 'hard to decipher', is pronounced as two syllables.

craft has been revived as a verb in the language of advertising (*a beautifully crafted antique-pine replica*) and in literary and other criticism (*performances crafted out of a shared language*).

crape, crêpe. *Crape* is used for a band of black silk or ornamental silk worn as a sign of mourning, and *crêpe* is used for other gauze-like fabrics having a wrinkled surface and in *crêpe paper.*

crash. Since the 1950s, *crash* has been used attributively (before a noun) to denote something such as a course or programme that is done or undertaken urgently or quickly, e.g. *a crash course in Rus-*

sian or *a crash diet*. In this use, *crash* seems to be unaffected by possible associations of collision and violence (or indeed of computer failure), though *a crash course in driving skills* might come dangerously close to suggesting them.

crayfish, a 16c alteration of an earlier word *crevis* (or *crevisse*), is the usual word in Britain for a small lobster-like freshwater crustacean. Americans call them *crawfish*, and Australians and New Zealanders tend to abbreviate the word to *cray* (as in *cray-fishing* and *cray-pot*).

credence, credit, credibility.

1 In general use, *credence* means 'belief, trustful acceptance', and is used mainly in the expression *to give* (or *lend*) *credence to*, which means 'believe, trust': *The radicality of these changes . . . had lent credence to the set of beliefs described above*—Dædalus, 1979.

2 The phrase *to give credit to* once meant much the same as *to give credence to*, i.e. 'to believe', but in current use it is more likely to be used in the form *to give a person credit for* (something), meaning to ascribe some good quality to them: *You chaps do tend to give the rest of us credit for perceptions about your work that we don't . . . always have*—John Wain, 1953.

3 *Credibility* shares some of the meaning of both *credence* and *credit* in that belief lies at the heart of its meaning, but it is used rather to mean 'the condition of being credible or believable': *The empirical basis of theory is fundamental to its reliability and its validity and, in the end, its credibility*—P. H. Mann, 1985. This meaning, now largely confined to special domains such as religion

and philosophy, has been overshadowed by an extended meaning 'reputation, status': *It was clear to the [American] President that his credibility was on the line with the leaders in Hanoi*—Guardian, 1970 | *By then, however, the fatal damage to the Prime Minister's credibility will have been done*—Today, 1992. Such credibility is regularly *enhanced*, *established*, *gained*, *lost*, *maintained*, and so on.

The overlap between the older and the newer meaning can be seen in the following example: *A major French archaeological discovery that was declared fraudulent by many prehistorians in the 1920's has now regained credibility as a result of dating studies conducted at three independent laboratories*—Scientific American, 1975.

4 Two special uses of *credibility* that have arisen recently are *credibility gap*, meaning 'an apparent difference between what is said and what is true' (*Official American statements are no longer taken on trust . . . . The phenomenon . . . is called the 'credibility gap'*—Guardian, 1966) and, in BrE, *street credibility* (often reduced informally to *street cred*), meaning 'acceptability among fashionable young urban people' (*Springsteen's street credibility is the core of his effectiveness. His striking working-class imagery is within everyone's experience*—Washington Post, 1980).

credible, creditable, credulous.

Credible means 'able to be believed', with reference to people or statements: *I stand on the balcony, apparently musing on this very credible story, but really wondering how soon we can step back inside*—R. James, 1989 | *Was it credible that Elise should have a car accident that involved no other vehicle, no jay-walking pedestrian, no treacherous roads?*—K. Kingston,

1993. It also has an extended meaning 'convincing, having substance', comparable to that of *credibility*: *The Secretary of State repeated several times that we need such a scale of weaponry to provide what he calls a credible deterrent—Hansard*, 1992. *Creditable* means 'bringing credit; deserving praise': *The company produced a creditable performance, particularly when compared with the results of many of its competitors—Daily Telegraph*, 1992. *Credulous* means 'too ready to believe, gullible': *It could be argued that the very incomprehensibility of the modern world has made us even more credulous—*J. Empson, 1989.

creole. A *creole* is a language formed from the contact of a European language (especially English, French, or Portuguese) with another (especially African) language. Unlike a PIDGIN, which is an improvised language used mainly by traders who do not have a language in common, a *creole* is more developed and can be a mother tongue. The term *creole* is applied to a wide range of languages, including the original languages spoken by black slaves in the US; English-based creoles such as Krio (in Sierra Leone), Guyanese, and Gullah; French-based creoles in Haiti and the Ivory Coast, and Portuguese-based creoles in Brazil and Cape Verde.

crêpe see CRAPE.

crescendo. 1 A *crescendo*, which in Italian means 'growing' (from Latin *crescere* 'to grow'), is originally a term in music for a gradual increases in loudness or force, or a passage played in this way. From this it developed an extended meaning referring to other cumulative increases in force or effect: *His second-*

*in-command at the Embassy . . . was unrattled by the crescendo of disaster to the allied cause—*J. Colville, 1976. In the 1920s, and apparently first in AmE, it developed further to mean the result rather than the process of increasing, and has been widely used as a synonym for *peak* or *climax*, notably in phrases such as *reach* (or *rise to*) *a crescendo*: *It was in relation to the annual increment arrangements of the civil service pay system that your attack reached its crescendo of unfairness—Economist*, 1975. The newer use lies in disputed territory, and is likely to prevail as the more commonly required meaning, despite the availability of alternatives such as *apogee, climax, culmination, peak, pinnacle,* and *summit.*

2 The plural is *crescendos*. *Crescendo* is occasionally used as a verb meaning 'to increase in loudness or intensity', and has inflected forms *crescendoes, crescendoed, crescendoing.*

cretin, now pronounced **kret**-in, was originally used to mean (in current terminology) 'a person who is deformed and mentally retarded as the result of a thyroid deficiency' and is etymologically related to the word *Christian*. Its dominant meaning in general use now (first recorded in the 1930s) is 'a fool, one who behaves stupidly'. This use is widely regarded as offensive.

crevasse, crevice are both derived from a Latin root *crepare* meaning 'to break with a crash'. A *crevasse* is a deep open crack or fissure in a glacier; in AmE it is also used to mean a breach in a river embankment. A *crevice* is a narrow cleft or opening, usually one in the surface of anything solid such as rock or a building.

crick, rick. Both words are commonly used of strains or sprains of the neck, back, joints, etc. *Crick* appeared earlier (15c as a noun, though not until 19c as a verb); *rick* is apparently of dialect origin and is first recorded as a verb in about 1800 and as a noun in the mid-19c. A variant form *wrick* has now fallen out of use.

cringe, meaning 'to shrink back in fear', has inflected forms *cringed, cringing*.

cripple, meaning 'a person who is permanently lame' is now regarded as offensive. Use *disabled person* instead.

crisis. 1 The word is derived via Latin from a Greek root meaning 'turning point', and should strictly refer to a moment rather than a continuing process, so that uses such as *a prolonged crisis* are arguably self-contradictory. However, a word as useful as *crisis* will not allow itself to be straitjacketed in this way, and many examples of the disputed use will be found: *The continuing and ever occurring crisis in the inner-cities, where large numbers of people are trapped in a cycle of poverty*—Black Panther, 1973 | *Pakistan, despite its gas resources, has an ongoing energy crisis*—D. Hedley, 1986. Some element of change should be present in the meaning (*The death of his father . . . triggers off a crisis for him too, producing a temporary breakdown, dismissal from his job, separation from his wife, the lot*—Times, 1970); and the word should not be used as an enfeebled synonym of words such as *difficulty, dilemma, problem*, and *quandary* (*Scott Lithgow . . . were desperate for staff throughout the crisis*—Economist, 1975 | *The crisis at strike-torn Leyland deepened*—Belfast Telegraph, 1977 | *To make matters worse a crisis*

in the Council came to a head—W. Green, 1988).

2 *Crisis* is often used with a defining word, either an adjective or an attributive noun as in *economic crisis, energy crisis, food crisis, identity crisis, refugee crisis*, etc. It has also come to be used with the redundant addition of *situation*, a use that should be avoided: ☒ *Unless catchment areas are re-drawn Lord Williams's school will go through a crisis situation for at least five years*—Oxford Times, 1978.

3 The plural *crises* is often found in uses that are contrary to expectation on a strict evaluation of the word's meaning: *Three simultaneous crises . . . that seemed worrisomely different from those of the past*—Newsweek, 1973.

criterion, meaning 'a principle or standard by which something is judged', has a plural *criteria*. This plural form is often taken to be singular, a use that is not standard: *Any call coming in . . . could be answered . . . , that's all the criteria is*—conversation recorded in British National Corpus. The following examples illustrate correct uses of the singular and plural: *The Ottoman Empire . . . was a multinational state, . . . the criterion of differentiation among its subjects was religion and not nationality*—A. Mango, 1971 | *Some possible criteria for this area of work are listed below*—J. Thorpe, 1989. In order to render *criteria* effectively singular, a collective such as *set* can be used: *However, we may wish to use a different set of criteria*—A. Lawton et al., 1991.

criticism in everyday use means 'finding fault', although strictly *criticism* can be favourable as well as unfavourable. The sense is more neutral in terms such as *literary criticism* and *textual criticism*.

critique is pronounced with stress on the second syllable, and means 'a critical essay or analysis'. Fowler (1926) said of the noun that 'there is some hope of it dying out', and offered the alternatives *review, criticism*, and *notice*. Nonetheless, *critique* remains in use, albeit in contexts that justify Fowler's implied accusation of pretentiousness: *This melange of stroboscopic graphics, jingles and one-liner critiques—Art Line*, 1989.

crochet, meaning a type of handicraft, is pronounced **kroh**-shay as a noun and a verb. The verb has inflected forms *crocheted, crocheting*, with the *t* remaining silent in both.

crocus, the flower, has plural forms *crocuses* (several flowers) and *crocus* (used collectively). *Croci* is limited to technical contexts.

crow *verb*, meaning 'to make the sound of a cock' and 'to boast', has past forms *crowed* (more usual) and *crew* (only in the first meaning, often in allusion to the cock in the New Testament account of Christ's betrayal). The past participle is always *crowed*.

crown. When *the Crown* is used to mean 'the office of the monarch', it should be treated as grammatically neuter and not as the gender of the king or queen: *The Crown can only act on the advice of its* [not *her* or *his*] *Ministers*.

crucial. 1 *Crucial* means 'decisive, critical', and is often used as a more effective and more expressive alternative for *important* or *significant*: *There are four crucial stages in cheesemaking*—J. G. Davis, 1976 | *I understand that you must edit letters, but the crucial point on*

avoiding sexist language was omitted—*Today's Horse*, 1991.

2 The same thing has happened to the adverb *crucially*, which is sometimes used as a synonym of 'importantly', and even of 'very' or 'extremely': *At this juncture, two crucially fundamental questions now emerge—Guardian*, 1989 | *Crucially, he promised to undertake an immediate and fundamental review of the tax—Parliamentary Affairs*, 1991.

cruel has the forms *crueller, cruellest* in BrE and *crueler, cruelest* in AmE.

crumby, crummy. When the reference is to actual crumbs, as in a crumby loaf or a crumby tablecloth, use *crumby*. When the meaning is 'dirty, squalid; inferior, worthless', use *crummy*.

-ction see -XION.

cubic, cubical. *Cubical* means only 'shaped like a cube', whereas *cubic* has other meanings as well, as in *cubic equation, cubic measure, cubic metre*, etc., and also the meaning 'cube-shaped' in technical applications such as *cubic alum*.

cui bono? This Latin phrase literally means 'to whom (is it) a benefit?', i.e. in English 'who stands to gain (from an act or circumstance)?', with the implication that this person is responsible for it. As Fowler (1926) pointed out, it does not mean 'to what purpose?' or 'what is the good?'.

cul-de-sac is pronounced **kul**-də-sak and should be printed in roman type.

cullender see COLANDER.

cult. 1 In the meaning 'a particular form or system of religious worship', especially with reference to ritual and ceremony, *cult* dates from the 17c. In the 19c, archaeologists applied the term to primitive practices which they did not think worthy of the name *religion*; hence *cult* acquired unfavourable connotations and is objected to by many whose activities are now described by it.

2 *Cult* has also developed extended meanings: (1) 'a devotion or homage to a person or thing', as in *the cult of beauty* and *the Wordsworth cult*, (2) in the 20c, 'a popular fashion followed by a specific section of society': *The eastern cult for junk food may be having a remarkable effect on the health and appearance of Japan's youngsters—Times*, 1986. In a further extension, *cult* is commonly used attributively (before a noun) to denote something that has a special following, as in *cult drama, cult film, cult object*, etc.

cultivable, cultivatable are both used in the meaning 'capable of being cultivated'; the first is more comfortable and was preferred by Fowler (1926).

cultivated, cultured are both used to mean 'having refined tastes and manners and a good education', but they part company in other meanings. *Cultivated* distinguishes a crop raised in a garden from one growing wild; and *cultured* is used of pearls (also called *culture pearls*) formed under controlled conditions.

culture. 1 Here is a word that has had mixed fortunes in the 20c, and means all things to all men. There are about 10,000 examples of it (including the plural form and compounds such as *culture-bound*) in the 100-million-word British National Corpus (language database) in diverse meanings generally related to the *OED*'s definition 'the civilization, customs, artistic achievements, etc., of a people, especially at a certain stage of its development or history'. In many of these examples *culture* is used generically and not in relation to any particular people or time: *For him spiritual and political ideas were becoming more and more inseparable in his concern with 'culture' as a whole*—R. Crawford, 1990. In others it has very specific reference, and is often preceded by a defining adjective or noun: *Unofficial sources report that the two organisations aimed to research and develop Mongol culture—Amnesty*, 1992.

2 The word has also developed more limited reference within a broader 'culture', as in *drugs culture, pop culture, youth culture*, etc.: *The miners' strike revealed the range of new movements and organisations which have been arenas . . . for the development of working-class culture and working-class consciousness*—T. Lovett, 1988 | *It was, nonetheless, a film that tried to solicit an understanding of the emerging drug culture*—J. Parker, 1991 | *Pop music and its link with youth culture should be an important field of study in media education—Action*, 1991.

3 After 1914 *culture* came into contact with the German word *Kultur*, and from it assumed, in British eyes, connotations of arrogance and supposed ethnic superiority; and it was mocked by some who tended to distort the spelling (*culchah*, etc.) to indicate that the acquisition of cultured ways implied an absurd degree of affectation or vulgarity. In the 20c, significant combinations of the word have been *culture shock*, meaning 'the feeling of disorientation experienced by a person suddenly subjected to an unfamiliar culture or way of life', *culture-specific*, meaning 'peculiar to a particular cultural environment', and *culture vulture*, meaning 'a person eager to acquire culture'. In 1956, the novelist and essayist C. P. Snow launched a topic of discussion that is likely to last indefinitely by coining the resonant phrase *the two cultures* to denote the arts and sciences as being somehow alien to one another. For so seemingly calm a word, the currents and conflicts it produces are paradoxical.

cum. This Latin preposition meaning 'with', apart from its use in Latin loan-phrases such as *cum grano salis* ('with a grain of salt'), has been used for several centuries in place-names such as *Horton-cum-Studley*. Its principal use since the 19c has been as a combining word used to indicate a dual nature or function, as in *kitchen-cum-dining-room* (usually with hyphens). The productive nature of this use can be seen in numerous examples, e.g.: *'Do you work there?' 'Yes, as a sort of administrator cum priest.'*—J. Higgins, 1985.

cumulative, accumulative are both used in the meaning 'formed or increasing by successive additions', although *cumulative* is now more usual (as in *cumulative arguments, effect, evidence, force*, etc.). *Accumulative* is however still found, and by virtue of its form has stronger associations with the process of *accumulating*: *Explanations of whatever kind are not universal answers, merely part of a progressive and accumulative act of learning and knowing*—G. Watson, 1991.

cuneiform, meaning 'ancient wedge-shaped writing', is now normally pronounced as three syllables in BrE, i.e. **kyoo**-ni-fawm, and as four in AmE, i.e. kyoo-**nay**-i-fawm.

cupful. In the plural, care should be taken to distinguish *cupfuls* from *cups full*. A *cupful* is a measure, and so *three cupfuls* is a quantity regarded in terms of a cup; *three cups full* denotes the actual cups, as in *three cups full of water*.

cupola, meaning 'a rounded dome on a roof', is pronounced **kyoo**-pə-lə. The plural is *cupolas*.

curb, kerb. In BrE, *curb* is a noun meaning 'a check or restraint' and a verb meaning 'to restrain'. As a noun it also means 'a strap fastened to a bit on a horse', and 'a fender round a hearth'. In AmE, *curb* has these meanings and is also 'a stone edging to a pavement (*sidewalk*)', which in BrE is spelt *kerb*.

curio is a 19c familiar abbreviation of *curiosity*, and means 'a rare or unusual object or person'. The plural is *curios*.

curriculum, meaning 'a course of study', has a plural *curricula*. A *curriculum vitae* (abbreviated to *CV* or *c.v.*) is a brief account of a person's education and professional experience. The plural is *curricula vitae* (*curricula vitarum* is pedantic), although *CVs* gets round this awkwardness.

curtsy, meaning a woman's or girl's formal greeting, is spelt *curtsy* not *curtsey*. Its plural is *curtsies*, and as a verb it has inflected forms *curtsies, curtsied, curtsying*.

cute started out in the 18c as a shortened form of *acute* in the meaning 'quick-witted, clever'; for a while it was often written with an apostrophe, and will be found that way in Dickens. This meaning has died out in BrE but is still a feature of AmE. In AmE, beginning in the 1830s, a new informal meaning emerged, 'attractive, charming, pretty (often in a mannered or amusing way)'. It is now very common in AmE as a general term of approbation rather analogous to *nice*, and can refer to activities and practically anything else as well as people and things: *Yes, Lisa runs a little gym in the West Palm. We all go there to work out. Isn't that cute?*—P. Booth, 1986. In BrE, this use is much more self-conscious, and is generally limited to babies and other small things with quaintly attractive characteristics.

cybernetics. 1 The term was introduced in 1948 by Norbert Wiener, meaning 'the theory or study of communication and control in living organisms or machines'. The word was derived from the Greek word *kubernetes* 'steersman'. It spread rapidly to refer to organisms treated as if they were machines, to observed similarities between neural activity and the electronic devices of modern communications, and so on.

2 A by-product of the word is the use of the first element *cyber-* in a wide range of computer terms: a *cybercafé* is a café equipped with terminals to access the Internet, *cyberphobia* is an ab-

normal fear of computers, *cyberpunk* is a style of science fiction, and *cyberspace* is the environment of *virtual reality*, a hallucinatory illusion of being elsewhere as created by special equipment controlled by a computer program.

Cyclops, a mythological one-eyed giant, is pronounced **siy**-klops, and its plural is *Cyclopes*, pronounced **siy**-kloh-peez.

Cymric, meaning Welsh, is pronounced **kim**-rik.

cynic, cynical. *Cynical* is the adjective form used in the meaning 'doubting human sincerity or integrity' and has developed a further meaning 'disregarding normal rules or standards', as in *a cynical foul*, *a cynical tackle*, etc. *Cynic* is used with direct reference to the Greek philosophers who bore this name.

cynosure, meaning 'a centre of attraction or admiration', is pronounced **sin**-ə-syooə or **siyn**-ə-syooə. Its earlier meaning 'guiding star' related to its use as the name of a constellation, and the current meaning is immortalized by Milton's phrase *The Cynosure of neighbouring Eyes* in 'L'Allegro' (1632).

cypher see CIPHER.

czar see TSAR.

Czech is now the settled (Polish) form of the adjective relating to Czechoslovakia (now two States, the Czech Republic and Slovakia).

Dd

dado, meaning the lower part of the wall of a room, or the plinth of a column, has a plural *dados*.

dais, meaning 'a low platform', is pronounced as two syllables, **day**-is.

dampen was once regarded as an Americanism, but is now established as a variant of *damp* (verb) in BrE, especially in figurative uses: *Everyone ignored the snow that had failed to dampen the impact of John F. Kennedy's brilliant oratory*—Jeffrey Archer, 1979 | *In that way, she argued, speculation about the marriage would be dampened rather than intensified—Today*, 1992 | (literal) *Most weights of watercolour paper are dampened and stretched before painting—The Artist*, 1993.

dangling participles see PARTI-CIPLES 3.

dare *verb*. **1** *Dare* is an example of a so-called semi-modal auxiliary verb, because, like the modal verbs *can, may, should*, etc., it is used in certain special ways, but unlike these fully modal verbs it can also behave like an ordinary verb. Its special characteristics are (1) use with a so-called 'bare' infinitive without *to* (*I'm not sure that I dare answer*), (2) use in the negative and in questions without *do* (*I dare not answer* | *Dare I answer?*), although in practice interrogative forms are normally confined to *how dare you, he, they*, etc., as discussed in 6 below, (3) a third person singular form *dare* without addition of *s* (*He says he dare not answer*). Note that in all these uses *dare* is an auxiliary verb followed by an infinitive without *to*.

2 *Dare* is also used as an ordinary verb, with or without a following *to*-infinitive, forming negatives and questions with *do*, and having a third person singular form *dares*: *They would not dare to come* | *Do you dare to contradict me?* | *I don't dare to answer* | *He dares to answer* | *Tell me if you dare*. In practice, not all these options are used, and some constructions sound more natural than others. For example, *I don't dare to answer* is perfectly grammatical, but *I dare not answer* is more idiomatic, at least in everyday English. In the present tense, *dare* behaves as a modal verb much more often than as an ordinary verb.

3 As a modal verb, *dare* is sometimes used in the past without inflection. Though formerly condemned (by the *OED* among others) as 'careless', the practice is common in writing as well as speech: *'Yes, yes,' she stuttered, then 'thank you', as an afterthought. She dare not look at his face*—M. Duckworth, 1960.

4 It is also noticeable that *dare* occurs more frequently in negative constructions and in questions, or preceded by *if*. As we have seen, the negative form can be *dare not* or *do* (etc.) *not dare*; and *dare not* is contracted to *daren't* in informal use (*I daren't answer*). The past *dared not* is rarely if ever contracted to *darednt*.

5 Further examples follow of *dare* used as a modal verb and as an auxiliary verb: (modal) *He hates only because he dare not love*—J. M. Coetzee, 1977 | *I dare not speak these dreams to any person*—Garrison Keillor, 1986 | *No one dared defy the group by going out at the last moment*—Ian McEwan, 1986 | (ordinary) *Marcus wouldn't dare to tell a lie like that unless it was true*—R. Hill, 1970 | *I did not dare to look down*—B. Rubens, 1985 | *How do they dare to be different?*—New Yorker, 1987 (This construction is needed to avoid the special meaning of *how dare they . . . ?*) | *She no longer dared to go into these shadowy apartments*—Anita Brookner, 1988.

6 There are two other special uses of *dare*: (1) in the phrases *how dare you* (etc.) *. . . ?* and *don't (you) dare . . .* , both normally followed by a bare infinitive (*How dare he dismiss Duke Ellington as a mere 'tunesmith'!*—Gramophone, 1976 | *How dare you come in without knocking?*—R. Dahl, 1984 | *Now you sit down there and don't you dare even look at anybody till I get back*—Kingsley Amis, 1988), and (2) in the phrase *I dare say* (or *I daresay*, as one word), meaning 'it is probable', normally followed by a *that*-clause (often with omission of *that*) (*I daresay I'll come back to it, in the fullness of time*—Penelope Lively, 1987).

7 Finally, there is the use of *dare* with an object, meaning 'to challenge or defy someone (to do something)', followed by a *to*-infinitive: *He looked round the table as if daring anyone to smile*—David Lodge, 1988.

dash. 1 There are, in formal printing at least, two types of dash: the en-rule (–) and the em-rule (—). An en-rule is twice the length of a hyphen, and an em-rule is twice the length of an en-rule. Most word-processing programs are able to distinguish the two lengths of rule, but in ordinary writing no distinction is usually made (and many people are not even aware of one).

2 The shorter en-rule has two principal uses: (1) to separate a range of dates, as in *pages 34–6* and *the 1939–45 war*, and (2) to join the names of joint authors and suchlike, as in *the Temple–Hardcastle project* and *Lloyd–Jones, 1939* (as a citation; *Lloyd-Jones*, with a hyphen, would be a single double-barrelled name).

3 The longer em-rule is the more familiar in everyday use, and corresponds to what most people understand by the term *dash*. Its principal uses are: (1) a single dash used to introduce an explanation or expansion of what comes before it (*It is a kind of irony of history that I should write about the French Revolution in the very country where it has had the least impact—I mean England, of course*—Encounter, 1990), and (2) a pair of dashes used to indicate asides and parentheses, forming a more distinct break than commas would (*Helen has only seen her father once in her adult life and—until her flight from Grassdale—her brother is a virtual stranger to her*—J. Sutherland, 1996). The use of a dash to stand for a coarse word (e.g. *f—*) in reported speech is much less common than it used to be, because public acceptance of these words spelt out is that much greater.

dastardly, like COWARDLY, is often used in a manner described by Fowler (1926) as inappropriate because it describes actions that, however reprehensible and brutal they may be, at least require boldness and courage. Acts of terrorism, however despicable, should not be described as *dastardly*.

data. 1 Fowler, writing before the computer age, declared uncompromisingly that '*data* is plural only', and pointed to the singular *datum*, which he conceded even then to be comparatively rare. For much of the time, *data* is used in contexts in which a conscious choice between singular and plural is not necessary: *Written sources provide systematic periodic data that can show trends and provide other relevant facts*—J. Waters et al., 1989. In some technical contexts (such as *sense-data* in philosophy), in which the information is regarded as several items, the plural is still usual; but in general use there is a marked tendency towards the singular after about 1970, under the influence of computing (see below), and most examples of the plural have to be sought from an earlier date: *It is no wonder if some authors have gone so far as to think that the sense-data have no spatial worth at all*—William James, 1890 | *Most of the data concerning shock and vibration on airplanes are classified*—Macduff and Curreri, 1958 | *The data come from fairly high doses of radiation*—Scientific American, 1972.

2 After about 1970, the primary meaning of *data* passed to the domain of computing, in which the information concerned is normally regarded as a unit, so that *data* is treated as singular and used with words such as *its*, *this*, and *much*, rather than *their*, *these*, and *many* (which now sound pedantic and even precious in this connection). This tendency is having a major impact on more gen-

eral use. If the sentence in the quotations of 1958 and 1972 above were written today, the verbs would almost certainly be *is* rather than *are* and *comes* rather than *come*. Examples of singular use: *They have done little to analyse and interpret this data*—*Computer Weekly*, 1971 | *Data is stored on a disk . . . as minute patches of magnetism*—P. Laurie, 1985 | *Everything that is happening to Mount St Helens is a 'classroom' experience for geologists and scientists scrambling to gather as much data as they can*—*New Scientist*, 1980 | *This data is open to a variety of interpretations*—T. Harris, 1993. The plural, however, also continues to be used to emphasize the plural implications of the word *data*: *The data . . . are mapped so that each class has, as far as possible, an equal number of countries*—P. M. Mather, 1991.

datable is spelt this way, not *dateable*. See -ABLE, -IBLE.

dates. The recommended style for BrE is *5 June 2001*, with no comma between the month and year. However, many newspapers, as well as American practice generally, prefer the style *June 5 2001* or *June 5, 2001*. In numerical notation, there is an important difference of practice on the two sides of the Atlantic: *5/6/01* means 5 June 2001 in Britain and 6 May 2001 in North America.

daughter-in-law means one's son's wife. The plural is *daughters-in-law*.

day, month, week, year are singular in expressions such as *a three-day week* and *a two-month term*.

day and age. The phrase *in this day and age* is a cliché. It slid into the language in the 1940s, although a film called *This Day and Age*, released in 1933, is not certainly the source. It should be avoided in favour of more straightforward terms such as *nowadays* or *at the present time*.

de- is a highly active suffix in current English, forming verbs and their derivatives. Notable 20c examples (with date of first record indicated) include: *debrief* (1942), *decaffeinate* (1927), *decertify* (1918), *decommunize* (1980), *de-emphasize* (1938), *de-escalate* (1964), *denet* (1962), *deregulate* (1964, with *deregulation* 1963). Note that a hyphen is usual when the second element begins with an *e*; in other cases it is optional.

dead letter, in general use, is properly a rule or regulation that is no longer observed; for example, capital punishment is a dead letter when it remains on the statute book although it is not used. The term should not be applied to aspects of life that have simply passed out of fashion, such as steam engines and cinema organs.

deaf mute is now regarded as derogatory because it implies an incapacity to communicate. It is safer to use neutral terms such *as profoundly deaf*.

deal noun. The phrase *a deal*, used for *a good deal* or *a great deal*, is now mainly confined to informal or dialectal use (*The decision saved him a deal of trouble*). A *great deal* and *a good deal* should not be used to mean 'a large number' of countable things (⊠ *A great deal of people have complained*); in these cases use *a great many*.

Dear, as part of a formal greeting at the beginning of a letter, was introduced in the 15c in vari-

ous formulas. *Dear Sir* and *Dear Madam* have become the most formal types, with *Dear Mr Jones* and *Dear Mrs/Miss/Ms Jones* serving as more socially neutral alternatives. Increasingly people are using the full name as in *Dear John Smith* or *Dear Jane Smith*, or (especially in circular letters) a descriptive name as in *Dear Customer* or *Dear Colleague*, in order to avoid the need for a title, which is a welcome tendency.

dear, dearly. You *love* someone *dearly* (i.e. very much), whereas you *buy* or *sell* something, or something *costs* you, *dear* or *dearly*.

dearth rapidly extended its meaning from its 13c restriction to food, to refer to a scarcity of anything: *Unable to find what she needed in 'romantic' novels, Letty had turned to biographies, of which there was no dearth*—Barbara Pym, 1977.

débâcle, pronounced day-**bah**-kəl, should properly be spelt with accents in place, although it is often written and printed without them.

debar, disbar. *Debar* means 'to exclude from admission or a right', as in *They were debarred from entering*, whereas *disbar* has the more specific meaning 'to deprive (a barrister) from the right to practise'. Both words double the *r* in inflection.

debatable is spelt this way, not *debateable*. See -ABLE, -IBLE.

debouch is pronounced di-**bowch** to rhyme with *pouch*.

debris is usually spelt without an accent, and is pronounced

deb-ri, although də-**bree** is normal in AmE.

debut is usually spelt without an accent, and is pronounced **day**-byoo.

debutant, debutante are pronounced **deb**- or **dayb**-, and are normally spelt without accents. A *debutant* is a male performer, and a *debutante* a female performer, appearing in public for the first time. The other meaning of *debutante*, a young woman making her social debut, is passing into history.

deca-, deci-. In the metric system, *deca-* means multiplied by 10, so that a *decalitre* is 10 litres, and *deci-* means divided by 10, so that a *decilitre* is a tenth of a litre or 100 ml.

decade. The preferred pronunciation is **dek**-ayd, although di-**kayd**, sounding like *decayed*, is increasingly heard.

deceptively. 1 *His voice was deceptively innocent, and she was led right into the trap*—E. Rees, 1992. Was his voice innocent or not? The answer seems to be that the appearance was of innocence whereas the reality was of something more sinister, and *deceptively* is therefore being used in the same way as *apparently* or *misleadingly*. This balance of meanings is more obvious when *deceptively* is used with words such as *appear, seem*, etc.: *Bill, who rarely played more than five minutes in any game because of a heart condition, was one of that rare breed who made the art of football look deceptively simple*—M. Gist, 1993.

2 But *deceptively* does not readily accompany an adjective that denotes something unfavourable or unwelcome, in the way that the more neutral word *apparently* does. When the appearance is unfavourable and the reality is favourable *deceptively* still seems to accompany the favourable adjective, as in the following example which is an echo of familiar estate agents' jargon: *Manoeuvring down the narrow steps into the boat, and turning into the airy and deceptively spacious lounge, Birbeck was greeted by Branson and Al Clark*—M. Brown, 1989. In this case, the lounge is claimed to be spacious (favourable) but appears not to be (unfavourable, i.e. the reverse of the balance found in the earlier examples), but it is understandable that no one in these circumstances would want to say that the room is (for example) *deceptively cramped*. Here, the analogy is with *surprisingly* (which strengthens the meaning of the adjective) rather than with *apparently* (which reduces it). This second type of use is idiomatic rather than suspect, but for those who prefer a stronger element of logic in their language an alternative word such as *surprisingly* or *unexpectedly* might be preferable.

decided, decisive. 1 Both words have to do with decision and decision-making, and their meanings overlap; but there are clear differences. When used of people, *decided* means 'having clear opinions' and *decisive* means 'able to decide quickly'; when used of circumstances, *decided* means 'definite, unquestionable' and *decisive* means 'deciding an issue, conclusive'. There are contexts in which both words can be used, but the implications are different: a *decided victory* is one that is overwhelming, whereas a *decisive victory* is one that (whether overwhelming or not) has a definite effect on the course of a war.

A manager is *decided* when he or she has a definite opinion on a subject, and is *decisive* when he or she makes decisions promptly and effectively.

2 The corresponding adverbs are *decidedly* (= unquestionably, undeniably) and *decisively* (= with conclusive effect).

decimate has changed its meaning because the old one is no longer needed. Historically, *decimate* means 'to kill one person in ten', and had its origin in military punishments. As the need for this meaning diminished, a new one emerged, the now familiar one 'to kill or destroy a large number or proportion of (people or things)': *In killing Moss, they'd used sufficient ammunition to decimate a small army*—R. Perry, 1979 | *The forest has largely gone, decimated by a forest industry that is just now assaulting the final remains—Dædalus*, 1988 | *The populations of dolphins and porpoises in the Black Sea have been decimated*—M. Donoghue et al., 1990.

decor is usually spelt without an accent, and is pronounced **dek**-aw.

decoy has an unstable stress pattern as both a noun and a verb, with both syllables variously stressed.

decrease is pronounced with stress on the first syllable as a noun and on the second syllable as a verb.

decry, descry are related in origin but now have widely different meanings. To *decry* something is to belittle or disparage it (*She also decries the double standard that dictates what men can do, women can't*—*New Musical Express*, 1992); to *descry* something is a somewhat literary word meaning to catch

sight of it in the distance (*Her thoughts were brought to an abrupt end, as she descried two figures on their way up the path*—J. Ashe, 1993).

deducible, deductible. *Deducible* means 'able to be deduced or inferred'; *deductible* means 'that may be deducted from or taken off a total'. See -ABLE, -IBLE

deduction, induction. *Deduction* is the inferring of particular instances from known or observed evidence; *induction* is the inferring of a general rule from particular instances.

deem is a fairly formal word, often used in legal contexts, for 'judge, consider', and is followed either by a complement without *as* or by a *to*-infinitive: *He was a senior policeman, and as such deemed to be unflappable*—B. Mather, 1973 | *In Ireland what a man said was deemed more important than what he did*—*Times Literary Supplement*, 1980.

deep, deeply. *Deep* is used as an adverb both literally (*With the horses provided you could trek deep into the forest*—*Drive*, 1972) and figuratively (*He was soon deep in studies of . . . the biology of unicellular organisms*—*Microscopy*, 1973 | *Johnny was standing with his back to the window, his hands thrust deep into his pockets*—E. Nash, 1993). *Deeply* is normally used only as an intensifying adverb in combinations such as *deeply aware, deeply satisfying*, etc., and when the meaning is 'profoundly, thoroughly': *It is the deeply moving, contemporary story of a young man who wouldn't surrender to the System*—*Ottawa Journal*, 1973 | *Powell himself was said to be deeply bothered by that*—*New Yorker*, 1977 | *They had kissed and caressed, but it* *was deeply frustrating*—D. M. Thomas, 1990.

defect should be pronounced with stress on the first syllable as a noun (= fault, imperfection) and on the second syllable as a verb (= to go over to an enemy or rival).

defective, deficient. *Defective* means 'having a defect (= fault)', whereas *deficient* means 'having a deficiency (or lack)'. So *eyesight, components, goods, logic, mechanisms*, etc., can all be *defective* if they are not working properly; and *courage, diet, funds, protein, the water supply*, etc., can all be *deficient* if there is not enough of them. Neither word is used any longer in professional contexts relating to mental abnormality.

defence is the spelling in BrE, *defense* in AmE.

defer has the forms *deferred, deferring; deference* (= respect, with stress on the first syllable); *deferral* and *deferment* (postponement, both with stress on the second syllable).

deficient see DEFECTIVE.

definite article see THE.

definite, definitely have useful roles as emphasizing words, and should not be dismissed too readily as superfluous: *His expression was bland, unreadable, but there was a definite glint in his eye that made her pulse begin to race*—E. Richmond, 1991 | *And pickled onions had definitely been a bad idea*—S. Shepherd, 1988. Since the 1930s, *definitely* has come into widespread use informally as a strong affirmative reply meaning 'certainly, indeed': *'Would they recommend that the experiment is repeated another year?' 'Oh,*

definitely.'—*Sunday Times*, 1959. See also ABSOLUTELY.

definite, definitive both refer to things that are said or written. *Definite* means 'clear and distinct', whereas *definitive* means 'decisive, unconditional, final' and normally refers to an answer, verdict, treaty, etc. A *definitive text, book*, etc., is a printed work that is regarded as the best authority on its subject and likely to remain so. Only *definitive* has connotations of authority and conclusiveness: a *definite no* is a firm refusal, whereas a *definitive no* is an authoritative judgement that something is not the case.

deflection is now the normal form in BrE and AmE, not *deflexion*.

defuse, diffuse. It is surprising how often *diffuse* (correctly = to disperse) is used for *defuse* in its figurative meaning 'to remove tension or potential danger from (a crisis, etc.)'. Examples of this wrong use are: *An early cut in base rates, which would . . . diffuse the dispute between the Chancellor and the Prime Minister*—*Times*, 1988 | *The Scott report is a time-bomb stealthy politicians and officials are trying to diffuse*—*Guardian*, 1995. Since this mistake occurs most often in newspapers, we might suspect that close writing deadlines are the culprit here.

degree. In Sheridan's *The Rivals* (1775), we find *Assuredly, sir, your father is wrath to a degree*. This means 'your father is very cross'; the use survives in more florid modern English and was accepted by Fowler (1926) 'however illogical it seems'. But ambiguity now arises because *to a degree* also means 'to some extent' as well as 'to a great extent' and the context does not always determine which is meant: *W. J. Bryan was to a degree exceptional even in the USA*—P. Wiles, 1969. Confusion is avoided by qualifying the word *degree* in some way, as in *to a large degree | to a certain degree | to some degree | to an amazing degree* etc. A frequent (chiefly informal) phrase now is *to the nth degree* (a loan from mathematics).

deify, deity are now frequently pronounced **day-** as well as the traditional **dee-**, causing raised eyebrows in more conservative circles. *The Deity* (= God), is spelt with a capital initial.

déjà vu, meaning in French 'already seen' and hence 'an illusory feeling of having experienced a situation before', is recorded first (1903) in the language of psychology and spread rapidly and widely in general use. The parallel phrases relating to other senses, *déjà entendu* (= heard, 1965) and *déjà lu* (= read, 1960) still sound somewhat affected.

deliberative now means only (1) 'appointed for the purpose of deliberation or debate', (*The political bureau was now to consist of 400 members and would be a deliberative rather than an executive body*— *Keesings*, 1990), and (2) 'using deliberation' (*Some problem-solving will take the form of a deliberative weighing of consequences*—M. Leahy, 1991).

delimit see LIMIT.

delusion, illusion overlap in meaning because both are to do with things wrongly believed or thought for various reasons. There is, however, a distinguishing principle: a *delusion* is a

wrong belief regarded from the point of view of the person holding it (and has special uses in psychiatry, as in *delusions of grandeur*), whereas an *illusion* is a wrong belief or impression regarded externally. *Delusion*, unlike *illusion*, has a corresponding verb, *delude*, and the action of this verb is sometimes implicit in the choice between *delusion* and *illusion*. The following examples will help to clarify these points: (delusion) *He suffered from the delusion that everything smelled of cats*— Arthur Koestler, 1947 | *That was the way delusions started, thinking there was anti-Jewish feeling when there wasn't*—P. H. Newby, 1968 | *Amorous delusions concerning . . . a lecherously attentive neighbour and her kindly but pre-occupied husband*— Daily Telegraph, 1970 | (illusion) *In the world as we know it . . . freedom is largely an illusion*—J. M. Roberts, 1975 | *The illusion must be maintained that this was a purely Polish debate with no intrusion being made by the Soviet Union*—J. A. Mitchener, 1983 | *Alfred Crowther loved his first-born child, but he had no illusions about him*—B. T. Bradford, 1986.

de luxe is written as two words in BrE and pronounced də **luks** or (less often) , də **looks**. In AmE it tends to be written as one word, and variously pronounced.

demand. You demand something *from* or (less commonly) *of* someone (*She demanded ten pounds from him*), and you make a demand *on* someone *for* something (*There were constant demands on her for her comments*).

demi- is a less productive prefix than it used to be, being overshadowed by *semi-* and *half-* (and occasionally *hemi-* for words of Greek origin). It survives in a number of English words, some of them loanwords from French, e.g. *demigod, demi-monde, demi-pension, demisemiquaver, demitasse. Demijohn* (a size of bottle) is probably a corruption of French *dame-jeanne* (= Lady Jane).

demo is an informal shortening of *demonstration* in two meanings, (1) 'a public march or gathering in support of some cause', and (2) 'a practical explanation of something, e.g. a machine works'. In its common computing application, *demo* is often used attributively (before a noun) to mean 'demonstrating the capabilities of', as in *demo software | demo tape.*

demur, meaning 'to raise scruples or objections' has inflected forms *demurred, demurring.* It is normally used in negative contexts and without a complement (*When we asked them they did not demur*), although it is occasionally followed by *at* or *to* (*They did not demur at my suggestion*).

denote see CONNOTE.

denouement, meaning 'the final unravelling of a plot in a story, etc.', is usually printed in roman type without an accent.

dentures was originally a genteelism (first recorded in 1874) for *false teeth*, but is now standard in more formal use.

depart is now used intransitively (without an object) either without any complement or followed by *from* (a point of departure) or *for* (a destination). Its use with an object is restricted to the formal or literary phrase *depart this life*, meaning 'to die', but in AmE is more common in general use (*They departed the house at noon*),

being recorded in uses by J. K. Galbraith, Robert Craft, and others.

depend. 1 *Depend* in its main meaning is followed by *on* or *upon*: *It was quite wrong to come to depend too much upon one's children*—Penelope Fitzgerald, 1979 | *As grandfather grew older . . . he seemed to depend increasingly on my company*—J. Simms, 1982. It is also commonly used in the informal expression *you can depend on it/that* etc.: *I'll have a damn good try . . . You can depend on that*—A. Price, 1982.

2 The slightly archaic meaning 'to hang down', which is the word's etymological meaning, is still used in some literary contexts: *From a beam crossing the low ceiling depended a mobile, the property of Parker*—Elizabeth Bowen, 1968, but is not a feature of normal usage.

dependant, dependent. *Dependant* in BrE is a noun meaning 'a person who relies on another for financial support', and *dependent* is an adjective meaning 'depending or conditional on something or someone else' (with several special meanings). In AmE *dependent* is the usual form for the noun.

dependence, dependency. *Dependence* is 'a state of depending'; *dependency* can also mean this but is more usually 'something, especially a country or province, that is dependent on another'. The distinction has been somewhat blurred by the recent term *dependency culture*, meaning 'a way of life determined by being dependent on state benefits'.

depositary, depository. A *depositary* is a person or authority to whom something is entrusted, a trustee. A *depository* is (1) a storage place for furniture, books, etc., and (2) a source (normally a book or suchlike, occasionally a person) of wisdom or knowledge.

depot, pronounced **dep**-oh, is printed in roman type with no accents.

deprecate, depreciate. 1 The two words are similar in form and in current use overlap somewhat in meaning, but their origin is different. *Deprecate* is from Latin *deprecari* 'to prevent by prayer' and its primary current meaning is 'to express disapproval of (a person or thing)': *When news of this 'record' multiple birth emerged last weekend, few dared to deprecate it—Sunday Times, 1987. Depreciate* is from Latin *depretiare* 'to lower in value' and currently means (1) without an object, 'to become lower in value or price' (*Experience has shown me that their cars are more reliable and depreciate less—Mail on Sunday, 1985*), and (2) with an object, 'to undervalue, to disparage' (*Before this Wilde depreciated pity as a motive in art; now he embraced it—R. Ellmann, 1969*). It is in this last meaning that the overlap in meaning occurs, the intruder normally being *deprecate* in place of *depreciate: Dealers have felt a need to deprecate their own firms' values, to disassociate themselves from them—A. Davidson, 1989 | A talent that results in giving exquisite pleasure to collectors of memorabilia is to be admired, not deprecated—M. J. Staples, 1992.* As a result *depreciate* is being more and more confined to its financial meaning in relation to currencies, share values, etc.

2 This intrusion on the part of *deprecate* is reflected in the derivative adjectives *self-deprecating* and *self-deprecatory* meaning 'disparaging oneself', and the noun *self-deprecation*, where the meanings are closer to *deprecate* than *deprecate: Barton . . . smiled, and then his face changed again, the old, self-deprecating expression over it—*Susan Hill, 1971 | *Sadly he declined, saying in a charmingly self-deprecatory way that he doubted he had any views worth hearing—*L. Kennedy, 1990 | *Markby chuckled, his customary air of self-deprecation returning—*A. Granger, 1991. These forms and uses are now fully established, although *self-depreciation* is also occasionally found.

deprivation, meaning 'depriving or being deprived (of something)', is pronounced dep-ri**vay**-shən, with stress on the third syllable. It should be distinguished from *privation*, which means 'lack of the comforts or necessities of life'.

de rigueur is pronounced də ri-**ger**, is non-naturalized in English and is printed in italics.

derisive, derisory. Although their meanings have coincided since their first appearance in the 17c, in current use they are for the most part kept separate, *derisive* meaning 'scoffing, scornful' as in *derisive laughter* and *derisive remarks* and *derisory* meaning 'ridiculously small or insignificant' as in *a derisory pay offer* and *a derisory contribution*.

descendant, descendent. In BrE *descendant* is the noun and *descendent* is the adjective, but in AmE either form is used in both cases.

description. Fowler (1926) discouraged the use of *description* as an alternative to *kind* and *sort* in expressions such as *crimes of this* *description*, but the use has become well established and often seems appropriate if sometimes a little old-fashioned: *That's the first flying machine of any description that has ever landed on Muck*—B. Moore, 1972.

descriptive. As applied to language, the term denotes a concept of grammar as describing actual practice rather than laying down theoretical rules. See PRESCRIPTIVE.

desert, dessert. There are two unrelated words spelt *desert*: one, with stress on the first syllable, is the barren area of land, and the other, with stress on the second syllable, is what one deserves, as in *get one's just deserts*. The verb *desert*, meaning 'to abandon' and stressed on the second syllable, is related to the first of these words. Finally *dessert*, with two *s*'s and stressed on the second syllable, is a word for 'the sweet course of a meal'.

deserter is spelt *-er*, not *-or*.

deservedly is pronounced as four syllables.

desiccated, from Latin *siccus* meaning 'dry', is spelt in this way, not *dessicated*.

desideratum meaning 'something lacking or needed', is pronounced **-ah**-təm or **-ay**-təm and has the plural form *desiderata*.

designer has been since the 1960s a vogue word first used in the fashion world to denote articles bearing the name of a famous designer and therefore prestigious and expensive. In this use *designer* is used attributively (before a noun), as in *designer dress, jeans, shoes*, etc. The word then spread into much wider use

to signify anything regarded as fashionable or specially made, with all sorts of figurative applications: *He remembered thinking to himself; so it's finally happened—designer industrial action*—David Lodge, 1988 | *The Home Secretary . . . turned on 'designer violence' on the [television] screen*—Times, 1988 | *Designer stubble of the George Michael ilk has also run its bristly course*—Guardian, 1989. A *designer drug* is a synthetic compound made to simulate an existing illegal 'recreational' drug, and a *designer dyke* is a glamorous Lesbian: *Gay girls have become rather fashionable . . . and the opportunity to write about 'lipstick lesbianism' and 'designer dykes' has not gone unseized*—Daily Telegraph, 1995.

despatch see DISPATCH.

desperado is pronounced des-pə-**rah**-doh, and has the plural form *desperadoes*.

despicable. Pundits and usage gurus since Fowler (1926) have been urging us to pronounce *despicable* with the stress on the first syllable, but unsurprisingly usage has swung in favour of a more comfortable pattern with the stress on the second syllable.

despise must be spelt *-ise*, not *-ize*. See -ISE.

dessert see DESERT.

destruct. 1 This is a back-formation from *destruction*, formed as a specific alternative to *destroy* to denote a calculated action, originally with reference to space missiles that were malfunctioning, then in other military or related contexts, and later in figurative uses. The normal past tense is *destructed*. Like all so-called 'ergative' verbs, it can be used transitively (with an object) and intransitively (without an object): *At this point it was destroyed (or 'destructed' as the official explanation puts it) by remote control—Times*, 1958 | *This was the prevalent left view until Thatcher's third term destructed, and Labour triumphalism had one last go—New Statesman*, 1992. It is also used as a noun, normally in attributive position (before another noun), as in *destruct system*.

2 The reflexive form *self-destruct* appeared in the 1960s, and follows the same grammatical functions of *destruct*. It is also used figuratively: *Watergate came from within. The system itself has begun to self-destruct—Guardian*, 1973.

destructible is spelt *-ible*, not *-able*. See -ABLE, -IBLE.

détente should be spelt with an accent and printed in italics.

deter has inflected forms *deterred, deterring*, and also doubles the *r* in the derivative forms *deterrence* and *deterrent* (both pronounced with *-ter-* as in *ten*).

deteriorate should be pronounced with all five syllables articulated. Pronunciation as if it were *deteriate* is often heard but should be avoided. A similar problem occurs with *temporary* and other words.

determiner. A determiner is a word that goes before a noun and determines its status in some way, such as *a, the, this, all*, and *such*. A *predeterminer* occurs before another determiner (*all* the time) and a *postdeterminer* occurs after another determiner (*The only* one).

detract, distract. Both words are used transitively (with an object) followed by *from*; but their meanings are different. *Detract*, which (more than *distract*) is also used without an object, means 'to take away (a part of something), to diminish': *The tape element involved in the production of a disc record detracts very little from the overall quality these days—J. Earl*, 1971. *Distract* means 'to divert the attention of' with a person, the mind, etc. as the object: *These days find Paris in a sort of limbo . . . There is, it is true, the Tour de France to distract us in the weeks ahead—Listener*, 1972. *Detract* sometimes encroaches on *distract*, especially in the expression *detract attention from*, which was an accepted usage in the early 19c but should now be avoided in favour of *distract attention from*.

devil's advocate is someone who argues against a proposition or belief in order to test it. It should not be used to mean someone who supports a bad or wicked cause. Its origin lies in the Roman Catholic official (in Latin *advocatus diaboli*) who tests the case for canonization of a candidate for sainthood by preparing and arguing the case against it.

devise must be spelt *-ise*, not *-ize*. See -ISE.

devoid, meaning 'lacking', is followed by *of* and comes after the word it refers to: *The Council is devoid of any powers—radio broadcast*, 1976 | *The language is nearly devoid of metaphor—Observer*, 1980.

devolve is a verb of reviving fortunes in the age of political devolution. Its three principal uses are as follows: (1) you devolve powers, authority, etc., *on* or *upon* someone, (2) power, authority, etc., devolves *on* or *upon* someone, and (3) a right, benefit, etc., devolves *to* (or occasionally *on*) someone. The word appears frequently in the form *devolved* to refer to a body or its powers when these have been devolved by a national government: *Our increasing dependence on tourism calls for highly devolved decision-making—Glasgow Herald, 1986 | Public support for the national question is at an historic high, with 50% of Scots favouring a devolved assembly and 30% of Scots wanting a separate parliament—Marxism Today, 1986.* The back-formed verb *devolute* is occasionally found instead of *devolve.*

dexterous is preferable to *dextrous*. Both are pronounced **dek**-strəs.

diabolic, diabolical. *Diabolic* is used primarily with direct reference to the devil (as in Byron's *Satan . . . merely bent his diabolic brow an instant, 1822*), whereas *diabolical* is used mainly in its extended meanings 'bad, disgraceful, awful': *Asked our postman about communications between Tunisia and England. He said they were 'diabolical'—S. Townsend, 1982 | From my point of view that pitch was dangerous. In fact, it was diabolical—Observer, 1986.* However, *diabolical* is sometimes used in the first sense, especially when the rhythm of the sentence is improved by it.

diagnose is properly used to mean 'to make a diagnosis of' with the disease or problem as the object. Now, however, it is increasingly used with a person as object, usually followed by *as* with a verb participle: *He was diagnosed as having an anxiety neurosis—British Medical Journal, 1984 | A baby who was incorrectly diagnosed as having died before birth—T. Stuttaford, 1990.* At present, however, this use does not extend to things: you can diagnose clutch trouble in a car but you can't yet diagnose a car as having clutch trouble.

diagnosis has the plural form *diagnoses* (pronounced **-gnoh**-seez).

diagram *verb*, meaning 'to represent by means of a diagram,' has the forms *diagrammed, diagramming, diagrammatic.* In AmE the verbal forms are often *diagramed, diagraming.*

dial *verb* has inflected forms *dialled, dialling* in BrE and *dialed, dialing* in AmE.

dialect.
See box opposite

dialectal, dialectic, dialectical. In the 19c all three words were used to mean 'belonging to a dialect', but only *dialectal* now serves this purpose. *Dialectic* is a form of philosophical argument by question and answer, and *dialectical* is the adjective derived from it.

dialogue is a conversation between two or more people. The first element has nothing to do with *di-* meaning 'two', but is derived from Greek *dia-* meaning 'through, across'. It is now often used of the talking process involved in negotiations and discussions, for example between one country and another or between

dialect

is the language form of a particular region, and varies from the standard language in matters of vocabulary, grammar, and pronunciation. Some dialects are also related to social class and ethnic origin. The dialects of the United Kingdom are recorded in Joseph Wright's magnificent but now dated *English Dialect Dictionary* (1896–1905) and in *A Survey of English Dialects* (1962–8) edited by Harold Orton and others. There is also a *Linguistic Atlas of England* (1978), edited by Orton and others, and numerous monographs and glossaries published by local dialect societies. Although words and uses that are grammatical within a dialect do not normally enter the standard language, there are some common words and phrases that had their origins in dialect, as is shown in the table below. Care should be taken to avoid confusing a dialect with a variety: Scottish English, for example, is a variety and not a dialect.

Some common words and idioms of dialect or local origin

WORD	DATE	ORIGINAL MEANING
beach	16c	shingle, pebbles
binge	19c	(as verb) = to soak
bleak	16c	pale, colourless
cack-handed	19c	cack = excrement
clever	16c	nimble-handed, adroit
elevenses	18c	elevens = morning meal
feisty	19c	ficety (US) = aggressive
old-fashioned (as in *an old-fashioned look*)	20c	knowing, precocious
pal	17c	Romany = brother
poke (as in *a pig in a poke*)	ME	bag, sack
tab	ME	short broad strap etc.
wilt	17c	become limp, droop

Bleak and *clever* are recorded at an earlier date in meanings that are historically unconnected to the later ones. ME = Middle English

trade unions and management. In AmE it is frequently spelt *dialog*.

diarrhoea is spelt in this way in BrE and *diarrhea* in AmE.

dice is in origin the plural of *die* (as in *the die is cast*, meaning 'the decisive step has been taken'). *Dice* are also the small cubes bearing 1 to 6 spots on each face, used in games of chance; this form is also used for the singular (*He had a dice in his pocket*).

dichotomy means 'a division into two' (from Greek *dicho-* meaning 'apart' and *-tomos* meaning 'cutting'). The word has long-established meanings in technical domains such as logic, astronomy, and the life sciences; in the 20c it has moved into general use to mean 'a difference or split' (e.g. *a dichotomy of opinion*) and often implies a contrast or a paradoxical circumstance: *By a dichotomy familiar to us all, a woman requires her own baby to be perfectly normal, and at the same time superior to all other babies*—John Wyndham, 1957 | *The coffee-table featured a couple of Shakespeare texts and a copy of Time Out—an intriguing dichotomy*—Martin Amis, 1973.

dictate is pronounced with the stress on the first syllable as a noun (as in *the dictates of conscience*) and with the stress on the second syllable as a verb (as in *dictate a letter*).

didn't ought may be the result of a collision of the strange behaviour patterns of two modal verbs, *do* and *ought*, but its origins are in dialect and it features in literature only as a (sometimes stereotypical) representation of rustic or poorly educated speech: *And I hope none here will say I did anything I didn't ought. For I have only done my duty*—Michael Innes, 1942 | *You didn't ought to have let that fire out*—William Golding, 1954.

die *noun* see DICE.

die *verb*. When used with a complement, the normal uses are to die *of* a disease, old age, etc., to die *from* (or occasionally *of*) a wound, neglect, etc., and to die *for* (a cause). The modern (originally AmE) idiom *to die for*, meaning 'outstandingly good' and often used attributively (before a noun), is informal only: *Excellent Vietnamese fare, including to-die-for softshell crabs*—Post (Denver), 1995.

dietitian, meaning an authority on diet, is the recommended spelling, not *dietician*.

differ is widely used without any complement: *While their aims and activities differ slightly, all are clubs in the sense of recruiting members*—R. Brown, 1993. It can be followed by *from* in the meaning 'to be unlike': *These languages . . . differ from the Polish dialects discussed above*—Language, 1975 | *Most British school and college mathematics classrooms do not differ much from those of a hundred years ago*—D. Pimm, 1988. When it means 'to disagree (with someone)' it is either used independently (*We agreed to differ*) or followed by *with*, but this use is becoming much less common as *disagree* takes over from it: *Dissanayake . . . had subsequently differed with the President on such issues as the handling of the withdrawal of Indian troops from Sri Lanka*—Keesings, 1990.

different. 1 Fowler wrote in 1926 that insistence 'that *different* can only be followed by *from* and not by *to* is a superstition'. It is in fact a 20c superstition that refuses to go away, despite copious evidence for the use of *to* and *than* dating back to well before 1700. First of all we should recognize that for much of the time *different*, when used predicatively (after a verb) is used without any complement at all: *But tonight would have been different*—A. Wells, 1993. We may then put *than* aside for a moment and concentrate on *different from* and *different to*. The argument in favour of *from* is based on the relation of *different* to *differ* (which is followed by *from* in this meaning); but this is an artificial construction based on the principles of Latin and not English grammar, and is contradicted by the varying practice of *accord* (*with*) and *according* (*to*). English works by analogy, and here the influence comes from words that have the same function, such as *comparable*, *equivalent*, and *similar*.

2 There are indeed occasions when *from* is inelegant and *to* is more natural, especially when *different* is separated from its complement (e.g. by an adverbial phrase), as will be seen from following examples which illustrate both uses: (from) *Casual shacking up was quite different from holy matrimony*—M. Underwood, 1980 | *The Anglo-American approach to copyright was thought to be different from the approach taken by France and other European countries*—*New Yorker*, 1987 | *He's no different from my brother, in the end*—Nadine Gordimer, 1988 | *What makes chenille different from other carpets is that it's the product of two distinct processes*—E. Blair, 1990 | (to) *He looked no different at first to other boys Margaret had known*—M. Leland, 1986 | *I found that a meadow seen against the light was an entirely different tone of green to the same meadow facing the light*—*Scots Magazine*, 1986 | *They don't seem to be any different to us*—*Chicago Tribune*, 1989 | *Sound waves are very different to water waves but the length of a sound wave changes with its frequency in the same way*—J. Downer, 1989.

3 *Different than* is a more complex issue. It is better established in AmE than in BrE, especially when *different* is followed by a comparative clause: *It used to be they'd play at different times than on the U.S. stations, but not any more*—*Globe & Mail* (Toronto), 1977 | *This discrepancy is intriguing because most scallops have a very different mode of life than other species*—*Bulletin of the American Academy of Arts & Sciences*, 1987. BrE looks more strongly askance at this construction than it does on *different to*, and the objection can be

better justified on grounds of style than the objection to *to* can be justified on grounds of grammar. It is natural to want to avoid an awkward relative construction such as we find in Joyce Cary's much discussed sentence *I was a very different man in 1935 from what I was in 1916*; for some the answer is *I was a very different man in 1935 than I was in 1916*, but a little lateral thinking might steer us right round the problem by suggesting an alternative: *I was not the same man in 1935 as I had been in 1916*. One should not presume to rewrite Joyce Cary, but this kind of solution might do better for those who simply want to stay clear of linguistic mantraps.

4 The case for *to* and *than* is more compelling, as occasional alternatives to *from*, when *different* is used in an adverbial phrase such as *in a different sense*, and when they follow the adverb *differently*, where *from* can become uncomfortably cumbersome: *Sebastian was a drunkard in quite a different sense to myself*—Evelyn Waugh, 1945 | *A false sense of security which makes drivers behave quite differently on motorways than on ordinary roads*—*Daily Telegraph*, 1971 | *The lepidopteran proboscis is very differently constructed from that of the Diptera*—Proctor & Yeo, 1973.

5 Note that *different* is commonly found in everyday use as a convenient synonym for more austere words such as *distinct*, *separate*, *various*, etc.: ☒ *Children's perceptions of their sexual roles are built up from many different sources*—N. Tucker, 1981 | *After four or five different activities have been described, you read the list of activities*—R. McCall, 1992 | *For sociology graduates there are career opportunities in many different areas*—*Edinburgh undergraduate prospectus*, 1993. If the exact meanings of the other words given above are needed, use them; otherwise this use of *different* is a useful one.

differential is a noun and adjective with several technical and general meanings. As an adjective it is used principally in combinations such as *differential rates of interest*, which are not just different rates of interest but rates based on quantifiable differences (such as the type of investment). In the same way, a *differential* is a determining factor based on some difference, and is not the difference itself. Examples: (noun) *Differentials do exist between blue- and white-collar workers, but they appear to be narrower than in most Western companies*—B. Eccleston, 1989 | (adjective) *As a result the effects of differential mortality rates for men and women are exacerbated*—C. Ungerson, 1991. It should not be used to mean simply 'distinguishing' or 'making a difference', as in *A small event like mother-in-law coming to stay can have a differential impact on newly marrieds*—J. Mattinson et al., 1989

differently abled is a politically correct alternative for *disabled*. See POLITICAL CORRECTNESS.

diffuse see DEFUSE.

diffusible is spelt *-ible*, not *-able*. See -ABLE, -IBLE.

digest is pronounced with stress on the first syllable as a noun (meaning 'a summary') and with stress on the second syllable as a verb (meaning 'to absorb (food) in the body').

digraph is a combination of two letters which together represent a single speech sound, e.g. *dg* in *judge* and *ea* in *head*. Certain di-

graphs are printed as ligatures, in which the two letters are joined, e.g. æ.

dike see DYKE.

dilatation, dilation mean 'making or becoming wider' (from Latin *latus* meaning 'wide'). *Dilatation* is the normal word in medical contexts, whereas *dilation* is more usual in general use. The verb is *dilate*.

dilatory, meaning 'given to or causing delay', is pronounced **dil-ə-tə-ri**. The same stress pattern applies, rather more awkwardly, to the derivative forms *dilatorily* and *dilatoriness*.

dilemma is now more usually pronounced with the first syllable rhyming with *die*. The correct meaning is 'a choice between two undesirable alternatives' and has its origin in rhetoric and logic, where it relates to a special kind of argument involving two unfavourable choices. It should not be used as a mere synonym of *difficulty*, *problem*, and similar words, although overlap in meanings will often blur the distinction. Examples: (correct) *The dilemma is logically insoluble: we cannot sacrifice either freedom or the organization needed for its defence*—Isaiah Berlin, 1949 | *It is possible to raise only one cheer for user charges as a means of avoiding the dilemma of cutting public services or increasing taxes*—Times, 1976 | (questionable) *Every pontoon player will understand the dilemma of the Tory chiefs. They are undecided whether to stick or twist on a relatively modest hand of cards*—Guardian, 1972 | *He was caught in a dilemma, a choice between doing a show or going on a much-needed vacation*—D. Halberstam, 1979 | *Three corridors: one to the left, one ahead, one to the right*

. . . *'Dilemma. Left, right or centre?'—*
Dirk Bogarde, 1980. A moral *dilemma*
is a choice between two morally
questionable courses of action,
and its use is fairly self-
determining: *He . . . warned present and future White House aides to
be on the alert for . . . moral di-
lemmas that may arise while serving
a President—Time*, 1977.

dilettante, meaning 'someone
with superficial or affected knowledge of a subject', is spelt with
one *l* and two *t*s, and has plural
forms *dilettanti* or *dilettantes*.

dingo, a wild Australian dog,
has the plural form *dingoes*.

diocese is pronounced **diy**-ə-sis,
and the plural *dioceses* is pronounced either **diy**-ə-seez or (less
commonly) **diy**-ə-si-siz.

diphtheria, the bacterial disease, is spelt with -*ph*- and should
be pronounced dif-, not dip-.

diphthong, meaning a speech
sound in which the articulation
changes from one vowel to another, as in *coin, loud, pain, spoke,*
etc., is spelt with -*ph*- and should
be pronounced dif-, not dip-. Diphthongs are a common feature of
English pronunciation.

direct, directly. Because *direct* is
an adverb as well as an adjective,
it gets in the way of *directly,*
which is an adverb only. *Directly* is
used (1) before an adjective (*They
were directly responsible for the accident*), and (2) to mean 'immediately', both of time and position
(*I'll come directly | Directly after this,
he was taken away | The house is dir-
ectly opposite*). *Direct* is usual when
it means 'by a direct route' or
'without any intermediary' (*Some
flights go direct from Heathrow to Los*

*Angeles | You can buy them direct
from the manufacturer*). In informal
contexts, *directly* can be used as a
conjunction meaning 'as soon as,
the moment after' (*She came directly I called*).

direct object. In grammar, a direct object is the noun or pronoun
or phrase that is directly affected
by the action of a transitive verb.
In the sentence *They bought a new
house, a new house* is the direct object of the verb *bought*. See also
INDIRECT OBJECT, INTRANSITIVE
AND TRANSITIVE VERBS.

dirigible, meaning 'capable of
being guided', is spelt -*ible* not
-*able*. It is also used as a noun,
meaning 'a dirigible machine'.
See -ABLE, -IBLE.

dis- is an active prefix which
continues to form nouns, adjectives, adverbs, and verbs, with the
meaning 'not' or 'the reverse'
with reference to the meaning of
the word it is attached to. Notable 20c formations included *dis-
affiliation* (1926), *disarmingly*
(1901), *disincentive* (1946), *disinformation* (1955), *disquieten* (1921).
Note that *disfunctional* is a variant
of *dysfunctional* (formed on the
prefix *dys*- meaning 'bad, badly')
and is not connected with this
prefix *dis*-.

disassemble see DISSEMBLE.

disassociate, meaning 'to end
an association with', was passed
over by Fowler (1926) but was described by Gowers (1965) as a
needless variant of *dissociate*. It is
still found nonetheless, especially
when the reversal of *associate* is
emphatic: *Any other woman would
have disassociated herself, gone
where she wasn't known, changed
her name—A. L. Barker, 1987 | The*

Foreign Office at once issued a statement disassociating the Government from the idea—Spectator, 1988.

disastrous should be pronounced as three syllables (di-**zah**-strəs), not as four (di-**zah**-stə-rəs).

disbar see DEBAR.

disc, disk. The normal spelling in BrE changed from *disk* at the time of the original *OED* (1896) to *disc* by the time of *OED2* (1989); in AmE it has remained *disk*. In computer terminology, however, the American spelling is dominant everywhere (as in *hard disk, disk drive*, etc.), but in other technical applications, including *compact disc* and *disc camera*, it is spelt with a *c*, not *k*.

discernible is spelt -*ible*, not -*able*. See -ABLE, -IBLE.

disciplinary is pronounced with stress on the first or third syllable, depending partly on its position in a sentence.

disco is a shortened (and now standard) form of *discothèque*, meaning 'a club or party with recorded pop music for dancing'. The plural form is *discos*, and as a verb, meaning 'to dance at a disco', it has the forms *discoes, discoed, discoing*.

discomfit, discomfort. *Discomfit* in current English means 'to thwart the plans of' (its original meaning) or 'to embarrass or disconcert'. In its weaker second meaning, in which it occurs most often in the form *discomfited*, it overlaps with the unrelated word *discomfort*, which means 'to make uneasy', and in the normal flow of speech it is not always possible—for speaker or hearer—to distinguish them. Examples: (discomfit) *I should have corrected her,*

but, discomfited, missed the right moment—Alison Lurie, 1969 | *Widger was not wholly without Schadenfreude at seeing his informative colleague discomfited for once*—Edmund Crispin, 1977 | *He turned away from her, discomfited at her glance*—L. Appignanesi, 1992 | (discomfort) *His Section's Mediterranean operations, where his cheerful courage discomforted the Germans and Italians, are dealt with in later chapters*—J. Ladd, 1979 | *The show, entitled 'Banality', was eerie, discomforting, and seemed to offend nearly everyone*—The Face, 1990.

discontent, meaning 'lack of contentment', is pronounced with the stress on the last syllable. Shakespeare's famous opening lines from *Richard III, Now is the winter of our discontent Made glorious summer by this sun of York*, have provided one of the most prolific of modern political clichés, *winter of discontent*, first used with reference to industrial unrest in Britain in 1978–9.

discount is pronounced with stress on the first syllable as a noun, and with stress on the second syllable as a verb.

discourse is pronounced with stress on the first syllable as a noun, and with stress on the second syllable as a verb.

discover, invent. To *discover* something is to find something that was hidden or not known; to *invent* something is to devise it by human effort: Halley *discovered* a comet and Galileo *invented* a telescope. Information as well as physical things can be *discovered*, and in this case a *that*-clause is common: *They discovered that they had been underpaid for months.* Similarly, excuses, stories, etc., can be *invented*, although a *that-*clause is not permissible.

discreet, discrete have the same origin in the Latin verb *discernere* meaning 'to sift', but their meanings are very different. *Discreet* means 'circumspect in speech or action', can be used of people or things, and is common as an adverb *discreetly*: *A public telephone stood in one corner of the discreetly lit foyer*—R. Busby, 1971 | *I noticed a few discreet establishments that looked as unauthentic, or as authentic according to your viewpoint, as New York's massage parlours*—*Times*, 1972. *Discrete* means 'distinct, separate': *Notwithstanding the vagueness of its aims, social work became sanctified as a discrete discipline under the Social Services Act of 1970*—*Times Literary Supplement*, 1980.

discus has the plural form *discuses*.

discussible is spelt *-ible*, not *-able*. See -ABLE, -IBLE.

disenfranchise, disfranchise, meaning 'to deprive of a vote', have both been in the language for several centuries. At present *disenfranchise* is the more common of the two. Both verbs should be spelt *-ise*, not *-ize*. See -ISE.

disguise *verb* is spelt *-ise*, not *-ize*. See -ISE.

disinformation, a more sinister equivalent of *propaganda*, is first attested in 1939 in relation to a German 'Disinformation Service'. Since then it has usually been applied to the activities of various intelligence groups during the cold war: *One technique of the Central Intelligence Agency . . . is disinformation . . . The Agency has expensive facilities for producing fake documents and other means for misleading foreigners*—*New Republic*, 1975.

disingenuous, meaning 'insincere, having secret motives', is the opposite of *ingenuous* meaning 'innocent, honest', and is applied to people and their actions: *The somewhat disingenuous slogan of 'ban the bomb'*—Harold Macmillan, 1971 | *I should be disingenuous if I pretended not to be flattered*—William Golding, 1982 | *Every feminist critic has encountered the archly disingenuous question: 'What exactly is feminist criticism?'*—B. Bergonzi, 1990 | *'I thought Amy wasn't here much,' said Theodora disingenuously*—D. M. Greenwood, 1991.

disinterest. 1 The noun is 17c and has two current meanings corresponding to those of the more commonly used word DISINTERESTED. These are (1) impartiality, (2) lack of interest. A third meaning, 'something contrary to one's advantage', is now virtually obsolete. The first meaning is found in earlier writing (*We here see Morris working, with entire disinterest, at his work*—*Saturday Review*, 1896), but the second is now far more common, despite the controversy attached to the corresponding meaning of *disinterested* (*The general reaction . . . was a mixture of curiosity, disinterest, fear, and embarrassment*—M. Morse, 1965 | *He misread my quietude . . . as either agreement or disagreement. It was neither. Pure, unadulterated disinterest*—Chinua Achebe, 1987 | *Despite British radio's disinterest in new music, and the reduced influence of the music press, I believe real talent will eventually get through*—N. York, 1991). At present the best course is to avoid the word in this meaning, either by using the more explicit phrase *lack of interest* or by rephrasing. (A form *uninterest* is occasionally found but is not generally current: *She had no idea . . . whether all men went through periods of uninterest*—Sebastian Faulks, 1989.)

2 The verb *disinterest*, meaning 'to rid of interest or concern' is marked 'now rare' in the OED but there are signs of its revival: *I try to disinterest myself from politics*—Aldous Huxley, 1923.

disinterested. **1** The use of *disinterested* to mean 'uninterested', although not a problem to Fowler (1926), is a keyword in current debates about correct usage. Those who rage most furiously are not always aware, however, that the word has changed its principal meaning several times during the nearly four centuries of its existence. It began by meaning 'not interested', then about 1650 developed the meaning 'impartial, unbiased', and has more recently tended to revert to its older meaning. These meanings reflect the different meanings of *interest*, as differently used in *They showed no interest in the idea* and *They have an interest in the business*.

2 The alternative word *uninterested* has had an opposite history, originally meaning 'impartial' and later meaning 'not interested', although it shows no sign of returning to its earlier meaning. The problem then lies with *disinterested*. Informed opinion is divided into those who believe that a useful distinction, between *disinterested* = impartial and *uninterested* = not interested, is being eroded, and those who are content to let *disinterested* serve as a synonym of *uninterested* as long as other words are available for the other meaning (*impartial, neu-*

tral, objective, unbiased, unprejudiced).

3 The following examples of *disinterested* show the strong presence of both meanings in current usage: (= impartial) *Many competent and disinterested experts on world poverty often stress the sterility of the East–West confrontation*—Encounter, 1981 | *She could imagine the coroner's disinterested voice*—J. Bedford, 1984 | *But of course none of the observers of twelfth-century England was disinterested*—Antonia Fraser, 1988 | *The doctor ran her hands round again, with the same disinterested precision*—Sara Maitland, 1990 | *The giant palms lining the road inspected me disinterestedly as I coasted along trying to find the Alcade Apartments*—P. Chester, 1990 | (= not interested: note that in this meaning *disinterested* is often followed by *in*, on the analogy of *uninterested*) *Washington ensured that he would appear to be what in fact he was, a republican gentleman disinterested in power*—Times Literary Supplement, 1988 | *Many women complain of feeling chronically tired, tied to the home, unattractive, disinterested in sex and generally overwhelmed during early parenthood*—J. Mattinson et al., 1989 | *She remains stubbornly neat and unadorned, disinterested in fashion*—S. Johnson, 1990 (Australia).

4 The recommendation must be to restrict *disinterested* to the meaning 'impartial' and to use alternative words when necessary to avoid possible misunderstanding. *Uninterested* remains the standard and recommended form in the meaning 'lacking interest': *I wouldn't say that—he was totally uninterested in both of us*—Graham Greene, 1980 | *He gave . . . a certain impression of being uninterested in people except at an agreeably superficial level*—D. Fraser, 1982 | *To* *viewers who are uninterested in polit-ics, it was worse than the World Cup—Observer*, 1990.

disk see DISC.

dislike *verb*. The normal con-struction is with an object, which can be a noun (*We dislike modern art*) or a verbal noun (*They dislike being absent*). It is non-standard to follow *dislike* with a *to*-infinitive, although this is sometimes found: *She was hounded by a fear of imminent poverty that made her dis-like to spend any money at all*—B. Guest, 1985.

dismissible is spelt *-ible*, not *-able*. See -ABLE, -IBLE.

disorient, disorientate. Both verbs have a long history (*disorient* being first recorded in 1655, *dis-orientate* in 1704) and both are still in use meaning 'to confuse (someone) as to whereabouts'. In most contexts *disorient*, being shorter, is preferable. The noun is *disorientation*.

disparate is in regular use in two main meanings, (1) 'essen-tially different or diverse in kind' (*disparate creeds | disparate modes of thought*) and (2) 'unequal' (*people of disparate ages | countries of disparate size*). The first mean-ing is the more common, al-though they tend to overlap. *Disparate* can qualify a singular (usually collective) noun or a plural noun: *Most of the conglom-erates which were made up of a dis-parate collection of businesses have failed*—D. Oates et al., 1989 | *Ma-chines can keep the disparate parts of such a system co-ordinated much better than men can*—*Economist*, 1991.

dispatch is the preferred form, not *despatch* (which was first re-corded, probably in error, by Dr Johnson).

dispel means 'to drive away in different directions, to disperse', and is used literally (*dispel clouds | dispel fog* etc.) and with general-ized abstract nouns (*dispel fear | notions | dispel suspicions*). It is not idiomatic to use *dispel* with an entity preceded by *a* or *an* that cannot be regarded as divisible (🗷 *dispel an accusation | dispel a ru-mour*); in these cases alternatives such as *rebut, refute*, etc. should be used.

dispensable is spelt *-able*, not *-ible*. See -ABLE, -IBLE.

dispenser is spelt *-er*, not *-or*.

dispersal, dispersion are both used to mean 'dispersing, spread-ing', but in non-technical mean-ings *dispersal* refers more to the process and *dispersion* to the re-sult. The following examples show the difference of emphasis: *More efficient dispersal of sulphur di-oxide at source cannot be regarded as an acceptable long term solution*—I. M. Campbell, 1977 | *Un-like the dispersals of the teacher-training college libraries, . . . those from the older Universities are fre-quently discussed and the causes and problems are widely realised*—W. J. West, 1992 | *In Yugoslavia, . . . there is a wide dispersion of incomes be-tween different regions.*—H. Lydall, 1989 | *It is wrong . . . to poison the sea with materials whose dispersion is difficult to control*—*Economist*, 1993.

disposable is spelt *-able*, not *-ible*. See -ABLE, -IBLE.

disposal, disposition. In gen-eral, *disposal* is the noun corres-ponding to *dispose of* (= get rid of) and *disposition* corresponds to *dispose* (= arrange). So *the disposition of the furniture* refers to the way the furniture is laid out, whereas *the disposal of the furniture* refers to its removal. *Disposal* also occurs in the fixed expression *at one's disposal*, and *disposition* has the special meaning 'temperament, natural tendency'.

disputable is now normally pronounced with the stress on the second syllable.

dispute is pronounced with the stress on the second syllable both as a noun and as a verb. A tendency to stress the noun on the first syllable, especially by northern trade-union leaders in the 1970s and 1980s has not established itself in standard English.

dissect means 'to cut into pieces', not 'to cut into two'; in other words, it is formed on the prefix *dis-*, not *di-*. The pronunciation is therefore di-**sekt**, not diy-**sekt**, although the second is often heard, probably under the influence of *bisect*.

dissemble means 'to pretend; to disguise or conceal' and should not be used to mean 'to take apart' as if it were a shorter form of *disassemble*. Example of correct use: *One of nature's innocents. He couldn't dissemble if he tried*—P. O'Donnell, 1971.

dissociate is first recorded in 1623, slightly later than its variant *disassociate*, and is now the more favoured form. It is followed by *from* and is often used reflexively (with *oneself* etc.): *The mother immediately dissociated herself from this conversation*—V. Glendenning, 1989 | *He is at pains to dissociate Reagan's party from the one he helped steer to victory in*

1968—*New York Review of Books*, 1990.

dissoluble, dissolvable are both pronounced with the stress on their second syllables. *Dissoluble* is the general word meaning 'capable of being separated into elements or atoms' and *dissolvable* is normally restricted to its meaning 'able to be dissolved in liquid'.

distensible means 'capable of being distended or stretched'; the alternative form *distendible* is now obsolete.

distil is now spelt with one *l* in BrE and with two *l*s in AmE. The inflections in both varieties are *distilled, distilling*, and the noun derivatives are *distillation, distiller*, and *distillery*.

distinct, distinctive. 1 Both words are related to the verb *distinguish*, but *distinct* means essentially 'separate, different' (*The word has several distinct meanings*) or 'unmistakable, decided' (*She has a distinct impression of being watched*), and is closer to *distinguishable*, whereas *distinctive* means 'characteristic, identifying' (*The bird has distinctive black and white wing markings*) and is closer to *distinguishing*. *Distinct* is often followed by *from* (*Holiness is distinct from goodness*), and this construction is common in the prepositional phrase *as distinct from*.

2 Examples of both words: (distinct) *Scrambling, as distinct from fell walking and rock climbing, is a Cinderella of a sport*—Guardian Weekly, 1978 | *It was a comparatively shabby office . . . Euram Marketing gave a distinct impression of watching the pennies*—G. Markstein, 1981 | *Software designers have used two* *distinct methods in their attempt to provide the perfect package*—Micro Software Magazine, 1982 | *I can still hear her distinct, rather emphatic, very self-assured speech*—R. Cobb, 1983 | (distinctive) *Everyone who knew the Temple School will remember the distinctive smell of Freddie's office*—Penelope Fitzgerald, 1982 | *Her main 'discovery' was the way in which Marx had challenged all previous political traditions*—D. May, 1986 | *Smooth, wedge-shaped styling makes for a distinctive appearance*—Times, 1980.

distinctly, as in *distinctly interesting*, belongs to the outer realms of Fowler's LOST CAUSES as a 1920s vogue word he much despised, less on linguistic grounds than because of the condescending attitude it revealed in the user, especially when used in combination with an otherwise complimentary word such as *fine* or *majestic*. Fowler had a point, and he would probably find confirmation of his opinion in more recent use, which often coyly distances the user from what is being said: *That night the singing was distinctly husky and out of tune*—J. B. Morton, 1974 | *He had a distinctly Arabic look about him, slicked-down black hair*—N. Thornburg, 1976 | *Religious references . . . to the Virgin Mary behaving in a way that is distinctly vampirish have been glossed over*—N. Tucker, 1981.

distribute should be pronounced with the stress on the second syllable, although stress on the first syllable is increasingly heard.

distributive in grammar means 'referring to each individual of a number or class'. Distributive adjectives and pronouns are words such as *each, every, either, neither*. A distributive plural is one that corresponds to individuals separately rather than jointly, as in *They wear gowns on formal occasions*, meaning each person wears one gown. In such contexts a singular noun is often idiomatic, and one could equally say *They wear a gown on formal occasions*.

distributor is spelt -*or* in all its meanings, not -*er*.

distrust, mistrust are largely interchangeable both as nouns and as verbs, although *distrust* is more common. Examples: (distrust) *He was labelled as a diehard and a bigot, when he actually distrusted the diehards and was himself distrusted by the bigots*—J. Ramsden, 1978 | *Just as quickly came the deep bitter distrust of all white people*—M. Darke, 1989 | (mistrust) *He didn't mistrust her exactly, there was just something he couldn't get to the bottom of*—Ann Pilling, 1987 | *Pornography and a fear of rape play a huge part in girls' mistrust of their own bodies*—J. Dawson, 1990.

ditransitive. A ditransitive verb is one that appears to have two objects, as in *He gave the baby a bottle* (= He gave a bottle to the baby; although suppression of a preposition is less clear when pronouns are involved as in *He gave her a bottle* and in idiomatic uses such as *He gave the girl a kiss*) and *They envied him his good fortune*.

diurnal is not an ordinary synonym of *daily* but has special technical meanings (especially in medicine and the life sciences) opposed to *nocturnal*: *Melatonin controls diurnal and seasonal adjustments of activity in many species*—Nature, 1970 | *During the last two hundred years, the European continent has seen a period of intensifying* persecution of the diurnal birds of prey—M. Bijleveld, 1974.

dive *verb*. In BrE the standard past tense is *dived*. In the 19c *dove* occurred in British and American dialect use and it remains a regular use alongside *dived* in northern parts of America and in Canada. It appears to have been first used in print by Longfellow (1855): *Straight into the river Kwasind Plunged as if he were an otter, Dove as if he were a beaver.* A modern American example: *The plane ducked and dove, the lights went out—New Yorker*, 1989.

diverse, divers. Both words once shared the meaning now confined to *diverse*, i.e. 'varied, unalike', qualifying singular and plural nouns, as in *Why is it so diverse, so varied in its character?—J. Houston*, 1990 | *Can a single author cover the diverse techniques of physical biochemistry?—New Scientist*, 1991. *Divers* now means 'several, sundry' without the notion of variety: *Evelyn Underhill (author of divers fat books on mysticism)—D. Davie*, 1991.

divest. The traditional uses of *divest* as a somewhat formal word meaning 'to undress' and, in the reflexive form *divest oneself of*, 'to dispossess oneself of', have been joined since the 1950s, first in AmE and then elsewhere, by the financial meanings 'to sell off (a subsidiary company)' and 'to cease to hold (an investment)'. The corresponding noun is *divestment*: *A 1966 decree requiring Von's Grocery Stores to divest a certain number of required stores . . . resulted in divestment of its forty least profitable outlets—New York Law Journal*, 1973 | *She advises American people to divest their investments in*

South Africa—*Christian Science Monitor*, 1986.

divisible is the current word meaning 'able to be divided', not normally *dividable*.

divorcee is the established word in either gender for someone who has been divorced. The French forms *divorcé* and *divorcée* are also used for a man and a woman respectively, and are useful when a gender-specific term is needed.

do *verb*. **1 GENERAL.** *Do* is one of the most productive and complex verbs in English, although a great deal of its use comes naturally to speakers of English as a first language. Essentially, *do* has two functions: (1) as an ordinary verb (*I am doing my work*), and (2) as an auxiliary verb forming tenses and aspects of other verbs (*I do like swimming* | *What do you think?*).

2 AS AN ORDINARY VERB. *Do* is used as an ordinary verb, with or without an object, in a vast range of meanings connected with activity of all kinds. The following examples are typical but not comprehensive: *I'll see what the children are doing* (= carry out, perform) | *Shall we do a casserole?* (= make) | *She did chemistry at university* (= studied) | *The garden needs doing* (= deal with, attend to) | *Have you done your teeth?* (= clean) | *Do as I do* (= behave, act) | *The school is doing Macbeth this year* (= perform) | *We did 100 m.p.h.* (= reach, achieve). There are also many colloquial uses which are best kept for informal conversation, e.g.: *We'll do the art gallery tomorrow* (= visit) | *They were done for shoplifting* (= prosecuted); and idiomatic expressions (*It'll do no harm* | *A hat does nothing for me* | *This will do us fine* etc.)

3 AS AN AUXILIARY VERB. In this role, *do* serves several key functions in relation to other verbs:

▶ **a** Forming negative statements (either as *do not* or as *don't*) and questions in which the main verb is a plain infinitive without *to*: *They do not want to come | I don't like it much | Do they want to come? | Don't you like it much? | Do they not want to come?*

▶ **b** Forming stronger or more emphatic positive statements: *I do like your garden | If you do come, you can stay with us | We did enjoy ourselves | Do remember the shops are closed tomorrow.*

▶ **c** Forming constructions in which the subject follows the verb (inversion): *Never did he want to try that again | Only after a long wait did he get to see the doctor | So angry did this make him that he had to leave the room.*

▶ **d** In so-called 'tag questions': *They don't like dancing, do they? | We met at the party, didn't we?*

▶ **e** In constructions in which *do* (or *do so*) stands for a main verb to avoid having to repeat it (called a *substitutive* function): *My wife likes travelling much more than I do | We said we'd buy one if you did too | We get on well and have done [so] for years | 'He said I could doss down here.' 'He couldn't have done.'* Note that uses of *do* following another auxiliary verb, as in the last example, are less common in AmE (which prefers *We get on well and have for years*).

▶ **f** There is also the emphatic construction, not recorded before the 18c, in which *do* (normally *does* or *did*) stands at the head of a subordinate phrase: *She likes the old books, Dickens and Jane Austen, does my old lady*—Kingsley Amis, 1988 | *He does have a sense of humour does Mr Marr*—Nigel Williams, 1992. This use is clearly conversa-

tional and should not be used in more formal contexts.

4 *DON'T HAVE = HAVEN'T GOT.* *Don't have* and *do you have* are more usual in AmE than the corresponding BrE *haven't got* and *have you got*, as in the following pairs of examples: (AmE) *I don't have any money* | (BrE) *I haven't got any money* | (AmE) *Do you have the time?* | (BrE) *Have you got the time?* *Don't have* is spreading into other varieties of English but still retains its American flavour: *We don't have any beer. Just red wine.*— *New Yorker*, 1986 (US) | *But you don't have a car*—M. Duckworth, 1986 (New Zealand) | *We don't have that kind of thing in my house, man*—A. Brink, 1988 (South Africa) | *'Don't you have central heating?' Clare asked*—F. King, 1988 (UK).

Question: Have you got a room for the night? Answer: Yes, we do. This apparently illogical use of *do*, replacing *have* as the auxiliary verb, arises because the question implicitly answered is *Do you have a room for the night?* It is a common pattern in AmE, and causes less surprise to British speakers now than formerly, since it has also become a feature of BrE. Note, finally, that Fowler's argument (1926) for rejecting *do have* and *don't have* in uses referring to particular instances (i.e. ✘ *Do you have a newspaper?* [at this moment] as opposed to *Do you have sugar* [habitually]?) was one of his weaker propositions and ignored the force of American usage.

5 CONTRACTED FORMS. The contracted forms *don't* (= do not), *didn't* (= did not), and *doesn't* (= does not), though not recorded in print before the 17c, are now customary in the representation of speech, and are gradually spreading into less formal business English, although it is best to avoid them in descriptive prose and in any writing intended for recipients not known to the writer.

6 I DON'T THINK. This is so idiomatic that its slight illogicality, once the cause of disapproval, now goes unnoticed. When you say *I don't think I've ever met anyone like you*, you mean to say *I think I've never met anyone like you*; but the second alternative, though possible, is far less natural in ordinary conversation.

7 NON-STANDARD USES. There are three non-standard uses of *do* which should be mentioned:

▶ **a** *done* = *did*. This is common in regional and uneducated speech in Britain and elsewhere: *I think it done him good* —Mark Twain, 1873 | *I never done anybody any harm* —Listener, 1969.

▶ **b** *don't* = *doesn't*: *He don't do much work*. This is generally regarded as illiterate.

▶ **c** *done* (= have already) is confined to American dialect: *I don't know what you need with another boy. You done got four* —E. T. Wallace, 1945.

do *noun*. The plural form is *dos* or *do's*.

do (the musical note). Use DOH.

dock in BrE is an artificially enclosed body of water for the loading, unloading, and repair of ships; in the plural it means 'a dockyard'. In AmE, however, a *dock* is a ship's berth or wharf.

docudrama is a word first recorded in AmE in 1961 for a dramatized documentary film, and it has since spread into BrE as, no doubt, will other *docu-*words such as *docusoap* (1990) and *docutainment* (1983; see also INFO-TAINMENT).

dodo has the plural form *dodos*.

dogged is pronounced as one syllable when the meaning is as in *He was dogged by misfortune* and as two syllables (**dog**-id) when the meaning is as in *He is a dogged fighter* (= tenacious, determined).

doh is the preferred spelling for the musical note, not *do*.

doily, meaning 'a napkin', is spelt like this, not *doiley* or *doyly*. It is named after a 17c London draper called *Doiley*.

doll's house is the normal form in BrE, but *dollhouse* is more usual in AmE.

Domesday, or in full *Domesday Book*, is the record of the lands of England made on the orders of William I in 1086. It is pronounced with the first syllable as in *doom*, and is a Middle English variant of the word *doomsday* meaning 'the day of the Last Judgement' (because the book was to be a final authority).

dominate, domineer. *Dominate* means primarily 'to exercise control or influence over' and is used transitively (with an object). *Domineer* is a more judgemental word meaning 'to behave in an arrogant and overbearing way' and is often used with *over* or in the adjectival form *domineering*: *The term ballbuster . . . is a graphic, forceful expletive, typically applied to a domineering female* —Verbatim, 1975.

domino has the plural form *dominoes*.

donate, meaning 'to give (money etc.) voluntarily', is a back-formation from *donation* and spread rapidly from American to British usage: *She could donate cer-*

tain organs to assist in research or spare-part surgery—Barbara Pym, 1977 | *The Silver Wink, donated by Prince Philip, is awarded to the winner of an annual elimination tournament* [in tiddlywinks] *for universities*—F. R. Shapiro, 1979.

doomsday see DOMESDAY.

double entendre means 'a word or phrase open to two interpretations, one usually *risqué* or indelicate'. The equivalent term in French is *double entente*, which is also occasionally used in the same sense in English.

double negative. 1 *He never did no harm to no one*—*The Archers* (radio broadcast), 1987. This, and other double negative constructions, can easily be found in all varieties of English used throughout the world. It is commonly associated with poorly educated East London English and Black English spoken in the US: *I don't take no money from no white folks*—*Chicago Tribune*, 1990.

2 It surprises many people, for whom double negatives are self-evidently wrong, to know that they were once an integral feature of standard English, and are to be found in Chaucer, Shakespeare, and other writers up to the 17c. For reasons that are no longer discoverable, the logic then changed: instead of compounding each other, a sequence of negatives came to be regarded as self-cancelling; in other words, an arithmetical argument replaced a linguistic one. Thereafter, playwrights put double negatives into the conversation of vulgar speakers, and 18c grammarians roundly condemned them.

3 In current English, a type of double negative is used with in-

tentional cancelling effect, as a kind of figure of speech as in *It has not gone unnoticed* (= It has been noticed). On the other hand, double negatives used to reinforce each other are taken as sure signs of a poor education and are rarely tolerated in normal speech. However, since attitudes have changed remarkably in the past on this issue, they may well change again.

4 Double negatives also occur, especially in speech, in uses of the type *You can't not go* (= you cannot consider not going, i.e. you have to go), in which *not go* is effectively a unified concept expressed in a verb phrase.

double passive see PASSIVE 2B.

double possessive. This is a construction such as *a friend of my father's* and *an admirer of hers*, in which the possessive state is indicated by *of* and the possessive form of the noun *father* or pronoun *hers*. It is well established in English alongside the simpler form (*a friend of my father*), and is useful in avoiding ambiguity by distinguishing between (for example) *a picture of the king* (= an actual portrait of the king) and *a picture of the king's* (= a picture owned by the king). Use of the double possessive is normally limited to nouns and pronouns denoting people, and so you would not normally say (for example) *an admirer of the British Museum's*. The use is also less idiomatic with nouns, as distinct from pronouns, when the relationship implied by *of* is not fully possessive, as in *an admirer of my mother* (= someone who admires my mother) as compared with *an admirer of my mother's* (= an admirer my mother has). But you would always say *an admirer of hers* and not *an admirer of her*.

double subject. This is a name for a construction in which a noun subject is followed by a supporting pronoun, as in Longfellow's *The skipper he stood beside the helm.* The OED describes this use as 'common in ballad style and now in illiterate speech'. Examples: *From time to time I clean. Mrs Pollypot she don't like cleaning.*—Mary Wesley, 1983 | *My cousin he didn't go to college*—Jessica Williams (citing a second-language learner), 1987.

doubling of final consonants in inflection.
See box opposite

doubt *verb.* **1** *I doubt whether he'll come* and *I doubt if he'll come* are the standard constructions when *doubt* is used in the affirmative to mean 'think it unlikely'. When *doubt* is used in the negative to mean 'think it likely', a *that*-clause is normal: *I don't doubt that he'll come.* The logic behind this difference is that when *doubt* is in the affirmative it implies uncertainty in the following clause (which is consistent with use of *whether* or *if*), whereas when it is used in the negative it implies probability in the following clause (which is more consistent with *that*).

2 This rationale lies behind the objection many people have to the increasing 20c use of *doubt* in the affirmative followed by a *that*-clause or by an object clause without a conjunction. This is commonly regarded as an Americanism, but it is attested in BrE use at the end of the 19c. Examples: (with *that*) *Schiller doubted that a poetic measure could be formed capable of holding Goethe's* *plan*—B. Taylor, 1871 | *I doubt that the White House is responsible for this rash of tittle-tattle*—Alistair Cooke, 1981 | *I doubt that the okapi which died . . . would agree with Mark Twain that 'Wagner is not as bad as he sounds'*—Independent, 1994 | (with object clause) *He doubted Ferrari would sue him*—New Yorker, 1986 | *I doubt there was anything really wrong with him*—Anita Brookner, 1992.

doubtful, dubious. **1** The constructions that follow *doubtful* correspond to the pattern outlined for *doubt* above, with *whether* and *if* still dominant but a *that*-clause now increasingly common: *It is doubtful that in the right-to-life controversy the rights of the unborn child will be inviolate*—A. E. Wilkerson, 1973 | *It is doubtful whether the Peloponnesian detachment was dispatched during the actual celebration of the Olympic games*—Classical Quarterly, 1976 | *Murray was doubtful as to whether this would be enough*—N. Tranter, 1987 | *Even if Amelia McLean had made more ambitious claims, it is doubtful whether anyone would have listened to her*—S. Reynolds, 1989 | *It was doubtful if Midge would ever again sleep in their old bedroom*—D. Rutherford, 1990 | *It seems doubtful that such an item would have been produced much after c.1550*—J. Litten, 1991.

2 *Doubtful* and *dubious* overlap in meaning but they should not be confused. *Doubtful* implies uncertainty about facts, whereas *dubious* implies suspicion about value or genuineness. Both words can be used of people or situations, but *dubious* is not normally followed by any of the constructions described above in relation to *doubt* and *doubtful*. The following examples (in addition to those already given) will clarify

doubling of final consonants in inflection

The table below explains the differing practice in English shown by the forms *hotter, enrolled, offered, targeted*, in which the root word (*hot, enrol, offer, target*) ends in a single consonant. Practice can also differ with the same word in BrE (e.g. *traveller*) and AmE (e.g. *traveler*). A key factor is the position of the stress in each case, and it is therefore useful to distinguish between words of one syllable and words of more than one syllable. The inflections and suffixes which affect the spelling in these ways are: *-ed* and *-ing* (in verbs); *-er* and *-est* (in adjectives); *-er* (forming agent nouns such as *traveller*); and *-y* (forming adjectives such as *rickety* or adverbs such as *initially*).

1 WORDS OF ONE SYLLABLE. Words ending in a single consonant double the consonant when adding any of the suffixes given above:

VERBS

beg	begged	begging	beggar
clap	clapped	clapping	
dab	dabbed	dabbing	
squat	squatted	squatting	squatter
throb	throbbed	throbbing	
rub	rubbed	rubbing	

An exception is *bus* (verb, = take people by bus), which has forms *bused, busing*.

ADJECTIVES

fat	fatter	fattest	fatty
glad	gladder	gladdest	
wet	wetter	wettest	

When the final consonant is *w*, *x*, or *y* this is not doubled:

VERBS

tow	towed	towing
vex	vexed	vexing
toy	toyed	toying

When the final consonant is preceded by more than one vowel (other than *u* in *qu*), the consonant is not normally doubled:

VERBS

boil	boiled	boiling	boiler
clean	cleaned	cleaning	cleaner
squeal	squealed	squealing	squealer

ADJECTIVES

clean	cleaner	cleanest	cleanly
loud	louder	loudest	loudly

▶

► doubling of final consonants in inflection
continued

2 WORDS OF MORE THAN ONE SYLLABLE. Words ending in a single consonant double the consonant when the stress is placed on the final syllable:

VERBS

allot	allotted	allotting	
begin		beginning	beginner
occur	occurred	occurring	occurrence
prefer	preferred	preferring	preference [*sic*]

Note the change of stress in *preference*, which affects the spelling. But the same exception as above applies to *w*, *x*, and *y*:

VERBS

guffaw	guffawed	guffawing
relax	relaxed	relaxing
array	arrayed	arraying

Words that are not stressed on the final syllable do not double the consonant unless it is an *l*:

VERBS

audit	audited	auditing	auditor
ballot	balloted	balloting	
benefit	benefited	benefiting	
bias	biased	biasing	
bigot	bigoted		
blanket	blanketed	blanketing	
budget	budgeted	budgeting	
carpet	carpeted	carpeting	
chirrup	chirruped	chirruping	
cosset	cosseted	cosseting	
crochet	crocheted	crocheting	
ferret	ferreted	ferreting	
fillet	filleted	filleting	
focus	focused	focusing	
gallop	galloped	galloping	
gossip	gossiped	gossiping	
hiccup	hiccuped	hiccuping	
leaflet	leafleted	leafleting	
market	marketed	marketing	
offer	offered	offering	
picket	picketed	picketing	
plummet	plummeted	plummeting	
profit	profited	profiting	
ricochet	ricocheted	ricocheting	

►

▶ doubling of final consonants in inflection
continued

VERBS *CONTINUED*

rivet	riveted	riveting	
rocket	rocketed	rocketing	
target	targeted	targeting	
thicken	thickened	thickening	
trumpet	trumpeted	trumpeting	
visit	visited	visiting	visitor
vomit	vomited	vomiting	

Exceptions in BrE:

input		inputting	
output		outputting	
kidnap	kidnapped	kidnapping	kidnapper
worship	worshipped	worshipping	worshipper

In AmE the forms are usually *kidnaped*, *worshiping*, etc.
In BrE words ending in *t* in the above list are the ones most likely to appear with a doubled consonant (under the influence of *fitted*, *fitting*), i.e. *budgetted*, *leafletting*, etc. *Focus* also sometimes inflects *focussed*, *focussing*. However, it is best to keep to the basic rule in these cases too.

Words ending in -*l* normally double the *l* regardless of where the stress is placed in the word:

VERBS

annul	annulled	annulling	
appal	appalled	appalling	
cancel	cancelled	cancelling	
channel	channelled	channelling	
chisel	chiselled	chiselling	
counsel	counselled	counselling	counsellor
dial	dialled	dialling	
dishevel	dishevelled	dishevelling	
enrol	enrolled	enrolling	
extol	extolled	extolling	
fulfil	fulfilled	fulfilling	
grovel	grovelled	grovelling	groveller
impel	impelled	impelling	
initial	initialled	initialling	
instil	instilled	instilling	
label	labelled	labelling	
level	levelled	levelling	leveller
libel	libelled	libelling	
marshal	marshalled	marshalling	
model	modelled	modelling	
panel	panelled	panelling	

▶

▶ **doubling of final consonants in inflection**
continued

VERBS CONTINUED			
quarrel	quarrelled	quarrelling	
revel	revelled	revelling	reveller
rival	rivalled	rivalling	
shovel	shovelled	shovelling	
travel	travelled	travelling	traveller
tunnel	tunnelled	tunnelling	

ADJECTIVES		
cruel	crueller	cruellest

Exceptions:

VERBS		
appeal	appealed	appealing
conceal	concealed	concealing
reveal	revealed	revealing
parallel	paralleled	paralleling

In AmE the final -l is not usually doubled:

	BrE (always)	AmE (usually)
cancel	cancelled	canceled
	cancelling	canceling
cruel	crueller	crueler
	cruelly	cruelly [sic]
dial	dialled	dialed
	dialling	dialing
duel	duelling	dueling
jewel	jeweller	jeweler
	jewellery	jewelry [sic]
label	labelled	labeled
	labelling	labeling
marvel	marvelled	marveled
	marvelling	marveling
travel	travelled	traveled
	travelling	traveling
	traveller	traveler

the differences between *doubtful* and *dubious*: (doubtful) *We're always a little doubtful about statements that have to be forced out of witnesses by revealing the extent of our prior information*—R. Hill, 1987 | *'Are you sure?' she said doubtfully*—T. Pratchett, 1990 | *If your tap water is of doubtful quality then you must be prepared to remedy the situation or use rain water instead*—Practical Fishkeeping, 1992 | *Then meeting Sophie's anxious gaze, she said briskly, 'Now don't look so doubtful.'*—M.

Bowring, 1993 | (dubious) *We still had the dubious privilege of representing two 'resting' actors*—M. Babson, 1971 | *Dreaming of luxury, of the quick buck dubiously acquired*—R. Barnard, 1980 | *Christine was a little dubious about Judith using brown eyeshadow, worrying that her eyes might end up looking bloodshot*—She, 1989 | *The right of people to know the human cost was overruled on the dubious grounds that this information could help the enemy*—Action, 1991.

doubtless, no doubt, undoubtedly, doubtlessly. 1 Fowler (1926) rightly noted that *doubtless* and *no doubt* convey probability rather than certainty about what follows, so that *They are doubtless* [or *no doubt*] *guilty* and *No doubt he* [or *He doubtless*] *meant well* connote no more than strong belief and reassurance respectively. If real conviction is intended, it is important to use *undoubtedly* or *without* (*a* or *any*) *doubt*, as is shown by substituting them in the example already given: *They are undoubtedly* [or *without doubt*] *guilty*.

2 *Doubtlessly*, for long made unnecessary by the adverbial role of *doubtless*, is beginning to reappear, at least in the US: *The current argument . . . doubtlessly offers a cogent and easily understood explanation for the current deadlock in East–West relations*—Washington Post, 1984.

dour, meaning 'severe, stern', is pronounced in BrE to rhyme with *tour* and not with *sour*, although the second pronunciation is common in AmE and Australian English.

douse, dowse. Three verbs are involved here: (1) *douse*, pronounced like the noun *house*,

meaning 'to doff (a hat etc.)', (2) *douse*, pronounced like the first one and possibly related to it, meaning 'to plunge into water', and (3) *dowse*, pronounced like the verb *house*, meaning 'to use a divining-rod to search for underground water or minerals'.

dove see DIVE.

down- is a productive 20c prefix forming verbs, e.g. *downface* (first recorded in 1909), *downgrade* (1930), *download* (in computing, 1980), *downplay* (1968), *downpoint* (1946), *downscale* (1945), *downsize* (1975), *downturn* (1909; also as a noun, 1926). Many of these are reversals of existing phrasal verbs (e.g. *play down, scale down*), but by no means all of them are (e.g. there is no form *size down* and *turn down* normally has a different meaning).

down-market, an adjective denoting the inferior end of the market, is so well established that it is surprising to find that its first record in the *OED* dates from no earlier than 1970.

downsize, meaning 'to reduce in size or scale', is first recorded in the 1970s with reference to the manufacture of smaller and more economical motor cars. In the US in the early 1980s it rapidly acquired its now primary meaning, in the euphemistic jargon of business management, of reducing the personnel of an organization by redundancies and other drastic measures: *Decline in demand for certain products and other factors 'make it imperative to downsize the business'*—Washington Post, 1983. It behaves like a so-called ergative verb in being used as an intransitive with the object made the subject: *New York* hospitals 'will downsize'—New York Times, 1986.

downstairs, downstair. Downstairs is the normal form for both the adjective (the downstairs lavatory) and the adverb (go downstairs). Downstair is occasionally found as an adjective, but not as an adverb.

down to, up to. 1 When referring to people and their actions, down to suggests obligation or responsibility whereas up to suggests opportunity. If you say It is up to them you imply that they have a choice about how to act, whereas if you say It is down to them you imply that they are responsible for acting or having acted in some way. Examples: The boom in Gucci and Pucci and . . . Lacoste 'names' on clothes, bags and other ornamentation is all down to the Yuppies—Sunday Telegraph, 1985 | It all came to a head when we lost 3–0 to Derby and, if I'm honest, all three goals were down to me—Today, 1992. The origin of this use is possibly connected with the phrase put down to, which has a similar meaning: My remarks . . . should be put down to my own lack of sympathy with the scientistic vision which Thomas upholds—Times Literary Supplement, 1980 | If that change can be put down to one man it is Bob Brett, who took over coaching duties . . . in February last year—Tennis World, 1992.

2 Down to and up to are used interchangeably in the meaning 'until' (up to the 19th century or down to the 19th century), except that the viewpoint is slightly different, up to being essentially forward-looking and down to retrospective.

downward, downwards. The only form for the adjective is downward (in a downward direction), but downward and downwards are both used for the adverb, with a preference for downwards in BrE: She ferreted in her bag; then held it up mouth downwards—Virginia Woolf, 1922 | Every time he looked downward he grew dizzy—J. M. Coetzee, 1983 | The fact that commissioners' careers only seem to go downwards after they leave Brussels has a negative effect on morale—EuroBusiness, 1989.

dowry, dower. The two words have a common origin (via French) in Latin dare 'to give', but now mean different things: a dowry (the more common word) is the property or money brought by a bride to her husband, and a dower is a widow's share of her husband's estate.

dowse see DOUSE.

dozen is a collective noun used in two ways, (1) as dozen, preceded by a numeral, meaning a unit of twelve (two dozen eggs), and (2) as dozens, in informal use, meaning 'very many' (We made dozens of mistakes).

drachm is a British unit of weight or measure formerly used in pharmacy, equivalent to one-eighth of an ounce (60 grains), or one eighth of a fluid ounce (60 minims) in liquid measure. The abbreviation is dr. See also DRAM.

drachma, the monetary unit of Greece (ancient and modern), has the plural form drachmas.

draft, draught. Draft, originally a phonetic respelling of draught, is used for (1) a preliminary sketch or version (She made a first draft of her speech), (2) a written order for payment by a bank, (3) a military detachment. A drafts-

man is someone who drafts documents. *Draught* is used in all other common meanings (game of *draughts*, a current of air, a ships' displacement, beer on *draught*, a dose of liquid medicine, a *draught*-horse). In AmE, *draft* is used for all these meanings and the game of *draughts* is called *checkers*.

dram is (1) a small drink of spirits, and (2) another spelling of DRACHM.

drank see DRINK.

drawing should not be pronounced with an intrusive -*r*- as if it were spelt *drawring*.

dream. For the past tense and past participle *dreamt* and *dreamed* are both used: *dreamed* is pronounced dreemd (and occasionally dremt) and *dreamt* is pronounced dremt. *Dreamt* appears to be somewhat more common in BrE than in AmE; and *dreamed* tends to be used more for emphasis and in poetry.

drier *noun* see DRYER.

drier, driest, drily are the comparative (= more dry) and superlative (= most dry) forms, and the adverb form, of *dry*.

drink. Notwithstanding a great deal of change over centuries of use, the standard forms in current use are *drank* for the past tense (*They drank tea*) and *drunk* for the past participle (*They had drunk tea*). See also DRUNK, DRUNKEN.

drink-driving is the form in BrE for the legal offence of driving a vehicle with an excess of alcohol in the blood; in AmE it is *drunk-driving*. The corresponding forms

for the offender are *drink-driver* and *drunk-driver*.

driving licence is the form in BrE, and *driver's license* is the form in AmE.

drunk, drunken. In general *drunk* is used predicatively (after a verb: *He arrived drunk*) and *drunken* is used attributively (before a noun: *We have a drunken landlord*). There is sometimes a slight difference in meaning, *drunk* referring to a particular occasion and *drunken* suggesting habit. *Drunken* also qualifies nouns for circumstances and events as well as people (*A drunken brawl ensued*). *Drunk* is used as a noun, meaning 'a person who is drunk'.

dry see DRIER, DRIEST, DRILY.

dryer is the preferred spelling for the noun meaning 'a machine or device that dries clothes, hair, etc.', not *drier*.

dual. Fowler (1926) described *dual* and (with better reason) *dualistic* as 'words of the learned kind', and warned against using them when alternatives such as *double*, *two*, and *twofold* were available. The danger was illusory, however, and *dual* causes no difficulty. In practice it has tended to form fairly fixed compounds, for example *dual carriageway* (first recorded in 1933), *dual control* (1913), *dual nationality* (1961), *dual personality* (1905), and *dual-purpose* (adjective, 1914).

due to. 1 The use of *due to* is one of the key topics of discussion in debates about correct usage, along with *infer/imply* and the split infinitive. As an adjective meaning 'owing, payable, attributable, (of an event etc.)

intended to happen or arrive' and so on, *due* + (optional) *to* causes little difficulty, and the following examples are unexceptionable: *Pay Caesar what is due to Caesar, and pay God what is due to God—New English Bible*, 1961 | *Incorrect speed is generally due to a worn idler wheel—Reader's Digest Repair Manual*, 1972 | *It was due to start at four o'clock, but didn't begin until twenty past—*William Trevor, 1976 | *Part of her happiness, her unaltered sense of her own superiority, was due to a sense of virginity preserved—*Anita Brookner, 1988. In all these uses, *due* is an adjective with a complement formed by the preposition *to* or by a *to*-infinitive, and they are compositional rather than idiomatic.

2 A problem arises when *due to* is used as a fixed prepositional phrase, on the analogy of *owing to* (which no one objects to in this way, for some reason), in which there is no noun or pronoun antecedent that *due* can be regarded as qualifying and no linking verb such as *be* or *become*. The purist view of the matter is that *There was a delay due to bad weather* is acceptable because *due* qualifies *delay*, whereas ✖ *The train was delayed due to bad weather* is unacceptable because *due* is grammatically unattached. (In some cases, it should be noted, the sentence can be construed either way, underlining the weakness of basing judgements about usage on close grammatical analysis: *Out in the countryside, two million people are at risk of starvation, due to the failure of the harvest—Independent*, 1996.) At present it is prudent to avoid this use of *due to* and to use alternatives such as *owing to, because of,* or *on account of*. However, *due to* is in strong pursuit of *owing to* and

will undoubtedly become standard in the 21c, if only because analogy is a powerful force and *due to* has the considerable advantage of convenience over its more awkward rival.

3 Examples of the disputed use: *Due to the incidence of Christmas and New Year statutory holidays it has been necessary to rearrange certain collection days—Alyn and Deeside Observer*, 1976 | *Michael . . . hated mathematics at school, mainly due to the teacher—Times Educational Supplement*, 1987 | *In the past 25 years the population has trebled due to the building program—East Yorkshire Village Book*, 1991 | *Cocaine smuggling charges against a well-known actress were dropped in 1988 due to legal bungling—Scottish Daily Mail*, 1998.

4 *DUE TO THE FACT THAT.* In this expression *the fact that* is used to turn a prepositional phrase into a conjunction. It can be awkward in use, and is often avoided by substituting *because*: *That this slippage is so slight is due to the fact that* [substitute *because*] *the other Enterprise staff have worked a great deal of extra time—Annual Report*, 1993. In some cases, however, this substitution does not work well, especially when there is a strong link between *due* and an antecedent noun, as in the following examples: *The success of the tampon is partly due to the fact that it is hidden—*Germaine Greer, 1970 | *Part of this frisson . . . is undoubtedly due to the fact that woman as a whole has been seen as a pacifying influence throughout their history—*Antonia Fraser, 1988.

dumb. **1** *Dumb* now has such strong connotations of stupidity and low intelligence that its original meaning, 'not able to speak', is often regarded as offensive. To be safe, it is better to use neutral terms such as *speech-impaired*.

2 The ailing fortunes of *dumb* as a verb have been revived by the emergence in the late 1990s of a new phrasal verb *dumb down*, meaning 'to make more simple or less intellectually demanding'. It has an irresistible immediacy of meaning and nuance: *Your headline 'Lords defy Straw over cannabis' . . . is another illustration of how sub-editors in search of a story dumb down serious debate—Guardian*, 1998. A new noun *dumbdown* (no hyphen, for simplicity) is eagerly awaited.

dumbfound, dumbfounded, meaning 'to nonplus, nonplussed', are formed on *dumb* and *confound* and should be spelt with a *-b-*.

dunno, a phonetic representation of *I don't know*, is first recorded in 1842 and is widely used in fiction and drama in illiterate or highly informal speech: *'Now it's back the way it used to be.' 'Why? . . . ' 'Dunno, sweet. Do not know.'—New Yorker*, 1986.

dustbin is the normal word in BrE for a rubbish bin, although *dustman* has largely been replaced by *refuse collector*. Neither *dustbin* nor *dustman* is used in AmE or in other varieties of English.

Dutch see NETHERLANDS.

duteous, dutiful. Both words mean 'observing one's duty' and

date from the 16c; Shakespeare used both, though with a preference for *duteous. Dutiful* is now standard.

dutiable see -ABLE, -IBLE.

dwarf. The traditional plural in BrE is *dwarfs*, although *dwarves* is increasingly found, perhaps under the influence of J. R. R. Tolkien, who used it regularly. In general use meaning 'a person of abnormally small stature', alternative terms such as *person of restricted growth*, though more awkward, are now preferable.

dwell in the meaning 'live, reside', is largely limited to literary contexts or special effect. The past and past participle is *dwelt*, not *dwelled*.

dye *verb* meaning 'to colour with dye', has the forms *dyes, dyed, dyeing*, to avoid confusion with the forms of *die* (*dies, died, dying*).

dyke, dike. In the meaning 'embankment', *dyke* is the preferred form. This is also true of the different (slang) word *dyke*, meaning 'a lesbian'.

dynamo has the plural form *dynamos*.

dynast, dynasty are pronounced **din-** in BrE and **diyn-** in AmE.

dysentery is pronounced in BrE as three syllables, and in AmE as four syllables, with stress on the first in both cases.

Ee

each. **1 SINGULAR OR PLURAL.**
Each is treated as singular when
it stands by itself as a pronoun,
when it comes before a singular
noun (*each house*), and when it is
followed by *of* and a plural noun
(*each of the houses*): *Each group is
responsible for its own quality
control*—A. Francis, 1986 | *Each of
the two key fobs has its own snap
fastening*—Sunday Express, 1981 | *Al-
most all accidents start with a simple
error on the part of the pilot that
leads to a chain of events, each of
which makes the situation worse*—D.
Piggott, 1991 | *What the treaty did
not do was to make the two king-
doms of France and England one;
they were to remain separate, each
with its own legal and administrative
identity*—C. Allmand, 1991. When
each follows and qualifies a plural
noun or pronoun, it is treated as
a plural since it is the noun or
pronoun and not *each* that determines the singular or plural status of the sentence: *They each
carry several newspapers, a whole
crop of the day's papers and the
Sundays*—Tom Stoppard, 1976 | *In
the last four beats of the third bar
. . . the voices each have slight differences in note-lengths and the placing
of syllables*—R. Brindle Smith, 1986.

2 EACH AND EVERY. This is regarded as a cliché and is best reserved for special effect as in
Sylvia Plath's allegory of the fig-
tree representing life: *I wanted
each and every one of them, but
choosing one meant losing all the
rest*—The Bell Jar, 1963.

3 EACH OTHER. The belief that
each other refers to two people or

things and *one another* to more
than two is a superstition already
rejected by Fowler (1926). Historical usage shows that there is no
basis for such a restriction, and
many contrary examples can be
found from good writers: (each
other referring to more than two)
*We took off in a motorcade traveling
at a speed of close to 100 miles per
hour with cars tailgating each other*—
Henry Kissinger, 1982 | *Everybody
knew each other or about each
other*—Anita Brookner, 1983 | *KHAD,
The Russians themselves, foreign
governments, the competing Afghan
political parties in exile—all spy on
each other*—New Yorker, 1987 | (one
another referring to two) *He and
Gussy were evidently very fond of
one another*—A. N. Wilson, 1978 |
*There is no such thing as complete
harmony between two people, however much they profess to love one
another*—Nadine Gordimer, 1987.

4 For the differences between
each and *every*, see EVERY.

early on is first recorded in BrE
in 1928 and only later in AmE. It
is a kind of back-formation from
earlier on, itself modelled on *later
on* (first recorded 1822). *Early on*
and *earlier on* are both now common in both BrE and AmE: *The
BBC recognised early on that there
was money to be made from selling
archive programmes on video*—New
Scientist, 1983 | *Early on, he puts a
coin in a newspaper vending-
machine*—New Yorker, 1987 | *Earlier
on, religion had supplied a drug
which most of the clergy were quite
ready to administer*—V. G. Kiernan,
1990.

earn has a past and past participle form *earned* (*They earned £200 a week | earned income*), although *earnt* is found from time to time in newspapers, reflecting its pronunciation and by analogy with *learnt*: *Ray and Alan Mitchell once worked gruelling hours and earnt good money as contract plumbers in London*—*Independent*, 1992.

earth is spelt with a capital initial (*Earth*) when it is regarded as a planet of the solar system. Like *Mars, Venus*, etc., it is then used without the (but note *the planet Earth*).

earthen, earthly, earthy. *Earthen* is used only in the physical sense 'made of earth' (either soil, or clay as in *earthenware*): *No city or government wants to build earthen structures or allow them to be built*—*New Scientist*, 1971. *Earthly* has two meanings, (1) denoting the earth or human life on earth, as distinct from *heavenly* (*They set themselves the difficult task of disentangling this cosmic dust from the earthly sort*—*Economist*, 1991) and (2) as an intensifying word in informal use in negative contexts (*A trainee is no earthly use in here at all*—M. Frayn, 1969). *Earthy* means (1) 'of or like the earth or soil', (2) figuratively, 'somewhat coarse or crude': *My friend Lindsey said I was consumed with earthy desires and unable to reach the higher planes*—S. Rowbotham, 1985 | *In one direction only a little earthy bank separates me from the edge of the ocean*—R. Sale et al., 1991 | *I'd been the typical first-year art-school person, entrenched in one style that was really landscapey—all earthy colours and shapes*—*Country Living*, 1991.

east, eastern, easterly *adjectives*. What is said here applies equally to *north, south*, and *west*, and their corresponding forms. *East* denotes physical position (*on the east side of town*) and is spelt with a capital initial (East) when forming part of a recognized name (*New York's East Side*), whereas *eastern* denotes regional and cultural association (*eastern forms of art*). *Easterly* is used chiefly of a wind blowing from the east (*an easterly wind | from an easterly direction*), and also of movement towards the east or a position achieved by this movement (*We took an easterly course | the most easterly part of the constellation*).

eastward, eastwards. The only form for the adjective is *eastward* (*in an eastward direction*), but *eastward* and *eastwards* are both used for the adverb, with a preference for *eastwards* in BrE: *Traffic snarled eastwards along Brompton Road at a snail's pace*—G. F. Newman, 1970.

easy is established as an adverb in fixed expressions such as *take it easy, have it easy, go easy on, easy does it*, and *stand easy*. Otherwise its use as an adverb is non-standard, though common informally in BrE as well as AmE: *We'd get a confession out of him easy as blinking*—R. Rankin, 1993. The main use of *easily* is in the meanings 'by far, by a wide margin', as in *The home team won easily*, and 'very probably' (*It could easily rain*).

eatable, edible. *Eatable* means 'fit to be eaten' and is normally applied to food, whereas *edible* means 'suitable for eating' and is often contrasted with what is poisonous or harmful (e.g. *edible mushrooms | edible snails*).

ebullient is pronounced with the second syllable as in *bulb*, not as in *bull*.

echelon. Gowers (1965) regarded the meaning 'a level or rank in an organization or in society' as a slipshod extension of the original English meaning 'a military formation of parallel rows'. Both meanings are in use, but the extended meaning is by far the more common. The word is derived from French (ultimately from *échelle* meaning 'ladder'), and it has developed in the same way in that language too.

echo has the plural form *echoes*. As a verb, it has inflected forms *echoes, echoed, echoing*.

ecology has spread rapidly in the 20c from technical to general use to mean 'the study of the interaction of people with their natural environment'. An earlier spelling *oecology*, reflecting its origin in the Greek word *oikos* meaning 'house' (the same root as in *economy*), is hardly ever used. *Ecology* has also produced the prolific prefix *eco-*, as in *eco-catastrophe* (1969), *eco-correct* (1994), *eco-friendly* (1989), *ecopolitics* (1973), *eco-terrorist* (1988), etc.

economic, economical. 1 These are both adjectives answering to the word *economy*: *economic* in the meanings 'relating to economics' and 'frugal, characterized by good economy', and *economical* in the meaning 'sparing in the use of resources'. An *economic cost* is one that is practical and makes good business sense, whereas an *economical cost* is one that is modest and not excessive.

2 The phrase *economical with the truth*, meaning 'saying just as much as is needed or relevant', is a political cliché of our times, recalling earlier notions of Burke and others that 'in the exercise of all virtues, there is an economy of truth'. In its present form it alludes to events of 1986, when the British Cabinet Secretary Sir Robert Armstrong, giving evidence during the 'Spycatcher' trial (in which the British government sought to prevent the publication of a book of that name by a former MI5 employee), referred to a former statement in the following way: *It contains a misleading impression, not a lie. It was being economical with the truth.* Phrases such as this are not easily forgotten, and allusive references abound, e.g.: *The world is full of minimisers: civil servants are economical with the truth, engineers want to cut down the weight of aircraft, bees use as little wax as possible—New Scientist*, 1994.

ecstasy is spelt *-asy*, not *-acy*. The drugs meaning is first recorded in the US in 1985 and is often spelt with a capital initial (*Ecstasy*).

ecu, ECU. Both forms are in use for the European currency unit, although the first is likely to prevail when the currency is established. Pronunciation differs between **ek**-yoo and **ayk**-yoo.

ecumenical, meaning 'relating to the whole Christian world', is spelt *ecu-* and not (as formerly) *oecu-*. The root is Greek *oikoumenē* 'the inhabited world'. The first syllable is pronounced either **ek-** or **eek-**.

-ed and -'d. The adjectival form *-'d* is often added instead of the more usual *-ed* when the root word ends in a fully pronounced vowel, e.g. *subpoena'd, shanghai'd*. Practice varies, however, and forms such as *antennaed, concer-*

tinaed, and *shampooed* are commonly found.

-ed see -T AND -ED.

-edly. 1 The suffix occurs in a number of familiar words such as *advisedly, allegedly, assuredly, deservedly*, and *unreservedly*, of which some date back to the 14c but most date from the 17c to 19c. In a lengthy article, Fowler (1926) listed these along with many highly abstruse and idiosyncratic forms that were unlikely to survive, such as *admiredly, ascertainedly, harassedly, incensedly*, and *statedly*, some of which were not even entered in the *OED*. There are also a few 20c forms, including *painedly, unashamedly*, and (not mentioned by Fowler) *reportedly*.

2 Normally *-edly* is pronounced as two additional syllables, even when the *-ed* element is not separately pronounced in the root words; this is true of all the words listed in the first sentence of the previous paragraph. That is to say, *advisedly, assuredly*, and *deservedly* are pronounced as four syllables, and *fixedly* and *markedly* as three. Formations from adjectives follow this rule only when *-ed* is pronounced as a separate syllable in the adjective, as in *cold-bloodedly* and *high-handedly* (four syllables), but not in *frenziedly, hurriedly*, and *shame-facedly* (three syllables).

3 A few awkward cases remain. One wonders how Browning would have pronounced *starchedly* in his *Red Cotton Night-Cap Country* (1873); and how D. H. Lawrence would have pronounced *painedly* in his *England, My England* (1921); and indeed how the *OED* editors articulated to themselves the forms *admiredly, depressedly, labouredly*, and *veiledly* when they set them down as part of the language. Many of these, however, are used too rarely to cause any real problem.

educable, educible. *Educable* is the adjective formed from *educate*, and *educible* the adjective formed from *educe* (= bring out, develop). See -ABLE, -IBLE.

-ee is an active suffix originally drawn from Old French words denoting the recipient of a grant or the like, as in *lessee* and *patentee*. In more recent formations, *-ee* denotes (1) the recipient of an action, often corresponding to an agent-noun in *-er* or *-or* (*addressee, amputee, employee, trainee*), (2) in a few cases, a person who performs an action or is associated with it (*attendee* = a participant at a conference or meeting, *escapee, refugee, standee* = a standing passenger). A few are peculiar to AmE, e.g. *enrollee* and *retiree*. The *-ee* in *bootee* and a few other words is a separate suffix of obscure origin; that in *goatee, jamboree, marquee*, and *settee*, is yet another (or possibly more than one).

-eer is a suffix first recorded in the 17c, replacing an earlier (French) form *-ier*. One of its first occurrences is in *mountaineer* (first used in Shakespeare's *The Tempest*, 1610, in the meaning 'one who lives in the mountains'). In more recent use, it has taken on disparaging connotations, as in *pamphleteer* (1642), *profiteer* (1912), *racketeer* (1928), and *marketeer* (originally 1832 in a neutral sense, now a person engaged in marketing in the sense of 'product promotion'). There are many derivatives in *-eering*, e.g. *buccaneering* (1758), *electioneering* (1760), *privateering* (1664), and associated verbs, some of them independently formed (e.g. *electioneer*, 1789) and others as back-formations (e.g. *mountaineer*, 1892).

effect *noun and verb* see AFFECT.

effective, effectual, efficacious, efficient.

1 All these words mean 'having an effect' of some kind, but with different applications and shades of meaning. *Effective* means 'having a definite or desired effect' that is actual rather than theoretical: *The toothbrush is undoubtedly the most effective weapon in the fight against bacterial plaque*—Daily Telegraph, 1971 | *She is most effective as a live performer of her own material*—New Yorker, 1975. *Effectual* means 'capable of producing the required result or effect', independent of a personal agent, and is often more theoretical than actual: *The rich ought to have an effectual barrier in the constitution against being robbed, plundered, and murdered, as well as the poor*—A. Arblaster, 1987 | *The rim of my hat, while effectually shading my eyes, did not obstruct my vision*—J. Davidson, 1991. A person cannot be described as *effectual* although he or she can be described as *ineffectual*, i.e. 'lacking the ability to produce results': *The Rangers' problems stemmed from the habit that . . . the team's general manager . . . had of hiring ineffectual cronies to coach the club*—New York Times, 1979.

2 *Efficacious* applies only to things, and means 'producing or sure to produce the required effect': *It is perhaps dubious to argue that a prayer or worship becomes more efficacious if more people join in*—S. Lamont, 1989 | *How can I persuade them, when they go to the bar, that a Perrier or a tonic water might be just as efficacious as alcoholic liquor?*—S. J. Carne, 1990. *Efficient* refers to a person's or thing's capacity to do work and produce results with minimum effort and cost: *You police spies don't seem to be a very efficient bunch, letting an old man be drowned while you are supposed to be keeping a watch on him*—G. Sims, 1973 | *Older systems can be improved with modern, efficient components and controls can be added to improve fuel economy*—Ideal Home, 1991. In recent use, *efficient* is sometimes preceded by an attributive noun that defines the scope of the efficiency: *Why not spend some of that money on improving public transport schemes—more energy efficient, safer and less polluting?*—C. Wheater et al., 1990.

effete is a 17c word originally meaning 'worn out by bearing offspring' (from Latin *fetus*) with reference to animals. It rapidly developed the transferred meaning '(of a material substance) that has lost its special quality or virtue', and by the late 18c was being applied to persons or systems that had lost their effectiveness. In the 20c it has come to be applied to effeminate men, though not, despite its etymology, to women who are or look as if they are past child-bearing age: *'Do you mind if I sit down?' asked the young man in effete, accented English*—R. Kee, 1991. It is still commonly used of ineffective institutions: *Somehow the whole fabric of society is softening, becoming effete*—R. Harrison, 1991.

e.g. is short for Latin *exempli gratia* and means 'for example'. It should be distinguished from *i.e.*, from Latin *id est*, which means 'that is to say'. In other words, *e.g.* illustrates whereas *i.e.* explains.

ego has the plural form *egos*.

egoism, egotism. **1** Both are 18c words for 'preoccupation with oneself' in various ways. There is no etymological difference to affect their meanings, and the intrusive -t- in *egotism* is unexplained. When Fowler wrote about these words (1926), *egotism* was the more popular form, and his prediction that *egoism* would oust it has not been fulfilled. It is useful to maintain a distinction: *egotism* is the general word for excessive self-centredness, whereas *egoism* is a more technical word in ethics and metaphysics for theories which treat the self as the basis of morality and sense-perception. In an extended meaning, *egotism* also means self-seeking conceit, whereas *egoism* is a more straightforward preoccupation with the self and an excessive use of *I*. The meanings are however so close that they will not stay apart in ordinary usage, nor will those of the corresponding personal designations *egoist* and *egotist* (although strictly an *egoist* is someone who subscribes to a type of morality based on the importance of the self and an *egotist* is a self-seeker) and of the adjectival forms *egoistic | egoistical* and *egotistic | egotistical.*

2 Some examples follow: (*egoism* and its derivatives) *I have never gone out of my way for man, woman, or child. I am the complete egoist*—Vita Sackville-West, 1931 | *How much of us will be recognisable in the pages of the history books of 2066? This egoist's niggle spiralled up into my mind*—New Statesman, 1966 | *He can retain his insights into another person, and use them in choices of means, without abandoning his long-term egoistic ends for the altruistic goals to which he briefly felt himself drawn*—A. C. Graham, 1985 | *He* [sc.

C. S. Lewis] *writes about it in unforgettably dramatic terms and with the sublime egoism (to use the word purely, with no pejorative sense) of a man alone with God*—A. N. Wilson, 1990 | *Hutcheson thought of himself as defending the reality of moral distinctions, and the genuineness of a morally good benevolence which was not egoistically based*—T. L. S. Sprigg, 1990 | (*egotism* and its derivatives) *Nothing so confirms an egotism as thinking well of oneself*—Aldous Huxley, 1939 | *He was continually talking about himself and his relation to the world about him, a quality which created the unfortunate impression that he was simply a blatant egotist*—H. Miller, 1957 | *To justify or to condemn them in public is a squalid piece of egotism when it will hurt the living*—C. Day Lewis, 1960 | *I had always thought him to be egotistical and attention-seeking*—D. M. Thomas, 1990 | *It amazed her that she'd ever believed herself in love with him, that she'd deluded herself into seeing his arrogance and his egotism as positive qualities*—S. Marton, 1993.

egregious. Of its two opposed meanings, 'remarkably good, distinguished' (as in Marlowe's *egregious viceroys of these eastern parts* in *Tamburlaine*) and 'remarkably bad', only the second is now in use, although it is also used to mean 'exceptional, unusual' more neutrally. The word comes from Latin *grex* meaning 'flock', and originally meant 'towering above the flock', i.e. 'prominent'. Modern examples: (with bad overtones) *His habit of surrounding himself with stooges and sycophants inevitably led to the debacle after an egregiously fraudulent election*—Washington Post, 1960 | *It may well be the case that an egregious idiocy has formed the basis of a political tradition*—Twentieth Century British

History, 1991 | *I have waited a long time to catch The Economist out on an egregious factual error—Economist*, 1993 | (neutral) *The inside is unified and austere, apart from an egregious baroque reredos, with a barrel vault*, [etc.]—J. Sturrock, 1988 | *He was truly egregious but a kind man and a good skipper—Dictionary of National Biography*, 1993.

eighties. This information is put here because *eighties* occurs first alphabetically, but it applies equally to *nineties*, *twenties*, *thirties*, and so on. These words, whether denoting decades or the years of a person's life, are spelt without an initial apostrophe, i.e. *eighties*, not *'eighties*.

either. 1 PRONUNCIATION. The pronunciations *iy*-dhə and *ee*-dhə are about equally common.

2 PARTS OF SPEECH. *Either* functions in two ways: as an adjective or pronoun, and as an adverb or conjunction. In all these uses, it means essentially 'one or other of two'; when more than two alternatives are involved an alternative word (such as *any*) or construction is often needed, at least in more formal contexts. (This aspect is discussed further in section 3 below.)

▶ **a** ADJECTIVE AND PRONOUN. *Either* means 'one or the other of two' (*Either book will serve the purpose* | *Either of you can go*) or 'each of two' (*We sat down on either side of the table*).

▶ **b** ADVERB AND CONJUNCTION. The basic meaning is 'as one possibility or alternative', and is normally balanced by *or* (*You may have either tea or coffee* | *Either come in or go out, but don't just stand there*). The position of *either* and *or* should be such that the

grammatical structures are correctly balanced, as in *Either I will go with John or I will stay here with you* but not in ✖ *Either I will go with John or stay here with you*. It is also used with a negative, normally at the end of a clause or sentence (*She didn't want to come, either* | *There is no time to lose either*).

3 EITHER WITH MORE THAN TWO. The essential duality of *either* is shown by the following example: *We either rely on our children to translate for us or we can try to catch up—Illustrated London News*, 1980. If the number of alternatives is extended to more than two, opinion is divided about the elegance and even the acceptability of the results; in general a greater tolerance is necessary in conversational English, but in formal English it is advisable to restrict *either* to contexts in which there are only two possibilities. In the case of the adjective and pronoun use, *either* should be replaced by *any* when a choice from more than two is involved (*Any of the books will serve the purpose*). It should be noted, however, that *any* can mean one or more than one, and so *any one* should be used when this is the meaning (*Answer any one of the following three questions*).

4 SINGULAR OR PLURAL AFTER EITHER. Normally *either* governs a singular verb (*Has either of you seen my pen?* | *Either John or Peter has got it*), but with the type *either of* (+ plural) a plural construction is sometimes used to emphasize the plurality of the statement as a whole, especially in inverted questions when the verb comes first (*Have either of you two ladies received an anonymous letter?—* A. E. W. Mason, 1924). Notional and grammatical agreement are in conflict in informal uses such as *Either John or Jane avert their eyes when I try to take their photograph*. When one of the alternatives is singular and the other plural, normal usage is to make the verb agree with the one closer to it (*Either the twins or their mother is responsible for this*). See also NEITHER.

ejector is spelt -*or*, not -*er*.

eke out. Fowler (1926) wanted to limit the use of this phrasal verb to refer to things that can be made to last longer or go further, i.e. a supply: 'you can eke out your income or a scanty subsistence with odd jobs or by fishing, but you cannot eke out a living or a miserable existence.' The use which he rejected has nonetheless been standard since the 19c, and it is futile to object to it: *Some runaway slaves . . . contrived to eke out a subsistence*—Darwin, 1845 | *He lived with his parents until their death, and thereafter eked out a marginal living as a messenger*—Oliver Sacks, 1985.

elder, eldest, older, oldest.
1 *Elder* and *eldest* mean the same as *older* and *oldest* but they are much narrower in their range of use, being applicable only to people and only as nouns or attributive adjectives (before nouns). You can say *his elder brother | her sister is the eldest | John is my eldest son | *but you cannot say ⊠ *John is elder than Paul | *⊠ *Which one is eldest? | Who has the elder car?* In these cases, *older* or *oldest* has to be used, as it can also in the cases where *elder* and *eldest* are legitimate.

2 *Elder* has special uses in *elder hand* (in cards), *elder* (= senior) *partner*, and *elder statesman*, and

(as a noun) is the title of lay officers of the Presbyterian Church.

elector is spelt -*or* not -*er*.

electric, electrical. In most contexts *electric* is the natural choice, especially to describe a device that works by electricity (*electric blanket | electric kettle*). *Electrical* is reserved for contexts in which the meaning is, more generally, 'relating to or concerned with electricity', as in *electrical engineering*.

elegant variation is the name Fowler (1926) gave to a celebrated article, nearly six columns long, on misguided avoidance of repetition which leads the user into stylistic traps that are anything but elegant, such as using *women* and *ladies*, *cases* and *instances*, or *have, possess*, and *own* in parallel uses in the same sentence, for example *The total number of farming properties is 250,000; of these only 800 **have** more than 600 acres; 1,600 **possess** between 300 and 600 acres, while 116,000 **own** less than eight acres apiece*. Another kind of variation is represented by the sentence *We much **regret** to say that there were very **regrettable** incidents at both the mills*. Although he found fault with Thackeray (*careering during the season from one great dinner of twenty **covers** to another of eighteen **guests***), Fowler's main targets were 'minor novelists and reporters'. A modern type of elegant (or not so elegant) variation occurs frequently in journalism, and involves the substitution of a general description for a specific name, for example: *Today **Mother Teresa** announced she is so moved by the plight of the Romanian children she is going to do something about it. **The Nobel Peace***

prize winner will open a mission in Bucharest to care for the children.

elegy, eulogy. An *elegy* was originally a lament for the dead, of which literary examples are Milton's *Lycidas* (1637) and Shelley's *Adonais* (1821). In the course of time, it came to mean any sorrowful poem or one written in the metre associated with elegies, as in Gray's *Elegy Written in a Country Churchyard* (1751). A *eulogy* was originally a speech honouring a dead person, and has come to mean more generally anything formally written or spoken as a personal tribute.

elemental, elementary. Elemental refers primarily to the forces of nature and in particular to the ancient belief in the 'four elements' of earth, water, air, and fire, as in *elemental fire | elemental forces | elemental spirits |* etc. Elementary, on the other hand, means 'rudimentary, introductory', as in *elementary school | elementary mathematics |* etc. In modern physics, elementary means 'not able to be decomposed', as in *elementary particle.*

elevator is the word used in AmE and sometimes elsewhere for what in BrE is called *lift*. However, Americans as well as Britons use the word *ski-lift* for the device that carries skiers up a slope.

elicit, illicit. Confusion arises occasionally because both words are pronounced the same way (i-**lis**-it). *Elicit* is a verb meaning 'to draw out or evoke (an answer, admission, etc.)' whereas *illicit* is an adjective meaning 'unlawful, forbidden'.

eligible, illegible. These are more likely to be confused in casual speech than in considered writing. *Eligible* means 'fit or entitled to be chosen' (*eligible for a pension*) or 'desirable, suitable' (*an eligible bachelor*). *Illegible* means '(of writing) not clear enough to read'.

ellipsis. 1 MEANING. Ellipsis is the omission from a sentence of words which are normally needed to complete the grammatical construction or meaning. It occurs most often in everyday speech, in expressions such as *Told you so* (= I told you so) and *Sounds fine to me* (= It *or* that sounds fine to me), and also occurs regularly in all kinds of spoken and written English.

2 IDIOMATIC ELLIPSIS. Ordinary English grammar normally calls for the omission of certain elements, especially when they might otherwise be repeated from a previous occurrence in the same sentence. Examples are the definite article (*He heard the whirr and ⋀ click of machinery*), the infinitive marker *to* (*I was forced to leave and ⋀ give up my work at the hospital*), the subject of a verb (*I just pick up wood in a leisurely way, ⋀ stack it and ⋀ slowly rake the bark into heaps*), and the verb itself after *to* (*Knowledge didn't really advance, it only seemed to ⋀*) or after an auxiliary verb (*We must ⋀ and will rectify the situation*). More complex forms of ellipsis occur in literature, often for special effect: *Henriques knew they would eat his tongue for wisdom, ⋀ his heart for courage and for fertility ⋀ make their women chew his genitals*—N. Shakespeare, 1989. Other examples are given by S. Greenbaum, *Oxford English Grammar* (1996), 77–8.

3 UNACCEPTABLE TYPES. The extent to which English allows words to be omitted in these ways is determined by what can reasonably be supplied by the hearer or reader from the rest of the sentence, without causing ambiguity or confusion. Ellipsis is not possible when the omitted word is not identical in form and function to its role where it is present, as in ⊠ *No state has* ∧ *or can adopt such measures*, in which the word to be supplied is *adopted*, not *adopt*. Nor is it permitted when there is a change from active to passive in an omitted verb, as in *Our officials ought to manage things better than they have been*, in which the word to be supplied is *managed*, not *manage*; nor again when the construction changes, as in *The paintings of Monet are as good* ∧ *or better than those of van Gogh*, which should read . . . *are as good as or better than those of van Gogh*. Less obviously wrong, but best avoided, are cases where number (singular / plural) changes, as in Fowler's characteristically gruesome example *The ring-leader was hanged and his followers* ∧ *imprisoned* (with ellipsis of *were*).

4 OMISSION OF *THAT* IN RELATIVE CLAUSES. See THAT 3B.

5 ELLIPSIS IN NON-STANDARD SPEECH. Ellipsis of auxiliary verbs such as *can*, *do*, and *have* is a feature of non-standard speech in AmE: *Well how you expect to get anywhere, how you expect to learn anything?*—E. L. Doctorow, 1989 | *Watergate, man. Where you been?*—M. Doane, 1988.

6 PUNCTUATION MARK. *Ellipsis* is also used to mean a punctuation mark consisting of (usually) three full points to mark either a pause or the intentional omission of words (for example in quoting). When the omission comes at the end of a sentence, it is normal to add a fourth point to mark the full stop.

else. **1** The usual possessive forms are *anybody else's*, *someone else's*, etc., and not (for example) *anybody's else*, although this was used until the mid-19c: *They look to me like someone else's, to be frank*—Penelope Lively, 1987 | *English feudalism was like anyone else's*—London Review of Books, 1988.

2 In questions, *else* invariably follows an interrogative pronoun, as in *What else did he say?* Postponement of *else* to the end of the sentence, as in *What did he say else?*, although possible up to the early part of the 20c, is no longer grammatical.

3 Thus use of *else* as a conjunction to mean 'otherwise, if not', which is common in literature since the Middle Ages, now seems archaic but is still found in informal speech: *Fortunately it* [sc. a staircase] *was not spiral, else I would have succumbed to vertigo*—B. Rubens, 1985.

elusive, illusory. The confusion here has been greatly reduced by the virtual disappearance from the scene of the forms *elusory* and *illusive*. This leaves *elusive* as the adjective from *elude*, meaning 'difficult to grasp (physically or mentally)', and *illusory* as the adjective corresponding to *illusion*, meaning 'deceptive, not real or actual'. Examples of each: *Preparations are now complete and they set off in a few days' time to try and capture that elusive denizen of the deep*—the Loch Ness Monster—Stornoway Gazette, 1971 | *I must warn you that paper profits are often illusory*—D. Westheimer, 1973.

e-mail, short for *electronic mail*, is a term that has become rapidly familiar with the advance of technology over the last ten years or so. It is often spelt with a hyphen, presumably to afford some extra status to the prefix *e*, although this has not shown much sign yet of forming other words of this kind. Its grammatical behaviour follows that of *mail*, i.e. it is a noun and a verb; you can *e-mail* messages and you can *e-mail* people.

embargo has the plural form *embargoes*.

embarrass, embarrassment are spelt with two *r*s and two *s*'s.

embed is spelt *em-*, not *im-*.

emigrant, immigrant, migrant.
1 An *emigrant* is someone who leaves his or her home country to live in another country; and an *immigrant* is one who comes to live in a country from abroad. The same person is therefore an *emigrant* on going through the exit gate at a port or airport and is an *immigrant* when given permission to take up residence in the country of arrival. The corresponding verbs are *emigrate* and *immigrate*. (Note one *m* in *emigrant* etc. and two *m*s in *immigrant* etc.)

2 A *migrant* is either (a) a migrating animal or bird, or (b) in Australia and New Zealand, an immigrant. An *émigré* (French = having emigrated) is a political emigrant, originally one from France during the French Revolution.

emote is a back-formation meaning 'to express emotion'. It is first recorded in America in 1917, and has been largely restricted to the language of ballet and theatre critics and to photography: *The female sitter had to emote in some way, either by dressing up or by gazing with drooping head into a bowl of flowers—Amateur Photographer*, 1970 | *How are you going to get up and emote in front of an audience?—L. S. Schwartz*, 1989.

emotional, emotive. *Emotional* and *emotive* both mean 'connected with or appealing to the emotions', but *emotional* is the word more often used in the neutral sense 'relating to emotions' whereas *emotive* has a stronger sense of 'causing emotion': *In this oppressive society women need the care and emotional support of other women—A. Wilson*, 1988 | *The whole subject of removing children from their parents was no less emotive for them than for other members of the community—R. Black*, 1992. *Emotional*, but not *emotive*, also means 'easily affected by emotion' with reference to people (*All of us get elated and emotional as we stroll through a pine grove on a hot summer day when the old trees fill the air with their pungent fragrance—P. Heselton*, 1991). *Emotive* is more commonly used of words or behaviour that tends to arouse emotions, and often qualifies words such as *issue, language, topic*, etc. (*He was just firing a smokescreen of emotive words and phrases—Gavin Lyall*, 1982), whereas *emotional* describes feeling and actions that involve emotion in themselves (*From a good script will emerge a film in which every scene carries an emotional charge—J. Park*, 1990). However, the considerable overlap in meaning is shown by the fact that the two words could be exchanged in the last two examples without causing any major difference to the way they are understood.

empathy. **1** This is originally a term used in psychology and aesthetics meaning 'the power of identifying oneself mentally with (and so fully comprehending) a person or object of contemplation'. In general use it tends to replace *sympathy* or *feeling for* when these words are sometimes more appropriate; *sympathy* can be felt without the element of personal experience that is implied by *empathy*: *Seeing our sadness, our empathy with the pain she was surely suffering, she said, 'What's wrong with you all?'* —A. Davis, 1975 | *It was a hard life, and Byron recounts it with empathy and gusto*—Anthony Burgess, 1986. It also gained some currency from educationists who established a fashion for teaching history by getting pupils to feel *empathy* for (or *empathizing* with) people of other ages, as an antidote to preoccupation with political history. But all that has changed again.

2 The corresponding adjective is either *empathic* (probably the more usual form) or *empathetic*.

employee has replaced *employé* (feminine *employée*) as the dominant form in BrE for someone who is employed. In AmE the alternative form is *employe*, pronounced as three syllables and usually stressed on the second.

emporium is a formal word for a large retail store or a centre of commerce. The principal plural form is *emporia*, although *emporiums* is increasingly found.

empower, empowerment. *Empower* is a 17c verb meaning 'to give power or authority to'. In the 1970s it acquired a new meaning, 'to make (someone) able to do something', implying the freedom to adopt moral values and principles of one's choice as advocated by members of the New Age movement and others. A person who is *self-empowered* is able to act independently of the constraints imposed by conventional values: *These self-empowered individuals are motivated by teamwork and developing broader skills rather than just achieving conventional status*—*Independent*, 1995. The corresponding nouns are *empowerment* and *self-empowerment*.

-en adjectives. The practice of adding -*en* to nouns denoting a substance, as in *golden*, *silken*, and *woollen*, dates from Old English. From the earliest time, however, and especially from the 16c, there has been a tendency to use the corresponding noun attributively (before another noun), as in *a gold* [not *golden*] *brooch* and *silk* [not *silken*] *curtains*. By this process, forms in -*en* have been enabled to develop figurative meanings, so that we are now much more likely to encounter *brazen impudence* than *brazen rods*, *leaden skies* rather than *a leaden roof*, and *a silken touch* rather than *silken curtains*.

enamel has the forms *enamelled*, *enamelling* in BrE and *enameled*, *enameling* in AmE.

enamour is commonly used in the form *be enamoured of*, or sometimes *be enamoured with*, usually in negative or ironic contexts: *I am not so much enamoured of the first and third subjects*—Dickens, 1866 | *Not all feminists were so enamoured with such tactics*—F. Mort, 1987 | *He was also not enamoured of the music, although he later found it much more enjoyable*—M. Hodkinson, 1990. The US spelling is *enamor*.

en bloc, meaning 'as a whole', was adopted into English in the later 19c, and is now normally regarded as naturalized, i.e. printed in ordinary Roman type.

enclose is the correct form for the word meaning 'to close in, include, etc.', not *inclose*.

encomium, meaning 'a formal expression of praise', has the plural form *encomiums* or occasionally *encomia*.

encrust, meaning 'to cover with a crust', is preferable to *incrust*.

encyclopaedia, encyclopedia. This word is first recorded in English in the 16c, and was adopted from a late Latin word which in turn was based on a supposedly corrupted form of a Greek term meaning 'general education' in the arts and sciences. The form *encyclopedia* is now very common in book titles, especially of books of general information as distinct from books on special areas of knowledge, where the older form *encyclopaedia* is still holding its own.

endeavour is the spelling for the noun and verb in BrE, *endeavor* in AmE. See FORMAL WORDS.

ended, ending. *Figures for the period ending | ended 31 December.* In referring to periods of time, *ended* is used to denote the terminal date when the time is in the past, and *ending* when the time is in the future or (in current use) in the past; so *ending* is never wrong. The word used of the initial date is always *beginning*, never *begun*.

endemic, epidemic. An *endemic* disease is one that is regularly or only found among a particular people or in a particular region, whereas an *epidemic* disease is a temporary but widespread outbreak of a disease. *Epidemic*, but not *endemic*, also functions (more usually) as a noun. Both words have extended meanings in relation to things other than diseases: *It is among managerial and professional workers that sponging, skiving and malingering is epidemic*—New Society, 1975 | *Recurrent energy crises are endemic in African agricultural societies*—G. T. Nurse, 1985.

end of the day. *At the end of the day* is one of the less attractive 20c clichés. It is first recorded in 1974 and means no more than 'eventually, when all's said and done': *But, at the end of the day, it is an amateur sport and everyone is free to put as much or as little into the game as he chooses*—B. Beaumont, 1982.

endorse, in its modern marketing meaning 'to give one's approval to (a product)' was labelled by the *Concise Oxford Dictionary* in 1914 as 'vulgar in advertisements'. Its original meaning is 'to write on the back of (a document)', from Latin *dorsum* 'back', with various applications in law and commerce. In the 19c it came to mean 'to support (an opinion)', from which the use in advertising developed.

end product, end result. These have both been criticized for containing an element of redundancy, since both a product and a result must necessarily come at the end, but they are well established. *End product* was first used in chemistry by Rutherford to describe 'a stable, non-radioactive nuclide that is the final product of a radioactive series' (*OED*).

enforce is the correct spelling, not *inforce* (which however survives in *reinforce*). Its typical grammatical objects are such things as a law, an action, a person's wish, etc. Occasionally an older construction is found with a person as object followed by a *to*-infinitive, on the analogy of *force* (*Are the companies legally enforced to complete the forms?*—radio broadcast, 1978).

enforceable is the correct spelling, not *enforcable*.

England, English see BRITAIN.

English worldwide. English is used as a first language by an estimated 350 million people, and as a second language by over 400 million people (estimates vary widely.) There are many varieties and styles of English in different parts of the world; see the separate entries for AMERICAN ENGLISH, AUSTRALIAN ENGLISH, BLACK ENGLISH, DIALECT, ESTUARY ENGLISH, STANDARD ENGLISH. The diversity of English is reflected in the title of a recent (1998) book by Tom McArthur, *The English Languages* (plural).

enhance means 'to improve or intensify (something already good)' and is used typically with reference to achievements, reputations, values, etc. It is not used with a person as object; *The book enhanced his reputation* is correct, but *The publication of his book enhanced him* is not.

enjoin. 1 *Enjoin* has meanings connected with commanding and issuing instructions, and is typically used in three constructions: (1) you enjoin a person *to* do something, (2) you enjoin something *on* a person, and (3) you enjoin *that* something should happen. Fowler (1926) wrote that the first of these 'is not recommended', but his reasons were not convincing even then and this construction is now too common and useful to be objected to: *The church had enjoined the faithful to say an Ave Maria*—Barry Unsworth, 1985.

2 In an almost opposite meaning, in use in legal language since the 16c, *enjoin* means 'to prohibit or forbid'; in this meaning it can refer to a person or thing, and is followed by *from*: *The Al-Fayed brothers . . . sought to enjoin the Observer from publishing the results of its continuing enquiries*—Observer, 1986 | *Because the Times by now had been enjoined from publication*—Bulletin of the American Academy of Arts and Sciences, 1989.

enjoy continues to be used with reference to things that are the complete opposite of enjoyable (such as ill health or a poor reputation), despite its identification as a 'catachrestic' (incorrect) use in the OED: *Despite the jokey reputation that middle-class British hotels enjoy, they compare very well indeed for comfort with their European and US counterparts*—Homes & Gardens, 1970 | *The Japanese Prime Minister . . . enjoys an even lower popularity-rating . . . than President Nixon*—Listener, 1974. This use is no more than an apparently illogical development of meaning characteristic of all languages, and it is well established.

enormity, enormousness.
1 Both words are derived from Latin *e norma* meaning 'out of the ordinary', and both originally had meanings associated with wicked and criminal aspects of abnormality. *Enormity* (15c) is older than *enormousness* (17c), and its first recorded meanings are 'a breach of the law, a crime'. Both words have also been used unexceptionably at different times to mean what *enormousness* now

means, 'very great size', but by the end of the 19c *enormity* was confined again to its special meaning, 'great wickedness', as in *The enormity of the crime shocked everyone*, and to its concrete use as in *The regime inflicted many enormities on its opponents*. This distinction continues to be defended by many advocates of careful usage in most contexts.

2 Because *enormousness* is such an awkward word, and alternatives such as *hugeness* and *immensity* are not much better, *enormity* is beginning to compete with it again (especially in AmE) in contexts that have nothing to do with wickedness, depravity, and suchlike, but these uses are likely to attract disapproval: ✖ *A wide-angle lens captures the enormity of the Barbican Centre, London's new arts complex*—*Times*, 1982 | ✖ *The enormity of such open spaces momentarily alarms her*—Susan Johnson, 1990 (Australia) | ✖ *Menzies was wilting under the enormity of the work*—D. Craig, 1991.

3 In the examples that follow, *enormity* is used correctly according to the criterion given above: *Hanging would seem quite a lenient sentence considering the enormity of his crime in those harsh old days*—R. Long, 1990 | *I did not know then that one frequently fails to live up to the enormity of death*—Anita Brookner, 1990 | *The enormities of the Hitler regime and the Holocaust opened up many fields of research into the workings of minds*—J. Lawson, 1991. There is a practical point to be made, that generalized use of *enormity*, given its special meaning, can lead to ambiguity in contexts such as *We all recognize the enormity of their achievement*, when the achievement in question might anyway be open to different interpretations. However,

meanings legitimately overlap in sentences such as the following: *She tried to be a strength for her daughter, but was overwhelmed by the enormity of what was happening to them all*—R. Black, 1992.

enough, sufficient, sufficiently. 1 *Enough* functions as both an adjective and an adverb, whereas *sufficient* requires modification as *sufficiently*. As an adjective (or modifier), *enough* will normally serve, but *sufficient* is more idiomatic when a more qualitative point is being made. For example, in the sentence *It was not sufficient for the tribunal merely to establish by whose hand information . . . was improperly leaked*—*Daily Telegraph*, 1971, *sufficient* implies a stronger element of disapproval of the inadequacy than would be the case if *enough* had been used. *Enough* also has two grammatical characteristics that are not shared by *sufficient*: (1) *enough* cannot be used with mass nouns denoting quantity, such as *number, supply*, etc., preceded by the indefinite article; you can say *a sufficient number* but not ✖ *an enough number*, and (2) *enough* can be placed postpositively (after the word it qualifies), as in *They have money enough for a holiday* and *They do not have a large enough house*, which places a greater emphasis on the commodity or attribute in question.

2 Choice between *enough* and *sufficiently* when they are used as adverbs is normally determined by the degree of formality needed, *sufficiently* being the more formal. The main grammatical difference between them is that *enough* is placed after the word it qualifies when this is an adjective or another adverb: *He was not firm enough* and *She did not sing well enough* but *He was not sufficiently* *firm* and *She did not sing sufficiently well*. There is no difference in use when they qualify verbs or clauses: *They are not working enough* and *They are not working sufficiently*.

enquire, enquiry, inquire, inquiry. The forms in *en-* and *in-* have long been largely interchangeable. At present the *in-* forms are dominant in all meanings in AmE, whereas in BrE there is a tendency to prefer the *in-* forms for official or formal types of investigation and (to a lesser extent) the *en-* forms for routine or general types of information-seeking. The differences in BrE are seen in these typical collocations: (formal investigation) *inquiry agent | judicial inquiry | a committee to inquire into child abuse |* (general information-seeking) *| I enquired after her health | There were several enquiries about the job | Try directory enquiries.*

enrol is spelt with one *l* and is inflected with two *l*s in *enrolled, enrolling, enroller*, but there is only one *l* in *enrolment*. In AmE, there are two *l*s in all these forms, including *enroll* itself.

ensure see ASSURE.

enterprise is spelt *-ise*, not *-ize*.

enthral is spelt with one *l* and is inflected with two *l*s in *enthralled, enthralling*, but there is only one *l* in *enthralment*. In AmE, there are two *l*s in all these forms, including *enthrall* itself; and there is a variant *inthrall*.

enthuse is a 19c back-formation meaning 'to show enthusiasm' or 'cause enthusiasm in', and is used with and without an object; you can enthuse people, enthuse *over* something, or simply en

thuse. Although regarded with disfavour by those for whom verb back-formations are second-class words, it is here to stay, and serves a useful purpose.

entitled means 'having a right or claim to' and should not be used as a synonym of *liable* (to a penalty), as in *Germany suffered bitterly and was entitled to suffer for what she had done*. Here *was entitled to* should be replaced by *deserved to*.

entrench, meaning 'to establish firmly', is spelt *en-*, not *in-*.

envelop, envelope. *Envelop* (with stress on the second syllable) is the form for the verb, meaning 'to wrap up, surround, etc.', and it inflects *envelops, enveloped, enveloping*. *Envelope* (with stress on the first syllable, now normally pronounced **en-** rather than **on-**) is the form for the noun, meaning 'a container for a letter, etc.'.

-en verbs from adjectives. *See box overleaf*

environs, meaning 'the surrounding area of a place', is a plural noun and should be pronounced in-**viy**-rənz, with the same pattern as in *environment*.

envisage, envision. 1 *Envisage* is an early 19c loanword from French, meaning at first 'to look in the face of' and then (its current meaning) 'to have a mental picture of (something yet to happen)'. Fowler (1926) dismissed it as an 'undesirable Gallicism' and recommended as alternatives the words *face, confront, contemplate, recognize, realize, view,* and *regard*. Gowers (1965) added *imagine, intend,* and *visualize* to the list of words for which *envisage* was 'a

-en verbs from adjectives

1 There are about fifty verbs ending in *-en* (e.g. *cheapen, harden*) which have been formed from adjectives. The table given below shows that this process of verb formation was at its most productive in Middle English and in the early modern period up to about 1700. There is only one possible pair before the Norman Conquest (11c), namely the Old English antecedents of *fast* and *fasten*, but the relation of these two words to one another is not at all straightforward. The table also shows representative examples of (1) adjectives (such as *blind*) which function as verbs without adding *-en*, (2) adjectives which have two verb forms in current use (such as *smooth*), (3) adjectives (such as *hot*, *long*, and *strong*) which resort to cognates (*heat*, *lengthen*, and *strengthen*), and (4) adjectives (such as *cold*) which have no corresponding verb form at all. Dates refer to forms in the preceding columns, and are of the formation of the word, whether or not in the meaning(s) now current.

2 Other verbs, such as *enfeeble*, *enlarge*, and *enrich* (all ME), were formed by adding the prefix *en-* rather than the suffix *-en*.

3 Nearly all the *-en* verbs which came into existence in the 16c and 17c joined or replaced words that were spelt in the same away as the adjective. For example, *deep* already existed as a verb in the Anglo-Saxon period, and *deepen* did not join it and compete with it until the 16c.

4 By 1700 the productive power of the suffix had largely disappeared. The 18c produced only *broaden*, *madden*, and *tighten*; the 19c only *coarsen*, *quieten*, *smarten*, and *tauten*; and the most recent is *neaten* (1898).

ADJECTIVE	VERB 1	DATE	VERB 2	DATE	VERB 3	DATE
black	black	ME	blacken	ME		
bright			brighten	OE		
broad			broaden	18c		
cheap			cheapen	16c		
coarse			coarsen	19c		
cold						
damp	damp	ME	dampen	16c		
dark			darken	ME		
dead			deaden	17c		
deaf			deafen	16c		
deep			deepen	16c		
fast			fasten	OE		
fat			fatten	16c		
flat	flat	16c	flatten	17c		
foul	foul	OE				

▶

▶ -en verbs from adjectives
continued

ADJECTIVE	VERB 1	DATE	VERB 2	DATE	VERB 3	DATE
fresh			freshen	17c		
glad			gladden	ME		
good						
hard			harden	ME		
hot	hot	OE			heat	OE
lame	lame	ME				
less			lessen	ME		
light (= not heavy)			lighten	ME		
light (shining)	light	OE	lighten	ME		
like			liken	ME		
long					lengthen	ME
loose	loose	ME	loosen	ME		
mad			madden	18c		
moist			moisten	16c		
neat			neaten	19c		
quick			quicken	ME		
quiet	quiet	ME	quieten	19c		
red			redden	17c		
ripe			ripen	ME		
rough	rough	15c	roughen	16c		
sad			sadden	ME		
sharp			sharpen	ME		
short			shorten	ME		
sick			sicken	ME		
slack			slacken	16c		
smart			smarten	19c		
smooth	smooth	ME	smoothen	17c		
soften			soften	ME		
stiff			stiffen	15c		
still	still	OE				
stout			stouten	19c		
straight			straighten	16c		
strong					strengthen	ME
sweet			sweeten	ME		
taut			tauten	19c		
thick			thicken	ME		
tight			tighten	18c		
tough			toughen	16c		
weak			weaken	ME		
wet	wet	OE				
white			whiten	ME		
wide			widen	17c		
worse			worsen	ME		

pretentious substitute'. None of these will always quite serve, however, and only some of them can be substituted for *envisage* in its common construction followed by a verbal noun (*We do not envisage leaving just yet*).

2 Neither Fowler not Gowers noticed the arrival, first in Britain (1921) and then more assertively in America, of the closely synonymous word *envision*, meaning 'to see or foresee as in a vision'. The evidence of current use shows that *envision* is strongly favoured in AmE and *envisage* in BrE, but the division is not absolute. Examples: (envisage) *The best scenario . . . that we can envisage is one in which all those who want to do formal work will have an opportunity of doing two or three days a week—Journal of the Royal Society of Arts*, 1980 | *So mother envisaged us all here, gathered round staring down in this ghastly way—*Penelope Lively, 1989 | *Mr King spoke . . . more diplomatically, emphasizing that he did not envisage any 'immediate' change in force levels—Times*, 1990 | (envision) *They envision themselves wearing berets . . . and crawling about the rubble, throwing Molotov cocktails—Melody Maker*, 1968 | *His blackest hypochondria had never envisioned quite so miserable a Catastrophe—*Lytton Strachey, 1921 | *He did not envision any basic change in the social structure or the standard of living – Bulletin of the American Academy*, 1989 | *It may be only the stuff of newspaper editorials, of course, to envision a strategy in which the United Nations takes decisive action—Sunday Times*, 1990.

eon is an American spelling of AEON.

epic. **1** *Epic* is a term traditionally applied (first as an adjective, later as a noun) to narrative

poems that celebrate the achievements of the heroes of history or legend, such as the *Iliad*, the *Odyssey*, Virgil's *Aeneid*, Milton's *Paradise Lost*, the *Chanson de Roland*, the Old English elegiac poem *Beowulf*, and the Hindu *Mahābhārata* and *Rāmāyana*. The name normally applied to Old Norse narrative poems of this kind is *saga*.

2 The word has been extended in more recent usage to refer to any major literary work, theatrical performance, or (especially) film, which has some claim to be regarded as exceptional in terms of its length, subject matter, or scale of treatment: *I want very much to see the Birth of a Nation, which is said to be a really great film, an epic in pictures—*Aldous Huxley, 1916 | *Talking of films, Meier is still working on his wild, underground epic, Snowball, as well as producing a new Hollywood movie called MM—Face*, 1992. It has also gone full circle in acquiring a new adjectival meaning 'great, heroic' in various applications when used attributively (before a noun): *The Communists' Red Army had just completed its epic Long March from the Southeast to its new headquarters at Yenan—Time*, 1977 | *In his epic landscape of Jerusalem executed in April of 1830, Roberts draws the Holy City in silhouette—*R. Fisk, 1991 | *Nigel Benn and Chris Eubank came face-to-face for the first time in 25 months since their epic world title fight—Today*, 1992.

epidemic see ENDEMIC.

epigram, epigraph. Both words come from the same Greek roots meaning 'to write (or written) on'. *Epigram* is slightly earlier (16c) and has two principal meanings in current use, (1) a short poem with a witty or ingenious ending, and (2) a terse or pungent saying. A third meaning, a dedicatory or explanatory inscription on a building, tomb, coin, etc., is now obsolete and is supplied by *epigraph*, which also means a short quotation or pithy sentence put at the beginning of a book, chapter, etc., as a foretaste of the leading idea or sentiment to be found in the work.

episcopalian means 'belonging or referring to an episcopal church', i.e. a church founded on the principle of government by bishops. It refers primarily to the Anglican Church in Scotland and the US, which has elected bishops; in this context it is spelt with a capital initial, *Episcopalian*.

epistle refers primarily to the letters of the New Testament, e.g. the Epistle of St Paul the Apostle to the Romans. It is sometimes used ironically or whimsically to mean a letter of any kind: *The whole tenor of the epistle is that of one elite talking to another without reference to . . . those who have paid . . . Yuk—It*, 1970.

epithet. An *epithet* is an adjective indicating some quality or attribute (good or bad) which the speaker or writer (or the verdict of history) regards as characteristic of a person or thing, eg *Charles the Bold, Ethelred the Unready, Philip the Good, William the Silent*, and many figures (*Alexander, Alfred, Peter, Pompey*, etc.) called *the Great*. An *epithet* can also be a noun used as a significant title or appellation, e.g. *William the Conqueror, Vlad the Impaler*. In more casual use, *epithet* simply means 'description' or 'name': *The epithets of liar, racist and worse hurled at the vice president just won't stick—Washington Times*, 1988.

epitome, pronounced as four syllables (i-**pit**-ə-mi), is derived from a Greek word literally meaning 'to cut into'. It has two main meanings in English, (1) a person or thing typically representing a quality or class (*Little did he dream when he designed the polka dot that one day it would become the epitome of fashion—New Yorker*, 1970), and (2) a summary or shorter version of something written (*The book . . . is not intended to be popular. No doubt a lively epitome will one day be made for general reading—*Evelyn Waugh, 1956).

epoch. 1 An *epoch* is the beginning of a distinctive period in the history of something or someone, whereas an *era* is a period of history characterized by particular circumstances or by a particular series of events. A *period* is a more general term for a distinct portion of time in relation to a person's life or to human history and an *aeon* is an immeasurable length of time often used in more rhetorical contexts. In geology, the three terms *epoch, era*, and *period* have special meanings: *era* denotes the largest unit of time, a *period* is a division of this, and an *epoch* is a subdivision of a *period*.

2 The adjective *epoch-making* is first recorded in the 19c (Coleridge had used *epoch-forming* in 1816), and is now widely used to mean 'remarkable, significant' as well as (more appropriately) 'historic': *Not an epoch-making or path-breaking book—Times Literary Supplement*, 1973 | *This was an epoch-making moment in the history of Egypt, like the day a dam bursts—*N. Barber, 1984.

eponym, eponymous. 1 An *eponym* is a person after whom

something is named, such as a building, an institution, an organization, a machine, a product, or a process. Examples include: *Alzheimer's disease*, from Alois *Alzheimer*, 1864–1915, German neurologist; *Braille*, from Louis *Braille*, 1809–52, French inventor; *diesel*, from Rudolf *Diesel*, 1858–1913, German engineer; *mackintosh*, from Charles *Macintosh*, 1766–1843 (with a change of spelling); *Morse code*, from S. F. B. *Morse*, 1791–1872, American inventor; *sandwich*, from the 4th Earl of *Sandwich*, 1718–92.

2 The adjective *eponymous* is used in the following way: *Beowulf* is the *eponymous* hero of the Old English poem of that name; *Emma* is the *eponymous* heroine of the novel *Emma* by Jane Austen; and *Robinson Crusoe* is the *eponymous* hero of *The Life and Strange and Surprising Adventures of Robinson Crusoe* by Daniel Defoe.

equable, equitable. Both words come from Latin *aequus* meaning 'equal', but their meanings are different. *Equable* means 'even and moderate, regular' and is typically used with words such as *climate*, *disposition*, and *temperament*. It denotes avoidance of extremes as well as avoidance of change. *Equitable* means 'just, fair' (usually with reference to several parties involved), and is typically used with words such as *agreement*, *settlement*, and *solution*.

equal. 1 As a verb, *equal* has inflected forms *equalled, equalling* in BrE and *equaled, equaling* in AmE.

2 As an adjective, *equal* is followed by *to* (*The square on the hypotenuse is equal to the sum of the squares on the other two sides*), whereas the verb takes a direct object without *to* (*The square on*

the hypotenuse equals the sum of the squares on the other two sides). *Equal to* also had the meaning 'fit for, able to deal with' (*I hope I shall be equal to the challenge*—P. Street, 1990); when it is followed by a verb this should be a verbal noun, not an infinitive (*They are not equal to performing* [✖ *to perform*] *the task*).

3 Ellipsis (omission) of *to* should be avoided in phrases such as *equal to* or *greater than*, as in *Their budget must be equal to or greater than the minimum total cost of supplying the expected output*—B. C. Smith, 1988. See ELLIPSIS.

4 *Equal* is often regarded as an absolute that cannot be qualified by words such as *very, more, rather*, etc. However, this rule does not apply to all its meanings, and it is legitimate to say, for example, *They wanted a more equal allocation of resources*, in which *equal* means 'fair' as much as 'divided equally'. There is also George Orwell's famous line *All animals are equal but some animals are more equal than others*—*Animal Farm*, 1945, which is often recalled allusively in uses such as the following: *All victims are equal. None are more equal than others.*—John Le Carré, 1989.

equally. Fowler (1926) condemned the use of *equally as* (*They are equally as good*) as an 'illiterate tautology', preferring either (*They are equally good*) or (*They are as good*). Another unexceptionable possibility, which goes some way to providing the sentence balance that *equally* gives, is *They are just as good*.

equilibrium is pronounced with the first syllable either ek- or eek-. The plural form (not often needed) is *equilibria* or *equilibriums*.

equip has inflected forms *equipped, equipping*. The noun form is *equipment*.

era see EPOCH.

-er and -est forms of adjectives and adverbs. 1 GENERAL.
This article deals with the forms of the comparative and superlative of adjectives and adverbs, either by inflection (*larger, largest; happier, happiest*) or by using *more* and *most* (*more usual; most unfortunately*). It also deals in outline with the rules for using the various forms available. See also the articles on ADJECTIVE and ADVERB.

2 ADJECTIVES THAT HAVE *-ER* AND *-EST* FORMS. The adjectives that take *-er* and *-est* in preference to (or as well as) *more* and *most* are:

▶ **a** words of one syllable (*fast, hard, rich, wise*, etc.).

▶ **b** words of two syllables ending in *-y* and *-ly* (*angry, early, happy, holy, lazy, likely, lively, tacky*, etc.) and corresponding negative forms in *un-* when these exist (*unhappy, unlikely*, etc.). Words ending in *-y* change the *y* to *i* (*angrier, earliest*, etc.). In some cases only the *-est* form is used (e.g. *unholiest* but *more unholy*).

▶ **c** words of two syllables ending in *-le* (*able, humble, noble, simple*, etc.).

▶ **d** words of two syllables ending in *-ow* (*mellow, narrow, shallow*, etc.).

▶ **e** some words of two syllables ending in *-er* (*bitter, clever, slender, tender*, etc., but not *eager*). In some cases only the *-est* form is used (e.g. *bitterest* but *more bitter*).

▶ **f** some words of two syllables pronounced with the stress on the second syllable (*polite, profound*, etc., but not *antique, bizarre, secure*, etc.).

▶ **g** other words of two syllables that do not belong to any classi-fiable group (e.g. *common, cruel, pleasant, quiet*); some words can take *-er* and *-est* although the forms sound somewhat less natural (e.g. *awkward, crooked*).

Adjectives of three or more syllables need to use forms with *more* and *most* (*more beautiful, most interesting*, etc.).

3 ADVERBS THAT HAVE *-ER* AND *-EST* FORMS. The adverbs that take *-er* and *-est* in preference to (or as well as) *more* and *most* are:

▶ **a** adverbs that are not formed with *-ly* but are identical in form to corresponding adjectives (e.g. *runs faster, hits hardest, hold it tighter*).

▶ **b** some independent adverbs (e.g. *often* and *soon*).

Adverbs in *-ly* formed from adjectives (e.g. *richly, softly, wisely*) generally do not have forms in *-er* and *-est* but appear as *more softly, most wisely*, etc. The phrase *easier said than done* is a special case, in that there is no equivalent use as an adverb of the simple form *easy*.

4 CHOICE OF FORMS. With adjectives and adverbs of one syllable it is usually less natural to use *more* and *most* when forms in *-er* and *-est* are available, although there are exceptions that are not readily explained: *The job was harder than they thought* sounds less idiomatic in the form *The job was more hard than they thought*, but *We felt gladder after seeing the children* sounds equally idiomatic in the form *We felt more glad after seeing the children*. With adjectives of two syllables it is often possible to form comparatives and superlatives both by *-er* and *-est* forms and with *more* and *most*. For example, the sentences *He was most unhappy when he was on his own* and *He was unhappiest when he was on his own* are both idiomatic, although the first but not the second can mean 'extremely unhappy' as well as 'most unhappy (of all)', in accordance with the different meanings of *most*.

5 USAGE WITH AND WITHOUT *THE*. Comparative and superlative forms are used as adjectives without *the*, and comparatives can be followed by *than* (e.g. *John is taller than his mother*). They are also used as quasi-nouns (or absolute adjectives) preceded by *the* (e.g. *John is the tallest of the children*). Superlatives have a special function, without *the*, to express strength of meaning in uses such as *Darkest Africa* and *to speak with deepest emotion*.

6 SUPERLATIVES IN COMPARISON OF TWO. The comparative forms are meant to compare two persons or things and superlative forms more than two, and it is normally ungrammatical to use the superlative in the role of the comparative, as in *The largest of the two*, although this is commonly found in spoken and written English. Use of the superlative is however idiomatic in certain fixed expressions, such as *Put your best foot forward | May the best man win | Mother knows best*, in which the comparison may effectively be of two but the idiom is sufficiently generalized to weaken strict duality.

7 LITERARY USES. Some unconventional and ungrammatical formations are found as stylistic devices in literature, e.g. Shakespeare's *easiliest, freelier, proudlier, wiselier*, Charles Lamb's *harshlier, kindlier, proudlier*, Tennyson's *darklier, gladlier, looselier, plainlier*, George Eliot's *neatliest*, and Lewis Carroll's *curiouser*. See also ADJECTIVE 3. Other formations are occasionally used for comic effect, e.g. *admirablest, loathsomer, peacefulest*,

wholesomer. Such devices belong to the category of special usage that makes exceptions to normal grammatical rules.

-er and -or. These suffixes form agent nouns denoting either a person or a thing that performs the action denoted by the word's stem; this is sometimes a word in its own right and sometimes not, e.g. *dispenser, farmer, maker, porter, sailor, suitor*. In theory, *-er* can be added to any English verb to form an agent noun; but in practice both *-er* and *-or* forms are used, sometimes as active English suffixes and sometimes as elements borrowed with the word as a whole (e.g. *doctor* from Old French *doctour* from Latin *doctor*). Choice between the two suffixes is purely historical and does not have any principled distinction. Note however that some agent nouns exist in two forms, e.g. *adviser* and *advisor* (the second probably influenced by *advisory*).

When *-er* is added to verbs ending in a consonant + *-y*, the *y* is normally changed to *i*, as in *carrier, occupier*, etc. Exceptions are *flyer*, which is now more usual than *flier*, and *drier*, which alternates with *dryer*.

-er and -re (noun and verb endings) see -RE AND -ER.

eraser is spelt *-er*, not *-or*. See -ER AND -OR.

ere, pronounced like *air* and meaning 'before', has been in continuous use as a preposition and conjunction from the Old English period. Now it is only used for archaic effect or in poetry, but it refuses to disappear altogether: *And time seemed finished ere the ship passed by*—Edwin Muir, 1925 | *I would give you a gift ere we go, at your own choosing*—

J. R. R. Tolkien, 1954 | *In that cluster of villages, London by name, Ere slabs are too tall and we Cockneys too few*—John Betjeman, 1958 | *No thriftful scrutiny was drawn When, ere creation's mighty dawn, Thou plannedst man's abode*—P. Falvury, 1968.

ergative is a term for a type of verb of action or movement in which the object of the verb can become the subject of the same verb used intransitively (without an object), as in *They closed the door | The door closed*. There are many verbs of this type, including *change, close, cook, finish, move, open, shut, slide*. Some languages, such as Eskimo and Basque, have a special case for nouns used as the subject of ergative verbs.

erotica, meaning 'erotic literature and art' is a plural noun, and any verb it governs should be plural (*Erotica are much in evidence in the world of videos*), although it is often treated as a singular mass noun: *None of Minton's erotic drawings have resurfaced, even today when erotica has become much sought after*—F. Spalding, 1991. In many uses number is not explicit: *Above the pulp-line . . . lies the world of erotica, of sexual writing with literary pretensions or genuine claims*—George Steiner, 1967.

err, meaning 'to do wrong', is pronounced as in *her. Errant*, meaning 'doing wrong', is pronounced with the first syllable as in *merry*.

erratum, meaning 'an error (in printed matter)' is pronounced i-**rah**-təm. It is a singular noun, with a plural *errata. Errata* should not be used as a singular noun on the analogy of *agenda*; if a singular is needed, a phrase such as *list of errata* is preferable.

ersatz is a German loanword meaning 'a substitute or imitation' and is first recorded in English in 1875. It is still used, often in attributive position (before a noun, e.g. *ersatz coffee | an ersatz culture*), and is pronounced in a somewhat non-naturalized manner as **er**-zutz or **er**-sutz.

erstwhile is a word that dates from Old English, and is still occasionally found, mainly as an adjective meaning 'of old, former': *Many erstwhile Green Line travellers were doubtless driving their own cars*—K. Warren, 1980.

escalate is a 1920s back-formation from *escalator* (first recorded in 1900), and has burst the bounds of meaning that a word for a moving staircase might be expected to impose. Not surprisingly, *escalate* is now rarely used in its first meaning 'to travel on an escalator'. By the 1950s, it had come into regular use to mean 'to increase or develop rapidly by stages', chiefly in the context of military and political conflict. Typical examples from that time (the first intransitive, the second transitive, i.e. with an object) are: *The possibility of local wars 'escalating into all-out atomic wars'*—Manchester Guardian, 1959 | *Using tactical nuclear weapons which would be likely to escalate hostilities into a global nuclear war*—Economist, 1961. In more recent use, *escalate* continues to be used in such contexts but has extended beyond them: *Only a tiny percentage of cannabis-smokers escalate to heroin*—Listener, 1967 | *The police more often came under physical attack and began to respond with a steadily escalating counter-violence*—Liberty and Legislation, 1989 | *Her previous calm gave way to*

terror that escalated until it threatened to overwhelm her—E. Blair,
1990 | 'Iraq is not interested in escal-
ating the situation or creating any crisis,' he told BBC Radio 4's Today
programme—Today, 1992.

escape *verb and noun.* There are
three significant 20c uses, the
first two of the verb and the
third of the noun:

1 In intransitive use (without
an object), to describe astronauts
overcoming gravity and leaving
the earth's atmosphere: *A space-
ship will escape from Earth at 11.2
kilometres a second—Journal of the
British Interplanetary Society*, 1949.

2 In transitive use (with an object), to mean 'to escape from (a
place)', both of astronauts as in
the previous paragraph and in
other contexts, such as escape
from a convent in the following
example: *It transpires she may have
escaped Santa Clara to look for a
well-known terrorist*—N. Shakespeare,
1989. This is a revival of an older
use and shows an obvious relation to more standard transitive
uses as in escaping *danger*, *arrest*,
criticism, *suspicion*, and other unwelcome circumstances.

3 In computing, *escape* is a
noun denoting a function (and
keyboard key) that ends an operation or affects a following sequence of commands in some
way. For anyone who has fallen
into any of the engulfing traps
that computer technology can lay
for the unwary, the notion of *escape* provides a potent image.

escapee is first recorded in use
by Walt Whitman, who refers to
southern escapees in a memoir
(1875–6) of his experiences as a
hospital visitor during the American Civil War. It has come in for
much adverse criticism from

those who think that *escaper* (on
the analogy of *deserter*) is the
form called for, but the word is
established and is supported by
other forms such as *refugee*. It
also accords well with the active
use of the past participle (which
is passive in form), as in *an escaped prisoner*. See -EE.

escort is pronounced with the
stress on the first syllable as a
noun and on the second as a
verb.

Eskimo has the plural form *Eski-
mos*, but *Eskimo* also is used as a
collective. The Eskimo term *Inuit*
(the plural of *inuk* meaning 'person') is preferred by the people
themselves.

**especial, especially, special,
specially. 1** There is no longer
any great difficulty with *especial*
because *special* has all but driven
it out, although it is still used occasionally to refer principally to
exceptional personal qualities or
attributes as in *your especial
charm*. The adverbs *specially* and *especially* present a much bigger
problem, because each continues
to the usurp the role of the other
quite extensively. Essentially, the
difference is this: *especially* means
'chiefly, much more than in other
cases' and can qualify adjectives
and adverbs as well as verbs,
whereas *specially* means 'for a special or specific purpose' and
qualifies verbs, participial adjectives formed from verbs (as in
specially made), and occasionally
(when it encroaches on *especially*,
as described at 3 below) adjectives.

2 The following examples show
this distinction: (especially) *The
sumo wrestlers are not especially tall,
but they are especially big*—C. James,
1978 | *Ancient woods . . . are espe-*

*cially important for wildlife—Times,
1982 | Insist on listening to some
music, preferably piano music that
shows up wow and flutter especially
well—Listener, 1982 | The transfer of
Britain's most sophisticated technolo-
gies (especially in laser and micro-
computing) . . . will have appalling
effects on the British economy—City
Limits, 1986 | (specially) This fine
piano was made specially for us—
Chicago Tribune, 1977 | I gathered
these specially in bud, because I
thought it would be nice to see them
open out in the warmth of the
house—D. Madden, 1988 | A poll,
specially commissioned by London
Weekend Television, examined the attitudes of different age groups to
wealth distribution—F. Field, 1989.*

3 The meanings of the two
words come closest when qualifying an immediately following adjective, as in the following
examples in which each word is
virtually interchangeable for the
other, although *especially* is still
the more correct: *It's a pretty an-
onymous mark. Not one I'm specially
proud of, either*—Penelope Lively,
1991 | *The function of the criminal
law, as we see it, is . . . to provide
sufficient safeguards against exploitation or corruption of others, particularly those who are specially
vulnerable because they are young,
weak in body or mind or
inexperienced*—T. Newburn, 1992.
Specially more usually encroaches
on *especially*, but sometimes *especially* is the offender: ☒ *These
Pakistani garments are created especially for the wearer by a joint effort
of the women of the family.* —A. Wilson, 1988.

espresso, a name for strong
black Italian coffee (from a word
meaning 'pressed out'), is spelt
with initial *es-* not *ex-* (a variant
erroneously influenced by English
express).

Esq. This abbreviation is a 16c
shortening, as a written form of
address, of *esquire*, which originally denoted 'a young aspirant to
knighthood who attended and
served a knight', and was later
extended to refer to other classes
of men including peers, lawyers,
and so on. By the mid-20c *Esq.*
had become a courtesy designation, principally in correspondence, with no significance as to
rank. When *Esq.* is used, it follows
the name and replaces any prefixed title (*Mr, Dr, Capt.*, etc.) that
would otherwise be used. With
one exception (US lawyers ad-
dressing themselves), its use is restricted to Britain, and even here
it is dying out as other conventions come into use.

-esque is a suffix forming adjectives, and corresponds to French
-esque or Italian *-esco* (from the
medieval Latin ending *-iscus*). In
English it occurs in words derived
from Italian and French, e.g. *gro-
tesque, picaresque, picturesque,* and
is an active suffix added to personal names to form adjectives
meaning 'in the style of . . . ', e.g.
*Audenesque, Disneyesque, Schumann-
esque.* (It will be noticed that such
words would only awkwardly
make alternative forms in *-ian*).

-ess. 1 This suffix forms nouns
denoting female persons or animals, and was adopted in Middle
English from the Old French
form *-esse* (from late Latin *-issa*).
The first wave of *-ess* words in
English (*countess, duchess, empress,
hostess, mistress, princess,* etc.) were
all imported in their entirety
from French. From this beginning, *-ess* rapidly became an active suffix added to words that
already existed in English, e.g.
Jewess (14c, Wyclif), *patroness* (15c),

poetess (16c, Tyndale); and it supplanted the older native female suffix *-ster*, which now survives only in *spinster*. These words were formed by substituting *-ess* for *-er* in words such as *adulterer | adulteress*, or by adding *-ess* to the stem of words such as *author | authoress*. In some cases, a feminine form predated a corresponding masculine form; for example, *sorceress* (14c, Chaucer) is attested before *sorcerer* (1526, Tyndale). Some words required modification or refinement, producing (for example) *governess* in place of the earlier *governeresse* and *ambassadress* instead of the (unrecorded) alternative *ambassadoress*.

2 The *OED* records over 100 words in *-ess* formed from Middle English to about 1850, some merely fanciful or now obsolete (e.g. *entertainess, farmeress, vicaress*) but others still in regular use (e.g. *ambassadress, heiress, mayoress*).

3 In the 20c, the feminist and politically correct movements have had a devastating effect on the fortunes of many *-ess* words, and have effectively brought the life of *-ess* as an active suffix to an end. Those regarded as especially offensive are (on racial grounds) *Jewess* and *Negress*, and (on gender grounds) occupational terms such as *actress, air hostess, authoress, manageress, poetess, proprietress, stewardess, waitress*, all of which have yielded to gender-neutral alternatives, either the traditional masculine forms (*actor, author, manager, poet, proprietor, waiter*) or specially devised forms (*flight attendant, waitperson*). Other words continue unchallenged, among them *abbess, adulteress, adventuress, ambassadress, duchess, goddess, governess, heiress, murderess, postmistress, princess, songstress*. Some of these are unalterable titles,

others are not simply female equivalents of the masculine form (e.g. an *ambassadress* is the wife of an *ambassador*; a *mayoress* is the wife of a *mayor*, and in both cases a female office-holder would be called by the *-or* forms), and others are encountered too rarely (or only in special contexts such as fiction) to cause disquiet.

4 A further limitation on the use of many *-ess* forms is that they cannot be followed by *of* to identify them in relation to a work or achievement; instead of *the authoress of Persuasion* you have to say *the author of Persuasion*. It is possible, however, to say *the goddess of love*, in which *of* plays a somewhat different role.

Essex. This name of one of the English Home Counties conjures up, in the expressions *Essex man* and *Essex girl*, a 1980s image of the brash, amoral, self-made right-wing young businessman lacking all refinement and cultural interest, and his promiscuous, materialistic girlfriend: *Essex man lies unheeded and unloved in the gutter of political history—Economist*, 1995 | *An alarming tale of Essex girl jokes and sexual innuendo—Independent on Sunday*, 1995. It remains to be seen how long these names, which are closely tied up with the materialistic political climate of the 1980s, continue in use.

-est (forming superlatives of adjectives and adverbs) see -ER AND -EST FORMS.

Establishment. *The Establishment* (with a capital *E*) means 'the group in society exercising authority or influence, and seen as resisting change' and, by extension, 'any influential or controlling group' as in *the literary* *establishment.* This concentration of a previously somewhat vague range of meaning was due largely to an article by the journalist Henry Fairlie published in *The Spectator* in 1955, where he defined the term as referring not only to 'the centres of official power—though they are certainly part of it—but rather the whole matrix of official and social relations within which power is exercised'. The term *Establishment* had been applied earlier to the ecclesiastical system also known as the *established Church,* i.e. the Church of England and the corresponding churches in other parts of the United Kingdom.

estate. 1 The meaning of *estate* in the term *three estates of the realm* is a historical one, 'an order or class forming part of the body politic'. The *three estates* are the Lords Spiritual (i.e. the heads of the Church), the Lords Temporal (i.e. the peerage), and the Commons. The terms dates from the 15c. and has been used of similar institutions in other countries. A misuse, noted by the *OED,* which identifies the three elements as the Crown, the House of Lords, and the House of Commons, is first recorded as early as 1559. A *fourth estate,* the newspaper press, was added (possibly by Edmund Burke) in the early 19c.

2 *Estate* meaning 'a landed property' is first recorded in the late 18c. In the 20c this has been supplemented by a meaning well noted by C. S. Lewis in his *Studies in Words* (1960): *When I was a boy estate had as its dominant meaning 'land belonging to a large landowner', but the meaning 'land covered with small houses' is dominant now.*

3 *Estate car* is a general term in BrE for a kind of car that has the internal accommodation extended into the rear with a door at the back. The equivalent term in AmE is *station wagon.*

esthete, esthetic are American spellings of AESTHETE, AESTHETIC.

estimable means 'worthy of esteem, admirable'. *Estimatable* is the form required for the meaning 'capable of being estimated', although it does not seem to be much used (there is one occurrence only in the 100-million word British National Corpus).

estimation. 1 Fowler described the use of *estimation* in the phrase *in my estimation* (= in my opinion) as 'illiterate', a verdict which is negated by several centuries of use in this meaning: *The dearest of men in my estimation*—E. W. Lane, 1841 | *It was about this time that Martin took a great slump in Maria's estimation*—J. London, 1909.

2 *Estimation,* in addition to the meaning just discussed, is the process of forming a judgement or calculation, as distinct from *estimate* (noun), which is the result of the process, i.e. (1) an approximate decision about cost, size, value, etc., or (2) the cost or size itself, as in *The total estimate comes to £500.*

Estuary English is the name for a variety of informal and allegedly classless English spoken in the area of the Thames Estuary, i.e. London and parts of the Home Counties (notably Essex). The term was coined in 1984 by a London scholar named David Rosewarne. As well as peculiarities of vocabulary (such as *cheers* for *thank you* and *mate* for *friend*), the most recognizable features of Estuary English are phonetic: the replacement of *t* by a glottal stop in words such as *butter* and *water,* the replacement of *l* by a sound like *w* in words such as *full* and *ball-game*, and other features described more fully in books such as Paul Coggle's *Do You Speak Estuary?* (1993).

et al. is an abbreviation of Latin *et alii* (= and other people) or *et alia* (= and other things), and is used to avoid listing a long sequence of names, only the first or the first few being given, as in *Smith, Jones, et al.* It is regularly used in bibliographical citation for works having several authors, and is printed in roman or italic type according to the particular style in use. It is appropriately used for references to people; for other categories *etc.* is preferable.

etc. 1 This is an abbreviation of the Latin phrase *et cetera* meaning 'and other things of the same kind', and is pronounced et **set**-ə-rə or et **set**-rə, despite the temptation to articulate the first syllable ek on the analogy of words such as *ecstasy* and *excellence*.

2 It means 'and so on' or 'and the rest', and can refer to people or things or both. Practice varies regarding the punctuation that precedes and follows *etc.*, but in general it is best to treat it as if it were 'and so on', i.e. precede it by a comma when it comes after two or more items already separated by commas (*We need pencils, paper, etc.*), but not when it comes after a single item or two items without a comma (*We need paper etc.* | *We need some pencil and paper etc.*). It should be followed by a comma when a comma would be used in the case of 'and so on' (*We need pencils, paper, etc., as well as a desk to work on*).

3 Since *etc.* includes 'and' in its element *et*, it is illiterate to write

and etc. (or & etc.). The form *&c*, though once common (and used by Fowler in ordinary writing), is now out of fashion.

ethics, morals. 1 Both terms are concerned with the practice of right and wrong. The *Concise Oxford Dictionary* (1995) defines *ethics* as 'the science of morals in human conduct'; what this means is that morals forms the basis of abstract principles whereas ethics are the application of these principles in human activity, especially in specific areas of activity such as law and medicine (*professional ethics*).

2 Of the corresponding adjectives, *ethical* describes what is right or wrong in terms of an accepted code of behaviour, whereas *moral* describes what is right or wrong in principle, as affecting human behaviour generally: *The various moral systems of the world may include many of the same moral ideas—*G. A. & A. G. Theodorson, 1970 | *They believe in the moral superiority of primitive over civilised man—Daily Telegraph*, 1972 | *It is neither easy nor ethical to perch with notebook or video camera over spontaneous scenes of human mating or aggression—New Scientist*, 1983 | *Condoning surrogacy as a solution is surely not justified on either ethical or practical grounds—Financial Times*, 1985. *Moral* also occurs in a few fixed expressions such as *moral certainty* (= strong probability), *moral courage*, *moral majority,* and *moral support*, and here means 'having a psychological effect associated with confidence in a right action'.

ethnic is now principally used to denote a section of a community having distinct racial, cultural, religious, or linguistic characteristics not shared by the rest of the community. *Ethnic* is typically used to describe clothing, dance, music, and other customs that distinguish such people: *The Radio Authority has helpfully decreed that classical music, light orchestra and non-amplified jazz, folk, country and ethnic music aren't pop—Times Educational Supplement*, 1991 | *Vegetarian dishes in various ethnic cuisines—Mexican, Thai, Indian, Italian, Japanese, Middle Eastern, etc.— New Musical Express*, 1991. An *ethnic minority* (first recorded in 1945) is a section of a community that forms a minority within a larger community, for example Sikhs, Muslims, and West Indian people in Britain. In a further development of the term, people are described as being (for example) *ethnic Turks* when they are of Turkish origin but living in a country other than Turkey; in recent times we have heard a great deal about *ethnic Vietnamese* in Cambodia and *ethnic Albanians* in Serbia: *The ethnic Albanian ministers had been tendering their resignations one by one since late March— Keesings*, 1990.

ethnic cleansing. This unfortunate euphemism, highly reminiscent of the *final solution* and other expressions to do with the suppression of peoples, is first recorded in 1991 in connection with events in Yugoslavia that have continued through the 1990s. It means 'the mass expulsion or extermination of people from a minority ethnic or religious group within a certain area': *The area has a large number of towns and villages, many emptied of Muslims and Croats in three years of ethnic cleansing—Times*, 1995.

ethnic names and stereotypes. 1 SLANG NAMES FOR PEOPLE. These range from the neutral or affectionate (*Brit* = someone British, *Mick* = an Irishman) via the category of often though not always derogatory (*Limey* (in America) = someone British, *Yank* (in Britain) = an American) to the invariably offensive (*dago* = Spaniard, *Yid* = Jew). Across this range much depends on the relationship between the user of the term and the hearer. Most offensive of all in current use are *Nigger* for a black-skinned person (so offensive that pressure groups in the US want to see it removed from dictionaries) and *Paki* for a person from Pakistan or the Indian subcontinent generally. The origin of some terms is obscured or forgotten; many have to do with trivialized conceptions of supposed habits (*Frog* = Frenchman, from the practice of eating frog's legs in France, *Kraut* = German, from the eating of sauerkraut in Germany, etc.), others are fanciful formations (*Pommy* (in Australia) = English immigrant, from *pomegranate* as a word-play on *immigrant*), and others again develop folk etymologies (e.g. *wog* = foreigner, supposedly an acronym of *westernized* (or *wily*) *oriental gentleman* but more likely a shortening of *golliwog*). Some are of unknown origin (e.g. *kike*, AmE = Jew). A fuller account of this topic will be found in the *Oxford Companion to the English Language* (1992), 381–4, from which much of this material is drawn.

2 STEREOTYPES. Ethnic stereotypes have long featured as a component of idiom in many languages, and these often have more to do with popular conception than historical truth. Increased sensitivity to unfavourable ethnic description in the 20c has led to a strong disapproval of many terms, such as *street Arab* and *young Turk*. Most notorious of all has been the use of *Jew* as an opprobrious term for 'a mean or grasping person', a historical use which arose from the association of Jews with medieval money-lending and was duly recorded in successive editions of the *Concise Oxford Dictionary* but dropped (on grounds of lack of currency) from the ninth edition (1995).

-ette is a suffix corresponding to an Old French form *-ette* and is found in English (mostly from the 19c) in four types of noun, either as an active suffix or as part of a word adopted from French:

1 diminutive words, e.g. *chemisette* (= a small chemise, 1807), *cigarette* (= small cigar, 1842), *novelette* (= a short novel, 1820), *pipette* (= a small pipe, 1839), *statuette* (= a small statue, 1843). Formations of the 20c include *kitchenette* (= a small kitchen, 1910), *launderette* (which is not just a diminutive but means a special kind of self-service laundry, 1949), *diskette* (= a small computer disk), *superette* (= a small supermarket, chiefly AmE and Australian, 1938). In some words, such as *launderette* and *serviette* (originally Scottish, and reintroduced into standard English in the 19c: see U AND NON-U), *-ette* is not strictly a diminutive, but is best considered in this category.

2 feminine words, a usage launched in a spectacular way with the word *suffragette* (1906), a female supporter of, and active campaigner for, women's right to vote. No word of this kind coined since has had the same resonance. The American scholar H. L. Mencken (writing in 1921) noted

the appearance of a string of ephemeral formations including *conductorette* and *farmerette*, but the only one to attain any permanent currency was *usherette* (1925): *What the hell are you holding that torch for as if you were a bloody usherette?*—A. N. Wilson, 1990. This, together with *undergraduette* (1919, and see below) and *majorette* (AmE, in *drum majorette*, 1938), represent a distinct anticlimax after a promising start. A trickle of trivial words continued in the post-war years, until the suffix was taken up by male chauvinist magazine writers in the 1980s to form depreciatory and often hostile terms for women such as *bimbette, hackette, snoopette, undergraduette* (a revival of the 1919 word), *whizzette*, and even *womanette*.

3 names of fabrics, some but not all imitations of something else, e.g. *muslinette* (1787, the first recorded), *leatherette* (1880), *flannelette* (1882), *stockingette* (1824, now more usually written as *stockinet*), and *winceyette* (1922, a lightweight cotton fabric for nightclothes, from wincey, itself an alteration of woolsey in linsey-woolsey).

4 names of commercial foods. American newspapers in the 1990s have been carrying advertisements for *Clubettes* (= bite-size crackers), *Creamettes* (= a type of pasta), *Croutettes* (= a stuffing mix), and *Toastettes* (= a kind of tart). The model for these tradenames is possibly the word *croquette* (first recorded in 1706), a term borrowed from French and meaning 'a fried breaded roll or ball of mashed potato or minced meat'.

etymology. **1** *Etymology* is the study of the history and derivation of words, and *an etymology* is the history of a particular word. Most dictionaries of concise size and larger give detailed accounts of a word's sources, which can be from other English words (e.g. newspaper) or from other languages (e.g. *kiosk* via French from Persian). Some words borrowed from other languages have been assimilated to English-looking forms; for example Spanish *cucaracha* has given us *cockroach* by assimilation with the English words *cock* and *roach* (see ASSIMILATION).

2 The vast majority of English words (apart from those made from existing English words) are derived from Old English (Anglo-Saxon), from Norse languages, or from a late form of Latin via French words that came into English after the Norman Conquest in 1066. A succinct account of the main sources of English words is given in the *Concise Oxford Dictionary* (1995), ix-xii, to which the reader is referred for further information. It is disappointing for many people that the origins of some quite familiar and important words remain obscure or unknown. The histories of *boy* and *girl* are unknown before Middle English, *dog* has no identified Germanic cognates, many informal or slang words, such as *bamboozle, caboodle, cagey, clobber, gimmick, jiff,* and *posh,* have no verified origins, despite spurious claims made for some of them (such as the supposed 'port outward starboard home' origin of *posh*), and some words that appear to be made up of distinctive elements, for example *contraption* and *theodolite,* are also doubtful or unknown in origin.

3 Certain words, possibly including some of those in the last paragraph, are onomatopoeic, i.e.

they represent a sound with which their meanings are associated, such as *clang, plonk,* and *thwack*; and a few words that are less obviously connected with sounds, such as *blizzard* and *jumble,* also belong to this class.

4 The word *etymology* itself comes from a Greek word *etymon* meaning 'true'. However, the etymology of a word represents its original meaning rather than its true meaning in any judgemental sense. Appeals to etymology to defend the use of words against change in meaning (as for example with DECIMATE), though commonly made, are usually futile, since few words in the core vocabulary of English now mean what they used to mean, as the complex history of *nice* demonstrates.

eulogy see ELEGY.

euphemism.
See box overleaf

euphuism (not to be confused with *euphemism*: see the preceding entry) is an affected or high-flown style of writing or speaking, originally applied to work of the late 16c and early 17c written in imitation of John Lyly's *Euphues* (pronounced **yoo**-fyoo-eez 1578–80). The name is derived from Greek *euphues* meaning 'well-endowed by nature'.

Eurasian is a term (noun and adjective) first used in the 19c for a person of mixed European and Asian (especially Indian) parentage.

Euro-. 1 *Euro-,* shortened to *Eur-* before certain vowels, is one of the more productive combining forms of the 20c, as a linguistic reflection of far-reaching political and economic developments

euphemism

is the use of a milder or vaguer word or phrase in place of one that might seem too a harsh or direct in a particular context, and *a euphemism* is such a word or phrase. The most productive subjects for euphemism are bodily functions, sexual activity, death, politics, and violence. Euphemisms in these and other areas of language use are given in the table below.

WORD OR PHRASE	COMMON EUPHEMISMS
lavatory	bog (slang), comfort station, convenience, little boys' room, little house, loo, restroom (AmE), washroom (AmE), water closet (WC)
urinate	have a tinkle (slang), pass water, relieve oneself, spend a penny, take a leak (slang)
have sexual intercourse with	make love to, sleep with
prostitute	call girl, fallen woman, street-walker
die	depart this life, give up the ghost, kick the bucket (slang), pass away, pass on
kill	do way with, remove, take out, terminate
redundancy	downsizing, rationalizing, restructuring, slimming down

Examples of phrasal euphemism are *collateral damage* (= accidental destruction of non-military areas), *ethnic cleansing* (= mass expulsion or extermination of ethnic minorities), *final solution* (= Nazi extermination of European Jews), *friendly fire* (= killing of soldiers on one's own side), *helping the police with their inquiries* (= under interrogation and imminent arrest), *pacification* (= evacuation and destruction of villages in war), and (facetiously) *tired and emotional* (= drunk).

across Europe. The form is first used in the 1950s in hyphened combinations such as *Euro-African* and *Euro-American*, and in the institutional names *Eurovision* (1951, a network of European broadcasting organizations) and *Euratom* (1956, = European Atomic Energy Community). The first generalized words are *Euro-dollar* (1960, a dollar held outside the US, though not necessarily in Europe), the disparaging *Eurocrat* (= European bureaucrat, 1961), and the not much more favourable *Eurocentric* (= regarded in European terms, 1963). The first uses related to Europe (or Western Europe) generally, and this meaning continues in formations such as *Euromissile* (1979) and *Eurostrategic* (1977), whereas many terms that arose in the 1960s and since refer more specifically to the European Community (now Union) in relation to the UK's potential and later actual membership, especially the notorious *Eurosceptic* (1986) and its antonym *Europhile*, both used as adjectives and nouns, and other irreverent formations including *Eurobabble* (1986, in a US source) and *Eurojargon*.

2 Like many prolific combining forms, *Euro-* has succeeded in detaching itself and going into orbit as a word in its own right:

The Euro terrorists announced . . .
that they had set up a 'Western Euro-
pean Revolutionary offensive'—
Evening Standard, 1987 | *The name*
Britannia had been dropped from the
deal because its nationalistic conno-
tations could have obvious draw-
backs in a pan-Euro
venture—European Investor, 1990. It
remains to be seen what will be
the linguistic consequences of
choosing *Euro* (or *euro*) as the
name for the new common currency of the European Union.

evade see AVOID.

evasion, evasiveness. *Evasive-*
ness is the quality a person has of
being *evasive*, whereas *evasion* is
the process or result of this quality, or an instance of it: *He has*
been in the trenches too long not to
be a master at mixing sincerity with
evasiveness—Rolling Stone, 1977 |
Never before can so many decent, ex-
plicit words have utterly altered their
meaning to conceal an evasion or
untruth—Sunday Times, 1977. *Evasion*
has a special meaning in relation
to legal obligations, and differs
from *avoidance* in denoting illegal-
ity: *He'd been had up for offering*
bribes to council employees: the
whole story had been ridiculous, tales
of . . . call girls and twenty-pound
notes, of tax evasion and porno-
*movies—*Margaret Drabble, 1977. See
also AVOID.

eve means 'the evening or day
before' (as in *Christmas Eve*) and,
in figurative use, also means 'the
time just before an event' (as in
the eve of the election). In the following examples, *eve* is literal in
the first two phrases, is figurative
in the third, and may be either
in the last two: *On Christmas Eve* |
on the Eve of St Agnes | *on the eve*
of great developments | *on the eve of*
the battle | *on the eve of departure*.

The meaning in particular cases
is often clear from the context.

even is normally placed immediately before the word or phrase
that it qualifies: *Doctors must pur-*
sue costly and even dangerous inves-
tigations | *She is talking even more*
loudly | *He even enrolled in a busi-*
ness studies course. In some cases
even qualifies an entire subordinate clause: *Even if my watch is right*
we shall be late. When *even* qualifies a verb formed with an auxiliary or modal verb (*can, do, have,*
might, etc.), it is placed between
the auxiliary verb and the infinitive (*He had even managed to laugh*
at it | *I did not even bother to read*
it) and this is also the case when
even qualifies the complement of
the verb *It might even cost £100.* In
informal contexts involving negatives, *even* sometimes comes at
the end of a sentence: *They didn't*
want anything to eat, or a drink even.

evenness is spelt with two *n*s.

event. 1 *In the event of* is a somewhat awkward prepositional
phrase used in BrE to mean 'if
such-and-such (should happen)'. It
is followed by a noun or verbal
noun: *The 12 members of the Basle*
central bankers' club have made re-
ciprocal arrangements to make short-
term loans to each other in the event
of any currency coming under severe
pressure—Times, 1968 | *Every*
manned space flight . . . has a back-
up crew, to replace the prime crew in
*the event of illness or death—*R. Turn-
ill, 1970. The expression has
picked up some bad vibes from
its extended form *in the unlikely*
event, familiar to air travellers
from its euphemistic reference to
danger: *In the unlikely event of a*
landing on water . . . .

2 In AmE, and in the language
of law and business also in BrE,

the phrase is *in the event* (*that*), used as a conjunction: *A metal tubular structure over the cockpit which protects the driver in the event the car overturns* —Publications of the American Dialect Society, 1964. | *Parties should consider at the outset the payment of their advisers' fees in the event that the transaction aborts* —D. J. Cooke, 1993.

eventuality, eventuate. Both words date from the 18c and have had their fair share of criticism. *Eventuate* was derided by De Quincy (1834) as 'Yankeeish' and by Dean Alford (1864) as 'another horrible word', and Fowler (1926) castigated both as 'flabby journalese', leaving a string of 'characteristic specimens' to speak for themselves. It is undeniable that *result* or *come about*, or sometimes simply *happen*, are often preferable alternatives: *It had been intended to have educated Saudi women dealing with the public at the exhibition, but . . . this had not eventuated* —Times, 1986 | *Many of the things we worry about never eventuate* —D. Rowe, 1987. *Eventuality* has been less fiercely attacked, although it is often a mere synonym for circumstance, event, or possibility: *Although he had been ordered not to destroy it, Harmel was prepared for the eventuality* —C. Ryan, 1974 | *Of course, different situations demand different reactions and one cannot plan for every eventuality* —P. Mann, 1982.

ever. 1 AS INTENSIFIER. In informal conversation *ever* is sometimes used as an intensifier immediately after an interrogative word such as *who, what, why*, etc.: *Who ever can that be?* | *What ever did you say to him?* | *Why ever should you think that?* These uses should be distinguished from the one-word forms *whoever, whatever*, etc., which are relative pronouns: *I'll do whatever you want.* See WHATEVER, WHAT EVER; WHOEVER, WHO EVER.

2 *DID YOU EVER?* This expression is informal only, and has a distinct Victorian ring: *'And where is she now?' 'In a studio.' . . . 'Did you ever!' said Mrs. Fanshaw* —Peel City Guardian, 1892 | *Cody! Out there is the middle of nowhere, by sheer coincidence, Cody Tull! . . . 'Well did you ever.'* —A. Tyler, 1982.

3 EVER SO. An older use after *if* or *though* with the meaning 'at all, in any degree' now sounds archaic and has almost disappeared: *Though Sir Peter's ill humour may vex me ever so, it never shall provoke me* —Sheridan, 1777. It is now overshadowed by the same phrase used (since the mid-19c) in positive contexts as an intensive meaning 'vastly, immensely': *It's the greatest idea, and I'm ever so grateful* —J. Leland, 1987 | *He's done ever so well out there. He's a fashion photographer, has his own studio.* — David Lodge, 1991. This use is largely restricted to conversational English.

every. 1 DIFFERENCES BETWEEN *EACH* AND *EVERY*. Both words denote all the people or things in a group, and both normally govern a singular verb (for some exceptions see EACH). But *each* is a pronoun (as in *I'll take three of each*) as well as an adjective (or determiner), whereas *every* is only an adjective (or determiner); you cannot say ☒ *I'll take three of every*, although you can say *I'll take three of every kind. Each* can refer to two or more items, whereas *every* can only refer to three or more. The meaning is also slightly different in that *each* regards the people or things concerned separately, whereas *every* regards them collectively.

2 TYPICAL USES OF *EVERY*. *Every* is used (1) with singular countable nouns to denote three or more (*It would be quite impossible to prosecute every motorist | The new version is better in every way | The company has a training day for every new employee | They have every right to be here*), (2) with some abstract uncountable nouns referring to a feeling or attitude (*We have every sympathy for their case | I have every confidence in you*), (3) with nouns of time to form adverbial phrases denoting frequency (*She comes every day | We get an extra day off every three weeks | We see them in town every now and then*), (4) with numbers to denote distribution (*They investigate one case in every ten | The police were stopping every third car*). When a possessive pronoun precedes a noun, *every* comes between them: *She'll look after your every need.*

3 *EVERY SINGLE, EVERY OTHER*. *Single* serves as an intensifier after every (*I was able to hear every single word*), and *other* denotes alternate items in a group (*Every other house had a garage*).

4 *EVERY ONE*. As two words, *every one* can refer to people or things, and each word retains its distinct meaning (*When we cut up the apples, every one of them was rotten*). Written as one word, *every-one* refers only to people: see EVERYONE.

everybody has been written as one word since the 19c, and alternates with *everyone* with no difference in meaning. Both words take a singular verb, but pronouns in the continuation of the sentence are often plural to denote neutrality of gender: *Every-body seems to recover their*

spirits—Ruskin, 1866 | *Everybody has a right to describe their own party machine as they choose*—Winston Churchill, 1954 | *'There's a bus waiting outside the terminal to take everybody to their hotels,' said Linda*—David Lodge, 1991. See AGREEMENT 4.

everyday is written as one word when it is used as an adjective in attributive position (before a noun): *They were wearing everyday clothes*. As an adverbial phrase, every day is written as two words: *She goes shopping nearly every day.*

everyone, as an indefinite pronoun meaning the same as *everybody*, is now regularly spelt as one word. This convention is surprisingly recent (20c); the *OED* (in 1894) preferred *every one* (two words), while Fowler (1926) presented a spirited argument in favour of the linked form *everyone*. As with *everybody*, *everyone* takes a singular verb but can be followed by a plural pronoun or possessive in the continuation of the sentence to denote neutrality of gender: *Everyone then looked about them silently, in suspense and expectation*—W. H. Mallock, 1877 | *Everyone was absorbed in their own business*—A. Motion, 1989 | *The classical allegories look like surreal school outings in which everyone got to take their clothes off, and then was sorry*—M. Vaizey, 1991. See AGREEMENT 4. Unlike *every one* written as two words (see EVERY 4), *everyone* refers only to people.

everyplace is a modern AmE synonym of *everywhere*: *Although, like everyplace else, the White Elephant had engaged a corps of college students*—Saturday Review, 1976.

every time, used as an adverbial phrase and conjunction, should

be written as two words: *It hap-
pens every time | Every time they
come, there's an argument.* It is
sometimes found as one word,
but this is incorrect: ☒ *Everytime I
see a new line on my face, I'm also
hysterically thinking it's all over—The
Face*, 1990.

evidence *verb.* This verb, meaning 'to serve as evidence of' or 'to
attest' (*The closer links with the London company were evidenced by the
acquisition of LGOC-type buses and
equipment*—K. Warren, 1980) and,
more loosely, 'to indicate' (*Everything he was and did evidenced
distinction*—Nadine Gordimer, 1990),
is decidedly awkward and is not
often found in everyday use.
Other more comfortable words
are available (e.g. *attest, demon-
strate, exhibit, indicate, show*) and
are usually preferable.

evilly, the adverb from *evil,* is
spelt with two *l*s.

evince is used mainly in formal
English (or, as Fowler put it, by
'those who like a full-dress word
better than a plain one') to mean
'to show or make evident (a quality or feeling)'. One might add
that it is usually found in the
company of other full-dress
words: *Nobody he passed evinced
the slightest interest in him or
seemed to constitute any kind of
threat*—J. Leland, 1987 | *They con-
stantly evince a smug hermeticism
that is graceless and slight*—*Times,*
1987.

ex-, used as a prefix meaning
'former', causes no difficulty
when it is attached to single
words (*ex-convict | ex-president |
ex-lover*). Fowler's objection to its
use with noun phrases (*ex-Lord
Mayor | ex-Prime Minister*) as 'patent
yet prevalent absurdities', is uncharacteristically pedantic, and

the eye easily accommodates
most expression of this kind. In
more awkward cases, especially
where further hyphenation is involved, *former* is always available
(*a former trade-union leader*). *Ex-* has
a special use in *ex-directory,* meaning 'not listed in a (telephone)
directory', in *ex-dividend,* meaning
'before payment of a dividend',
and in *ex-VAT,* meaning 'before
VAT has been added'.

exalt, exult. The two words are
not related and have different
meanings which can be confused
because of their closeness of
form. *Exalt* (pronounced ig-**zawlt**)
means 'to praise highly', and is
often used in the participial form
exalted, meaning 'grand, noble',
with reference to status, ideals,
etc.: *No member of your Government
should consider his position to be
more important and exalted than that
of the Paramount Chief*—*Rand Daily
Mail,* 1917. *Exult* (pronounced
ig-**zult**) means 'to feel great joy or
triumph', and is common in its
adjectival form *exultant: Alice could
hardly prevent herself from openly
exulting*—Doris Lessing, 1986 | *As the
camera pulled back on the last shot
and credits were shown on the
screen, the tension in the studio re-
laxed, replaced by an exultant
mood*—S. Conran, 1992. The meanings come very close in the corresponding nouns, *exaltation* =
expression of praise, and *exult-
ation* = expression of joy.

exceedingly, excessively. Both
words came into use in the late
15c. *Exceedingly* (16c in its current
meaning) means 'very, extremely',
and is now used only with adjectives and adverbs (most often
well): *His room was exceedingly
cold*—P. Fitzgerald, 1982 | *Judd was
doing exceedingly well as an air
cadet*—C. Lorrimer, 1993. *Excessively*

has a much stronger meaning 'too, by too much', and is used with verbs as well as adjectives and adverbs: *She may exercise excessively, spending hours each day in the gymnasium*—Abraham & Llewellyn-Jones, 1984 | *In Enid Blyton's work, this excessively simple world picture is carried to extremes*—N. Tucker, 1981.

excellent can be qualified by *quite* or *most*, which are adverbs with absolute meaning, but not by *very* or *more*, which are grading adverbs: *The quite excellent British Museum Press, which is managing to produce some twenty scholarly titles this season*—Art Newspaper, 1992.

except. 1 Use as a conjunction is now archaic, as in the famous passage in Psalms (AV, 127:1): *Except the Lord build the house, they labour in vaine that build it* (in more modern translations this is rendered *Unless the Lord builds the house . . .*).

2 *Except* should not normally be used by itself to mean 'except that' or 'but', although this is common informally and in conversation: *The day he turned 18, Trojan moved into his own council flat in Caledonian Road. Except he didn't like it*—The Face, 1987.

3 *Except for*, as in *They all came except for James*, is also somewhat informal, and is best avoided when *except* alone will do: *They all came except James*. At the beginning of a sentence, however, *except for* is needed: *Except for James, everyone brought a gift with them*.

excepting is correctly used as a preposition instead of *except* when it follows *not* (or another negative) or *always*: *His comprehensive knowledge of the Lakes stood above that of all the men of his time, not excepting Wordsworth*—J. Sloss

et al., 1984. An alternative, though less usual, construction is . . . *Wordsworth not excepted*. Examples of uses in which *except* would be preferable are: ⊠ *Faith had left all her jewellery, excepting mother's pearl and ruby eternity ring, to Dorothea Shottery*—Susan Hill, 1969 | ⊠ *These processes, excepting that of population growth, are largely unexplored*—P. Blaikie, 1987.

exception. The proverb *the exception proves the rule* means 'the existence of an exception shows that a rule exists in those cases that are not exceptions'. It should not be used to mean 'the exception becomes the rule', although this is often found.

exceptional, exceptionable.
1 These adjectives relate to different meanings of exception. *Exceptional* means 'unusual, not typical', i.e. 'forming an exception' in a favourable sense: *Schizophrenes are often held to be people of exceptional charm*—D. Cory, 1977 | *You could get an exceptional trade-in price for your old car*—Sunday Express, 1980. *Exceptionable* means 'to which exception may be taken', i.e. 'open to objection': *Prince later wrote to Gould when he was in Australia, complaining that Alfred Newton had been 'far, far too complimentary' about Lear's part in the publication, 'particularly when we know that most of the subscribers are of the opinion that his plates are almost the only exceptionable part of your work*—I. Tree, 1991. It is more often used in the negative form *unexceptionable*, meaning 'not open to objection, perfectly satisfactory'.

2 In the following examples, *exceptionable* seems to be used in error for other words, *exceptional* in the first example, and *acceptable* in the second: *The establishment Whigs . . . came to argue that*

excessively | executive 230

resistance was only allowable in exceptionable circumstances, such as those of 1688—T. Harris, 1993 | *The three point nine million pounds was effectively a minimum exceptionable level and it was within this figure they required the one point six million on minor works and footways to be increased to two million pounds*—record of meeting, 1992.

excessively see EXCEEDINGLY.

exchangeable is spelt with three *e*s.

excise is spelt *-ise*, not *-ize*. As a noun and verb in the 'tax' meaning, it is pronounced with the stress on the first syllable; as a verb meaning 'to remove by cutting' it is pronounced with stress on the second syllable.

excitable is spelt without an *e* in the middle.

exclamation mark. In ordinary writing, the exclamation mark (!) should be used sparingly, and in particular should not be used to add a spurious sense of drama or sensation to writing that is otherwise undramatic or unsensational, or to signal the humorous intent of a comment whose humour might otherwise go unrecognized. There are a number of established uses:

1 To mark a command or warning: *Go to your room! | Be careful!*.

2 To indicate the expression of a strong feeling of absurdity, surprise, approval, dislike, regret, etc., especially after *how* or *what*: *What a suggestion! | How awful! | Aren't they odd! | What a good idea! | They are revolting! | I hate you!*.

3 To express a wish or feeling of regret: *I'd love to come! | If only I had known!*.

4 To indicate someone calling out or shouting: *Outside Edith's house, someone knocked. 'Edith!' | 'You're only shielding her.' ' Shielding her!' His voice rose to a shriek.*

Many literary uses can be found in the *Oxford Dictionary of Quotations*. The following are a few representative examples: *I weep for Adonais—he is dead! O, weep for Adonais!*—Shelley, 1821 | *Yet still the blood is strong, the heart is Highland, And we in dreams behold the Hebrides!*—J. Galt, 1829 (translated in *Blackwood's Magazine*) | *Nearer, my God, to Thee, Nearer to Thee!*—S. F. Adams, 1841 | *Oh, to be in England Now that April's there . . . While the chaffinch sings in the orchard bough In England—now!*—Robert Browning, 1845 | *Fools! For I also had my hour; One far fierce hour and sweet*—G. K. Chesterton, 1900 | *What a queer thing Life is! So unlike anything else, don't you know, if you see what I mean.*—P. G. Wodehouse, 1919 | *Six days of the week it* [sc. *work*] *soils With its sickening poison—Just for paying a few bills! That's out of proportion*—Philip Larkin, 1955.

excusable is spelt without an *e* in the middle.

executive in general use denotes one of three branches of government of which the other two are the *legislative* and the *judicial*. In the UK, it also denotes a rank of civil servant above *administrative* and *clerical*, and in the UK and US it means a high officer with important duties in a business organization. In attributive use (before a noun) *executive* has developed a meaning used in marketing to describe anything promoted as suitable for use by executives, i.e. luxurious or exclusive: *You can quaff from 'executive bars' . . . in 'executive suites' and top up from 'executive ice machines' on* *'executive floors' . . . We have . . . luxuriated over 'executive menus' (smoked salmon is an extra with the 'executive breakfast'), and I once gratefully pocketed my 'complimentary executive gifts'.*—Lucinda Lambton, *Listener*, 1989.

executor, meaning an official appointed to carry out the terms of a will, is pronounced with the stress on the second syllable. It should be distinguished from *executioner*, an official who carries out a sentence of death.

exercise, both as a noun and a verb, is spelt *-ise*, not *-ize*, and has only one *c*.

exhaustible is spelt *-ible*, not *-able*. See -ABLE, -IBLE.

exhaustive, exhausting. Both words are derived from the verb *exhaust*, but relate to different meanings. *Exhaustive* relates to the meaning 'use up the whole of' (as in *exhausting a supply*) and means 'thorough or comprehensive': *We have all read the Steering Committee's exhaustive report*—D. Meiring, 1979. *Exhausting* relates to the meaning 'to tire (a person)' and means 'extremely tiring' or 'draining of strength': *He's known as the studio's resident Romeo, with a social life and a string of girlfriends which must be exhausting rather than exhilarating*—*Leicester Chronicle*, 1976.

exigent, exiguous. Both words are related to Latin *exigere* in its two meanings 'to enforce payment of' and 'to weigh exactly'. *Exigent* corresponds to the first of these meanings and means 'exacting' or 'urgent': *He was a man whose personal life, though occasionally exigent, never became a siren song*—A. S. Byatt, 1988 | *The*

exigent journalist Lynn Barber, in her collection of interviews Mostly Men, singles him out as the sole male representative of a type she describes as 'nice, straightforward, feet on the ground'.—*She*, 1989. *Exiguous* corresponds to the second meaning and means 'very small, scanty': *She gulped it down, paid the exiguous dispensing fee, and left the premises*—E. R. Taylor, 1991. | *The description of the facts is somewhat exiguous*—*Weekly Law Reports*, 1992.

exit. In stage directions the correct style is *Exit Macbeth* (when one person leaves the stage) and *Exeunt Banquo and Fleance* (when more than one person leaves). The two forms are the third person singular and third person plural present tense of the Latin verb *exire* 'to go out'.

-ex, -ix.
See box overleaf

ex officio is a Latin phrase meaning 'by virtue of one's office or status' (*The principal is ex officio a member of the board of governors*). It is spelt with a hyphen when used attributively (before a noun, as in *an ex-officio member of the committee*).

exorcize, meaning 'to expel (an evil spirit or influence)' is preferably spelt *-ize*, although *-ise* is common.

exoteric, exotic. Both words are derived ultimately from Greek *exō* meaning 'outside'. *Exoteric* is the opposite of *esoteric*, and means 'intended for people generally'; *exotic* means 'coming from or associated with a foreign country', often with connotations of the remarkable or bizarre, as in *exotic dances*.

-ex, -ix

Naturalized Latin nouns ending in *-ex* and *-ix* vary in their plural forms, sometimes (as English words) adding *-es* and sometimes (as Latin words) changing the ending to *-ices*. The following table lists the most important words and their plural forms.

SINGULAR	PRINCIPAL MEANING	PLURAL
apex	highest point (technical)	apexes apices
appendix	supplement in book (medical)	appendices appendixes
codex	manuscript in book form	codices
cortex	outer part of an organ	cortices
duplex	apartment on two floors (AmE)	duplexes
helix	spiral curve	helices
ilex	tree or shrub	ilexes
index	list in book (technical)	indexes indices
matrix	mould, grid structure, etc.	matrices *or* matrixes
murex	mollusc	murices
radix	number or symbol	radices
silex	quartz or flint	*no plural*
simplex	thing in its simplest form	simplexes
vertex	highest point	vertices *or* vertexes
vortex	mass of whirling fluid	vortices *or* vortexes

expandable, expansible are two forms of the derivative of *expand*. See -ABLE, -IBLE.

expect was the object of much criticism during the 19c when it was used to mean 'to suppose, surmise', as in *I expect you'd like a drink*. Fowler, however, regarded it as a natural extension of meaning and wrote (1926) that 'it seems needless purism to resist it'. This view has been supported by the weight of usage, especially in spoken English.

expedience, expediency. Both forms are in use in the meaning 'fitness, suitability, advantage', although *expediency* is much more common. The rhythm of the sentence often determines which is used: *The present mentality on the island emphasises short cuts, expedience and disdain for professional standard—New Scientist, 1991 | At the time there was a case to be made for the new policy satisfying the demands both of expediency and humanity—K. Tidrick, 1992.*

expiry, expiration. The primary meaning of *expiry* is 'the end of the validity or duration of something', as in *on expiry of the lease at the end of the month*. It is also a rather formal or euphemistic word for 'death'. *Expiration* can have these meanings, although much more often it means 'the act of breathing out', which *expiry* cannot be used to mean. Both words are derived from Latin *expirare* meaning 'to breathe out'.

expletive is pronounced ik-**splee**-tiv, with the stress on the second syllable, for both the noun (meaning 'an oath or swear word') and the adjective (meaning 'filling out a sentence, line of verse, etc.').

exploit is pronounced with the stress on the first syllable as a noun (meaning 'a bold or daring feat') and with the stress on the second syllable as a verb (meaning 'to take selfish advantage of').

export is pronounced with the stress on the first syllable as a noun and with the stress on the second syllable as a verb.

exposé, meaning 'a revealing of something discreditable', is pronounced as three syllables and is printed in roman type with an accent on the final e. The accent is sometimes omitted in AmE.

exposition is sharply distinguished in meaning from *exposé*. Its main meanings are (1) an explanation or interpretation of something difficult, (2) an explanatory article or treatise, and (3) a public exhibition.

ex post facto is a legal phrase meaning 'with retrospective action or force', as in *increasing its guilt* ex post facto / ex post facto *laws*. Strictly speaking, as Fowler (1926) noted, the spelling should be *ex postfacto* (meaning 'on the basis of the later enactment'), but the phrase has been written as three words since the 17c.

expressible is spelt *-ible*, not *-able*. See -ABLE, -IBLE.

exquisite. The position of the stress has been moving over the last two centuries from the first syllable, which used to be the rule, to the second, which is now very common. Neither Fowler (1926) nor Gowers (1965) made any comment, but there are many who continue to prefer the older stress pattern despite its awkwardness.

extant used to mean just 'existing', so that heresy, fashion, roads, etc. could all be extant. Now, it means 'continuing to exist', i.e. having withstood the ravages of time, so that ancient texts, fossils, old churches, etc. are the kinds of thing now described as *extant*.

extempore, pronounced as four syllables, means 'spoken or done without preparation', and can be used as an adverb or an adjective. It is preferable to the cumbersome alternatives *extemporaneous(ly)* and *extemporary / extemporarily*. *Impromptu* means much the same, conveying perhaps a greater element of spontaneity.

extend. Fowler (1926) and others have castigated the use of *extend* to mean 'to give, to offer' in expressions such as *extend a welcome*. Fowler wrote that 'extend in this sense has done its development in America, and has come to use full-grown via the newspapers—a bad record'. Few would object to its use today, which is common: *Sincere thanks were extended to all those who contributed to the success of the exhibition—Middlesborough Catholic Voice*, 1992 / *An open invitation is extended to Mr Amos to attend meetings of the Village Association committee—record of meeting, undated.

extendable, extendible, extensible are three equally legitimate forms derived from the verb *extend*. See -ABLE, -IBLE.

extenuate means 'to lessen or reduce the seriousness of (guilt or an offence)' and usually occurs in the participial form *extenuating*: *Poverty and desperation are extenuating factors in Bangladesh, but not in the United States—New Yorker*, 1973 | *The law itself, framed as it is in terms of strict liability, is not concerned with any niceties which might be provoked by extenuating circumstances—K. Hawkins, 1993.*

exterior, external, extraneous, extrinsic. 1 The four words are related, and all have meanings based on *outside*. *Exterior* and *external* both refer to the outside of things in contrast to the inside (*Most manufacturers describe their exterior wall paints as masonry paint—Do It Yourself Magazine*, 1991), and medicine is for *external use* when it is applied to the outside of the body; but *exterior* is generally physical only, whereas *external* is also applied in abstract or figurative meanings (*Changes in staff, changes in curriculum and increasing external demands making planning a chancy business—M. Sullivan*, 1991); the *external world* is the world beyond one's perception. As a noun, however, *exterior* has the abstract meaning 'the outward or apparent behaviour or demeanour of a person': *How about your pal Ivan? Does he have sensitive feelings under that Neanderthal exterior?—D. Ramsay*, 1973 | *Bob, who hides a sparky humour behind a grizzled exterior, said tenants who were taking his beers were doing it on a 'belligerent, sod-the-brewer basis'—What's brewing?*, 1991. *External* is used as a noun generally in the plural to mean 'the outward aspects or circumstances': *The place has all the appropriate externals, chimneys choked with ivy, windows with jasmine, worm-eaten shutters, mossy thatch—P. Tris-*

tam, 1989 | *Eventually he found all forms of religion involving 'externals' and ordinances unsatisfying—Dictionary of National Biography*, 1993.

2 Something that is *extraneous* is introduced or added from outside and is foreign to the object or entity in which it finds itself. Uses are both physical and abstract: *Several other insects attach extraneous objects or material to themselves, but for very different reasons—M. & T. Birkhead*, 1989 | *The best public art . . . is architectural art, the enrichment of buildings at which the Victorians excelled rather than extraneous pieces of sculpture and other items dotted around the streets—Daily Telegraph*, 1992 | *A moment later any extraneous thoughts were driven from his mind—I. Watson*, 1993. *Extraneous* points are irrelevant matters brought into a discussion to which they do not properly belong. Something that is *extrinsic* is not an essential and inherent part of the thing in question, and is often contrasted with *intrinsic*: *Motivation may be considered as either intrinsic or extrinsic; intrinsic motives include those of exploration and curiosity, and extrinsic those of status and social approval—B. O'Connell*, 1973 | *Your personal belongings may be frugal and of little extrinsic value, but when they are lost or stolen, the cost of replacement can be surprisingly high—S. Meredeen*, 1988.

extol, meaning 'to praise enthusiastically', is spelt *-ol* in BrE and has inflected forms *extolled, extolling*. In AmE *extol* and *extoll* (with the same inflections) are both in use.

extraordinary is normally pronounced ik-**straw**-di-nə-ri as five syllables, not six, the *a* being

merged into the following *or* to
form one syllable.

extraterritorial, meaning 'situated or having force outside a
country's territory', has prevailed
over the variant form *exterritorial*.

extrinsic see EXTERIOR.

extrovert, meaning 'outgoing
and sociable' (also used as a noun
to denote such a person), is now
usually spelt *extro-* (on the analogy of *introvert* and *controvert*), although *extra-* is the better (and
slightly earlier) formation, and
the one used by Jung when writing in English.

exult see EXALT.

-ey and -y in adjectives. The
normal suffix used to form adjectives from nouns is *-y*, as in *dusty,
earthy, messy*. Nouns ending in a
single consonant preceded by a
single vowel normally double the
consonant: *fatty, funny, nutty*. Some
adjectives are formed from verbs
rather than nouns: *chewy, fiddly,*

runny. When the root ends in *-e*
this is normally suppressed: *bony,
chancy, crazy, hasty, nosy, shady*, etc.
Some adjectives, however, are
formed with *-ey*:

1 Those formed from nouns
ending in *-y*: *clayey, skyey*. Note
that *cagey* (also *cagy*) and *phoney*
(also *phony*) are both of unknown
etymology, and do not belong to
this category. *Fiddly* is formed on
the verb *fiddle*, not the noun.

2 Those formed from nouns
ending in *-ue*: *bluey, gluey*.

3 *Holey*, meaning 'full of holes',
is spelt *-ey* to distinguish it from
the adjective *holy* = sacred.

eye *verb* has inflected forms *eyes,
eyed, eyeing*.

eyot (an islet) see AIT.

eyrie, meaning 'nest of a bird of
prey', is the preferred spelling,
not *aerie, aery*, or *eyry*. The word is
probably derived via medieval
Latin from an Old French word
aire meaning 'lair of wild animals'.

Ff

fabulous originally meant 'mythical, legendary', but already in the 17c its meaning was extended to refer to anything astonishing or incredible, whether or not it belonged to fable or legend. The word enjoyed a revival in America and Britain in the 50s and 60s in the weakened sense 'marvellous, wonderful', and spawned a shortened form *fab*. *Fab* now sounds dated, but *fabulous* is still very much in use in this meaning: *Miss Mitchell, looking, one must admit, fabulous, played down her frenzy*—Cambridge Review, 1959 | *She stretched her stockinged toes towards the blazing logs. 'Daddy, this fire's simply fab.'*—Times, 1963 | *Trueman puffed at a cigarette and said he looked fabulous*—A. Ross, 1963 | *That's a fab idea. I think I will*—B. T. Bradford, 1983 | *He thought she looked fabulous, just like a dream*—R. Ingalis, 1987. The principal usage of these words has always been with young people, and is likely to remain so despite the more recent appearance of much racier words.

façade, meaning the outward aspect of something (both physical and abstract), should be spelt with a cedilla, although the word is otherwise fully naturalized.

face up to, meaning 'to confront, accept bravely' (normally with a non-personal object), was first noted in America and Britain in the early 1920s, and at first provoked great criticism, Eric Partridge (1942) objecting to it as 'a needless expression, the result of the tendency to add false props to words that can stand by themselves'. The fury has long subsided, and the expression is listed in the *Concise Oxford Dictionary* (1990) without any limiting label. Examples of recent use: *He won't face up, can't face up, to them being gone*—K. Hulme, 1984 | *Why don't you simply face up to the past?*—Kazuo Ishiguro, 1986 | *These are problems which it is a major responsibility of government to face up to*—Parliamentary Affairs, 1991.

facile pronounced **fas**-iyl, means 'easy, smooth, effortless' with reference to people or what they do, and there is always a derogatory implication of something too easily achieved and of little value. A *facile speaker* is one for whom speaking comes easily and who therefore speaks glibly (rather than persuasively), and a *facile task* is one that is easily done but hardly worthwhile. If these connotations are not intended, a synonym such as (with reference to people) *able, accomplished, fluent,* etc. or (with reference to achievements) *effortless, fluent, natural,* etc., should be used instead.

facilitate, meaning 'to make easy or feasible' should have as its object a task or operation (including a verbal noun in *-ing*), not a person: *The more expensive short-wave receivers include . . . additional features . . . which facilitate accurate tuning*—BBC Handbook, 1962 | *They often used hypnosis to facilitate recall*—A. Storr, 1979 | *The door kept open between them to facilitate communication*—R. Cobb, 1983.

facility, faculty. 1 *Facility* (from Latin *facilis* meaning 'easy') means 'ease or ready ability to do something, aptitude': *Firstborn children have greater verbal facility, and there is evidence that they have more successful relationships with their teachers—Journal of Genetic Psychology*, 1973. It also has a concrete meaning which has proliferated greatly in the 20c, of 'something that provides an amenity or service', used in the singular or plural and referring either to the provision of an amenity (as in the third example) or to the amenity itself: *Other recreational facilities include two lighted tennis courts, a swimming pool and a jogging trail—Philadelphia Inquirer*, 1976 | *What about gays, one asks, and will there be facilities for them to relate significantly to each other?—Sunday Telegraph*, 1980 | *The channel will also have the facility for shopping from the armchair at the touch of a switch, now termed 'teleshopping'—Times*, 1983 | *Other features include sound facilities—Which Micro*, 1984 | *You don't need a generously proportioned tub to fit a spa or whirlpool bath facility—Do It Yourself*, 1990. A common use is in finance and banking, to denote an arrangement such as a loan or overdraft: *If you want credit, a bank facility is usually better value than even a good dealer can offer—Opera Now*, 1990.

2 *Faculty* means 'an aptitude or ability to do something' in the sense of an inborn or inherent power rather than a proficiency developed (for example) by practice. The *faculty of language* is the natural ability of humans to speak, whereas a *facility for language* is an individual's particular skill in speaking.

fact. 1 The expression *the fact that* has long had an important

function in enabling clauses to behave like nouns: *Some studies give attention to the fact that non-smokers cannot avoid inhaling smoke when breathing smoky air—*G. Richardson, 1971 | *The fact that I am gay is written down in black and white—Gay News*, 1978 | *Ethnic minorities will hopefully be tempted into the force by the fact that a black and female PC is given a starring role in the film—Guardian*, 1984 | *The fact that Nixon was willing to make his chastisement public suggests . . . that the President at least understands 'the parameters of the problem'—Time*, 1970. When standing at the head of a sentence (as in the second and fourth examples), the words *the fact* can sometimes be omitted without harming grammatical integrity, but a degree of emphasis or focusing is lost. On the other hand verbs that can be complemented by a *that*-clause do not need to be linked by *the fact that*, so that the sentence ⊠ *We acknowledge the fact that mistakes have been made* can be rephrased as *We acknowledge that mistakes have been made*, and ⊠ *They convinced him of the fact that it was right* can be rephrased as *They convinced him that it was right*. The phrases *owing to the fact that* and *despite the fact that* can normally be replaced by *because* and *although* respectively, thereby producing a more economical and clearer structure. For *due to the fact that* see DUE TO 4.

2 *Fact* is used in a number of idioms: *in fact, as a matter of fact, in point of fact, the fact is*, etc. These often serve to assist the rhythm and continuity of speech, but can easily become overused and redundant in written material.

factious, factitious, fractious. *Factious* means 'characterized by faction or dissension', as in *factious quarrelling*, whereas *factitious* means 'contrived, artificial', as in *factitious reasoning*; the words are related in their connection with Latin *facere* 'to do' but there is no overlap in meaning. *Fractious* has nothing to do with either but is sometimes confused with *factious*; it means 'irritable, peevish', as in *a fractious child*. See also FICTIONAL, FICTITIOUS.

factor, aside from its technical senses, means 'a fact or circumstance that contributes to a result', and the notion of cause lies at the heart of its use, as in Gladstone's sentence (1878) *The first factor in the making of a nation is its religion*. A modern example of its proper use is: *Other factors can alter the Earth's climate from millennium to millennium and decade to decade*—C. Tudge, 1991. In recent years, however, *factor* has become widely used in a weakened meaning 'consideration, aspect, feature' with little or no notion of causality: *A very important factor in the teaching of tennis is the value of practice once the lesson is over*— *Tennis World*, 1991. A new use dating from the 1980s involves a preceding noun as a defining word (e.g. *the Falklands factor*) to denote an event which is considered to have a significant effect on the fortunes or politics of a country, political party, etc.: *With the Libyan Legacy taking over from the Falklands Factor, the only question about Thursday's local elections is the extent of Labour's gains*—*Observer*, 1986. The *feel-good factor* is a feeling of material security in society; it is slowly yielding to the *feel-bad factor*.

The flagging fortunes of *factor* as a verb have been boosted with the evolution of the phrasal verb *factor in*, meaning 'to include (a

factor) in an assessment, plan, etc.': *All the political and military variables should be factored in before Israel decides on a response*—*Los Angeles Times*, 1991. It is chiefly used in AmE but is rapidly spreading to British use, and *factor out* is also occasionally found.

faculty see FACILITY.

faeces, meaning 'excrement', is pronounced **fee**-seez and is spelt with -*ae*- in BrE but -*e*- in AmE. The corresponding adjectival forms are *faecal* and *fecal* (pronounced with a hard *c*).

fag, faggot. In BrE a *fag* is a colloquial word for (1) a piece of drudgery or a wearisome or unwelcome task, (2) a cigarette, and (3) a junior pupil at a public school who runs errands for a senior. In BrE a *faggot* is a ball or roll of seasoned chopped meat that is baked or fried, and in BrE and AmE it is a bundle of sticks or twigs bound together as fuel. In AmE both *fag* and *faggot* are slang words for a male homosexual.

faint, feint. Both words come from the same Old English root. *Faint* is used as an adjective meaning 'indistinct, pale' or 'feeling dizzy', as a noun meaning 'a loss of consciousness', and as a verb meaning 'to lose consciousness'. *Feint* is used as a noun meaning 'a sham attack or blow as a diversion', as a verb meaning 'to make a feint', and (since the 19c) as an adjective denoting faint lines on ruled paper.

fair, fairly *adverbs. Fair* is used in its ordinary meaning 'in a fair manner' in several fixed expressions, e.g. *to bid fair, to play fair, fair between the eyes*. In dialect use and in some non-British varieties it is used to mean 'completely, fully, really', as in *It fair gets me down*. It should be remembered that *fairly* has several meanings: (1) in a fair manner (*He treated me fairly*); (2) moderately, to a noticeable degree (*The path is fairly narrow | a fairly good translation*); (3) utterly, completely (*He was fairly beside himself*). In some contexts it is difficult to know (as with *quite*) whether the meaning is 2 or 3, although in speech intonation can clarify which is meant.

fait accompli, pronounced fayt ə-kom-**plee**, means 'a settled arrangement or circumstance that cannot be altered'. It is normally printed in italic type.

faithfully. For *Yours faithfully*, see LETTER FORMS.

fall and *autumn* are used on both sides of the Atlantic as the name for the third season of the year, although in everyday use *autumn* is standard in BrE and *fall* in AmE. *Fall* is a shortening of the phrase *fall of the year* or *fall of the leaf*, and was in British use from the 16c until about 1800. The word *autumn* dates from the 14c, and comes from Latin *autumnus*, but the ultimate origin is obscure.

false analogy see ANALOGY.

falsehood, falseness, falsity. The three words, all to do with departure from the truth or what is true, have a considerable overlap in meaning and are sometimes interchangeable. *Falsehood* is the intentional telling of an untruth, and a *falsehood* is a lie or untruth. *Falseness* and *falsity* are both used more broadly to mean 'deceitfulness or unfaithfulness' or an instance of either. Examples: *A half-truth was a falsehood,*

and it remained a falsehood even when you'd told it in the belief that it was the whole truth—Aldous Huxley, 1939 | *As it had always been, truth and falsehood were inextricably intertwined in that statement*—S. Naipaul, 1980 | *The engagement had probably not been a complete falsity, a piece of acting*—Humphrey Carpenter, 1982 | *Reason cannot decide the truth or falsity of what is revealed in such cases, but can decide whether the revelation is genuine*—R. S. Woolhouse, 1988 | *The biggest danger in diplomacy is falseness, dishonesty and lack of credibility*—D. Freemantle, 1988 | *Speaking for a generation of American and British intellectuals, Seldes condemned American movies for their 'falseness' but saw that it was 'the falseness of the McKinley era'*—P. Stead, 1989 | *His falsity and hollowness are not just the opposite of the true and the wholesome, but threaten to undermine it*—J. Dollimore, 1991.

famed is a literary word meaning 'made famous', and is found (for example) in Shakespeare and Byron, often followed by *for* (the cause of the fame): *The English, for example, were famed for their assumptions of innate superiority*—J. Wormald, 1991 | *Many in and after the Second World War were to ponder the strange, radical genius of famed humility of social origin and ambiguous political stance*—G. Watson, 1991 | *Once famed as 'Baghdad by the Bay' in the days when such an appellation was a compliment, San Francisco has gone the way of many major U.S. cities*—Daily Telegraph, 1992. It is not a mere synonym of *famous*, although it is often found with that meaning, especially in newspaper writing: *In her famed speech on election night 1987, . . . she announced that 'we've got a big job to do in some of those inner* *cities'*—B. Pimlott, 1991 | *John Parkinson offers a tribute to a famed astronaut*—New Scientist, 1991.

fan, fanatic, fanatical. *Fanatic* is common as a noun meaning 'a person having excessive or misguided enthusiasm for something'; as an adjective it has largely given way to *fanatical*: *He was a fanatical worker, often doing thirteen or fourteen hours a day*—A. Thwaite, 1984. The abbreviated form *fan*, meaning 'a keen supporter', occurs in an isolated use in AmE as early as 1682, though not again until the late 19c when it became part of the ritual language of baseball, and then passed into general use in AmE, BrE, and elsewhere in the 20c in the senses 'a supporter, an admirer' (of a person or thing). *Fan mail* is first recorded in 1924, *fan letter* in 1932, and *fan club* in 1941, and other combinations are in use, including *fanzine* (= fan magazine), first recorded in 1951.

fantastic. 1 *Fantastic* is one of the most popular 20c colloquial terms for 'excellent, very enjoyable'. It is first recorded with this meaning in the 1930s and is now used in all sorts of contexts: *Oh, Val, isn't it fantastic? . . . It's amazing, isn't it?*—Margery Allingham, 1938 | *'This is my favourite place,' Jeremy shouts to her above the music, 'fantastic girls here, really alive and witty'*—M. Wandor et al., 1978 | *In the March issue of the Clothes Show Magazine, Wella offered our readers the fantastic opportunity to win a complete hair makeover*—Clothes Show, 1991 | *Then suddenly I get a call saying, 'We are going on the road,' so I was in and it was fantastic*—Guitarist, 1992. The adverb *fantastically* is also common as a general intensifier: *He's fan-*

tastically good-looking—Iris Murdoch, 1989 | *'We are doing fantastically well,' insisted a spokeswoman*—Today, 1992.

 2 Both *fantastic* and *fantastically* meanwhile continue to be used in their more literal meanings connected with fantasy and imagination, albeit somewhat compromised by the newer meanings: *We gazed in wonderment at the fantastic shape of the small island of Tindholmur as we passed*—B. Tulloch, 1991 | *De Quincey frequently dreamt of a fantastically elaborate and labyrinthine building*—R. Castleden, 1993.

fantasy, phantasy. 1 The *OED*, echoed by Fowler (1926), tried to assert a distinction between these two spellings, the first reflecting the Greek spelling and the second the more immediate French source of the word, 'the predominant sense of the former being "caprice, whim, fanciful invention", while that of the latter is "imagination, visionary notion" '. In modern use there is no such distinction, and *fantasy* prevails in all meanings.

 2 The use of *fantasy* in attributive position (before a noun) is relatively recent. *Fantasy world* dates from 1920, and C. Day Lewis appears to have been the first to use *fantasy life* (but his hyphen is not now usual): *It is said that an only child develops a particularly vivid fantasy-life*—Buried Day, 1960. In the 1980s came a new development with the invention, first in America and then in Britain, of a game called *fantasy football*, in which participants choose an imaginary team made up of real-life players; the actual performance of these players determines the fortunes of the fantasy team and ultimately the winner of the game. It will be interesting

to see what impact this use has on the word *fantasy*.

far. 1 *FAR FROM* + **NOUN.** This is a common way of expressing denial or rejection of a proposition: *The American dream seems as far from reality as my Communist dream—Guardian*, 1986. Its function as metaphor is more strongly evident in the variant form *far removed from*: *The trial will seem far removed from the red-light districts and suburbs where Sutcliffe struck—Observer*, 1981.

2 *(SO) FAR FROM* —*ING.* This construction, first recorded in the 17c, is used to reject or deny one proposition and assert another. The use of *so* was still current in 1926, when Fowler cited the example *So far from 'running' the Conciliation Bill, the Suffragettes only reluctantly consented to it. So* is still used for emphasis, but in general use it has tended to drop out of the construction: *Far from there being any noticeable improvement in the quality of relationships as practised among freaks, I would say there has been a distinct deterioration—Ink*, 1971 | *The crowd of students . . . far from being calmed by the duplicated communication which the registrar had delivered had become wild and agitated—*J. Mann, 1975.

3 *FAR-FLUNG.* This quite modern word (first recorded in 1895) calls to mind Kipling's *Recessional* (1897): *God of our fathers, known of old, Lord of our far-flung battle-line.* Fowler (1926) wrote of 'its emotional value . . . as a vogue-word. The lands are distant; they are not far-flung; but what matter? *Far-flung* is a signal that our blood is to be stirred.' The *far-flung Empire* has been replaced by less stirring concepts, but the rich flavour of the adjective remains as a reminder of past grandeur.

4 *AS FAR AS* | *SO FAR AS.* When used in contexts referring to physical distance, *as* and *so* were once freely interchangeable: *I can take you as far as York* or *I can take you so far as York.* In current use, *as far as* is used, and the option with *so* is obsolete. In adverbial clauses of the type *as far as . . . is concerned* or *as far as . . . goes*, the verbs *is* (or *are*) *concerned* and *goes* (or *go*) should not be omitted: *Young girls must be made to realise that boys of the same age have a 'tiger in their tank' as far as sexual desire goes—New Zealand Tablet*, 1971 | *The old pals act will operate as far as the press is concerned—*T. Heald, 1975. The expression *as far as I am concerned* is commonly used as a kind of emotional disclaimer: *It makes me a bit sick actually and they can keep their mag as far as I am concerned—Guardian*, 1973 | *I started out with some idea of serving the community and bunk like that, and now the community can get on with it as far as I'm concerned—*J. Bingham, 1975. See also IN SO FAR AS.

5 *GENERAL USES.* Far is regularly used before comparatives and before *too* + adjective: *The people of Garston have suffered far too long from the planning blight that has caused serious deterioration in the area—Liverpool Echo*, 1976 | *Hard disks are made to a far higher degree of precision, using an aluminium platter that is extremely finely ground—Times*, 1982 | *It turns out to be a far more interesting car to drive than its Japanese clones—Australian Financial Review*, 1984. It also occurs in many idioms, *far and away, far be it from me, far and near, go too far, so far so good*, etc., for which a large modern dictionary should be consulted.

farrago, meaning 'a confused mess or muddle', comes from a

Latin word meaning 'mixed fodder' (from *far* = corn), and is normally used in abstract senses. The plural form is *farragos* in BrE and *farragoes* in AmE.

farther, further. 1 GENERAL. *Further* is the older form, being recorded in Old English and probably related to our word *forth*, while *farther* is a Middle English variant of *further*; from this stage the two words came to be used as the comparative of *far*, and by the 17c had entirely replaced the other Middle English forms *farrer* and *ferrer*. *Farther* is related only coincidentally in form to *far*, although this coincidence seems to have influenced its use. It is never wrong to use *further* and *furthest*, whereas *farther* and *farthest* are restricted in use, and in cases where there is a choice *further* and *furthest* still tend to be more common.

2 USE OF *FARTHER*, *FARTHEST*. The principal role of *farther* is in expressing physical distance, corresponding more closely to the notion of 'more far' and 'most far': *The gulls rose in front of him and floated out and settled again a little farther on*—Virginia Woolf, 1922 | *And now the prince is scouring the farthest reaches of the globe for his bride*—J. M. Coetzee, 1977 (South Africa) | *Most DIY owners find that five to ten miles is the farthest they want to travel*—Today's Horse, 1991. This apparent preference may be carried over into uses that represent degree rather than physical distance, but within the context of a wider distance metaphor: *'Why, Lord, no honey!' I told her. 'It's the farthest thing from my mind.'*—Lee Smith, 1983 (US) | *Kasparov simply saw farther, 'much, much farther', than the machine*—New York Times Magazine, 1990.

3 USE OF *FURTHER*, *FURTHEST*. *Further* and *furthest* are more usual when the meaning is one of degree rather than physical distance: *He . . . found English currency confusing and the driver sought to confuse him further*—Evelyn Waugh, 1961 | *It seeks the furthest extension of the educationally valuable among the masses*—Encounter, 1987 | *In the case of her friendship with Flaubert she went one decade further and became a mother-substitute*—Economist, 1993.

4 OTHER EVIDENCE. The following examples show that the pattern is not totally consistent, with *further* (in particular) being used in ways associated with *farther* and (less so) vice versa: *This was the lower fountain, furthest from the house*—A. S. Byatt, 1987 | *'You get a lot farther using your nose than your palate,' Patty says about wine-tasting*—New Yorker, 1987 | *The New Delhi station which did appear, somewhat further away, was a functional monstrosity in concrete and steel*—J. Richards et al., 1988 | *One, Lewis Holt, actually worked in Fleming's laboratory, and took the purification a stage farther than any of the previous workers*—M. Weatherall, 1990 | *The ferryman pointed to a thatched, low-roofed timbered hut further along the shoreline*—P. C. Doherty, 1991. Overall, the evidence shows a somewhat stronger presence of *farther* and *farthest* in AmE, but American usage guides do not normally reflect this tendency in their guidance.

5 SPECIAL USES. There are some uses that are exclusive to *further*:

▶a When used as a sentence adverb: *Further, shameful as it might be to admit it, the idea of the play had started to interest him rather*—Kingsley Amis, 1958 | *Further, firms' employment policies may be discrim-*

inatory even when they appear not to be—J. Urry et al., 1993.

▶ **b** When it is an adjective meaning 'additional' or an adverb meaning 'additionally' or 'also': *He wrote for booklets containing further particulars of almost every device he saw advertised*—Elizabeth Bowen, 1949 | *Dundee's modern shopping precinct has now been further decorated with paint-sprayed gang slogans*—*Scotsman*, 1973 | *The apartment was further defended by a police lock*—J. Aiken, 1975 | *The person in custody is required . . . to appear again at a police station at a certain time for further questioning*—*Daily Telegraph*, 1976 | *Brush with the beaten egg white and bake for a further 5 to 10 min until they're crisp and golden*—*Ideal Home*, 1991.

▶ **c** In certain fixed expressions in which *further* is an adjective, e.g. *further education*.

▶ **d** In the formal expressions (1) *further to*, used especially in business correspondence to refer to matters raised previously: *Further to our letter of 20 August . . .* , and (2) *until further notice*.

▶ **e** In the compound adverb *furthermore*.

▶ **f** As a verb meaning 'to favour or promote (an idea, scheme, etc.)': *No city has done more than Coventry since the war to further the cause of internationalism*—*Times*, 1973 | *There has been greater emphasis by unions upon legislative enactment to further their general objectives*—R. Bean, 1992.

Fascism, Fascist. When Fowler wrote in 1926, Mussolini had not long been established in power, and the future of these words, and their Italian counterparts *fascismo* and *fascista*, was uncertain. He suspended judgement on their anglicization 'till we know whether the things are to be tem-porary or permanent in England'. The concepts are still very much with us, the English words are still pronounced in an Italian manner with the central consonant as *sh* (**fash**-izm / **fash**-ist), and the Italian forms are not used at all except in the special contexts of Italian history.

fatal, fateful. Both words have to do with the workings of fate, and their complex histories, fully explored by the *OED*, have often intertwined. Fowler (1926) wrote a fond defence of the special meaning of *fateful*, 'having far-reaching consequences', which (unlike *fatal*) might be good or neutral as well as bad: *In summing up 1934 we can see, in the light of what was to come, that it was a fateful year'*—J. F. Kennedy, 1940 | *The fateful sequence of events had started with a malfunction in the main pumps supplying cooling water to the reactor's core*—C. Aubrey, 1991. *Fatal* means 'causing death' (as in *fatal accident*), and can refer to inanimate things and situations as well as to those able to suffer actual death: *Even when your trump suit is solid, it may still be fatal to touch it too early*—*Country Life*, 1976 | *The existence of these private but non-fee-paying schools will have a deeply depressing, if not fatal, effect on other schools in the area*—M. Warnock, 1989 | *Until he faces up to his own fatal flaws, he has no hope of conquering them*—*Today*, 1992. The closest synonyms to *fatal* in this meaning are *catastrophic, disastrous, ruinous*.

father-in-law means one's wife's or husband's father. The plural is *fathers-in-law*.

fathom, a unit of measurement of depth, is unchanged in the plural when preceded by a number, i.e. *six fathom deep* but *several fathoms deep*.

fatwa. A *fatwa* (from Arabic *fatā* 'to instruct by a legal decision') is a legal ruling given by an Islamic religious leader. It came dramatically to western attention in 1989 when by such a ruling Iran's Ayatollah Khomeini called for the death of the writer Salman Rushdie for publishing *The Satanic Verses* (1988), which many Muslims considered blasphemous. *Fatwa* is already undergoing extensions of meaning, and is erroneously used to mean 'sentence of death' (which, in the case of Rushdie, it means only in effect). The plural in English contexts is *fatwas*, and the use of a verb form is also recorded: *Unlike many writers and artists, Chahine hadn't been fatwaed, but he felt threatened nevertheless—New Yorker*, 1995.

faucet is a late Middle English word meaning 'a tap for drawing liquor from a barrel or cask'. In BrE it survives in technical uses (often combined with *spigot*), but in domestic use it has given way entirely to *tap*. In AmE, *faucet* is in widespread use for an ordinary water tap, but its distribution is uneven, with *spigot* in use in the south and *cock* and *tap* also in use.

fault *verb*. *To fault*, meaning 'to blame, find fault with', has been criticized as an awkward verbalization by some 20c usage guides, especially in America, though not by Fowler (1926), nor by Gowers (1965) who declared supportively that it was enjoying a revival. The use dates from the 16c and is now fully established: *Martita wasn't too keen on Fay Compton I gathered (though she couldn't fault her perfect diction)*—Alec Guinness, 1985.

fauna, flora, meaning respectively the animal life and plant life of a particular time or region, are derived from the names of Roman goddesses and are singular (uncountable) nouns. The plural forms, though rarely needed, are *faunas* and *floras* (occasionally *faunae* and *florae*).

faux pas, meaning 'a minor blunder or indiscretion', is pronounced foh **pah** and is printed in italic type. The plural form is the same, pronounced foh **pahz**.

favour, favourable, favourite are the normal BrE spellings, as distinct from *favor, favorable, favorite* in AmE.

fax is first recorded in 1948 as a shortened form of *facsimile* (*process*, etc.) and quickly established itself in the standard language as a noun and verb, especially during the 1980s when *fax machines* came into widespread use. The word has been accepted much more readily than *pix* (= pictures) and *sox* (= socks), presumably because no comfortable alternative exists, *facsimile transmission* being too technical and awkward for ordinary use.

fay, fey. *Fay* is a literary word for *fairy*. Used attributively (before a noun), it has the meaning 'fairy-like': *When she made formal use of figures in her landscapes, they were somewhat mannered, almost fay children—Listener*, 1962. *Fey* is an unrelated word of great antiquity originally meaning 'fated to die soon', a meaning it still has in Scottish English. In due course it came to denote a kind of frenzied excitement associated with impending death, and in extended use it means 'strange, other-worldly; elfin, whimsical': *She's got that fey look as though she's had breakfast with a leprechaun*—D. Burnham, 1969. In this last meaning it makes close contact with *fay*, but properly used *fey* still has implications of imminent death and the supernatural, whereas *fay* inhabits the land of dreams. In speech, of course, there is no explicit distinction.

faze means 'to disconcert, disturb' and is used informally in mainly negative contexts: *It is a pretty daunting prospect going on stage for forty minutes but it does not seem to have fazed her*—S. Stone, 1989 | *The one thing I am not going to do is look remotely fazed or ruffled*—E. Galford, 1993. It is in origin a 19c AmE variant of the ancient verb *feeze* 'to drive off, to frighten away' and has nothing to do with the ordinary verb *phase*, although this spelling is sometimes used in the US.

fearful, fearsome. 1 *Fearful* means 'full of fear; frightened, apprehensive', usually with reference to something specific, and is normally followed by *of* or by a clause introduced by *that* or *lest*: *There are parochial or communal parties which . . . are fearful of absorption into larger units*—Economist, 1981 | *Eisenhower's official policy was to remain aloof, fearful that any direct intervention would make Castro a martyr*—N. Miller, 1989 | *He became very fearful of cars, buses and stairs, eventually shutting himself in his room, with the curtains drawn, for 14 months*—Guardian, 1989 | *She stood outside looking up at a creamy moon, fearful lest some bat might fly into her hair*—Julian Barnes, 1990. It is also used with reference to feelings and circumstances that are characterized by great fear:

His mother had brought him up to hold priests in fearful reverence—G. McCaughrean, 1987, and in the weakened meaning 'unpleasant', with reference to things and situations: *In fact it had been very hard-bought, some of the winnings, taking fearful tolls of nerve, straining every atom of him*—Nicolas Freeling, 1972 | *On the Left Bank, with a fearful expenditure of lives, the German all-out offensive had bought possession of two hills of secondary importance*—A. Horne, 1993.

2 *Fearsome* means 'appalling or frightening, especially in appearance': *Ichiro continued to regard me with the most fearsome look*—Kazuo Ishiguro, 1986 | *Rhododendrons . . . have become a fearsome forest weed, preventing the growth of other plants*—Outdoor Action, 1989 | *Despite their fearsome reputation, however, killer whales have never been known to attack humans without the provocation of a bullet or harpoon*—M. Donoghue et al., 1990.

feasible. The key to the use of this word, and the problems associated with it, lies in its relation to the different meanings of *possible*. *Feasible* has three main uses, two unexceptionable and one controversial, all associated with different aspects of possibility:

1 With reference to ideas, projects, etc., 'capable of being done, practicable': *Changes became feasible over a period of time*—Harold Wilson, 1976 | *There was no question that a tunnel was technically feasible, but I wanted to know what the economics would be*—N. Fowler, 1991 | *Clearly, it is not feasible to have cameras covering the whole of the track.*—Hansard, 1992.

2 With reference to people and things generally, 'capable of being used or dealt with successfully': *The sixties should see them* [sc. labour-saving devices] *put into commercial production in sufficient quantity to make them financially feasible—Sunday Times*, 1960 | *The new semi-automated test could at last make massive screening programmes for cervical cancer economically feasible—New Scientist*, 1991.

These first two meaning are often hard to distinguish, although essentially the first refers to actions and processes whereas the second refers to what is being dealt with or considered; they are given separately in the OED but are combined in the *Concise Oxford Dictionary*. Perhaps only compilers of dictionaries attempt to see a difference.

3 With reference to a theory, proposition, etc., 'able or likely to be the case': *Had he not assumed the initiative it was feasible she would have given a reason to keep them out*—L. Grant-Adamson, 1989. This third, and controversial, meaning comes closest to being a synonym of *possible* (in its meaning 'able to be the case' rather than 'able to be done') or *probable*, and Fowler urged strongly that when these words can be substituted without affecting the meaning they should be. The examples he gave, unattributed but probably from newspapers, were: *Witness said it was quite feasible* [better *possible*] *that if he had had night binoculars he would have seen the iceberg earlier* and *We ourselves believe that this is the most feasible* [better *probable*] *explanation of the tradition*.

Each case must be treated on its merits, but when the context requires the sense of likelihood or probability (as in the 1989 example above) rather than practicality it is prudent to test first whether *possible* or *probable* might not be the more satisfactory word

(this will occur most often in constructions of the type *It is feasible that . . .*), and to use *feasible* only if both the other words seem unnatural or unidiomatic.

feature *verb*. Fowler (1926) warned against the extension of the meaning 'to give special prominence to' which he identified as originating in cinema announcements. He cited an unattributed example of 1924: *Boys' school and college outfits, men's footwear and undergarments, as well as . . . , are also featured*, and urged the use of *display* or *exhibit* instead. But his words went unheeded, and the verb *feature* is now in regular use both transitively (with an object, as in the example just given) or intransitively (without an object): *I was to have my name featured for the first time at the top of the bill*—Charles Chaplin, 1964 | *Libraries and the youth service feature prominently in many of the local authority cuts—Times*, 1976 | *Student concerts featuring him as composer and pianist*—R. Hayman, 1981.

February should be pronounced with both *r*s fully articulated. It is now common, especially in AmE, to hear the word pronounced as if it were *Febuary* (and it is occasionally spelt that way too, which is a great deal worse).

federation, confederation, confederacy. *Federation* and *confederation* are the more precise constitutional terms, a *federation* being a union of federal states and a *confederation* being a union of states in alliance. *Confederacy* is a looser term for an organization of states such as the southern states of the US which seceded from the Union in 1860–1, thus

precipitating the American Civil
War.

feedback developed its meaning
in general use, 'information
about something from the people
that have used it or been involved in it', in the 1960s: *They
would like feedback from the last
issue, articles from individuals and
groups giving a socialist-feminist analysis of activities—Women's Report,
1976 | The aim of marking is . . . to
give constructive feedback so that the
students' work steadily improves—
Electronic Publishing,* 1991. Earlier
technical uses in electronics and
biology date from earlier in the
20c.

feel *verb.* **1** *Feel* is followed by an
adjective to denote the nature of
a feeling, whether physical or
emotional: *I'm feeling cold | They
began to feel afraid.* For *to feel bad,*
see BAD 1.

2 Occasional, but misguided,
opposition has been expressed to
the use of feel in the intuitive
meaning 'to think, believe, consider' or, as the *OED* puts it, 'to
apprehend or recognize the truth
of (something) on grounds not
distinctly perceived; to have an
emotional conviction of (a fact)'.
The use goes back to Shakespeare
(*Garlands . . . which I feel I am not
worthy yet to wear—Henry VIII*
IV.ii.91, and has been current ever
since in standard use. Modern examples: *But perhaps it was a little
flat somehow, Elizabeth felt. And
really she would like to go—*Virginia
Woolf, 1925 | *If Pascal had been a
novelist, we feel, this is the method
and the tone he would have used—*
Graham Greene, 1969 | *Many gays ei-
ther were in therapy or felt they
should be—*E. White, 1980.

feel-good, feel-bad. We have
had the *feel-good factor* and *feel-*

goodism since 1977, when the *New
York Times* reported that *the latest
aberration in the American pursuit of
happiness is the feelgood movement.*
The word had been used earlier
in *Dr Feelgood,* a term for a physician who provided short-term
palliatives rather than effective
cures. In the 1990s, the term feel-
good factor came increasingly to
be associated with material pros-
perity as a political and social
factor. The antidote to all this is
the *feel-bad factor,* which dates
from the early 1990s: *We're all so
insecure about our short-term contracts and our feel-bad factors that
we're terrified of appearing keen to
leave the office—Guardian,* 1995. No
other set of words encapsulates
so well the swinging emotional
moods of peoples in the nineties.

feint see FAINT.

fellow, in its meaning 'belonging to the same class or activity'
used attributively (before a noun),
is sometimes hyphened and
sometimes written as a separate
word: *fellow citizen* or *fellow-citizen.*
The modern tendency is to spell
such combinations as two words
except when the second element
is an agent noun (as in *fellow-
traveller*) or when the combination
is a verb (*to fellow-travel*).

female, feminine. 1 GENERAL.
Female is used as an adjective,
contrasting with the etymologically unrelated word *male,* to designate the sex of humans and
animals that can bear offspring
and to designate plants that are
fruit-bearing. *Feminine* is used
only of humans and has two additional meanings: (1) denoting
characteristics or qualities associated with women, and (2) contrasted with *masculine* and *neuter,*
denoting a class of grammatical

gender. Both words also have technical meanings in various domains. In broad terms *female* is used principally to indicate the sex of a person, animal or plant, whereas *feminine* is used of characteristics regarded as typical of women, i.e. beauty, gentleness, delicacy, softness, etc. See also WOMANLY, WOMANISH.

2 FEMALE AS A NOUN. *Female* has a long history in the meaning 'a female person'; 'a woman or girl', but despite this several 19c usage guides advised against the use on the grounds that it was unsuitable to apply the same term to animals and human beings. The *OED* (in 1895) said of *female* used as a synonym for *woman* that 'the simple use is now commonly avoided by good writers, except with contemptuous implication'. This observation holds good in our gender-sensitive age, and it would be difficult to contemplate *female* being used in this way without some degree of disparagement being intended or understood: *He had no option now but to speak to his landlady in the morning about letting this homeless female have his bed for the night*—M. J. Staples, 1992. The use is best reserved for use in natural history and for occasions when a general or neutral term is needed (for example, in technical writing) to include both *woman* and *girl*, or to avoid the social distinctions still sometimes inherent in *woman* and *lady*: *More than 55 females, from babies to elderly women, have been killed during the first year of the Uprising*—Spare Rib, 1989 | *Young white females are by far the most common users of crisis and suicide prevention facilities*—K. Hawton et al., 1990.

feminine designations. For most agent nouns and nouns in-

dicating occupation no distinction is made between masculine and feminine: *clerk, cook, councillor, counsellor, cyclist, doctor, lecturer, martyr, motorist, nurse, oculist, palmist, president, pupil, secretary, singer, teacher, typist*, etc. A few, such as *actress, hostess*, and *usherette*, exist in feminine forms; forms in -*mistress* corresponding to the masculine -*master* (e.g. *postmistress, schoolmistress*) have fallen out of use. There is still some expectation that some occupations will be held by a man (e.g. *chef*) and that others will be held by a woman (e.g. *secretary*), but these barriers are falling fast. In practice, if there is a need to be specific about the gender of an occupational or agent noun, a feminine noun such as *woman, lady*, or *girl* is sometimes used (*woman driver, lady doctor*, etc.), although this too can offend sensitivities because corresponding male designations are only occasionally used in contexts in which the occupation has strong female associations (*male nurse, male typist*, etc.). The circumstances of these uses illustrate well the tensions between linguistic convention and social progress. See also -ESS, -ETTE, -MAN, -PERSON, -TRIX, -WOMAN, GENDER NEUTRALITY.

feminineness, feminism, femininity. These are the only survivors from a whole host of 19c formations which also included *feminacy, feminality, feminility*, and *femininitude* (the last a nonce-word used in 1878). *Feminineness* and *femininity* have much the same meaning, 'the fact or quality of being feminine', whereas *feminism* rapidly developed a special meaning 'advocacy of the rights of women on the grounds of equality of the sexes', a meaning which it has retained with increased force in the later part of the 20c.

feral, ferial. Both words are usually pronounced with the first syllable as in *ferret* rather than *fear*, although the second form is occasionally heard. *Feral* means 'wild' (from Latin *ferus* 'wild') and is commonly applied to animals in a wild state after escape from captivity. *Ferial* (from Latin *feriae* 'holiday') is an ecclesiastical term denoting a day not appointed for a festival or feast.

ferment, foment. 1 *Ferment* is pronounced with the stress on the first syllable as a noun and with the stress on the second syllable as a verb.

2 As verbs, *ferment* and *foment* are often confused because they are pronounced approximately the same way and their uses overlap in their figurative meanings. To *ferment* means literally 'to effervesce or cause to effervesce' (from Latin *fervēre* meaning 'to boil') and figuratively 'to excite or become excited'; and so it can be transitive (with an object) or intransitive: you can *ferment* trouble or trouble can *ferment*. *Foment* means literally 'to bathe with warm or medicated liquid' (from Latin *fomentum* meaning 'poultice') and figuratively 'to instigate or stir up' (especially trouble). *Foment* is only transitive: you can *foment* trouble but trouble cannot *foment*. Examples: *Gladstone's complaint in 1874 that the opposition fomented by the Daily News had been 'one main cause' of the weakness of his late government was, of course, a simplism—Times Literary Supplement*, 1977 | *Such protestations ferment a running sore which breeds contempt for the authorities—Nonesuch* (Bristol), 1991 | *He hosted the meetings where the rebellion was fomented which ousted Mrs Thatcher from power—Today*, 1992.

ferrule, ferule. *Ferrule*, also spelt *ferrel*, is the ring or cup used to strengthen the end of a walking-stick or umbrella, and is derived from Latin *ferrum* meaning 'iron'. A *ferule*, also spelt *ferula*, is a flat implement formerly used for beating schoolchildren, and is derived from Latin *ferula* meaning 'giant fennel'.

fervent, fervid. Both words mean 'ardent, intense' with reference to speech, feelings, etc. There are two significant difference in their use: (1) *fervent* but not *fervid* is also used of people (*a fervent supporter of free entrance to museums*), and (2) *fervent* has positive connotations whereas *fervid* can sound depreciatory, rather like the difference between *warm* and *feverish* as applied to feelings. Examples: (fervent) *There is no doubt that trade unionists were fervently hostile to the actions of Franco*—K. Laybourn, 1990 | *Every available wall space was covered with graffiti and fervent slogans*—T. Strong, 1990 | *That they shared, along with all other participants in the crusade, a fervent devotion, a conviction that their sins would be forgiven, is certain*—J. Dunbabin, 1991 | (fervid) *While a fervid interest in sex overpowered other girls, she listened to their confidences unmoved*—C. Brayfield, 1990 | *I'm afraid your rather fervid imagination is running away with you*—E. Rees, 1992 | *As in every war men confronted with death who had forgotten, or never knew how, began to pray fervidly*—A. Horne, 1993.

fertile. The standard pronunciation now is -tiyl in BrE and -təl in AmE.

fervour is spelt *-our* in BrE and *fervor* in AmE.

-fest is a new suffix derived from the German word *Fest* meaning 'festival, celebration'. It occurred first in AmE in the late 19c in the word *gabfest* meaning 'a gathering for talking' and spread rapidly to produce other words such as *talk fest, shooting fest, liquor fest*, etc. It has also spread to BrE in formations such as *discofest, filmfest, funfest, rockfest*, etc.

festal, festive. Both words are derived from the Latin words *festum* meaning 'feast' and *festus* meaning 'joyful', and mean 'in the nature of a feast or festival'. *Festive* is much the more common, and is the one generally chosen when the meaning is 'cheerful, joyous, celebratory': *A room can look festive and jolly without being overwhelmed by lots of gaudy decorations—Ideal Home*, 1991. *Festal* lies somewhat closer to its etymological connection with festivals: *It was eaten with a spoon and served on festal days as part of the main course—Good Food*, 1992. The *festive season* is a way of describing Christmas, and *festive* also occurs with words such as *air, atmosphere, mood*, and *occasion*.

fetal see FOETUS.

fête should be spelt with the circumflex in place, although it has disappeared in many forms of computer setting.

fetid, meaning 'stinking', is normally pronounced **fet**-id, occasionally **feet**-id. The spelling *fet-*, rather than *foet-*, is now dominant.

fetish. 1 *Fetish*, meaning 'a thing evoking special respect' (and more precise meanings in anthropology and psychology), is now pronounced **fet**-ish. The word is a 17c adoption of French *fétiche*, and was originally an African object or amulet having magical power, although the word itself is not of African origin.

2 Fowler (1926) extended the use of fetish as a term for 'current literary rules misapplied or unduly revered'. These included the SPLIT INFINITIVE, insistence on *from* after DIFFERENT, aversion to putting a PREPOSITION at the end of a sentence, and the idea that two consecutive metaphors are necessarily 'mixed' (see METAPHOR AND SIMILE 2). To these may now be added the use of HOPEFULLY as a SENTENCE ADVERB, insistence that NONE is always singular, and insistence that AGENDA, DATA, and other such words are always plural. (Capital letters indicate items that will be found as other entries in this book.)

fetus see FOETUS.

few. *Few* may be used with or without preceding *a*, although the sense is slightly different. *There were few seats left* means there were not many (and is negative in implication), whereas *There were a few seats left* means that some were still left (and is positive in implication).

2 For *comparatively few*, see COMPARATIVELY.

fewer, less. 1 As a general guide, *fewer* is used with plural nouns (*fewer books*) and collective nouns (*fewer people*) and indicates number, whereas *less* is used with singular nouns and indicates amount (*less money | less happiness*). However, there is an extensive no man's land between these two positions. To begin with, *less* can be idiomatically used with plural nouns when these denote something closer to an amount than a numerical quantity, as with distances, periods of time, ages, and sums of money: *less than 5 miles to go | less than six weeks | children less than three years old | less than £100*. Supermarket checkouts are correct when the signs they display read *12 items or less* (which refers to a total amount), and are misguidedly pedantic when they read *12 items or fewer*. School examiners often invite candidates to write a summary of a passage of prose in *fifty words or less*. In some borderline cases it is more idiomatic to use *less* when *fewer* would put an unwelcome emphasis on the numerical quantity rather than the cumulative effect of the total: *. . . unashamedly rejoiced in having had in his house at one time no less than five Nobel Prize Winners*— Margaret Drabble, 1987. But *less* should be avoided when it qualifies an otherwise unqualified plural noun: *I shall care about less things*—Penelope Fitzgerald, 1980 | *We had been given less men . . . to perform a holding action—Paintball Games*, 1989.

fey see FAY.

fiancé, fiancée. The first is masculine and the second is feminine. Both words are pronounced fi-**on**-say.

fiasco has the plural form *fiascos*.

fiat. The legal term, meaning 'an authorization or order', is pronounced **fly**-at. The make of car (*Fiat*) is pronounced **fee**-at.

fibre is the spelling in BrE and *fiber* in AmE.

fictional, fictitious. *Fictional* means 'occurring in fiction', i.e. in a piece of literature, whereas *fictitious* means 'invented, unreal; not genuine'. So *Oliver Twist* is a *fictional* name when it refers to Dickens's character, and a *fictitious* name when someone uses it as a false or assumed name instead of their own. Similarly, events are *fictional* when described in a work of fiction, and *fictitious* when invented in ordinary life.

fiddle. As a verb, *fiddle* is more in demand to convey the meaning of cheating than of playing the violin, and it is mainly as a noun that the musical sense survives. So the situation is still as described by Gowers (1965): 'A violinist will speak of his instrument as a *fiddle*, but not of his playing as *fiddling* or of himself as a *fiddler*.'

fidget as a verb has inflections *fidgeted, fidgeting*.

field. In the meaning 'an area of operation or activity, a subject of study', *field* tends to be overused, and it is advisable to be aware of available synonyms. The most commonly needed are (for fields of study) *sphere, subject, area, discipline, domain*, (for areas of operation or responsibility) *area, province, department, line, speciality, responsibility*, (sometimes) *territory*. These also need to be use with care, for fear of avoiding the hackneyed only to adopt an alternative that is precious or stilted, as can happen with *department* and *territory*, or still worse *métier*, for example.

fifties see EIGHTIES.

figure. 1 Both the noun and the verb are pronounced **fig**-ə in BrE but **fig**-yə in AmE. The derivative forms *figural*, *figuration*, and *figurine* have the -y-sound in both BrE and AmE; but *figurative* (**fig**-ə-rə-tiv) lacks it in BrE.

2 As a verb, *figure* is used, especially in AmE and often with *out*, to mean 'work out, calculate, think'. To *figure on* something is to plan it or take it for granted, and in AmE something *figures* when it makes sense or seems likely. All these uses are informal only.

figure of speech is any of several recognized linguistic devices used to make language lively or more colourful, such as META-PHOR and SIMILE.

fillers are words such as *actually, you know, in fact, really,* and *I mean,* and pause markers such as *er* and *um,* that have little or no meaning and are merely used to help maintain a flow, and sometimes improve sentence balance, in conversational English. Their routine use is quite legitimate, and everyday discourse would be unnatural without them.

finable, meaning 'liable to a fine', is spelt this way, not *fineable.*

final clause, in grammar, is a clause that states a purpose, especially when introduced by a formula such as *to, in order to, in order that, so as to, in the hope that,* etc.: *He turned on the plane's radio, in order to hear the traffic controller—New Yorker,* 1972 | *The Labour administration massaged the basis of the calculation of the exchange rate . . . so as to make the situation appear better—Daily Telegraph,* 1982 | *Clerks double-book their barristers in the hope that one of the cases will be settled before*

getting to court—Economist, 1983 | *In order to fully understand an alarm reaction it is useful to think back many thousands of years to the time of the caveman—S. Enright et al.,* 1990.

finale, meaning the last part of something, is pronounced as three syllables (fi-**nah**-li).

finalize, as a synonym of *complete* or *finish,* came into use in the 1920s in Australia and New Zealand, then in the US and, in the 1930s, in Britain. It was widely denounced by usage pundits such as Partridge and Gowers as an unnecessary addition; but it often has a stronger sense of effective conclusion than is conveyed by *complete* or *finish: Arrangements have also been finalized for the establishment of a ranching scheme at Jaldesa—Inside Kenya Today,* 1971.

fine toothcomb see TOOTHCOMB.

finger. The fingers are now usually numbered without including the thumb, so that the *first finger* is the index finger, the *second finger* is the middle finger, the *third finger* is the ring finger, and the *fourth finger* is the little finger. In the marriage service, however, the ring finger is called the *fourth,* not the *third.*

fiord see FJORD.

fire *verb,* meaning 'to dismiss from a job', has its origins in AmE in the 1880s, when it was also used as a phrasal verb to *fire out.* Fowler (1926) entered both forms without much comment apart from mentioning their American origin; by the time Gowers wrote (1965), only the simple verb *fire* was used, and he noted that it was 'still an American colloquialism, though making headway among us at the expense of the verb to *sack*'. As it turns out, *fire* stands alongside *sack* as one of two words used regularly and unexceptionably in informal English.

firm *adverb* is used mainly in two fixed expressions, to *stand firm* and to *hold firm to*. In all other contexts the natural adverbial form is *firmly*: *The bracket was firmly fixed to the wall.*

first. 1 When used with a number, *first* (like *last*) normally precedes it, as in *the first three cars*. This practice dates from the 16c, when first came to be regarded more as an adjective than as a noun; before that time, it was common to say *the two* (or *three,* etc.) *first . . . .* In current use, the order *the three first cars* would suggest three cars that came first in three races, and not the three cars that came first, second, and third in the same race.

2 In listing a sequence of points or topics, there is a convention that the first item is introduced by *first*, not *firstly*, although the continuation can be *secondly, thirdly, fourthly,* etc. The reason for this is that *first* early on had a role as an adverb, and the use of *firstly*, though established by the 17c, was felt to be an unnecessary affectation. Today this rule seems little more than a superstition, and various sequences are in use: *first . . . , secondly . . . , thirdly; firstly . . . , secondly . . . , thirdly . . . ; firstly . . . , second . . . , third . . .* Of these, the first two options are both acceptable, but the third should be avoided.

first name see CHRISTIAN NAME.

firth is the standard spelling for an estuary or inlet of the sea. In the past (notably in the work of Cowper and Tennyson), it was changed by a process called METATHESIS to *frith*, but this form is no longer in normal use.

fish. The plural form is normally *fish* (*nets full of fish | They caught seven fish yesterday*); but *fishes* is sometimes used to emphasize a plural rather than a collective concept and to denote kinds of fish: *feed the fishes | food fishes like cod and flounder.* In biblical allusions, *fishes* is used rather than *fish: five loaves and two small fishes.*

fit *verb.* In BrE the past tense and past participle are *fitted* in all meanings: *The dress fitted well | The dress fitted her well | We've fitted a new lock to the front door.* In some parts of the US, *fit* also is used in the first two of these three meanings: *His head fit snugly into his collar like a shell into a canister*—D. Pinckney, 1992 | *Many questions were put; none fit*—*Bulletin of the American Academy,* 1994.

fix. The meanings of the verb, which is first recorded in the 15c, and the noun, not recorded until the early 19c, do not correspond very well.

1 *noun.* ▸**a** The earliest meaning of the noun is 'a difficulty, predicament, dilemma', which is originally AmE but was soon used in BrE as well, for example in a letter written by Charlotte Brontë in 1839: *It so happens that I can get no conveyance . . . so I am in a fix.* This meaning remains common in BrE, although it still has a slight American flavour: *Since she had vowed to remain celibate, she was in rather a fix when her father planned to marry her to the King of Sicily*—B. Cottle, 1983 | *The patient* *will indeed be in a fix from which he may find it hard to extricate himself*—C. Rycroft, 1985.

▶**b** From the 1930s in the US, a dose of a narcotic drug came to be called a *fix-up* and then a *fix*, and this use (only *fix*) spread into BrE in the 1950s with the increased circulation of hard drugs such as heroin: *A weird scene where the dope peddlers gather to beat up Johnny, who gets more into debt with each 'fix'*—Oxford Mail, 1958 | *He needed her as a drug addict needs his fix*—Iris Murdoch, 1985. From this drugs meaning other figurative meanings soon developed: *Many people seem addicted to exercise and get depressed if they don't get their daily fix*—Guardian, 1984 | *For them conventional war has been lived through—and they think nuclear weapons are a cheap fix to deter it*—Green Magazine, 1990.

▶**c** A *quick fix* is a hasty remedy that deals with a difficulty in the short term; the expression is recorded first in a hyphenated adjectival form from the 1950s: *Quick-fix reflectors and diffusers, heavy duty bi-pin lampholders*—Architectural Review, 1959 | *The most recent 'quick-fix', suggests the committee, is desalting*—New Scientist, 1966 | *He is urged to make quick-fix tax cuts and get the economy moving*—National Observer (US), 1976.

2 *verb.* There are three uses of the verb, all American in origin and one still exclusively so, that call for comment.

▶**a** (Also to *fix up*.) 'To prepare (food or drink).' *You must fix me a drink*, Fanny Trollope said in her *Domestic Manners of the Americans* (1839); and Bret Harte, an American writer, wrote in a work of 1891, *Mother'll fix you suthin' hot.* The use is familiar in BrE, but is

still regarded as an Americanism: *When I am quite exhausted, go and cook a meal, fix a drink*—Nina Bawden, 1981.

▶**b** (Also to *fix up*.) 'To mend or repair (something broken or not working).' This meaning is first recorded in AmE in the late 18c, and has spread to other varieties of English: *Other men would have fixed that fuse in a few seconds*—News of the World, 1990.

▶**c** The informal American expression *to be fixing to* (do something), meaning 'to be about to or preparing to' (do it), first recorded in 1716, is still hardly ever encountered outside the US: *If you're after Lily, she come in here while ago and tole me she was fixin' to git married*—E. Welty, c.1980.

fixation was used from the 17c with the general meaning 'the action of fixing'. Its current meaning of 'obsession, fixed idea' is a legacy of the use in Freudian psychosexual theory: *Don has this very definite fixation that I am going to bang up our . . . new car*—E.J. Barr, 1973 | *He adds his voice to those condemning the modern fixation on fitness at the expense of honing cricket skills*—Wisden Cricket Monthly, 1992. It also has technical uses in chemistry and medicine.

fixedly is pronounced as three syllables. See -EDLY.

fixedness, fixity. Both are 17c words with a range of meanings to do with abstract senses of fixing and being fixed, but *fixedness* is now used much less often than *fixity*: *Beaten into a fixity of revolutionary purpose, the peasants will have no more of it*—Times Literary Supplement, 1984 | *A film that seemed able to contemplate death ends up by denying even the fixedness of character*—Independent, 1990

| What distinguishes perversion is its quality of desperation and fixity—New York Times, 1991.

fjord is the recommended spelling for the Norwegian sea inlet, not *fiord*.

flaccid. The recommended pronunciation is **flak**-sid, not **flas**-id.

flagrant see BLATANT.

flair, meaning 'an instinct for what is excellent, a talent', was adopted into English from French in the late 19c. It should be distinguished from the unrelated noun and verb *flare* meaning 'a dazzling flame of light' etc., which is 16c and of unknown origin.

flamboyant is now used mainly in abstract senses 'showy, ostentatious'. It was adopted in the early 19c by architects to denote decoration marked by wavy flamelike lines. It is connected in origin with the French word *flamber* meaning 'to burn'.

flamingo has plural forms *flamingos* (preferred) or *flamingoes*.

flammable, meaning 'easily set on fire', was revived in modern use (in BrE by the British Standards Institution) and used together with the noun *flammability* in place of *inflammable* and *inflammability* (which have the same meaning) in order to avoid the possibility that the *in-* forms might suggest a negative meaning 'not easily set on fire'. The negative forms now recommended are *non-flammable* and *non-flammability*.

flannel has inflected forms *flannelled, flannelling* in BrE and *flaneled flaneling* in AmE. *Flannelette*, a napped cotton fabric imitating

flannel, is spelt *-l-* in both varieties.

flare see FLAIR.

flat, flatly. The dominant adverbial form *flatly* is always used figuratively, as in *flatly contradicting* and *flatly refusing*. *Flat* is used in fixed expressions such as *flat broke* and *turn something down flat*, and to mean 'exactly and no more' as in *two minutes flat*. *Flat* is only semi-adverbial, and mainly adjectival, in uses such as *The ladder was standing flat against the wall*.

flatways, flatwise both mean 'with the flat side (and not the edge) uppermost or foremost'. Both forms have been in use from the 17c, but *flatways* is now dominant, especially in AmE: *Just cut in half flatwise, apply the topping and slip into a 450 F oven—Washington Times*, 1989.

flaunt, flout. The two words are unrelated. To *flaunt* means 'to display ostentatiously': *Women should have it both ways—they should be able to flaunt their sexuality and be taken seriously—E. Wurtzel*, 1998. To *flout* means 'to show contempt for (a rule, the law, etc.)': *Countries engage in covert activities because they do not want to flout the rules openly—Encounter*, 1987. The confusion, apart from the similarities of sound, may be due to the notion of conspicuousness common to both actions, and it is noteworthy that *flaunt* is used mistakenly to mean *flout* but the reverse does not occur: ☒ *By flaunting these rules, Hongkong and Shanghai have challenged the Bank's authority—Daily Telegraph*, 1981 | ☒ *The union continued its campaign against Sunday trading, targeting shops which flaunted regulations—Times*, 1989.

flautist, flutist. *Flutist* is the older term (17c) for a player of the flute, and is still preferred in AmE. *Flautist* was adapted from the Italian word *flautista* in 1860, and is now the more usual form in BrE.

flavour is spelt *-our* in BrE and *flavor* in AmE. In BrE the derivatives (*flavouring, flavoursome,* etc.) are also spelt *-our* except *flavorous*.

fledgling is the recommended spelling, not *fledgeling*.

flee, meaning 'to run away, escape' is most often used in its past tense *fled. Flee* has a somewhat literary or romantic flavour: *The fourteenth Dalai Lama . . . has lived in exile in the Indian Himalayas since 1959, when Khamba rebels persuaded him to flee from Lhasa—* Times, 1973.

fleshy, fleshly. The distinction in current use is much the same as between *earthy* and *earthly. Fleshy* relates to flesh in its physical sense and means primarily 'plump, fat' (e.g. *fleshy hands | fleshy fruit*), whereas *fleshly* relates to the allusive senses of flesh, and means 'carnal, sensual, sexual' (e.g. *fleshly desires | fleshly thoughts*).

fleur-de-lis, a heraldic lily, is spelt this way for preference rather than *fleur-de-lys* or *flower-de-luce* (which occurs in AmE). It is pronounced fler-də-**lee**, and the plural is *fleurs-de-lis*, pronounced the same way.

flier see FLYER.

floatation see FLOTATION.

floor, storey. In Britain the *storey* at ground level is called the *ground floor*. A *single-storey* house is one with a *ground floor* only; a two-storey house has a *ground floor* with a *first floor* above it; a three-storey house has a *second floor* above the first, and so on. In America, the floor at ground level is called the *first floor;* the British *first floor* is the *second floor,* and so on. Cellars, basements, and mezzanine floors are not counted in either reckoning.

flora see FAUNA.

floruit, pronounced flor-oo-it, is a Latin third-person singular verb in the past tense meaning 'he or she flourished'. In English it is used with a following designation of date to indicate when a writer, painter, etc., is believed to have been alive and working, e.g. *floruit 1750.*

flotation is now the dominant spelling for the word meaning 'the process of launching or financing a business or commercial enterprise'. It has replaced the earlier form *floatation*, on the analogy of words such as *flotilla, flotsam*, etc.

flotsam and jetsam. The traditional distinction between goods found afloat at sea (*flotsam*) and goods found on land after being cast ashore (*jetsam*) is not historically straightforward, and is now largely theoretical since the words are invariably used together. *Jetsam* (late 16c) is recorded slightly earlier than *flotsam* (early 17c), and is a form of *jettison* meaning 'to throw overboard'. Flotsam is derived from an Anglo-French word related to *float*.

flounder, founder. These two words are easily confused because their form and meanings are both close. The physical meaning of *flounder* is 'to struggle in mud or while wading' and hence 'to stumble or move clumsily', and from these meanings developed the abstract sense 'to perform a task badly or without knowledge; to be out of one's depth'. The corresponding meanings of *founder* are (physical) with reference to a ship, 'to fill with water and sink', and (abstract) with reference to a plan, scheme, intention, etc., 'to come to nothing, to fail'. In the abstract senses, where the confusion mostly lies, it is therefore normally people who *flounder* and plans and relationships (and suchlike) that *founder*. In practice the use of both words in their physical meanings as part of a larger metaphor (as in the 1980 example that follows) tends to blur the boundaries between literal and metaphorical use. The following examples will help to clarify the differences between *flounder* and *founder*: (flounder) *The family physician bucks the case to a psychosomaticist, who flounders in jargon*—Time, 1971 | *His early and unexpected death was a cruel setback which left the College floundering in indecision over the choice of a suitable successor*—E. Cotchin, 1990 | *'You'll feel better later on,' he floundered*—H. Forrester, 1990 | (founder) *I wanted to leave England . . . I did not intend to be aboard when that particular Titanic finally foundered in a sea of bureaucracy*—K. Hagenbach, 1980 | *Without . . . help, the marriage may founder, thus providing . . . another dire example to romantic young people that 'arranged marriages are best'*—P. Caplan, 1985 | *While these approaches may have a grain of truth in them, they founder in the evidence of women's actual political activity*—J. Urry et al., 1993.

flu, a 19c shortening of *influenza*, is used (with or without *the*) as

often as the full form, except in more formal contexts. The older form 'flu (with initial apostrophe) has dropped out of use.

flunkey, a (usually derogatory) term for a liveried servant or (in extended use) a toady, is the preferred spelling, not *flunky*. The plural is *flunkeys*.

flutist see FLAUTIST.

fly. 1 The noun is used as a collective in special names for various small flies or aphids that trouble gardeners, such as *fruit fly* and *greenfly*. These accordingly function as singular nouns (with plural *-flies*) and collective plurals: *It is easy to see that would-be DIY funeral undertakers would be as welcome as a swarm of greenfly at the Chelsea flower show*—J. Spottiswoode, 1991.

2 The perfect form of the verb can be *is* (or *are*) *flown* as well as *has* (or *have*) *flown* when the meaning is 'escape'.

flyer, flier. *Flyer* is the preferred spelling in all meanings of this agent noun formed from the verb *fly*. *Flier* is more common in AmE.

fob off. There are two ways of using this phrasal verb, either with the person or the thing as the object. You can fob someone off *with* something (or just fob someone off, with no further complement stated), or you can fob something off *on* someone; in both cases someone is deceived into accepting something inferior or unwelcome. The first construction seems to be more common: *She tried to fob him off tactfully at first, but then he became brutal*—D. M. Thomas, 1990 | *Do not allow yourself to be fobbed off without getting the information you need*—G.

Brandreth et al., 1992 | *They were instructed to fob them off with promises in order to get them back to work as quickly as possible*—M. Almond, 1992 | *There is no 'mass audience' of uncritical couch potatoes ready to be fobbed off with any old rubbish*—East Anglian Daily Times, 1993 | (on construction) *Aghast at the roll-call of drunks, adulterers and pederasts that Central Office had fobbed off upon him,* [etc.]—J. Paxman, 1990.

fo'c'sle is a much reduced form of *forecastle*, the forward part of a ship where the crew has its quarters. In both spellings the word is pronounced **fohk**-səl.

focus. The noun has plural forms *focuses* in general use and *foci* (**foh**-siy) in technical use, and the verb has inflected forms *focuses, focused, focusing*, although some printing styles prefer forms with -*ss*-.

foetid see FETID.

foetus, fetus. Medical usage in Britain and the US favours *fetus*, following the word's origin in Latin *fetus* 'offspring'. In AmE this spelling is preferred generally, but *foetus* still prevails in non-medical use in BrE. Because this preference is largely based on a misconception that the -*e*- spelling is some kind of Americanism, the -*oe*- spelling is likely to continue obstinately in use, but in the fullness of time the cards are stacked in favour of *fetus*. Meanwhile, the corresponding adjective is *fetal* in AmE and medical usage and *foetal* in general BrE use.

fogey, fogy. This occurs mainly in the expressions *old* (and now also *young*) *fogey*. *Fogy* was formerly the dominant spelling;

Thackeray and Charles Kingsley, for example, wrote about *old fogies*, implying a singular form *fogy*. But with the more recent arrival of the *young fogey* ('a young person with conservative tastes and attitudes'), the spelling with -*ey* (plural -*eys*) is now more common.

foist has meanings similar to FOB OFF, but it is not followed by *off* and is not used in this meaning with a person as its object; you can foist something *on* someone but you cannot foist someone (off) *with* something: *I'm not about to foist something on the public just for the sake of releasing something*—Record Mirror, 1982.

An older use with a person or thing as object followed by *in* or *into*, meaning 'to introduce surreptitiously', is now found only rarely. It was once a favourite of scholars referring to the introduction of false readings into texts; Bulwer-Lytton wrote in 1936 of *interpolations . . . supposed to be foisted into the Odyssey.*

folio has the plural form *folios*.

folk as an ordinary word for people in general is tending to fall out of use in BrE, except in northern parts of the country and occasionally elsewhere to denote a greater degree of affection than the word *people* does: *Even folk who know little about Scotland have probably heard of the Trossachs*—Scottish World, 1989 | *What Ursula brought home every week made all the difference to the old folk*—David Lodge, 1991. It also survives strongly in certain specific uses:

1 As the last element of compounds and fixed expressions, or qualified by an adjective, as in *menfolk, north-country folk, towns-*

folk, womenfolk. In general use, however, even these are beginning to sound somewhat jocular or precious.

2 In the plural (usually *folks*) to mean 'one's parents or relatives': *That really messes us up if my folks try to get hold of me*—L. Duncan, 1978 | *The folks wouldn't like it too much*—R. J. Conley, 1986. *Folks* is also used as a light-hearted form of address to an audience by public entertainers, and this is sometimes imitated for special effect by journalists and writers: *Yes, folks, in 1990, 2,245 people were murdered in the city of New York*—Bernard Levin, 1991.

3 In the singular as an elliptical form of the term *folk music* (see 4 below).

4 In attributive combinations in which *folk* is joined to a second word, some of the combinations being loan translations from German, e.g. *folk-dance, folk-dancing, folk memory, folk music, folk-singer, folk-song, folk-tale, folkways*; and especially in *folklore*.

folk etymology is 'a popular modifying of the form of a word or phrase in order to make it seem to be derived from a more familiar word'. Examples are *cockroach* (from Spanish *cucaracha*), *sparrow-grass* (a dialect and colloquial name for *asparagus*), and *hiccough* (a later spelling of *hiccup* under the mistaken impression that the second syllable was related to *cough*).

following has long been used as a participial adjective either qualifying a noun, as in *for the following reasons*, or by itself as a quasi-noun, as in *The following are my reasons*. From this has developed a use of *following* as a quasi-preposition independent of any noun: *Used car prices are going up, following the Budget*—*Observer*, 1968. This use was not a problem for Fowler (1926) but Gowers (1965) condemned it in cases where the connection between the two events is 'merely temporal' and the preposition *after* would serve. In the example just given, there is a strong element of consequence, and so the use of *following* is perhaps justified, but this is not so in the example that follows, in which *after* could have been used with no loss of meaning: *Members are invited to take tea in the Convocation Coffee House . . . following the meeting*—University announcement, Oxford, 1991. In some cases there is even a possibility of ambiguity with other meanings of *following*: *Police have arrested a man following extensive inquiries*.

font see FOUNT.

foot. The normal plural form *feet* alternates with *foot* when used as a unit of measurement: *She is six feet/foot tall* | *a plank ten feet/foot long*. When such a phrase is used attributively (before a noun), a hyphen is normally placed between the numeral and *foot*, as in *a 12-foot dinghy*. When the number of inches is also given, *foot* is more common than *feet*: *He is six foot eight*.

for. 1 As a coordinating conjunction introducing a clause that gives a reason or explanation, *for* has two features of use not shared by *because* and *since*: (1) it cannot come at the beginning of a sentence but must follow a main clause: *He picked his way down carefully, step by step, for the steps were narrow*—G. Greene, 1988, and (2) it is normally preceded by a comma, except occasionally when the sentence is short: *It was* gloomy and damp, for the sun could hardly shine through the tops of the trees—New Yorker, 1989 | I wanted a setting for my own little life, for I did not think that I should know too many people—Anita Brookner, 1990 | (comma omitted) He did not cry any more for it did not help—D. Matthee, 1986. In most uses, for is rather more formal in effect than either because or since.

2 In AmE for is used to introduce a subordinate clause after certain verbs: I didn't intend for you to find out—J. McInerney, 1985 | I can't afford for that bike to break down—New Yorker, 1986. In BrE other constructions would be used instead; for example intend would be followed by a that-clause.

for- and fore-. The prefix for- occurs in a number of words formed in Old English, such as forbid, forgive, and forsake. It is not an active prefix in the sense of being used to form new words. Fore-, on the other hand, is a prefix native to English and is widely used to form verbs and nouns from existing words in the general meanings 'before, in front' with regard both to space and to time, e.g. forearm, foreshorten, foretell. Special care should be taken to distinguish between words that exist in both for- and fore-forms; see the separate entries for FORBEAR, FOREBEAR; FORGO, FOREGO.

forbear, forebear. 1 Forbear is a verb (pronounced with the stress on the second syllable) meaning 'to abstain from, go without' and is usually followed by to + infinitive or from + verb in -ing: He did not enquire after their progress and Nutty forbore to mention it—K. M. Peyton, 1988 | Naturally he couldn't forbear from upsetting me—Will Self,

1993. Its past form is forbore and its past participle is forborn.

2 Forebear is a noun (pronounced with the stress on the first syllable) meaning 'an ancestor': Henry Carew had chosen the Church as some of his forebears had done—T. Hayden, 1991 | The main myth being punctured . . . is the old erroneous view that humanity evolved gradually over the aeons from an ape forebear—New Scientist, 1991. Forebear is also used figuratively: Heseltine may not prove as co-operative as his DTI forebears—Marketing Week, 1992. The situation is complicated somewhat by the fact that most dictionaries allow forbear as a variant of forebear, but the advice here is to maintain the distinction.

forbid. 1 The past tense is forbade, although forbad is occasionally used and cannot be said to be wrong. The pronunciation of forbade is fə-**bayd** or (as if it were forbad) fə-**bad**.

2 Forbid can be followed by a noun (often a verbal noun): Cars are forbidden on the beach | We decided to forbid smoking altogether. When forbid has a personal object it is normally followed by to + infinitive: I forbid you to go | We were forbidden to go. A construction with object + from + verb in -ing is also found, on the analogy of prevent and prohibit: He overcame the barrier known as the 'colour line' which effectively forbade blacks from boxing whites —E. Cashmore, 1982 | Current laws forbid a company from operating a reactor even after it has been built—New Scientist, 1991. Fowler (1926) regarded this construction as 'unidiomatic' but it has been in use since the 16c and is likely to remain so since the analogies are powerful. This construction is occasionally used with omission of *from* (*The petition asked the king to forbid villeins sending their children to school*—S. J. Curtis, 1948 | *She'd far rather have enjoyed the company of her contemporaries and, in fact, Colonel Goreng didn't forbid her consorting with them*—Timothy Mo, 1991), but this can be regarded as non-standard. (In the 1991 example, *consorting* may be a verbal noun qualified by possessive *her*).

forceful, forcible. 1 Fowler (1926) identified the difference in meaning as follows: 'while forcible conveys that force rather than something else is present, forceful conveys that much as opposed to little force is used or shown; compare *forcible ejection* with *a forceful personality*.' He then went on to say that the more important consideration than difference in meaning was the need to use one (*forcible*) as the natural regular word and reserve the other (*forceful*) for 'poetical or other abnormal use'. His conclusion was that otherwise, 'we shall shortly find ourselves with a pair of exact synonyms either of which could well be spared instead of a pair serving different purposes'. In practice, the two words are kept apart fairly comfortably, and Fowler's prescriptions and predictions were wide of the mark; neither is the 'ordinary' word any more than the other. The principal use of *forceful* is in the meaning 'vigorous, powerful', whereas *forcible* means primarily 'done by or using force'. *Forceful* can be used of people as well as actions, whereas *forcible* is used only of actions.

2 Examples: (forceful) *It might be easier to . . . start again from scratch, crystallizing a lifetime's experience into a hundred forceful pages?*—Iris Murdoch, 1976 | *He was strong and*

his resources of stamina enabled him to play just as forcefully in the final ten minutes of a game as in the first ten—S. Studd, 1981 | *She said she tried to push him off, but he was too forceful*—Independent, 1989 | *John McLeish, himself a forceful character, felt as if he had been put through a wringer*—J. Neel, 1991 | (forcible) *He favoured the forcible sterilization of criminals, diseased and insane persons, and 'worthless race-types'*—J. R. Baker, 1971 | *Section 47 of the National Assistance Act 1948 allows for the forcible removal from their own homes of elderly people who are not mentally ill*—O. Stevenson et al., 1990 | *They will wish to see sovereign rights and self-government restored to those who have been forcibly deprived of them*—W. Jackson, 1990.

forceps. The plural is the same.

fore. *To the fore* was originally a Scottish and Anglo-Irish phrase meaning 'at hand, available, surviving'. It came into English literary use during the 19c, and in current standard English means 'into view, to the front'. A person is said to have *come to the fore* when he or she has become prominent in some way.

forebear see FORBEAR.

forecast is pronounced with the stress on the first syllable both as a noun and as a verb. As a past form and past participle, *forecast* (identical to the form of the present tense) has more or less ousted *forecasted*.

forecastle see FO'C'SLE.

foregather see FORGATHER.

forego see FORGO.

foregoing means 'preceding, previously mentioned' and is

used as an adjective corresponding to the verb *forego* = to precede, especially in writing to
refer to points made in earlier
parts of the text: *If the foregoing
representation of Jesus Christ can be
accepted, it would be the end of the
mysticism surrounding him*—W. E.
Gale, 1988 | *All the foregoing are
drawn from documents employed by
the author in various studies*—J.
Campbell-Kease, 1989.

foregone means 'previous, completed' and is used mainly in the
expression *foregone conclusion*,
meaning 'an easily foreseen or
predictable result': *The privatisa-
tion of the BBC and the race down-
market of ITV would then be a
foregone conclusion*—*Listener*, 1984.

forehead. The pronunciation
faw-hed, reflecting the word's
spelling, is now much more usual
than **fo**-rid, which was once favoured and is still recommended
by some dictionaries.

foreign words and phrases.
Fowler (1926), in an article entitled 'foreign danger', warned
that 'those who use words or
phrases belonging to languages
with which they have little or no
acquaintance do so at their peril'.
He was thinking primarily of
so-called 'non-naturalized' expressions that are customarily put in
italics in printed matter so as to
alert the reader to the presence
of something unusual. Some of
these expressions tend to retain
the grammatical behaviour of the
languages from which they were
borrowed, notably in the formations of plural forms, so that the
plural of *curriculum vitae* (see CUR-
RICULUM), for example, can cause
some initial difficulty (it has to
be *curricula vitae*, unless one re-
sorts to *CVs*). Further difficulty is

caused by uncertainty as to
whether a word is naturalized or
not; REFERENDUM has the plural
form *referenda* if it is not naturalized and *referendums* if it is (and
for those in doubt about this one,
naturalized forms ultimately, and
rightly, prevail). Problems also
occur when the meaning in English changes from that in the
source language, or when mistaken meanings are applied, as
with CUI BONO?. For other examples of foreign words and
phrases, see the separate entries
for items in bold italics throughout the book, including BÊTE
NOIRE; BONNE BOUCHE; CORPUS DE-
LICTI; DE RIGUEUR; DÉTENTE;
DOUBLE ENTENDRE; EX OFFICIO;
FAIT ACCOMPLI; FAUX PAS; IBID.; IN-
GÉNUE; INTER ALIA; JEU D'ESPRIT;
LAISSEZ-ALLER; LAISSEZ-FAIRE; MA-
TÉRIEL; MODUS OPERANDI; MODUS
VIVENDI; PETITIO PRINCIPII; PIÈCE
DE RÉSISTANCE; PIED-À-TERRE;
PIETÀ; PIS ALLER; POST HOC, ERGO
PROPTER HOC; RAISON D'ÊTRE; RE-
DUCTIO AD ABSURDUM; SINE QUA
NON; ULTRA VIRES.

forename see CHRISTIAN NAME.

forensic means 'connected with
courts of law' (from Latin *forum*
meaning 'public square' where
among other things judicial business was done), and should not
be used as a general word for
'technical, scientific'. *Forensic evidence* means 'evidence presented
in connection with a legal trial'
and is usually, though not necessarily, medical or technical evidence; a *forensic scientist* is a
scientist employed by a police department. Informally, *forensic* is
also used elliptically to mean 'a
forensic department or unit': *Perhaps the boys at forensic had made a
gaff*—M. Maguire, 1976.

for ever, forever. This is written as two separate words in BrE (but often as one word in AmE) when the meaning is 'for all future time' (*He said he would love her for ever*) and as one word when the meaning is 'always, continually' (*They are forever complaining*).

foreword, preface. *Preface* is the traditional word (first recorded in the 14c) for the author's introductory remarks at the beginning of a book, normally dealing with the practicalities of the book's development and making due acknowledgements rather than introducing its content (which in some cases is done by an *Introduction*). *Foreword* is a 19c word (originally used as a term in philology) for an introductory section of a literary work, and practice has varied between use of this term and *Preface*. More recently, publishers have sometimes favoured the inclusion of both a *Foreword* (usually written by a distinguished or authoritative person other than the author) as well as a *Preface* written by the author. In such cases, the *Foreword* is placed first.

for free, for real. These two phrases, originally Americanisms, are regularly used in BrE, often in a jocular manner and with quotation marks in print: *Two pilots have in fact done the job 'for real'—both Sqn Ldr Marshall and Flt Lt Dave Fischer have put Harriers down on the deck of HMS Bulwark—RAF News*, 1977 | *I'd love a research assistant, but you have to pay for them. And most people want me to do things for free!*—C. Tickell, 1991.

forgather is the recommended spelling for this word meaning 'to assemble, meet together', rather than *foregather*, which is also

found by association with the prefix *fore-* (see FOR- AND FORE-). It is a 16c Scottish loanword from Dutch *vergaderen* used in the same sense.

forge has a derivative form *forgeable*, with an *e* in the middle.

forget has the inflected form *forgetting* and the derivative form *forgettable*, both with -*tt*-.

forgive has a derivative form *forgivable*, without an *e* in the middle.

forgo, forego. Both words are pronounced with the stress on the second syllable. *Forgo* means 'to go without, abstain from'; *forego* means 'to go before, precede' and occurs principally in the forms FOREGOING and FOREGONE (see the separate entries for these, and FOR- AND FORE-).

forgot, as a past participle used instead of *forgotten*, is limited to archaic and dialect language, and to use in some forms of AmE.

forlorn hope now means only 'a faint hope, an enterprise which has little hope of success', but its form has nothing to do with the English word *hope*. It was a 16c adaptation of Dutch *verloren hoop*, literally meaning 'lost troop', and in English originally meant 'a picked body of men detached to lead an attack'. The current figurative use, first recorded in 1641, has driven out all memory of the original meaning.

formality, formalism. The first is the ordinary noun corresponding to *formal*: *formality* is primarily the observance of rules and conventions, *a formality* is something that has to be done by convention (often with implications of superfluousness: *The interview* *was a mere formality*), and *formalities* are customary procedures. The word in all these uses often has a dismissive tone. *Formalism*, first recorded in 1840, has meanings based on the notion of 'excessive adherence to prescribed forms' and is used in various technical applications in theology, mathematics, linguistics, and the arts.

formal words. Fowler (1926) aptly identified words 'that are not the plain English for what is meant' and characterized choice between different words for the same thing in terms of the clothes we choose: 'we tell our thoughts, like our children, to put on their hats and coats before they go out.' The examples he gave now sound dated ('We think of our soldiers as *plucky fellows*, but call them in the bulletins *valiant troops*'), but the message is as vivid as ever. *Peruse* is more formal than *read*, *purchase* than *buy*, *luncheon* than *lunch*, *endeavour* than *try*, *evince* than *show*; and *purloin* is more formal (or, often, more jocular) than *steal*. As is the case with most of these, formal words can be turned on their heads and made to look silly in trivial or jocular use. Different modes of writing and speaking call for different levels of vocabulary. At one extreme there is the language of legal documents, business, and academic monographs; at the other there is the language of everyday conversation, with a broad range of styles in between. The language of broadcasting and journalism, in particular, has become a great deal less formal in recent years, to such an extent as to cause unease among those who mistakenly identify formality, or the lack of it, with standards of English.

format is pronounced **faw**-mat, and as a verb has inflected forms *formatted, formatting*. The verb dates from the 1960s and is mostly used in the context of computing.

former, latter. 1 These two words are used contrastively (as *the former* and *the latter*) to refer to the first and second respectively of two people or things previously mentioned; in this role they are used attributively (before a noun) or, more usually, absolutely (with no noun following). *Former* has an important and extremely common additional meaning, for which *latter* has no corresponding meaning, 'having been previously but no longer', as in *the former Miss America | his former employers | The former East Germany*. When another adjective or qualifier is present, *former* normally comes after it to ensure association with the noun: *In England the death of a 71 year-old former process worker at ICI is being investigated*—Nature, 1974.

2 For the meaning of *former* contrasted with *latter*, there are several points of usage to consider:

▶ **a** In their contrastive uses, *former* and *latter* are more often used without a following noun: *The relationship between capitalist and non-capitalist modes is one of exploitation, in which the former creams off the surplus from the latter*—T. Cubitt, 1988. They are occasionally used attributively (*No one mentioned the latter point and only four teachers the former*—D. Pimm, 1988), but care needs to be taken in these cases to avoid possible ambiguity with the 'having been previously' meaning of *for-*

mer: the sentence *I am sure the former view will prevail* needs its context to clarify whether it is an earlier view or the first of two views that is intended.

▶ **b** *Former* (in particular) and *latter* should only be used in writing when they are close to their antecedents, so that the reader is not forced to search back over earlier passages in order to establish the identity of the persons or things referred to.

▶ **c** When more than two people or things are involved, *former* and *latter* should not be used; either *first* and *last* should be used, or the sentence should be rephrased: ☒ *Though her bibliography includes Hecht, Snyder, and Daiches, she omits the latter's first name* [correct to . . . *Daiches' first name*]— *Modern Language Notes*, 1957.

▶ **d** When *former* and *latter* refer to something in the plural, they are regarded as plural in turn: *The former describe events which are possible if not mundane, while the latter are metaphors*—J. Empson, 1989.

formidable. The standard pronunciation is with the stress on the first syllable, although the word is often heard with the stress on the second syllable.

formula. In general contexts the plural form is *formulas*, and in chemistry and mathematics it is *formulae*, pronounced -lee. *Formulae* is more common in general use in AmE than in BrE.

for real see FOR FREE.

forsake, meaning 'to give up, go without', is spelt *for-* not *fore-*, and has inflected forms *forsook*, *forsaken*. See FOR- AND FORE-.

forte. There are two distinct though related words with this

spelling. One (pronounced **faw**-tay or **faw**-ti) comes directly from Latin *fortis* meaning 'strong' and means 'a person's strong point'. The plural, if needed, is *fortes*. The other (pronounced **faw**-ti) comes via Italian *forte* and is an instruction in music to play a passage loudly or strongly. It is also used as a noun meaning such a passage, and the plural is again *fortes*.

forth. The phrase *and so forth* is a less common and somewhat more literary alternative for *and so on*, used after the enumeration of items that could be continued further. There is no difference in meaning, despite the associations of assertiveness that *forth* has in expressions such as *go forth* and *set forth*.

forties see EIGHTIES.

fortuitous. 1 The *OED* and all reputable dictionaries show this to be a word with only one meaning, 'caused by chance, accidental'. Addison wrote in the *Spectator* in 1712 that *the highest Degree of* [*wisdom*] *which Man can possess, is by no means equal to fortuitous Events*. It is first recorded in the 17c, and was used for nearly three centuries without difficulty. But about 1920 it started to get in the way of the older (Middle English) word *fortunate*, which is also connected with the working of chance and more specifically with the good effects of chance. (Whether this confusion was due to a double association with *fortunate* and *propitious* cannot now be determined; but *propitious* is sometimes the word called for rather than *fortunate*.) In an example given by Fowler (1926), the word required is *fortunate* but the word used is *fortuitous*: *I must say I should not have expected so fortuitous a termination of a somewhat daring experiment*. This encroachment is restricted to events and circumstances; with reference to people, *fortunate* remains unthreatened so far: *I was fortunate in being on the spot to take this photograph—Country Life*, 1971.

2 Modern examples of *fortuitous* used to mean 'fortunate' or 'fortunately coincidental' are: *Ellen Orford in the poem is a middle-aged woman and it was fortuitous for me that I was about the right age* [to sing the role]—Joan Cross, 1983 | *King successfully persuaded them to lend the collection for the exhibition . . . A move which proved fortuitous for the future of the national music collection—Independent*, 1995. An unwelcome effect of this confusion is that it is not always possible to know which meaning is intended in a particular use of *fortuitous*, since in many cases an event can happen equally by plain chance or by good chance: *The choice was not altogether fortuitous*—M. Freeland, 1990 | *I had already made up my mind to join the South African tour when it happened, so it was fortuitous in a way—Today*, 1992. *Fortuitous* is too useful in its primary meaning for this uncertainty to be acceptable, and care should be taken not to use it when *fortunate* or a similar word such as *propitious* is the word intended. In the following examples, *fortuitous* is used in its proper sense: *His presence was not fortuitous. He has a role to play; and you will see him again—*A. Brink, 1979 | *Quite fortuitously, Morse lights upon a set of college rooms which he had no original intention of visiting—*Colin Dexter, 1983 | *In some instances death is caused fortuitously—*M. Jefferson, 1992.

forum has the plural form *forums*.

forward, forwards. 1 For the adjective, the correct form in standard English is *forward*: *It has four forward gears and reverse controlled by a speed-sensing governor—Daily Telegraph*, 1971 | *Already clouds of steam were rising, obscuring the forward view—*D. Rutherford, 1990 | *The aggressor's own forward momentum even strengthens the force of the counter-blow against him—*P. Lewis, 1991. In addition to its directional meanings, *forward* has the meaning 'bold in manner, precocious': *Any child who requested a book by title he at once designated as 'forward' or 'lippy'—*R. Roberts, 1971.

2 For the adverb, choice between the two forms is even less clear-cut than in the case with *backward* and *backwards*. The *OED* (in 1897) attempted to distinguish *forward* as having a meaning that 'expresses a definite direction viewed in contrast with other directions', but doubts about this were expressed already by Fowler (1926, but evidently writing in about 1917). In some fixed expressions *forward* is either preferred or obligatory: *backwards and forwards* (preferred), *come forward* (obligatory), *look forward* (*to*; obligatory), *put forward* (= propose; obligatory). In some other meanings there is a preference for *forward*: 'to the front, into prominence' (*Hugh stepped forward. 'It's me, don't be frightened.'—*Mary Wesley, 1983 | *Her mind refused to bring any such memory forward—*E. Jolley, 1985 (Australia) | *Then Nigel Carew drew his sabre and thrust it into the hand of his youthful son and pushed him forward—*T. Hayden, 1991), 'in advance, ahead' (*Civilian volunteers from the town* *carried sacks of grenades forward to the men in action*—J. Ladd, 1979), 'onward so as to make progress' (*Rossi expressed surprise that the Commission was 'apparently no further forward than in 1984'*—C. Rose, 1990 | *He had continually to be looking at his watch and calculating whether they were forward enough*—G. E. Evans, 1993), 'towards the future, continuously onwards' (*The overall feeling is that the Jockey Club is genuinely concerned with helping the industry move forward*—Independent, 1989).

3 The most common occurrence of *forwards* is in meanings denoting straightforward movement towards the front: *A control stick adjusted the airflow from the fan, to make the craft hover or go forwards*—Motoring Which?, 1970 | *Certain single-celled organisms are propelled forwards in the water*—New Scientist, 1971 | *Then he leaned forwards and touched Colin's forearm*—Ian McEwan, 1981 | *It was Amelia who came forwards*—K. Newman, 1990 | *The opponent sees the opening and moves forwards to sweep or punch you*—D. Mitchell, 1991. In all these examples, however, *forward* would be at least as natural (except perhaps in the 1990 example, in which the use of *forwards* emphasizes the physical action not always present in the expression *come forward*); in general *forward* occurs significantly more often as an adverb than does *forwards*, both in BrE and in AmE.

foul, foully. The normal adverb from *foul* is *foully* (pronounced with both ls): *Jerome had done foully, but not so foully as he himself and all here believed*—Ellis Peters, 1993. The older form *foul* survives in the quasi-adverbial expressions *foul-mouthed* and *to fall foul of*.

fount, font. These are the traditional British and American spellings respectively of the term meaning 'a set of printing type of one size or face'. *Font* is now also used in BrE, and is rapidly ousting *fount*. Both words are only remotely connected with *fount* meaning 'fountain, source' (see next entry) and *font* meaning 'a basin for water in a church'.

fount, fountain. *Fount* is a shortening of *fountain* (compare *mount* and *mountain*) and is mainly used in poetry and for special effect. It also occurs with the meaning 'source, origin' in phrases such as the *fount of all wisdom, knowledge*, etc.

fowl. The collective use of the singular form is now largely restricted to compounds such as *guineafowl* and *wildfowl*.

foyer, meaning 'the entrance hall in a theatre, etc.', is pronounced **foy**-ay.

fracas, meaning 'a noisy disturbance', is pronounced **frak**-ah in BrE and **fray**-kəs in AmE. Its plural form is also *fracas*, pronounced **frak**-ahz and **fray**-kəs respectively.

fraction in general use means 'a very small part': *Teaching loads at white schools often are only a fraction the size of those at black schools*—Saturday Review (US), 1971. This use is idiomatic despite the pedantic objection occasionally heard that a fraction can be nine-tenths as much as one-tenth. In some cases, however, the point is reinforced by an adjective such as *small* or *tiny*: *The tax deduction for having a company car is a tiny fraction of its real value*—Guardian, 1979. See also PERCENTAGE.

fractious see FACTIOUS.

fragile, frail. 1 *Fragile* is pronounced **fraj**-iyl in BrE and **fraj**-əl in AmE.

2 *Fragile* is normally used of things being easily broken, whereas *frail* is normally used of people being infirm or in poor physical condition: *The lectern at the Guildhall is a classic example of one that looks beautiful but is too small and fragile to use*—H. Thomas & L. Gill, 1989 | *After Charlotte's death in 1943, the villagers all noticed how extraordinarily frail and sunken Shaw looked*—National Trust Magazine, 1990. There is an overlap in meaning created by the figurative use of both words in the sense 'weak, easily overturned': *OPEC last week managed to preserve its fragile unity*—Observer, 1985 | *The drinking, drug-taking and the high-pitched battles soon toppled the frail structure of their romance*—J. Rose, 1990 | *Our international institutions are frail, fragile and tend to be powerless*—D. Adamson, 1990. In general, *fragile* tends to be used more often than *frail* in this meaning, whereas *frail* alone has the meaning 'morally weak, easily yielding to temptation'.

fragmentary should be pronounced with the stress on the first syllable.

framework. Sir Ernest Gowers (1965) was greatly offended by what he saw as the overuse of the expression *within* (or *in*) *the framework of*, meaning broadly 'in the context of'. Presumably he grew tired of reading it in successions of official Civil Service memos and reports, and he devoted a lengthy article to discouraging its use; but his judgement that 'it has become so trite that the very sight of it may nauseate the sensitive reader' is personal rather than objective. It is also listed among the 'clichés and modish and inflated diction' in the *Oxford Guide to English Usage* (1994). It is true that effective images like this one can lose power through constant use, but it is difficult to find evidence of excessive use in the case under review, and it is hard to fault examples such as the following: *The exercise of justice is only possible within the framework of established institutions which command respect*—Roger Scruton, 1980 | *The qualities that make a good diplomat . . . a willingness to work within the framework of civilised courtesies*—M. Binyon in *Times*, 1991.

Frankenstein, in Mary Shelley's Gothic tale, is the name of the creator of a monster and is not the monster itself. In allusive use since the late 19c, however, the word has been used as if it referred to the monster and not its creator: *There are now growing indications that the Nationalists in South Africa have created a political Frankenstein which is pointing the way to a non-White political revival*—Daily Telegraph, 1971 | *Indoctrinated mass organizations . . . could, critics charged, easily prove a Frankenstein*—Soldier of Fortune, 1990. The allusions in these case should be to a *Frankenstein's monster*.

frantically is the correct form of the adverb from *frantic*, not *franticly*.

free gift is recorded from 1909 and has persisted in use in advertising and marketing circles, despite its evident tautology.

freeman, free man. A *free man* is a man who is free in general senses (literally or metaphorically). A *freeman* is (1) a person who is granted the freedom of a city, or (2) in historical uses, a person who is not a slave or serf.

free rein, meaning 'unrestricted scope for action', is spelt this way, not *free reign* (as if it were connected with *reign* = rule). The following example should be corrected accordingly: ☒ *If they are given free reign to invest and produce they will grow*—New Yorker, 1987.

French words and phrases used in English.
See box overleaf

frequentative. Frequentative verbs express repeated or continuous action and are formed with certain suffixes, in English principally -*er* and -*le*. Examples are *chatter, clamber, flicker, flitter, glitter, slumber*; *crackle, dazzle, paddle, sparkle, wriggle*.

fresco, meaning a type of wall-painting, has plural forms *frescos* (preferred) and *frescoes*.

friar, monk. A *friar* is a member of a mendicant (i.e. living on alms) or originally mendicant religious order of men, especially the Augustinians, Carmelites, Dominicans, and Franciscans, who live among the people and do good works. A *monk* can include these, but properly denotes a member of a religious community living apart under vows of poverty, chastity, and obedience.

Friday (and other days of the week).
Friday, being the first day of the week alphabetically, is chosen to make this point, which also applies to the other six. The suppression of *on* in adverbial ref-

erences to days of the week (*See you Friday | He normally eats fish Fridays*) is spreading to BrE from America, but the process is not complete and the use remains informal in Britain, especially in the singular. Only an American would say or write that something 'happened Friday' instead of 'happened last Friday', or to give a real example: *Noriega . . . said Monday the U.S. Southern Command in Panama . . . threatens the Central American nation*—USA Today, 1988.

friendlily is available as an adverb from *friendly* but because of its awkwardness it is rarely used: *The women . . . still addressed him friendlily*—William Trevor, 1980 | *All this was friendlily presented*—Roy Jenkins, 1991. The phrasal alternative *in a friendly way* (or *manner*) often serves better.

frier see FRYER.

frith see FIRTH.

frock was originally a male garment, especially the mantle of a monk or priest. Discarded by men, the word came back into favour in the 19c as a synonym of *gown* or *dress* for women or girls. Fowler described it as a vogue-word used 'especially for a dress regarded from the decorative point of view'. It is still in use but has a distinct period flavour and can be disparaging or facetious. A recent (1998) advertisement for a sports car shows the car with a supermodel in an elegant designer dress standing beside it. The caption reads 'our latest model . . . and Claudia Schiffer in a frock'.

frolic *verb* has inflected forms *frolicked, frolicking*.

French words and phrases used in English

1 English has been receptive to words and phrases from French for several centuries. The process has been continuous although there are two periods of special importance: the years after the Norman Conquest (11c), and the time of the French Enlightenment (18c) when movements in science and philosophy exposed gaps in the vocabulary of English (much as the French computing industry and media are absorbing English words at the moment). Many words from these periods have now been fully assimilated into English and behave like English words with no hint of foreignness (e.g. *button, glory, ounce, place, prime, uncle*, etc.). In the 19c, moral and other sensitivities sought refuge in the alien flavour of French in expressions such as *affaire de cœur* (first recorded in English in 1809), *crime passionnel* (1910), and *ménage à trois* (1891), and in the domains of art, literature, food, and wine French was felt to have an appropriacy corresponding to perceived national stereotypes.

2 The process of assimilation into English is illustrated by the noun *abandon*, meaning 'surrender to natural impulses', which entered the language early in the 19c. It was first printed in italics as a foreign word and pronounced in the French manner with a nasalized final syllable. By the early 20c it was printed in ordinary roman type as an English word (in James Joyce's *Ulysses*, for example), and about the same time, or a little later (after Daniel Jones's *English Pronouncing Dictionary* of 1917), it acquired the anglicized pronunciation that is now familiar, aided by the pre-existence of the fully assimilated verb. Hundreds of French loanwords had a similar history between the time of their adoption into English and their complete assimilation, and others are in the process of doing so. In the assimilation process, accents constitute the most persistent features of the original language when these are present. Even the most fully assimilated words, such as *café* and *façade*, tend to retain their accents, probably as an orthographic support for a still partly French pronunciation. Pronunciation in fact, as these two words show, is usually the least reliable guide to the degree of a word's assimilation.

3 The table below lists a selection of French words and phrases to illustrate four levels of adoption into English: A = printed in italic type and pronounced in a French manner (with some modification, e.g. in the articulation of *r*, the introduction of the indeterminate schwa sound (ə) for unaccented vowels, and the elimination of nasalized sounds); B = Gallicisms mainly confined to literary or scholarly use; C = printed in roman type but retaining some features of the French pronunciation; D = fully anglicized and printed in Roman type.

▶

▶ French words and phrases used in English

continued

WORD / PHRASE	APPROXIMATE MEANING	DATE	CATEGORY
affaire de cœur	love affair	19c	A
à merveille	wonderfully	18c	B
arrière-pensée	ulterior motive	19c	B
au fond	basically	18c	B
au pied de lettre	literally	18c	B
baroque	of 17c and 18c art	18c	D
billet-doux	love letter	17c	C
bizarre	strange	17c	D
blasé	indifferent	19c	C
brunette	brown	16c	D
cachet	sign of prestige	17c	D
café	coffee house	19c	C
camembert	cheese	19c	C
cartel	association of manufacturers	16c	D
charlatan	sham, fraud	17c	D
clairvoyant	one who foresees	17c	D
crime passionnel	crime of passion	20c	A
déjà vu	already seen	20c	C
éclair	cake	19c	D
enfant terrible	unconventional person	19c	A
escargot	edible snail	19c	C
esprit de corps	team spirit	18c	A
esprit de l'escalier	inspiration too late	20c	B
gigolo	paid escort or lover	20c	D
laissez-faire	non-interference	19c	A
mayonnaise	thick sauce	19c	D
ménage à trois	household of three	19c	A
nom de guerre	name assumed in war	17c	A
nom de plume	pen-name	19c	C
pièce de résistance	most remarkable item	18c	A
point d'appui	strategic point	19c	B
sobriquet	nickname	17c	C
soi-disant	so-called	18c	B
son et lumière	sound and light effects	20c	A
touché	word used to concede a point	20c	C
tour de force	feat of skill	19c	C
tournedos	cut of beef	19c	C

from. Avoid the mixture of styles shown in the type *He was chairman of the board from 1979–1985*. This should be expressed either *He was chairman of the board 1979–1985* or *He was chairman of the board from 1979 to 1985*. See also BETWEEN 3.

from whence, from hence.

1 Although widely disapproved of on the grounds that *from* is redundant, *from whence* has a long and distinguished history of use in questions (*From whence these Murmurs, and this change of mind*—Dryden, 1697) and in indirect questions or as a conjunction introducing a relative clause (*No man can say from whence the greater danger to order arises*—F. Harrison, 1867). The phrase with from continues to be used in modern literature: *When they show the captive a picture of the City of London, that he may know from whence they come, he displays no interest*—Penelope Lively, 1991 | *Dark clouds had gathered over the hills to the north, from whence came the lucky changeling folk in times long past*—S. Koea, 1994 (New Zealand). The modern uses have mostly to do with people's origins and can be justified stylistically as archaisms (cf. *Thys felowe, we knowe not from whence he ys*—Tyndale, 1526). In general use, if *whence* has to be used, it is best used without *from*; but of course the problem can be avoided altogether by rephrasing in a way that is in any case more natural in modern English: *. . . so that he can know where they come from*.

2 The *OED* gives numerous examples, dating from the 14c to the 19c, of the use of *from hence*. A typical 19c example is *From hence I was conducted up a staircase to a suite of apartments*—W. Irving,

1820. In the 20c this use is best avoided.

fruition has only an indirect connection with *fruit*, but the false association led it astray in the 19c. Its current meaning 'fulfilment, the realization of aims' (especially in the phrase *come to fruition*) dates from then; before that it meant 'enjoyment' (from the Latin deponent verb *frui* 'to enjoy'), a meaning which is still listed in dictionaries of current English though hardly much used.

fryer is the preferred spelling for the agent noun meaning 'a person or thing that fries', not *frier*.

frying-pan is the usual term in BrE, but in AmE it alternates with *frypan* and *skillet*.

-fs, -ves.
See box opposite

fuchsia, the plant, is correctly spelt this way (after the 16c German botanist Leonhard *Fuchs*), not *fuschia*, although this is sometimes erroneously used (and encouraged by the word's pronunciation, **fyoo**-shə).

fuel *verb* has inflected forms *fuelled, fuelling* in BrE and *fueled, fueling* in AmE.

-ful is a suffix forming nouns that denote amounts, as in *cupful, handful, mouthful,* etc. In many cases these nouns develop meanings that are remote from the word that forms the first element; for example, a *handful* means 'a small number' as well as 'an amount that can be held in the hand'. The plurals of these words is *cupfuls, handfuls, mouthfuls,* etc.

-fs, -ves

Nouns ending in *-f* and *-fe* have plural forms as shown in the table below:

NOUN	-FS PLURAL	-VES PLURAL	VERB FORM
beef	beefs (= kinds of beef)	beeves (=oxen)	
belief	beliefs		
calf		calves	calve, calved
dwarf	dwarfs	dwarves (see entry)	dwarf, dwarfed
elf		elves	
half		halves	halve, halved
handkerchief	handkerchiefs		
hoof	hoofs	hooves (see entry)	hoof, hoofed
knife		knives	knife, knifed
leaf		leaves	leaf, leafed
life		lives	live, lived
loaf		loaves	loaf, loafed
oaf	oafs		
proof	proofs		prove, proved
roof	roofs	rooves (see entry)	roof, roofed
scarf	scarfs	scarves (see entry)	
self		selves	
sheaf		sheaves	sheave, sheaved
shelf		shelves	shelve, shelved
staff	staffs	staves (music)	staff, staffed
thief		thieves	thieve, thieved
turf	turfs	turves (see entry)	turf, turfed
wharf	wharfs	wharves	
wife		wives	
wolf		wolves	wolf, wolfed

fulcrum is pronounced **fuhl**-krəm or **ful**-krəm and has plural forms *fulcra* or *fulcrums*.

fulfil is the BrE spelling; in AmE it alternates with *fulfill*. The inflections in both varieties are *fulfilled*, *fulfilling*.

full survives as an adverb only in the phrases *full well* (as in *You know full well what I mean*) and *full in the face* (as in *The ball hit him full in the face*). Other uses (e.g. *full early, full fain*) are now somewhat literary or archaic; in Shakespeare's *Full fathom five thy Father lies* (*Tempest* I.ii.399), the meaning is 'fully, quite' and refers to the number.

fullness is spelt with two *l*s, but the form *fulness* occurs in 19c and earlier printed works.

full stop. 1 The principal use of the full stop (also called *point, full point,* and *period*) is to mark the end of a sentence that is a statement (as in this sentence). This applies to sentences when they are not complete statements or contain ellipsis (see SENTENCE), as in the opening of Dickens's *Bleak House* (1852–3): *London. Michaelmas term lately over, and the Lord Chancellor sitting in Lincoln's Hall. Implacable November weather*. If the sentence is a question or exclamation, the mark used is the QUESTION MARK or EXCLAMATION MARK, which include a full stop in their forms.

2 The full stop is also used to mark abbreviations and contractions, although this use is diminishing, partly as a matter of printing style and partly because many abbreviations have become more familiar and no longer need identification. The distinction between abbreviations (e.g. *I.o.W.* = Isle of Wight) and contractions (e.g. *Dr* = Doctor), though arguably a useful one, has been rapidly eroded by this process, so that shortenings of various kinds are printed and written without full stops, e.g. *BBC, DPhil, etc, ie, IoW, Mr, Ms, pm* (= post meridiem), *St* (= Saint or Street), etc. The style recommended here is somewhat more conservative than this, dropping full stops in initialisms that are all capital letters (e.g. *BBC, NNW* = north-north-west, *TUC*), in many contractions (*Dr, Mr*, etc.), and in acronyms that are pronounced as words (e.g. *Anzac, Nato*), but retaining them in lower-case initialisms such as *a.m., e.g.* and *i.e.*, in mixed styles such as *D.Phil.* and *M.Sc.*, and in shortened words such as *Oct.* (= October) and *Tues.* (= Tuesday). The important point, however, is to achieve consistency within a particular piece of writing or printing. Some shortenings have a greater need of full stops to avoid possible ambiguity with other words in some contexts,

e.g. *a.m.* (= ante meridiem), *no.* (= number).

3 If an abbreviation with a full stop comes at the end of a sentence, another full stop is not added when the full stop of the abbreviation is the last character: *Bring your own pens, pencils, rulers, etc.* but *Bring your own things (pens, pencils, rulers, etc.)*.

4 Full stops are routinely used between units of money (£11.99, $27.50), before decimals (10.5%), and between hours and minutes (10.30 a.m.; AmE 10:30 a.m.).

fulsome. 1 The first meaning of *fulsome* was 'copious, abundant', but it had lost this along with other meanings by the 16c and acquired an unfavourable sense 'excessive, cloying', especially with reference to praise or flattery. This meaning has remained the dominant one until the second half of the 20c, when *fulsome* began to be used in favourable meanings, so that *fulsome praise* meant high or lavish praise rather than excessive or nauseating praise. This new use, more common in AmE but increasingly found in BrE too, should be avoided, because the adverse meaning is still much in use and there is a danger of unfortunate misunderstanding. Examples of the erroneous use: ✘ *That very fulsome tribute to Mrs Shirley Williams by the PM*—radio broadcast, 1979 | ✘ *I got a very fulsome apology from the President of Iraq*—Ronald Reagan, quoted on NBC News, 1987. An example of the correct use is: *Walks surefootedly through the minefield that separates fulsome idolatry from condescending anecdotal chit-chat*—Times Literary Supplement, 1977.

2 *Fulsome* is also occasionally used to mean 'full-figured', with reference to a woman's figure, by fashion writers who analyse the word as consisting of *full* + *-some* as in *handsome, wholesome*, etc.: *I am warned that these particular cassocks will only fit either the exceptionally petite or the handsomely fulsome—Daily Telegraph*, 1985.

fun, first recorded in 1700 and stigmatized by Dr Johnson as a 'low cant word' (i.e. ephemeral jargon), has long hovered on the brink of adjectival status (*It was really fun*) and more recently has taken a step further in informal attributive uses such as *We had a fun time* or *That would be a fun thing to do*. It still has a way to go, however, since it cannot yet be qualified by intensifying adverbs such as *very* or *extremely* (use of *great* instead gives away the noun's disguise), and lacks the comparative and superlative inflections that a single-syllable adjective normally has (although *more fun* as in *This sounds more fun* is legitimate; *funner* and *funnest* are beginning to appear in youth slang in AmE).

function. 1 The noun has a number of technical meanings in mathematics and (now) in computing, and has acquired general meanings that caused Fowler (1926) to categorize it as a POPULARIZED TECHNICALITY. As a noun, it is often used somewhat pretentiously in meanings for which other words would serve as well: (1) *role, duty,* or *responsibility* (*This function is now discharged by departmental select committees*—H. Calvert, 1985), (2) *use* or *purpose* (*Identify the main functions of a hedge before deciding its composition—Gardeners' World*, 1991), (3) *action, activity,* or *performance* (*He was embarrassed about the nature of his illness and reluctant to discuss his bowel function with anyone*—J. Merchant et al.,

1989), (4) *capacity, facility,* or *operation* (especially with a preceding word: *In some countries major social consumption functions are controlled by the central government and social investment functions by local governments*—P. Dunleavy 1987), or (5) *party* or *gathering* (*It was not the kind of function to which Nat was accustomed to go, but his father's employer . . . pressed a ticket on him*—Frederic Raphael, 1960).

2 As a verb, *function* often substitutes unnecessarily for more workaday words such as *act, operate, think,* or *work*: *Excessive heat may make us feel 'stupid' and unable to function mentally*—U. Markham, 1991. The phrase *to be a function of* is a direct borrowing from mathematics, and usually means little more than *to be caused by*: *This suggests that, in part, the housewife's dissatisfaction with her work is a function of downward social mobility*—A. Oakley, 1990.

3 There is a place for *function* as a formal and technical word, but in general use the alternatives suggested above are usually worth considering.

functional. In addition to its special meanings in medicine and psychology, the primary meanings of *functional* are (1) 'designed or intended to be practical rather than attractive', a synonym of *utilitarian*, and (2) 'having a function, working'. In the 1990s the word has been used in the second meaning to describe a type of food, originated in Japan, that contains health-promoting additives instead of the conventionally harmful ones: *Functional foods are sometimes wrongly referred to in the media as 'miracle foods', implying they are something of a panacea, negating the *need for a healthy diet'—Grocer,* 1996.

funerary, funeral, funereal. *Funerary* is the standard adjective in the neutral meaning 'of or used at a funeral or funerals', as in *funerary ashes, funerary urn,* etc. It dates from the late 17c and has replaced *funeral,* which was originally an adjective but became predominantly a noun from the 16c onwards (in uses such as *funeral expenses* and *funeral rites* it is a noun used attributively and not an adjective). *Funereal,* which is first recorded in 1725, has a special judgemental meaning 'appropriate to a funeral', either 'deadly slow' (like a funeral procession) or 'gloomy, dreary, dismal': *Her mother and brother had departed to the kitchen from where Wexford could hear their muted whisperings and the funereally careful clink of cups*—Ruth Rendell, 1981 | *Karl nodded and began to walk slowly up the steps, Erika by his side, moving at a funereal pace*—P. Carter, 1986 | *Even with Donald there, Aileen thought, the place had a funereal silence about it*—C. F. Roe, 1992.

fungus has the plural form *fungi,* pronounced **fung**-giy or **fun**-jiy, although *funguses* is sometimes used, especially to mean 'types of fungus'. The adjectival forms are *fungal* and *fungous,* and *fungus* itself is sometimes used attributively (before a noun, as in *a fungus disease*).

funnel *verb* has inflected forms *funnelled, funnelling* in BrE and *funneled, funneling* in AmE.

funny is used in two primary meanings: (1) amusing, comical

(as in *a funny joke*), (2) strange, hard to explain (as in *a funny look*). Since the 1930s, as first recorded in a novel by Ian Hay, meaning (1) has come to be called *funny-ha-ha* and meaning (2) *funny-peculiar.*

furore, meaning 'an uproar, an outbreak of fury', is pronounced as three syllables. The word is spelt *furor* in AmE and pronounced **fyoo**-raw.

further, furthest see FARTHER.

fuse. There are two distinct words: (1) the one meaning 'a device for igniting a bomb' is 17c from Latin *fusus* 'spindle', and (2) the one meaning 'a device or component for protecting an electric circuit' is 19c, derived from the earlier verb meaning 'to melt'. The first of these words, but not the second, is usually spelt *fuze* in AmE.

-fy. This suffix forming English verbs corresponds to French *-fier* and Latin *-ficare.* It occurs from the 15c onwards in words either borrowed whole from French or modelled on French forms (e.g. *beautify, classify, horrify, pacify*), and is also an active suffix occasionally forming new (often somewhat jocular) words such as *bullify* (18c = to make into a bully), *Frenchify* (16c), and *ladify* (17c). These words have inflections in *-ifies, -ified, -ifying.* When there is a choice of spelling between *-ify* and *-yfy* (as with *countrify/-yfy* and *ladify/-yfy*) the spelling in *-ify* is preferable. A small group of words end in *-efy* (e.g *liquefy, stupefy*) and inflect *-efies, -efied, -efying.*

Gg

gabardine. This is the recommended spelling for the word meaning 'a smooth durable cloth' or a raincoat made from it. The form *gaberdine* is used with historical reference to the smock worn by almsmen and beggars, and by Jews on the Elizabethan stage, as in Shakespeare's *Merchant of Venice* I.iii.111 (Shylock): *You call me misbeliever, cut-throat, dog, And spit upon my Jewish gaberdine.*

Gaelic, pronounced **gal**-ik or **gay**-lik, denotes any of the modern Celtic languages spoken in Ireland (Irish Gaelic), Scotland (Scottish Gaelic), and the Isle of Man (Manx). There are two main varieties that were ancestors of these languages: Brythonic (or *P-Celtic*), also the indigenous language of Wales and Cornwall and taken by Britons to Brittany, and Goidelic (or *Q-Celtic*), which spread from Ireland into the Isle of Man and Scotland.

gala is normally pronounced **gah**-lə but the traditional pronunciation, as recorded in the *OED* (1899) and as used in the Durham Miners' Gala, is **gay**-lə. Both pronunciations are in use in AmE. The plural form is *galas*.

gallant is pronounced **gal**-ənt in the ordinary meaning 'brave', and gə-**lant** in the special meaning 'attentive to women, amorous' and the related noun 'lover or paramour'. Fowler thought that these two uses were, even then (1926), 'perhaps moribund', but they persist, usually in fic-tional or romantic contexts rather than in everyday language.

galley has the plural form *galleys*.

Gallicisms. Fowler (1926) used this term to describe what he called 'borrowings of various kinds from French in which the borrower stops short of using French words without disguise'. That is to say, they are words that have been assimilated in various ways, or in some cases translated, into English. While acknowledging their established contribution to English vocabulary, he gave a warning not to use them as a kind of affectation derived from their foreignness. There are three principal types of Gallicisms; Fowler was thinking especially of the third:

1 French words which have been adapted to suit the ordinary conventions of English by dropping accents or substituting English endings, e.g. *actuality* (from French *actualité*) and *redaction* (from French *rédaction*). See also FRENCH WORDS AND PHRASES USED IN ENGLISH.

2 Mismatches, i.e. words that do not mean in English what they mean in French; for example, *papier mâché* is literally 'chewed paper' and does not exist in this meaning in French (the equivalent is *carton-pâte*), *duvet* in English means 'a continental quilt' but in French means 'a sleeping-bag', and *cagoule*, which in English means 'a windproof outdoor garment with a hood', in

French means a monk's hood or 'a child's balaclava'. Some food terms have different meanings in the two languages: *fromage frais,* which is now widely seen in British supermarkets, is what in French is called *fromage blanc, fromage frais* being a fresh unmatured type of cheese.

3 Loan translations, i.e. expressions adopted from French in a more or less literally translated form, e.g. *gilded youth* (from French *jeunesse dorée*), *jump* (or *leap) to the eyes* (French *sauter aux yeux*), *marriage of convenience* (French *mariage de convenance*), and *that goes without saying* (French *cela va sans dire*).

gallop meaning 'to go at a fast pace', has inflected forms *galloped, galloping.*

gallows has been treated since the 16c as a singular noun, with a (rarely used) plural *gallowses. Gallows humour* means 'grim and ironical humour'.

galore, meaning 'in plenty', comes after the word it qualifies (*bargains galore in our spring sale*). It is derived from Irish *go leór* meaning 'to sufficiency, enough'.

galosh, meaning 'a waterproof overshoe', is normally used in the plural *galoshes.* This spelling is preferred to the variant *golosh.*

gambit, in its generalized meaning 'an opening move in a conversation, meeting, set of negotiations, etc.', is a technical term taken from chess (see POPULARIZED TECHNICALITIES), where the meaning is 'an opening in which a player sacrifices a piece or pawn to secure an advantage'. In the extension of meaning, the notion of sacrifice has largely disappeared: *Liza was attractive and*

her response to some of his occasional conversational gambits on the way home had been interesting and unusual—P. Street, 1990 | *These questions are often opening gambits for a negotiation of some sort*—P. Davies, 1991.

gambol, meaning 'to skip or frolic playfully', has inflected forms *gambolled, gambolling.* In AmE the forms *gamboled, gamboling* are also used.

gamut. In music, *gamut* properly means 'the note G at the pitch now indicated by the lowest line of the bass staff'. From this it was extended eventually to mean 'the whole series of notes used in medieval or modern music', and this has given rise to the generalized meaning 'the whole series or range or scope of anything' which chiefly occurs in the expression *run the gamut* (= experience the whole range of): *The audience for science fiction now runs the gamut from the high school 'trekkie' to the serious literary scholar*—book catalogue, 1983. The word is formed from medieval Latin *gamma* (= the note G) + *ut*, the first of six arbitrary names forming the hexachord (*ut, re, mi, fa, sol, la*); these were said to be taken from the initial letters of a sequence of Latin words in the office hymn for St John the Baptist's day.

gantry is spelt in this way when it refers to any of various structures supporting a crane, set of railway signals, space rocket, etc. In the meaning 'a wooden stand for barrels', it is also spelt *gauntry* and pronounced **gawn**-tri.

gaol, gaoler, see JAIL, JAILER.

gap is widely used as the second element of expressions denoting 'a divergence in views, sympathies, development, etc.' Those recorded in the *OED* include *credibility gap* (first recorded in 1966), *dollar gap* (1948), *export gap* (1952), *generation gap* (1967), *missile gap* (1959), and *technology gap* (1967).

garage. The standard pronunciation in BrE is **ga**-rahzh, although some speakers say **ga**-rij or (with the stress on the second syllable) gə-**rahzh**. The dominant pronunciations in AmE are gə-**rahzh** and gə-**rahj**.

garrotte is the customary spelling for the word (verb and noun) to do with killing by strangulation. In AmE the dominant spelling is *garrote* (with inflections *garroted, garroting*), although other forms are also found.

gas. The plural of the noun is *gases*, but the verb has inflected forms *gasses, gassed, gassing*. *Gas*, short for *gasoline*, is the most usual word in AmE for BrE *petrol*, and permeates BrE in colloquial expressions such as *step on the gas*.

gaseous. The dominant pronunciation in standard English is **gas**-i-əs; **gay**-si-əs is now only rarely heard.

gasoline is the AmE term for what in BrE is called *petrol*, a volatile liquid obtained from petroleum. This spelling is preferred to *gasolene*, but the word is normally used in its shortened form *gas*. See GAS.

-gate is a suffix taken from the name *Watergate*, a building in Washington DC containing the headquarters of the Democratic Party, which was the centre of a break-in and political scandal in 1972. The suffix is used in various combinations to denote an actual or alleged scandal that is in some way comparable. Examples are *Dallasgate* (1975), *Koreagate* (1976), *Irangate* (1986, referring to secret US sales of arms to Iran), and most recently *Monicagate* (1998, referring to a sexual scandal involving Monica Lewinsky and President Bill Clinton). These formations are a godsend to journalists wishing to instil the breath of scandal into short eye-catching headlines.

gateau, a loanword from French meaning 'a rich cake', has the plural form *gateaus*, or occasionally *gateaux*.

gauge is spelt in this way, not *guage*.

gauntlet. There are two distinct words here: (1) 'a stout glove' used in the expression *throw down the gauntlet* (= accept a challenge), from an Old French diminutive of *gant* meaning 'glove', and (2) used in the phrase *run the gauntlet* (= undergo a punishment or ordeal), assimilated from an earlier form *gantlope*, of Swedish origin. The second word is sometimes spelt *gantlet* in AmE.

gay. 1 *There is no historical case for homosexual ownership of 'gay'. So can we have our word back, please.'*—Paul Johnson, 1995. This typifies the reaction of many people to this major change, occurring from the mid-20c but with occasional earlier evidence, in the use of a basic English word. At this time, the homosexual community made it clear that they wanted to be called *gay* instead of *homosexual* or any of the other derogatory names including *fag, faggot, fairy, homo,* *pansy*, and *queer*. The first substantial evidence is from the 1950s: *In a way it was an odd threesome. It occurred to me that Esther rather hung round our two gay boys*—E. Lambert, 1951. The historical basis for this use of *gay* is sometimes sought in earlier meanings: (17c) 'addicted to social pleasures and dissipations' (as in *gay dog* and *gay Lothario*) and (19c) '(said of a woman) leading an immoral life, living by prostitution'. But these older and hardly favourable meanings constitute dubious precedents, and in all probability the connection was impressionistic rather than analytical. Whatever the case, the new meaning looks here to stay, and dictionaries of current English tend to list it first of the several meanings of *gay*. There are a number of points to be made in defence of the new meaning: it is useful to have a word that is not offensive; the traditional meaning of *gay* was in any case acquiring something of a period flavour; and there are plenty of synonyms available: *merry, jolly, cheerful, happy, high-spirited, lively*, and others that can be found in a good thesaurus.

2 *Gay* is also used in the meaning 'intended for, used by, or associated with homosexuals' (as in *gay bar* and *gay politics*), and as a noun: *What about gays, one asks, and will there be facilities for them to relate significantly to each other?*—*Sunday Telegraph*, 1985. Unlike the adjectival use, however, the noun *gay* usually denotes male homosexuals only, and the phrase *lesbians and gays* (usually in that order) is used to show clearly that both sexes are meant: *Venues and services staffed by lesbians and gays are invaluable in maintaining a sense of community*—P. Lincoln & T. Kaufmann, 1991 | *One end result has been an increase in the extent to which gays and lesbians have been subjected to physical violence*—J. Dollimore, 1991. The *gay gene* is a slang term for DNA sequences which can predispose an individual to homosexuality.

3 It should be mentioned that, despite all the inhibitions reviewed above, the traditional meaning of *gay* is still alive and well for some writers: *She had lived a very gay life in London, when she was on the stage*—Nina Bawden, 1991 | *But she disobeyed him, brought the baby out, and he had never found her so gay, so welcoming*—Marina Warner, 1992.

gazebo, pronounced gə-**zee**-boh and meaning 'a small glass building designed to give a wide view', has the plural form *gazebos*. The word is 18c, and is thought to be a fanciful formation on *gaze*, as if it were a Latin future verb meaning 'I will gaze (at the view)'.

geezer is a (now somewhat dated) slang term for a person, usually a man. It is a late-19c adaptation of *guiser* meaning 'mummer', reflecting a dialect pronunciation.

gelatin, gelatine. *Gelatin* (pronounced **jel**-ə-tin) is the customary form in chemical use, and in AmE in all uses, but *gelatine* (pronounced **jel**-ə-teen) is common in BrE in contexts to do with the preparation of food.

gender. 1 Since the 14c the word has been primarily a grammatical term denoting groups of nouns in terms of their being masculine, feminine, or neuter. In the earliest form of English (Old English or Anglo-Saxon, *c*. 740 to 1066), nouns fell into three classes, masculine, feminine, and neuter: *stān* (stone) was masculine, *giefu* (gift) was feminine, and *scip* (ship) was neuter. The definite article and most adjectives varied to accord with the gender of the accompanying noun, as they still do in other languages. By the end of the 11c, this system was lost. In modern English grammatical gender exists only in the singular personal pronouns *he, she, it, his, hers, its,* etc., and in some feminine endings such as *-ess, -ette* (imported from French), and *-ine*.

2 Although nouns associated with female and male persons and animals are generally feminine or masculine as appropriate, grammatical gender and sexual gender do not have a complete correspondence in any language, which accounts for some of the anomalies that can cause offence in our modern gender-sensitive age (e.g. in referring to vehicles as *she*).

3 The evidence in the *OED* shows that the term *gender* was also used as a term meaning 'the sex of a person', although the *OED* editors (1899) marked this as 'now only jocular'. Since the 1960s this meaning has come back into regular use, especially among feminists, to emphasize 'the social and cultural, as opposed to the biological, distinctions between the sexes' (*OED2*, 1989). This revival, which is a useful one, has given rise to many new compound expressions, including *gender gap, gender identity, gender language, gender model, gender role,* and *gender-specific*; and academic disciplines now include the field of *gender studies*.

gender-neutrality. 1 In English, explicit grammatical gender is chiefly confined to the third-person singular personal pronouns, *he, she, it, his, hers, its,* etc. From earliest times until about the 1960s it was unquestionably acceptable to use the pronoun *he* (and *him, himself, his*) with indefinite reference to denote a person of either sex, especially after indefinite pronouns and determiners such as *anybody, anyone, each, every,* etc., after gender-neutral nouns such as *person, individual,* and *speaker,* and in fixed expressions such as *every man for himself* and *one man one vote*. The feminist movement has greatly intensified sensitivities in this area, and alternative devices often have to be found. When a gender-neutral pronoun or determiner (i.e. one that is free of grammatical gender) is needed, the options usually adopted are *he or she* (or *his or her,* etc.), or the plural forms *they, their, themselves,* etc.: *Each client should take the advice of their estate agent, who will take into account the style of the property,* [etc.]—*Real Property Guide* (Edinburgh), 1995 | *Anyone who involves themselves in such issues does so for their own salvation—Big Issue,* 1998. (This use of plural pronouns is not new, but a revival of a practice dating from the 16c.) An alternative strategy is to rephrase the sentence, for example by couching the whole thing in the plural; by this device the 1995 example above becomes *Clients should take the advice of their estate agents . . .* , although the loss of singular focus can sometimes blur the sense (as, perhaps, in this example).

2 Artificial devices, including the use of composite forms such as *s/he, hesh, wself,* etc., have not found general currency, partly because they are difficult to articulate and are only possible in writing. A reflexive pronoun *themself* is occasionally found and is likely to become more common, but at present it is non-standard: *It is not an actor pretending to be Reagan or Thatcher, it is, in grotesque form, the person themself*—I. Hislop, 1984 | *Someone in a neutral mood can devote themself solely to problem solving*—Independent, 1995.

genealogy, meaning '(the study of) a person's line of descent', is derived from a Greek word *genea* meaning 'race, generation'. The existence of so many words ending in -*ology* (*archaeology, psychology, sociology,* etc.) and the influence of its own derivative word *genealogical* (with a stressed -*o*-), traps some people into pronouncing *genealogy* as if it too ended in -*ology*, and even into spelling it that way.

generator is spelt -*or* in all its meanings, not -*er*.

genie, meaning 'a spirit of Arabian folklore', is pronounced **jee**-ni and has the plural form *genii*, pronounced **jee**-ni-iy. See also GENIUS.

genius, meaning 'a person of great intellectual power', has the plural form *geniuses*, not *genii*, which is the plural of GENIE.

gent (= gentleman). Apart from its use in commercial circles (e.g. *gents' outfitters*) and (in the UK) the colloquial euphemism the Gents, meaning a men's lavatory, this shortening is mainly used to indicate sociability, courtesy, etc., e.g. *He's a perfect gent.*

genteel. Its primary meaning is 'affectedly or ostentatiously refined or stylish', but it is often used ironically to mean 'of or appropriate to the upper classes'.

genteelism. Fowler (1926) described *genteelism* as 'the substituting, for the ordinary natural word that first suggests itself to the mind, of a synonym that is thought to be less soiled by the lips of the common herd, less familiar, less plebeian, less vulgar, less improper'. It is euphemism taken a stage further by virtue of the inappropriate social context into which the substitute word is placed. Fowler's list included items that would now be considered normal or even preferable, such as *assist* for *help, close* for *shut, mirror* for *looking-glass,* and *stomach* for *belly.* Others, such as *anent* for *about* and *domestic* for *servant,* have fallen out of use or are no longer socially relevant. A few might be thought valid as genteelisms: e.g. *carafe* for *waterbottle, edifice* for *building, endeavour* for *try, expectorate* for *spit, inquire* for *ask, lingerie* for *underclothing, peruse* for *read, perspire* for *sweat,* and *sufficient* for *enough.* To these may be added *dentures* for *false teeth, desire* for *want, hard of hearing* for *deaf, lounge* for *sitting-room,* and *retire for the night* for *go to bed.* See also U AND NON-U.

genteelly, the adverb from *genteel,* is spelt and pronounced with two ls.

gentle. The phrase *the gentle art,* which was used with clever irony by the American painter James McNeill Whistler in his title *The Gentle Art of Making Enemies* (1890), had already become a cliché by the time Fowler wrote (1926). As well as being used allusively in titles, e.g. *The Gentle Art of Singing* (1927), it occurs in general contexts: *Grant took full advantage of the lunchtime lull in traffic, and in derestricted areas excelled himself in the gentle art of speed with safety—*

Josephine Tey, 1936 | *Hype is an American word for the gentle art of getting a tune into the pop charts without actually selling any records—Sunday Times, 1968. The gentle art* is also an affectionate name for the sport of angling.

gentleman. The word *gentleman*, formerly a term indicating social class, has largely fallen out of use in this meaning with the gradual erosion of class distinctions. It survives as a form of address (usually as *ladies and gentlemen*), in the phrase *gentleman's agreement* (an informal agreement not binding in law) and as a term of general polite reference, especially in public (*I have a question from the gentleman in the second row*). The designation *gentlemen* is still occasionally seen on signs for public lavatories, but *men* is more usual. The feminine form *gentlewoman*, meaning 'a woman of good birth or breeding' has almost entirely fallen out of use except as an archaism.

genuflection, meaning 'a bending of the knee', is the preferred spelling, although *genuflexion* is also in use.

genuine is pronounced **jen**-yuh-in in BrE. In AmE the pronunciation **jen**-yuh-iyn is widespread (sometimes for humorous effect) but non-standard.

genus, the term for a taxonomic grouping in biology, is pronounced **jee**-nəs. The plural is *genera*, pronounced **jen**-ə-rə.

geographic, geographical. Both forms have a long history, *geographic* being first recorded in 1630 and *geographical* in 1559. The longer form is dominant in BrE, but *geographic* alternates with it more frequently in AmE.

geometric, geometrical. As with the preceding words, the longer form is about a century older than the shorter one (1552 and 1630 respectively). In this case, the shorter form is dominant in fixed collocations in BrE (*geometric mean, geometric progression, geometric tracery*, etc.), but in general contexts the choice seems to depend on the rhythm and balance of the sentence. In AmE *geometric* seems to be more usual both in fixed collocations and in general contexts.

German words used in English.
See box overleaf

gerrymander meaning 'to manipulate election districts unfairly', is originally a US word formed from the name of Elbridge Gerry, governor of Massachusetts in 1812. His name was pronounced with a hard initial *g*, and the word was at first pronounced likewise, but pronunciation with a soft *g* (j-) is now standard in both AmE and BrE.

gerund see VERBAL NOUN.

gesticulation, gesture. 1 *Gesture* is a somewhat older word (15c) than *gesticulation* (16c), and both are related to Latin *gestus* meaning 'action'. In current use they overlap in their meanings to do with movement of the body or parts of the body as a mode of expression, and it is the degree of animation that governs the choice, *gesticulation* indicating a much more theatrical movement of the arms or body. The extended meaning of *gesture*, 'a friendly action intended to evoke a positive response', first came into English as recently as the early 20c: *The gift of your Medal of Honour to a British comrade in arms*

German words used in English

English has been steadily adopting words from German for several centuries, although there are fewer loans of phrases than there are from French. There are sometimes changes of form (e.g. *kaput*) or changes of meaning (e.g. *spiel*). The table below shows the more important loans, with their dates of first appearance in print and their meaning, together with an indication of whether they have been naturalized in English (i.e. are printed in roman type and regarded as English words) or non-naturalized:

WORD	MEANING	DATE	NATURALIZED
angst	guilty anxiety	1944	yes
blitz	sudden attack	1939	yes
echt	authentic	1916	no
edelweis	Alpine plant	1862	yes
ersatz	artificial, imitation	1875	yes
kaput	broken, not working	1895	yes
kindergarten	children's nursery	1852	yes
kitsch	garish or gaudy art	1926	yes
poltergeist	mischievous ghost	1848	yes
quartz	mineral	1765	yes
rucksack	type of bag	1866	yes
schadenfreude	enjoyment of another's misfortune	1895	no
spiel	glib talk	1896	yes
ur-	original, earliest	1880s	yes
waltz	dance	1781	yes

. . . *is a gesture of friendly sympathy and good will which we will not forget*—Times, 1921 | *Flowers didn't occur to Sneed until he had arrived at the hospital, and there the gesture was pointless*—G. F. Newman, 1970.

2 A 20c neologism that extends this use is *gesture politics*, defined as 'political action which concentrates primarily on publicity value and influencing public opinion'. It is normally used with connotations of disapproval: *There is no room for gesture politics. If we want to open debate about the future and our constitution, that is fine*—Daily Mail, 1995.

get. 1 RANGE OF USE. *Get* is one of the most frequently used and most productive words in English. Often it has virtually no meaning in itself and draws its meaning almost entirely from its context, especially in idiomatic uses such as *get to bed, get dressed, get home, get the flu, get a letter, get a new hat, get going, get rich, get one's feet wet, get a train*, and so on. It will be seen from these examples as an all-purpose substitute for a whole range of verbs including *arrive, become, buy, catch, collect, obtain, receive*, etc. *Get* also has a highly productive role in forming idiomatic phrasal verbs such as *get along, get at, get away, get away with, get back, get by, get down to, get on, get out, get over, get through, get together*, etc.

2 SUPPOSED OVERUSE. The view that *get* is an overused word and should be avoided in good English is a superstition. It was not a problem for either Fowler (1926) or Gowers (1965), whose entries on this word dealt with different aspects of its use. There are some uses that should be recognized as informal, e.g. *We got along fine* might be better expressed as *We were on good terms* in more formal contexts and *What are you getting at?* as *What are you suggesting* [or *implying*]?, but there is no advantage in *I received a letter this morning* over *I got a letter this morning* nor in *She's gone to collect her post* over *She's gone to get her post.* Many idiomatic phrases involving *get*, such as *get away with* and *get down to*, are effectively neutral in terms of register and can be used in virtually any context.

3 HAVE GOT = POSSESS. This was one of the issues that Fowler and Gowers dealt with, as mentioned above. Fowler wrote that '*have got* for *possess* or *have* is good colloquial English but not good literary English', and Gowers suggested that 'the intrusion of *got* into a construction in which *have* alone is enough originated in our habit of eliding *have*. *I have it* and *he has it* are clear statements, but if we elide we must insert *got* to avoid the absurdity of *I've it* and the even greater absurdity of *he's it*.' In negative contexts and questions, BrE *have* (or *had*) *not got* and *have* (or *had*) *you got?* is as common as (and somewhat less formal than) *do* (or *did*) *not have*, and *do* (or *did*) *you have?*, but the second alternative is the usual form in AmE.

4 The neologism *get a life*, meaning 'to start living a fuller or more interesting existence', is informal only: *The aristocracy is having to make some hard decisions: whether to pretend that the twentieth century never happened or to jump ship, join the middle class and get a life—Tatler*, 1993.

5 See also GOT, GOTTEN.

get-at-able, meaning 'accessible, attainable', is recorded from the late 18c, and is now more common than the older form COME-AT-ABLE.

geyser. The pronunciation in both its main meanings ('hot spring' and 'heating apparatus') is now **gee**-zə, although **giy**-zə is also used for the 'hot spring' meaning. In America and New Zealand, where the 'heater' meaning is not used, the pronunciation is uniformly **giy**-zə.

ghastlily, the adverb from *ghastly*, is best avoided as being too awkward to say.

ghetto has the plural form *ghettos*.

ghoul, meaning (1) 'an evil spirit' and (2) 'a person morbidly interested in death', is pronounced gool.

gibber, gibberish are pronounced **jib**-ə-.

gibbous, meaning 'convex, protuberant', especially with reference to the moon, is pronounced **gib**-əs.

gibe, jibe. The first spelling is recommended for the verb meaning 'to jeer, mock'. See also (the sailing term) GYBE.

gigolo, meaning 'a woman's paid escort or lover', is pronounced **zhig**-ə-loh or **jig**-ə-loh, and has the plural form *gigolos*.

gild, meaning 'to cover thinly with gold', has a past participle *gilded* (*The porcelain is gilded by a magma of gold*), but the adjectival form is either *gilt* (*gilt tooling | gilt-edged securities*) or *gilded* (*gilded youth*). This word should be distinguished from the noun *guild* (with *u*), meaning 'a medieval association of craftsmen or merchants'.

gild the lily, meaning 'to try to improve what is already as beautiful as it can be', is a not quite accurate quotation from Shakespeare, *King John* IV.ii.11: *To gilde refined Gold, to paint the Lilly; To throw a perfume on the Violet,* [etc.].

gill. The word for 'the respiratory organ in fishes' is pronounced gil, and the word for 'a unit of liquid measure' is pronounced jil.

gimmick, a word of unknown origin meaning 'a trick or device, especially to attract publicity or trade', entered AmE in the 1920s, appearing first in glossaries and then in writers such as James Thurber (1948). Few other words have shared the speed with which it has passed from being a slang word to being a part of normal English.

gingerly is now used primarily as an adverb meaning 'in a careful or cautious manner' (*He descends gingerly from the cab—New Yorker*, 1990); formerly it meant 'elegantly, daintily'. Its use as an adjective meaning 'showing great care or caution' is now less common than it once was.

gipsy see GYPSY.

gird. The normal past tense and past participle of the verb meaning 'to encircle or secure with a band or belt' is *girded*, but *girt* has been in use as recently as the 19c and is still used as an archaism, especially in adjectival compounds such as *sea-girt*.

girl is falling out of use as a term applied to adult women, partly under pressure from the feminist movement and partly because some of the institutions with which the word is associated in this use have become obsolete, for example the employment of female domestic servants (who were called *girls* whatever their age). However, the use remains active in several contexts: in referring to a regular female companion as a *girl* or *girlfriend*; in titles of books and films (e.g. Kingsley Amis's *Take a Girl Like You*, 1960, and Helen Gurley Brown's *Sex and the Single Girl*, 1962), in the lyrics of popular songs (e.g. *Diamonds are a girl's best friend*, Leo Robin, 1949; *Thank you girl*, Lennon & McCartney, 1964), in the expressions *glamour girl, cover girl, page three girl*, etc., and in the plural use of *the girls* to refer to a group of young women friends, analogous to *the boys*. In general use, however, *woman* or *young woman* are to be preferred. See LADY, WOMAN.

girlie has been used as an adjective since the 1920s to refer colloquially to entertainment and magazines that include pictures of naked or scantily dressed young women. It is spelt *girlie*, not *girly*.

girt see GIRD.

given, given that. These are used as a preposition and conjunction (introducing a subordinate clause) respectively with the meaning '(it being) granted or assumed (that)'. The history of their use shows them to be free of the need to be attached to a particular subject, and so they are not so-called 'unattached participles' (see PARTICIPLES 3, 4). In the following modern examples, *given* is grammatically free of the subject of the main clause in each case: (preposition) *He didn't think that, given her ambitions and temperament, she would enjoy it*—A. West, 1984 | *Given the world around us, that would be unhelpful, to say the least*—Times, 1992 | (conjunction) *Given how busy the Spanish monarchs were in the 1480s, it's a wonder they gave Columbus any notice at all*—Chicago Tribune, 1988 | *Given that the government shies away from a graduate tax, student loans are the next best way of ensuring that students who benefit from higher education foot some of the bill*—Economist, 1991.

given name see CHRISTIAN NAME.

glacial, glacier. The standard pronunciations in BrE are **glay**-shəl and **glas**-eer respectively; in AmE they are **glay**-shəl and **glay**-shər.

gladiolus is pronounced gla-di-**oh**-ləs, and the plural form is *gladioli*, pronounced gla-di-**oh**-liy.

glamour is spelt *-our* in BrE and either *-our* or *-or* in AmE. The word is originally Scottish, and was brought into general literary use by Walter Scott about 1830. It is an alteration of the word *grammar* (or more strictly, of the old form *gramarye*) with the meaning 'occult learning, magic, necromancy'. It then passed into standard English and meant 'a delusive or alluring charm'; nearly a century later, in the 1930s, it acquired its main current meaning, first in AmE and then in BrE and elsewhere, relating to the charm

or physical allure of a person (usually a woman).

glance, glimpse. A *glance* (which can be followed by *at*, *into*, *over*, or *through*) is a brief look (*He cast a doting glance at his wife*—M. Underwood, 1973 | *Karen and Jill exchanged glances of not-quite-mock despair*—M. Babson, 1975), whereas a *glimpse* (which is usually followed by *of*) is what is seen by taking a glance rather than the glance itself (*The automatic roof light gave me a quick glimpse of two men, then the driver reached up to switch it off*—A. Ross, 1970). There is a corresponding difference in the use of the verbs: *He glanced down at the face of his gold Rolex*—W. Wager, 1970 | *Under the best conditions it might be possible with glasses to glimpse the red supergiant star Antares*—Daily Telegraph, 1973.

glasses is the usual term in both BrE and AmE for what are also called in BrE (though not in AmE) *spectacles*. In AmE *eyeglasses* is often used in the same meaning, but this has long fallen out of use in Britain.

glassful. In the plural, care should be taken to distinguish *glassfuls* from *glasses full*. A *glassful* is an amount contained in a glass, and *three glassfuls* (e.g. of water) means three times this amount, though not necessarily held in three glasses. *Three glasses full* (of water) means three different glasses each full of water. Note that there is no form *glassesful*. See also CUPFUL.

glimpse see GLANCE.

global has developed its meaning from the original simple meaning 'spherical, round' to 'all-inclusive' in abstract senses (19c) and, more recently, 'world-wide, involving the whole world', as in *global warfare* and the *global village* (coined by Marshall McLuhan in 1960 to denote the effective shrinking of the world by virtue of advanced communications), and especially in *global warming*, a term that became established in the 1980s to mean 'an increase in the temperature of the earth's atmosphere thought to be caused by the greenhouse effect'. In computer technology from the 1960s onwards, *global* means 'operating on the whole of a file or program', so that a *global change* made to an item is one that affects every occurrence in that item.

glue *verb* has inflections *glues, glued, gluing*; the adjective is *gluey*.

glycerine is spelt *-ine* in BrE and *-in* in AmE. In technical writing *glycerol* (same meaning) is used.

gn-. English words beginning in *gn-* are pronounced with the initial g silent, i.e. *gnat* and *gnostic* are pronounced nat and **nos**-tik respectively. Exceptions are the food-term *gnocchi* (a 19c loanword from Italian), which is pronounced **nyo**-ki, and the animal name *gnu* (from a South African language), which is sometimes pronounced nyoo as well as noo.

gnaw. The past tense and past participle are *gnawed*. *Gnawn* is sometimes found in print and is given in dictionaries, but it has an archaic or poetic ring: *From crock of bone-dry crusts and mouse-gnawn cheese*—Walter de la Mare, 1921.

go. 1 The noun has the plural form *goes*.

2 There are five uses of the verb that call for comment:

▶ **a** *IT GOES WITHOUT SAYING.* This is a naturalized Gallicism (see GALLICISMS), from French *cela va sans dire*. Native English equivalents are *needless to say, of course,* and others, which some people prefer.

▶ **b** *GO* + **BARE INFINITIVE.** The construction *go* + infinitive without *to* was the primary construction until the 17c, occurring many times in Shakespeare (e.g. *He is walked up to the top of the hill. I'll go seek him*—1 *Henry IV* II.ii.10). Although this construction survives in AmE (e.g. *I'll go put your lovely flowers in water*—John Updike, 1986), in BrE it is now confined to a few fixed expressions such as *let him go hang (for all I care)*. In BrE the current constructions are *go + and* + infinitive or *go + to*-infinitive: *Let's go and see that film at the local*—K. Benton, 1976 | *You go to buy a car, offering your Old Faithful in part-exchange*—*Drive*, 1977 | *She . . . said she would go and turn the sprinkler off herself*—*New Yorker*, 1986.

▶ **c** *GO* + *AND.* The combination *go + and* + infinitive often has special meanings, e.g. (1) 'to be so foolish, unreasonable, or unlucky as to': *You herd cattle all day, you come to despise them, and pretty soon . . . you have gone and shot one*—Garrison Keillor, 1990, and (2) as an instruction in the imperative: *It's late, child . . . Go and get some sleep*—J. M. Coetzee, 1977 (South Africa).

▶ **d** *GO* = **SAY.** The use in question here is illustrated by the following example: *Butch and I were discussing this problem, and Butch goes, 'But you promised you'd do it.' Then I go, 'Well, I changed my mind.'*—*Chicago Tribune*, 1989. Go is always used in this way with past reference (though very often in the present tense, as here). It may be regarded as an extension of the meaning that refers to a thing making a sound, as in cows going moo and bells going dong, and a transitional stage between names of sounds and reported speech can be discerned in the evidence given by the OED (*Additions Series* II, 1993): *He was roused by a loud shouting of the post-boy on the leader. 'Yo-yo-yo-yo-yoe,' went the first boy. 'Yo-yo-yo-yoe,' went the second*—Dickens, 1836 | *She was a dear little dickey bird, 'Chip, chip, chip,' she went*—*Illustrated Victorian Songbook*, 1895. The extended use in reported speech is especially common in school and youth language, and is also heard in conversational adult use.

▶ e **GO FOR IT.** In 1987, the (American) cox of the Oxford boat in the University Boat Race wore a shirt with the slogan *Go for it* displayed on the back, thereby signalling the arrival in Britain of this popular American phrase of the 1980s: *I told her about Scott* [sc. a boyfriend]. *Eileen said, 'Go for it, Andrea!'*—*New Yorker*, 1986. It may be seen as an extension of the meaning of *go* illustrated by uses such as *I could go for you in a big way*, i.e. 'be enthusiastic about, be enamoured of'.

gobbledegook.

1 The term, though not the concept, was unknown to Fowler (1926); Gowers (1965) knew it, but like Fowler put his material in an entry called *jargon. Gobbledegook* (or *gobbledygook*) is the extensive use of unintelligible jargon in printed information that is intended for a general readership. Jargon within particular fields of study, such as computing or linguistics, is quite legitimate; it becomes *gobbledegook* when ordinary people not experienced in those domains are expected to understand it. The term is first recorded in America in 1944, and was probably coined as a representation of a turkey-cock's gobble.

2 The following passage from an American policy document about transport plans (as reported in a Chicago newspaper of 1995) shows gobbledegook in its most potent form: *While EPA* [*the Environmental Protection Agency*] *will solicit comments on other options, the supplemental notice of proposed rulemaking on transportation conformity will propose to require conformity determinations only in the metropolitan planning areas (the urbanized area and the contiguous area(s) likely to become urbanized within 20 years) or attainment areas which have exceeded 85 percent of the ozone, CO, NO2, PM-10 annual, or PM-10 24-hour NAAQS within the last three, two, one, three, and three years respectively.* Doubtless the statement made good sense to members of the EPA, and its accuracy is not in question. The fault lies in its inability to make any more than laborious sense to the general public to whom it was addressed.

3 Dr James Le Fanu, medical correspondent of the *Daily Telegraph*, reported (in 1995) a much more worrying case of the result of a cervical smear test sent to a patient in the following form: *The results of your test showed early cell changes (mild dyskaryosis suggesting CIN I) and wart virus changes.* The patient was advised to have a repeat test in six months, but no further explanation was offered. She turned to Dr Le Fanu, and he translated it for her as follows: *There are some funny-looking cells ('dyskaryosis') which may or may not indicate the very earliest signs of pre-*

cancerous change ('suggesting CIN I') which almost always returns to normal with no treatment. However, when associated with evidence of infection with the wart virus, it is slightly more likely to progress up through grades CIN II and III—at which point something may need to be done, hence the need for a further test in six months' time. Dr Le Fanu concluded that until those responsible for sending such reports to women include a translation of what they mean, 'tens of thousands of women every year . . . will continue to be unduly and unforgivably frightened'.

4 Other areas of information that are vulnerable to gobbledegook include law, social services, welfare, taxation, banking, local government, and technical subjects. In some domains, especially law, complex language arises from a need to achieve detailed precision and to avoid the ambiguity or uncertainty that can result from using everyday language. Efforts are being made to improve the clarity of public documentation, and have been furthered by the work of writers such as George Orwell, Sir Ernest Gowers (*The Complete Plain Words*, 1954 and later editions), and others, by writers of several manuals entitled *Plain English for Lawyers*, and by the work of the Plain English Society (see M. Cutts, *The Plain English Guide*, 1995).

5 See also JARGON, OFFICIALESE, PLAIN ENGLISH.

gold, golden. Of these adjectives, *gold* is used more often to denote something made of gold (*gold ring* | *gold watch*), whereas *golden* is used of colours and in abstract and figurative meanings referring to wealth generally

(*golden hair* | *golden retriever* | *golden goose* | *golden handshake*).

golliwog, meaning 'a black-faced brightly dressed soft doll with fuzzy hair' was first used as *Golliwogg*, the name of a doll character in books by the American writer B. Upton from 1895. It is now regarded as offensive, because of its stereotypical racial allusions.

good survives as an adverb only in non-standard AmE, e.g.: *I'm looking after the place good*—Maurice Gee, 1994. The use in *feel good* (which is current in BrE and AmE) is adjectival, not adverbial: *I didn't feel too good the next day*—S. Wall, 1991.

goodbye is spelt as one word and (as a noun) has the plural form *goodbyes*. The AmE variant *good-by* has the plural form *good-bys*.

good will, goodwill. *Good will* means 'the intention and hope that good will result' (and is hyphened in attributive position, i.e. before a noun as in *a good-will gesture*); *goodwill* is 'the established reputation of a business etc. as enhancing its value'.

gossip has inflections *gossiped*, *gossiping*; the adjective is *gossipy*.

got. The past and past participle of *get* is as productive of idiom as the verb as a whole. Some noteworthy uses are informal and verge on the non-standard:
  ▶**a** Use with *to*-infinitive, meaning 'to have an opportunity to': *This was considered a bonus for me, because I got to sit in the front*—F. Kidman, 1988 (New Zealand) | *We got to see exactly what happens to the green when we were taken out on the floor of MRQ*—New Yorker, 1989.

▶ **b** Elliptical for *have got* = possess: *What you got in that jar, Alvie?*—M. Eldridge, 1984 (Australia) | *I can't get my head around it, Sharon. Suddenly I got three fathers*—*Times*, 1987 | *Right now, we got nine cops in the Miami police department being tried for murder*—*The Face*, 1987 (US speaker).

▶ **c** *Got to*, elliptical for *have got to* = must: *We just got to live. Isn't that so?*—A. Fugard, 1980 (South Africa, black speaker) | *'We got to help these people,' he says, 'any way we can.'*—*Newsweek*, 1990.

▶ **d** Use of *got to be* to mean 'came round to being': *It got to be 11 p.m. We left the way we had come*—*New Yorker*, 1989.

gotten. 1 Few uses mark out the Americanness of a person more readily than their natural use of *got* and *gotten* as alternative past participles of *get*. (These uses are also spreading to Australia and New Zealand, as some of the examples given below will show.) *Gotten* is no longer used in Britain (except in *ill-gotten*), although it was once in regular use. In AmE, it is used only when the meaning is 'have (or has) obtained or acquired', i.e. when it denotes coming into possession; when the meaning is 'have (or has) in one's possession', i.e. when it denotes the fact of possession now, *got* is used. The difference can be seen by comparing the two sentences *We have gotten an apartment in Manhattan*, which means we have recently acquired it, and *We have got an apartment in Manhattan*, which means we have one available to us (as well as a house in Boston, for example). BrE uses *got* in both cases, with consequent ambiguity in some cases. Examples: *An army friend . . . had gotten us tickets for a Tchaikovsky*

extravaganza—Philip Roth, 1979 | *Have you gotten your paper the last couple of Sundays?*—*New Yorker*, 1986.

2 *Gotten* is also used when the meaning is 'have (or has) become, come, developed, etc.', i.e. when a notion of progression is involved: *Has my reputation in town gotten that bad?*—T. Winton, 1985 (Australia) | *Been sewn up for a long time and the locals have gotten used to the idea*—T. Winton, 1985 (Australia) | *'You have gotten close to the whirlpool,' Fleda said*—J. Urquhart, 1986 | *This last year and a half I've gotten to fill out a lot of forms*—John Updike, 1986 | *People in the USA have gotten much healthier in the past 30 years*—*USA Today*, 1988 | *It had gotten too quiet in the neighbourhood*—T. McGuane, 1989 | *They may have finally gotten rid of Sir Robert* [Muldoon] *from under their feet,* [etc.]—*NZ Herald*, 1991.

3 *Got*, not *gotten*, is used in the expression *have* (or *has*) *got to* = must; for example, if you say *I have gotten to leave this evening* you mean you have made arrangements to leave, not that you are obliged to leave.

gourmand, gourmet. The older of these two historically unrelated loanwords from French is *gourmand*, which came into English in the 15c, first as an adjective meaning 'greedy, fond of eating' and later as a noun denoting such a person, which remains its primary meaning. In the 18c it developed the meaning that *gourmet* (early 19c) was to have, i.e. 'a judge of good eating'. In current use, *gourmand* is confined to its original noun meaning and *gourmet* continues to be used in the one meaning it has always had. *Gourmet*, unlike *gourmand*, is also used attributively (before a

noun), as in *gourmet food* and
gourmet meal.

government. Note the *n* in the
middle of this word, which
should be pronounced as well as
written.

Governor-General. The recom-
mended plural form is *Governors-
General*, although *Governor-
Generals* is also found.

graceful, gracious. Both words
are derived from Latin *gratia*
meaning 'the quality of being
pleasing', but their meanings are
different. *Graceful* means 'having
or showing grace or elegance'
and is generally used of physical
appearance and movement (*a
graceful bow | graceful dances |
graceful lines*). *Gracious* means
'showing grace, kindly, courteous'
and refers to things that people
say and do rather than their
physical attributes (*a gracious re-
sponse | gracious acknowledgement*).
It also has the meaning 'characterized by elegance and wealth'
(*gracious wealth*). The adverb *graciously* occurs often in the meaning 'courteously, kindly': *'Oh, aye,
said Jock graciously, 'he's magic with
that mashie.'—Scotsman*, 1976.

gradable adjectives are adjectives that can vary in the intensity of their meaning, have
comparative and superlative
forms, and can be qualified by adverbs such as *very, too, fairly*, etc.
Greedy, large, patient, and *rich* are
all gradable, whereas *dead, female,
married*, and *rectangular* are non-
gradable or absolute adjectives.
See ADJECTIVE 4.

graduate *verb*. There is no problem with the ordinary intransitive meaning (without an object),
as in *He graduated from Yale in 1994*
and *She graduated last year*. The

newer AmE use with the name of
the university or college as kind
of adverbial with *from* omitted
(*He graduated Yale in 1994*, compare
He teaches school, in which *at* is
omitted) is more controversial,
and is not standard in BrE. Note
that in AmE *graduate* can refer to
completion of a high-school
course as well as of a university
degree.

graffiti is in the 1990s a plural
word requiring a plural construction, but its use is rapidly on the
move. Its singular is *graffito*,
which is hardly used. Before the
1960s *graffiti* was mainly used by
art historians and archaeologists
to refer to drawings or writing
scratched on the walls of ancient
buildings (notably at Pompeii).
Spray-can daubings since the
1960s have brought the word dramatically into general use, with
the result that *graffiti* is now
commonly used as a mass noun
like *confetti*: *That haunting graffiti in-
scribed on the approaches to Pad-
dington station—Times*, 1980 | *'I
don't need drugs,' the T-shirt graffiti
proclaims—Observer*, 1981. Some
writers on usage express a hope
for the resurgence of a singular
form *graffito*, but even this would
not cater for the mass use and
graffiti is likely to go the way of
confetti, spaghetti, not to mention
data and *media* and suchlike. For
now, however, *graffiti* should be
treated cautiously as the plural
noun it originally is.

grammar is the system by which
words are used together to form
meaningful utterances. It denotes
both the system as it is found to
exist in the use of a language
(also called *descriptive grammar*)
and the set of rules which form
the basis of the standard language, i.e. the variety of a lan-

grand compounds

Grand, which is derived via French from Latin *grandis* meaning 'full-grown', is used in combination with other words to form words denoting (1) rank (*grand duke*), (2) family relationships involving a gap of more than one generation (*grandmother*), and other items involving large size or status (*grand slam*). Most of these compounds are now spelt either as one word (especially the relationships) or as two, although some of the relationship terms are also written with a hyphen. The following table shows the principal items:

ranks	grandma	grand master (chess)
grand duchy	grandmother	Grand National
grand duchess	grand nephew	grand opera
grand duke	grand niece	grand piano
family relationships	grandpa	Grand Prix
grand aunt	grandparent	grand slam (sport, bridge)
grandchild	grandson	grandstand
grandad	grand uncle	grand total
granddaughter	*miscellaneous*	grand tour
grandfather	grand jury	grand unified theory (physics)

Terms denoting family relationships are spelt with a capital initial (e.g. *Grandma*) when used as a form of address in letters etc.

guage that is regarded as most socially acceptable at a given time (also called *prescriptive grammar*). See STANDARD ENGLISH.

grammatical agreement, concord see AGREEMENT.

grammatical gender see GENDER.

gram, gramme. The shorter form is now usual for the metric unit of mass. The abbreviation is *g* (without full point).

gramophone, a late-19c word formed by inversion of the older word *phonogram* (compare AmE *phonograph*), is now old-fashioned except with historical reference, having been replaced by *record-player* and largely superseded anyway by the development of the

CD player. In modern systems, the equipment for playing vinyl records is often called a *record deck* or simply a *deck*.

grand compounds.
See box above

granny, an affectionate name for *grandmother*, is spelt *-y*, not *-ie*, although the choice is more open in Scotland. It is spelt with a capital initial (*Granny*) when used as a form of address in letters etc. The plural form is *grannies*.

granted. 1 Like CONSIDERING and GIVEN, *granted* can be used as a preposition and (as *granted that*) conjunction that is grammatically free of the subject: *And, granted the initial assumptions . . . I think it stands the test*—A. White, 1965 | *Granted that Americans are* *not interested in Atlantic union, the emotional value to them of European union is enormous*—Listener, 1961. There is also an absolute use, which should only be used informally: *Granted, it was not hard to interest a security man, who apart from a regular soldier had the most boring job on earth*—Thomas Keneally, 1985 | *I somehow don't see life in an ordinary manner, not even this sere and monotonous existence in Africa; granted, it browns me off sometimes, but I do pretty well on the whole*—I. Young, 1990. See also PARTICIPLES 3, 4.

2 The common expression *take for granted* can be followed by a simple object or by a *that*-clause (often with a preceding *it*): *It was taken for granted that the astronauts would be brought down in the Bermuda 'recovery area' at 12.22 a.m.*—Listener, 1965 | *He took it all for granted, and would never have a clue just how blessed he was*—F. Cooper, 1991 | *Economists have taken it for granted that . . . creditors will in practice need to get most of the benefit from debt relief*—Economist, 1991 | *If she missed his letters for a few days, she would probably stop taking him for granted*—F. Pitt-Kethley, 1991.

gratis, meaning 'free of charge', is pronounced **grah**-tis or **gray**-tis in BrE and **grat**-is in AmE.

gratuity is a somewhat pretentious word for 'tip', and is usually found in printed form on restaurant menus and bills. It also refers (without the same pretension) to a bounty given in certain circumstances to servicemen and servicewomen when they are discharged.

gray is a common AmE variant of *grey*.

greasy is pronounced **gree**-si in its literal meaning 'smeared with grease' and **gree**-si or **gree**-zi when applied to an unctuous or smarmy person.

Great Britain see BRITAIN.

Grecian. The adjective *Grecian* has steadily retreated before the word *Greek*, and is now idiomatically restricted to describing architecture, facial outline (especially *Grecian nose*) and a soft low-cut slipper. It is no longer used at all as a noun. Otherwise *Greek* is the natural word (*Greek alphabet | Grecian language*). A third form, *Greekish*, was largely obsolete by the end of the 19c.

greenhouse effect. This important but often misunderstood term is defined by the *Concise Oxford Dictionary* (1995) as 'the trapping of the sun's warmth in the lower atmosphere caused by high levels of carbon dioxide and other gases more transparent to incoming solar radiation than to reflected infrared radiation.' See also *global warming*, under GLOBAL.

greenness, the quality of being green, is spelt with two *ns*.

grey is the dominant form in BrE, although *gray* is also used in AmE. In an unusually long note the *OED* (1901) recorded that 'an enquiry by Dr. Murray in Nov. 1893 elicited a large number of replies, from which it appeared that in Great Britain the form *grey* is the more frequent in use, notwithstanding the authority of Johnson and later English lexicographers who have all given the preference to *gray*'.

grid, griddle, gridiron. It would be natural to assume that *grid* was the original word, *griddle* ('a circular iron plate that is heated by a fire or by other means for baking, toasting, etc.') a diminutive of it, and *gridiron* ('a cooking utensil of metal bars for broiling or grilling') a compound form based on it. However, the *OED* shows that *griddle* and *gridiron* were the original terms (both 13c) and that *grid* is a recent (19c) back-formation from *gridiron*.

grievous, meaning 'severe, causing grief or suffering' (as in *grievous bodily harm*), is sometimes wrongly pronounced as if it were *grievious*, and even spelt this way.

griffin, griffon, gryphon. A *griffin* (also spelt many other ways, e.g. *griffon* and, e.g. by Lewis Carroll, *gryphon*) is 'a fabulous creature with an eagle's head and wings and a lion's body'. A *griffon* is (1) a small dog like a terrier, and (2) a large vulture. All three uses represent variants of the same word, which is derived from Greek *gryps* referring to the fabulous creature.

grill, grille. In BrE a *grill* is a device for cooking food, and the food itself. A *grille* is a metal grid protecting the radiator of a motor vehicle; this too is sometimes spelt *grill*.

grimace, meaning 'a distortion of the face' or 'to make a grimace', is most commonly stressed (especially when a verb) on the second syllable, as gri-**mays**. First-syllable stress, as **grim**-əs, is also used, especially in AmE.

grimy, meaning 'covered in grime, dirty', is spelt *grimy*, not *grimey*. The comparative and superlative forms are *grimier*, *grimiest*.

groin, groyne. The *groin* is the part of the body between the belly and thigh; a *groyne* (AmE *groin*) is a low wall or timber framework built out from a seashore to prevent beach erosion.

grotto has the plural form *grottoes*.

ground, grounds. Both the singular and the plural are used in the expressions *on the ground* (or *grounds*) *that*, and *grounds* is more common in the expression *grounds for* (complaint etc.): *Occupations that various insurance companies consider to be grounds for rejection of applications for auto insurance . . . included . . . paperhangers, . . . sports coaches and assistants, travelling salesmen, . . . and doctors* — New Yorker, 1975 | *The Post Office tried to register the name Viewdata for its product but this was refused on the ground that it was too all-embracing a title* — Guardian, 1979 | *Fundamentalist Jews are limbering up to oppose the plan on the grounds that it will depict scenes from the New Testament as well as the Old* — Daily Telegraph, 1985.

group names of animals (e.g. *a pride of lions*) see PROPER TERMS.

grovel, meaning 'to behave obsequiously', has inflected forms *grovelled*, *grovelling*, and in AmE also *groveled*, *groveling*.

groyne see GROIN.

gruelling, meaning 'extremely arduous or demanding', is spelt with two *l*s in BrE and also as *grueling* in AmE.

gryphon see GRIFFIN.

guano, meaning 'fertilizer made from bird dung', is pronounced **gwah**-noh, and has the plural form *guanos* (in the sense 'types of guano').

guarantee, guaranty. The two words have close meanings relating to the fulfilment of a legal obligation. *Guarantee* is used for the verb, and also for the noun when the obligation relates to the quality of a product or service, whereas *guaranty* is a noun only, is mostly restricted to legal and commercial contexts, and refers primarily to undertakings to pay a debt if the person or party primarily responsible defaults.

guarantor is a person, bank, etc., that gives a guarantee or guaranty.

guerrilla is the recommended spelling in English for the word meaning 'a member of an independent fighting force', not the common variant *guerilla*. It is pronounced gə-**ril**-ə, like *gorilla* (the animal).

guess. The informal use of *I guess* meaning 'I think it likely, I suppose' developed in America in the late 18c from the standard use of the phrase meaning 'it is my opinion or hypothesis (that)'. The Americanness of the informal use has been marked throughout the 19c and much of the 20c, and it still has the flavour of an Americanism, but it is now widespread throughout the English-speaking world: *No, I guess I don't look at him very much*—Gore Vidal, 1955 | *Martha. You remember them now? George. Yes, I guess so, Martha*—Edward Albee, 1962 | *I guess it takes a long time to grow up*—M. Sarton, 1978 | *I guess you're supposed to think to yourself that you're in a garden*—R. Ingalls, 1985. Use of *I guess* as a tag at the end of a statement is characteristic of AmE: *He would have been watching the returns in the Senate elections I guess*—A. Broinowski, 1973.

guest has developed a wide range of uses in which payment may or may not be involved (as it is with *paying guests* and *guest workers*). The development of attributive uses (before a noun) that go well beyond the core meaning of *guest* may be seen in *guest artist, guest beer, guest speaker, guest star, guest worker, guest writer,* and others.

guild see GILD.

guillemot, the name of a bird, is pronounced **gil**-i-mot.

gulf, bay. In their meanings to do with the sealine, *bay* is the ordinary word, whereas *gulf* is chiefly reserved as a name for a large or notable stretch of sea (as in *the Persian Gulf* which is also known as *the Gulf*) and implies a deeper recess and a narrower width of entrance.

gullible, meaning 'easily fooled or cheated', is spelt *-ible* not *-able*.

gunwale, meaning 'the upper edge of a ship's side', is pronounced **gun**-əl.

gusseted, meaning 'having gussets' (in meanings connected with clothing and architecture), is spelt with one *t*, not two.

guts, meaning 'courage or determination', is more forceful and less neutral than either of these words. It is now only slightly informal, although it is more so in idiomatic expressions such as *hate a person's guts* and *work one's guts out* (in which *guts* has a more literal meaning within a broader metaphor).

guttural is a non-technical term denoting a consonant produced in the throat or by the back of the tongue and the soft palate, for example k and hard g.

guy, in informal use, means 'a (primarily male) person' in BrE and (especially in the phrase *you guys*) 'a person (of either sex)' in AmE. In BrE it is fast replacing *chap*, which now sounds dated. This use with reference to people established itself in North America towards the end of the 19c and has made steady progress in Britain and other parts of the English-speaking world, especially Australia and New Zealand. Examples: *You guys all belong in the same ballpark*—Observer, 1970 | *I'm just as romantic as the next guy, and always was*—John Lennon, 1980 | *She was a regular guy, a good sport and a fine actress*—quoted in *American Speech*, 1983 | *I could see John by the bar talking to some guys*—New Yorker, 1989.

gybe *noun and verb*. This sailing term is spelt *gybe* in BrE and *jibe* in AmE. See also GIBE.

gymnasium. The preferred plural form is *gymnasiums*, although *gymnasia* is widely used. In Germany and Scandinavia the word (pronounced gim-**nah**-zi-əm) also means 'a school that prepares pupils for university entrance'.

gynaecology, meaning 'the physiological study of women', is pronounced with a hard initial g. The spelling is *-ae-* in BrE and *-e-* (*gynecology*) in AmE.

gypsy, gipsy. The term has both ethnic and general reference: either to a member of dark-skinned nomadic people of Hindu origin and associated with Egypt (hence the name) or a person who adopts the same mode of life. The recommended spelling is *gypsy* or (to emphasize ethnic status) *Gypsy*. The *OED* gave priority to *gipsy*, but this spelling is far less usual now.

Hh

h. 1 The sound of *h* (aitch) at the beginning words such as *have* and *house* and in the middle of words such as *ahead* and *behave* is known technically as a voiceless glottal fricative. In Britain, the presence or absence of this sound in speech is one of the key factors in the social evaluation of an individual's use of language or, as the *OED* expressed it, it 'has come to be regarded as a kind of shibboleth of social position'. Dropping initial *h*, in particular, is associated with the working-class and poorly educated speech of East London, so that there is no difference between the sounds of (for example) *hedge* and *edge*, *hill* and *ill*, and *high* and *eye*.

2 Dropping one's aitches may be a sign of uneducated speech, but standard speakers do not always notice that certain function words (e.g. *has, have, had*), pronouns, and possessives tend to lose their initial h sounds when these occur in unstressed positions in rapid speech, e.g. *She shoved him into her car*, in which *him* is articulated as *im* and *her* as *er*. Until the beginning of the 20c, words containing the letters *wh* (e.g. *what, whistle, nowhere*) were regularly pronounced with the h sound intact by most RP (received pronunciation) speakers in England as well as other parts of Britain and America. But the *Concise Oxford Dictionary* (1995) and most other dictionaries of current English give an unaspirated w sound in their phonetics for all this class of words, reflecting the fact that the aspiration of *wh* has largely disappeared from spoken standard English in England, so that there is no audible difference between the sounds of (for example) *whales* and *Wales*, *where* and *wear*, and *whit* and *wit*.

3 The use of *an* instead of *a* as the form of the indefinite article before words beginning with an unstressed but lightly aspirated *h* (e.g. *an habitual complaint | an historic occasion*) is in decline: see A, AN 2.

habitué, meaning 'a habitual visitor or resident', is now printed in roman type and pronounced in an anglicized manner as hə-**bit**-yoo-ay. The plural is *habitués*, pronounced hə-**bit**-yoo-ayz.

hackneyed, meaning 'made commonplace or trite by overuse', is spelt *-eyed*. For *hackneyed phrases*, see CLICHÉS.

had. 1 *HAD BETTER*. See BETTER 1.

2 *HAD HAVE*. This occurs with unreal (or unfulfilled) propositions in the past, constructed either with *if* (or an equivalent construction) as in the sentence *If I had have known, I would have said something* or with a verb expressing an unfulfilled intention, such as wish: *I wish you'd have kept quiet*. Though now associated with dialect and informal usage, the construction can be traced back in print to the 15c, e.g. *Had not he have be* [= been], *we shold never have retorned*—Malory, 1470–85. In a discussion of this issue in the journal *English Today* (1986), Professor Frank Palmer commented that 'there is a problem with past unreal, because it needs to mark past tense twice, once for time and once for unreality'. Another correspondent pointed out the type *had + a- + verb* as shown in the first part of a sentence in Galsworthy's *Strife* (1909): *If we'd a-known that before, we'd not a-started out with you so early*, which is distinct from the substitution of *of* for *have* in American regional use: *It was four o'clock in the morning ten, and if we'd of raised the blinds we'd of seen daylight.*—Scott Fitzgerald, 1925. The upshot is that constructions of this type, of which *had have* is the most common in BrE, should be avoided in more formal speech.

3 HAD RATHER. The type *I had rather* is as idiomatic as, though much less common than, *I would rather*, and in its contracted form *I'd rather* is indistinguishable. In historical terms it was formed on the analogy of the now archaic type *I had liefer* meaning 'I should hold it dearer': *I had rather err with Plato than be right with Horace*—Shelley, 1819 | *I had rather gaze on a new ice age than these familiar things*—Jeanette Winterson, 1985.

haemo-, hemo-. This combining form derived from Greek *haima* meaning 'blood' occurs in words such as (BrE) *haemoglobin, haemophilia, haemorrhage*, etc. In AmE they are written *hemo-*. Note the two *r*s in *haemorrhage*.

hair-brained is an erroneous variant (first recorded in 1581 and still found) of *hare-brained*, meaning 'rash, wild'.

hairdo, meaning 'the style or styling of a woman's hair', is informal only. The plural form is *hairdos*.

hale is the spelling in the expression *hale and hearty*. It comes from an Old English word *hāl* meaning (and related to) 'whole'.

half. 1 *Half* functions as a noun or pronoun (*the first half of the year* | *I've still got half*), an adjective (*a half share*) or predeterminer (i.e. placed before another determiner such as *the*, *half the audience*), and an adverb (*He'll come half way* | *I'm half inclined to agree*).

2 When *half* is followed by a singular noun (with or without *of* between), the verb is also singular, and when the noun is plural the verb is plural: *Half of the country is employed in agriculture* | *Half the people like the idea* | *Half that amount is enough.* Occasionally, by the principle of 'notional agreement', the type half (of) + collective noun can correctly be used with a plural noun: *Nearly half (of) the population lose at least half their teeth before they reach the age of 40.*

3 In some phrases concerned with quantities, measures of time, etc., the position of *half* is variable in the relation to the following *a* or *an*, e.g. *I'll have half a pint* (no hyphen) or *I'll have a half-pint* (with a hyphen). In most cases, however, the type *half a year, half a million dollars*, etc., is more usual. Repetition of the article, as in ⊠ *It took a half an hour*, is nonstandard.

hallo see HELLO.

Hallowe'en is spelt with an apostrophe and pronounced hal-oh-**een**.

halo has the plural form *haloes*.

handful has the plural form *handfuls*. See -FUL.

handicap as a verb has inflected forms *handicapped, handicapping*.

handkerchief. The recommended plural is *handkerchiefs*, not *handkerchieves*.

handsome is applied equally to men and women who are, as Dr Johnson put it, 'beautiful with dignity'. In current use there is a tendency to use the term of women only when they are middle-aged or elderly.

hanged, hung. In standard usage, the past tense and past participle of *hang* is *hanged* with reference to capital punishment and *hung* in other meanings. So curtains and pictures are *hung* but a convicted murderer is (or was) *hanged*. The distinction can be traced back ultimately to the existence of two separate words, one Old English and the other Old Norse. *Hung* is occasionally used in the meaning of *hanged*, especially in regional and dialect use.

hangar, hanger. A *hangar* is a large shed for housing aircraft; a *hanger* (in full *coat-hanger*) is a light frame with a hook for hanging clothes. Both are pronounced **hang**-ə, without the middle *g* sounded.

hanger-on, meaning 'an unwelcome follower or dependant', has the plural form *hangers-on.*

hara-kiri, meaning 'Japanese ritual suicide' is spelt with a hyphen.

harass. There are two pitfalls with this word meaning 'to trouble or annoy repeatedly' and its derivatives *harassing, harassment*, etc. One is the spelling, with only one *r* (unlike *embarrass*); the other is the pronunciation, which should be **ha**-rəs with the stress on the first syllable, although hə-**ras** with second-syllable stress is spreading rapidly from AmE to BrE and will probably prevail in the end.

harbour is spelt *-our* in BrE and *harbor* in AmE.

hard. 1 HARD AND HARDLY. The normal adverb from *hard* is *hard*, as in *They are working hard* and *Don't hit it so hard*. *Hardly* has a special use, meaning 'scarcely' (as in *We hardly know them*) and 'only with difficulty' (as in *She could hardly speak*).

  2 HARDLY . . . WHEN . . . AND HARDLY . . . THAN . . . The standard construction is *hardly . . . when . . .* : *Hardly had the two children been freed when they* [sc. a rescue team] *were on the spot, having covered the ground in a snow-tractor—Country Life*, 1971. The construction with *than*, though increasingly common and perhaps suggested by the analogy of *no sooner . . . than . . .* , is nonstandard: ⊠ *Hardly had the chalky jet stream dissipated above the horizon than it was time for another jetaway get-away to points west—American Square Dance*, 1991.

  3 CAN'T HARDLY. Since *hardly* already has a negative or restricting force, use of another negative (as in *I can't hardly believe it*) is incorrect: ⊠ *Mom just loaded us with fried chicken and I can't hardly walk—New Yorker*, 1988 | ⊠ *No, Swedon can't write anything. He can't hardly write his own pawn-tickets—Penelope Fitzgerald*, 1990.

hard words.
See box opposite

hare-brained, meaning 'rash, wild', is spelt *hare-*, not *hair-*.

harem, an Arabic word denoting the women living separately in a Muslim household, is spelt this

hard words

is a semi-technical term for what it immediately suggests, long and difficult words that are often derived from Latinate rather than English sources, such as *rebarbative* (= repellent) and *nugatory* (= futile, trifling). The first English dictionaries devoted much space to hard words, explaining words of foreign origin in terms of native English words. The following list is drawn from Robert Cawdrey's *Table Alphabeticall* of 1604:

agnition	acknowledgement	Latin *gnoscere* 'to know'
carminate	to card wool	Latin *carmen* 'a card for wool'
combure	to burn up	Latin *comburere* 'to burn up, consume'
deambulation	a walking abroad	Latin *ambulare* 'to walk'
enarration	exposition or commentary	Latin *narrare* 'to relate'

All these words are now obsolete. The following, from the *New Shorter Oxford English Dictionary* (1993), are still in use:

claustration	enclosure, confinement	Latin *claustrum* 'enclosed space'
coriaceous	like leather	Latin *corium* 'leather'
edulcorate	purify	Latin *dulcis* 'sweet'
evasible	able to be evaded	French (as *table*)
idoneous	apt, suitable	Latin *idoneus* 'apt'
infraction	act of breaking an agreement	Latin *frangere* 'to break'
straticulate	arranged in thin layers	Latin *stratum* 'laid down'
tergiversation	equivocation, betrayal	Latin *tergum* 'back' and *vertere* 'to turn'
velleity	a mere wish	Latin *velle* 'to wish'

way in English. It is usually pronounced **hah**-reem, although pronunciation with the second-syllable stress is also heard. In AmE the stress is on the first syllable, which is pronounced either as in *hair* or as in *hat*.

have. 1 For the type ⊠ *No state has ʌ or can adopt such measures*, see ELLIPSIS 3.

2 In a sentence of the type *Some Labour MPs would have preferred to have wound up the Session before rising*, the present infinitive is preferable, i.e. *Some Labour MPs would have preferred to wind up the Session before rising*, although the perfect infinitive is sometimes found when the past nature of the unperformed action is being emphasized. Examples: *Fish, who had decent feelings, would have preferred to be pawed in privacy*—J. I. M. Stewart, 1975 | *I would have preferred to have seen an accompanying annotated sketch so that the plant zonations could be easily recognised*—Birds, 1981.

3 *HAVE TO* AND *HAVE GOT TO*. In the meaning 'must', *have to* normally denotes habitual or continuing necessity (*I have to wear contact lenses*) whereas *have got to* denotes immediate or temporary necessity (*I've got to catch a train in half an hour*). In the past tense, *had to* is much more usual than *had got to*: *In addition to his normal day's work in the library, he had to care for a complete invalid, shop on the way home, . . . and then translate demanding tomes until one or two o'clock in the morning*—D. Murphy, 1979 | *He knew . . . that in order not to lose control irretrievably of his life he had to hold on to his job*—William Boyd, 1981. The only available perfect and pluperfect forms are *have had to* and *had had to*: *They like the feeling that they have had to fight other men for possession. That is what it is all about, really*—Anita Brookner, 1984 | *Turning the other cheek was for girls who hadn't had to give blow jobs to tramps in exchange for a few pieces of candy*—P. Booth, 1986.

4 For *don't have* = *haven't got* and *do you have* = *have you got*, see DO 4.

5 For *had have*, see HAD 2.

haver, meaning 'to hesitate', is originally Scottish. This meaning spread south of the border in the 20c, but in its other meanings 'to talk foolishly' and (as a plural noun *havers*) 'nonsense' it is still anchored in the north.

he. 1 For *he* or *him* after the verb *be*, see CASES 2A.

2 For the expression *he or she*, see GENDER-NEUTRALITY.

heading, headed. In BrE the expression meaning 'to be going in a particular direction' is *to be heading for* (in physical and figurative contexts, e.g. *heading for trouble*). In AmE *to be headed for* is also common and this form is beginning to appear in BrE and other varieties of English: *You're bloody cheerful . . . for a bloke that's*

headed for a number one reaming [= reprimand] *from the CO*—J. Charlton, 1976 | *They were headed for the perilous North Channel . . . if they survived the wolfpacks*—D. Grant, 1980 | *Deng Xiaoping barreled on down the capitalist road last week—but he might be headed for a collision*—*Bulletin* (Sydney), 1984 | *They were all headed for Ralph's house*—*New Yorker*, 1991.

headline language see JOURNALESE.

headquarters can legitimately be used either as a singular (*a large headquarters in Paris*) or as a plural (*The firm's headquarters are in Paris*). The singular more often denotes the physical premises and the plural the institution in its broader sense.

head up. This phrasal verb has passed rapidly from AmE to British use, and means 'to take charge of (an enterprise or group of people)'. There is not a great deal of difference in meaning between *head up* and the simple verb *head*, except that *head up* has stronger implications of *taking* charge as distinct from *being* in charge.

heaps. *There was heaps of time*— Mary Wesley, 1983 represents the normal colloquial idiom when the word following *heaps of* is a singular or mass noun (and the same is true of *loads of*, *lots of*, *masses of*, and similar expressions). But when the following noun is plural the verb should be plural too: *'Heaps of people do say it* [sc. 'bloody']. *Even on television.' 'But not on schools programmes.'*— C. Storr, 1971. Note that *heaps* is plural in all cases when it is being used literally rather than idiomatically: *Great heaps of* *cumulo-nimbus cloud were boiling up*—Dick Francis, 1970.

heave. The past tense and past participle is *heaved* in its ordinary meanings 'to lift, haul, throw, etc.' and 'to utter (a sigh)', and *hove* (1) when the meaning is 'come into view' (*She hove around the Minister's flank with the effect of an apparition*—Thomas Keneally, 1980), and (2) in nautical usage (*The hip hove to | The anchor was hove up*).

hectic. 1 The meaning that is now the dominant one, 'busy and confused', is fairly recent (early 20c) and has developed in the same way as the figurative meaning of *feverish*. *Hectic* was originally an adjective or noun referring to the kind of fever that accompanied consumption (*For like the hectic in my blood he rages*—Shakespeare, *Hamlet* IV.iii.80); its physical use declined with the decline in occurrence of the disease itself, but fevers are still with us. An early figurative use occurs in Kipling: *Didn't I say we never met in pup-pup-puris naturalibus, if I may so put it, without a remarkably hectic day ahead of us?*—*Traffics & Discoveries*, 1904. Modern examples follow (note that *hectic* often comes before a period of time): *At times, though, in these hectic weeks of organization, . . . it seemed we should never make our deadline for packing all our gear ready to go to India*—Chris Bonington, 1971 | *It might be that you are having a hectic day at work and you feel that things are getting to you, or you might be stuck in a traffic jam with your pulse racing*—S. Spindler, 1991 | *After the hectic activity of summer, I look forward to doing more relaxed boating and fishing trips in early autumn*—B. Tulloch, 1991.

2 The adverb from *hectic* is *hectically*: *Hectically she scrabbled for something constructive to say*—R. Ash, 1993. Note also that *hectic* is still occasionally used in its medical sense: *The hectic face on the thin neck rose too sharply out of the collar of a silk blouse*—Anita Brookner, 1990.

hegemony, meaning 'political leadership of a group of states', is pronounced hi-**jem**-ə-ni or hi-**gem**-ə-ni, with the g either hard or soft and with the stress on the second syllable.

hegira, the term denoting Muhammad's departure from Mecca in AD 622 and used for dates in the Muslim era, is pronounced **hej**-i-rə in BrE and in AmE more commonly hə-**jiy**-rə. The spelling *hejira* is occasionally found.

he, him see CASES 2A.

heifer, meaning 'a cow that has not born a calf', is spelt this way.

heinous, meaning 'extremely wicked', is pronounced **hee**-nəs.

heir. An *heir apparent* is an heir whose claim cannot be set aside by the birth of another heir. An *heir presumptive* is an heir whose claim may be set aside if another heir with a stronger claim is born. *Heir apparent* is often used now of a person regarded as likely to succeed to the position held by the head of a political party, business organization, etc.

helix, pronounced **hee**-liks and meaning 'a spiral or coiled curve', has the plural form *helices*, pronounced **hel**-i-seez, or occasionally *helixes*.

Hellene, Hellenic are the noun and adjective respectively referring to the people and culture of

Greece, ancient and modern. They are normally used in the context of the history, literature, and archaeology of Greek lands. *Hellene* is pronounced **hel**-een and *Hellenic* is pronounced he-**len**-ik or he-**lee**-nik.

hello, hallo, hullo. There is a bewildering array of spellings and stress patterns with this greeting word; or they would be bewildering if anyone ever worried about them. In speech, the stress alters instinctively, and to list the variations would be as pointless as counting the hairs of one's head. The spelling preferred is *hello*; *hallo* is more common in BrE than in AmE; and *hullo* is now the least usual, despite being the first recorded (in 1864). The noun has the plural form *hellos* (etc.); and the verb (meaning 'to say *hello*') has inflected forms *helloes, helloed, helloing.*

helmeted, meaning 'wearing a helmet', is spelt *-eted.*

help *verb. Help* is one of the oldest words in English, going back to the time of King Alfred (9c). It has two principal meanings in current English: 'to assist' (*Can I help you?*) and 'to prevent' (*I can't help it*). The connection between these two apparently unrelated sets of meanings lies in the use of *help* in the context of dealing with disease and misfortune, in which the interrelated notions of providing help and of preventing suffering are more clearly perceptible. (For a fuller account, see the *OED* entry, one of the most interesting and complex in the language.) There are three issues to explore with help, the first two connected with the 'assist' meaning and the third with the 'prevent' meaning:

1 *CANNOT HELP BUT.* This use is illustrated by the example *She could not help but notice that all the passengers on the bus were pensioners*—S. Mackay, 1984. The construction used here is common, and is a fusion of two other typical constructions: *She could not but notice . . .* and *She could not help noticing . . . .* It is preferable to use either of these constructions in more formal contexts, although the fused construction is common informally and is likely to become more so.

2 *MORE THAN* [OR *AS LITTLE* ETC. *AS*] *I CAN HELP.* This idiom is illustrated by the examples *Don't sneeze more than you can help* and *Sneeze as little as you can help.* Fowler, in an uncharacteristically weak and rambling article (1926), found this construction indefensible and corrected the examples to *Don't sneeze more than you must* and *Sneeze as little as you can.* These emendations are unexceptionable in themselves, but correcting idiom on the grounds of logic is a futile exercise.

3 *HELP* + *TO*-INFINITIVE. The construction *help someone to do something* (as in *He helped me to dig out my driveway*) has been shortened since the time of Shakespeare to *help someone do something* (*He helped me dig out my driveway*). Shakespeare used both constructions, omitting *to* when *help* is itself preceded by *to*: *The day will come that thou shalt wish for me To help thee curse this poisonous bunch-backed toad*—Richard III I.iii.247. The reluctance to repeat *to* accounts for some but not all of the following modern examples, which are taken from several varieties of English: (*to* omitted) *The purpose is as much to help the actors discover their roles as to work out cinematically-effective*

moves—*Daily Telegraph*, 1970 | *Our
every deed must help make us
acceptable*—*Times*, 1986 | *I had
helped her carry it to her bedroom*—
Garrison Keillor, 1986 (US) | *One of
my housemates . . . offered to help
me move in*—*New Yorker*, 1986 |
*Mandy helped him choose something
for Claire*—C. K. Stead, 1986 (New
Zealand) | *When he is done he in-
structs Ria to help him pull the wire
tight*—S. Johnson, 1990 (Australia) |
(*to* included) *It may help us to con-
ceive of our predicament if we imagine . . .* [etc.]—*Dædalus*, 1986 (US)
| *The levees were helping to aggra-
vate the problem they were meant to
solve*—*New Yorker*, 1987 | (*to* re-
peated) *An interpersonal relationship
in which one person (the counselor)
attempts to help another (the coun-
selee) to understand and cope with
problems*—*Encyclopedia of Psych-
ology*, 1972 (US) | *If a male employee
asks for time off to stay at home with
his sick wife to help to look after her
and the kids, the affiliative manager
agrees*—*Harvard Business Review*,
1976 | *She allowed Pearl to help her
to stack up her hair*—Iris Murdoch,
1983. There does not seem to be
any distinction in preferences between AmE and BrE or the other
major varieties of English.

hence. For the use of *from hence*,
see FROM WHENCE, FROM HENCE.

hendiadys, pronounced hen-**diy**-
ə-dis, is derived from a Greek
phrase meaning 'one by means of
two'. It is a figure of speech in
which a single complex idea is
expressed by two words connected by a conjunction (usually
and), for example *nice and easy,
good and ready.*

he or she see GENDER-
NEUTRALITY.

her should not be used as the
subject of a clause in standard

English, although the use is
found in some regional and dialect usage: ⊠ *Her and Kitty didn't
have much to do with each other
anymore*—N. Virtue, 1990.

here. The type *this here friend of
mine* and *these here bicycles* is confined to uneducated speech, but
here placed after the noun is
standard: *your friend here* | *these bi-
cycles here.*

here is, here are. The normal
agreement rules apply in most
cases, i.e. *Here is* [or *Here's*] *my
ticket* and *Here are my tickets*. However, in spontaneous discourse a
sentence such as *Here's some
flowers for you* is idiomatic and acceptable.

hereby, herewith. These two
formal words are the strongest
survivors of a group of words
that also includes *herein, hereof,
hereto, heretofore,* and *hereunder,*
and even they are restricted to
the contexts of legal and business
correspondence or to humorous
imitations of them: *I hereby prom-
ise never to smoke again* | *Herewith I
enclose a cheque to cover my sub-
scription*. The other words are
mainly confined to legal language
and are rapidly being forced out
in the interests of PLAIN ENGLISH.

hero has the plural form *heroes*.

heroin, heroine. Both words are
pronounced the same way, **her**-
oh-in. The first is the drug and
the second is the principal
woman in a novel, play, etc. Despite their closeness of form and
pronunciation, they manage to
stay out of each other's way.

hers. This possessive pronoun, as
used in *The blame is not mine but
hers*, is written without an apostrophe. *Hers* is wrongly used in

the following example and should be replaced by *her*: ⊠ *Hers and my children got together for a party*. (The error is obvious if the sentence is simplified by the removal of *and my*.)

herself, himself, itself. These pronouns have two primary roles, (1) as reflexives (*He was talking about himself | Mary was looking at herself in the mirror | He made himself a cup of coffee*), and (2) as emphatic words in apposition to a noun or pronoun (*The supervisor herself called | The lock itself is still working*). *Himself* is still used as a gender-neutral pronoun despite the weakening of this role with the simple pronoun *he*, probably because the alternatives available for *he* are more complex when applied to *himself*: *None of us was willing to commit himself to a clear-cut opinion*—R. Linder, 1955 | *In this way the casual viewer . . . is liable to come away with the impression that here is an anti-Semite attempting to denazify himself*—*Daily Telegraph*, 1970 | *This problem faced by the teacher who sees himself as deliverer of prepacked information is admirably expressed by Caldwell Cook*—H. Pluckrose, 1987 | *The investigator himself may not know whether these effects have occurred*—A. Ashworth, 1992.

hesitance, hesitancy, hesitation. All three words are first recorded in English in the early 17c, and the story since then has been one of advancement for *hesitation* and of sharp retreat for the other two, especially for *hesitance* although this occurs occasionally. There is a residual distinction between *hesitancy* and *hesitation*; the first denotes a tendency, whereas the second denotes a fact or action (and occurs in the plural): (hesitancy, hesitance) *He under-*

stood the hesitancy of many landlords to rent to male rather than female students—*Daily Colonist* (Victoria, B.C.), 1973 | *An examination of the client's hesitance, however, indicates that he is not at all sure about the terminology and that he may simply be echoing the wording of the charge*—J. Citron, 1989 | *He was reluctant to begin and his hesitancy made her look questioningly at him*—T. Hayden, 1991 | (hesitation) *He had driven the Deputy Director . . . half mad with his hesitation, his recycled arguments for accepting and not accepting*—D. Bloodworth, 1978 | *Women have trouble communicating in a 'male' language and the result is hesitations, false starts, and so on*—D. Cameron, 1992. *Hesitation* but not *hesitancy* is used in the idiomatic phrases *not have a moment's hesitation* and *without hesitation*: *When Granpa asked me what I wanted for my fifteenth birthday I replied without a moment's hesitation, 'My own barrow.'*—Jeffrey Archer, 1991 | *When in 1974 I was flattered by an invitation to make a T V appearance as the Dimbleby lecturer, I accepted without hesitation*—A. Goodman, 1993.

hew, a literary word meaning 'to chop or cut', has a past form *hewed* and past participles *hewn* or *hewed*.

hiccup has inflected forms *hiccuped*, *hiccuping*. The spelling *hiccough*, formed by false association with *cough*, has nothing to recommend it.

hierarchic, hierarchical. *Hierarchical* is more common, but the choice of form seems to depend on the rhythm of the sentence rather than on any other factor.

high, highly. *High* is used as an adverb to mean 'far up, aloft' and in figurative uses in which allusion to physical height is the metaphor: *Most surfaces were piled high with magazines | The junior executive is aiming high | Feelings were running high*. Highly is used to mean (1) 'very, extremely' before adjectives and participial adjectives (*It was highly amusing | a new wave of highly talented intellectuals*), and (2) as an intensifier with verbs such as *praise, speak, think*, etc. when denoting favourable opinion (*She spoke highly of her tutor | I think quite highly of the latest efforts*). Note also the phrase *high and low*, as in *He searched high and low for the lost ring*.

hike, meaning 'an increase (in prices, wages, etc.)' is fairly recent (first recorded in 1931) and has spread rapidly from AmE, especially to the informal language of British journalism: *The oil industry is still accommodating itself to its new size following the 1979 price hike*—D. Hedley, 1986 | *An announcement by Argentina's President Carlos Menem rescinding a planned threefold hike in the duties on paper imported for book production was greeted with delight by hundreds of publishers* —Bookseller, 1993 | *Football fans hit by big ticket price hike*—headline in *Independent*, 1998.

him should not be used as the subject of a clause in standard English, although the use is found in some regional and dialect usage: ⊠ *Him and Carol lived too high, kept buying stuff they couldn't nohow afford*—Truman Capote, 1965.

him or her see GENDER-NEUTRALITY.

himself see HERSELF.

hindsight. At first used to mean 'the backsight of a rifle', since the later part of the 19c it has

been used in an abstract sense 'wisdom or knowledge after the event', especially in the phrase *in* (or *with*) *hindsight*: *With hindsight, it was probably the best thing that could have happened to him, otherwise he would no doubt have ended up as a Bomber Pilot*—J. Beech, 1989 | *In hindsight, if I had been aware of the exact nature of the Foreign Legion, . . . I would have been much more hesitant about joining*—C. Jennings, 1990.

hinge. The present participle is better spelt *hingeing* to clarify the sound of the soft g.

hippo, hippopotamus. The respective plural forms are *hippos* and *hippopotamuses*.

his. For *his or her* see GENDER-NEUTRALITY. For the use of *his* to refer back to *one*, see ONE.

hisself is non-standard for *himself*, and arises from the tendency to regard *self* as a noun and to place possessive pronouns and adjectives in front of it (e.g. *his very self*).

historic, historical. Both words are used to mean 'of or concerning history, belonging to the past rather than the present', but *historical* is the more objective word denoting something that happened in the past, whereas *historic* describes not simply what belongs to the past but what has an important role in the past, i.e. it means 'famous or important with regard to history'. A *historical* treaty is one that took place (as opposed to one that is fictitious); a *historic* treaty is one that is of great importance in history (as opposed to one that is insignificant). *Historic* is often used with reference to buildings and monuments: *The president of the*

Historic Houses Association . . . plays down too much euphoria over the Chancellor's proposed substitution of inheritance tax for capital transfer tax—Daily Telegraph, 1986 | *After visiting the Hayward Gallery I spent a half-hour just gazing along the river line, the historic buildings sharp in the clear, cold, sunny air*—D. M. Thomas, 1990. When the meanings are confused, it is usually *historic* that is used when *historical* would be more appropriate: *Extinct volcanoes are those that have not erupted in historic time, whereas active volcanoes have been seen to erupt*—M. A. Summerfield, 1991 | *It may involve the use of relevant historic documents*—R. Brooks, 1993.

historic present is a term used of narrative that is put in the present tense for dramatic effect, although it is describing events in the past. For example: *She had no notion of how welcome she would be. But Raymond* **opens** *the door before she can touch the bell, and he* **hugs** *her around the shoulders and* **kisses** *her twice*—A. Munro, 1989.

hither, meaning 'to or toward this place', is an ancient word that existed in Old English. In current English it is restricted, except for formal or archaic uses, to a number of fixed phrases: *hither and thither* or *hither and yon* (= in various directions), and *come-hither*, used adjectivally to mean 'enticing, flirtatious', as in *a come-hither look*.

HIV. Since the abbreviation stands for 'human immunodeficiency *virus*', the word *virus* is strictly redundant in the phrase *HIV virus*, although this is now established usage.

hoard, horde. A *hoard* is a large stock or store of money or accumulated objects (in archaeology,

for example); a *horde* is a large collection of people or animals, and is used in the singular or plural, often disparagingly: *A horde of football fans attempt to lure into their bedrooms a pair of tarts by arrangement with the pimpish day porter*—Daily Telegraph, 1976 | *By shooting a gun numerous times and flashing a sun-gun, we persuaded hordes of bats to fly round the cave*—Listener, 1976.

hoe *verb* has inflected forms *hoes, hoed, hoeing.*

hoi polloi. The normal construction is *the hoi polloi*, meaning 'the masses, the common people'. The fact that *hoi* in the original Greek expression (literally 'the many') already means 'the' is therefore ignored; objection to this now seems pedantic, is countered by the weight of usage (Dryden, Byron, and others, not to mention W. S. Gilbert), and itself ignores the need for naturalness in English, since omission of *the* would usually be awkward. Examples: (with *the*) *Nothing like a yacht to ensure your privacy and not having to mix with the hoi polloi*—Jeffrey Archer, 1991 | *As trains and coaches and carriage excursions organised by Thomas Cook were deemed to be for the hoi polloi, the party had decided to take their own carriages*—A. Myers, 1991 | (without *the*) *Seat-holders were let in through side doors while hoi polloi had to come in through the front in the hope of getting what they could*—J. Munson, 1991.

hoist, meaning 'to raise or haul up', has past and past participle forms *hoisted*. Historically *hoist* is a participial form of an earlier verb *hoise* (with the same meaning), and it survives in this form in the expression *hoist with one's*

own petard, meaning literally
'blown up by one's own bomb'
and hence 'adversely affected by
one's own bad schemes for
others'.

holey, meaning 'full of holes', is
spelt *-ey* to distinguish it in writing and print from the adjective
holy meaning 'sacred'.

Holland see NETHERLANDS.

home. 1 As an adverb, *home* has
many idiomatic uses as in *come
home* and *go home, see someone
home, drive a nail* (or *point*) *home*,
etc. When the meaning is 'in his
or her home' the British preference is to use *at home* (*He stayed at
home* | *Is Jane at home?*) whereas
AmE prefers *home* by itself (*He
stayed home* | *Is Jane home?*).

2 As a noun, *home* means 'the
place where one lives', and when
referring to the building is distinguished from *house* in designating
residential function as well as
physical existence: *The well secured
home probably includes an entry-
phone, grilles, . . . and an alarm—
Financial Times*, 1982. It is usual to
say *in the privacy of one's own home*
rather than *one's own house*, and
estate agents tend to prefer *home*
as having a more personal sound.
In AmE, *home* is used much more
freely where in BrE *house* would
be used: *In Beverly Hills and Bel Air,
we saw the homes (never called
houses) of Jane Withers, Greer Gar-
son, and Barbra Streisand—Guardian*,
1973.

3 As a verb, used chiefly of
pigeons and in the phrasal verb
home in on, home has inflections
homed, homing.

homely. The connotations of
this word as applied to a person
(usually a woman) are favourable
in BrE, in which it means 'simple, unpretentious' and disparaging in AmE, in which it means
'unattractive, dowdy'.

homo-, homoeo-. These two
prefixes are derived from the
Greek words *homos* meaning
'same' and *homoios* meaning 'of
the same kind', and this difference in meaning is reflected in
the English words formed on
them, e.g. *homosexuality* denotes
sexual attraction towards the
same sex and *homoeopathy* denotes
treatment of disease by using
small doses of drugs that have
the *same kind* of effect as the disease itself. Words in *homo-* are
pronounced either hom- or hohm-,
whereas words in *homoeo-* are
more usually pronounced hom-.
In AmE, *homeo-* is the more usual
spelling.

homogeneity, meaning 'being
of the same kind', is better pronounced -ji-**nee**-i-ti than -ji-**nay**-i-ti,
i.e. with the stressed syllable having the sound of *bee*, not *bay*.

**homogeneous, homoge-
nous.** *Homogeneous* is pronounced
with the stress on the third syllable and means 'of the same
kind': *The most common way of
grouping was to sort the children by
ability . . . and to make the groups as
homogeneous as possible*—R. Alexander, 1992. The word *homogenous*
(stressed on the second syllable)
was formerly used in biology to
mean 'having a common descent', but has been largely superseded by *homogenetic*, so as to
become a loose cannon colliding
frequently with *homogeneous*:
⊠ *The community was not homogenous, but made up of a multitude of
different groups with different attitudes and beliefs—Guardian*, 1989.
Homogeneous is still the correct

word to use. The adjective *homogenized*, denoting milk that has been treated so that the cream does not separate, is related in form but not in meaning.

homograph, homonym, homophone. *Homonym* is a generic term for a word having the same spelling or sound as another word but a different meaning. Homonyms are either *homographs*, words written the same way (e.g. *bat* denoting either an implement or an animal and *entrance* meaning either 'a way into a place' or 'to beguile') or *homophones*, words pronounced the same way but (usually) not spelt the same way (e.g. *pair* and *pear*, *hoard* and *horde*, *right* and *write*).

homosexual, pronounced either hom- or hohm-, is still the term used in more formal contexts, although *gay* is become more widely used and is often heard (for example) in news broadcasts.

Hon. is an abbreviation of (1) *honourable*, especially in parliamentary contexts (*The Hon. Member for Lincoln*) and as a courtesy title given to sons and daughters of members of the nobility and to civic dignitaries such as the Lord Mayor of London (the correct form is with the first name in full, e.g. *The Hon. James Brown*), and (2) *honorary*, as in *The Hon. Secretary*. For full details see *Debrett's Correct Form* or other manuals dealing with forms of address.

honeyed is recommended in preference to *honied*.

honorarium, meaning a voluntary payment made for professional services instead of a formal fee, is pronounced with the third syllable as in *air*. The plural form

is *honorariums* (preferably) or *honoraria*.

honour, honourable are spelt -*our* in BrE and *honor, honorable* in AmE.

hoof has a plural from *hooves* (more usual) or *hoofs*.

hope. Apart from the expression *to live in hopes*, the use of the plural noun in phrases such as *to be in hopes, in the hopes that*, etc., is more characteristic of AmE than of BrE: *He never said a kind word to them, and they worked like dogs in hopes of hearing one*—Garrison Keillor, 1989. The normal BrE equivalent is *in the hope of* (or *in the hope that*): *Clerks double-book their barristers in the hope that one of the cases will be settled before getting to court*—*Economist*, 1983.

hopefully. 1 This (now controversial) adverb has been used since the 17c as a straightforward adverb of manner: *As lovers do, as lovers will, they travelled hopefully to Paris*—Maurice Gee, 1985 | *Out on the corridor, Nurse Bodkin was hovering hopefully near a suspended piece of mistletoe*—E. McGrath, 1990. According to the evidence of the *OED*, the controversial use of *hopefully* as a sentence adverb sprang up, after an isolated use in 1932, in the 1960s, first in AmE and almost immediately in BrE: *We asked her when she expected to move into her new apartment, and she answered, 'Hopefully on Tuesday.'*—*New Yorker*, 1965 | *The cost of developing a new 'Dash 50' series of engines, that hopefully will power Lockheed's 'extended range' jet, is put at around £75 million*—*Daily Telegraph*, 1970 | *I want a bigger range to choose from and hopefully this role will help me*—S. Stone, 1989.

2 Like *thankfully*, *hopefully* stands apart from the routine sentence adverbs *clearly, frankly, happily, luckily, normally, sadly, unfortunately*, etc., because the rationale of its formation differs and it cannot be resolved grammatically into a phrase such as *in a hopeful way* or *to a hopeful extent*. The argument based on ambiguity, however, is less compelling; sentences of the type *They are working hopefully towards a solution of the problem* will normally be clear enough either from intonation (in speech) or from context. For more on this issue in its context, see SENTENCE ADVERBS.

3 The recommendation must be to use these meanings of *hopefully* and *thankfully* with caution; they are here to stay but strong rearguard actions continue to be fought over them. And *hopefully*, in particular, can sound irritating.

horde see HOARD.

horrid. *Horrid* may be seen as the least emphatic in a series of adjectives meaning 'disagreeable' which proceed with increasing severity to *horrible* and *horrifying*. *Horrendous* and *horrific*, once stronger still than any of these, have lost much of their power through overuse in popular fiction, film, and broadcasting. In older literature, references to *horrid spears, mountain peaks, thickets*, etc., reflect a now obsolete meaning 'bristling, shaggy, rough'.

hospitable should be pronounced with the stress on the first syllable, although second-syllable stress is common.

hospitalize, meaning 'to send or admit (a patient) to hospital', first recorded in 1901, is regarded with some suspicion in BrE, but is standard in AmE.

host *verb*. This is first recorded in the 15c, and is not a modern verbalization of the noun. For this reason, objection to the use of *host* meaning 'to act as host or compère of (a television show)' is somewhat misconceived, although it is often prudent to use readily available alternatives such as *present, introduce*, or *compère*.

house see HOME.

how come? This colloquial American phrase, meaning 'how is it (or did it happen) that?', was first noted in the mid-19c, and still has strong North American associations, although no one in Britain would fail to understand it: '*How come you're still thin?*' *she asked with amusement*—A. Munro, 1989.

however. **1** When *ever* is being used as an intensive after the interrogative adverb *how*, as in *How ever did you do it?*, the two words should always be written separately.

2 *However*, in the meaning 'nevertheless', has many possible positions in a clause. If it is put at the beginning, it should be followed by a comma: *I should be angry if the situation were not so farcical. However, I had a certain delight in some of the talk*—William Golding, 1980. This use should be distinguished from *however* used at the beginning of a sentence as an ordinary adverb meaning 'no matter how', which is not followed by a comma: *However confident he may be that he has outgeneralled a woman, a man likes to have reassurance on the point from a knowledgeable third party*—P. G. Wodehouse, 1973. In mid-sentence, *however* is preceded and followed by commas. The choice of position depends on the word being emphasized, which is normally the one that comes immediately before *however*: *Parry, however, had had an alibi which Mr Wilkes is confident that he has broken*—Daily Telegraph, 1984 | *Even with the stimulatory measures, however, the deficit does not seem likely to be excessive in the years to come*—Times, 1981. It is preceded by a comma when it occurs at the end of a sentence: *The presence of a girl in a group of tipsy young men keeps them in check, however*—Lancashire Life, 1978.

3 There are two erroneous uses to guard against: (1) *however* as a simple substitute for *but*: ⊠ *They came for dinner, however they left before ten* and (2) a sentence allowed to run on when *however* should have a capital letter and start a new sentence: ⊠ *Resources for doing so are not available, however, the matter will be reviewed at a later date.*

hullo see HELLO.

human, humane, humanitarian. 1 The notion that *human* should only be used as an adjective and that *human being* should be used for the noun is found in some older usage books (though not Fowler, 1926) but is not supported by the weight of usage. Many examples of *human* as a noun will be found in *OED*2, to which may be added: *There rose before his inward sight the picture of a human at once heroic and sick*—William Golding, 1954 | *Behind the mental subterfuges . . . by which humans escape from reality lies a deep sense of inadequacy*—English, 1989 | *The human got in and, still holding the box with exaggerated care,*

placed it on its knees—T. Pratchett, 1992.

2 As an adjective, *human* is used predominantly as a classifying word in non-judgemental contexts, qualifying words such as *body, eye, life, mind, nature, race, rights,* and *voice*. The difference between *human* and *humane* in their judgemental meanings is that *human* denotes a generalized quality that distinguishes (actual or ideal) human behaviour from that of non-humans, whereas *humane* denotes a quality as it affects treatment of other people: (human) *When he pushed the postern closed behind him she stepped back into the gateway, eyeing him with very human caution*—J. Byrne, 1993 | (humane) *This is only a temporary solution and there have been many attempts to organise more humane working systems*—W. T. Singleton, 1989 | *Most academic criminologists had tended to regard the advances of rehabilitation in the penal process as being a beneficial and humane trend*—B. Roshier, 1989. Note, however, that *humane* is used with reference to animals as well as people: *There is a range of attitudes including the position of those who can accept whaling in principle if it can be made more humane in practice*—Animal Welfare, 1992 | *They believe in a humane rearing system for livestock, which is mindful of the needs of the animal in question*—C. Wheater et al., 1990.

3 Another adjective to be considered in this context is *humanitarian*, a 19c word that was originally a noun used in theological contexts. From the 1850s it has had the adjectival meaning 'practising humanity or humane action', and it is a common word in modern contexts of international aid and support: *Reports from Jordan indicated that Iraqi busi-*

nessmen fearful of incurring penalties were no longer prepared even to transport food and essential humanitarian supplies to Iraq—Keesings, 1990.

humankind. First recorded in the 17c as an occasional variant of *mankind*, *humankind* has gathered strength in the 20c, largely because it serves well as a gender-neutral term for the human race: *One single species—humankind—is putting the Earth at risk—BBC Wildlife,* 1990.

humour is spelt *-our* in BrE and *humor* in AmE, and the same distinction applies to the derivative *humourless* | *humorless*. *Humorous* and *humorist*, however, are spelt the same way in both varieties.

hybrid formations are words made up of elements belonging to different languages. They vary widely in the degree of irregularity they represent, from the routine addition of English prefixes and suffixes to stems from French (*bemuse, besiege, genuineness*) or vice versa (*breakage, disbelieve, readable*) to the merging of major word elements with different origins, as with *bureaucracy* (18c, from French *bureau* and Greek *-kratia* 'rule'), *coastal* (19c, from English *coast* and the Latin-derived suffix *-al*: see LOST CAUSES), *gullible* (19c, from English *gull* 'to deceive' and the Latin-derived suffix *-ible*), *speedometer* (20c, from English *speed* and the Greek-derived combining form *-ometer*), and *television* (20c, from Greek *tele-* 'far' and *vision*, a word of Latin origin). Some so-called blends and portmanteau words are in effect hybrids, e.g. *breathalyser* (20c, from English *breath* and Greek-derived *analyse*) and *workaholic* (20c, from English

work and *alcoholic*, a word derived via French from Arabic). In a language as eclectic in its origins as modern English the formation of such hybrids is natural and inevitable, and it is difficult to discern a sustainable principle behind the occasional objections that are made in the letter columns of the broadsheet newspapers to formations of this kind.

hyena is spelt *-e-*, not (as formerly) *-ae-*, and has the plural form *hyenas*.

hygiene, hygienic are spelt *-ie-* and pronounced respectively **hiy**-jeen and hiy-**jee**-nik. The Greek word from which these words are ultimately derived is the first word (an adjective) of *hugieinē technē*; 'art of health'.

hyper-, hypo-. These prefixes are derived from Greek prepositions *huper* and *hupo* meaning 'over, above' and 'under, below' respectively. In English, *hyperthermia* means 'abnormally high body temperature' and *hypothermia* means 'abnormally low body temperature'; *hypertension* means 'abnormally high blood pressure' and *hypotension* means 'abnormally low blood pressure'. Both prefixes are usually pronounced in the same way (**hiy**-pə), and the meaning may have to be clarified by the context in which they are used. In other words the prefix does not correspond so closely to sense; for example, *hypochondria* means 'excessive anxiety about one's health' (suggesting *hyper-* rather than *hypo-*) and is derived from a Greek word meaning 'the soft parts of the body below the ribs', where such feelings were thought to arise. *Hypercritical* duly means 'excessively critical', but *hypocritical* and *hypocrisy* (pronounced hip-, not hiyp-) are derived from a Greek word *hupokrisis* meaning 'acting a part, pretence'.

hyperbole, pronounced hiy-**per**-bə-li, is a figure of speech involving an exaggerated statement that is not meant to be taken literally, e.g. *a thousand apologies*. It should not be confused with *hyperbola*, pronounced hiy-**per**-bə-lə, a term in geometry.

hypercorrection is a modern (20c) term for the application of a grammatical rule, especially in sensitive areas of usage, in a case where it is not appropriate. Examples are (1) the use of a pronoun form *I, he*, etc., instead of *me, him*, etc., e.g. ✖ *It is time for you and I to have a talk* on the analogy of *It is time you and I had a talk*, and (2) use of *as* instead of *like* as a preposition, e.g. ✖ *He talks as a fool*, influenced by the preference for *as* when used as a conjunction: *He talks as a fool talks*.

hyphen. In print, a hyphen is half the length of a dash; unlike the dash, it has the purpose of linking words and word elements rather than separating them. Beyond this apparently simple rule, in the world of real usage, lies chaos (Fowler's word, 1926), especially when use of the hyphen is governed by contextual discretion rather than clear-cut rules. The following paragraphs describe the main uses of the hyphen, beginning with the more routine and ending with the least straightforward:

1 To join two or more words so as to form a single expression, e.g. *ear-ring, get-at-able*, and words having a grammatical relationship which form a compound, e.g. *load-bearing, punch-drunk*. The routine use of the hyphen to connect two nouns to form a compound word is diminishing in favour of one-word forms, especially when the elements are of one syllable and present no problems of form or pronunciation, as in *birdsong, eardrum*, and *playgroup*, and in some longer formations such as *figurehead, nationwide*, and even (despite the clash of vowels) *radioisotope*, which is entered in this form in the *OED*. However, a hyphen is often necessary to separate two similar consonant or vowel sounds in a word, e.g. *breast-stroke, co-opt, fast-talk, sword-dance, Ross-shire*. In the area of choice between spelling as one word with hyphen and as two words, the second option is now widely favoured, especially when the first noun acts as a straightforward modifier of the second, as in *filling station* and *house plant*. Different house styles in publishing and journalism have different preferences in many of these cases.

2 To clarify the meaning of a compound that is normally spelt as separate words, when it is used attributively (before a noun): *an up-to-date record | the well-known man*; but *the record is up to date | The man is well known*; also (with no ambiguity) *prettily furnished rooms*.

3 To join a prefix to a name or designation, e.g. *anti-Christian, ex-husband*. There is no satisfactory way of dealing with the type *ex-Prime Minister*, in which the second element is itself a compound, except to rely on the tendency of readers to use their knowledge of the world to choose the natural meaning, i.e. 'former Prime Minister' (which makes sense) rather than 'Minister who was once Prime' (which is nonsense). A second hyphen, e.g. *ex-Prime-Minister*, is not recommended.

4 To avoid ambiguity by separating a prefix from the main word, e.g. to distinguish *re-cover* (= provide with a new cover) from *recover* and *re-sign* (= sign again) from *resign*.

5 To represent a common second element in all but the last word of a list, e.g. *two-, three-, or fourfold*.

6 To clarify meanings in groups of words when the associations are not clear or when several possible associations may be inferred. This is the area of usage that involves the greatest initiative and discretion on the part of the writer, and it is also the area to which Fowler devoted most of his attention. The best way of offering guidance is to give examples in which careful hyphenation prevents misunderstanding: *The library is reducing its purchase of hard-covered books | Twenty-odd people came to the meeting | The group was warned about the dangers of extra-marital sex | There will be special classes for French-speaking children*.

7 The hyphen is also used in printing to divide a word that comes at the end of a line and is too long to fit completely. The principle here is a different one, because the hyphen does not form a permanent part of the spelling. Printers have sets of rules about where to divide words; for example, between consonants as in *splen-dour* and between vowels as in *appreci-ate*, and

words of one syllable should not be divided at all, even quite long ones such as *queues* and *rhythm*.

hyphen, hyphenate, *verbs.* Both words mean 'to spell (a word or phrase) with a hyphen'. This book uses *hyphen*, following the practice of the successive *OED* editors C. T. Onions and R. W. Burchfield, although *hyphenate* is more common in general usage.

hypo- see HYPER-.

hypocritical, hypercritical see HYPER-, HYPO-.

hyponym, hypernym. In linguistics, a *hyponym* of a given term is a more specific term in the same domain; e.g. *spaniel* is a hyponym of *dog*, and *bag*, *box*, and *cup* are hyponyms of *container*. A *hypernym* is a more general term, so that *dog* is the hypernym of *spaniel*, and *container* of *bag*, *box*, and *cup*. Because the two words can sound the same in speech, the alternative term *superordinate* is often used instead of *hypernym*.

hypothecate, hypothesize. The correct word for 'to form a hypothesis' is *hypothesize*, and it is used with or without an object or with a *that*-clause: *Quick to learn, quick to grasp concepts and to hypothesize, they need the best minds to provide appropriate support and challenge*—J. Spink, 1989 | *It was then decided to hypothesize a particular market situation for a single product line*—C. Tomkins, 1991 | *I hypothesise that if I move and turn the lamp in a particular way I will get the result I want*—W. T. Singleton, 1989. *Hypothecate*, which is sometimes wrongly used in this meaning, correctly means 'to give as a pledge or security' (from Greek *hupothēkē*; 'deposit') especially in the context of taxation in which the money raised is used for a special purpose: *An alternative scheme for financing the NHS involves the removing of finance from general taxation and the introduction of a health stamp or hypothecated tax*—P. Hardy, 1991.

hypothesis, meaning 'something proposed as a basis for reasoning', has the plural form hypotheses, pronounced -seez.

I. 1 *I*, the first person pronoun representing the speaker (or writer), is a shortening of earlier forms *ic, ich, ik*, etc., and has been written as a capital letter at least since the development of printing imposed uniformity in the 15c.

2 Popular preoccupation with the correctness (or hypercorrectness) of '*John and I*' (rather than '*John and me*') as an answer to questions such as *Who do you mean?* has led to an absurd proliferation of the use of *I* where *me* is correct because the pronoun is governed by a verb or preposition. The best known case, *between you and I*, is discussed at the entry for BETWEEN (section 5). Other types are shown by the following examples: ✖ *I think she disapproved of Beth and I, just quietly*—S. Johnson, 1990 (Australia) / ✖ *'What is it?' asked Lemprière. 'Part of you and I,' said Septimus*—L. Norfolk, 1991 / ✖ *. . . after seeing you and I lingering over a late breakfast*—Chicago Tribune, 1991. The fallacy of these uses can readily be seen by isolating the pronoun and removing the noun it is paired with in each sentence, e.g. ✖ *I think she disapproved of I, just quietly*.

i before e. The traditional spelling rule '*i* before *e* except after *c*' should be extended to include the statement 'when the combination is pronounced -ee-', as in *believe, brief, fiend, hygiene, priest, siege*, and in *ceiling, deceive, conceit, receipt, receive*, etc. The extension to the rule is necessary in order to take account of words such as

beige, freight, neighbour, sleigh, veil, vein, weigh (all pronounced -ay-), *eiderdown, feisty, height, heist, kaleidoscope, sleight* (all pronounced -iy-), and words in which the *i* and *e* are pronounced as separate vowels, e.g. *holier, occupier*. This leaves *caffeine, protein*, and *seize* as the most important exceptions to the rule as qualified.

ibid. is a shortening of Latin *ibidem* 'in the same place' and is used principally in printed matter to indicate a reference to a source already mentioned.

-ible see -ABLE, -IBLE.

-ic, -ical adjectives. 1 There are three main situations: (1) cases where only an adjective ending in *-ic* is available (e.g. *alcoholic, basic, dramatic, linguistic, patriotic, public*), (2) cases where only an adjective ending in *-ical* is available (e.g. *chemical, practical, radical*), and (3) cases where adjectives ending in *-ic* and *-ical* are available, often with a difference in meaning (e.g. *classic / classical, comic / comical, economic / economical, historic / historical*) but sometimes with no difference in meaning (e.g. *geographic / geographical, problematic / problematical*). Pairs that represent a difference in meaning are discussed as separate entries. When there is no difference in meaning, choice is often determined by considerations of idiom and sentence rhythm. Assertions relating to regional distinctions (e.g. that *-ic* forms are more common in AmE) lack adequate statistical support.

2 With one exception, all these adjectives, whether they end in *-ic* or *-ical* or both, form adverbs in *-ically* (*basically, dramatically, geometrically, practically,* etc.). The exception is *public*, which has an adverb form *publicly*.

-ics. 1 There are a few names of arts or of branches of study that end in *-ic*, of which the most important in general use are *logic, magic, music,* and *rhetoric*. Otherwise the normal ending for terms of this kind is *-ics*: *acoustics, classics, economics, ethics, mathematics, obstetrics, physics,* and many others. (In some cases a singular noun exists with a different meaning: a *classic* is something of acknowledged fame or quality, an *ethic* is a set of moral principles, and a *statistic* is an item of statistical data.) Although these are plural forms, they take singular verbs when they are the name of a subject and a plural verb when they are used generally: compare *Economics is her main interest* and *The economics of the foreign aid are extremely complex.*

2 Another class of nouns in *-ics* corresponds to adjectives in *-ic* or *-ical*, e.g. *heroics, hysterics, tactics,* and these are treated as regular plurals, e.g. *Heroics are out of place.*

idea. *Idea* is followed by *of* + noun (or verbal noun) when the meaning is 'notion, concept' (*It's not my idea of having a good time*) and by a *to-*infinitive when after a construction with the verb *be* (*The idea is to get the ball in the hole*).

ideology was first used in the later 18c in the meaning 'the science of ideas', and has since filled a much-needed role as a term free of religious and spiritual connotations to denote 'a system of ideas forming the basis of an economic or political theory', as in *capitalist ideology.*

idiom in the context of language has two principal meanings: (1) the manner of expression that characterizes a language, and (2) a group of words that has a meaning not deducible from the individual words. The first can therefore be seen as the sum total of all the instances of the second. Examples of idioms in the concrete second meaning are *over the moon, under the weather, might as well,* and *hard put to it.* The adjective *idiomatic* draws on both these meanings in denoting what is natural and customary in the use of a language; as Fowler recognized (1926), 'grammar and idiom are separate categories', so that a mode of expression can be idiomatic or grammatical or both or neither. Fowler's various examples are still valid and useful: *It was not me* and *There is heaps of material* are idiomatic but ungrammatical, *The distinction leaps to the eyes* and *a hardly earned income* are grammatical but unidiomatic, *He was promoted captain* and *She all but capsized* are both grammatical and idiomatic, and *You would not go for to do it* is neither.

idiosyncrasy, meaning 'an individual's particular habit or mode of behaviour', is derived from the Greek words *idio-* 'own, peculiar', *sun* 'together', and *krasis* 'mixture' and so its etymological meaning is 'a peculiar mixing together'. It is wrong to spell it *-cracy,* as if it were connected with words such as *democracy* and *autocracy.*

i.e. is short for Latin *id est* and means 'that is to say'. It should be distinguished from *e.g.,* from

Latin *exempli gratia*, which means 'for example'. In other words, *i.e.* explains whereas *e.g.* illustrates.

-ie, -y. 1 These suffixes are used in pet-names and diminutives. There is often a free choice between *-ie* and *-y*, except that *-y* is always used in the pet-names *baby, daddy, ducky, granny, hubby, mummy,* and *sonny,* and in the diminutives *bunny, fatty, kitty, nappy,* and *teddy,* and *-ie* is always used in the diminutives *bookie, girlie, goalie,* and *nightie,* and is the preferred form in a number of words associated with Scotland (*beastie, kiltie, laddie, lassie,* etc.). In other cases (*dearie | deary, goalie | goaly, nightie | nighty,* etc.), it is largely a matter of individual preference or of a particular printing style. Spellings of individual words will be found in the current edition of the *Concise Oxford Dictionary.* The plural forms of all these words end in *-ies.*

2 Spelling of personal names (*Jamie, Katie, Molly, Sally, Willie,* etc.) is not a matter of choice but of the form favoured by the bearer of a particular name.

if. 1 *If* is followed by the subjunctive form *were* (instead of *was*) when the condition it introduces is hypothetical or impossible to fulfil, as in *If I were younger, I'd travel the world. Was* is used (1) informally in such cases (*If I was younger, I'd travel the world*), and (2) to indicate past tense in which the condition is capable of fulfilment (*If I was younger, I wasn't any wiser*). Use of the subjunctive form *be* (instead of *am, is,* or *are*) is now decidedly old-fashioned: *If this be true, all is not lost.* See SUBJUNCTIVE MOOD.

2 *If* and *whether* are both used to introduce noun clauses as in *Tell me if|whether you can come,* but

whether is regarded as somewhat more formal and is preferable in avoiding possible ambiguity (in the sentence just given, a possible interpretation, though not the natural one, when *if* is used is 'If you can come, tell me (some other thing)'.

3 *If* and *though* are both possible in constructions of the type *a cheap, if|though risky method,* although again there is sometimes a small risk of ambiguity in the use of *if.*

4 *If* is sometimes used in a clause without any continuation, either as a way of making a strong assertion or as a polite request. This use is normally limited to conversation: *Well, if that isn't the best thing I've heard since I was home*—Compton Mackenzie, 1919 | *'I've got to leave this morning, so if you'll make out my bill, please?'*—Colin Dexter, 1983 | *'There's your tea. Drink it.' . . . 'If I could have another lump of sugar.'*—Graham Greene, 1988.

if and when. *If and when the law catches up with them, I hope it has it in for them*—*Punch,* 1967. This phrase (along with *as and when* and *unless and until*) almost belongs to the category of the Fowlers' LOST CAUSES, but not quite. They wrote of it in *The King's English* (1906), 'this formula has enjoyed more popularity than it deserves; either "when" or "if" by itself would almost always give the meaning', and gave several examples to support their case, making an exception of the following quotation from Gladstone: *If and when it was done, it was done so to speak judicially,* in which the force of both *if* and *when* is needed. Significantly, this was their only example in the past tense; all the other examples referred to future time. While it is true that *if* alone (when there is doubt) or *when* alone (when there is no doubt) would often serve, there are contexts in which a point needs to be made with regard both to the likelihood of occurrence and to the time of it: *Many drugs will be given if and when needed, probably with no obvious rhythm*—J. M. Waterhouse et al., 1990. The expression is especially popular with lawyers because at the very least it makes the same point doubly effective.

ignoramus, meaning 'an ignorant person', has the plural form *ignoramuses*. It was originally a law term from the Latin word meaning 'we do not know', and so the ending has nothing to do with Latin nouns in *-us*.

-ile. Many nouns and adjectives ending in *-ile* (*docile, domicile, facile, fertile, fragile, missile, mobile, sterile, virile*, etc.) are pronounced -iyl in BrE and -əl in AmE. The main exceptions are *automobile* and *imbecile*, which are usually pronounced -eel in both varieties, and *profile*, which is pronounced -iyl in both varieties, as (with some variation) are the statistical terms *decile, percentile*, and *quartile*.

ilk is a word that arouses passions when it is used to mean 'kind or sort': *Fifteen years a faithful husband, that was his ilk*—Saul Bellow, 1987. *Ilk* arrived at this meaning by a strange route: originally it meant 'same' (Old English *ilca*), but was pushed aside in this role by the arrival in the Middle English period of *same* (from Old Norse). In Scotland from the 15c, the phrase *of that ilk* emerged with the meaning 'of the same place, territorial designation, or name', to denote the

names of landed families, e.g. *Guthrie of that Ilk* = Guthrie of (a place also called) Guthrie. The Scottish use was rapidly misunderstood south of the border and by the 18c the word *ilk* had acquired the meaning 'family, class' and hence 'kind or sort', and we are back at the point where we started. Although there is much evidence of the spread of the popular use, it should be borne in mind that it can sound absurd to anyone (not necessarily Scottish) who is familiar with the word's historical usage. Examples: *Her husband's employment was not of the ilk of the typical man on the job on the coast*—A. Kennedy, 1986 (New Zealand) | *Rambo and Rocky and their ilk are the mere tip of a vast iceberg*—Encounter, 1987 | *I'm being flippant. Irresponsible in the well-known propensity of my ilk*—Kingsley Amis, 1988.

ill, sick. *Ill* and *sick* share responsibilities in peculiar ways, and are not always interchangeable. To begin with, *ill* is more usually predicative (placed after a verb, as in *She was ill*), whereas *sick* occurs naturally in attributive position (before a noun, as in *She was a sick woman*) as well as predicatively (as in *She was sick*), and in compounds such as *sick leave* and *sick room*). *Ill* is used attributively only in the broader sense 'out of health' (*He was an ill man when I last saw him*), in the extended meanings 'faulty, unskilful' (*ill judgement | ill management*), in idioms and proverbs (*do an ill turn to | It's an ill wind that blows nobody any good*). It also occurs adverbially in compounds (*ill-behaved | ill-considered*). In BrE, *to be sick* and *to feel sick* have the special meanings 'to vomit' and 'to be inclined to vomit', and to underline the anomalies of the two words a person can *look ill* and then *report* (or *go*) *sick*. In varieties of English other than BrE, the overlaps in meaning and usage vary considerably, and in some varieties there is little difference other than the more formal nature of the word *ill*. In AmE, the meaning 'vomiting' is normally supplied by the phrase *sick to* (or *at*) *one's stomach*.

illegal, illegitimate, illicit, unlawful.
The different meanings of these words correspond to the meanings of *legal, legitimate, licit* (now rarely used), and *lawful*. Something is *illegal* when it is in all circumstances against the law, *illicit* when it is in some circumstances against the law or prohibited in some way, and *illegitimate* when it is contrary to custom or common justice as well as (or instead of) contrary to the law. *Unlawful* is a somewhat old-fashioned word for *illegal* and refers to divine as well as human law. See further at LEGAL, LAWFUL.

illegible, unreadable.
In current use what is *illegible* is not clear enough to be decipherable (as in *illegible handwriting*), and what is *unreadable* can be physically read but is too dull to be worth reading or too difficult to be understood.

illicit
see ELICIT; ILLEGAL.

illiteracies.
This was a term used by Fowler (1926) to denote examples of 'a kind of offence against the literary idiom that is not easily named' and identified its chief habitat as the correspondence columns of the newspapers. The instances he gave included *aggravating* (= annoying), *between . . . or . . .* instead of *between . . . and . . .* , *however* for *how ever* in the type ⊠ *However did you*

find out?, like used as a conjunction (⊠ *If I could think like you do*), frequent use of split infinitives (⊠ *Am ready to categorically affirm*), *think to* (= remember to, as in ⊠ *I did not think to tell them,*), and *individual* to mean 'person'. In 1965 Gowers added three more instances: *between you and I*, likewise used as a conjunction (⊠ *Its tendency to wobble . . . likewise its limited powers of execution*), and *neither* with a plural verb (⊠ *For two reasons neither of which are noticed by Plato*). Some of these illiteracies may still be so called, notably, as explained elsewhere, *between you and I* (see BETWEEN 5) and *however* for *how ever*. In other cases, time has moved on, and the *Concise Oxford Dictionary* gives many of the castigated uses with the much milder warning 'colloquial' or 'disputed' rather than 'illiterate'.

illiterate, innumerate.
Illiterate (16c) means 'unable to read or write' or 'poorly educated'; *innumerate* (20c) means 'having no knowledge of or aptitude for the principles of mathematics'. The corresponding positive forms *literate* and *numerate* date from about the same times, although *numerate* is attested much earlier (15c) in a now obsolete meaning 'numbered, counted'.

illusion
see DELUSION.

illusive, illusory
see ELUSIVE.

image
is an old word (13c) derived from Latin *imago* meaning 'copy, likeness, picture' and in all its meanings suggests a real or mental picture. Since the late 1950s it has been used by marketeers, advertisers, and (more recently) political spin-doctors to mean 'a concept or impression

created in the minds of the public about a particular person, product, institution, etc.': *The first task of the public relations man, on taking over a business client, is to 're-engineer' his image to include something besides the production of goods*—J. K. Galbraith, 1958 | *In contrast to the image of police work as exciting and dangerous . . ., patrolling was invariably boring and somewhat aimless*—I. Marsh, 1992 | *It is important, too, that close attention is paid to image building (e.g. banks and insurance companies must be seen to be stable, reliable institutions, but with a friendly, non-intimidating attitude—an image which banks in particular have spent a lot of money fostering over the past decade)*.—G. Lancaster et al., 1992.

imaginable, meaning 'able to be imagined', is spelt without an *e* in the middle.

imaginary, imaginative. *Imaginary* means 'existing only in the imagination, not real', whereas *imaginative* means 'having or showing a high degree of imagination'. Both words can be applied to people as well as things; an *imaginary* person is one who does not really exist (e.g. is fictitious), whereas an *imaginative* person is one who is creative or inventive.

imbalance is a surprisingly recent word (19c), first used as a technical term in ophthalmology and now used generally in many contexts: *The imbalance in the world's financial system has become grotesque*—*Times*, 1969 | *The marked increase in the average salary reflects both the imbalance of supply and demand for health workers*—*Scientific American*, 1973 | *Teaching implies an imbalance of knowledge, otherwise it would not be necessary*—B. Bergonzi, 1990.

imbroglio, an originally Italian word meaning 'a confused or complicated situation', has the plural form *imbroglios*.

imbue see INFUSE.

imitate has a derivative form *imitable* meaning 'able to be imitated'.

immanent see IMMINENT.

immediately has been used informally since the early 19c, especially in BrE, as a conjunction equivalent to *immediately after*: *I starting writing 'Jill' immediately I left Oxford*—Philip Larkin, 1983 | *Immediately I heard the front door I switched off his computer*—Nigel Williams, 1992.

immigrant see EMIGRANT.

imminent, immanent. The more common word *imminent*, derived from the Latin word *minēre* 'to threaten', means 'about to happen' and has connotations of threat or danger. *Immanent*, derived from the Latin word *manēre* 'to remain', means 'indwelling, inherent' and is chiefly used in theology to denote the divine presence throughout the universe.

immoral, amoral. Both words are applied to people, to people's actions, and to standards of behaviour. *Immoral* means 'morally wrong, wicked', whereas *amoral* means 'having no morals', i.e. 'outside the scope of morality' and is strictly neutral in meaning, although in practice both words are used judgementally. Examples: (amoral) *Children are first amoral . . . then enter a pre-moral stage, when social and authoritarian factors are the main restraints*—M. E. Wood, 1973 | *For someone who appeared so gleefully wicked and* *amoral, Cleo seemed surprisingly dim when it came to character judgment*—C. Storm, 1993 | (immoral) *This view takes into account the general view that crime is or ought to be those actions which are considered so immoral or damaging that they should be subject to punishment*—J. D. Rogers, 1987 | *Simon criticised Jesus for allowing such an immoral woman to touch him*—R. Cooper, 1990.

immovable is spelt without an *e* in the middle, and the usual meaning is 'unyielding, unwilling to change one's mind'.

immune is followed by *to* or *from*. When the reference is to disease or some other form of harm or danger, *to* is more usual, and when *from* is used it is more often in the context of legal liabilities, but these distinctions are far from clear-cut and both constructions are found regardless of context, with *to* somewhat more common than *from*: (to) *Each country will be concerned to maintain the invulnerability of its submarine-based strategic missiles, which are essentially immune to attack from land-based weapons*— *Scientific American*, 1972 | *A situation could arise where harmful bacteria, having become immune to disinfectants, survive to cause illness which cannot be treated by antibiotics*—R. North, 1985 | *They came from a variety of schools and backgrounds and it is difficult to believe that their pupils are more immune to racial prejudice than those mentioned above*—D. Pimm, 1988 | (from) *Those who have a commitment to the Christian faith are not thereby immune from depression*—M. Batchelor, 1988 | *The laws affecting the common land were supervised by Down Drivers, themselves not immune from prosecution*—M. Lister, 1988 | *Real*

diamonds have a quite distinctive, soapy texture to the surface and are immune from water—Frederick Forsyth, 1989.

immunity, impunity. In non-medical contexts *immunity* means 'freedom or exemption from an obligation, penalty, or unfavourable circumstance' and like *immune* can be followed by *to* or *from*: *Balder was a son of the most senior god, Odin, and one version of the legend says he was blessed with the gift of immunity from harm*—H. Hauxwell et al., 1989 | *A common question is whether people should be tested before vaccination for existing immunity to HBV and/or after inoculation to determine whether the vaccination was successful*—*The Embalmer*, 1993. *Impunity* has the more limited meaning 'exemption from punishment or from the injurious consequences of an action', is not followed by *to* or *from*, and is used chiefly in the phrase *with impunity*: *In our dreams we can do with impunity things we would like to do in real life but cannot*—*make love with a Hollywood sex symbol or murder our boss*—J. Grant, 1990.

impact. The literal meaning of the noun is 'the action of one body coming forcibly into contact with another', and refers to physical collision. The figurative meaning 'strong effect or influence' is justifiable when there is a corresponding figurative notion of a collision (*the impact of Christianity on social justice*), but it is questionable when the meaning is no more than 'effect, impression' (*the impact of new policing methods on the crime figures*). The verb, which is pronounced with the stress on the second syllable, is older than the noun in its physical meaning ('press closely into or in something'). Intransitive uses began to appear in the 20c, and in 1962 it was reported in a work called *Basic Astronautics* that a Soviet space rocket *had impacted onto the Moon's surface.* About the same time figurative uses began to proliferate, corresponding to the figurative meaning of the noun: *The Magazine . . . is not the place for consideration of national or international events except in so far as they impact on* Oxford—*Oxford Magazine,* 1956. There has been continued opposition to these uses, both in Britain and in America. When there is so much hostility, it is prudent to use more familiar synonyms, such as *effect, influence,* and *impression* for the noun and *affect, influence,* or *have an effect on* for the verb.

impassable, impassible. *Impassable* means 'that cannot be traversed' and refers to roads, stretches of countryside, etc. *Impassible* means 'incapable of feeling emotion' or 'incapable of suffering injury', and is pronounced with the second syllable as in *passive* rather than as in *pass.*

impasse, meaning 'a deadlock, or position from which progress is impossible', is pronounced many different ways, but the recommended pronunciations are am-**pahs** and **am**-pas.

impeach in BrE means 'to charge with a crime against the State, especially treason', and in AmE means 'to charge (the holder of a public office) with misconduct'. What it does not mean is 'to dismiss from office'.

impel has inflected forms *impelled, impelling.*

imperial, imperious. *Imperial* means 'relating to an empire or emperor' and hence 'characteristic of an emperor, supreme in authority'. *Imperious* is a more judgemental word and means 'overbearing, domineering'.

imperialism. This word is first attested in the 19c, when it reflected the British politics of the time and denoted what was seen as the benevolent spirit or principle of empire. In the 20c, it came to be used disparagingly, first by the Communist bloc with reference to the US and the Western powers generally, and then conversely to refer to the imperial system or policies of the USSR in the countries over which it held sway. Imperialism now seems to be a largely historical concept, although the word is still used in political writing of the continuing or potential imperial policies of certain countries.

imperil, meaning 'to put at risk, to endanger', has inflected forms *imperilled, imperilling* in BrE and *imperiled, imperiling* in AmE.

impersonal verb. In current English this term is restricted to verbs used in the third person singular with indefinite *it* as subject, e.g. *it is snowing, when it rains.*

impinge, meaning 'to have an effect (on)', has a present participle *impingeing,* with *e* to preserve the soft sound of the *g.*

implement, as a verb, is a useful word used first in Scotland in the sense 'to put (a treaty, agreement, etc.) into effect', a meaning it still has in general usage. In the 20c its use has been greatly extended to cover any kind of idea, policy, proposal, suggestion, etc., as a general synonym for *carry out*, *effect*, *fulfil*, and other words. Although objections are sometimes raised to this use, it is well established and is often a better word than any of these synonyms might at first seem to be. It also has the advantage of a ready noun form *implementation*.

imply see INFER.

import. The noun is pronounced with the stress on the first syllable, and the verb with the stress on the second syllable.

important, importantly. Both words have a special elliptical use dating from the 1930s, in which one or other stands by itself (or qualified by *more*, *most*, etc.) as a kind of sentence adverb: *Perhaps more importantly, income not applied to exclusively charitable purposes is not exempt from taxation—Times*, 1972 | *But, more important, a linked policy can be encashed—surrendered—before maturity date—Daily Telegraph*, 1973 | *But most important of all, we begin by giving you the training you need—Scientific American*, 1973 | *More important, Mr Deng gave China a new revolutionary vision in the decade of reform from 1978—Economist*, 1991 | *The reason is twofold: he has an unassuming nature, but more importantly, his achievements are the fruits of hobbies—New Scientist*, 1991. The use of (*more* etc.) *importantly* is sometimes criticized on the grounds that (*more* etc.) *important* (elliptical for *what is more important*) is adequate, but both words are commonly used in this way and *importantly* conforms more closely than *important* does to the regular type of sentence adverb.

impostor is the recommended spelling, not *imposter*.

impracticable, impractical.
These two words have related meanings to do with the impossibility of doing something, and correspond to the positive forms PRACTICABLE, PRACTICAL. *Impractical* is a relatively recent (19c) word and means the same as *unpractical*, i.e. 'not practical or realistic'; it can also be used of a person, with the meaning 'lacking the ability to do practical things', and usually has a general application. *Impracticable* means 'not able to be carried out, not feasible', and is more usually applied to particular cases. In practice, however, the two words are close enough in meaning to run the frequent risk of getting in each other's way: *In the end the scheme was abandoned as impracticable—*J. F. Lehmann, 1960 | *As his arms were full of books it would have been impracticable for him to wave—*J. I. M. Stewart, 1974 | *I have always been ridiculously impractical . . . I cannot repair a fuse—*F. Howerd, 1974 | *Her plans were so impractical that someone like me was necessary to point this out—*Anita Brookner, 1987.

impresario, meaning 'an organizer of public entertainments', has the plural form *impresarios*.

imprint is pronounced with the stress on the first syllable as a noun and on the second syllable as a verb.

improbable see PROBABLE.

impromptu, as a noun meaning 'an extempore speech or performance' or 'a short piece of instrumental music', has the plural form *impromptus*.

improvable, meaning 'able to be improved', is spelt without an *e* in the middle.

improvise is spelt -*ise*, not -*ize*.

impunity see IMMUNITY.

in. 1 Use of *in* instead of *for* with reference to past time (*We have not spoken in more than a year*) has spread from AmE to BrE. It is used in contexts that are explicitly or implicitly negative, and as such is a revival of an older English use: *To Westminster Hall, where I have not been . . . in some months*—Samuel Pepys, 1669. More recent examples are: *Mark had never been near his house in a year*—Compton Mackenzie, 1924 | *The first bridge across the Bosphorus in 2,300 years . . . is now being built*—*Daily Telegraph*, 1971.

2 In meanings to do with place, in certain contexts AmE uses *on* or *at* where BrE uses *in*: *a store on Fifth Avenue* | *They are all in school now.*

3 See also the separate entries for INASMUCH AS, IN ORDER THAT, IN SO FAR AS, IN THAT.

in- and un-. 1 Both prefixes are used to make negative forms of adjectives and nouns; *in-* is Latin in origin and is no longer active in making new words, whereas *un-* is English in origin and is a living prefix. Historically, some words have existed in both *in-* and *un-* forms, but one or other of them normally drops out in the end, so that (for example) *unability* gave way to *inability* in the 18c, although *unable* and not *inable* is the corresponding adjective. Other mismatches occur with the pairs *imbalance* | *unbalanced*, *uncomprehending* | *incomprehensible*, *indigestible* | *undigested*, *indisputable* | *undisputed*, *indistinguishable* | *undistinguished*, *unseparated* | *inseparable*, *instability* | *unstable*, and others.

2 Choice between *un-* and *in-* forms is not normally a problem for native speakers of English, with occasional exceptions such as *inadvisable* (= not advised) | *unadvisable* = (of a person) not open to advice, *inarguable* | *unarguable* (both in use), *incommunicative* | *uncommunicative* (both in use), *inconsolable* | *unconsolable* (the first now preferred), *indecipherable* | *undecipherable* (both in use), *inhuman* (= brutal, unfeeling) | *unhuman* (not human), *insupportable* (= intolerable) | *unsupportable* (= indefensible), and others.

3 Note that *in-* is not used to form negative forms of verbs, whereas *un-* is (*undo*, *unmask*, *unsettle*, etc.).

inapt, inept. These two words are often confused because they overlap in their basic meanings 'inappropriate, unsuitable' and 'unskilful'. *Inapt* tends to mean rather the first of these, and applies only to actions and circumstances, whereas *inept* means rather the second, is much more common, and applies to people as well as actions: *In this respect, the oft-quoted cathedral metaphor is not inapt*—J. Richards et al., 1988 | *She believes it would be politically inept to cut such training programmes at a time when the jobless total is rising fast*—*Today*, 1992 | *Nicholas was inept at all forms of promiscuity except gossip*—*Esquire*, 1992. So if you say that a person's reply is *inapt* and *inept*, you mean that it was both inappropriate and clumsily expressed.

inartistic see UNARTISTIC.

inasmuch as is a rather formal and awkward expression meaning 'to the extent that, in so far as' or more simply 'in view of the fact that, since'. The preferred style is two words (as here) rather than four, since this underlines the unity of the expression. Examples: (first meaning) *Inasmuch as she could be pleased, the idea of this marriage pleased her*—C. Blackwood, 1977 | *These provisions apply only inasmuch as trade between Member States is affected*—D. I. Bainbridge, 1993 | (second meaning) *Inasmuch as Gray was Perdita's father, he was to be treated with a reasonable degree of respect*—B. Guest, 1985 | *He predeceased Sir Nelson, which made my task a little easier, inasmuch as it was not necessary for me to carry out complicated inquiries in India*—E. V. Thomson, 1992.

in back of see BACK.

inchoate means 'undeveloped' or 'just begun' and is derived from the Latin word *choare* 'to begin': *It was obviously necessary that we should continue our still inchoate discussion over a drink*— D. M. Davin, 1975 | *She is not allowed to express her real, if inchoate, feelings for Robert Marlin*—T. Tanner, 1986. It should be distinguished from *incoherent*, which means 'lacking logic or consistency', and *chaotic*, which means 'having no order, utterly confused', both of which words tend to be used in similar contexts.

incidentally is spelt this way and not (as the pronunciation in rapid speech might suggest) *incidently*. Its usual role is as a sentence adverb marking a new stage in speech (or sometimes writing) and it does not always carry its full weight of meaning 'as an unconnected remark', the following matter often being a continuation of what went before: *The man who shot her, incidentally, is called Lord Lichfield*—*just one of the names dropped thuddingly at

every opportunity—*Daily Telegraph,* 1976 | *Incidentally, thanks to Tommy Hands, I nearly became a landlord myself*—A. J. P. Taylor, 1983.

incident, incidental *adjectives.* *Incident* has been almost entirely replaced as an adjective in the 20c by *incidental*, so that a sentence such as *Those in the highest station have their incident cares and troubles* now sounds decidedly dated. This freeing of *incident* from its older role as an adjective has coincided with its greatly increased use as a noun with the meaning 'a particular episode or distinct event receiving general attention', a use in which it can refer to a wide range of events from the most important (terrorist attacks, leakages of radiation from nuclear power stations, and so on) to the most minor or trivial (domestic arguments, demonstrations at meetings, traffic mishaps, etc.). In police use it has a special application reflected in the compound forms *incident book*, *incident room*, etc., in which *incident* is not an adjective but the noun used attributively.

incise, meaning 'to cut into, engrave', is spelt *-ise*, not *-ize*. The noun derivative is *incisor* (usually meaning a front tooth), not *-er*.

incline is pronounced with the stress on the first syllable as a noun (meaning 'a slope') and with the stress on the second syllable as a verb (as in *be inclined to*).

inclose is not the correct form: see ENCLOSE.

include, comprise. Like *comprise*, *include* has the whole as its subject and its parts as the object. The difference is that *comprise* generally denotes the whole set of parts whereas *include* can be selective, so that if a house *comprises* two living rooms, two bedrooms, a kitchen, and a bathroom, there are six rooms in all, whereas if the house *includes* these rooms there may be others as well. *Include* is often used to single out a particular item or subset, in which case *comprise* is again inappropriate: *The Serbian forces attacking Sarajevo are units of the former Federal army: they do not include regiments still stationed in Zagreb.* See also COMPRISE.

including. There is evidence, both in BrE and in AmE, of *including* used with a prepositional phrase introduced by a word such as *by, in, to*, etc.: *Copies of this notice are being distributed on a wide scale including to overseas establishments*—radio broadcast, 1990 | *We find free speech under assault throughout the United States, including on some college campuses*—International Herald Tribune, 1991 | *Pensions disappeared [when my partner died] and I faced a huge tax bill—including on a half share of our house, which we owned jointly*—Independent, 1998.

incognito, when used as a noun meaning either 'a secret identity' or 'a person with a secret identity', has the plural form *incognitos.*

incommunicado, meaning 'having no communication with others', is spelt with two *m*s.

incomparable, meaning 'matchless, without an equal', is pronounced with the stress on the second syllable.

in connection with see CONNECTION.

inconsequent, inconsequential. The two words overlap considerably in meaning. Both are used to mean 'not following naturally; lacking logical sequence', but when, for example, an argument is a disconnected one it would normally be described as *inconsequent*, whereas *inconsequential* would imply that it is of no importance.

inconsiderateness, inconsideration. Both words mean 'thoughtlessness towards others', but the phrase *lack of consideration* is more common and less awkward than either.

inconsolable is now preferred to *unconsolable*. See IN- AND UN-.

increase is pronounced with the stress on the first syllable as a noun, and with the stress on the second syllable as a verb.

incrust see ENCRUST, which is the preferred form.

incubator, meaning 'a device for keeping a baby at a constant temperature', is spelt -*or* not -*er*.

incubus, meaning 'a male demon believed to have sexual intercourse with sleeping women' and hence 'a nightmare', has the plural form *incubuses.*

inculcate means 'to urge or impress (an idea, fact, etc.) on someone' and is derived from the Latin word *inculcare* 'to stamp with the heel' (Latin *calx*). It has the fact or idea as its object, optionally followed by *in, on,* or *upon*: *What Solzhenitsyn writes about ideological rituality, about the harmful waste of millions of people's time and efforts on this chatter that inculcates twaddle and hypocrisy, is indisputable*—Times, 1974 | *I have tried to inculcate in my pupils an atti-*

tude of intelligent laziness—Guardian, 1989. Use with the person as object, on the analogy of *indoctrinate*, is also found but is not generally considered standard: *They will also try to inculcate you with a spurious respect for a 'culture' which not only fails to distinguish between what is good and what is profitable* [etc.]*—Punch*, 1992.

incur, meaning 'to suffer or experience', has inflected forms *incurred, incurring*.

indecipherable see IN- AND UN-.

indefinite article see A, AN.

indent is pronounced with the stress on the first syllable as a noun and with the stress on the second syllable as a verb.

index. In general use the plural is normally *indexes*, but in mathematical and scientific contexts it is *indices*.

Indian. In BrE an *Indian* is first and foremost a native or national of India. In the American context its use arose from the mistaken belief of Columbus and other voyagers who reached the east coast of America in the 15c and 16c that they had reached India by a new route. *Indian* and *Red Indian* are now regarded as old-fashioned and inappropriate, and more reminiscent of stereotypical images of the Wild West than of contemporary America. *American Indian*, or preferably *Native American*, should be used instead.

indict, meaning 'to accuse formally', is pronounced in-**diyt**, and the same pronunciation applies to its derivatives *indictable* and *indictment*.

indigestible is spelt in-.

indirect object. 1 In grammar, an indirect object is a person or thing named as the recipient of the direct object of a transitive (or more strictly, DITRANSITIVE) verb. In the sentences *I gave my sister a book* and *I gave her a book*, *my sister* and *her* are the indirect objects. It will be seen that in this type the indirect object usually precedes the direct object. When both direct and indirect objects are pronouns, the reverse order is sometimes found (*I gave it her back*).

2 An alternative to this ditransitive construction is to use a preposition (usually *to* or *for*) before the indirect object with the indirect object then following the direct object (*I gave a book to my sister | I handed the book to her | I handed it to her*).

3 Verbs other than those of giving can have indirect objects, e.g. *Tell me the truth* (in which *me* is the indirect object) | *He cooks his wife a hot meal every evening* (in which *his wife* is the indirect object). See also DIRECT OBJECT, INTRANSITIVE AND TRANSITIVE VERBS.

indirect question. An indirect question is a question put into reported form. For example, *What do they want to do?* is a direct question and its indirect form is *I asked them what they wanted to do*. When the direct question calls for an answer 'yes' or 'no', the indirect form is introduced by *if* or *whether*: (direct) *Do you want to go for a walk?* | (indirect) *I'll ask them whether they want to go for walk*. It should be noted that indirect questions follow the word order of statements and are not followed by a question mark; it is wrong to say, for example, ✗ *I asked them what did they want to do?* or ✗ *Tell me how old are you?*

indirect speech see REPORTED SPEECH.

indispensable is spelt *-able*, not *-ible*. See -ABLE, -IBLE.

indisputable is pronounced with the stress on the third syllable. See also IN-, UN-.

indissoluble, meaning 'unable to be dissolved', is pronounced with the stress on the third syllable.

indistinguishable is spelt *-able*, not *-ible*.

individual. When used as a noun, *individual* should denote a single person in contrast with a group of people or with society as a whole: *the role of the individual in the community | She continues to treat them as individuals.* It is less satisfactory, and can often sound quaint or affected, when used simply as a synonym for *person*, and in this use it is normally restricted to jocular or disparaging contexts: *There was an odd individual standing by the door | Individuals arrived in their own cars.*

indivisible, meaning 'unable to be divided', is spelt *-ible*, not *-able*. See -ABLE, -IBLE.

indoor, indoors. The adjective is *indoor* (*indoor games*) and is a shortening of an earlier form *within-door. Indoors* is an adverb (*Let's go indoors now*) and represents an earlier form *within doors.*

induction see DEDUCTION.

industrial action is an established term (first recorded as recently as 1971 in the *OED*) denoting various kinds of industrial protest including strikes, working to rule, overtime bans, etc. The word *action*, paradoxical though it may seem, refers to the activity of protest and has a precedent in the term *political action* (late 19c).

inedible, uneatable. *Inedible* means 'not suitable for eating', whereas *uneatable* refers to food and means 'not fit to be eaten' because of its condition rather than its nature.

ineffective, ineffectual. *Ineffective* means 'not producing any effect' and normally refers to actions or processes. *Ineffectual* often refers to people, and means 'lacking the ability to produce results'. The distinctions are more fully discussed at EFFECTIVE.

inequity, iniquity. These two words are related in form, meaning, and derivation. *Inequity* is the opposite of *equity* and means 'inequality, unfairness, injustice': *The city cannot do what is most needed: join its suburban neighbours in a regional government that . . . evens out the huge inequities in school financing and municipal services—Economist,* 1993. *Iniquity* means 'gross injustice, wickedness: It is easy for a well-fed Englishwoman like myself to shake with anger about the futility of war, to protest about the iniquity of racial prejudice—M. & L. Hoy,* 1991. In some uses I suspect that *iniquity* has been used when *inequity* was meant, but it rarely happens the other way round: *I suggest this iniquity be removed as soon as possible—Daily Telegraph,* 1992.

infamous see NOTORIOUS.

infectious see CONTAGIOUS.

infer, imply. 1 The only point noted by Fowler (1926) was that the inflected forms of *infer* are *in-*

ferred and *inferring*, and this is thankfully still true (but note *inferable* or *inferrable*, with one r or two, and *inference* with only one r). Fowler made no comment on the meaning of *infer*, and it was left to Gowers (1965) to add a short note to the effect that 'the use of *infer* for *imply* is sadly common—so common that some dictionaries give *imply* as one of the definitions of *infer* without comment'. The *Concise Oxford Dictionary* (1995) labels this meaning 'disputed' and gives as the primary meanings of the two words: (*infer*) 'to deduce or conclude from facts or reasoning', (*imply*) 'to suggest the truth or existence of (something not expressly asserted), to insinuate or hint'. The problem lies in the fact that deduction and suggestion can often be seen as part of the same process. It is nearly always *infer* that encroaches on *imply* (but see paragraph 3 below for clarification of 'nearly'), and the *OED* puts the issue in its historical context by giving examples dating from the 16c onwards.

2 The following examples show in three groups the correct meanings of both words and then the disputed meaning of *infer*: (*imply* correctly used) *Vast stretches of abandoned concrete underfoot imply that someone once had plans for this land*—New Yorker, 1986 | *I wouldn't want to imply that lead is the most important factor in children's intelligence*—radio broadcast, 1987 | (*infer* correctly used) *You would have been able to infer from the room alone the nature of those who lived in it*—D. M. Davin, 1979 | *No reference to any living person is intended or should be inferred*—Saul Bellow, 1987 | (*infer* used for *imply*) *I can't stand fellas who infer things about good clean-living Australian sheilas*—Private Eye, 1970 | *These were the ones who had made a slightly sulky entrance (inferring rebellion), and had then proceeded to sit on the floor*—M. Bracewell, 1989.

3 The only domain in which *imply* is used where *infer* might be expected is in legal language, in which the inference and the conclusion are regarded as part of the same process, as the following extract shows: *When a possessory interest in property is conveyed, a court may imply from the circumstances that the parties also intended to grant or reserve an easement as well despite their failure to say so in the deed*. Otherwise, it is *infer* that has broken the bounds of logic and is on the loose in the arena of idiom.

inferable see INFER 1.

inferior is not a true comparative (like *lower*, for example) and is followed by *to*, not *than*: *When we are together there's no competition; neither of us feels better than or inferior to the other*—J. Dawson, 1990. When used attributively (before a noun), it means 'of poor quality' rather than 'less good'. *I have had to put up with inferior accommodation, lousy food and paltry pocket money*—M. & L. Hoy, 1991.

inferno has the plural form *infernos*.

infinite, infinitely are derived from the Latin word *infinitus* meaning 'without limit' (Latin *finis* 'end'), and this is the proper meaning of these words in English. In practice, however, they tend to be used in the weaker senses 'very great' and 'very much'; this use is acceptable in informal English but is best replaced in more formal contexts by alternatives such as *extensive*, *vast, substantial, considerable, immense, enormous,* or in some cases even simply *great* or *huge* (or their adverbial equivalents). Examples: *The infinite variety of Chinese food, with classic dishes such as Peking duck and shark's fin soup—Country Life,* 1973 | *It seems to me infinitely more absurd . . . not to want to see the best in this line that civilisation has to offer—Church Times,* 1976. When smallness of size or number is meant, *infinitesimal* and *infinitesimally* are preferable, when one of the simpler words given above will not do: *Brailsford . . . judged it more harshly: 'a blind alley which won't bring us even infinitesimally nearer to peace.'—*J. Hinton, 1989 | *She worked crouching down, and the infinitesimal pace of her labours made her feel like an ant, toiling away earnestly at a microscopic task—*J. Rogers, 1990.

infinitive. The infinitive of a verb is its simplest uninflected form, and the form that appears as the headword in dictionaries. When used in sentences, there are two basic kinds of infinitive: (1) the bare infinitive, identical to the form just mentioned, which is used with auxiliary verbs such as *can, may, shall, should, will, would,* etc., with the so-called semi-modal verbs *dare, help,* and *need,* and after idiomatic expressions such as *had better* (*I had better* **wait**), (2) the *to*-infinitive, in which the base form is preceded by the particle *to,* which is used with verbs such as *expect, have, hope, want,* etc., in expressions of purpose (*To call* attention, ring the bell), in idiomatic expressions such as *to be honest, to put it mildly, so to speak,* etc., and to form noun phrases which can be the subjects of other verbs (*To err is human*). When a second infini-

tive follows a *to*-infinitive, this is often expressed as a bare infinitive without another *to: I want* **to go** *to the library and* **get** *a book.*

inflammable, inflammatory. *Inflammable* has the same meaning, i.e. 'easily set on fire', as *flammable,* which is now preferred in official advisory contexts: see FLAMMABLE. *Inflammatory* means 'tending to cause inflammation (of the body)' and figuratively (especially in the context of speeches, leaflets, etc.) 'tending to cause anger'.

inflatable, which since the 1950s has been used as a noun as well as an adjective, is spelt without an *e* in the middle.

inflection. 1 Inflection is the process by which words change their form by the addition of suffixes or other means in accordance with their grammatical role. Inflection of nouns usually involves the addition of *-s* or *-es* to form plurals (*book* | *books, church* | *churches*); of verbs, the addition of *-s* or *-es, -ed,* and *-ing* to form third-person present-tense forms (*want* | *wants*), past tenses (*wanted*), past participles (*wanted*), and present participles (*wanting*); and of adjectives, to form comparative and superlative forms, the addition of *-er* and *-est,* sometimes with modification of the stem as in *happier, happiest.*

2 In the context of phonetics, inflection means 'modulation (i.e. adjusting the tone or pitch) of the voice'.

3 The alternative spelling *inflexion* applies to both meanings, but it is considered old-fashioned and Oxford style prefers *inflection.*

inflexible is spelt *-ible,* not *-able.* See -ABLE, -IBLE.

inflict, afflict. Both words are concerned with the suffering of unpleasant circumstances, but they have different constructions. *Inflict* has the unpleasantness as object, and *afflict* the victim: *It was he who had inflicted an appendectomy of doubtful necessity on Harry forty-two years ago*—R. Goddard, 1990 | *And finally there are abstract fears which afflict a great many*—the *'might be' fears*—Woman, 1991. *Afflict* is often used in the passive, followed by *with* or *by*: *Most commanders would have been afflicted with convenient deafness at that moment, but Davout rounded on the speaker at once*—R. Butters, 1991 | *The obvious fact that people of comfortable circumstance live peacefully together and those afflicted by poverty do not goes largely unnoticed*—New Statesman, 1992.

inform is a formal equivalent of *tell* and is generally limited to official contexts. It is followed by *of* or a *that*-clause (*The police informed them of their rights* | *An announcement informed us that the train was about to arrive*), but (unlike *tell*) does not have the instructional meaning followed by *to* (⊠ *Please inform them to wait outside*).

informant, informer. An *informant* is a neutral term for someone who gives information, especially about language, culture, etc. to a linguist or anthropologist. An *informer* is someone who gives information against another person to the authorities, and it has sinister or unfavourable overtones.

infotainment, first recorded in the US in the 1980s, means 'broadcast material that seeks to inform and entertain'. It belongs to a group of media-related portmanteau words of the late 20c: see also DOCUDRAMA.

infringe, meaning 'to violate (a rule or law)', has inflected forms *infringed, infringing*. In current use it is used both transitively (with an object, e.g. *The players were penalized for infringing the off-side rule*) and intransitively followed by *on* or *upon*, with the more general meaning 'encroach on, threaten': *The measure threatens to infringe upon and restrict our right to travel in certain countries.*

infuse. When using the word in its physical meaning, you can *infuse* (a plant, herb, etc.) in a liquid in order to extract its properties, or (by a linguistic process that Fowler called 'object-shuffling') you can *infuse* (a liquid) by inserting something in it. The figurative meanings of *infuse* behave in corresponding ways: you can *infuse* (a quality or attribute) into a person or thing or you can *infuse* (a person or thing) with a quality or attribute. Examples: *Joanna Trollope's latest delicious novel . . . focuses on two men, lifelong friends of sixtysomething, whose younger women infuse them both with seemingly eternal vigour*—She, 1989 | *He did his best to infuse good humour into his voice*—H. Forrester, 1990. *Imbue* could be used in the second construction with the same meaning: *A girl imbued with such qualities would be very special and extremely dangerous*—R. Hamilton, 1993.

-ing forms. The suffix *-ing* is added to verbs to form VERBAL NOUNS (***Smoking*** *damages your health*) and PARTICIPLES (*The house had a **smoking** chimney*).

ingenious, ingenuous. These two words are distantly related and both have undergone a major shift in meaning. *Ingenious* came into English via French from a Latin source derived from *ingenium* 'cleverness'; it originally meant 'intellectual, talented', but the meaning gradually weakened and its current sense is less complimentary and even depreciatory, '(of a person) clever, showing aptitude for devising curious devices' and '(of a device or machine) cleverly contrived': *There were the ingenious hand-made toys, the shadow-puppets manipulated on sticks*—H. Trevelyan, 1971 | *I see . . . that some ingenious person . . . has videotaped my television series*—Brian Aldiss, 1980. *Ingenuous*, by contrast, is derived from Latin *ingenuus* 'freeborn' and originally meant 'befitting a free man, noble in character', eventually weakening in sense to mean 'open, frank, candid': *She smiled ingenuously and the openness of her face seemed to ease his bad temper a little*—S. Wood, 1993 | *Mr Getty arrived half an hour late with the ingenuous excuse that he had miscalculated how long it would take him to walk from the Ritz to Boodles Club in St James's Street*—*Art Newspaper*, 1992. The noun *ingenuity* was originally a derivative of *ingenuous* but was usurped by *ingenious* in the 16c, so that in current use *ingenuity* corresponds to *ingenious*, and *ingenuousness* corresponds to *ingenuous*. See also DISINGENUOUS.

ingénue, meaning 'an innocent or unsophisticated young woman', is first recorded in English in Thackeray's *Vanity Fair* (1848). It is still usually printed in italics (sometimes without the accent) and pronounced in a French manner.

ingrained is the normal spelling for the word meaning 'deeply rooted, inveterate' or (in physical senses) 'deeply embedded'.

ingratiate, a 17c Latinate loanword, is now normally used reflexively (with *oneself* etc.) in the meaning 'to render oneself agreeable to someone, to bring oneself into favour with someone': *The child glared at me so fiercely that I tried to ingratiate myself by asking who was her favourite composer*—M. Dibdin, 1991. The non-reflexive use is not standard: ⊠ *He was going to pretend that his limp was cured, and that would ingratiate him with Matta, help him set his trap*—R. Campbell, 1993. (A better alternative in this example would be *commend him to*.) *Ingratiate* occurs frequently in the adjectival form *ingratiating*: *He was a typical British Council smoothie, with a fatuous grin and an ingratiating manner*—James Kirkup, 1991.

inherent is pronounced with the second syllable as in either *heron* or *here*, with a preference for the first of these.

inheritor, meaning 'a person who inherits', is spelt *-or*, not *-er*. It can be used of both a man and a woman.

inhuman, inhumane. The difference in meaning between these two words corresponds to that between *human* and *humane* (see HUMAN, HUMANE). *Inhuman* means 'lacking the qualities proper to human behaviour; cruel, brutal', whereas *inhumane* denotes a lack of feeling or compassion as it affects treatment of other people. Both words can be used of people, actions, or attitudes. Examples: (inhuman) *The West German branch of Amnesty International . . . called for an investigation into . . . inhuman torture of political prisoners*—*Athens News*, 1973 | *Claudia could see that locking up a Masai for a crime he did not* *understand was cruel and inhuman*—J. Cartwright, 1993 / (inhumane) *They have, after all, been traditionally concerned with restricting the use of weapons which are considered indiscriminate or inhumane*—J. Dewar et al., 1986 / *He was by no means an inhumane individual; he was a loving father, he was faithful to his wife for many years and to his mistress until death*—E. Acton, 1992.

initial, as a verb meaning 'to mark or sign with one's initials', has inflected forms *initialled, initialling* in BrE and *initialed, initialing* in AmE.

initialisms see ABBREVIATIONS 3.

initiate, meaning 'to instruct (a person) in some piece of knowledge', has the person as object and not the item of knowledge. You can *initiate* someone *in* something but you cannot *initiate* something *into* someone. The correct word for the second construction is *instil*.

-in-law is added to the name of a relation to denote relationship by marriage (*mother-in-law, son-in-law*, etc.). Plurals are formed by adding -s to the main element, e.g. *mothers-in-law. In-laws* is used colloquially to refer to such relations generally; it is only idiomatic in the plural.

innings. In cricket, *innings* is both singular (*the first innings*) and plural (*the best of his three innings*). In AmE, the word used in baseball has a singular form *inning* and a plural form *innings*.

innuendo, meaning 'an indirectly disparaging hint or remark', has the plural form *innuendoes*. The word is derived from a Latin gerund (verbal noun) meaning 'by

nodding at', i.e. 'by pointing to, by meaning'. In English it was originally used in legal contexts to introduce an explanatory aside or comment, rather like *i.e.*, meaning 'that is to say'; then it came to be used as a noun denoting the aside itself, from which the current meaning developed.

innumerate see ILLITERATE.

inoculate, meaning 'to inject with a vaccine', is spelt with one *n*. See also VACCINATE.

in order for. This allows a looser construction than IN ORDER THAT and avoids attendant problems with the mood and type of the following verb: *In order for this to work, the change from symmetry to broken symmetry must have taken place very slowly inside the bubble*— Stephen Hawking, 1988. This construction should be distinguished from the expression in order meaning 'acceptable, allowable as a procedure', which can be followed by *for: Is it in order for us to ring up your father and ask him to dine?*—Ngaio Marsh, 1977.

in order that. 1 Historically, *in order that* has been rather more restricted in terms of the grammatical construction that follows than has the rather less formal alternative *so that*. Fowler, writing in 1926, regarded use of the subjunctive (*in order that nothing be forgotten*) as archaic, use of the modal verbs *may* and *might* as the regular construction (*in order that nothing might be forgotten*), the use of *shall* and *should* as permissible in some contexts (*in order that nothing should be forgotten*), and the use of *can, could, will*, and *would* as 'undoubtedly wrong' (*in order that nothing can be forgotten | in order that nothing would be forgotten | etc.*). It is doubtful whether Fowler was correct in terms of usage even in his own day. Today, with electronic language data available to check our intuitions about language, the facts are (1) that the subjunctive is increasingly used and is therefore by no means archaic, and (2) the modal verbs, including *can* and *could*, *shall* and *should* (though rarely *will* and *would*), as well as *may* and *might*, are freely used when the context calls for them, although the *could*, *should*, and *would* forms are more common in each pair, and (3) that in order to avoid these problems many people are resorting to the alternative *in order for . . . to . . .* (see 4 below).

2 Examples of usage over the last sixty years or so will put the grammatical range in perspective:

(may, might) *Stabilisation of wages is an urgent necessity in order that the industry might enjoy continued peace—World's Paper Trade Review*, 1922 | *A suitable block-and-tackle is essential in order that the boat may be hauled far enough up the shore to be safe from 'rafting' ice—Discovery*, 1935 | *The cutting of benefits to mothers who do not give the names of their children's father . . . in order that they may be made financially accountable—Rouge*, 1990 | *He always insisted upon a certain reserve in order that the artist might give 'full measure' on the stage—Dancing Times*, 1990.

(can, could) *The motor should be wound up fully for each record played, in order that the turntable can rotate at its normal and even speed—P. A. Scholes*, 1921 | *The Telematics Programme . . . looks at users' needs and requirements in order that entire networks can talk to each other ready for 1992—Practical Computing*, 1990 | *In order that the oligomer could be deprotected easily, 'PAC amidites' were used in the synthesis—Nucleic Acids Research*, 1990.

(shall, should) *What factor . . . must be present in order that the implicate should be dependent in being on the implicans—D. J. B. Hawkins*, 1937 | *In order that he shall be said to make a moral judgement, his attitude must be 'universalisable'—A. E. Duncan-Jones*, 1952.

(do) *I can only hope that such methodology will be adopted by teachers new to media work in order that learning about the media does not become a bookcover here and a story-board there with little attempt at a coherent conceptual context—Times Educational Supplement*, 1990.

(subjunctive) *It is necessary to overcome this stability in order that a chemical reaction take place—Chemical Reviews*, 1952 | *In order that he be regularly scared by Authority, he should present himself every six months to the Service's Legal Adviser—J. Le Carré*, 1989.

3 Use of the subjunctive is often awkward in negative constructions because the modal verb *do* is not available, but negative examples are found: *Paulin vacillates in his claims in order that he not have to meet the responsibilities of arguing any of them out—London Review of Books*, 1990. This use is regular in AmE.

4 When the subject of the purpose clause is the same as that of the main clause, the alternative and simpler expression *in order to* is available (see IN ORDER TO). When it is not the same (as in most of the examples given above), the looser construction *in order for . . . to . . .* has become much more common (see IN ORDER FOR).

in order to. This expression of purpose, which is in origin a complex preposition, has been in use since the 16c. In current use it is formed with a *to*-infinitive to mean 'with the purpose of (doing), with a view to': *Rozanov . . . had taken a sharp right-hand turn in order to avoid going along the road*—Iris Murdoch, 1983 | *The SDP . . . wants to reform the unions in order to bring them back in*— *Times*, 1986. Use of the simpler preposition *to* instead of *in order to* is often preferred when the rhythm and emphasis of the sentence allow it, and this is sometimes less formal in effect: *The path takes an unscheduled turn to miss a big tree*—C. K. Stead, 1986 | *We both came here to get other people out of trouble*—Anita Brookner, 1986. The presence of a different kind of *to*-infinitive in the vicinity (as in the 1986 *Times* example) may sometimes be a factor in preferring the longer form *in order to*.

input, now pronounced with the stress on the first syllable both as a noun and as a verb, has defied the linguistic obsolescence that might have been apparent to the *OED* editors and assumed a new life in the domains of statistics, psychology, electronics, and (especially, since the late 1940s) computing. In all these, the essential meaning is (for the noun) 'information or data put into a system' and (for the verb) 'to enter (information or data) in a system'. The past and past participle forms of the verb are either *input* or *inputted*, and the present participle is *inputting*.

inquire, inquiry see ENQUIRE.

insanitary, unsanitary. *Insanitary* is more usual word in BrE and means 'not sanitary' in the sense 'dirty, unhealthy'; both

forms are used in this meaning in AmE. Fowler (1926) proposed a more neutral meaning for un-sanitary, i.e. 'lacking and not needing provision for sanitation' without implications for health.

inside of, meaning 'in less than (a period of time)' as in *It'll be finished inside of three days*, is a colloquial expression first recorded in AmE in the 1830s. It has made its way into other varieties of English, and is now heard informally in BrE, though its Americanness is still apparent. A related though now dated expression found in BrE is *for the inside of*, which has the somewhat different meaning 'for the most part of': *At first Isabel had only meant to stay away for the inside of a week*— L. P. Hartley, 1955.

insidious, invidious. Since both words involve doing or threatening harm, their closeness of form causes them to be commonly confused. *Insidious* (from Latin *insidiae* 'ambush') means 'proceeding inconspicuously but harmfully' (*An insidious form of sexism pervades most biographies of famous women, a tendency to treat women's work as peripheral to their lives*—Ms, 1973), whereas *invidious* (from Latin *invidia* 'envy') means 'likely to excite resentment or indignation' (*I hope it is not invidious . . . to single out here the museums for mention*— *Oxford University Gazette*, 1984). So *insidious* has more to do with the process and *invidious* more to do with its effect.

insightful, meaning 'showing insight or understanding', is first recorded in a work by John Galsworthy in 1907. Since then it has become an omnipresent word of catch-all praise in many kinds of writing in which the writer, one may suppose, has no precise idea of the compliment he or she is paying: *She created a film which was memorable, intriguing and moving, a warm and insightful reconstruction of a vanished age—Listener*, 1982 | *It was a wonderful insightful exhibition—Modern Painters*, 1988. The problem with this overused word is that it depends so heavily on *insight*, which fails to support it with any corresponding force of meaning.

insignia, meaning 'badges or distinguishing marks of office', is in origin a plural of Latin *insigne*, although this form is rarely used in English. *Insignia* may be used either as a plural noun or as a singular (mass) noun, e.g. either *Their insignia were worn on their coats* or *Their insignia was worn on their coats*. It should not be used as a countable noun, i.e. preceded by *an* or used in the plural: ⊠ *They wore an insignia on their coats* | ⊠ *They wore insignias on their coats.*

insist takes several constructions in current English in the meaning 'to assert as a demand': you can *insist on* something (or *on doing* something), you can *insist that* something *be* done (subjunctive, with *that* optionally omitted, or with *should* as an alternative), or you can simply *insist* (with no complement). Examples: *Tony insisted that she accompany him to a meeting of the Literary Society—*A. S. Byatt, 1985 | *And I, maliciously, insisted he take the most comfortable chair—Penelope Lively*, 1987 | *Henry had not wanted to bring Louisa on the expedition but she had cried to go, and the adults insisted that she not be left behind—L. Clarke*, 1989 | *The family received me very warmly and Signora Ugolotti insisted that I should have something to eat—W.*

Newby, 1991. When *insist* means 'assert as a fact or truth', it is followed by a *that*-clause with an ordinary indicative (i.e. not subjunctive) verb: *The girls insist that it is their fundamental right to wear their scarves at all times—Guardian*, 1989.

in so far as, meaning 'to the extent that', should be written as four words, although it is also found in the form *insofar as* and occasionally *in-so-far as*; but in all forms the *as* is detached: *Enforcement, insofar as salaries are concerned, is costing nothing—Times*, 1969 | *The exercise of reviewing his life was proving monstrous in so far as it revealed the places in which it had gone irredeemably wrong—Anita Brookner*, 1988. It is a rather formal phrase, and can often be replaced by *as far as* or recast with little loss of meaning in a simpler construction with *since* or *because* (as in the 1988 example just given).

insoluble, unsolvable. *Insoluble* relates to the meanings of *dissolve* as well as *solve*, and therefore refers to difficulties, questions, and problems that cannot be answered as well as to substances that cannot be absorbed in liquid. *Unsolvable* is more limited in range, corresponding only to the first of these meanings.

inspector is spelt -*or*, not -*er*.

install is spelt with two *l*s and has inflected forms *installed*, *installing*. The noun is *instalment* in BrE and *installment* in AmE.

instantly, instantaneously. *Instantly* means 'immediately' and refers to the point at which something happens, whereas *instantaneously* means 'in an instant' and refers to the (imperceptibly

short) period of time that something takes: *He pressed the override
switch and the computer came in-
stantly to life*—A. Haig, 1974 | *Her
throat had been slashed viciously,
and she must have died almost
instantaneously*—R. Long, 1990. The
result can often be the same, but
the difference of emphasis is
worth bearing in mind.

instigate properly means 'to
bring about by excitement or persuasion, to foment or provoke',
and usually refers to an antisocial
or discreditable action: . . . *a radical association that . . . instigated
campus riots that succeeded in clos-
ing down a number of universities
over a period of months in 1969*—
New Yorker, 1975 Because of its
similarity of form to *institute*, it is
sometimes wrongly used in the
neutral meaning 'to start, set up':
*Departments . . . should ensure that
all staff are made aware of their obligations under the legislations, and
instigate appropriate actions to ensure compliance*—UK Treasury circular, 1991. With so many synonyms
available, *instigate* is best restricted to its traditional role.

instil is spelt with one *l* in BrE
and as *instill* in AmE. The inflected forms are *instilled, instilling*
in both varieties. The non-
physical meaning is 'to introduce
(a feeling, idea, etc.) into a person's mind': *They believed, quite
wrongly, that to instil a sense of guilt
into me would ultimately be for my
good*—R. Hitchcock, 1989. It should
not be used with the person as
object, tempting though this
sometimes is in passive use:
⊠ *During the war my mother and
brother and I went to Norfolk, and
there I was instilled with a love of the
countryside – Sunday Express*, 1986.
In this construction, the alterna-

tives *imbue, infuse*, and *inspire* are
available. See INFUSE.

instinct see INTUITION.

instinctive, instinctual. The
normal adjective from *instinct* in
everyday use is *instinctive*, which
can refer to people and animals
or to their behaviour and actions.
Instinctual is used mainly in technical contexts such as psychology
and psycholinguistics, and is
modelled on other forms such as
conceptual and *habitual*, which
seem to afford it an extra authority not shared by the more generalized word *instinctive*.

institute, institution. Both
words are used with reference to
organizations and societies set up
to pursue some specific literary,
scientific, legal, or social purpose,
and choice usually depends on
the form already used for a particular name. The earliest *institute*
mentioned in the *OED* is the *Mech-
anics' Institute* (established in
1823), and the earliest institution
is the *Royal Masonic Benevolent Institution* (founded in 1798). Famous recent examples include the
Women's Institute (first established
in Canada in 1897 and then extended to other countries in the
early 20c) and the *British Standards Institution* (the UK national
body on standards, established in
the 20c). In the generalized meaning 'something established by law
or custom', as applied for example in the UK to the monarchy, the Grand National, the
last night of the Proms, etc.,
(though no longer to capital punishment and the Workhouse,
which featured in Fowler's 1926
list), *institution* is the only word
used.

instructor is spelt *-or*, not *-er*.

insubstantial has ousted *unsubstantial* for the word meaning 'lacking substance or solidity'.

insufficient is a useful word because *enough* has no corresponding negative form, but *not enough* is often more natural and usually less formal-sounding. Another alternative in some contexts is *inadequate*, which can refer to quantity as well as quality.

insupportable, unsupportable see IN- AND UN-.

insurance see ASSURE, ASSURANCE.

insure see ASSURE, ENSURE.

intaglio, an originally Italian word meaning 'an engraved design or gem', is pronounced in-**tah**-li-oh or in-**tal**-yoh and has the plural form *intaglios*.

integral is both a noun (used in mathematics) and an adjective (meaning 'forming a whole' or 'necessary to the completeness of a whole'). As a noun it is pronounced with the stress on the first syllable; as an adjective it may be pronounced with the stress on the first or the second syllable, although the first is often preferred.

integrate essentially means 'to make whole' and is widely used of bringing separate or disparate elements together to form a unity. Since the late 1940s it has been used to refer to the social absorption of distinct groups, especially ethnically or culturally different peoples or disadvantaged elements. In this meaning it is used both transitively (with an object) and (less often) intransitively: *Those children who came knowing some English integrated well—New Statesman*, 1966 |

Old people, sick people and isolated people need access to a telephone if they are to be fully integrated with the rest of society—Nature, 1972 | *From these beginnings developed the startling and revolutionary notion that in residential areas traffic and people should not be segregated but instead should be integrated—R. Rolley*, 1990. The noun *integration* has developed a corresponding meaning, and those who favour it are known as *integrationists: In the work of black authors who are integrationists a tacitly separatist or ethnically independent element appears frequently—Black Scholar*, 1971.

intelligent, intellectual. As adjectives, these words both refer to the capacity of people to think. A person is *intelligent* who has quick understanding and an ability to apply thought processes effectively. (It is sometimes contrasted with *clever*, which is more concerned with the manipulation of thought for its own sake than with its useful application.) A person is *intellectual* (or *an intellectual*, for it is also a noun) who thinks and acts predominantly to serve the pursuit of knowledge and the appreciation of fine things in literature and the arts, and is less concerned with the mundane and material aspects of life. However, the notion of the intellectual unable to slice bread or drive a car has to be regarded as a somewhat dated (or never valid) stereotype.

intelligentsia is a singular noun meaning 'the class of intellectuals regarded as possessing culture and political initiative'. The form of the word is Russian, and it was originally applied disparagingly in pre-revolutionary Russia. In a weakened sense, it also means 'people doing intellectual work'.

intend. **1** *Intend* is followed in standard usage by a *to*-infinitive (*We intend to go* | *We intended you to go*), by a verbal noun (*We intend going*), or by a *that*-clause (*We intended that you should go*). In the passive, it is followed by *for* in the meaning 'be meant or designed for' (*These are intended for children*). Non-standard constructions include the type ☒ *He didn't intend for Wales to lose*, which should be expressed as *He didn't intend that Wales should lose*, and the informal AmE type *Don't pick up a magazine unless you intend on buying it*, which should be expressed as *Don't pick up a magazine unless you intend buying* [*or intend to buy*] *it*.

2 The participial form *intended*, meaning 'the person one intends to marry', now sounds a dated and precious genteelism. It may be too late for a natural word to emerge (*fiancé(e)* is an overt loanword, *lover* is too explicit and may not always be appropriate, and *friend* is a patent evasion) now that social attitudes have broadened the terminological base well beyond the conventions of marriage.

intense, intensive. In the broad meaning 'existing in a high degree, extreme' as applied to feelings and qualities, *intense* is the word to use. (It also applies to people, in the sense 'apt to feel strong emotion'.) *Intensive*, which used to share aspects of the non-personal meaning of *intense*, is now reserved for the special meaning 'directed to a single point or objective, thorough, vigorous': *The country has suffered from intensive over-planning—Times, 1977.* Special applications include the

terms *intensive care* (of medical treatment, in this form from the 1960s) and *labour-intensive* ('needing a large workforce', 1950s).

intensifier in grammar is a class of adverbs that amplify or add emphasis to a gradable adjective (i.e. an adjective with a meaning capable of a range of force), such as *extremely, greatly, highly,* and *very.* Some adjectives are also classed as intensifiers, for example *complete* as in *a **complete** fool, single* as in *not a **single** word, sure* as in *a **sure** sign,* and *whole* as in *a **whole** month.*

intensive see INTENSE. It is also an older term for INTENSIFIER.

intention is followed either by *of* + verbal noun or by a *to*-infinitive, the first of these being somewhat more common and the second influenced by the verb *intend: I have no intention—no present intention—of standing for Parliament*—Harold Macmillan, 1979 | *He went to Cambridge to read Natural Science, with the intention of becoming a geologist*—H. Carpenter, 1981 | *He has given notice of his intention to turn up this evening*—Kingsley Amis, 1980 | *It was probably all the worry over his unfeeling attitude, his intention to evict her, that had rekindled the dream in the first place*—A. Murray, 1993.

inter, intern. *Inter* (with the stress on the second syllable) means 'to bury (a corpse)' and has inflected forms *interred, interring.* *Intern* means 'to arrest and confine (an alien) in time of war'. See also INTERMENT, INTERNMENT.

inter-, intra-. *Inter-* is a combining form meaning 'between, among' (*intercity* | *interlinear*) or 'mutually, reciprocally' (*interbreed*

| *intermix*), whereas *intra-* forms adjectives and means 'on the inside, within' (*intramural* | *intravenous*).

inter alia is Latin for 'among other things'. Since *alia* is neuter plural it does not normally refer to people. The Latin equivalent would be *inter alios*, but this is never used. The English alternative *among others* does not have this restriction and is preferable in general use.

interceptor, meaning 'a person or thing (especially an aircraft) that intercepts', is spelt *-or*, not *-er*.

interchange is pronounced with the stress on the first syllable as a noun and with the stress on the third syllable as a verb.

interchangeable is spelt with an *e* in the middle to preserve the soft sound of the *g*.

intercourse. The use of this word as short for *sexual intercourse* (first recorded in 1798 but not common before the 20c) has made it difficult to use it in its general meaning 'communication or dealings between individuals, nations, etc.', and a sentence such as the following from Elphinstone's *History of India* (1841) might now be subject to misunderstanding: *The intercourse between those princes was highly characteristic of Asiatic despots.* Even the phrase *social intercourse*, unambiguous though it is in print, can cause uncertainty when heard in the run of ordinary conversation.

interdependence, interdependency. Both forms are in use with no difference in meaning, but *interdependence* is more common.

interest is now normally pronounced **in**-trist or **in**-trest, with the first *e* unpronounced. The same applies to the derivative words *interested, interesting*, etc.

interestingly is recorded as a SENTENCE ADVERB from the 1960s, and is now common: *Interestingly, what exercises Lord Chalfont is not the existence of nuclear weapons, an existence which, he says, cannot be repealed*—Martin Amis, 1987.

interface. The use of this word was transformed between the publication of the original *OED* entry in 1901 and that of the updated entry in *OED2* in 1989. To the earlier editors it meant simply 'a surface lying between two portions of matter or space, and forming their common boundary'. In the 1960s, two disciplines adopted it for their own special use and effectively rivalled each other in their efforts to propel it into vogue use: the computer industry and that special branch of sociology known as communications theory, represented especially by the Canadian critic and theorist Marshall MacLuhan (*The Gutenberg Galaxy*, 1962). Now, an *interface* was, on the one hand, 'an apparatus designed to connect two scientific instruments, devices, etc., so that they can be operated jointly' and, on the other, 'a point where interaction occurs between two systems, processes, subjects, etc'. Its vogue status was assured when it was applied ever more widely to the relations between business development and marketing systems, lecturers and students, unions and management, and other areas of public life: *The issue of insanity as a defense in criminal cases . . . is at the interface of medicine, law and ethics*—*Scientific American,*

1972. McLuhan was also responsible for the first use of *interface* as a verb, meaning 'to come into interaction with', first recorded in 1967, and a corresponding use in computing soon followed. There are signs that the onslaught from this word has abated somewhat in the 1990s, leaving it to be used more effectively in technical domains. This is fortunate, when more familiar (and usually more precise) alternatives, such as (for the noun) *boundary, contact, link, liaison, meeting point, interaction*, and (for the verb) *communicate, have contact with, interact*, are readily available to cater for the general meanings.

interior, internal. The differences in meaning and usage between these two words correspond to those between *exterior* and *external* (see EXTERIOR, EXTERNAL). *Interior* is a noun as well as an adjective and refers in physical senses to the inside of things in contrast to the outside, whereas *internal* is primarily an adjective and is also applied in abstract or figurative meanings: *The courageous, determined and almost unique efforts of former Police Commissioner C.S. to root out internal graft backfired—Hongkong Standard*, 1977 | *Politicisation of religion means the internal transformation of the faith itself—Listener*, 1978. With reference to the body, *internal injuries* are those sustained by the inside organs, and medicine for *internal use* is meant to be swallowed. The word is also used occasionally as a noun in the plural to mean 'intrinsic qualities' and in various technical applications.

interlocutor, meaning 'a person who takes part in a dialogue or conversation', is spelt *-or*, not *-er*,

and is pronounced with the stress on the third syllable.

interment, internment. *Interment* means 'the burial of a corpse', whereas *internment* means 'the confinement of aliens in time of war'. See also INTER, INTERN.

intermezzo, as used in the contexts of music and drama, has the plural form *intermezzos*.

intermission, meaning 'an interval between parts of a play, film, etc.', is American in origin but is now as widely used in BrE as the traditional word *interval*.

intermittent, meaning 'occurring at intervals', is spelt *-ent*.

in terms of. *When John Major emerged as a possible candidate to lead the Conservative party, one was struck by his engaging artlessness in terms of class—Daily Telegraph*, 1991. The Oxford philosopher Michael Dummett (1993) awarded this complex preposition the distinction of being 'the lowest point so far in the present degradation of the English language', when used as an all-purpose connector as in the example just given. Extreme though this opinion may be, the use it condemns is a far departure from the original (18c) use of the phrase as an expression of a precise mathematical relation. In its now predominant generalized use, *in terms of* should state a particular specifying relation: *The impact of Ibsen . . . did much to revitalize the degenerate English theatre and force it to think in terms of living ideas and contemporary realities—J. Mulgan & D. M. Davin*, 1947 | *Justifying space in terms of material wealth is as ridiculous as saying that man went to the Moon* *merely to be able to return with vel-cro zips and non-stick frying-pans*—New Scientist, 1991. When the meaning intended is as vague as 'in relation to', 'concerning', or even 'of' (as in the example given at the beginning), these expressions are preferable.

intern is pronounced with the stress on the second syllable as a verb (see INTER) and with the stress on the first syllable as a noun (also spelt *interne*, meaning 'a recent graduate in medicine' or 'a person working as an apprentice in one of the professions', principally American use).

international community. This expression has found favour in recent years with politicians and journalists, and one can see why. It is a convenient catch-all phrase invoked when international support for a policy or action is needed (or, more often, assumed), much as 'public opinion' is invoked in domestic politics. In neither case is any specific attribution or verification possible; yet both empty phrases sound impressive. The earliest evidence in the *OED* dates from the late 1950s and shows the expression to have originated in legal language: *Could the papacy . . . be properly regarded as a member of the international community of the law of nations?*—R. A. Graham, 1959. Recent examples : *Pretoria sees the Eminent Persons Group as a useful channel of communication with the ANC and the international community*—Financial Times, 1986 | *The way in which Saddam Hussein still behaves is unacceptable to us, to the United Nations and to the international community, and we shall continue to keep pressure on him*—Hansard, 1992.

internecine. Dr Johnson had a hand in changing the use of this

word, which its Latin origin shows to mean 'characterized by great slaughter'. He mistakenly understood the prefix *inter-* to denote reciprocal or mutual action and defined *internecine* as 'endeavouring mutual destruction', thereby setting the word on the way to its primary current meaning. Despite the objections of the more fervent purists, who invoke the word's pre-Johnsonian credentials, it is used in its later meaning with reference to physical war and killing and has developed an extended or trivialized meaning applied to the battles of the boardroom and other areas of business and public life: *The electorate . . . finally gagged on their traditional roughage of internecine strife*—Times, 1974 | *He was on edge, engaged in flaming rows, head-blasting music mayhem and internecine squabbling with his garage band compadres Crazy Horse*—New Musical Express, 1991.

Internet has a capital *I*.

internment see INTERMENT.

interpersonal, once the preserve of psychologists, has crept into the language of the curriculum vitae, in which no applicant's credentials are adequate without an endorsement of his or her *interpersonal skills*, i.e. the ability to deal effectively with other people. It is also widely used by sociologists to refer to the ways in which people treat each other in everyday life: *The social workers in their study appeared to be more aware than the psychiatrists of the relevance of interpersonal and family problems*—K. Hawton et al., 1990.

interpretative, interpretive. The preferred form for this word meaning 'serving to interpret or explain' is *interpretative*, on the analogy of *authoritative*, *qualitative*, and *quantitative*: *You may be wondering why I am rabbiting on about interpretative processes when the theme of this article is how to build a bracket clock—Practical Woodworking*, 1990. However, *interpretive* is also found, perhaps reinforced by the tendency to articulate both words in this way in rapid speech: *Chinese culture has undergone major interpretive phases in recent decades—Dædalus*, 1991.

interregnum, meaning 'an interval when normal government is suspended', has the plural form *interregnums*.

intestinal, meaning 'relating to the intestines', is pronounced with the stress on the second syllable (in-**tes**-ti-nəl, preferably) or on the third syllable (in-tes-**tiy**-nəl, increasingly in BrE).

in that, which is difficult to analyse grammatically, is effectively a conjunction, but it is not easy to find in dictionaries. Shakespeare used it: *Let him die, in that he is a Fox—2 Henry VI* iii.i.257. Fowler (1926) regarded it as obsolescent (becoming obsolete) and warned against the misuse that idiomatic expressions are liable to on their way out of the language. But Fowler's judgement was at fault, and the examples he gave were not typical of usage, and so he was tilting at windmills. The expression still has a place at the core of everyday usage and means rather more than is conveyed by *because*: *They work like disks in that they can be partially erased—Management Computing*, 1990 | *The vessels . . . are unusual in that they have no engine room—Ships Monthly*, 1991.

in the circumstances see CIR-CUMSTANCE.

into, in to. 1 *Into* is written as one word when the meaning is unified in expressing motion towards or to within a destination (*He walked into a tree | She put her hand into his*). However, when *in* and *to* retain their separate roles, it is important to write them as separate words, usually when *to* is not connected with *in* but is part of a following *to*-infinitive or refers forward to a noun or phrase: *People dropped in to see them | He accompanied her in to dinner | They were listening in to our conversation.*

2 The recent (1960s) use of *into* meaning 'involved in or knowledgeable about' (usually as a transitory interest), is informal only: *First I was into Zen, then I was into peace, then I was into love, then I was into freedom, then I was into religion. Now I'm into money—New Yorker*, 1971.

intra- see INTER-.

intransitive and transitive verbs. A verb is transitive when it 'takes an object', i.e. it has a following word or phrase which the action of the verb affects (*They **lit** a fire*), and is intransitive when it does not take an object (*We **arrived** at noon*). Some verbs are always or predominantly transitive (*assure, bury, deny, put*); others are always or predominantly intransitive (especially verbs of motion such as *arrive, come, go*, etc.); and others are sometimes transitive and sometimes intransitive (for example, *move* is transitive in the sentence *Go and **move** the car* and intransitive in the sentence *The car **moved** down the road*, and *cook* is respectively intransitive and transitive in the sentences *I like to cook* and *I'm going to cook the breakfast*). Some verbs appear to have two objects, which in traditional grammar are called *direct* and *indirect*: in the sentence *They **gave** her an apple*, *apple* is the direct object (= what they gave) and *her* is the indirect object (= the person who got the apple). See also DIRECT OBJECT, DITRANSITIVE, INDIRECT OBJECT.

intransitive past participles.
Most past participles are of transitive verbs and, when used as adjectives, denote an action performed on the noun or phrase they qualify; for example, the phrase *a **polished** table* denotes the state of the table as having been polished. However, some verbs that are intransitive nonetheless form past participles which are used as adjectives, as in *an **escaped** prisoner* (= a prisoner who has escaped), *a **failed** writer* (= a writer who has failed), ***fallen** leaves* (= leaves that have fallen), and *a **grown** man* (= a man who has grown up, *not* a man who has been grown). In these cases the nouns or phrases they qualify are the subjects rather than the objects of the corresponding verbs. See PARTICIPLES.

intrigue *verb*. 1 The inflected
forms are *intrigued, intriguing*.

2 The predominant current meaning is 'to arouse the curiosity of; to fascinate'. When Fowler wrote (1926) this was a fairly new sense (first attested in the 1890s) and the need for what he regarded as an affected Gallicism puzzled him when an apparent wealth of synonyms, including *fascinate, mystify, interest,* and *puzzle, perplex* (he could also have mentioned *absorb, captivate, enchant,* and *enthral*), was already available. But none of these has

quite the same element of the mildly sinister or elusive that *intrigue* draws from its other meanings, past and present (principally the still current one 'to carry on an underhand plot'). Like some of the synonyms mentioned, *intrigue* is commonly used in its participial form *intriguing*. Examples: *Even more intriguing than the sociology of fashion is its psychology*—Observer, 1974 | *We are in turn sympathetic, intrigued, shocked, entertained—but oh the yearning for the world she magically conjured*—A. Huth, 1992.

intrinsic means 'inherent, essen-
tial, belonging naturally' and is the opposite of *extrinsic*: *The study of portraits on coins is . . . as much about the political factors that influenced them as about their intrinsic or moral interest*—A. Burnett, 1991. See EXTERIOR 2. The corresponding adverb is *intrinsically*.

intrusive r is the insertion of
the sound of an unwritten *r* between one vowel sound and another, as in *draw-r-ing* for *drawing* and *umbrella-r-organization* for *umbrella organization*. Though much criticized, it is common even in received pronunciation and follows the pattern of linking *r* in words ending in an *r* that is only sounded when a vowel follows, as in *far away* (see LINKING R).

intuit, an 18c back-formation
from *intuition*, means 'to know or deduce intuitively', and is a mainly literary or technical word: *Maud decided she intuited something terrible about Cropper's imagination from all this*—A. S. Byatt, 1990.

intuition, instinct. The two
words overlap in meaning, and the *OED* indeed uses *intuition* in one of its definitions of *instinct*.

Both refer to intellectual activity and both denote processes in which knowledge is apprehended without using any process of reasoning. An important difference, however, is that *intuition* is confined to humans whereas *instinct* is attributable to the animal world at large. In extended meanings, *intuition* means 'immediate insight' into a fact or feeling (as in the notorious phrase *a woman's intuition*), and *instinct* means 'unconscious skill' (*an instinct for getting the best deal*); these meanings too refuse to stay apart. Examples: (intuition) *A student's intuition moves far more swiftly than can an instruction manual, and I believe that self-tuition is the finest form of education*—R. Brindle Smith, 1986 | *Whatever that small voice of intuition was telling her about her destiny, common-sense decreed that the Prince already had a full hand of potential suitors*—A. Morton, 1993 | (instinct) *Blythswood Square, once home of the infamous poisoner Madaleine Smith, and latterly, numerous other ladies with hearts of loose change and the instincts of a blushing tarantula*—E. Chisnall, 1989 | *Running out was totally unprofessional, but she had acted purely on instinct*—J. Evans, 1993.

Inuit see ESKIMO.

invalid is pronounced with the stress on the second syllable as an adjective (meaning 'not valid') and with the stress on the first syllable as a noun (meaning 'a person affected by disease or injury').

inveigle. The recommended pronunciation of this verb meaning 'to entice or persuade by guile' is in-**vay**-gəl rather than the alternative in-**vee**-gəl.

inventor is spelt -*or*, not -*er*.

inventory, meaning 'an official list of goods etc.', is pronounced **in**-vən-tə-ri in BrE and **in**-vən-taw-ri in AmE.

inversion. In grammar, *inversion* is the process by which the normal order of words, with the subject followed by the verb and then by the object or complement (if any) as in *We play football on Saturdays* is broken by putting the subject after the verb (as in questions: *Do you play football on Saturdays?*) or by putting the complement (or part of it) first in the sentence, often for emphasis (*On Saturdays, we play football*). Other regular forms of inversion, usually requiring little conscious effort by native speakers, occur as follows:

1 In direct speech, the subject and the verb (*say, cry, shout,* etc.) that identify the spoken words are optionally inverted: *'Hey!' **shouted Mrs. House,** who sat inside with her jumpsuit around her knees*— New Yorker, 1992.

2 After negatives placed in initial position for emphasis, the subject and verb are routinely inverted: *Yet never before **had I seen** anything so scarlet and so black*— J. M. Coetzee, 1990.

3 After initially placed *so* followed by an adjective, the subject and verb are inverted: *He had hardly been aware, so nervous **was he,** of what he had been saying*— Peter Carey, 1988.

4 In a sentence in which a statement is followed by a reinforcing form of do: *She enjoyed a laugh, **did Lilian***—Margaret Drabble, 1987.

5 In declarations beginning with an adverb, when the subject of a following intransitive verb is a noun: *Here **comes the train*** but *Here **they come***.

6 In condition clauses with omission of *if* or *whether*: ***Were this done**, we would retain a separate Bar with skill*—*Times*, 1986 | *Statistically, afterworlds*—***be they** Christian, Greek, Pharaonic*—*must be populated almost entirely by children*—Penelope Lively, 1987.

7 In certain types of comparison involving a statement after *than*: *Poland's power structure included neither more nor fewer Jews than **did the power structure** in Rumania or in Hungary*—*Dædalus*, 1987.

8 Words are placed first for special effect in poetry and rhetorical writing: ***His soul** proud science never taught to stray*—Pope | ***Trusting** she had been, she who had been reared in the bosom of suspicion*—Margaret Drabble, 1987. This has spilled over into more informal usage, in which the effect is awkward rather than striking and should be avoided except in conversation: ***Great literature** it's not, but . . . it's short, pithy*—*The Face*, 1987.

inverted commas see QUOTATION MARKS.

investigator is spelt *-or*, not *-er*.

investor is spelt *-or*, not *-er*.

invincible, meaning 'that cannot be defeated', is spelt *-ible*, not *-able*. See -ABLE, -IBLE.

invisible is spelt *-ible*, not *-able*. See -ABLE, -IBLE.

invite *noun* (with the stress on the first syllable). This is a good example of a word that has been in more or less continuous use since the 17c but has not attained the acceptability afforded to its rival, *invitation*. Dr Johnson must have known it but did not include it in his Dictionary (1755), nor did Charles Richardson in 1863. It was admitted with a 'colloquial' label to the OED (1901) and its failure to gain respectability was noted by Fowler (1926), who commented that 'it is less recognized as an English word than *bike*'. Seventy years on, things have hardly changed, and the general consensus seems to be that as a noun *invite* belongs to the informal or even comic realms of language use: *The four detectives didn't await an invite into the house*—G. F. Newman, 1970 | *He scoffs, indicating the dodgier invites entreating his attendance at this or that launch*—*Sunday Express Magazine*, 1987 | *He knows a particularly good printer who did the invites for his cousin's wedding*—*Precision Marketing*, 1989.

involve. 1 This heavily used word has extended its meaning from the notion of envelopment or entanglement (it is derived from the Latin word *involvere* meaning 'to enwrap') to less precise forms of connection, as in *What does the work involve?* and *No other vehicle was involved* (in police descriptions of one-vehicle accidents). Resistance to this natural development in meaning belongs to the domain of LOST CAUSES.

2 The participial form *involving* used as a quasi-preposition is often better replaced by a simpler word: *A collision took place involving a private motor vehicle and a lorry* (use *between*) | *There was no reduction last year in the number of cases involving cruelty to horses* (use *of*).

inward, inwards. The only form for the adjective is *inward* (*the inward route*), but *inward* and *inwards* are both used for the adverb, with a preference for *in-wards* in BrE: *Our instructor starts us on snowplough turns (with the tips of the skis pointing inwards)—Observer*, 1978.

iodine, the chemical element and the antiseptic made from it, is pronounced either **iy**-ə-deen or **iy**-ə-din. In AmE it is also pronounced **iy**-ə-diyn.

-ion, -ment, -ness. These three suffixes are all used to form nouns; *-ion* and *-ment* represent Latin elements via Old French and are normally added to verbs to form nouns of action (*abridgement, excision*) or state (*contentment, vexation*), whereas *-ness* is an Old English form, is normally added to adjectives to form nouns of state (*bitterness, happiness*) or instances of a state or quality (*a kindness*), and is the most active suffix in forming new words. Regarding *-ion* and *-ment*, the choice is largely determined by the forms already existing in Old French, although some nouns were formed on existing English verbs (e.g. *acknowledgement, amazement, fulfilment*). Some verbs have given rise to more than one form, usually with a difference in meaning (e.g. *commission* and *commitment* from *commit, excitation* and *excitement* from *excite*).

Iranian is pronounced i-**ray**-ni-ən in BrE, and i-**ray**-ni-ən, i-**rah**-ni-ən, or iy-**ray**-ni-ən in AmE.

irascible, meaning 'irritable, hot-tempered', is spelt *-ible*, not *-able*. See -ABLE, -IBLE.

iridescent, meaning 'showing gleaming colours, rainbow-like', is spelt with one *r*, being derived from the Latin word *iris* (stem *irid-*) meaning 'rainbow'.

iron curtain. The phrase had its origin in the 18c with reference to a safety device lowered in theatres between the stage and the auditorium. Its figurative use referring to any impenetrable barrier evolved in the early 19c and it acquired its classic meaning in the 20c when used of the East-European sphere of influence exercised in the postwar years by the Soviet Union. The locus classicus (though not the first use, which was in 1920) was a speech given by Winston Churchill in the US in 1946: *From Stettin, in the Baltic, to Trieste, in the Adriatic, an iron curtain has descended across the Continent*. Although the term has developed various allusive uses (*I don't want the United States to appear like an 'Iron Curtain' to the Vietnamese—Freedomways*, 1967), the dismantling of the Berlin Wall in 1989 and the collapse of the Soviet Union has caused it to lose its potency except as a vivid historical reminder.

ironic, ironical, ironically. For the adjective, choice between *ironic* and *ironical* seems to be determined largely by sentence rhythm. Both words properly mean 'of the nature of irony', i.e. implying the opposite of what is literally or normally meant by a word, look, etc.: *She gave an ironical laugh as she looked at Guy—*Olivia Manning, 1977. In this sentence, *ironical* shows that the laugh was marking something other than the usual humour. Both words, however, are now increasingly used to mean simply 'odd, strange, paradoxical', and the same is true of the corresponding adverb *ironically*: *It is paradoxical, 'ironical' as people say today, that the constitution should bestow this power on someone who laments constitutionitis in others—*

Observer, 1987 | *It is ironic that such a beautiful orderly house should be the setting of our messy little farce*—S. Mason, 1990 | *Ironically the bombing of London was a blessing to the youthful generations that followed*—I. &. P. Opie, 1969 | *Ironically enough, the Israeli role in both remains crucial*—*Sanity*, 1991. These uses, which are surely established despite frequent criticism of them, perhaps contain an echo of the concept of *dramatic irony*, in which an audience is made aware of an act or circumstance that affects the action on stage (or screen) in a way that is unknown to one or more of the participants in the drama.

iron out is a common phrasal verb, American in origin and used informally to mean 'to remove (difficulties etc.)'. As the physical image is still fairly near the surface, it is prudent to avoid contexts that might sound incongruous. Gowers (1965) pointed out the absurdity of ironing out bottlenecks, and to this may be added the following from the computer age: *The new computer was delivered . . . last week. . . . Ironing out the bugs will probably take until the new year*—*Guardian*, 1971.

irony. In the ordinary use of language *irony* means primarily 'an expression of meaning by use of words that have an opposite literal meaning or tendency'. When we look out of the window at the pouring rain and exclaim 'What a lovely day!', we are using a trivial form of irony. Literary forms of irony include (1) *dramatic irony*, in which an audience is taken into the writer's confidence and is made aware of more than the participating characters know, and (2) so-called *Socratic irony* (after the Greek philosopher Soc-

rates, who used it), in which a participant in a discussion falsely purports to be ignorant of a matter in order to elicit a particular response from the other participants. A fuller historical account of irony in language will be found in the *Oxford Companion to the English Language* (1992), p. 532.

irreducible, meaning 'that cannot be reduced', is spelt *-ible*, not *-able*. See -ABLE, -IBLE.

irrefutable, meaning 'that cannot be refuted', should be pronounced with the stress on the second syllable, although pronunciation with stress on the third syllable is gaining ground.

irregardless is in origin probably a blend of *irrespective* and *regardless*. It is sometimes found in humorous contexts and is nonstandard.

irrelevance, irrelevancy. Both words are in use and there is no distinction in their meaning, but *irrelevance* is more common.

irreparable, irrepairable. *Irreparable*, meaning 'that cannot be recovered or made good', is pronounced with the stress on the second syllable, and is used of circumstances and relationships, typically qualifying words such as *consequences, loss, harm,* and *damage*. The word used to describe physical objects, machines, etc., that cannot be repaired is *irrepairable* (or *unrepairable, not repairable, beyond repair*), pronounced with the stress on the third syllable as in *repair*; but *irreparable damage* is the normal expression whether or not the damage is physical: *These people were supposed to be making us fit and instead they were doing irreparable damage to my heart and lungs*—

J. Herriott, 1977. | *The strikers had defied a decree . . . to end the strike, which he said was causing irreparable damage to the economy*—Keesings, 1990.

irreplaceable, meaning 'that cannot be replaced', is spelt *-able* and with an *e* in the middle to preserve the soft sound of the *c*. See -ABLE, -IBLE.

irrepressible, meaning 'that cannot be restrained', is spelt *-ible*, not *-able*. See -ABLE, -IBLE.

irresistible, meaning 'that cannot be resisted', is spelt *-ible*, not *-able*. See -ABLE, -IBLE.

irrespective of. This expression is variously regarded by grammarians as an adjective plus a preposition, an adverbial phrase (alternative to *irrespectively of*, which is also found though much less often), or a complex preposition. The difficulty of classification arises because of the detached way in which the expression is used, undermining the status of *irrespective* as an adjective: *People sometimes judge actions to be right irrespective of their consequences*—A. J. Ayer, 1972 | *The beginner in chess, who tries to follow his plans irrespective of his partner's countermoves, will soon go down in defeat*—Bruno Bettelheim, 1987.

irresponsible is spelt *-ible*, not *-able*. See -ABLE, -IBLE.

irreversible, meaning 'that cannot be changed or undone', is spelt *-ible*, not *-able*. See -ABLE, -IBLE.

irrevocable, meaning 'that cannot be changed or recalled', is pronounced with the stress on the second syllable.

irridescent is an erroneous spelling of IRIDESCENT.

is. 1 For general points of usage see BE. Some common and interesting idiomatic uses of *is* are given here.

2 For *is* after a compound subject, as in *Fish and chips is my favourite meal*, see AGREEMENT 3. For problems of agreement between subject and complement when one is singular and the other is plural, as in *More nurses is the next item on the agenda*, see AGREEMENT 5.

3 . . . IS WHAT . . . OR . . . IS HOW . . . FOLLOWING A STATEMENT. *One never knows with these lefties, is what I always say*—A. Brink, 1988 | *You step up to him and you cart him all over the park, is what you do*—S. Fry, 1990. This use, as the contexts of these examples show, is highly informal.

4 IS NOTHING TO DO WITH. This construction, as an alternative to *has nothing to do with*, was defended by Fowler (1926) as the more natural choice in everyday speech 'when we . . . are not in the mood for weighing words in the scales of grammar', is found in the 19c (*This is nothing to do with your life*—H. S. Merriman, 1896), but is less common than the construction with *have* in current use to judge by the evidence in the British National Corpus and in the *OED*.

5 —IS —. *Let anyone repeat, as often as he pleases, that 'the will is the will'*—Locke, 1690 | *A man's a man for a' that*—Burns, 1790 | *Home is home though it is never so homely*—Charles Lamb, 1823. These older literary uses are echoed in 20c occurrences: *A job's a job, that was the thing*—Maurice Gee, 1985 | *She worried about Colin's wrist in the cast but a trip out was a trip out, and* the day mustn't be spoiled—N. Virtue, 1990. Occasionally the word is is repeated (echoing Gertrude Stein's *Rose is a rose is a rose is a rose, is a rose . . . —Sacred Emily*, 1913): *There is only one art form common to all sorts and conditions of people: the poster . . . A hoarding is a hoarding is a hoarding—Guardian*, 1970.

6 POSTPONED AND REPEATED IS. This somewhat informal use dates from the early 19c: *He's a sad pickle, is Sam!*—M. Mitford, 1828 | *Yes, he is true to type, is Mr Heard*—Ronald Knox, 1932.

7 . . . IS ALL. *No one's interested, is all*—M. Doane, 1988. This idiomatic expression, used for emphasis at the end of a sentence, sounds dialectal but is found in standard (especially American) works of fiction.

-ise as a verbal ending is sometimes optional as an alternative to *-ize* (*baptise, prioritise*) and is sometimes obligatory because of a word's origin (*advertise, compromise, exercise*). See more fully at -IZE.

island, isle. The two words are etymologically unconnected. *Island* is derived from an Old English word *īgland*, which is a combination of *īg* (itself meaning 'island') and *land*; *isle* is a reduced form of *insula*, the Latin word for 'island'.

-ism and -ity. These noun-forming suffixes are derived via Old French from the Latin noun endings *-ismus* and *-itas*. The suffix *-ism* forms nouns of action based on verbs or adjectives (*baptism, criticism, heroism*), and has a number of special meanings: (1) a political or religious movement or system of thought (*atheism, Buddhism, realism*), (2) a pathological condition (*alcoholism, Parkinson-*

ism), (3) a special feature or peculiarity of language (*Americanism, Gallicism*), (4) a basis of prejudice or discrimination (a 20c development first apparent in *racism*, and more recently in *sexism, ageism, speciesism*, etc.). The suffix *-ity* has the special role of forming abstract nouns from comparative forms (*inferiority, majority*) but in general has the more limited meaning 'a quality or condition, or an instance of it' (*authority, humility, purity*). Some words have produced nouns (with different meanings) in both *-ism* and *-ity* (*liberalism | liberality, modernism | modernity, realism | reality*, etc.).

issue *verb*. The use reflected in the sentences *They issued them with passports* and (perhaps more typically) *They were issued with passports* is military in origin and in its general application (on the analogy of *provide* and *supply*) was disapproved of by Fowler (1926). It has nonetheless become well established during the 20c, at least in BrE although it occurs less often in AmE (*People in Russia's second city . . . are issued with coupons which entitle them to basic foodstuffs at subsidized state prices—Chicago Tribune*, 1991).

-ist is a suffix forming nouns and adjectives corresponding to various kinds of noun in *-ism* (*atheist, Buddhist, evangelist, racist, sexist*), nouns denoting a person engaged in some activity or pursuit (*archaeologist, balloonist, cyclist, economist*). Some words have an alternative form in *-alist* (*agriculturalist | agriculturist, educationalist | educationist*) and in these cases both forms are correct.

italics. Italics are *a style of sloping type, like this*, and are used for a number of special purposes, principally:

TITLES OF BOOKS, FILMS, WORKS OF ART, ETC.: *David Copperfield, Gone with the Wind, Mona Lisa.*

TITLES OF LONG POEMS: *Paradise Lost.*

NAMES OF NEWSPAPERS ETC.: *Daily Express, Radio Times.*

NAMES OF SHIPS AND VEHICLES: *Ark Royal, Concorde.*

FOREIGN WORDS AND PHRASES: *amour propre, ne plus ultra* (see FOREIGN WORDS AND PHRASES).

FOR EMPHASIS: 'Oh, come on, it can't be *that* bad.'

For other uses see *Hart's Rules*, 23–8. In writing, italics are shown by underlining.

itch *verb. Itch* is recorded with the transitive meaning 'to cause to itch' from the 16c, but in BrE is now usually informal only, although it is still standard in AmE. Some examples are poetic: *The thick super-salty water of the Mediterranean, which tires and itches the naked eye*—R. Campbell, 1951 / *The dice already itch me in my pocket*—Louis MacNeice, 1951. Another transitive meaning, mainly down-market AmE, is 'to scratch (a part of the body)', as in *Don't itch your leg*—Chicago Tribune, 1991.

-ite. The adjectival ending is derived chiefly from Latin past participles in *-itus.* The length of the Latin *i* varied, but no longer directly influences the pronunciation in English (*definite* with short *i* and *recondite* with long *i* were not so in Latin, for example). The *-ite* in *anthracite, dynamite, Jacobite,* etc., is a different form, and is always pronounced with a long *i.*

it is I, it is me see CASES 2A.

itself see HERSELF.

its, it's. *Its* is the possessive form of *it* (*The cat licked its paws*) and *it's* is a shortened form of *it is* (*It's raining again*) or occasionally *it has* (*I don't know if it's come*).

-ize, -ise in verbs.
See box overleaf

-ize, -ise in verbs

1 SPELLING. The primary rule is that all words of the type *authorize/authorise, civilize/civilise, legalize/legalise*, where there is a choice of ending, may be legitimately spelt with either *-ize* or *-ise* throughout the English-speaking world (except in America, where *-ize* is always used). Oxford University Press and other publishing houses (including *The Times* until recently) prefer *-ize*; Cambridge University Press and others prefer *-ise*.

The reason there is a choice is that the *-ize* ending, which corresponds to the Greek verbal ending *-izo* (whether or not the particular verb existed in Greek in the same form), has come to English in many cases via Latin and French sources, and in French the spelling has been adapted to *-ise*. A key word showing the line of descent is *baptize*, which answers to Gk βαπτίζω and Latin *baptizo*; the French have opted for *baptiser*, and a large proportion of English writers and publishers have followed suit by writing the word as *baptise*. People are generally aware of the choice, but often mistakenly regard the *-ize* ending as an Americanism; and they find it especially hard to countenance in words which do not have corresponding nouns in *-ation* but other forms in which the letter *s* features, such as *criticize* (*criticism*), *hypnotize* (*hypnosis*), and *emphasize* (*emphasis*).

It is important to note that there are some words in which there is no choice: they have to be spelt with *-ise* because they come from words in which the relevant elements are *-cise*, *-mise*, *-prise*, *-vise*, or other forms unconnected with *-izo/-iso*. The most important of these words are given in the table below:

VERBS THAT MUST BE SPELT WITH -ISE

advertise	despise	improvise
advise	devise	incise
apprise	dis(en)franchise	merchandise
arise	disguise	prise (open)
chastise	enfranchise	revise
circumcise	enterprise	supervise
comprise	excise	surmise
compromise	exercise	surprise
demise	franchise	televise

The AmE spelling of *analyse, catalyse*, etc., as *analyze, catalyze*, etc., is also a separate matter: see -YSE, -YZE.

2 STATUS OF SUCH VERBS. The oldest English verb in *-ize* is *baptize* (13c), mentioned above. Other examples over the centuries are *authorize* (14c), *characterize* (16c), *civilize* (17c), *fossilize* (18c), and

▶

▶ -ize, -ise in verbs
continued

terrorize (19c). Apart from the spelling question, there is a widespread belief that there are too many new verbs of this kind. Objections have been raised to *finalize* and *prioritize* and (with more reason) *hospitalize* and *permanentize*. Forms not attested before 1950 include, in addition to those given in the table below, a whole lot of forms beginning with *re-* including *resensitize* and *retribalize*, and noun derivatives such as *institutionalization* and *privatization*. However, these words represent a small proportion of new words and meanings in English, even among verbs, and it is significant that fewer than ten words in *-ization* or *-ize* are entered in each of the two editions (1991 and 1997) of the *Oxford Dictionary of New Words*, out of a vocabulary total of 2000 items in each. There are many opportunities for ad hoc or nonce formations, and some examples are given in the table. All have their uses on occasions and will come and go as needed without becoming part of the permanent stock of language.

Words in -ize, -ization, or -izer recorded after 1950.
Nonce and ad hoc forms are marked with an asterisk

WORD	COMMENT OR SOURCE
annualize	
capsulize	
computerize	
condomize*	*Newsweek*, 1987
denuclearize	
disasterize*	
funeralize*	recorded as obsolete in the 17c and now revived
invisibleize*	Iris Murdoch, 1991
liquidizer	a machine
marketization*	
modularize	
operationalize	
peripheralization*	
privatize	
psychedelicize*	2 citations in the *OED*
rehospitalization*	
remobilize	
ruggedize	'to make rugged'
technologize	
texturize	
transistorize	common in the 50s and 60s

▶

▶ -ize, -ise in verbs
continued

WORD	COMMENT OR SOURCE
trivializer	a person
weaponization*	

3 VERDICT. English has always been highly productive in forming new verbs to represent actions and processes related to social and material developments. Many of these have used suffixes such as *-ize* and *-ify*. Some of the 20c newcomers will drop by the wayside; others will survive into the 21c and beyond, despite the occasional creasing of brows. Together they provide significant linguistic insights into social change.

Jj

jacket *verb*, meaning 'to cover with a jacket', has inflected forms *jacketed*, *jacketing*, with one *t*.

jail, jailer is now more common than *gaol*, *gaoler* in BrE and is the dominant spelling in AmE. It is the preferred spelling, except in historical contexts in which the *gaol*-forms might be more appropriate.

Jap, a colloquial shortening of *Japanese*, is used as a noun and adjective with strong derogatory overtones. It is less common now than it was in the postwar period, and there are signs that it is falling into disuse.

jargon. 1 HISTORY OF THE TERM. The *OED* gives several meanings for *jargon*, all except one mostly derogatory in connotation. The prevailing current senses of the word are (1) 'words or expressions used by a particular group or profession', and (2) 'incomprehensible talk, gibberish', with the second regarded as arising conceptually out of the first, although this is not how the meanings evolved historically. The exception just mentioned is the meaning 'the inarticulate utterance of birds', which is the oldest sense, is found in Chaucer, and as the *OED* notes 'has been revived in modern [i.e. 19c] literature', e.g. by Longfellow: *With beast and bird the forest rings, Each in his jargon cries or sings—Return of Spring* 6. Both meanings given above developed (apart from an isolated Middle English use of the second) in the 17c; there is a good ex-ample in the notice 'Bookseller to Reader' published with Swift's *Tale of a Tub* (1704): *If I should go about to tell the reader, by what accident I became master of these papers, it would, in this unbelieving age, pass for little more than the cant or jargon of the trade.*

2 JARGON IN THE RIGHT PLACE. Every profession and sphere of activity develops its own jargon to enable its members or participants to communicate effectively with one another; medicine, law, gastronomy, sociology, and (most recently) computing are well-known examples. The following example is drawn from a work of literary criticism: *The view of the text . . . has been seriously challenged in recent years, mainly by structuralist and semiological schools of criticism. According to these, the text has no within, beneath or behind where hidden meanings might be secreted. Attention is instead focused exclusively on the processes and structures of the text and on the ways in which these produce meanings, positions of intelligibility for the reader or the specific effects of realism, defamiliarisation or whatever*—T. Bennett, 1982. It will be seen from this example that jargon consists of ordinary words used in special ways as well as specially devised words (such as *defamiliarisation*). Jargon often arises from a need for precision, when terms that would be acceptable in general contexts are not precise enough in specialized use, combined with a need for concision in order to avoid having to repeat lengthy expressions that are likely to recur in a piece of writing. When the archaeologist Colin Renfrew calls the driving out of a people from their normal territory a *constrained population displacement*, he is using a term devised to summarize an argued proposition without having to repeat lengthy explanations each time.

3 JARGON IN THE WRONG PLACE. Examples are given in the entry for GOBBLEDEGOOK of jargon misused, when it is intended to be intelligible to the public at large or to people who are not members of the profession or activity concerned. In the *Plain English Guide* (1995), Martin Cutts quotes the following example of jargon used by a housing association in letters to its tenants explaining why modernization work has been delayed: *Find attached a draft programme for the anticipated commencement date on your property and we anticipate that the work will take three or four days to complete. Your next contact will be by the contractor . . . who will contact you individually about a week prior to the start at your house. If you anticipate any problems with access arrangements or require any further information, please do not hesitate to call . . . [etc.].* Cutts rewrites this section of the letter as follows, removing the jargon and simplifying the structure to produce a version that is not only much clearer but more reassuring to the reader when reassurance is the intention of the letter: *I attach a programme which shows the likely starting date for work on your property. We expect the work will take three or four days to complete. You will hear next from the contractor . . . who will contact you about a week before work at your house begins. Please call . . . if you think the contractor will have any*

problems with access to your house, or if you need any more information.

jehad see JIHAD.

jejune is pronounced ji-**joon**. It properly means 'meagre, scanty; dull or uninteresting' and is used primarily of ideas or arguments. It is derived from the Latin word *jejunus* meaning 'fasting', and originally meant 'without food' in English. The writer Kingsley Amis has famously defended the traditional meaning of *jejune* against users of a newer meaning 'puerile, childish, naïve', which arose towards the end of the 19c by a somewhat bizarre association with *juvenile*: *Mother seemed jejune, at times, with her enthusiasms and her sense of mission*—M. Howard, 1982. Although this use is quite common, it should be avoided in favour of readily available alternatives such as *childish, infantile*, or *juvenile*, and *innocent, guileless, ingenuous*, or *naïve*.

jetsam see FLOTSAM AND JETSAM.

jettison in current use is a verb meaning 'to discard' and refers to physical things as well as abstract (e.g. ideas). Its origins are as a noun in maritime law, meaning 'the action of throwing goods overboard, especially to lighten a ship in distress'. Its verb inflections are *jettisoned, jettisoning*.

jeu d'esprit, meaning 'a witty or humorous trifle', is pronounced zher des-**pree** and is printed in italics. It has the plural form *jeux d'esprit* (pronounced the same).

Jew. The use of *Jew* in its opprobrious meaning 'a person who is mean or drives a hard bargain', and the corresponding verb *to jew*, are thankfully disappearing from the language, although occasional uses are found in print. These uses, first recorded in the time of Shakespeare, have caused deep offence and have been the cause of great embarrassment to historical lexicographers who have had to record them. Robert Burchfield, the *OED* editor, has described the problem in a study of controversial vocabulary which appeared in *Unlocking the English Language* (1989), 83–108.

jewel has inflected forms *jewelled*, *jewelling*, and the derivative form *jeweller*. In AmE the usual forms are *jeweled*, *jeweling*, and *jeweler*.

jewellery should be pronounced **joo**-əl-ri, not **joo**-lə-ri (as in *foolery*). The form *jewelry* is usual in AmE and is sometimes used in BrE.

Jewess, though in use since the 14c, now has derogatory overtones (for racial reasons and because of gender sensitivity) and should be avoided, although Jewish people are said to use it among themselves.

jibe see GIBE; GYBE.

jihad, meaning 'a holy war undertaken by Muslims against unbelievers', is pronounced **jee**-hahd, and is preferably spelt this way rather than *jehad*.

jiu-jitsu see JU-JITSU.

jockey has the plural form *jockeys* as a noun, and as a verb (used especially in the expression *jockey for position*) has inflected forms *jockeys*, *jockeyed*, *jockeying*.

jollily, jolly *adverbs. Jolly* is used as a colloquial substitute for *very* (*A jolly good idea* | *You know jolly well*). The adverb meaning 'in a jolly manner' is *jollily*, although

awkwardness of articulation reduces its use when *in a jolly manner* (or *way*) is available instead.

journalese. Some words and uses are peculiar to the language of newspaper articles and, more especially, newspaper headlines. Examples are *probe* for 'investigation' or 'investigate' (*Hong Kong missing millions probe*), *quiz* for 'interrogate' (*Police quiz councillors over expenses fraud*), *package* for 'deal' (*Steel bosses offer new pay package*), and *swap* for 'transfer' in the medical sense (*Baby heart swap drama*). Combinations of nouns in headlines (as in the last example), use of the present tense, and use of a *to*-infinitive to denote future time, are common features: *Councillor planning action over go-go girl affair claim—Evening News* (Edinburgh), 1994 | *Sex cinema blaze man pleads guilty—Independent*, 1995 | *Premier to defy unions over £3.60 minimum wage—Daily Mail*, 1998. Puns, as the most concise form of written humour, feature prominently in headlines, e.g. *Hirst's sheep give Britain art failure—Independent*, 1998 (reporting an opinion poll which found that the 'pickled sheep' art of Damien Hirst was among least liked by British visitors to art galleries).

journey has the plural form *journeys*.

judgement, judgment. Both spellings are in use, and both are correct. *Judgement* is more common in general use in BrE, but *judgment* is dominant in legal contexts and in AmE.

judging by, judging from. Both forms are used with the meaning 'if we are to judge by . . . ' at the head of a clause and only loosely connected grammatically to the

main clause: *Untidy housewives
abound, judging by all the so-called
slatterns, trolly-mogs, slovens and
tosspots*—P. Wright, 1974 | *Judging
from her voice, she had been
crying*—M. Nabb, 1989 | *Fen for the
most part seemed absorbed in his
own thoughts, which, judging by his
expression, did not please him*—A.
Murray, 1993.

judicial, judicious. These two
words, both derived from the
Latin word *judex* meaning 'judge',
are easily confused although
their current meanings are distinct. *Judicial* means 'relating to
judges or legal processes' (*a judi-
cial inquiry | judicial separation*),
whereas *judicious* means 'sensible,
prudent; sound in judgement' in
general contexts (*judicious use of
time | a judicious plan of action*). A
judicial decision made by a judge
is one in accordance with the
law, whereas a *judicious* decision
(whether made by a judge or
some other person) is one that is
wise and discerning when all factors are taken into account.

ju-jitsu, the Japanese system of
unarmed combat, is preferably
spelt this way, not *jiu-jitsu*.

jumbo has the plural form *jum-
bos*.

junction, juncture. A *junction* is
a point at which two or more
things are joined, and usually refers to physical objects. It has the
special meaning of 'a point at
which roads or railway lines meet
or cross'. *Juncture* occurs principally in the expression *at this
juncture*, which properly denotes a
coincidence of events producing a
critical or dramatic moment but
in practice tends to mean simply
'at this moment, now': *The United
States came to Vietnam at a critical
juncture of Vietnamese history*—F.

Fitzgerald, 1972 | *At this juncture, the
opposing demands of two distinct
worlds were visited upon her*—C. G.
Wolff, 1977 | *Liz hoped that at this
juncture Shirley would go to bed*—
Margaret Drabble, 1987.

junta, a Spanish loanword meaning 'a political or military clique
taking power after a coup or revolution', is now pronounced in an
anglicized way as **jun**-tə. The
plural form is *juntas*.

juror, a member of a jury, is
spelt *-or*. A male juror is sometimes called a *juryman* and a female juror a *jurywoman*.

just *adverb.* **1** When it means 'a
little time ago', *just* is used differently in BrE and AmE. In BrE the
usual construction is with a perfect tense formed with *have*: *I have
just arrived home*, but in AmE the
verb is normally a simple past
form: *I just arrived home*. Care
needs to be taken to avoid misunderstanding, since *just* can also
mean 'only, simply' as in *They are
just good friends*. So a sentence
such as BrE *I have just seen my
brother* and, even more, AmE *I just
saw my brother* can mean either 'I
have recently seen my brother' or
'I have seen my brother and no
one else' (or, perhaps, 'I have seen
my brother and have done nothing else'). In speech, intonation
will usually clarify the meaning,
but in written English the difficulty may need to be resolved by
rephrasing.

2 The phrase *just now* has several meanings, and the primary
meaning can change from one
part of the English-speaking
world to another. The principal
possibilities are (1) with past reference, 'a short time ago' (*What
was it you were saying just now,
child?*—E. Jolley, 1985 | *When I re-*

turned to the house just now I sensed that something—unusual had occurred—S. Craven, 1993), (2) with a present continuous tense, 'at this moment' (Just now I'm going with a Catholic, who lives down in Armagh—F. Kippax, 1993), (3) with a simple present, 'at this time, right now', common generally with a negative (She cannot afford to think about her mother just now—J. Neale, 1993) but characteristically Scottish in positive use (But it's not just me, it's the whole of Scotland just now—M. Gray, 1989), (4) with a future tense in South African and Indian English, 'very shortly, in a little while' (The men on cell duty will do that just now—A. Sachs, 1966 (South Africa)).

juvenile has a neutral meaning 'relating to or associated with young people' (juvenile crime) and a derogatory meaning 'immature' (Behaving in a juvenile way).

Kk

keep. The construction *keep + object + from + -ing* verb is idiomatic in current English: *His hands held flat over his ears as if to keep his whole head from flying apart—*Martin Amis, 1978. The intransitive use of *keep + from + -ing* verb is recorded in the *OED* but is now mostly confined to AmE: *Maria cut the wheel to the left, to keep from hitting the cans—*T. Wolfe, 1987.

kerb is the standard BrE spelling of the word meaning 'stone edging to a pavement or raised path'. In AmE it is spelt *curb*: see CURB.

kick. 1 The word *kick* has provided some powerful metaphors over the years. In recent use, the image of starting a motorcycle by the downward thrust on a pedal (a *kick-start*) has been vividly applied figuratively to mean 'an impetus given to get a process started'. It is now more commonly used as a verb, 'to get (a process) started': *With lots of new ideas this high profile branch is an excellent place to kick-start your career—*advertisement in *The Grocer*, 1996.

2 A rather less appealing image, taken from the macho language of American business management, is the term *kick-ass*, used as an adjective to mean 'rough, aggressive, powerful': *His point is that 'the old kick-ass way of managing' is counter-productive—Times*, 1991. Best avoided, except in direct reference to those who get their own kick from this sort of thing.

kid, in its informal meaning 'child' (*He's only a kid | He came with his wife and kids*), has a long history, being first recorded in the 17c, but is still only suitable for more informal use. The verb *to kid*, meaning 'to trick or tease', is early 19c and possibly derived from this noun; it has the same level of informality.

kidnap has inflected forms *kidnapped*, *kidnapping* in BrE; in AmE the forms *kidnaped*, *kidnaping* are also used.

kidnapping see ABDUCTION.

kidney has the plural form *kidneys*.

kilo has the plural form *kilos*.

kilometre is spelt *-metre* in BrE and *-meter* in AmE. The word is better pronounced with the stress on the first syllable, in line with other words for measures such as *kilogram* and *millimetre*, although pronunciation with the stress on the second syllable, on the (less secure) analogy of words such as *barometer* and *speedometer*, is increasingly common and is standard in AmE and other non-British varieties.

kimono, meaning 'long loose Japanese robe', has the plural form *kimonos*, or occasionally (as in Japanese) *kimono*.

kin is now a rather old-fashioned term for one's relatives or family. It is mostly used in the fixed expressions *next of kin* and *kith and kin*.

kinda see KIND OF.

kindly, as used to introduce a formal request (*You are kindly requested to refrain from smoking | Kindly refrain from smoking*), now has a dated sound to it, and it is never quite clear who it is who is being *kind* (a point Fowler noticed in 1926). A modern alternative, often seen for example on notices in restaurants and taxis, uses the style *Thank you for not smoking*, which is thought to be more effective in its direct assumption of compliance.

kind of, sort of. 1 These expressions mean much the same, and share the same grammatical problems. (The issues raised here seem to occur less often in practice with the third alternative, *type of*.) There is less of a problem when *kind of* is preceded by *a* or *the*, which are invariable, but difficulties arise with *this, that, these,* and *those*. When followed by a singular noun, the correct form is (e.g.) *this kind* [or *sort*] *of house*, not *this kind* [or *sort*] *of a house*. When it is followed by a plural noun, many purists insist on making *kind* or *sort* plural as well, e.g. *these kinds* [or *sorts*] *of houses*. To say *this kind* [or *sort*] *of houses* is ungrammatical, but an alternative style *these kind* [or *sort*] *of houses* has been in use since the 14c. Although this too is ungrammatical on a normal interpretation and was questioned by the *OED*, its rationale lies in regarding *kind of* as an adjectival phrase qualifying the following noun (in this case, *houses*), with the demonstrative pronoun *these* or *those* also qualifying *houses* rather than qualifying *kind* (or *sort*). This type is now very common in colloquial contexts: *She was used to these kind of smells in the night-time bedclothes*—M. Duckworth, 1960 | *These sort of people are only inter-*

ested in lining their pockets—J. Leland, 1987. Alternatives are *these kinds* (or *sorts*) *of*—and—*of this kind* (or *sort*): *The pressure here is to consider the . . . circumstances which do, in fact, coerce people in these sorts of ways*—M. Whitford et al., 1989 | *The present tax rules can in practice effectively discourage demergers of this kind*—*Times*, 1980.

2 In AmE, *kind of a* is often used informally where in BrE it would be *a kind of*: *We're kind of a middle-aged Sonny and Cher*—*Washington Post*, 1973.

3 *Kind of* and *sort of* also occur as adverbial phrases in informal contexts, especially in AmE: *All these rich bastards driving up the property values have kind of made it impossible for everyone else*—*New Yorker*, 1987 | *He just sort of glanced at the photos and then carried on talking*—N. Watts, 1990.

4 The uses shown in paragraphs 2 and 3 are characteristically American and should not be used in more formal speech or writing. An even more informal written form is *kinda*, which represents the sound of *kind of* in rapid speech: *That little chap must have been really desperate to take that kinda crap*—Caris Davis, 1989 | *There was this real weirdo in here, rifling about the desks, wearing some kinda disguise*—S. James, 1993. Again the association is chiefly American, and is non-standard.

knee-jerk is a popularized technicality taken from the physical meaning 'a sudden involuntary kick caused by a blow on the tendon just below the knee when the leg is hanging loose'. It is now popular among politicians, broadcasters, etc., especially in the phrase *knee-jerk reaction*, as an adjective meaning 'instant and barely considered': *The* [*motor*] *industry's . . . knee-jerk support for road construction and its opposition to tighter air pollution standards have not endeared it to the public*—Times, 1991 | *The Braer disaster produced a knee-jerk reaction among many hoping to improve safety standards at sea*—East Anglian, 1993.

kneel. The past and past participle form *knelt* is now more common than *kneeled* in all varieties of English: *Some of the recruits knelt to pray before retiring, presumably for strength*—Anthony Burgess, 1987.

knife. The plural form of the noun is *knives*, but the inflected forms of the verb are *knifes, knifed, knifing*.

knit. The past tense and past participle form of the verb in its main meaning is *knitted* (*a knitted scarf*). In figurative meanings, *knitted* and *knit* are both used (*She knit/knitted her brows* | *a close-knit group*).

knock up. Care needs to be taken with this phrasal verb, which in BrE means 'to wake by knocking on the door' and in AmE means 'to make pregnant'.

know. The expression *you know*, inserted parenthetically in a sentence in speech, sometimes has real meaning, e.g. in introducing extra information that the hearer is likely to know already, but generally it is a meaningless sentence-filler like *I mean: People get the wrong idea, thinking we might be, you know, glamorous or brilliant or something*—Sunday Times, 1974.

know-how, meaning 'technical expertness or practical knowledge', is first recorded in print in AmE in 1838, but did not come into widespread use until about a century later. It is now established in both Britain and America, and is acceptable in all but the most formal contexts.

knowing. *We won't lunch till late, knowing her*—Mary Wesley, 1983. This use as an unattached participle is well established and unexceptionable.

knowledgeable is spelt with an *e* in the middle.

Koran, the sacred book of Islam, is normally spelt this way in English contexts, although the form *Quran* or *Qur'an*, a closer transliteration of the Arabic original (meaning 'recitation'), is also found.

kosher, meaning 'fulfilling the requirements of Jewish law', is pronounced **koh**-shə.

kowtow, meaning 'to act obsequiously', is pronounced with each syllable to rhyme with *cow*, and is no longer spelt *ko-tow*.

kudos, meaning 'glory, renown' (usually in connection with a particular event or achievement), is a (19c) singular noun derived from a Greek noun with the same meaning. Its occasional use in the 20c as if it were plural, with even a singular back-formation *kudo*, is non-standard verging on the illiterate: *This did not win Mr. Eisenhower many kudos in the press*—Wall Street Journal, 1963 | *A kudo to Life for a fine story on baseball's spring training*—Life, 1963.

lab is an established and acceptable short form of *laboratory* in all but the most formal contexts.

label *verb* has inflected forms *labelled*, *labelling* in BrE and *labeled*, *labeling* in AmE.

laboratory is pronounced with the stress on the second syllable in BrE and with the stress on the first syllable (and the final syllable like *Tory*) in AmE.

labour is the standard spelling in BrE, whereas *labor* is the standard form in AmE.

lack *verb*. The use with *for* meaning 'to be short of something' in negative contexts seems to have originated in the 19c: *If you are inclined to undertake the search, I have so provided that you will not lack for means*—Rider Haggard, 1887 | *Here's hoping he'll never lack for friends*—Mark Twain, 1892 | *You get a lower standard of trim, but you don't lack for much in the way of essential equipment*—Which? Car Buying Guide, 1987 |*'I can see by those here present that Samuel did not lack for friends,' said the priest who now filled the place of Father Michael*—P. Bryers, 1993.

lackey, meaning 'an obsequious parasite', has the plural form *lackeys*.

lacquer *verb* has inflected forms *lacquered*, *lacquering*.

ladleful has the plural form *ladlefuls*.

lady, woman. The division of usage between these two words is complex and is caught up in issues of social class. In George Meredith's *Evan Harrington* (1861), the heroine, Rose Jocelyn, is rhetorically asked, *Would you rather be called a true English lady than a true English woman, Rose?*, and it is still the case that *lady* denotes social standing and refinement and is the female equivalent of *gentleman*, whereas *woman* is the normal word that is generally neutral in tone but in some contexts can sound over-direct or discourteous (*Which of you women is Mrs Jones?*). As well as its use as a title, *lady* is used in certain fixed expressions, such as *lady of the house*, *the Ladies* (or *Ladies'*, a women's public lavatory), a *lady's man*, and others, and in the form of address *ladies and gentlemen*. In AmE, though less in BrE, *lady* has developed an informal meaning rather like *dame*, both as a form of address (*Where are you going, lady?*) and in third-person reference (*She's some lady*). *Lady* is still used with words denoting a profession (*lady doctor*), but in this use is beginning to sound affected and is fast giving way to *woman* (*woman doctor*). See also FEMININE DESIGNATIONS. It should finally be mentioned that the feminist movement generally disfavours *lady* as being socially and historically loaded, and prefers the more neutral *woman* despite its occasional bluntness of tone. This preference is likely to influence the future of the words' usage considerably.

laid, lain. *Laid* is the past and past participle of *lay*, whereas *lain* is the part participle of *lie*. See LAY, LIE.

laissez-aller, -faire, -passer.
The first means 'unconstrained freedom', the second 'abstention by people in authority from interference in the actions of individuals', and the third 'a pass or permit'. All three are normally printed in italics.

lama, llama. The form with one *l* is the Tibetan or Mongolian Buddhist monk, whereas the form with two *l*s is the South American animal. For obvious reasons, care should be taken in remembering which is which.

lamentable, meaning 'deplorable, regrettable', is correctly pronounced with the stress on the first syllable, not the second (though either is acceptable in AmE).

lamprey, the eel-like fish, has the plural form *lampreys*.

landward, landwards. As an adjective, *landward* is the correct form in all varieties of English (*a landward breeze*). As an adverb, *landwards* is the dominant form in BrE (*sail landwards*), whereas both forms are used in AmE. In Scottish use, *landward* as an adverb is used to mean 'towards the country as opposed to the town'.

large, largely. *Large* is used as an adverb with the verbs *bulk* and *loom* and in the phrase *by and large*. Otherwise *largely* is the normal adverb and means 'to a large extent' (*His failure was largely due to laziness*).

largesse is now the dominant form for this word meaning 'generosity' or 'money given freely', not *largess* as recommended by Fowler in 1926.

larva has the plural form *larvae*, pronounced **lah**-vee.

lasso is pronounced la-**soo** in BrE and **las**-oh in AmE. The plural form of the noun is *lassos* and the verb has inflected forms *lassoes, lassoed, lassoing*.

last. 1 When used with a number, *last* (like *first*) normally precedes it, as in *the last three cars*. See FIRST 1.

2 In listing a sequence of points or topics, *lastly* (or *finally*) is preferable to *last*, especially when the preceding items are introduced with numbers ending in *-ly*: *first* (or *firstly*) . . . , *secondly* . . . , *thirdly* . . . , *lastly* . . . For the choice between *first* and *firstly*, see FIRST 2.

last but not least. When Antony in Shakespeare's *Julius Caesar* (III.i.190) greets Caesar's assassins, he takes their hands in the order Brutus, Cinna, Casca, and Trebonius, and says to Trebonius: *Though last, not least in love, yours, good Trebonius*. Though used here (and elsewhere in Shakespeare) to good effect, this phrase is now a cliché and should be avoided except in the few cases when it has real meaning.

late, former, one-time, sometime. All these words are used occasionally (the first two a little more than that) to describe the earlier status of a person or thing. A *late husband* is one that is no longer alive, whereas a *former husband* (or *ex-husband*) is one that is no longer a husband (but is more likely than not still alive). *Sometime* is used more of the official function a person or thing has had, for example a building may be the *sometime* headquarters of the KGB; *former* and *one-time* are also possible here and would be more usual in everyday language. See also ERSTWHILE; FORMER, LATTER.

later on see EARLY ON.

lath, lathe. A *lath*, pronounced lahth, is a flat strip of wood. The plural is *laths*, pronounced lahths or occasionally lahdhz. A *lathe*, pronounced laydh, is a machine for shaping wood or metal, and has the plural form *lathes*, pronounced laydhz.

Latin plurals.
See box overleaf

latish, meaning 'somewhat late', is normally spelt without an *e* in the middle. See MUTE E.

latter is now used only in the phrase *the latter*, which contrasts with *the former* to refer to the second of two previously mentioned items so as to avoid lengthy repetition. See FORMER, LATTER.

laudable, laudatory. The essential difference is that *laudable* means 'deserving praise' whereas *laudatory* means 'expressing praise'. So an action or attitude that is *laudable* calls for a *laudatory* response.

lavatory, the standard word in the early part of the 20c for a receptacle for urination and defecation (and the room containing it), has tended to give way to alternatives such as *loo* (the usual middle-class word) and *toilet* (still non-U but the word mostly used in official contexts, on notices, etc.). See also U AND NON-U; TOILET.

laver, meaning 'edible seaweed', is pronounced **lah**-və.

lawful see LEGAL.

lawman, lawyer. *Lawman* is an informal lay term for a law-enforcement officer, often with historical reference, whereas a *lawyer* is a professional person practising law as a solicitor or barrister.

lay, lie. These two words cause confusion even to native speakers of English because their meanings are related and their forms overlap. *Lay* is a transitive verb, i.e. it takes an object, and means 'to place on a surface, to cause to rest on something'; its past form and past participle are both *laid* (examples: *Please lay it on the floor | The teacher laid the book on the desk | They had laid it on the floor*). *Lie* is intransitive, and means 'to rest or be positioned on a surface'; its past form is *lay* (i.e. identical with the present form of the other verb), its present participle is *lying*, and its past participle is *lain* (examples: *Go and lie on the bed | She went and lay on the bed | He is lying on the bed | The body had lain in the field for several days*). The principal mistakes in the use of these verbs are using *lay* for *lie*, *laid* for *lay* (past of *lie*), and *lain* for *laid*: ⊠ *We are going to lay* [read: *lie*] *under the stars by the sea*—Sun, 1990 | ⊠ *Standing in a semicircle, we had lain* [read: *laid*] *all our uniforms and possessions at our feet*—C. Jennings, 1990 | ⊠ *He chose a place between two snoring servants and laid* [read: *lay*] *down to sleep, oblivious to the figure watching him from the shadows*—P. C. Doherty, 1991.

lay-by, meaning in BrE 'an area by the side of an open road where vehicles may stop', has the plural form *lay-bys*.

Latin plurals

Plurals of Latin words used in English are formed according to the rules either of the source language (*apex/apices, stratum/strata*) or of the borrowing language (*gymnasium/gymnasiums, arena/arenas*). In some cases more than one form is in use, sometimes with a usage distinction (*appendix/appendices/appendixes, formula/formulae/formulas*) and sometimes with no clear distinction (*cactus/cacti/cactuses*). Words ending in *-is* usually follow the original Latin form (*basis/ bases, crisis/crises*) for reasons of euphony, and the same rule operates in other cases (*nucleus/nuclei*). A more alien form is the plural *-mata* of words ending in *-ma* in the singular (*lemma/lemmata, stigma/stigmata*). There are occasional surprises; for example we might expect the plural of *crux* to be (Latin) *cruces* but it is in fact more often (English) *cruxes*. There is a trap for the unwary with Latinate nouns ending in *-us* which cannot form plurals in *-i* for formal grammatical reasons: *hiatus* (a fourth-declension noun in Latin with a plural *hiatus*), *ignoramus* (a first-person plural verb in Latin, not a noun), *octopus* (a Romanized form of a Greek word *octopous*), *vademecum* (*cum* being a preposition meaning 'with'). The table below shows the types of plural that the more commonly used Latin words have in English; when there is more than one both are shown:

SINGULAR FORM	LATIN-TYPE PLURAL	ENGLISH PLURAL
addendum	addenda	
alga	algae	
apex	apices	apexes
appendix	appendices	appendixes
aquarium	aquaria	aquariums
arena		arenas
automaton	automata	automatons
basis	bases	
cactus	cacti	cactuses
codex	codices	
compendium	compendia	compendiums
corrigendum	corrigenda	
crematorium	crematoria	crematoriums
crisis	crises	
crux	cruces	cruxes
desideratum	desiderata	
encomium	encomia	encomiums
focus	foci	focuses
formula	formulae	formulas
genus	genera	
gymnasium	gymnasia	gymnasiums
helix	helices	helixes

▶

► **Latin plurals**
continued

SINGULAR FORM	LATIN-TYPE PLURAL	ENGLISH PLURAL
index	indices	indexes
lemma	lemmata	lemmas
matrix	matrices	matrixes
maximum	maxima	maximums
memorandum	memoranda	memorandums
miasma	miasmata	
minimum	minima	minimums
momentum	momenta	momentums
moratorium		moratoriums
nucleus	nuclei	
oasis	oases	
radix	radices	
referendum	referenda	referendums
stigma	stigmata	stigmas
stratum	strata	
thesis	theses	
vortex	vortices	vortexes

Further information will be found in the separate entries for some of these words.

---

lb., an abbreviation for *pound* (weight) is derived from Latin *libra* 'pound'. The plural form is *lb.* or *lbs*.

leadership. The established meanings 'the position of a leader' and 'the ability to lead' have been joined in the 20c by the meaning 'group of leaders': *A dinner for the heads of the Senate Committees and the Leadership on both sides and their wives*—Mrs L. B. Johnson, 1964 | *Following an LDP conference, the party leadership announced on Sept. 19 that it planned to break away from the coalition which had backed Aquino*—Keesings, 1990.

leading question. In law, a *leading question* is one which suggests an expected answer to the witness, and the use of such ques-

tions is strictly controlled by Judges' Rules. In general use the term is often extended to mean a 'loaded' or 'searching' question, i.e. one that will *lead* to other matters: *Following the end of the First World War, the leading question in the mining industry was whether or not the state would return the coal mines to their pre-war owners*—K. Laybourn, 1990.

lead, led. *Lead* is the present tense of the verb meaning 'to go in front', 'to take charge of', etc., and its past form is *led*. A common mistake is to use *lead* for the past form and pronounce it *led* in speech, probably on the false analogy of *read*: ⌧ *His idea was the one that lead to the solution of the mascara mystery*—Chicago Sun-Times, 1990.

leaf. The noun has the plural form *leaves*, and the verb has inflected forms *leafs, leafed, leafing* (*He was leafing through a book*).

-leafed, -leaved. Both forms are in use in combinations such as *broad-leafed/-leaved* and *four-leafed/-leaved*, but there is a preference for *-leaved* in current use.

leaflet. As a verb, meaning 'to distribute leaflets to', *leaflet* has inflected forms *leafleted, leafleting*.

leak *verb*. The transitive meaning 'to disclose (secret information) intentionally' is, apart from an isolated example of 1859, a 20c use, although the practice is doubtless a lot older. It is related to, if not a development of, the phrasal verb *to leak out*, which is first recorded in 1863.

lean *verb*. The past form and past participle are in BrE either *leaned* (pronounced leend or lent) or *leant* (pronounced lent) and usually *leaned* in AmE. Examples: *Georgia Rose . . . leaned forward and blew out every one of her candles*— Lee Smith, 1983 (US) | *Syl smiled back at me and leaned across and took my hand*—A. T. Ellis, 1987 | *His tone was weary, and he leant his head down on one hand*—Iris Murdoch, 1993.

leap *verb*. The past form and past participle are in both BrE and AmE either *leaped* (pronounced leept or lept) or *leapt* (pronounced lept). Examples: *I can't say that wretch I leaped in after was much of a loss to the human race*—P. Bailey, 1986 | *She had leapt on board the boat like a boy*—New Yorker, 1994.

learn *verb*. **1** The past form and past participle are in BrE either *learned* (pronounced lernd or lernt)

or *learnt* (pronounced lernt); *learned* is more usual as the past form and, in AmE, as both past form and past participle. Examples: *So, what was learned from this experience?*—Essays & Studies, 1987 | *A point that none of my bright young officers seem to have learnt at school*—B. L. Barder, 1987 | *Ideally, you should treat each child as an individual, with his own list of words to be learnt*—M. Torbe, 1988 | *She learned that the vessel had come, and was glad, for she said that the young man would speak for her*— Dorothy Dunnett, 1989.

2 The use of *learn* to mean 'to teach', though unexceptionable to writers of earlier ages such as Caxton, Spenser, Bunyan, and Johnson (1755), fell into disfavour around 1800 and appears in nonstandard contexts in 19c literature: *If she knows her letters it's the most she does—and them I learned her*—Dickens, 1865.

learned is pronounced as one syllable when it is the past and past participle of *learn*, and as two syllables (**ler**-nid) when it is an adjective meaning 'having or showing much knowledge'.

learning difficulties. This term became common in the 1980s to describe a wide range of abnormalities including Down's syndrome, dyslexia, and the complaint known as *attention deficit disorder*. In emphasizing the difficulty experienced rather than any perceived deficiency, it is considered less discriminatory than *mental handicap* and related terms, and is the standard term in official contexts in the UK.

lease on life. In BrE the idiom is *take a new lease of life*, whereas in AmE it is *take a new lease on life*.

least. 1 *Least of all* means 'especially not' and should only be used in negative contexts: *I am not going to try to play the role of prophet, least of all Jeremiah*—*Listener*, 1973.

2 Use *less*, not *least*, when contrasting two things: *The latter aircraft was the less pleasant to fly*—E. Brown, 1983 (an example that is exemplary with regard both to *less* and to *latter*).

leave, let. *Leave* is well on its way to forcing out *let* in certain idiomatic uses, especially in *leave/ let be* (*Will you leave/let me be? I'm trying to work*), *leave/let go* (*Please leave/let go of the handle*), and above all in *leave/let alone* when it means 'to refrain from disturbing, not interfere with' (*I'll leave/ let you alone to get on with it now*). *Leave alone* is the only possibility when the meaning is 'not to have dealings with' (*I wish you'd leave the matter alone*), and *let alone* is still dominant in the meaning 'still less, not to mention' (*They never buy a newspaper, let alone read one*).

leftward, leftwards. The only form of the adjective is *leftward* (*a leftward glance*). For the adverb, *leftward* and *leftwards* are used both in BrE and AmE (*turn leftward/leftwards*).

legalese is a fairly recent term (first recorded in 1914) for the complicated technical language used in legal documents. Legal language has become complex and difficult for the lay person to understand because of a need to be both precise and comprehensive in the points made; nonetheless, there is now a vigorous campaign in progress, led (in the UK) by the Plain English Campaign and (in the US) by the Plain English Forum and others, to simplify legal language in everyone's interests. These intentions are hardly new. Nearly 200 years ago, Thomas Jefferson, third president of the US, railed against statutes 'which from verbosity, their endless tautologies, their involutions of case within case, and parenthesis within parenthesis, and their multiplied efforts at certainty, by saids and aforesaids, by ors and ands, to make them more plain, are really rendered more perplexed and incomprehensible, not only to common readers, but to the lawyers themselves' (quoted in D. Mellinkoff, *The Language of the Law*, 1963). Tom McArthur, a well-known writer on language, reports in the *Oxford Companion to the English Language* (1992), 595, that 'in 1983, an English court ordered a law firm to pay £93,000 damages for unintentionally misleading a client by using "obscure" legal language in a letter of advice'. Martin Cutts, in the *Plain English Guide* (1995), devotes a chapter to lucid legal language, and gives examples of complex language rewritten in a simpler form. As well as indicating complexities of grammatical structure, he points to words and phrases that notoriously cause difficulty to those not versed in the law: *aforesaid, be empowered to, failure to comply with, forthwith, heretofore, in the event of, pursuant to, the said —, thereto*, and many others.

legal, lawful, legitimate, licit. 1 All four words share the basic meaning 'conforming to the law'. Something is *legal* when it is authorized by the law of the land, *legitimate* when it conforms to custom or common justice, and *lawful* (a more old-fashioned word) when it conforms to moral or divine law. *Legal* is the only choice in the neutral descriptive meaning 'relating to the law' (as in *legal language*), and *legitimate* alone has the meaning 'born of married parents'. *Licit*, which means much the same as *lawful*, is the least used of all these words, although *illicit* is somewhat more common. See also IL-LEGAL.

2 For *legitimate* as a verb, see LE-GITIMATE, LEGITIMIZE.

legible, readable. In current use *legible* means 'clear enough to be decipherable' (as in *legible handwriting*); *readable* can also have this sense but more often means 'well written and interesting to read'.

legislation, legislature. Both words date from the 17c. *Legislation* is the process of making laws, and the *legislature* is the body (or group of bodies) that makes them.

legitimate, legitimize. 1 As a verb, *legitimate* is pronounced with the last syllable as -ayt and means 'to make legitimate or legal'. It competes in both BrE and AmE with *legitimize*, which is the only form used in the meaning 'to make (a child) legitimate': *My companion had up his sleeve something that would legitimate his employing my Christian name*—J. I. M. Stewart, 1974 | *Had the baby been a boy, he would have seriously considered legitimizing the union*—E. Pizzey, 1983 | *You . . . forget the very people who legitimize your authority*—Chinua Achebe, 1987.

2 For *legitimate* as an adjective, see LEGAL.

leisure is pronounced **lezh**-ə in BrE and **leezh**-ə in AmE.

lend. 1 see LOAN. Use of *lend* for *borrow* (*May I lend your pen?*) occurs in some British dialects but is non-standard.

2 Use of *lend* as a noun occurs in British dialect use and colloquially in New Zealand, but is non-standard: *Could you give me the lend of a bob?*—Frank Sargeson, 1946 (New Zealand) | *Just ringing this feller to ask if I could have a lend of his gun*—J. Howker, 1985 (UK).

length should be pronounced with the g fully articulated, not as in *tenth*.

lengthways, lengthwise. For the adjective only *lengthwise* is used: *The driver was sleeping in a doubled-up lengthwise position*. For the adverb both forms are available: *a hollow tube split lengthways/lengthwise*.

lese-majesty, meaning 'treason' or 'an insult to a sovereign or ruler', is pronounced leez **maj**-is-ti. The French form *lèse majesté* is also used in English, and its pronunciation is closer to the French. The term no longer has any legal force in English, having been replaced by *treason*.

less. 1 For *less* and *fewer*, see FEWER.

2 For *much less*, see MUCH MORE, MUCH LESS.

3 *LESS* **AND** *LESSER*. *Less* is a comparative form of *little*, and is used with singular mass nouns to mean the opposite of *more*: *less butter* | *less noise*. It cannot be used with plural nouns (in which case FEWER is used), nor with a preceding *a* or *an* (in which case an alternative such as *lower* or *smaller* is used: *I want to pay less rent* but *I want to pay a lower rent*). *Lesser* is a so-called double comparative and means 'not so great

(i.e. important or significant) as the other or others'; it is preceded by *a* or *the* (*a lesser man than him | the lesser evil*). It is not used to refer to physical size or number; in these cases use *smaller*, *lower*, etc.: (*a smaller car | a lower price*).

-less. 1 This suffix dates back to Old English and is used to form adjectives from nouns (*doubtless, endless, powerless*). It has also been added to verbs with the meaning 'not affected by the action of the verb', although few of this type survive (*countless, dauntless, numberless* (possibly from the noun), *tireless*). As a living suffix it can now only be added to nouns.

2 A hyphen is used when the suffix is added to a noun ending in -*ll* (*wall-less, will-less*), but not when added to one ending in a single *l* (*soulless, tailless*).

lessee, lessor. The *lessee* is the person who holds a property by lease, and the *lessor* is the person who lets a property by lease.

lesser see LESS 3.

lest, despite its slightly archaic flavour, lives on in the language and is one of the mainstays of the subjunctive in English: *I shall say nothing about alcohol lest I be pilloried by publicans*—Julian Critchley, 1987. An alternative construction, especially after verbs of fearing or apprehension, is with *should*: *I can see you're in a fever lest slick Ben and his moll should get back . . . before you make your getaway*—Ngaio Marsh, 1962 | *And she also felt slightly nervous lest the large house should suddenly disgorge many other hidden residents*— Margaret Drabble, 1988. Use of the indicative is already evident, and often sounds perfectly natural

(the subjunctive is identifiable only in the third person singular anyway): *He would never have repeated the story lest it weakened our war effort*—A. N. Wilson, 1977.

let. 1 A pronoun that follows *let* in exhortations should be in the objective case (*me, him, her,* etc.) and not the subjective (*I, he, she,* etc.), since it is the object of *let*. Mistakes occur most often when there are two pronouns joined by *and* or when the pronoun is followed by a clause with *who*: ☒ *Let you and I say a few words about this unfortunate affair* (read *Let you and me . . .*) | *Let he who did this be severely punished* (read *Let him who . . .*).

2 The type *let us* (or *let's*) + infinitive is well established in English (*Let's hold more chat*— Shakespeare, 1588). More colloquial forms occur, especially in AmE: *Let's you and me duck out of here*— J. Macdonald, 1950, but these are considered non-standard. When *let* is used to introduce a firm request, rather than a casual suggestion, the two words should be written separately: *Let us try once more.*

3 The negative form of *let's* is *let's not* or (in BrE) *don't let's*. In AmE, *let's don't* is used informally.

letter forms. 1 Many of the more formal formulas for writing letters that were noted by Fowler (*Your obedient servant, Yours respectfully,* etc.) have disappeared even from business letters and the letter pages of the more traditional broadsheets newspapers. So too has the practice of addressing colleagues by their surnames only (*Dear Jones*). The standard forms of opening are: (1) to individuals *Dear Mr Smith | Mrs Jones | Ms Brown,* or (more informally) *Dear John | Jane.* The corresponding conclusion is normally *Yours sincerely* (with capital Y), or, in the case of people the writer knows well, *With kind regards*, *With best wishes*, or some variant or combination of these; (2) in personal correspondence more intimate forms such as *My dear John*, *My dearest Jane*, *My darling Jim*, etc, are used, with an appropriate conclusion such as *Yours ever*, *All love*, etc.; (2) in business and other more formal contexts, *Dear Sirs | Sir | Madam*, with the conclusion *Yours faithfully* or (somewhat less formally) *Yours truly*.

2 For forms of address in special cases such as bishops or members of the nobility, readers should consult the latest edition of a work such as *Debrett's Correct Form*.

leukaemia is the spelling for the disease in BrE, and *leukemia* in AmE.

level. 1 The phrase *at — level* is well established and has a useful role to play: *No work is at present supported at international level on oil seeds such as sunflower, safflower and rapeseed*—Nature, 1974 | *The Treasury took the lead in setting up official inter-departmental committees, some at permanent-secretary level*—Harold Wilson, 1976.

2 *Level playing field* is a vogue use of the 1980s and 1990s referring to a sphere of activity that offers no advantage to any particular side. It has achieved the status of cliché in record time, and the verbal plays are already being rammed down our throats, especially by journalists with column-inches to fill: *That is not a level playing field. It is not even just a home-field advantage. It is like asking their competitors to play ball in a swamp*—Washington Journalism Review, 1990.

3 For the verb, the inflected forms are *levelled*, *levelling* in BrE and *leveled*, *leveling* in AmE.

leverage. The first syllable is pronounced **leev** in BrE and **lev** in AmE.

liable, likely see APT.

liaise, liaison. The noun *liaison*, pronounced li-**ay**-zon in BrE and in various ways in AmE, became fully anglicized early in the 20c, replacing its nasalized final syllable with a normal one. Since the early 20c, it has had the meaning 'an illicit sexual relationship'; curiously the verb *liaise* has not developed a corresponding meaning but is restricted to military and business contexts and is a key word in management jargon in the sense 'cooperate or have direct dealings': *The coordinating nurse on each shift 'liaises' with the admissions office regarding bed availability*—Professional Nurse, 1992.

libel, slander. 1 *Libel* is a published false statement that is damaging to a person's reputation, whereas *slander* is a malicious false statement that is spoken about a person. In popular usage the terms are sometimes used interchangeably, but the difference should always be borne in mind. The legal issue has become more complicated in recent years now that uncertainty exists about how far the word *published* can be extended to cover email, Internet websites, and other forms of electronic (as distinct from print) media of communication.

2 As a verb, *libel* has inflected forms *libelled*, *libelling* in BrE and usually *libeled*, *libeling* in AmE.

licence, license. In BrE, the noun is spelt *licence* and the verb *license* (and so *licensed premises, licensing hours*, etc., although *licenced* is occasionally seen and can be justified on the ground that it is formed from the noun rather than the verb). In AmE, both the noun and the verb are spelt *license*.

lichee see LYCHEE.

lichen. The dominant pronunciation of the plant name is **liy**-kən (as *liken*), although **lich**-ən is also heard in BrE (though not in AmE).

lich-gate, meaning 'a roofed gateway to a churchyard', is spelt *lich-*, not *lych-*. It is derived from the Old English word *līc* meaning 'corpse', because the gateway was formerly used at burials for sheltering a coffin until the clergyman's arrival.

licorice see LIQUORICE.

lie see LAY, LIE.

lie, = tell an untruth, has inflected forms *lies, lied, lying*.

lien, meaning 'a right over another's property to protect a debt charged on that property', is pronounced **lee**-ən or leen.

lieutenant is pronounced lef-**ten**-ənt in BrE (but with the -f- sound usually omitted when referring to the navy) and loo-**ten**-ənt in AmE. The -f- sound in BrE may be due to a (pre-19c) reading of Old French *lieu* as *liev* or *lief*.

life. The plural is *lives* except that the art term *still life* has the plural form *still lifes*.

life cycle. The term is first recorded in 1873 in its biological meaning 'the series of changes in the life of an organism', and this is the only meaning given in the current edition (1999) of the *Concise Oxford Dictionary*. During the course of the 20c, however, it has developed extended meanings, and in the 1940s the anthropologist Margaret Mead wrote of the modern man: *Here he is, only in middle age, and his life is over . . . no new fields to conquer . . . So while he is not out of a job . . . the very nature of the life-cycle in America is such that he feels like an old man—Male and Female*, 1949. The term is now found in the context of other human activities involving origin, development, change, and eventual decline and death, such as business and economics: *In principle the task of the project manager is to plan, organize and lead a group of people to complete a project life cycle*—S. A. Bergen, 1990. This is a natural development of meaning when a cycle of events is involved, but care should be taken not to use the term in contexts in which the simple word *life* or another word such as *process* would do.

life insurance see ASSURE, ASSURANCE.

lifelong, livelong. *Lifelong* (19c) is a combination of *life* and *long*, and means 'lasting or continuing for a lifetime' (*his lifelong companion*). *Livelong*, pronounced **liv**-long, is a much older word (15c) and is a combination of *lief*, meaning 'dear, beloved', and *long*. It is a literary word used as an intensive or emotional form of *long* in describing periods of time (e.g. *the livelong day*).

lifestyle. The term will be familiar to modern readers in the meaning given in the *Concise Oxford Dictionary* (1995): 'the particular way of life of a person or group', although it has a much older, specialized meaning introduced to the language of psychology by the neurologist Alfred Adler in the 1920s. In recent years it has been absorbed into marketing jargon to mean 'the sum total of the behaviour patterns and likes and dislikes of particular customers or a section of the market' and has developed an attributive or adjectival use (i.e. coming before a noun): *The latest lifestyle choice for the vibrant elderly is the 'retirement village'—Independent*, 1995. In some contexts, *way of life*, or even just *life*, seems preferable to a word that has become so bogged down in promotional hype. The derivative word *lifestyler*, meaning 'someone with a special lifestyle' has an ephemeral ring but is occasionally found: *The centre is built on a hilltop amid a broadleaf wood and is home to a community of proselytising alternative lifestylers—Holiday Which?*, 1991.

ligature, in printing, is a pair of letters printed in a joined form, e.g. æ. See DIGRAPH.

light. 1 The phrase *in the light of*, meaning 'having regard to, considering', is more often heard in the form *in light of* in AmE: *In light of what you've told us, we have decided to leave earlier.*

2 In BrE the past tense and past participle of the verb are usually both *lit* (*We lit the fire when it grew dark* | *He had already lit his pipe* | *The streets are all well lit*), but *lighted* is also used when the use is adjectival and there is no qualifying adverb (*She had a lighted cigarette in her hand*). In AmE, *lighted* is often used in contexts where *lit* would be normal in BrE: *She*

lighted a candle and turned off the lamp—New Yorker, 1987.

lightning, lightening. *Lightning* is the spelling with reference to electrical flashes in the sky (*thunder and lightning*), whereas *lightening* is a form of the verb *lighten* (*the lightening of burdens*). *Lightning* is originally a contracted form of *lightening*.

like. 1 *LIKE* **AS A CONJUNCTION.** *Like* is used as a preposition in the sentence *Please try to write like me* and as a conjunction in the sentence *Please try to write like I do*. In the second sentence, *like* is used instead of *as*, and this use seems still to be one of the cardinal issues by which a person's awareness of what is correct or incorrect grammar is judged. Fowler (1926) wrote that 'every illiterate person uses this construction daily; it is the established way of putting the thing among all who have not been taught to avoid it'; and Evelyn Waugh wrote of his close friend and fellow writer Henry Green in the 1940s that 'only one thing disconcerted me . . . The proletarian grammar—the "likes" for "ases", the "bikes" for "bicycles"'.

Nonetheless, there is plenty of good evidence for this use. The *OED* gives examples from Shakespeare, Southey, William Morris, and other good writers. In more recent usage, *like* is often used as a conjunction in three principal ways; (1) with the verb repeated or a form of *do* replacing it (*They didn't talk like other people talked—*Martin Amis, 1981 | *I'm afraid it might happen to my baby like it happened to Jefferson—New Yorker*, 1987 | *The retsina flowed like the Arno did when it overflowed in 1966—Spectator*, 1987), (2) in AmE and Australian English, though less in BrE, to mean 'as if' or 'as though' / *wanted him born and now it feels like I don't want him*—E. Jolley, 1985 (Australia) | *She acts like she can't help it*—Lee Smith, 1987 (US), (3) replacing *as* in fixed or semi-fixed expressions such as *as I said*: *Like you say, you're a dead woman*—Mary Wesley, 1983 | *Like I said, I haven't seen Rudi for weeks*—Thomas Keneally, 1985.

Clearly, *like* continues to assert its right to be regarded as a conjunction, and there is little doubt that this right will be recognized in time. For the present, the advice has to be: when *as* (or *as if* or *as though*) can be substituted for *like*, use these alternatives, which are absolutely safe: *They didn't talk as other people talked* | *Now it feels as if I didn't want him.*

2 *LIKE* AS A PREPOSITION. There is, thank goodness, normally no problem with this use, in which *like* governs a noun or noun phrase and not a clause: *The Pope was confined like a prisoner in the Vatican*—R. Strange, 1986. A minor difficulty arises occasionally when *like* is used to mean 'such as', since it is not always clear whether the person or thing specified is included. For example, the title of Kingsley Amis's novel *Take a Girl Like You* (1960) could be taken to mean 'a girl, for example, you' or 'a girl resembling you'. To resolve the ambiguity, the book would have to be called *Take a Girl such as You*, which it understandably isn't.

3 USE OF *LIKE* AS A FILLER. In this use, *like* is added parenthetically to a statement. This is conversational only, and even then is often disapproved of as nonstandard: *Hayley was pleased. 'That's him. He's, like, got her hypnotized.'*—Maurice Gee, 1990.

4 *LIKE* IN IDIOMATIC PHRASES. This category includes phrases such as *like always, like anything, like fun, like mad*. These again belong only in informal conversational style: *They wept like anything to see Such quantities of sand*—Lewis Carroll, 1872 | *Skate was with him like always*—M. Doane, 1988.

like *verb*. *I should like* is normal in BrE and *I would like* in other varieties, although in practice the contracted form *I'd like* is common, especially in speech. These forms are followed either by a *to*-infinitive (*I should like to come too*) or by an object followed by a *to*-infinitive (*They would like us to come too*). The past form is *should* (or *would*) *have liked to*, and in this case the normal *to*-infinitive should follow, e.g. *I should have liked to come too*, not ✗ *I should have liked to have come too* (but *I should like to have come too* is also possible). The construction *like* + *for* + object + *to*-infinitive is largely confined to AmE: *I'd like very much for you to meet him*—New Yorker, 1988.

-like. In occasional or less familiar formations, and when the first part ends in *-l*, a hyphen is used (*cat-like, eel-like*), but more established combinations are spelt as one word (*childlike, lifelike, statesmanlike*).

likeable is the preferred form, not *likable*.

likely. 1 As an adverb, *likely* needs the support of a qualifying or intensifying word such as *more, quite*, or *very* (*They've quite likely left by now* | *It's more likely a toadstool*), whereas in AmE it often stands alone: *It is possible to predict that within a few years the microfiche likely will move into the* *study and home—Publishers' Weekly*, 1971.

2 For use of *apt*, *liable*, and *likely*, see APT.

likewise, like *also*, is used as an adverb and not a conjunction in standard English: *Go and do likewise | They likewise prefer reading*. In uses where it might be a conjunction, it normally needs the support of a genuine conjunction such as *and*: *A heated window, and likewise rear wipers, are essential*. It is, however, permissible for *likewise* to stand at the head of a sentence, where its role is still mainly adverbial: *St Paul's Cathedral is one of the most easily recognizable sights of London. Likewise the Eiffel Tower is one of the most easily recognizable sights of Paris.*

-lily. Few adjectives in *-ly* form adverbs in *-lily* because they are too awkward to use. As Fowler noted (1926), 'it is always possible to say *in a masterly manner, at a timely moment*, and the like, instead of *masterlily, timelily*'. Some adjectives in *-ly* retain the same form for the corresponding adverb, e.g. *kindly*. A few forms in *-lily* exist, all adjectives in which *-ly* is part of the stem rather than an adjectival ending: *holily, jollily, sillily, wilily*.

limey, limy. *Limey* is the adjective corresponding to the fruit called *lime*, whereas *limy* relates to the caustic alkaline substance. *Limey* (with a capital initial letter) is an AmE slang term for a person from Britain, and arose from the enforced consumption of lime-juice in the British navy.

limit, as a verb, has inflected forms *limited, limiting*. *Limit* means 'to put a limit on', i.e. 'restrict', whereas *delimit* means 'to determine the boundaries of', and is used with reference to territories, frontiers, etc.

lineament, liniment. *Lineament*, pronounced as four syllables with the first three like *linear*, means 'a distinctive feature of the face', and is normally used in the plural. *Liniment* (three syllables) is an embrocation.

lingo, a colloquial word for a language or the special vocabulary of a language, has the plural form *lingos*.

liniment see LINEAMENT.

linking r is the sounding of a normally silent *r* when a vowel sound follows, as in *a pair of gloves* and *pour out the tea*. This is quite correct, but see INTRUSIVE R.

liquefy, meaning 'to make liquid', is spelt *-efy*, not *-ify*. Its inflected forms are *liquefies, liquefied, liquefying*.

liqueur, the strong sweet alcoholic spirit, is spelt with two *us*.

liquidate, liquidize. *Liquidate* is the word used in business contexts and in the sense 'eliminate by killing'. *Liquidize* is a more recent word meaning 'to make liquid' (in physical senses) and is now principally used in the context of the kitchen liquidizer which blends ingredients and makes purées.

liquorice is the BrE spelling, and *licorice* the AmE spelling, of the word denoting a black root extract used as a sweet.

lira, the chief monetary unit of Italy, has the plural form *lire*, which in English is pronounced in the same way as the singular.

lit see LIGHT.

litany, liturgy. A *litany* (from Greek *litē* 'prayer') is a prayer couched in the form of a sequence of petitions. It has a figurative use in expressions such as a *litany of curses* or *woes*. A *liturgy* (from Greek *leitourgia* 'public service, public worship') is a prescribed form of worship, embracing many individual prayers and petitions.

litchi see LYCHEE.

literally. Few words have the capacity to cause such mirth: *My grandfather, King George VI, who had literally been catapulted onto the throne*—Prince Edward as quoted in *Private Eye*, 1998. There will always be occasions when this type of hilarity is best avoided; on the other hand, a little linguistic reflection will reveal a logical rigour behind a much derided use.

1 The literal (16c) meaning of *literally* is 'in a literal sense': *This was a china warehouse indeed, truly and literally to be called so*—Daniel Defoe, 1719. It is still used in this way, with reference to the meaning of individual words (with the word *mean* often explicitly present) and to the broader sense in which phrases and sentences are to be understood: *He . . . was literally too tired to move*—J. Gores, 1972 | *The cracker in Georgia cracker literally means a person who still cracks corn*—S. B. Flexner, 1982.

2 In the course of time, *literally* became caught up in the language of metaphor, in which English abounds, and we find this type of use: *Every day with me is literally another yesterday for it is exactly the same*—Pope, 1708. From this it is a short step for the word to become an intensifier contained wholly within metaphor: *For the last four years . . . I literally coined money*—F. A. Kemble, 1863. In other examples we can see the word half in and half out of the realm of metaphor: *Crabs and lobsters are literally to be found crawling round the floor waiting for an order*—*Good Food Guide*, 1973 (the creatures are physically crawling around the floor but are, we may assume, only metaphorically waiting for an order).

3 This historical development explains how the word has apparently reversed its meaning; in fact it has done no such thing but has been absorbed into the metaphor; once understood as part of the verbal image and not as external to it, the use makes good linguistic sense. It is doubtful though whether this rationale will satisfy those who see the developed meaning of *literally* as sloppy and inappropriate (which it rarely is) or as ludicrous (which it sometimes appears to be): *Most of the buildings on the corniche have literally been face-lifted*—*Blitz*, 1989 | *They* [sc. supermarkets] *can literally play God, even to the point of sending food back to the genetic drawing board for a redesign*—*Guardian*, 1995.

4 In another very common type, *literally* introduces a fixed expression or cliché that has some particular (often punning) relevance to the context: *We have lived in a wonderful variety of houses, including . . . a leaking gothic horror of a Victorian rectory in deepest Sussex that was literally falling to pieces*—*Medau News*, 1980 | *There is a catastrophic 'implosion' . . . followed by a shock-wave which literally blows the star apart in what is called a supernova outburst*—Patrick Moore, 1990 | *Today, Cerezo's letter to the villagers is literally carved in stone; a six-foot-high marble and stone replica stands opposite 13 rough wooden crosses, marking*

the spots where the villagers fell—
New Statesman, 1992.

5 The conclusion is: avoid using
literally when the effect might be
distracting or comic; but it can
be used to good effect in cases
where it reinforces a strong verbal image.

litotes, pronounced liy-**toh**-teez
or li-**toh**-teez, is a figure of speech
in which an assertion is made by
means of understatement or denial of an opposite, as when St
Paul declared that he was 'a citizen of *no mean* city' (Acts 21:39).
Typical modern examples include
not bad (= very good), *not uncom-
mon* (= quite frequent), and *it was
nothing* (as a statement dismissing
one's own achievement). *Litotes* is
therefore the opposite of HYPER-
BOLE or overstatement.

litre is the BrE spelling for the
metric unit, and *liter* the AmE
spelling.

liturgy see LITANY.

liveable is the preferred form,
not *livable*.

-lived see LONG-LIVED; SHORT-
LIVED.

livid. The meaning that is more
familiar today, 'furiously angry',
is a recent one not recorded before the 20c. The earlier (17c)
meaning, still in use, is 'of a bluish leaden colour; discoloured by
bruising': *A huge, livid, recently
healed scar ran along the right side
of his face*—P. Abrahams, 1985.

living-room see SITTING-ROOM.

llama see LAMA.

-l-, -ll-.
See box opposite

Lloyd's, Lloyds. The name of
the London society of under-
writers is spelt *Lloyd's* (also *Lloyd's
list, Lloyd's Register*), whereas the
name of the bank is *Lloyds Bank*
(no apostrophe).

loadstar, loadstone see LODE-
STAR, LODESTONE.

loaf. The plural form of the
noun is *loaves*; the third person
singular of the verb is *loafs*.

loan *verb.* In 19c British English,
loan was a standard alternative
for *lend*, but by the time Fowler
wrote (1926) *loan* had been largely
driven out by *lend*, although it
has continued in use in AmE. In
current use *loan* is mostly confined to non-British varieties of
English: *Delaney told him he could
loan him $50 a week*—Thomas Ken-
eally, 1985 (Australia) | *The problem
was how to stretch the small amount
of money he had been loaned by Herr
Pfuehl*—Anita Desai (India). But it is
used in BrE too in the context of
making something valuable (such
as a work of art) available by a
formal arrangement to an institution for a period: *It is part of the
Christ Church plate in the treasury
showcase, which also displays many
items loaned by parishes within the
diocese*—Christ Church Oxford: A Pit-
kin Guide, 1991 (an alternative,
more pleasing to some, is *on loan
from*). In normal contexts, however, *loan* is a so-called 'needless
variant' of *lend*.

loanword is a word adopted,
normally with little change in
form, from another language. Examples in English are *blitz* (from
German) and *locale* (from French;
see below).

loath, meaning 'averse, reluctant', as in *loath to comment*, is

-l-, -ll-

Much confusion is caused by differing spelling practice in BrE and AmE in verbs of two syllables pronounced with the stress on the second syllable, e.g. *enthrall/enthral* and *fulfil/fulfill*. Practice varies even within each variety of English; the following table lists the recommended spellings:

BrE	AmE
annul	annul
appal	appall
befall	befall
distil	distill
enrol	enroll
enthral	enthrall
extol	extol
fulfil	fulfill
install	install
instil	instill

The recommended spellings for nouns in *-ment* are:

BrE	AmE
annulment	annulment
enrolment	enrollment
enthralment	enthrallment
extolment	extolment
fulfilment	fulfillment
instalment	installment
instilment	instillment

For the spelling of inflected forms of verbs in -l (*appal, appalled, appalling*, etc.) see DOUBLING OF FINAL CONSONANTS IN INFLECTION.

spelt *loath*, not *loth*, and is pronounced lohth (like *both*). It should be distinguished from the verb *loathe* meaning 'to hate', which is pronounced lohdh. The adjective *loathsome*, meaning 'hateful, repulsive', is derived from *loathe* and is pronounced **lohdh**-səm.

locale, meaning 'a scene or locality, especially with reference to an event or occurrence taking place there', was adopted in the 18c from French in the form *local* and respelt in the 19c by writers such as Walter Scott to indicate that the stress lay on the second syllable (loh-**kahl**).

locate is an 18c Americanism that still has a transatlantic flavour, especially in its intransitive use (without an object) as in *Numerous industries have located in the area*. In BrE, this use is more common in the form *relocate*, also originally an Americanism (19c): *I am advising your colleague . . . to relocate*—Robert McCrum, 1991. In both varieties, *to be located* is a synonym for 'to be situated' (*The supermarket is located in the northern outskirts of the city*), but again its American sound can cause disquiet among British language purists.

locum tenens. To avoid having to pronounce the second word at all (**tee**-nenz is the preferred option), this term for 'a deputy standing in for a doctor or cleric' is best shortened to *locum* (pronounced **loh**-kəm). The plural then is *locums*. The plural of the full form is the somewhat unusable *locum tenentes*.

lodestar, lodestone are the preferred spellings, not *load-*.

loggia, a word of Italian origin meaning 'an open-sided gallery or arcade', is pronounced **loj**-ə, and has the plural form *loggias*.

lonelily, though good enough for Matthew Arnold (*The weird chipping of the woodpecker Rang lonelily and sharp*, 1852), is too awkward for everyday use, and is best replaced by the type 'in a lonely fashion'. See -LILY.

long. The conjunction *as long as* has two main meanings: (1) 'during the whole time that' (*You can stay as long as you like*), and (2) 'provided that, only if' (*You can stay as long as you help me*). In the second meaning, it is more likely to be preceded by a comma (*You can stay, as long as you help me*), and the shortened form *long as* is occasionally found in informal reported conversation: *'It's all right,' he said, 'long as you are here'—*Graham Greene, 1938.

longevity, meaning 'long life', is pronounced lon-**jev**-i-ti, not long-**gev**-i-ti.

longitude. The recommended pronunciation is **lon**-ji-tyood rather than **long**-gi-tyood. Beware of

pronouncing it, let alone spelling it, *longtitude*.

long-lived is pronounced long-**livd** in BrE and long-**liyvd** in AmE.

look. 1 NON-STANDARD USES. There are various idiomatic uses of *look* that are confined to particular parts of the English-speaking world and are not part of standard English: for example *look you* as a way of attracting attention, found in Shakespeare (*Why, look you, how you storm!—The Merchant of Venice* I.iii.140) and still used in Wales, *looky here* (an AmE variant of *look here*), and the colloquial AmE (20c) form *lookit* used with the meaning 'Look!' or 'Listen!'.

2 LOOK + TO-INFINITIVE. *I shall hereafter look to be treated as a person of respectability—*T. Huxley, 1900. This type, meaning 'to expect', has been in continuous use since the 16c but is beginning to sound dated and is falling into disuse. Still in regular use is a form of this in which the continuous tense is used (*am looking*, etc.) and the sense is more of hope or intention than of expectation: *I am looking to the government to help to solve the problem—*oral source, 1987 | *The home team will be looking to get a result against the visitors next Saturday—Times*, 1988. In a third type, *look + to*-infinitive means 'to look as if, to appear': *The owl looked to be encircled by six cloaked hitmen—*J. E. Maslow, 1982. Although there is a theoretical risk of ambiguity here, this does not seem to occur in practice.

3 LOOK + ADVERBS AND ADJECTIVES. The meaning we are concerned with here is 'appear, seem'. Uses with an adverb complement (as in Shakespeare's *The skies looke grimly*) are now virtually extinct. A possible exception is the phrase *to look well* (= to appear to be in good health), but even here *well* is virtually an adjective. Uses with adjectives are normal, as in *to look black, blue, cold, elderly, foolish, small, stupid*, etc.

4 LOOK LIKE + CLAUSE *You look to me . . . like you was made out of old wichetty grubs*—Patrick White, 1961 (Australia) | *Looks like your child's birthday is news again this year*—*Guardian*, 1973. For this construction, see LIKE 1.

loom large see LARGE, LARGELY.

loose, loosen. Both words involve removal of restraints, physical or otherwise. The difference is that *loose* releases or sets free whereas *loosen* only makes more loose (or less tight). To *loose* a prisoner from his bonds is to set him free; to *loosen* his bonds is to make them less tight although he remains a captive. Unwelcome things are *loosed on* people when people have to endure them: *Another miserable heritage of Watergate has been the bilge loosed on the public by . . . psychopathic jargoneers . . . and belly-achers*—*New York Law Journal*, 1973. See also LOSE.

Lord's, the name of the London cricket ground, is spelt with an apostrophe.

lose. The verb *lose* is occasionally written as *loose*, especially by writers in a hurry. The verb *loose* has a quite different meaning, and has enough problems of its own (see LOOSE, LOOSEN).

lose out, meaning 'to be unsuccessful', is recorded in AmE from the mid-19c and is now common in BrE as well. It has various shades of meaning, and is not simply a synonym for *lose*. Followed by *on*, it means 'not to get

a fair chance in': *Like most birds she didn't want to lose out on a nosh-up*—A. Draper, 1970. Followed by *to*, it means 'be defeated or worsted by': *The popular press, thrown off balance and uncertain of its role, lost out to the heavies and the provincials*—*Author*, 1971.

lost causes. Each generation has its own preoccupations about language, and the transitory nature of some of these tends to be overlooked. Some issues of current concern are listed at the entry for FETISH; these include the split infinitive, the ending of a sentence with a preposition, use of the sentence adverb *hopefully*, and the use of *from* after *different*. None of these concerns has any firm basis in grammar or language structure; the split infinitive, for example, is a 19c superstition. In the 18c, Dr Johnson disliked words that he classified as 'low words' (he did not use the term 'slang') such as *bogus, coax, joke, flog, prim, rogue, snob*, and *spree*; all these are now accepted items of general vocabulary. Among Fowler's strictures that we may now regard as lost causes are: *agenda* (use *agendum* for the singular), *belittle* (= disparage, an undesirable alien), *cachet* (should be 'expelled as an alien'), *data* (plural only), *caption* (in the sense 'title or heading': 'rare and might well be rarer'), *category* (use *class*), *clever* (= well-read or studious, 'much misused, especially in feminine conversation'), *coastal* and *tidal* (badly formed barbarisms), *conservative* (= moderate, cautious in estimating), *distinctly* (as in *distinctly interesting*), *malnutrition* ('a word to be avoided'), *negotiate* (= tackle successfully, an 'improper' sense), and *suchlike* (= the like, 'now usually left to the uneducated'). See also IF AND

WHEN. More recently, strictures on the use of *decimate* and *involve*, on the pronunciation of multi-syllable words such as *controversy* and *formidable*, and on newer words of mixed origin (such as *television*), have all joined the band of lost causes. To regard them in this way is a recognition of the force of language change, rather than a concession to declining standards.

lot. The phrases *a lot of* and *lots of* (*a lot of time* | *lots of people*) are common and highly versatile, being used freely with singular (mass) nouns and plural nouns. In positive contexts, *a lot of* is idiomatic (*There is a lot of time*) and *lots of* is informal; in negative contexts, *much* or *many* or *a great deal of* are usually better alternatives in more formal contexts (*We do not have much time*).

loud, loudly. *Loud* is occasionally used as an adverb, especially in semi-fixed expressions such as *loud and clear* (*I can hear you loud and clear*: *loudly and clearly* could also be used here, but would sound less natural). In other contexts it is used informally, but *loudly* is the better choice: *She spoke loud enough for the whole class to hear.*

louvre, meaning '(one of) a set of overlapping slats for ventilation', is spelt in this way in BrE and *louver* in AmE.

lovable is the preferred spelling, not *loveable*.

love. In literature of the 16c to 19c, the expression *to make love to* means 'to court, to be amorous towards' ('*Who's had the impudence to make love to my sister!' cried Harry*—George Meredith, 1861), whereas in modern literature it means 'to have sexual intercourse with'. This more specific meaning arose during the 20c, and has driven out the older meaning much as the sexual sense of *intercourse* has driven out, or at least compromised, all its other uses. Regard for the date of writing is therefore important on encountering the expression in print.

lovelily, despite a long history (first recorded *c*.1300) and use by great writers (*So lovelily the morning shone*—Byron, 1813), now seems too awkward for everyday use, and is best replaced by the type 'in a lovely manner'. See -LILY.

lovey, a colloquial form of address to a loved one or (in more recent use) to a theatrical colleague, is spelt in this way, not *lovy*.

low, lowly. *Low* is an adjective (*a low ceiling*) and adverb (*to aim low* | *to lie low*). *Lowly* is an adjective meaning 'humble, modest' (*of lowly station*); its use as an adverb is now largely confined to poetry.

lunch, luncheon. *Lunch* is now the standard word for a midday meal, and *luncheon* seems affectedly formal (although it is used, perhaps not surprisingly, in the commercial term *luncheon voucher*).

lunge, meaning 'to make a sudden movement forward', has the participial form *lunging*, not *lungeing*, which means 'exercising a horse with a long rope (or *lunge*)'.

luxuriant, luxurious. These two words, both connected with the word *luxury* (in turn derived from the Latin word *luxus* meaning 'abundance'), have got in each other's way since the 17c. Nonetheless, their meanings are distinct, as R. M. Ballantyne recognized in two uses in his *Coral Island* (1858): *The trees and bushes were very luxuriant | Altogether this was the most luxurious supper we had enjoyed for many a day.* Essentially, *luxurious*, the more general word, means 'rich or abundant in luxuries or comforts' whereas *luxuriant* has the specific meaning 'rich or abundant in foliage or vegetation'.

-ly forms adverbs (*boldly, quickly*; see ADVERB 2) and adjectives (*goodly, kindly*). Some adjectives form adverbs in *-ly* in addition to being used as adverbs themselves, always with distinctions in meaning (e.g. *dear | dearly, direct | directly, hard | hardly, right | rightly, tight | tightly*). See the entries for these words, and for other aspects see -EDLY; -LILY.

lychee (pronounced **liy**-chee), the name of a Chinese fruit, is spelt this way rather than *lichee* or *litchi*, although these forms are dominant in AmE (and are pronounced **lee**-chee).

lych-gate see LICH-GATE.

lyric, lyrical. *Lyric* is the adjective to use when referring to a type of poetry that expresses the poet's feelings in set forms such as an ode or sonnet (*lyric poet | lyric verses*). A *lyric* is a poem of this kind, and in modern use *lyrics* (plural) denotes the words of a popular song. *Lyrical* is occasionally used for the adjective *lyric* (as in Wordsworth's title *Lyrical Ballads*, 1798), but predominantly means 'using language appropriate to lyric poetry, and is therefore more allusive and descriptive. It is also used in the expression *wax lyrical*, meaning 'to talk in enthusiastic terms about something'.

Mm

macabre is pronounced mə-**kah**-brə, although it tends to sound like mə-**kah**-bə, with the last r lost, in rapid speech.

Macchiavellian, a noun and adjective denoting a politically devious schemer, is spelt with a capital initial letter and two ls.

machination, meaning 'scheming, laying plots', is pronounced mak-i-**nay**-shən or mash-i-**nay**-shən.

machismo, meaning 'a show of masculinity', is at an early stage of naturalization into English and its pronunciation varies between mə-**chiz**-moh and mə-**kiz**-moh.

macho is a shortened form of *machismo*, and is mostly used as an adjective meaning 'showily masculine, virile'.

mackintosh, the waterproof coat, is spelt with a *k*, although the inventor's name was Charles *Macintosh*. The shortened form *mac* is often used instead.

Mac-, Mc-. In English dictionaries and lists of names, it is usual to order all names spelt with these prefixes as if they were spelt *Mac-*, so that a user who is unsure of the spelling does not have a lengthy search. A typical sequence is therefore *Maccabees, McCarthyism, mace, macle, McNaughten rules, macramé*. In American practice, however, it is more usual to place names beginning with *Mc-* at their literal place in the sequence, i.e. after words in *mac-* and any in *mb-*, so that *Mc-* *Carthy* might appear more than twenty pages further on than *Macdonald*.

mad. The primary meaning of the adjective, 'suffering from mental illness', has been in continuous use since Old English, although it is no longer a part of medical usage. Its extended meaning 'foolish', as in *a mad undertaking*, is also Old English, the meaning 'angry' (common especially in AmE) is 14c, and the idiomatic uses as in *like mad* and *mad about football* both date from the 17c.

madam, madame. The English form *madam* is a now somewhat formal or affectedly courteous form of address to a woman (*Dear Madam | Madam Chairman | Can I help you, madam?*). When addressing royalty, the shorter form *ma'am* is used. *Madame*, pronounced mə-**dahm**, is the right form of address to a woman from any foreign nation (not necessarily French), and is also a term (should one be needed) for a woman brothel-keeper.

maelstrom, an originally Dutch word meaning 'a state of great confusion', is pronounced **mayl**-strəm.

maestro, meaning 'a distinguished musician or artist', is pronounced **miy**-stroh, and has plural forms *maestri* (**miy**-stri) or *maestros*.

Mafia, pronounced **maf**-i-ə, is spelt with a capital initial when it refers to the organized international body of criminals in Sicily, southern Italy, and the US; a member of the Mafia is a *Mafioso* (maf-i-**oh**-zoh), plural *Mafiosi* (maf-i-**oh**-zi). The form *mafia*, with small initial, is used in the extended meaning 'any group exerting a sinister hidden influence' (as in *the literary mafia*).

Magdalen, Magdalene. The names of the colleges in Oxford (*Magdalen*) and Cambridge (*Magdalene*) are pronounced **maw**-dlin. In the full biblical name *Mary Magdalene* (= of Magdala in Galilee), *Magdalene* is pronounced **mag**-də-lin or mag-də-**lee**-ni. The form *magdalen*, pronounced **mag**-də-lin, is used in the meanings 'a reformed prostitute' or 'a home for reformed prostitutes'.

Magi, as in *the three Magi*, is pronounced **may**-jiy. It is the plural of *magus* (**may**-gəs), which denotes a member of a priestly caste in ancient Persia.

magic, magical. The two words compete with one another in all the main senses, 'relating to magic', 'produced by or as if by magic', and 'wonderful', although *magic* is used exclusively in certain fixed expressions such as *magic lantern* and *magic square*. When used in its descriptive role, *magic* still behaves more like a noun than an adjective; otherwise, *magic* and *magical* are largely interchangeable, however close or remote the connection with magic and related phenomena: . . . *in the evenings, when the afterglow makes the whole valley magic*—J. Ashe, 1993 | *She had not been kissed for over two years and it was magical*—P. Wilson, 1993 | *The waters here are magically calm and peaceful*—B. King & A. Chambers, 1993. In the second half of the

20c, *magic* has come to be used informally both in attributive position (before a noun) and by itself as a term of enthusiastic approval (*We had a magic time | It's magic!*).

magma, meaning 'fluid material under the earth's surface', has the plural form *magmas* (no longer *magmata*).

Magna Carta is the usual spelling now for the famous English charter of 1215, although *Magna Charta*, once the dominant form, is still sometimes found, especially in AmE. Gowers (1965) reported that 'in a Bill introduced in 1946 authorizing the Trustees of the British Museum to lend a copy to the Library of Congress, *Charta* was the spelling used. But when the Bill reached committee stage in the House of Lords, the Lord Chancellor (Lord Jowitt) moved to substitute *Carta* and produced conclusive evidence that that was the correct spelling. The amendment was carried without a division; so *Carta* has now unimpeachable authority.' It should be mentioned that *Charta* and *Carta* are both valid forms in Latin.

magneto, a shortened form of *magneto-electric machine*, has the plural form *magnetos*.

magus see MAGI.

major is commonly used, especially in journalism, to mean 'important, significant', without any notion of comparison inherent in the word's origins. A political leader invariably gives a *major* speech, a reference book is published in a *major* new edition, and *major* accidents occur regularly on main roads and motorways. This use is too well established for it to be condemned, but *major* is better used when the element of comparison is present, so that a *major* work is important relative to other lesser works, a *major* road is contrasted with a minor one, and so on.

major-general has the plural form *major-generals*.

majority. We are concerned here with three related uses, two of them relatively straightforward and one that gives rise to a difficulty:

1 *MAJORITY* = 'A SUPERIORITY IN NUMBERS', especially in political contexts, 'the amount by which a winning vote exceeds the next': *The amendment was passed by a large majority | The labour candidate's majority was increased by 15%.* The verb following this use is always singular. (Note that in AmE, *majority* means the amount by which the winning vote exceeds *all* the others, i.e. what in BrE is called an *overall majority*; for the meaning given above *plurality* is used.)

2 *MAJORITY* = 'THE GREATER NUMBER OR PART'. *Any future Prime Minister to whom the donnish majority was prepared to give an honorary doctorate would be one whose policies found favour with them—Times, 1985 | The vast majority have now come to terms with their destiny—Encounter, 1987.* The verb following this use can be either singular or plural, depending on whether collectivity or individuality is the stronger notion.

3 *MAJORITY OF* + PLURAL NOUN. *The vast majority of Luxembourgers speak Letzeburgesch at home—Guardian, 1972 | A majority of them come from the Scheduled Castes—Times of India, 1972 | It is clear from opinion polls that the very large majority of people in Scotland wish to remain part of Britain—Times, 1976 | The majority of school buildings are dilapidated and decaying—Encounter, 1987.* The verb following this use is invariably plural, and the noun following *majority of* should always be plural; uses with singular nouns (*the majority of the work | the majority of the time*) are unidiomatic unless these are words such as *group, population,* etc. which denote a collection of individuals: *Gillray, in common with the vast majority of his public, did not want to take the Jacobin side—M. Billig, 1991 | The majority of the working population in the 1960s, around two-thirds of the labour force, was employed in service occupations—J. Allen et al., 1988.*

malapropisms. Fowler (1926) was right to point out that malapropisms, or 'the use of a word in mistake for one sounding similar', occur occasionally, as 'single spies, not in battalions, one in an article, perhaps, instead of four in a sentence', unlike the utterances of the eponymous Mrs Malaprop in Sheridan's *The Rivals* of 1775 in which they come thick and fast. Two modern examples: *One, a head of English, could not explain the function of an intransigent* [instead of *intransitive*] *verb and advised me to 'forget it'*—letter in *Sunday Times*, 1988 | *When she heard our Gloucester house was haunted, she uttered the immortal line, 'You'll have to get the vicar in to circumcise* [instead of *exorcise*] *it*—J. Cooper, 1991.

male, masculine, manly.
1 Both *male* and *masculine* entered the language from Old French in the 14c and rapidly took on distinct roles. *Male* is used as an adjective and noun, contrasting with the unrelated

word *female*, to designate the sex of humans, animals, and plants that can beget offspring by insemination or fertilization. *Masculine* is used only of humans and has two additional meanings: (1) denoting characteristics or qualities associated with men, and (2) contrasted with *feminine* and *neuter*, denoting a class of grammatical gender. Both words also have technical meanings in various domains. In broad terms *male* is used principally to indicate the sex of a person, animal or plant, whereas *masculine* is used of characteristics (once, and to some extent still) regarded as characteristic of men, especially physical strength, vigour, competitive assertiveness, etc. *Manly* (13c, originally referring to humans generally but now only to men) also has this meaning but is more positive and complimentary than *masculine*. As a noun, *male* does not carry the unfavourable implications of *female*, but is still best restricted to uses relating to the animal world. See FEMALE, FEMININE.

2 Two 20c uses of *male*, both largely promoted by the feminist movement, are in the terms *male chauvinist* (first recorded in 1970), meaning 'a man who is prejudiced against women', and *male menopause* (1949), meaning 'a crisis of potency, confidence, etc., said to afflict men in middle life'.

malicious, malign, malignant, malevolent. 1 All four words are connected with doing harm or evil (from Latin *malus*), but there are important differences. *Malicious* means 'intending to do harm' and is associated with people (or occasionally animals) and their actions: *The dog that destroys Gabriel Oak's sheep is over-enthusiastic, not malicious*—Margaret

Drabble, 1976. *Malignant* is used principally in medical contexts of life-threatening diseases and tumours; its more general meaning, 'feeling or showing intense ill will', is still found (*He would have a sensation of something malignant about to crush him*—G. Watson, 1991) but is now overshadowed by the technical use. The shorter form *malign* is used mostly of things that are evil in their nature or effects (*She was no longer the victim of chance, of a malign fate*—W. J. Burely, 1989); it has also been used in the medical sense as an opposite of *benign* but has largely given way to *malignant*. *Malevolent* means 'wishing harm to others' and refers rather to general disposition than to particular actions or conduct: *Trees were brooding presences, soughing incantations. Every bush hid an invisible force, frequently malevolent*—W. McIlvanney, 1975. *Malevolent* is often used of looks and sounds: *He had a nervous twitch which jerked at a muscle at the corner of his thin-lipped mouth and a malevolent stare*—A. Granger, 1991.

2 The corresponding nouns are *malice* (or *maliciousness*, which has more specific reference), *malignancy*, and *malevolence*. The noun *malignity* is derived from *malign* and has enjoyed substantial usage over several centuries in the meaning 'wicked ill will or hatred', which it still has although it is used much less than formerly: *His self-sufficient malignity* [is] *seemingly motiveless until the last pages of the book, when a tattooed number is noticed on his arm, and a casual remark—'I spent the war in Belsen'*—G. Watson, 1991.

mall, in the meanings 'a sheltered walk or promenade' and 'an enclosed shopping precinct', is increasingly heard in Britain in the form mawl (already familiar in America, Australia, and elsewhere), rather than mal. But mal is still obligatory in the London place-names *The Mall*, *Chiswick Mall*, and *Pall Mall*.

malnutrition belongs firmly to the list of Fowlerian LOST CAUSES. 'A word to be avoided,' wrote Fowler in 1926, as often as *under-feeding* will do the work. Alas for Fowler, *underfeeding* has not done its work, although the related form *underfed* is still going strong as an alternative for *malnourished*. It is interesting, though, that we are so ready to use the technical term in general contexts.

man has been used for centuries in the generalized meaning 'a human being (regardless of sex)', and is embedded deep in idiom and verbal imagery: *Man cannot live by bread alone* | *Every man for himself* | *Be one's own man* | etc. It is no use protesting that the gender phenomenon represented here is linguistic and not sexual, when changing social attitudes (shared by men as well as women) see it as an unacceptable outward sign of male dominance. There are alternatives available, though none of them is quite without awkwardness: *person* or *one* for *man* in the countable sense (*One cannot live by bread alone*), and *humanity* or *humankind* for *man* in the uncountable sense (*Humankind cannot live by bread alone*). As these examples show, however, it will be many years before such contrived substitutions will sound natural, and they probably never will. But in everyday language there is no reason not to respect gender sensitivities in language. See also SEXIST LANGUAGE.

-man, as a suffix in occupational words such as *chairman* and *craftsman*, is normally restricted now to male contexts in accordance with changing attitudes to the word MAN. When the person concerned is a woman, forms in *-woman* or *-person*, or some other gender-neutral term such as *police officer* for *policeman* and *firefighter* for *fireman*, are now commonly used instead.

manage has inflected forms *managed* and *managing*, and a derivative form *manageable*.

manageress see -ESS.

maneuver is an AmE variant of MANOEUVRE.

mango, the fruit, has plural forms *mangoes* (preferred) or *mangos*.

mangy, meaning 'having mange' or 'squalid, shabby', is spelt this way, not *mangey*.

-mania. The rapid turnover of occasional and ephemeral words formed with this suffix was noted by the *OED* and has continued in the 20c with forms such as *Beatlemania*, *Olliemania* (Oliver North, central figure in the US Iran Contra scandal of the later 1980s), and *technomania*. Corresponding forms in *-maniac* also continue to be found.

manifesto has the plural form *manifestos*.

manikin, meaning 'a dwarf', 'an artist's dummy', or 'an anatomical model', is spelt this way, not *mannikin* or *manakin*. A dressmaker's model is a *mannequin*.

Manila is the spelling for the capital of the Philippine Islands. The hemp and paper are both spelt *manila*, although *manilla* is sometimes found.

manipulate. The adjective derivatives are *manipulable* ('capable of being manipulated'; not *manipulatable*) and *manipulative* ('inclined to exploit unscrupulously').

mankind is pronounced with the stress on the second syllable when the meaning is 'the human species' and with the stress on the first syllable when the meaning is 'male people, as distinct from female'. In the first meaning, *humankind* is now often used instead. See SEXIST LANGUAGE.

mannequin see MANIKIN.

manner. The phrase *to the manner born* is now commonly used to mean 'naturally at ease in a given situation'. This use is informal only; the phrase is taken from Shakespeare, *Hamlet* I.iv.17, where it means 'destined by birth to follow a custom or way of life'.

manoeuvre has inflected forms *manoeuvred, manoeuvring*. The spelling in AmE is *maneuver*, with inflected forms *maneuvered, maneuvering*.

man-of-war has the plural form *men-of-war*.

manpower see SEXIST LANGUAGE.

manqué. In the meaning 'that might have been but is not', *manqué* is placed after the noun it refers to: *a poet manqué*.

mantel, mantle. *Mantel* is originally a variant of *mantle*, both forms are derived from the Latin word *mantellum* meaning 'cloak', and both have meanings to do with covering. *Mantle* has several uses, including 'cloak' (usually as worn by women) and the figurative meaning 'responsibility or authority' (especially regarded as passing from one person to another). *Mantel* has one meaning, usually in the longer form *mantelpiece* or *mantelshelf*, 'a shelf over a fireplace'.

many. 1 *Many*, like *much*, tends to sound more formal in positive contexts (*They have many friends*) than in negative ones (*They do not have many friends*). In conversation and less formal written English, *a lot of* (or, even more informally, *lots of*) is used instead in positive contexts.

2 The type *many a*, though notionally plural, always entails a singular construction: *Many a prostitute, whether she calls herself a . . . hostess, or a common whore, imagines that she is exploiting the male sex*—Germaine Greer, 1970.

Maori is pronounced as two syllables (**mow**-ri) and has the plural form *Maoris* in general usage, although Maoris themselves have been urging non-Maoris in New Zealand and elsewhere to use their own pronunciation of the name with three syllables (**mah**-aw-ri) and to adopt their plural form *Maori*, the same as the singular. The plural form is more likely to succeed than the pronunciation, since the two-syllable form is more natural to most speakers of English.

marathon, the name of the long-distance race and, by extension, a word for any lengthy or difficult task or undertaking, is derived from the name of the famous battle fought between Greeks (mainly Athenians and Plataeans) and Persians on the east coast of Attica in 490 BC. The length of the race (26 miles 385 yards or 42km 352m) is based on a relatively late tradition that the Athenian Pheidippides ran from Marathon to Athens *after* the battle with news of the Greek victory, whereas the primary source for these events, the 5c BC historian Herodotus, records that Pheidippides ran to appeal for support *before* the battle from Athens to Sparta (in southern Greece), a distance that represents a much more remarkable achievement.

marchioness see MARQUESS.

margarine. After a battle royal fought throughout the 20c between those who pronounce it with a 'soft' -j- sound (as in the shortened form *marge*) and those who favour a 'hard' -g- sound (as in *Margaret*), the first of these is now completely dominant, despite Fowler's objection (1926) that this was 'clearly wrong'. He based his view partly on the authority of the *OED* (which in its 2nd edition of 1989 still puts the 'hard' form first) and partly on the fact that the only other words in which g is 'soft' before a vowel other than e or i are *gaol* (and its derivatives) and *mortgagor*.

marginalize. To the editors of the *OED* around the turn of the century, this meant no more than 'to write marginal notes upon', and they marked it 'rare'. Since then it has been so transformed that the 1991 edition of the *Oxford Dictionary of New Words* described it (or, more precisely, its derivative *marginalization*) as 'one of the main social buzzwords of the eighties'. Increased awareness of the rights of underprivileged groups and minorities has given the word its new lease

of life in the meaning 'to treat (a person or group of people) as *marginal* and therefore unimportant'. The use of *marginal* reflected here is itself a 20c development, first in the sociological meaning 'partly belonging to two differing societies or cultures but not fully integrated into either' and then in the more general meaning 'of minor importance, insignificant'. Examples: *Society, taking its lead from the media and its politicians, begins to reject a whole class and marginalizes them in the job market*—C. Phillips, 1987 | *Until recently, children's books were regarded as marginal, less than serious as literature*—J. Briggs, 1989 | *It is not yet clear that the church's long years of marginalisation in our national life have been ended*—Independent, 1990 | *You work with what are often called 'marginalized' people, such as African-Americans and people of color*—Bomb, 1992.

markedly see -EDLY.

marquess, marquis. Both words are pronounced **mah**-kwis. A *marquess* is a British nobleman ranking between a duke and an earl, and a *marquis* is a foreign equivalent ranking between a duke and a count. A *marquise*, pronounced mah-**keez**, is the wife or widow of a marquis or a woman holding the rank of marquis in her own right. A *marchioness* is the wife or widow of a marquess, or a woman holding the rank of marquess in her own right.

marriageable is spelt with an e in the middle.

marshal. The verb has inflected forms *marshalled, marshalling* in BrE, and usually *marshaled, marshaling* in AmE.

marten, martin. A *marten* is an animal like a weasel, whereas a *martin* is a bird of the swallow family.

marvel. The verb has inflected forms *marvelled, marvelling* in BrE, and usually *marveled, marveling* in AmE.

marvellous is the spelling in BrE, but *marvelous* is more usual in AmE.

Mary. The plural form is *Marys* (as in *the two Marys*).

masculine see MALE.

massacre is spelt this way in BrE and AmE, and has inflected forms *massacres, massacred, massacring*.

massage is pronounced **mas**-ahzh or **mas**-ahj in BrE, and mə-**sahzh** in AmE. The agent nouns *masseur* and *masseuse* are pronounced with the stress on the second syllable in both BrE and AmE.

massive has become an over-used word in contexts that have little to do with mass: *A massive punt downfield from* [goalkeeper] *Parkes—Times*, 1975 | *Yet another massive stage project, now previewing at the Aldwych, where it officially opens on June 19—Times*, 1980. In many cases alternatives such as *immense, enormous, substantial, powerful, impressive*, or even *huge* or *large*, should be considered. In extended and figurative uses, *massive* is best reserved for contexts in which an image of vast size is appropriate: *Riot police looked on impassively . . . as a massive crowd of mourners . . . gave the clenched fist Marxist salute—Times*, 1977 | *The most important area on which to concentrate was the massive amount of water required by the production of textiles—Daily Telegraph*, 1992. But use one of the alternative words when the image is unreal or forced: ⊠ *Women have massive amounts of love invested in fathers, lovers and sons, and many of these women despise the systems their own men may be helping to sustain—*B. Cant et al., 1988.

masterful, masterly. Although both words have at some time in their history shared all the meanings involved here, they have settled down in more recent usage in such a way that *masterful* conveys meanings to do with dominance and power whereas *masterly* connotes skill and fine qualities: *His mentor was band leader Joe Loss. 'When Loss used a stick the bounce and freedom within a beat was masterly.'—Gramophone*, 1978 | *'Oh, I do like the way you talk to the waiters, so masterful,' sighed Esther—*S. Mackay, 1984. Fowler (1926) noted with regret that *masterful* was too often used for *masterly* (though not the other way round), and this is still the case: ⊠ *Johnny Hodges, Duke Ellington's masterful alto saxophonist—Daily Telegraph*, 1970 | ⊠ *There are just enough such slippages in this generally masterful book to suggest that Fish still has room for further self-revision—Times Literary Supplement*, 1990. We also find *masterfully* now and then doubling as an adverb for *masterly*, which lacks a single-word equivalent: ⊠ *For over twenty years, Hugo had masterfully deployed the metaphor of the wave—*A. Martin, 1991. The distinction is important since the two words are not so distinct in meaning that ambiguity can always be avoided.

mat see MATT.

materialize is first recorded in 1710 and its first meaning was transitive (with an object): to *ma-terialize* an idea was to realize it and to *materialize* a spirit was to make the spirit appear. Its intransitive use, now more familiar, dates from the late 19c, still in the context of spiritualism: *The . . . ghosts . . . gave dark séances and manifested and materialized—Harper's Magazine*, 1884. But in current use the sense has been generalized so much that it means little more than 'happen' or 'become available': *Plans do not always materialise in the anticipated way—*Barbara Pym, 1982 | *The alimony her ex-husband was supposed to pay never materialized—*R. Deacon, 1988. This use is acceptable in all but the most formal contexts.

matériel meaning 'material and equipment used in warfare (as distinct from personnel)', has not been fully naturalized in English and is printed in italics with an accent (although the accent is often omitted in Services' documents).

matey, an informal word meaning 'sociable', is spelt with an *e*, not *maty*.

math is the AmE abbreviation for *mathematics*; in BrE it is *maths*.

mathematics is treated as a singular noun when it is the name of a subject (*Mathematics is not my favourite activity*) and as a plural noun when it means 'the process of calculating' (*The mathematics of the problem are quite complex*).

maths see MATH.

matinée literally means 'morning' in French, but it now invariably means 'in the afternoon' (in French and English) when used to distinguish an afternoon film or

theatre performance from an evening performance. The accent is often dropped, especially in AmE.

matrix, meaning 'a mould in which something is shaped' (and other technical meanings), is pronounced **may**-triks and has the plural form *matrices* (**may**-tri-seez) or *matrixes*.

matt, meaning 'dull, without lustre', is spelt *matt* in BrE and either *mat* or (more usually) *matte* in AmE.

maty see MATEY.

mausoleum, meaning 'a grand tomb' (after that of the 4c BC king of Caria, Mausolus), has the plural form *mausoleums*.

maximum. The plural, though not often needed, is *maxima*, or informally *maximums*.

may, can see CAN.

may, might. 1 With reference to present or future possibility, *may* and *might* are both used, but with *may* the possibility is more open and with *might* it is more tentative or remote: (may) *The ACLU may have a strong case—Economist*, 1980 | *The cyclists may use up to 6,000 calories during a race—Times*, 1983 (might) *The news that the Met season might have to be cancelled . . . is an annual threat—Listener*, 1980 | *Some players get a 'buzz' from the game [of Space Invaders] and that might explain why they become addicted—Times*, 1983 | *What is a little surprising is that even the programme's adult representatives claim they don't quite know what a bonk might be—Today*, 1986.

2 With reference to possibility in the past, *may have* leaves it open whether an event or circumstance was actually the case, whereas *might have* implies that it was not, and is explicit that it was not when the statement is part of an unfulfilled condition introduced by *if* or by inversion (as in the 1983 *Daily Telegraph* example below): (may have) *It may have been an awful night . . . but the meat and potato pies were brill—Guardian*, 1983 | *Police say they're anxious to trace a car and a van which may have been used by the gang*—television news broadcast, 1993 | (might have) *'You might have been killed yourself.' 'Not much chance; the raid had already gone past us.'*—A. Crawley, 1983 | *Had the Liberal Yellow Book been published in 1920 our history might have been different—Daily Telegraph*, 1983 | *Once he had answered differently—might have said that the two things were different in kind—but now he was not so certain—D.* Wingrove, 1990. It is incorrect to use *may have* when the possibility it expresses is clearly not an actual one: *If some of the resources squandered this morning had been used more wisely, we may have been able to take steps to save his life—Scotsman*, 1989.

3 There are a few idiomatic uses of *might* and *might have* that are worth noting: *You might have said something!* (= you should have said something) | *Might I suggest . . . ?* (= a polite, now somewhat old-fashioned alternative for *May I . . . ?*). *Might have* is occasionally used with future reference, again with a suggestion of unlikely fulfilment: *By tomorrow, the weather might have changed*.

maybe, an adverb meaning 'perhaps', is such a familiar part of current standard English that it comes as a surprise to know that it fell out of use in the 19c to an extent that caused the *OED* to

label it 'archaic and dialect'. It has a somewhat informal air about it, admittedly, but it is used in a wide range of contexts, written and spoken, especially in AmE, and shares all the grammatical flexibility of *perhaps*: *Maybe a shotgun was all he had*—A. Munro, 1987 | *If you quote the Liberal opposition saying that they did, aren't you implying that they didn't? Maybe?—London Review of Books*, 1987. Note that *may be* is spelt as two words when it is a combination of the modal verb *may* and the verb *be*: compare *Maybe she's joking* (or *She's maybe joking*) and *She may be joking*.

me. 1 For idiomatic uses of *me*, see I. For the types *as good as I/me* and *better than I/me* see CASES 2B.

2 Informally, *me* commonly replaces *I* at the head of clauses when linked to a noun by *and*: *Me and the teacher are going to race tonight from the school to the store—*J. Crace, 1986. It would be awkward to say *I and the teacher*, and the alternative *the teacher and I*, though less awkward, has a formal sound that makes it less likely to occur in casual conversation. This use of *me* seems generally more acceptable than corresponding uses of *her, him, us,* and *them*.

meagre is spelt this way in BrE, and usually *meager* in AmE.

mean. 1 In the meaning 'to intend', *mean* can be followed by a *to*-infinitive (when the speaker intends to do something: *I meant to go*), by an object + *to*-infinitive (when the speaker intends someone else to do something: *I meant you to go*) and, more formally, by a *that*-clause with *should* (*I meant that you should go*). Use of *mean for* + object + *to*-infinitive (✗ *I meant for you to go*) is non-standard.

2 *I mean* is legitimately used to introduce an explanation of what has just been said: *He was a marvellous butler. I mean, if you went there he'd welcome you in the most graceful and polite and proper way—New Yorker*, 1986. In conversation it is increasingly heard as a sentence-filler, rather like *you know* (see KNOW): '*Only . . . very nice?' he asked woefully. 'Oh, it's great! I mean, it's fantastic!'—Los Angeles Times*, 1987. This use is informal only but, as so often, there are borderline uses that blur distinctions: *I wasn't interested in him. I mean, when you shoot juice, you lose the other thing*—H. C. Rae, 1972 | *I publish, I mean I have had published, a few what we used to call slim volumes of verse, um, poetry, you know*—Christopher Hampton, 1974. It is all too easy to point to extremes that no one would consider standard (*You know, like, uh, hey, man, I mean, cool, huh?*—L. Woidwode, 1992); the real difficulties lie in the greyer areas of usage.

3 In the passive, *to be meant* has for long had the sense 'to be destined (by providence), to have special significance': *When I need you, you are here. You must see how meant it all is*—Iris Murdoch, 1974. This use has been joined by another passive use in which *meant* followed by a *to*-infinitive means little more than 'supposed, thought, intended': *For today he was meant to be having dinner with Stephanie at the Dear Friends*—A. N. Wilson, 1986. This altered meaning is now so familiar that its relative newness (mostly 20c) can cause surprise.

meaningful. The journalist and literary critic Philip Howard wrote in 1978 that 'ongoing situations and meaningful dialogues are two popular pieces of jargon

. . . at present', and they still are. *Meaningful* is essentially the opposite of *meaningless*, i.e. 'having meaning', as in *a meaningful utterance*. But *meaning* has other meanings, which are reflected in other uses of *meaningful*, especially 'important, significant, noteworthy', so that things such as talks, tests, results, work, and even relationships can be called *meaningful*. There is some justification for using the word when the notion of something having meaning is present: *Chris and Jayne turned to each other with raised eyebrows and meaningful looks*—P. Hennessy, 1983. But alternatives such as *important, significant*, and *effective* should be considered when it is importance rather than meaning that is the issue: *If your new employer has offered to provide you with facilities for updating, make sure that this is included in your contract of employment, and that it is backed up with meaningful support and supervision*—A. Morton-Cooper, 1990.

meaningless fillers. This is a term used to describe phrases such as *um, er, I mean*, and *you know*, which are inserted spontaneously as asides into conversation in order to fill pauses and maintain the flow of speech.

means. 1 When the meaning is 'financial resources', *means* is treated as plural: *Their means are somewhat limited*. When the meaning is 'a way or method' it can operate as a singular noun (when preceded by a determiner such as *a, any*, or *every*) or as a plural noun (when preceded by a plural-marking word such as *all, many, several*, etc.): *Several means are available for indexing numbers not obtainable with standard plain indexing*—L. E. Doyle et al., 1961 |

They remained for her a means, and not an end, a bargaining power rather than a blessing—Margaret Drabble, 1967 | *Derek and I drove down there and shut off the whole barn, preventing all means of getting in or out*—J. Hadwick, 1991. When *means* is preceded by *the*, the following verb can be either singular or plural, depending on the sense intended: *Throughout my boyhood the normal means of passenger transport, if something more than a bicycle was required, was the cab*—Jo Grimond, 1979 | *Moreover, the means by which this end is achieved are remarkable*—Michael Foot, 1986.

2 The dual role of *means* in the 'way, method' sense is a survival or folk memory of an earlier time, when both the singular *mean* and the plural *means* were used. The singular use has dropped out, but the construction, attached to the plural, has survived.

meantime, meanwhile. 1 As a solitary adverb, *meantime* has largely given way to *meanwhile*, but is still occasionally found: *Meantime, melt the remaining butter in a saucepan*—Delia Smith, 1978. It is most often used in the phrase *in the meantime*, which is now normally written as three words instead of four: *The telephone will . . . redial the number you last called, even if you've hung up in the meantime*—Which?, 1987. Conversely, *meanwhile* is most often used by itself, and only occasionally in the variant phrase *in the meanwhile*: *The animals Mrs Murray cares for are always returned to the wild if possible. Meanwhile, they stay at her study centre*—Times, 1986 | *In the meanwhile, I'll just lie here, flat on my back, fingering my perfect bones*—J. Shute, 1992.

2 In recent use, *meanwhile* is commonly used in journalism and (especially) broadcasting as a means of resuming a main theme after a digression or aside: *Meanwhile, as we say in the trade, Motherwell go bottom [of the League table]*—Desmond Lynam, in a television broadcast, 1987. The use may owe its origins to the catchphrase *Meanwhile, back at the ranch*, used originally in captions to silent Western films and later as a voice-over in films with sound. This phrase too is common allusively in a wide range of contexts: *Meanwhile, back at the ranch, I have been browsing through the press coverage*—Guardian, 1986 | *Meanwhile back in the Commons, Mrs Thatcher tried to resist questions by saying the issues were sub judice*—Today, 1987.

measles is normally treated as a singular noun, although occasionally it is used as a plural, sometimes preceded by *the*: *The measles have left him feeling weak*.

medal has derivative forms *medalled, medallist* in BrE, and usually *medaled, medalist* in AmE.

media, in its modern meaning 'newspapers and broadcasting regarded collectively', is properly treated as a plural noun: *The media . . . impel a Prime Minister to seek stardom at the expense of the Cabinet*—New Yorker, 1977. It is increasingly used, especially by the media themselves, as a singular mass noun like *agenda* and *data*, but this use is not yet standard and should be avoided: *That's what the media's for: to be useful in positive ways*—The Face, 1992. Above all, never write *a media* or *the medias*. The word is often used in attributive position (before a noun): *The shock-horror world of the media men*—Times Literary Supplement, 1980.

medicine. The recommended pronunciation is as two syllables, i.e. **med**-sin, although a three-syllable form, **med**-i-sin, is common in Scotland and the USA and elsewhere.

medieval is the recommended spelling, not *mediaeval*. It is pronounced me-di-**ee**-vəl, with four syllables, although me-**dee**-vəl or mi-**dee**-vəl, with three syllables, is common in AmE.

Mediterranean is spelt with one *d*, one *t*, and two *r*s, as its derivation from the Latin words *medius* 'middle' and *terra* 'land' reminds us.

medium. In the spiritualist sense, the plural is *mediums*, and in the meaning 'means of mass communication' the plural is MEDIA, which has its own pattern of behaviour. In all other meanings (e.g. 'an agency or means of doing something'), *mediums* and *media* are both used.

mega-, a prefix meaning 'great', continues to be used in scientific and technical applications, often with the specific meaning 'denoting a factor of one million' (as in the computing unit *megabyte*). In the 20c it has taken on a much more informal role in words such as *megastar* and *megahit*, and has become detached in the form *mega*, meaning 'excellent' or (as an adverb) 'extremely' (*mega famous*).

meiosis, pronounced miy-**oh**-sis, is a figure of speech involving an emphatic understatement made for effect, as when something outstanding is described as 'rather good'. A literary example occurs in Shakespeare's *Romeo and Juliet*, where Mercutio refers to his *mortal hurt* (at the hands of Tybalt) with the words *Ay, ay, a scratch, a scratch* (III.i.93). A special form of meiosis involving negatives is called LITOTES.

melted, molten. As adjectives, *melted* is the normal word (*melted butter | melted ice | melted snow*). *Molten* is used only of materials melted at extreme heat (*molten lava | molten lead*).

membership. *Her acceptance of this role has . . . given enormous pleasure to the membership*—B. Grant, 1990. The use of *membership* to mean 'members collectively' (e.g. of a trade union) was noted by Gowers (1965) as 'now rife and corrupting other words'. Its use is normally restricted to official or reporting contexts, and in general use *membership* most commonly retains its traditional meanings 'the status of being a member' (*I must renew my membership*) or 'the number of members in an organization' (*Membership is down by 15% this year*).

memento, meaning 'a souvenir', should not be converted into the dubious formation *momento*. The plural form is *mementoes*.

memo, a shortening of *memorandum* and now the more usual form in general use, has the plural form *memos*.

memorabilia, meaning 'souvenirs of memorable events, people, etc.', is a plural noun, and should not be treated as singular: ☒ *We've got railway memorabilia and we're very proud of it*—*Best*, 1991.

memorandum has the plural form *memoranda* (recommended) or *memorandums*. In general business use in the meaning 'informal note or message', MEMO is more often used.

ménage, a somewhat literary word meaning 'the members of a household', is printed in roman type with the accent retained. The pronunciation is semi-naturalized, with the final consonant retaining its French form, so **may**-nahzh.

mendacity, mendicity. *Mendacity* (from Latin *mendax* 'lying') means 'habitual lying or deceiving', whereas *mendicity* (from Latin *mendicare* 'to beg') means 'the practice or habit of begging'. The words are ultimately related in having a common ancestor in the Latin word *mendum* meaning 'fault'.

-ment see -ION, -MENT, -NESS.

mental. The use of mental in expressions such as *mental hospital* and *mental patient*, recorded from the end of the 19c, has been replaced in the 20c by *psychiatric*.

mentality, in its meaning 'mental character or disposition', is now nearly always used with unfavourable connotations, although this was not always so: *I hate the triviality of journalism, you know, the sort of fluttering mentality that fills up the page*—Humphrey Carpenter, 1978 | *A kind of unacknowledged underground mentality had permeated all kinds of places*—Arthur Miller, 1987.

merchandise is spelt *-ise* (and normally pronounced *-iyz*) for both the noun and the verb. In AmE, the verb is often spelt with a final *-ize*.

meretricious, derived from Latin *meretrix* 'prostitute', means 'showily but falsely attractive':

She could view with contempt those of her fellow tourists who, after the Aegean, could excite themselves over the meretricious charms of Venice—Robert Liddell, 1986. It should not be confused with *meritorious* and other words connected with *merit*.

merit as a verb has inflected forms *merited, meriting*.

mésalliance (non-naturalized) normally means 'a marriage with a person of a lower social position', by contrast with the naturalized word *misalliance*, which is used of any unsuitable alliance, including an unsuitable marriage. Both words entered the language in the 18c.

Messrs., originally a contraction of French *Messieurs* 'gentlemen', was formerly common as a plural form of *Mr* in business and commercial use (e.g. *Messrs. Berkeley, Stratton & Co.*), but has now fallen into disuse in most parts of the English-speaking world, except in certain professions, notably law. There are certain technical limitations on its use that need to be guarded against; for example, it is not used with Limited Companies. If in doubt, consult *Debrett's Correct Form* or a similar manual on form.

meta-. In recent use this prefix has been borrowed from the term *metaphysics* and applied to other words with the meaning 'of a higher or second-order kind': a *metalanguage* is language used to describe language, *meta-history* is the study of the principles governing historical events, and *meta-mathematics* is concerned with the structure and formal properties of mathematics. This is a development that seems likely to continue.

metal, mettle. 1 Both are in origin the same word. In the 16c *mettle* began to move apart as a separate word used only in figurative meanings, of which the dominant one still current is 'ardent or spirited temperament; spirit, courage', as in the expressions *show one's mettle* and *be on one's mettle*.

2 The verb *metal* has inflected forms *metalled*, *metalling* in BrE, and usually *metaled*, *metaling* in AmE.

metallurgy, the science of metals, is pronounced with the stress on the second syllable in BrE, and with the stress on the first syllable in AmE.

metaphor and simile. 1 The difference between these two figures of speech, which together constitute a major element of English idiom, is largely one of form. A *simile* is a fanciful comparison couched in a form introduced by *as* or *like*, for example Byron's line *The Assyrian came down like the wolf on the fold*, whereas a *metaphor* directly equates the image with the person or thing it is compared to: *Achilles was a lion in the fight*. Many figurative uses of words (e.g. the *mouth* of a river, a *blanket* of fog, *music* to one's ears) and many idioms (e.g. *get the green light, have one foot in the grave, take the rough with the smooth*) can be seen as metaphors.

2 A type of metaphor that always arouses derision is the *mixed metaphor*, in which two incompatible images are combined: *He has been made a sacrificial lamb for taking the lid off a can of worms | In coal mines, mice are used as human guinea pigs.* (both examples from recent letters pages of *The Times*). A similar if less vivid kind of ab-surdity can be caused by combining figurative uses in which the corresponding physical senses merge to present an alternative picture, as in *taking concrete steps* (cited by Gowers) and *grass-roots consumers*. In the hurly-burly of rapid speech, such disasters are bound to occur, but they can be avoided in more considered or formal language use when there is time to reflect on what is being said.

metathesis, pronounced with the stress on the second syllable, is a term for the transposition of sounds or letters in a word, sometimes as a feature of a word's development (e.g *hasp* from Old English *hæpse*) and at other times as an erroneous process (e.g. *anenome* for *anemone*).

meter is the normal spelling in BrE and AmE for the measuring or recording instrument, and is the AmE spelling of the words in BrE spelt *metre* (unit of length and rhythm in poetry).

meticulous is derived from the Latin word *metus* 'fear', and in the 16c and 17c it had a corresponding meaning 'fearful, timid'. Then the word went out of use, only to reappear in the early 19c in a completely different sense, 'over-careful about details'. This was the meaning known to the Fowler brothers when they wrote *The King's English* at the turn of the century, and they didn't much care for it, classing it among the 'stiff, full-dress, literary, or out-of-the-way words'. Between then and now, it lost (almost completely, but not always quite) its connotations of excess, and settled down in the meaning it now has, 'careful, punctilious, precise'. If it differs at all from these synonyms, it is perhaps from a vestigial shadow of this strange past rather than any real distinction in meaning: *Utz has planned his own funeral with meticulous care*—Bruce Chatwin, 1988 | *Very many tedious hours were spent on the dull and routine tasks of listing, plotting on graphs, meticulously checking and classifying*—I. Young, 1990.

metonymy is a figure of speech in which an attribute or property is used to refer to the person or thing that has it, e.g. *the White House* for the American presidency and *the Crown* for the British monarchy. In the proverb *The pen is mightier than the sword*, *pen* and *sword*, by a process of metonymy, represent the written word and warfare respectively. See also SYNECDOCHE.

metope, a term in architecture for a square section from a Doric frieze, is generally pronounced **met**-ohp (two syllables), or occasionally but increasingly rarely, **met**-əpee (three syllables).

mettle see METAL.

mews, meaning 'a set of buildings around an open yard', is usually called *a mews* and is treated as a singular noun. (The word is originally the plural of *mew* meaning 'a cage for hawks'.) It is often used attributively (before a noun) to describe a building that is part of a mews: *He intended to make the mews house his operational headquarters*—M. Babson, 1974.

mezzanine, a low storey between two others (usually between the ground and first floors), is pronounced **met**-sə-neen or **mez**-sə-neen.

mickle, muckle. These are merely variants of the same word meaning 'a large amount', and so the proverb *Many a mickle makes a muckle* is, in its usual form, a meaningless corruption. The correct form is *Many a little* (or occasionally *pickle* = 'small amount') *makes a mickle*, which is recorded from the 13c. The corrupted form is first attested in the works of George Washington (late 18c).

micro- continues to be a highly productive prefix, with the following among many forms first recorded in the 20c: *microclimate, microdot, microearthquake, micro-event, microfilm, micro-oven, microsurgery, microsystem, microwave*. A fuller list will be found in OED2.

mid, meaning 'middle of', is normally joined by a hyphen to the following word, as in *mid-century | mid-fifteenth century*. Note that when the century is in attributive position (before a noun), two hyphens are needed: *a mid-fifteenth-century church*. Note that *mid-air* is spelt with a hyphen whatever its position in the sentence, despite Fowler's preference (1926) for *mid air*.

middling, middlingly. *Middling* has been used as an adjective in various senses since the 15c, but is now more commonly found as an adverb, a use attested from the 18c. In this role it competes with *middlingly*, which is recorded from the same date and was used by Dr Johnson in his definition of the word *indifferently*. Modern examples of each are: *He was middling tall and thin*—Dick Francis, 1981 | *Ivan Ilyich, who has a middlingly successful legal career and has become a judge, . . .* —A. N. Wilson, 1988.

midst is now most commonly used in the phrases *in the midst of* or *in our* (etc.) *midst*, meaning 'among, in the middle of'. Typical contexts are both physical and abstract: *There was . . . something sinister about this place, unhusbanded and yieldless in the midst of the abundant land all about*—R. Adams, 1974 | *In the midst of all the politico-religious dissension [in Ulster], one tends to overlook the general social problems*—D. Murphy, 1978.

midwifery. The dominant pronunciation in BrE is **mid**-wif-ri (three syllables) or **mid**-wif-ə-ri (four syllables), although **mid**-wiyf-ə-ri (with the second syllable as in *wife*) is also heard in AmE.

might see MAY, MIGHT.

migraine. The usual pronunciation in BrE is now **mee**-grayn, although now **miy**-grayn is also heard and is standard in AmE.

mil, a unit of measurement equal to one-thousandth of an inch (0.00254mm), is spelt without a full point.

mileage, with two *e*s, is the recommended spelling, not *milage*.

milieu, a somewhat literary word for one's environment or social surroundings, is pronounced mil-**yur**. The preferred plural form is *milieux* (pronounced mil-**yurz**).

militate, mitigate. The two words are sometimes confused (usually *mitigate* is used for *militate*) because both meanings are connected with having a reducing effect and their forms and rhythm are close. *Mitigate* is transitive (i.e. it takes an object) and means 'to make less intense or severe', whereas *militate* is intransitive and (followed by *against*)

means 'to have a contrary force or effect'. The following examples show the correct use of *militate* then *mitigate*, followed by an incorrect use of *mitigate* for *militate*: *The housing styles, narrowness of the streets and the location of the district vis-a-vis the rest of the city all militate against Neustadt becoming an environmentally attractive area overnight*—R. Rolley, 1990 | *A great yellow sun like a runaway balloon shone from a deep blue sky, and a cooling breeze from the lagoon mitigated the heat*—L. Wilkinson, 1992 | ⊠ *Parents are expected to make 'sensible arrangements' . . . that will not mitigate against the child's best interests*—L. Feldman, 1992. *Mitigate* is frequently used in the form *mitigating* with words such as *circumstance, effect, factor,* etc.: *The offence with which you are charged is so serious that despite your personal mitigating factors a non-custodial sentence cannot be justified*—television news broadcast, 1993.

millenarian see MILLENNIUM.

millenary, an adjective (and, less often, a noun) denoting a period of 1,000 years, is usually pronounced with the stress on the second syllable, although pronunciation with the stress on the first syllable is also heard and is the dominant form in AmE.

millennium, a period of 1,000 years, is spelt with two *l*s and two *n*s. The plural is *millenniums* (preferred) or occasionally *millennia*. For the problems of reckoning when a new millennium begins, see the remarks at CENTURY. Whatever the arguments put forward on the basis of strict reckoning, the natural celebratory point for a new millennium is at the end of the year 1999, 2999, and so on, and not the year following. The adjective *millenarian*, meaning 'relating to the millennium' or 'believing in the millennium' (in the theological sense of Christ's second coming), is paradoxically spelt with only one *n*, being derived not from Latin *annus* 'year' but from *milleni*, the distributive form (meaning 'every thousand') of *mille* 'thousand'.

million. When preceded by a numeral or a quantifying word such as *many* or *several*, the plural is *million* (unchanged: *twenty million people*), but *millions* is used when it is followed by *of* (*millions of times*). With *few*, the plural is idiomatically *million*, not *millions*, even when followed by *of* (*a few million of them*).

mimic. The inflected forms of the verb are *mimics*, *mimicked*, *mimicking*.

mind *verb*. *Mind you, if you think she behaved strangely, you should have seen me*—Martin Amis, 1984. This absolute use of the verb *mind*, calling attention to or emphasizing what the speaker is saying, is recorded in the *OED* from the early 19c (Coleridge, Browning, etc.), along with the shorter form *mind* (without *you*): *Well, all right, but you aren't to do anything, mind*—Doris Lessing, 1988. This use is conversational or informal only.

mine, historically an alternative to *my* in uses such as *mine ease* and *O lady mine!* and still used occasionally in this way in jocular use (*mine host*), is in general use limited to its role as a pronoun, either after *of* (*a friend of mine*) or after a verb (*This one is not mine*).

mineralogy, the study of minerals, is spelt *-alogy*, not *-ology*. (Compare GENEALOGY.)

minimum. The plural, though not often needed, is *minima*, or informally *minimums*.

miniscule is fast establishing itself as an adjective in its own right with the meaning 'very small, minute', although as a corruption (influenced by the prefix *mini-*) of MINUSCULE it is regarded as non-standard: *Riborg showed her a photograph album, with herself by a fjord in a miniscule bikini*—J. Bow, 1991. There is a case to be made for allowing *miniscule* to have its way and leaving *minuscule* to its own more technical devices, but since this is not the accepted procedure at present the best advice is to avoid the word altogether in this meaning and use any of several available synonyms such as *minute, tiny, microscopic, diminutive*, etc.

minister. In its ecclesiastical sense, *minister* is the term to use for a member of the clergy, especially in the Presbyterian and Nonconformist Churches. It also has a more hierarchical meaning, reflecting the word's origin in Latin *minister* meaning 'servant' (from *minus* 'lesser'), denoting a church official who assists the higher orders (e.g. deacon or subdeacon) in discharging their duties. Care should be taken before using the term as a simple synonym for *priest*.

minority. 1 *Minority* has meanings at the other end of the scale of magnitude from MAJORITY, and is likewise treated as a singular noun except when used with *of* and a plural noun, in which case it too is plural: *Only a minority of Germans (around a third of the population according to American surveys carried out in 1945) were prepared to* *concede that the war was lost*—I. Kershaw, 1989. In one respect, however, *minority* has gone its own way, namely in its widespread 20c use referring to any relatively small group of people who differ from others in the society of which they are a part in race, ethnic origin, language, religion, political persuasion, sexual orientation, or other matters that give rise to questions of social treatment or discrimination: *Flaubert always sides with minorities, with 'the Bedouin, the Heretic, the philosopher, the hermit, the Poet'*—Julian Barnes, 1985 | *Among specific measures provided for in the convention were the launch of at least one radio station and a television network broadcasting in minority languages*—*Keesings*, 1990. In this meaning *minority* has acquired some flexibility of use, giving rise to apparently paradoxical collocations such as *growing* or *increasing minority* (i.e. increasing in numbers and therefore becoming less rather than more truly a minority).

2 Running parallel to this, but in an opposite direction as regards meaning, has been the 20c use of *minority* as a quasi-adjective meaning 'of or for a minority', often with a favourable sense as in *minority interests* or *minority tastes* (generally = more exclusive or intellectual): *Drummond once told me that Radio 3 broadcasts to about 30 minority tastes, each of which is characterised by its intense dislike of the other 29*—*Daily Telegraph*, 1992. An early exponent of the idea of *minority culture* was the Cambridge academic F. R. Leavis, whose influential book *Mass Civilization and Minority Culture* was published in 1930. It is noteworthy that this use of *minority*,

in relation to culture, implies an element of superiority or privilege, whereas the other 20c use of *minority*, in relation to social position, implies one of inferiority or deprivation.

minus, in the meaning 'lacking, without', has been used informally since the mid-19c. The Fowler brothers, doubtless affected by their experiences at the front in the First World War, illustrated this use in the first edition of the *Concise Oxford Dictionary* with the gruesome example *He came back minus an arm*; *arm* was changed to *dog* in a later edition.

minuscule is originally a technical term in palaeography for a type of small letter, and then the cursive script developed from it. In attributive use (before a noun) it denotes this type of writing, and in extended use it has acquired the general meaning 'very small' but it always seems somewhat awkward in generalized meanings: *The facilities here were minimal—a cracked wash-basin, one minuscule bar of soap, and one off-white towel*—Colin Dexter, 1992. Not surprisingly, in this meaning the word has come under the influence of the prefix *mini-* to produce the altered (and not yet accepted) form MINISCULE (see separate entry).

minutiae, meaning 'minor details or trivia' is pronounced mi-**nyoo**-shi-iy and is a plural noun. The singular form *minutia* is hardly ever used.

mis- is a prefix with the meaning 'badly', 'wrongly'. Words formed with it do not need a hyphen, even when the stem begins with an *s*: *misbehave, miscarriage, miscount, mismanage, misshapen, misspelling, misspent*, etc.

misanthrope. A *misanthrope* is a hater of fellow human beings; a person who hates women is a *misogynist*. The corresponding concept nouns are *misanthropy* and *misogyny*; hatred of men is *misandry*. How significant it is that *misanthrope* dates from the 16c and *misogynist* from the early 17c, whereas *misandry* is recorded only from the 1940s (and *misandrist* is not yet recorded at all) must be left for others to determine.

mischievous. The erroneous pronunciation and spelling of this word as *mischievious* (four syllables) is one of the most commonly cited indications of poor use of language, and should be avoided.

misdemeanour is spelt *-our* in BrE and *misdemeanor* in AmE.

mislead has the form *misled* as its past tense and past participle.

misogynist, misogyny see MIS-ANTHROPE.

misquotations.
See box overleaf

Miss is used as the title of a girl or unmarried woman, or of a married woman who has retained her maiden name. The title MS (see separate entry) has since the 1950s been increasingly used as an alternative with reference to women regardless of marital status.

misshapen, misspelling, misspent see MIS-.

mitigate see MILITATE.

mitre is spelt in this way in BrE, and usually *miter* in AmE.

mixed metaphor see METAPHOR AND SIMILE 2.

mnemonic, pronounced ni-**mon**-ik, is a device, usually a rhyme or sequence of words, used to help remember some fact or group of facts, e.g. the initial letters of the mnemonic *Richard Of York Gave Battle In Vain* give the order of the colours of the spectrum (red, orange, yellow, green, blue, indigo, violet).

mobile see MOVABLE.

moccasin, a name of a snake and a type of soft leather shoe, is the recommended spelling, with two *c*s and one *s*.

modal verbs. Modal (or, more fully, modal auxiliary) verbs are used to express the mood (in the linguistic sense that distinguishes statements, commands, suppositions, questions, and so on) of other verbs. The principal verbs of this type are *can, could, may, might, must, ought, shall, will*. These verbs behave in special ways, of which the most important are (1) that they can form questions and negatives without the use of *do* (*Can I go? | You may not leave*), and (2) their third-person singular forms do not add *-s* (*She will | It must*). A group of other verbs that share some of these features, such as *dare* and *need*, are sometimes called *semi-modal*. Note that

misquotations

Many catchphrases and allusive expressions are based on altered forms of literary quotations. The proverb *Every dog has his day* is based on a 16c adage translated from the Dutch humanist Erasmus (1500) and was given currency by a line spoken by Shakespeare's Hamlet: *Let Hercules himself do what he may, The cat shall mew, and dog will have his day* — Shakespeare, *Hamlet*, v.i.286. The idiom *to escape by the skin of one's teeth* is an altered form of the Authorized Version of *Job* 19:20: *I am escaped with the skin of my teeth*. Idiom and allusion go their own way in language; however, it is important to give the correct form when the allusion is given as a quotation. The following table lists the correct forms of some of the more common literary extracts, with the popular versions alongside:

QUOTATION	POPULAR FORM	SOURCE
In the sweat of thy **face** *shalt thou eat bread*	by the sweat of one's **brow**	Bible, *Genesis* 3:19
I am escaped **with** *the skin of my teeth*	to escape **by** the skin of one's teeth	Bible, *Job* 19:20
To gild refined gold, to **paint** *the lily*	to **gild** the lily	Shakespeare, *King John*
A goodly apple rotten at the **heart**	rotten at the **core**	Shakespeare, *Merchant of Venice*
But yet I'll make assurance **double** *sure*	**doubly** sure	Shakespeare, *Macbeth*
Tomorrow to fresh **woods** *and pastures new*	fresh **fields** and pastures new	Milton, *Lycidas*
They kept the **noiseless** *tenor of their way*	the **even** tenor	Gray, *Elegy Written in a Country Church-Yard*
A little **learning** *is a dangerous thing*	a little **knowledge**	Pope, *Essay on Criticism*
The best laid **schemes** *o' mice an' men Gang aft a-gley*	the best-laid **plans**	Burns, 'To a Mouse'
Water, water, every where, **Nor any** *drop to drink*	**And not** a drop to drink	Coleridge, *The Rime of the Ancient Mariner*
I have nothing to offer but **blood, toil, tears and sweat**	**blood, sweat, and tears**	Winston Churchill, *Hansard*, 1940

be, do, and *have,* which behave somewhat differently, are not classed as modal verbs but as ordinary auxiliary verbs.

model as a verb has inflected forms *modelled, modelling* in BrE and usually *modeled, modeling* in AmE.

modus operandi, meaning 'a plan or method of working', is pronounced **moh**-dəs op-ə-**ran**-diy, and is printed in italic type.

modus vivendi means 'a way of living or coping', most often (in law) an arrangement by which parties to a dispute can carry on pending a settlement. It is pronounced moh-dəs vi-**ven**-diy, and is printed in italic type.

mogul is the spelling in the sense 'an important or influential person'. In its historical meaning with reference to the 16c–19c rulers of northern India, the form *Mughal* should be used.

Mohammed, Mohammedan. The preferred spellings are MUHAMMAD, MUHAMMADAN.

mold see MOULD.

molt see MOULT.

molten see MELTED.

moment. The phrase *at this moment in time* is a modern cliché (see CLICHÉS).

momentarily means 'for a moment, briefly' in BrE: *One MP . . . wondered momentarily if he had wandered into the Lords by mistake*— Times, 1975. In AmE it has this meaning and also the meaning 'at any moment, imminently': *Miss Loren had been delayed in traffic but would arrive momentarily*— New Yorker, 1970. These features of usage are comparable to PRESENTLY.

momently in current English has much the same meanings as those given for MOMENTARILY, although its use is confined to literary contexts: *She believes Alix will be there, and indeed momently she is*—Margaret Drabble, 1987 | *You acknowledge, however, momently, . . . that at least what I claim is true*— A. S. Byatt, 1990.

momento is an erroneous variant of MEMENTO.

momentum. The plural, though not often needed, is *momenta*, or informally *momentums*.

Monday see FRIDAY.

monetarism, monetarist, monetary. These are pronounced with the first syllable as **mun-** in BrE and as **mon-** in AmE.

moneyed, meaning 'wealthy', is spelt *-eyed*, not *monied*.

mongol, mongolism, mongoloid, terms formerly used for sufferers of what is now called *Down's syndrome*, are considered offensive and should be avoided.

Mongoloid, referring to peoples including those of east Asia and south-east Asia, is one of a set of terms used by 19c anthropologists to classify human races. They are now outdated and potentially offensive, and the names of specific peoples or nationalities should normally be used.

mongoose, the small animal like a civet, has the plural form *mongooses*.

moneys. The natural plural in the meaning 'sums of money' is *moneys*, but *monies* took hold in 19c accounting circles and has penetrated into ordinary usage: *Certain monies had been put aside for them*—Anita Brookner, 1988. Nonetheless, *moneys* is preferable.

monk see FRIAR.

monkey. The noun has the plural form *monkeys*, and the verb has inflected forms *monkeys, monkeyed, monkeying*.

monologue, soliloquy. Both words (the first Greek and the second Latin in origin) denote a single person's act of speaking or thinking aloud; *soliloquy* generally refers to dramatic utterances without consciousness of an audience, whereas *monologue* primarily means speech that is meant to be heard and is used especially of the discourse of a talker who monopolizes conversation, or to describe a performance or recitation by a single actor or speaker.

month see DAY.

mood is a term in grammar that identifies utterances as being statements, expressions of wish, commands, questions, etc. It is a variant of the word *mode*, and has nothing to do with the more familiar word *mood*. In English, moods are expressed by means of an auxiliary verb (*can*, *may*, etc.) called a MODAL VERB, or by the SUBJUNCTIVE MOOD.

moot. A *moot point* or *moot question* is a debatable or undecided one. The word is from Old English (from a verb *mōtian* meaning 'converse') and should not be confused with *mute* meaning 'silent'.

moral, morale. When Fowler wrote in the years following the First World War, *morale*, in the meaning 'mental attitude or bearing', was a word at the forefront of consciousness, but there was uncertainty as to form between *morale* (an early 19c respelling preserving the sound of the French word and distinguishing it from the other meanings of *moral*) and the spelling *moral*, reintroduced towards the end of the 19c for this meaning on the grounds that *morale* was artificial and not the form of the word in this meaning in French. In the fullness of time, the form *morale*, together with its French-like pronunciation, which Fowler recommended, has prevailed, and few today will realize that there was ever a problem. However, the

story affords a colourful glimpse of the interaction between two great languages.

moratorium, meaning 'a temporary suspension or prohibition', has the plural form *moratoriums*.

more. 1 For *more* and *most* used in the comparison of adjectives, see ADJECTIVE 3–4. With adverbs, *more* and *most* are normally used when the adverb is formed with *-ly* from an adjective, e.g. *more richly, more happily*: see -ER AND -EST FORMS. The use of double comparatives, e.g. *They are more happier now*, though once a feature of English style (and used for example by Shakespeare), has fallen out of use and is considered illiterate.

2 *MORE THAN ONE*. This phrase, though plural in form and meaning, conventionally takes a singular verb: *More than one doctor attends each patient*. However, if the number following *than* is higher than one, or if the phrase is couched in the form *more* + plural noun + *than*, then the whole phrase moves into the plural: *More than two doctors attend each patient | More doctors than one attend each patient*. The same happens if *more than one* is followed by *of* and a plural noun or pronoun: *More than one of the doctors attend each patient*.

3 *MANY MORE*. Care needs to be taken to avoid the ambiguity of constructions in which *many more* is followed by an adjective. In the sentence *Many more important tasks had to be done*, it is unclear whether *more* belongs with *many* or with *important*, i.e. whether all the tasks were important or only the additional ones. In speech, intonation usually clarifies the intended sense, but confusion can be caused when this kind of construction appears in written form.

4 THE MORE. *More* is preceded by *the* in certain idiomatic uses. *The* is optional in the type *She is the more intelligent of the two*, and obligatory in the set type *The more, the merrier*, and when preceded by *all* (*It is all the more interesting for being new*).

5 For *more important* and *more importantly*, see IMPORTANT, IMPORTANTLY.

mores, pronounced **maw**-reez and meaning 'characteristic customs of a place or people', is the plural of the Latin word *mos* 'custom'. It is treated as a plural noun in English: *It is in the context of specific family strategies and patterns that sexual mores developed and were transformed*—J. Weeks, 1992.

Mormon is the popular name for a member of the Church of Jesus Christ of Latter-Day Saints, a millenary religion founded in 1830 at Manchester. It is spelt with a capital initial letter.

morphology is the study of the structure and form of words. It includes both inflection (how words change their forms according to grammatical function, e.g. *come, comes, came*, etc.) and derivation (how one word is formed from another, e.g. *unhelpful* from *helpful* and *helpful* in turn from *help*).

mortgage. Note the spelling with *-t-*. The lender in a mortgage contract is called the *mortgagee*, and the borrower the *mortgager* (or in legal work, *mortgagor*).

Moslem. The preferred and more usual spelling is MUSLIM.

mosquito has the plural form *mosquitoes*.

most. 1 For *more* and *most* used in the comparison of adjectives, see ADJECTIVE 3–4. With adverbs, *more* and *most* are normally used when the adverb is formed with *-ly* from an adjective, e.g. *most richly, most happily*: see -ER AND -EST FORMS. The use of *most* with an already superlative form of adjective, e.g. *She is the most cleverest*, though once a feature of English style (occurring in Shakespeare and elsewhere), is considered illiterate in current usage. When the comparison is between two people or things, *more*, not *most*, should be used: *This is certainly the more interesting of your two proposals*.

2 As a noun, *most + of* is treated as singular or plural according to the number of the following noun or pronoun: *Most of his story is true | Most of them have nothing to say*.

3 The combination *most + adjective* often has an intensifying rather than superlative role: *She is a most remarkable woman. | This was the most wicked crime*.

4 For *most important* and *most importantly*, see IMPORTANT, IMPORTANTLY.

5 *Dewey knew no fear, would just roar on into most any species of difficulty*—T. R. Pearson, 1991. In this meaning, in use since the 16c first in Scotland and now chiefly in UK dialects and in AmE, *most* is a shortening of *almost* and therefore a distinct word, though often treated together with the main meanings of *most* in dictionaries.

mother-in-law means one's wife's or husband's mother. The plural is *mothers-in-law*.

Mother's Day. In Britain, this is another name for *Mothering Sunday*, the fourth Sunday in Lent, traditionally a day for honouring mothers with gifts. In America, *Mother's Day* is on the second Sunday in May.

motif is a mid-19c loanword from French with special meanings that distinguish it from *motive*, an earlier (14c) loanword from French. A *motif* is chiefly used to mean a dominant theme or distinctive feature in a literary work, and in music a melodic or rhythmic figure from which a longer passage is developed.

motivate, motivation. *Motivation* has a special meaning in psychology which the *OED* defines as 'the conscious or unconscious stimulus for action towards a desired goal provided by psychological or social factors; that which gives purpose or direction to behaviour'. Both it and the corresponding verb *motivate* have entered the language of business and industrial personnel management to denote the factors that induce employees to work well: *The really crucial skills, to the head-teacher charged with the responsibility of taking a school into this new territory, will be those of motivation, leadership and team-building*—T. Brighouse et al., 1991. From here it is a short step to over-generalized uses in which both words are little more than synonyms for *cause* (verb and noun) or *reason*: *The principal motivation for this comparison is to help decisions about the allocation of health care resources*—British Medical Journal, 1975 | *The farming achievements of the eighteenth and early nineteenth centuries were also motivated by the need for more food*—J. Purseglove, 1989.

motto has the plural form *mottoes*.

mould. There are three separate words spelt this way in BrE: a hollow container for making a shape, a fungous growth, and loose friable earth. All three have corresponding verbs. In AmE the spelling in all meanings is *mold*.

moult is the spelling in BrE for the verb meaning 'to shed feathers or hair etc.' and for the corresponding noun. In AmE the spelling is *molt*.

mouse. The plural in the traditional meaning is *mice*, but *mouses* is commonly heard in the computing world for the hand-held device which controls the movement of the cursor on the screen. The verb *mouse* meaning 'to hunt mice', used with reference to cats, is sometimes pronounced mowz.

moustache (with stress on the second syllable) is the normal spelling in BrE, but *mustache* (with stress on the first syllable) is more usual in AmE.

mouth is pronounced mowth as a noun (but plural mowdhz), and mowdh as a verb (also -mowdhd in combinations such as *foul-mouthed*).

mouthful has the plural form *mouthfuls*. See -FUL.

movable, mobile. *Movable* generally denotes that something can be moved by applying an external force to it, whereas *mobile* means that it has the ability to move or be moved as a special characteristic. A *mobile phone* is designed to be carried about, and a *mobile shop* is built into a vehicle so that it can be transported. *Mobile* is also used with special meanings as a noun (a decorative hanging structure, and = mobile phone). *Movable* has a special meaning in law to denote property that is regarded as personal to the owner rather than as a permanent fixture. Note that *movable* is normally spelt in this way, although *moveable* is the form often used in legal contexts.

mow. The past of the verb is *mowed*. The past participle is *mowed* or *mown* (*He has mowed | mown the grass*), but when used as an adjective *mown* is the only form used (*Mown grass*).

MP (= Member of Parliament) is now normally used without full points. The plural is *MPs* (no apostrophe) and the possessive forms are *MP's* (singular) and *MPs'* (plural).

Mr, Mrs are now normally used without a full point: *Mr and Mrs J. Smith*.

Ms, despite the derision that greeted its early uses in the 1950s (at first in America and soon after in Britain), is now established as a useful and practical title applied to a woman irrespective of marital status (*Ms J. Smith*). It is normally used without a full point. Although it was originally devised out of concern for social equality and promoted especially by the feminist movement, it has proved a blessing to everyone, men and women alike, in avoiding the need to research into or divine the personal circumstances of female addressees. There is, however, a snag: it is awkward to pronounce, məz and miz being the normal forms, neither of them satisfactory.

much. For the complementary uses of *much* and *very*, see VERY.

much more, much less, still more, still less. *The principles, much more the practice, need a good deal of scrutiny. I didn't even see him, still less talk to him.* Much more (or *still more*) is used when the grammatical form of the sentence is positive, and *much less* (or *still less*) when it is negative. Uncertainty arises when the form is positive but the sense is negative, as with adjectives in un- and words like *difficult*. In the sentence *It is difficult to establish all the facts, much less to reach a conclusion, much more* is strictly needed, not *much less*, but the result is awkward and an alternative such as *let alone* is often preferred.

muchly, once a serious adverb, is now only used humorously: *She stepped away from him as though evading her share in the pleasure. 'Thank you muchly,' he said.*—M. Keane, 1988.

mucus, mucous. *Mucus* is the noun for a slimy substance secreted by a gland, and *mucous* is the corresponding adjective (as in *mucous membrane*).

Muhammad, Muhammadan. The name of the founder of Islam is now spelt *Muhammad* in English, not *Mohammed*. The word for a follower of Islam (and the corresponding adjective) is *Muslim*; *Muhammadan* (a term often used in the past) is now considered offensive by Muslims themselves in suggesting that Muhammad and not Allah is the object of worship.

mulatto, meaning 'a person of mixed white and black parentage', has the plural form *mulattos*. The word is no longer actively used but is found in the works of earlier writers such as Defoe, Thackeray, and Stevenson. *Half-*

caste still survives but is often regarded as depreciatory if not offensive; *person of mixed descent*, though more unwieldy, is usually preferred.

mullah, meaning 'a Muslim learned in Islamic law', is spelt in this way.

mumps, the illness, is usually treated as a singular noun (*Mumps is common in young children*), and is sometimes used informally or locally with *the* (*When I was sick with the mumps, . . .* —Margaret Atwood, 1989).

municipal is pronounced with the stress on the second syllable.

muscle, mussel. *Muscle* is the fibrous body tissue, *mussel* the bivalve mollusc.

Muslim, pronounced **muhz**-lim, is the preferred spelling for a follower of Islam (and the corresponding adjective), not *Moslem* or other older forms. Note that MU-HAMMADAN is no longer acceptable in this meaning.

mussel see MUSCLE.

must. The use of *must* informally as a noun meaning 'something that must be done or had, or that should not be missed', dates from the 1890s in American use. In the earlier part of the 20c, it was often written in inverted commas as being not quite pukka in serious or supposedly serious contexts, and this practice still sometimes occurs: *A film and a song made the Trevi Fountain a 'must' for tourists*—*Guardian*, 1973. Now, the idiom has moved a stage further in being used attributively (before a noun: *This is a 'must' book*), and in the phrasal adjective *must-have* (in which *must*

is a verb, not a noun: *The latest must-have fashion accessory*).

mute e.
See box opposite

mutual. 1 *That done, our day of marriage shall be yours, One feast, one house, one mutual happiness.*— Shakespeare, *Two Gentlemen of Verona*, v.iv.170–1 . Until the 19c, *mutual* was used with little difficulty in two main meanings: (1) that reflected in Valentine's words just quoted from *Two Gentlemen*, i.e. 'common, shared by several', and (2) another, slightly older, meaning defined as 'experienced or done by each of two or more parties with reference to each other', i.e. more or less equivalent to the much more awkward word *reciprocal*; this meaning is also found in Shakespeare: *A contract of eternal bond of love, Confirmed by mutual joinder* [= joining] *of your hands*—*Twelfth Night*, v.i.154–5. Although the *OED* gives copious evidence for phrases of the type *our mutual friend* (first recorded in 1658, i.e. long before Dickens used it as a title), *our mutual acquaintance*, *our mutual opinion*, etc., the 19c grammarians decided on the basis largely of their Latin view of grammar and meaning that while 'the *mutual* love of husband and wife' is correct enough, 'a *mutual* friend of both husband and wife' is 'sheer nonsense' (Henry Alford, Dean of Canterbury, 1864). (How 'sheer nonsense' can be used of something that is readily understood itself makes no sense.)

2 The state of affairs now, at the turn of the 21c, is that most usage guides warn against the use of *mutual* to mean 'common, shared' when there is no element of reciprocal action or feeling, i.e. not just shared but acting in

mute e

The letter *e* is mute or silent at the end of words such as *excite*, *move*, *sale*, and *rare*. In adding suffixes to these words, the question arises whether the final *e* should be retained (as it is in *changeable*) or dropped (as it is more usually, e.g. in *excitable* and *latish*). Choice is partly a matter of convention from word to word and partly determined by principles, the most important of which are that final *-e* is retained when a suffix is added (1) when *e* preserves the soft sound of a preceding consonant (as in *change*), (2) when the presence of the *e* distinguishes the root from another word (e.g. *route* (= to send by a particular route) gives *routeing* to distinguish it from forms of the verb *rout*), and (3) when the suffix begins with a consonant (as in *judge* / *judgement* (although *judgment* is also used) and *change* / *changeling*). The following table illustrates the commonest types, and some of the examples represent others (in some cases many others) of the same type:

acknowledge	acknowledgement (occasionally acknowledgment)
age	ageing
blue	bluey
change	changeable, changeling, changing
dye	dyeing
excite	excitable
gauge	gaugeable
glue	gluey
hinge	hingeing
hire	hireling
judge	judgement (occasionally judgment)
late	latish
like	likeable, likely
love	lovable, loving
mouse	mousy
move	movable
notice	noticeable
rare	rarer
rate	rateable
route	routeing
sale	saleable
whole	wholly

both directions (and usually involving no more than two parties). But meaning is not that containable, and is not always obligingly resident in individual words. *Mutual* is the kind of word that draws its meaning from its surroundings: *On the whole even Marwan was pretty laissez-faire about a girl and a boy talking about subjects of mutual interest*—Nigel Williams, 1993 (the interest may not be two-way but the talking is.) Furthermore, anyone who insists on using *common* instead of *mutual* is not living in the real world: *common* has acquired so much ancillary meaning from the other work it has to do that it will almost invariably change or weaken the sense. So the recommendation must be twofold: (1) use *common* or *joint* (or, often better, *in common* or *jointly*) if it fits without any of its other meanings getting in the way and has the force of meaning needed, especially in cases where it may be significant that the action is not two-way (*They all had problems in common*), (2) otherwise use *mutual*, whether there is explicit reciprocal action or not: *Wilde and Yeats reviewed each other's work with mutual regard*—R. Ellmann, 1986 | *No camaraderie exists between mother and daughter, no sympathy born out of mutual suffering*—J. Berman, 1987.

3 The difference in usage between *mutual* and *reciprocal* was succinctly summed up by Fowler as follows: '*Mutual* regards the relation from both sides at once: *the mutual hatred of A and B*; never from one side only: not *B's mutual hatred of A*. Where *mutual* is correct, *reciprocal* would be so too: *the reciprocal hatred of A and B*; but *mutual* is usually preferred when it is possible. *Reciprocal* can also be applied to the second party's share alone: *B's reciprocal hatred of A. Reciprocal* is therefore often useful to supply the deficiencies of *mutual*.'

myriad, a somewhat literary word meaning 'an indefinitely great number' (from a Greek word meaning 'ten thousand'), is treated like *billion* and *million* in relation to a following noun, i.e. you can say either *a myriad stars* or *myriads of stars*. A third construction, *a myriad of stars*, is also found. Examples: *Acting as a walking/talking A-Z, directing traffic, dealing with accident victims and domestic disputes are several of the myriad activities that absorb police personnel*—M. Brogden, 1991 | *Crystals are made of myriads of layers of atoms (or equivalent), and each layer builds upon the layer below*—Richard Dawkins, 1991 | *The conditions are made up of a myriad of separate agreements, some going back to the 1920s*—A. Ferner, 1988.

myself has two main roles: (1) as a reflexive pronoun in which the object of the action is the same as the speaker (*I managed to restrain myself* | *I was put in a room by myself*), (2) as an emphatic pronoun reinforcing the simple pronoun *I* (*I began to feel guilty myself*). It should not be used as the subject of a verb, although this is sometimes found especially in compound subjects joined by *and*: ☒ *It wasn't that Peter and myself* [read: *Peter and I*] *were being singled out*—Fay Weldon, 1988. Nor should it be used as the object of a verb when the action is not reflexive and *me* would do as well: *Palme Dutt's nervousness communicated itself to Isaac and myself* [read: *to Isaac and me*]—Nigel Williams, 1985.

Nn

naff. The phrasal verb *naff off*, a euphemistic substitute for *fuck off*, first appeared in print in Keith Waterhouse's novel *Billy Liar* (1959), and Waterhouse himself insists that it was originally conscript service slang as an acronym of '*n*asty, *a*wful, *f*uck it'. It was brought into prominence in 1982 when Princess Anne used it to get rid of bothersome photographers. The adjective *naff*, which has a range of meanings roughly corresponding to 'unfashionable, tasteless, inept', is unrelated to the verb.

naïve, also written *naive* (without accent), is originally the feminine of the French word *naïf*, which is no longer used in English. It has never been fully naturalized in English and is generally pronounced in a quasi-French way nah-**eev** or niy-**eev**. The corresponding noun is *naïvety* or *naïveté*.

name. 1 The elliptical construction *name of*, short for *by the name of*, is now common informally: *Keep your eyes peeled for a customer on his own, name of Sheldrake*—David Lodge, 1991.

2 The idiom *you name it*, used informally as a colourful equivalent of 'etc.', is first found in print in the 1960s, and is now well established: *Whatever they choose to say, Directors, DG, Higher Command, War Cabinet, Prime Minister, you name it, I'm not sending my units back into Europe*—Penelope Fitzgerald, 1980.

3 The idiom *to name* someone or something *after* (or *for*) some-

one or something else has settled down in the 20c as *name after* in BrE and *name for* in AmE: *Wellington, who, as we all know, has a boot named after him*—Printing World, 1976 | *Each chapter is named for the element it recalls*—New Yorker, 1987. The American use occasionally creeps into British contexts, but one is always aware that it is not entirely natural there: *In a city* [sc. Melbourne] *named for a British prime minister, in a state named for a British queen, . . .* —Sunday Times Magazine, 1988.

napkin is preferred by Fowler (1926), Nancy Mitford, and others to *serviette*, which they judged to be a genteelism or 'non-U'.

nappy, a shortening of *napkin*, is the BrE term for what in AmE is called a *diaper* (pronounced **diy**-ə-pə).

narcissus. The plural form of the plant name is *narcissi*, pronounced nah-**sis**-iy, rather than the more awkward *narcissuses*.

nary. The colloquial or dialect expression *nary a* (= not a) was exclusively American until the 20c, when it began to appear in British works: *You can wander around the cavernous vaults of the Law Courts in the Strand these days and come across nary a person*—New Society, 1973.

nasal in phonetics denotes a sound produced with the breath passing through the nose, e.g. *m*, *n*, *ng*, or French *en*, *un*.

nationalize, naturalize. These two words are close enough in form and meaning to cause occasional bother. *Nationalize* means 'to take (an industry etc.) into state ownership', whereas *naturalize* means 'to admit (a foreign person) into citizenship of a country' and also 'to adopt (a foreign word or custom)'. The respective nouns are *nationalization* and *naturalization*.

native. 1 In many of its meanings, *native* is uncontroversial: *native speaker*, *native of Liverpool*, *native oak* are typical examples of uneventful usage. The danger signals start to sound when the word is used to mean 'an original inhabitant of a country', because of the notions of cultural inferiority that the word conveys. A writer called J. C. Furnan, writing in 1950 and quoted in the *OED*, typified the stereotype implicit in *native* usually as follows: *greedy for beads . . . and alcoholic drinks. Suspect of cannibalism. Addicted to drumbeating and lewd dancing. More or less naked. Sporadically treacherous. Probably polygamous and simultaneously promiscuous. Picturesque. Comic when trying to speak English or otherwise ape white ways.* In uses that are clearly humorous, there is less objection to *native: New York in the summer was too hot even for the natives.* Otherwise, it is better to use more neutral terms such as *aboriginal* or *original inhabitant*.

2 The adjective is less pejorative. The indigenous peoples of North America have been called *Native Americans* since the 1950s without causing offence, although *American Indians* is also used.

natter, meaning 'to chatter idly', is largely confined to BrE. It seems to be an alteration of an earlier dialectal word *gnatter*, which is of uncertain origin but like *natter* bore the meaning 'grumble'.

nature. The phrase *of a . . . nature*, with an adjective before *nature*, should be used sparingly and only when the adjective by itself will not serve for some reason. For example, *a theologian of an enigmatic nature* could easily be rephrased as *an enigmatic theologian*. In other cases, *kind* or *type* could be used more effectively than *nature: These results, minor as they are, are of a nature that has not been achieved in any other use of the computer for style analysis in music—Computer & Humanities,* 1970.

naught, nought. *Naught* is an archaic or literary word meaning 'nothing' and it survives chiefly in phrases such as *come to naught* or *set at naught*. In BrE *nought* is the term for the digit 0 (*zero* in AmE). The game called *noughts and crosses* in BrE is known as *tick-tack-toe* in AmE.

nausea. The recommended pronunciation is **naw**-zi-ə.

nauseated, nauseating, nauseous. 1 In Britain *nauseated* and *nauseating* (as parts of the verb *nauseate*) occasionally mean respectively 'affected by nausea' and 'causing nausea' in the physical sense but more often mean 'disgusted' and (especially) 'disgusting': (nauseated) *Aung San was nauseated by his persisting with the corrupt practices which had disfigured pre-war parliamentary politics—H. Tinker, 1987 | She had some brightly coloured blouses and dresses hanging in the cupboard, and the mere sight of them made her feel shaky and nauseated—C. F. Roe, 1990 | (nauseating) He opined that Band

Aid was diabolical and that Geldof was a 'nauseating character'—M. Middles, 1988 | *He woke up to the nauseating smell of burning skin and a roaring sound*—FlyPast, 1991 | *What a nauseating little Miss Perfect you are*—R. Goddard, 1993. *Nauseous* is used (1) to describe things that cause physical revulsion or feelings of disgust (*But that doesn't mean I have to be involved in this kind of nauseous business*—R. Harrison, 1991) and (2) to mean 'suffering from nausea' (*She suddenly felt nauseous, and went to the sink and heaved uncontrollably*—Q. Wilder, 1993).

2 In America, *nauseated* until recently only meant 'physically suffering from nausea', and *nauseous* strictly meant 'causing nausea'. However, this distinction has become blurred, and *nauseous* is now commonly used in the same way as the physical meaning of *nauseated*: *The water isn't as cold as I figured, but when the bottom of my pajama-leg gets wet, I get a little nauseous*—Transatlantic Review, 1977 | *Was the President nauseous when he slumped to the floor, or was there any vomiting?*—New York Times, 1992. Meanwhile the 'causing nausea' sense of *nauseous* is being replaced by *nauseating*.

naval, navel. *Naval* is the adjective relating to *navy*, and *navel* is the rounded knotty depression in the centre of the belly (also in *navel orange* etc.). The two words are unrelated.

nay is still in use as a somewhat rhetorical (and often affected) way of expressing the meaning 'and more than that . . . ': *One could not but notice how theatrical, nay operatic, the whole adornment of the church was*—Oxford Magazine, 1991. As a noun, *nay* means principally 'a no vote' in parliamentary divisions.

né see NÉE.

near, nearly. *Near* has almost fallen out of use as an adverb meaning 'almost', and *nearly* serves this purpose: *He was nearly dead with fright*. An exception is *near-perfect*: *Gunnell, captain of the British women's team, showed exactly how it should be done with what turned into a near-perfect performance*—Daily Mirror, 1992.

nearby, near by. When used as an adjective before a noun, it should be written as one word (*at a nearby hotel*), but as an adverb normally as two (*at a hotel near by*).

necessarily. The dominant pronunciation in BrE, which has been influenced by American practice, is with the stress on the third syllable; a first-syllable stress is often advocated by older speakers but whether they always use it themselves is questionable.

necessaries, necessities. Both words are well attested in the meaning 'the basic physical requirements of life, including food, warmth, and shelter': *I gathered up what few necessaries I could quickly lay my hands on—tobacco and papers, coffee, a can to cook in, and a couple of tin cups*—R. J. Conley, 1986 | *He needed to do some shopping for cleaning materials and other basic necessities and decided to go*—B. M. Gill, 1989.

née, né. *Née* is the feminine form of the French adjective meaning 'born' and is traditionally used to identify the maiden name of a married woman: *Mrs Ann Smith, née Jones*. In other cases it is used to denote the original name of a woman who has changed her name; in this use it also appears in the masculine form *né* to refer to a man who has done this and even to non-human name changes: *Diana Dors, née Diana Mary Fluck | Norman Charles, né Charles Norman Diggs | The Morning Star, né Daily Worker.*

need *verb.* **1** Like *dare*, *need* can behave in two ways: as an ordinary verb and as a modal auxiliary verb sharing some of the characteristics of the main modals including *can, may, might, should*, etc. As an ordinary verb, *need* is regular and can be followed by a simple object (*We need more bread*), a verbal noun (*The cupboard needs cleaning*), or a *to*-infinitive (*They need to see for themselves*). As a modal verb, it has certain grammatical restrictions: (1) it is only used with a so-called 'bare' infinitive without *to* (*I'm not sure you need answer*), (2) it is only used in the negative and in questions without *do* (*You need not answer | Need I answer?*), (3) the third person singular form is *need* without addition of *s* (*He says she need not answer*). Note that in many cases the modal use can alternatively be expressed by *need* as an ordinary verb, e.g. *He says she does not need to answer*, but the sense is then more one of neutrally stating a fact whereas the modal use normally expects a type of response (i.e. he does not want her to answer).

2 Some contextual examples follow: (modal use) *The Landlady need never know*—J. Frame, 1985 | *But need she lie? Was he just a boy?*—M. Leland, 1985 | *It need not only be children who can enjoy guessing games*—Spectator, 1988 | (ordinary use) *The K2 tragedy shows that much more needs to be done to bring home the lesson*—Times, 1986 | *She acted as if Strawberry needed to be cuddled*—New Yorker, 1988.

3 In its use as an ordinary verb in the meaning 'stand in want of', *need* can be followed by either a verbal noun (which is more common in speech) or a passive *to*-infinitive (*The car needs washing | The car needs to be washed*). A third type, *The car needs washed*, is primarily Scottish: *I walked round the cottage to see what needed done*—C. Burns, 1989.

needs, originally an adverb meaning 'of necessity, necessarily', survives in the somewhat literary phrase *needs must*: *If needs must, I'll spin them a yarn about you being one of my long-lost sons*—P. Bailey, 1986. The phrase alludes to the old proverb *Needs must when the devil drives* (and its variants).

ne'er is a literary (chiefly poetical) shortening of *never*, in regular use since the 13c but now rarely used except in the compound *ne'er-do-well* meaning 'a good-for-nothing'.

negative, an emphatic form of *no* used for clarity, has been extended since about the 1950s from the language of radio communication into general use: *'Any result of my application for the return of my typist?' 'Negative,' said Mr Oates*—Evelyn Waugh, 1961.

négligé, négligée. Both spellings are in use in English, and the accents are sometimes dropped. In the meaning 'a woman's light dressing-gown', the preferred form is *négligée*. The pronunciation of both forms is **neg**-li-zhay.

negligible is spelt *-ible*, not *negligeable.*

negotiate is one of Fowler's LOST CAUSES. In 1926 he strongly attacked its use in what he called 'its improper sense' of 'tackle successfully' as in negotiating bends, obstacles, etc., a use that is now well established.

Negro, Negress. *Negro* needs to be used with great caution, and *Negress* is no longer in favour at all (except among American Blacks themselves). The standard terms are now *black* (or *Black*) and (in America) *African-American*. The plural of *Negro* is *Negroes*.

Negroid, referring to the peoples of central and southern Africa, is one of a set of terms used by 19c anthropologists to classify human races. They are now outdated and potentially offensive, and the names of specific peoples or nationalities should normally be used.

neighbourhood. It is inadvisable to use the clumsy expression *in the neighbourhood of* (a sum or figure) when *roughly* or *about* would serve as well.

neither. 1 PRONUNCIATION. Both pronunciations, **niy**-dhə and **nee**-dhə, are about equally common.

2 PARTS OF SPEECH. *Neither* functions in two ways: as an adjective or pronoun, and as an adverb or conjunction.

▶ **a** ADJECTIVE AND PRONOUN. *Neither* means 'not the one nor the other (of two things)': *Neither child knew the answer | Neither wanted to stay | Neither of them is right.* When more than two items are involved, *no* is preferable for the adjective and *none* for the pronoun, although *neither* tends to be used informally especially for the pronoun. Normally *neither* governs a singular verb, but with the type

neither of (+ plural) a plural construction is sometimes used to emphasize the plurality of the statement as a whole: *Neither of them are suitable.*

▶ **b** ADVERB AND CONJUNCTION. *Neither* is regularly paired with *nor*, linking two subjects. If both subjects are singular and in the third person, the verb should normally be singular: *Neither its chairman, Sir Frederick Dainton, nor its chief executive, Kenneth Cooper, is planning any dramatic gestures*— Times, 1985. But a plural verb is also attested historically and is still often found, especially when the essential plurality that is always present in *neither* comes to the fore: *Neither search nor labour are necessary*—Dr Johnson, 1759 | *But neither Baker nor Bush are needed for that*—Newsweek, 1991. As an adverb, *neither* can be used with *nor* to link more than two items: *Buildings made of some translucent and subtly incandescent material, neither glass nor stone nor steel*—Penelope Lively, 1991. *Neither* is used as a quasi-conjunction in constructions of the informal type *He's had no breakfast. Neither did he want any*, in which it is a substitute for *nor*.

3 CHANGE OF NUMBER AND PERSON WITH *NEITHER . . . NOR . . .* Complications occur when the number (singular or plural) of the two subjects is different. If either of the subjects (especially the second) is plural, the verb is normally plural: *Neither the Conservative figures nor the evidence of Labour's recovery since 1983 produce any sense of inexorable movement in political fortunes*—Times, 1985. A mixture of persons is more difficult, and can normally only be resolved by rephrasing, so that (e.g.) *Neither you nor I am/are |is the right person* becomes *You are*

not the right person, and neither [or
nor] *am I.*

4 POSITION OF *NEITHER* AND *NOR*.
The position of *neither* and *nor*
should be such that the grammatical structures are correctly
balanced, as in *This suits neither
one purpose nor the other* but not
in ⊠ *This neither suits one purpose
nor the other.*

5 *NEITHER* FOLLOWED BY *OR*. Although the *OED* gives plenty of
literary evidence for *neither* followed by *or* rather than *nor* (e.g. *I
can neither tell how many we kill'd,
or how many we wounded*—Daniel
Defoe, 1719), in current usage this
is considered incorrect and
should be avoided.

6 *NEITHER* REPLACING *NOR*. When
nor follows a negative statement
(not necessarily one with *neither*)
and introduces a different grammatical subject, it can be replaced by *neither*: *Becky is killed
accidentally. The police don't care
much; neither does Henry's wife*—
Publishers Weekly, 1974.

nem. con., short for Latin *ne-
mine contradicente*, means 'with no
one dissenting' (from a vote or
decision). It does not mean the
same as *unanimously* since it can
also include abstentions, which
unanimously does not.

neologisms see NEW WORDS.

nerve-racking is the preferred
spelling in BrE, although AmE
also allows *nerve-wracking*.

-ness see -ION, -MENT, -NESS.

net. In the commercial meaning
'not subject to deduction', the
spelling is *net*, not *nett*.

**Netherlands, Low Countries,
Holland, Dutch.** *The Netherlands*
is the official name for the Kingdom of Holland; *Holland* (strictly

only a part of the Netherlands) is
used informally. The term *Low
Countries* includes Belgium and
Luxembourg as well as the Netherlands. *Dutch* is used as a noun
and adjective for the language
and people of the Netherlands,
and in certain familiar phrases
such as *Dutch courage* (= false courage got from alcohol) and *go
Dutch* (= pay individually).

neurosis has the plural form
neuroses, pronounced nyoo-**roh**-
seez.

never. As a negative adverb, *never*
refers primarily to repeated or
continuous non-occurrence over a
period of time: *They never answer
letters* | *It never rained at all last
month.* It should only be used informally to refer to one occasion,
when a simple negative would be
equally appropriate: *I phoned you
but you never rang back* [better, *you
didn't ring back*]; it is used with
similar meaning in a number of
fixed expressions such as *never
fear* and *well I never.* It is also used
idiomatically as an emphatic
negative with reference to future
time: *You'll never catch the train
now.* The emphatic form *never ever*
(sometimes with a comma between them) is also restricted to
informal contexts: *She continued, a
little too vehemently, 'I've never, ever
been bored'*—Maggie Gee, 1985.

nevertheless, nonetheless.
Both words mean 'in spite of
that' and are interchangeable.
They are both now normally written as one word.

news. *News is what a chap who
doesn't care much about anything
wants to read*—Evelyn Waugh, 1938.
News, though earlier a singular or
plural noun, has been treated
since the early 19c as singular:
Here is [not *are*] *the news.*

new words (also called *neolo-gisms*). It is always tempting, as much in the history of the language as in political and social history, to identify tendencies with centuries, but language change is a continuous process, and what is significant is the social and technological factors that have produced change. In the later part of the 20c, the most significant social and historical developments that have given rise to new words and meanings are as follows (necessarily a selective list with fairly crude divisions in which some items belong in more than one category):

SCIENCE AND TECHNOLOGY: *airglow, astrochemistry, cardphone, cash machine, cellphone, chaos theory, dark matter, digital compression, electronic banking* (and many other electronic phenomena), *genetic engineering, home shopping, meme, mobile phone, smart card, Switch* (method of payment), *tone dialling, voicemail*

COMPUTING: *access* (verb, as in accessing data; this has spread into general use), *boot* (verb, noun), *browser, bulletin board, bundle, CD-ROM, chipset, cut and paste, cyberspace, dataglove, dialogue box, directory, download, e-mail* (= electronic mail), *flaming, -friendly* (as a suffix as in *user-friendly*), *hacking, helpdesk, home page* (on the World Wide Web), *hypertext, information superhighway, Internet, laptop, log-on, millennium bug, motherboard, the Net, newsgroup, plug-and-play, scroll bar, search engine, shareware, software, standalone, surfing, upgradeability, virtual reality, virus,* (*World Wide*) *Web, zip.* [It will be noticed that most of these words are extended uses or modifications of basic items of core vocabulary.]

ENVIRONMENTAL ISSUES: *biodiversity, CFC* (= chlorofluorocarbon), *global warming, greenhouse effect,* *greenhouse gas, ozone depletion, ozone-friendly, zero-emission vehicle*

POPULAR CULTURE: *babe* (= attractive young woman), *bad hair day* (= day when everything goes wrong), *body piercing, crack* (= cocaine), *Ecstasy, lifestyle* (first recorded in the 1930s and adopted in marketing jargon in the 1980s), *lipstick Lesbian, recreational drug, smart drug*

POLITICS AND SOCIETY: *abuse* (as in *child abuse, narcotics abuse*), *acquaintance rape, cardboard city* (area of homeless people), *cash for questions, challenged* (PC term for a disability, as in *mentally challenged, physically challenged,* etc.), *change management, charisma, charm offensive, dependency culture, differently abled, double whammy, downshifting, downsizing, empowerment, Essex man, feel-good* (*factor*), *feminism* (a 19c word that has exploded in use in the 20c), *feng shui, fundholder, gap year* (between school and university), *gesture politics, glass ceiling* (barrier to personal advancement), *granny dumping, home shopping* (by means of a telecommunications link), *homophobia, human resources* (= personnel), *jobseeker, leaderene* (coined by the satirical magazine *Private Eye* to refer to Mrs Thatcher), *league table* (of schools' performance), *living will, loyalty card, mission statement* (= statement of a company's business principles), *nanny state, narco-terrorism, National Lottery, negative equity, New Age, New Labour, New Lad, outsourcing, pindown* (treatment of children in care), *pink pound, political correctness, power dressing, pro-active, ram-raiding, Reaganomics, reskilling, road rage, safe haven, serial monogamy, sexism* (and other words in -ism, e.g. *ableism, fattism, sizeism*), *sleaze, social chapter, speed bump, spin doctor* (= senior public relations officer to a politician), *stakeholder economy,* stressed out, subsidiarity, surrogate mother, teleworking, Thatcherism

INTERNATIONAL POLITICS: collateral damage, ethnic cleansing, Euroscepticism (and other Euro- words), fatwa, friendly fire, intifada, killing field (= place of mass slaughter), peace dividend, peace process, safe haven, velvet revolution

HEALTH AND MEDICINE: Aids (and Aids-related), attention deficit disorder, BSE (= bovine spongiform encephalitis), CJD (= Creutzfeld–Jakob disease), community care, dyspraxia, frozen embryo, functional food, interleukin (proteins), keyhole surgery, kinesiology, mad cow disease, ME (= myalgic encephalomyelitis), post-traumatic stress disorder, Prozac (antidepressant drug), RSI (= repetitive strain injury), SAD (= seasonal affective disorder), safe sex, sick building syndrome, trans-fatty acid, water birth

MEDIA AND COMMUNICATIONS: DAT (= digital audio tape), electronic publishing, infotainment, mini-series, multimedia, soundbite, supermodel

FOOD AND DRINK: alcopop (= alcoholic soft drink), ciabatta, decaf (= decaffeinated coffee), fajitas, foodie, functional food, nacho, tiramisu, tortilla

LEISURE: adventure game, Aga saga (= type of novel concerned with middle-class rural characters), arcade game, bungee jumping, CD (compact disc), edutainment, fantasy football, gangsta (dancing), golden goal, grunge (rock music), home cinema, jungle (music), karaoke, performance poetry, quality time, rollover, scratch card, snowboarding

GENERAL SLANG AND INFORMAL USES: anorak, attitude (= idiosyncratic attitude or outlook), dweeb, geek, gobsmacked, item (= romantic relationship), nerd, oick, saddo, spazz out, techie, wannabe (= someone with an ambition). It will be noticed how many of these are terms of personal abuse addressed to or used of people

CATCHPHRASES: back to basics (misconceived slogan for a return to honest principles), been there, done that (assertion of experience), economical with the truth, get a life, level playing field, move the goalposts, you name it.

next. As an adjective meaning 'immediately following', next normally precedes the noun it is governing (next time | the next three), but in denoting time it can follow the noun (on Friday next | in July next). Care needs to be taken in referring to a future day of the week, since usage differs. Generally, next Friday means the coming Friday of the same week, but if this is being said on a Thursday it might mean the Friday of the following week, since the immediately following Friday would then be referred to as tomorrow. In Scotland and parts of northern England, next Friday always means the Friday of the coming week, and to denote Friday of the same week this Friday would be used. If there is likely to be any doubt, it is better to be specific in some way, e.g. by adding the date or by saying, for example, Friday of this week or Friday week as appropriate.

nice. The word nice is the great cause célèbre of meaning change in English. In medieval and Renaissance literature, nice (derived from Latin nescius meaning 'ignorant') has a wide range of generally unfavourable meanings such as 'foolish, stupid' and 'wanton, loose-mannered', and in some cases it is not possible to be sure which meaning was intended. The meanings to do with precision and fine distinctions (as in a nice point) arose in the 16c, and are still in use, but they are now swamped by the generalized favourable use of nice to mean 'agreeable, pleasant': *Talk to her in your best, professorial manner, make her think how nice and kind you are*—Nina Bawden, 1989 | *All her furniture is second-hand and rather nice*—J. Rose, 1990 | *I have three children of my own now and I thought it would be nice to surprise them with the sugar mice on the tree, and also the chocolate cat*—Catherine Cookson, 1990. There is no doubt that *nice* is greatly overused in this meaning, and critics have some reason to call it a 'lazy word' (i.e. inducing laziness in its users). Many synonyms, often more apposite and stronger in meaning, are available (*good, pleasant, enjoyable, fine, agreeable, satisfying,* etc.) and it is often better to use them, but in conversation *nice* has established itself too well and too idiomatically for cautionary advice to have any real point: *I thought the shoulder of lamb would be much nicer and it looked nice and fresh!*—conversation recorded in British National Corpus, 1992.

nicety is pronounced **niy**-st-ti, as three syllables. Its primary meaning is 'a subtle distinction or detail' whereas *niceness* corresponds more generally to the meanings of *nice*.

niche. The usual pronunciation is neesh, in the French manner, although the anglicized form nich is also heard. In business jargon, *niche* (always pronounced neesh, of course) means 'a special section of the market' to which the marketing effort for goods or services may be specifically directed, and in this use the word has developed a range of attributive uses (i.e. before another noun) such as *niche market, niche product,*

and *niche player* (= a firm which exploits a niche): *The move completes the group's strategy of becoming a niche player in the new securities market after the big bang*—*Times,* 1986.

niece is one of the most commonly misspelt words in English.

nigger. The word is highly offensive when used by a white person with reference to a black, but it can apparently be used without offence (along with a respelt version *nigga*) by one black person referring to another, perhaps as a deliberate reclamation of the term by those who have suffered from it. Various phrases based on it, such as *nigger in the woodpile* and *work like a nigger,* have largely fallen out of use in ordinary language except in historical contexts.

-nik, a suffix derived from Yiddish and Russian and added to words to denote a person or thing associated with that word, has made some headway since it was given an initial boost by the Russian sputniks in the 1950s. First there was *beatnik* (1958, still the most celebrated and substantial of these words), then *no-goodnik* (1960), *protestnik* (1965) and *peacenik* (1965), both arising from opposition to the war in Vietnam, *computernik* (1966), and *refusenik* (1975, = a Jew refused permission to leave the Soviet Union). Apart from *beatnik*, they all have an ad hoc flavour about them.

nimby, an acronym for 'not in my back yard', was first used in the 1980s to refer to people who objected to the siting of something unpleasant in their own neighbourhood, without being opposed to its introduction in principle (as long as it was located somewhere else). The word, unlike others of the same kind, has endured.

nineties see EIGHTIES.

no. 1 *No* is used (1) as an adjective or (in the terminology of some linguists) negative determiner, with both singular and plural nouns, as in *no house | no children |* and *no food*, (2) as an adverb, as in *They were no wiser*, (3) as an interjection, as in *'Did you hear that?' 'No, I didn't.*, and (4) as a noun (with plural *noes*), meaning 'a denial' or 'a vote of *no*', as in *We won't take no for an answer* and *The noes have it* (meaning a parliamentary motion has been defeated). It is not often realized that there are two words involved here: the first meaning comes from a Middle English word related to *none*, while the other meanings are of Old English origin.

2 In the first meaning, *no* can be used to form a negative statement instead of *not*, e.g. *There are no wasps at this time of year* instead of *There aren't any wasps at this time of year.* But note the difference in implication between *He is not a teacher* (= he is something other than a teacher) and *He is no teacher* (= he is not suited to be a teacher).

3 The idiom *whether or no* is an established though now somewhat dated alternative for *whether or not*, and tends to be found in the pages of romantic fiction: *For whether or no she had been instrumental in the making of that despicable will, it was her presence here that had caused it to be made* — E. Bailey, 1993.

nobody, no one. Like *anybody* and *anyone*, these are largely interchangeable, but *no one* is written as two words because *noone* would be too awkward. In a use such as *No one person was responsible*, *no* and *one* retain their separate meanings instead of jointly forming a pronoun. Note that a possessive word referring back to *no one* (pronoun) is often a plural one: *No one likes to have their word doubted*: see GENDER-NEUTRALITY.

noisome means 'harmful, noxious' and has nothing to do with the word *noise*. It comes from a Middle English word *nay*, related to *annoy*.

nominative is a grammatical term denoting a noun or pronoun that is the subject of a verb or sentence, e.g. *house* in *The house stood on a hill*. See CASES.

nom de plume, pseudonym. A *nom de plume* (also in translated form *pen-name*) is a name assumed by an author to appear on the title-page of a book; a *pseudonym* is an name assumed more generally although this too is normally applied in authorial contexts.

non- is a prefix that makes negative forms (usually with a hyphen) of nouns and adjectives (mainly), e.g. *non-aggression, non-alcoholic, non-event,* and *non-union*. In another more recent type *non-* is added to a verb to form a word meaning 'that does not —', e.g. *non-iron, non-skid. Non-* is regularly used to form adjectives that are neutral in meaning when a form in *un-* or *in-* also exists with a special (normally unfavourable) meaning, as with *non-professional* (= not professional in status) as distinct from *unprofessional* (= not conforming to professional standards); others of this type include *non-effective, non-essential, non-human, non-natural,* and *non-scientific.*

nonchalance, nonchalant.
These are pronounced as English words, i.e. **non**-chə-ləns and **non**-chə-lənt.

non-count nouns see COUNTABLE NOUNS.

none, which is not a shortening of *no one* but a descendant of an Old English pronoun, may be followed by a singular or a plural verb, depending on the sense. When individuality is being emphasized, or when *none* refers to something that cannot be plural, a singular form is used: *A fear which we cannot know, which we cannot face, which none understands*—T. S. Eliot, 1935 | *She is rather difficult to describe physically, for none of her features is particularly striking*—David Lodge, 1962 | *None of this was a matter of treachery*—P. Wright, 1987. When collectivity is the dominant notion, a plural form is used: *None of our fundamental problems have been solved*—London Review of Books, 1987 | *Though she had many affairs, none were lighthearted romances*—New Yorker, 1987.

nonesuch see NONSUCH.

nonetheless see NEVERTHELESS.

non-flammable see FLAMMABLE.

nonpareil, meaning 'something or someone unrivalled or unique', is most commonly pronounced non-pə-**rayl**, although other pronunciations are also heard.

nonplus, meaning 'to perplex', has inflected forms *nonplussed,*

nonplussing, and in AmE also *nonplused, nonplusing.* In a recent development, *nonplussed* has come to mean 'unperturbed' (*'Out of power?' asked McCoy, trying to appear nonplussed*—D. Kramer-Rolls, 1990 (US)), the very opposite of the accepted meaning, probably by association with the prefix *non-,* which implies a negative meaning.

nonsense. Uses of *nonsense* as a countable noun (i.e. preceded by *a* or in the plural) have become common in the 20c, especially in BrE: *I knew you'd make a nonsense of it so I told Wallis to be ready to take over*—L. Cooper, 1960. | *I could only pray that the pathologist wouldn't come up with a time of death that made a nonsense of the alibi I was handing him*—V. McDermid, 1992.

non sequitur, meaning 'a conclusion that does not logically follow from the stated premiss or argument', is now normally printed in roman type.

nonsuch, nonesuch. *Nonsuch* (pronounced **nun**-such) is now the more usual form in both its main meanings, 'a person or thing that is unrivalled' and 'a plant with black pods'.

non-U see U AND NON-U.

non-white. Despite objections of cultural bias in assuming that 'white' is somehow normal and 'non-white' a departure from it, this is a standard term when general reference is needed.

no one see NOBODY.

no place, meaning 'nowhere', is still largely confined to AmE: *You're going no place until Herb gets* *here*—M. Pugh, 1969. It is sometimes written as one word.

no problem is recorded from the 1960s as an informal reply of assurance. The English playwright John Osborne missed the point (perhaps deliberately) when he wrote a few years ago: *Last week, on doctor's orders, I telephoned a pathology factory to organise a blood test. 'No problem.' How can they possibly know until I've had it? But I do hope they're right*—*Spectator*, 1992. It was the organization of the blood test, and not its outcome, that (at that stage at least) presented no problem, idiomatically if not actually.

nor. 1 For the use of *nor* after *neither*, see NEITHER. Note that *nor* can be repeated to introduce a third or further item: *The comment that receives the heartiest agreement concerns neither the war, nor the earthquake, nor the crime rate*—*Observer Magazine*, 1992.

2 *Nor* is sometimes used when there is no negative present or implied in the preceding clause: *Horned head-dresses have been found but they belonged to an earlier period. Nor did Viking warriors have decorated shields*—*Independent*, 1998.

normality, normalcy. In BrE *normality* is the usual word, and *normalcy* is regarded with disfavour although both words date from about the same time (mid-19c): *The morning passed slowly, uneventfully, and with a beguiling normality*—Anita Brookner, 1989. In AmE and in some other varieties, both words are used with about equal frequency: *. . . partly in order to tidy up, tidy the room and return it to normalcy*—Anita Desai, 1988 (India).

north, northern, northerly see EAST.

northward, northwards. The only form for the adjective is *northward* (*in a northward direction*), but *northward* and *northwards* are both used for the adverb, with a preference for *northwards* in BrE: *The advancing Allied armies . . . forced themselves northwards from the toe of Italy*—R. Perry, 1979.

nosy, meaning 'inquisitive', is spelt this way in preference to *nosey*.

not. 1 *Not* is used to form negative statements and questions, and is attached both to individual words and to whole clauses by means of their verbs, normally requiring the use of an auxiliary verb such as *do* or *have*: *We do not want to go* | *not usually* | *Not another one!*. For the use of *not* with so-called 'modal' verbs such as *can, may*, and 'semi-modals' such as *dare* and *need*, see MODAL VERB.

2 *NOT WITH ONLY.* Fowler (1926), in one of his more colourful images, wrote that '*not only* out of its place is like a tintack loose on the floor; it might have been most serviceable somewhere else, and is capable of giving acute pain where it is'. It is important to keep *not only* attached to the item to which it relates, so that in the sentence *Katherine's marriage not only kept her away, but at least two of Mr. March's cousins* (C. P. Snow), a stress on her will clarify the meaning in speech, but in writing the sentence needs to be rewritten as *Katherine's marriage kept not only her away, but . . .* When *not only* is followed by *but also* (or sometimes just *but*), the placing of the two elements again needs to be correctly balanced: *Those who can not only read*

and count, but can operate data processing machines as well . . . are said to be 'computerate'—Times, 1981 | On January 25, 1959, [Pope] John announced not only the convening of the Council but also a synod for the diocese of Rome—P. Hebblethwaite, 1984. In the following example, the positioning is so seriously awry as to be distracting: At present, businessmen are allowed to pass along to customers not only their increases in costs, but also to tack on their standard profit margins—Time, 1972 (the correct order is . . . are allowed not only to pass along to customers . . .).

3 NOT WITH AN INFINITIVE. The usual position of not when attached to a to-infinitive is before the to: He promised not to do it again | She tried not to think about it any more. Occasionally, and usually for a strong negative effect, not splits the infinitive, but this should be regarded as a literary device best avoided in normal writing and speech where the effect is more awkward: My advice to any woman who earns the reputation of being capable, is to not demonstrate her ability too much—Muriel Spark, 1988.

4 NOT IN THE TYPE NOT UNGRATEFUL, NOT UNNOTICED, ETC. This device, known as meiosis, is very common in English and even Fowler (1926), though he disliked it, recognized that it is well established: The presence of one of the . . . vans in the area had not passed unnoticed by the alert crew of a Berkshire County Police wireless prowl car—N. Lucas, 1967. Note that this type, with the second word positive in form and only negative in implication, is not the same as an explicit double negative, such as They didn't notice nothing, which is more generally condemned in current usage.

5 NOT REPEATED IN A SUBORDINATE CLAUSE. I shouldn't wonder if it didn't turn to snow. This type, in which not is wrongly placed in a subordinate clause as a mere echo of a negative in the main clause, should be avoided, although it is sometimes heard in informal speech. The correct form is I shouldn't wonder if it turned to snow.

noticeable is spelt with an e in the middle.

notorious, infamous. Both words refer to fame achieved by means that are disapproved of, but notorious stresses the fame achieved whereas infamous is more concerned with the nature of the act: A notorious property developer . . . was spooning sago pudding into his face—D. Jordan, 1973 | The scene of one of Drachenfels' most infamous atrocities, this chamber has been shunned by most of the few who have penetrated the Castle—C. Sargent, 1992.

nought see NAUGHT. In expressing the figure nought out loud in a sequence of digits, BrE normally uses 'o' (as if it were the letter) whereas in AmE 'zero' is more usual.

noun. A noun is a word that names a person or thing. Common nouns name persons or things which are not peculiar to one example, i.e. are of a general nature (bridge, girl, sugar, unhappiness), whereas proper nouns name persons or things of which there is only one example (Asia, Concorde, Dickens). Concrete nouns refer to physical things (bread, woman), and abstract nouns to concepts (greed, unhelpfulness). Some nouns are concrete and abstract in different meanings, e.g. cheek is concrete when it refers to part of the face and abstract when it means 'impertinence'.

noun and verb differences.
See box opposite

no way. *He said he wouldn't start up a gang today—no way.—New Yorker,* 1975. This 20c Americanism is now common in casual BrE speech, although its transatlantic origin is always near the surface: *I wrote back and said no way did I think that she ought to go into the unit*—D. Coulby et al., 1987. An intermediate stage can be seen in the expression *there is no way (that)* . . . : *The Doctor realises that there is no way the two teachers could have achieved all this*—J. Bentham, 1986.

nth. The popularized extension of the expression *to the nth degree* from the language of mathematics to general usage in the meaning 'to the utmost' has continued despite Fowler's disapproval of it (1926): *Leonard could be fastidious to the nth degree in completing his own work—he has always said that he works 'one word at a time'*—L. S. Dorman et al., 1990.

nubile. The original Latin meaning of *nubilis*, '(of females) of an age suitable for marriage', has given way in the 20c to the meaning 'sexually attractive', making the earlier sense somewhat awkward to use, except with intentional ambiguity.

nuclear should be pronounced **nyook**-li-ə, and not as if it were spelt *nucular*, although this is occasionally heard, in AmE (famously by President Eisenhower in the 1950s) rather more than in BrE.

nucleus has the plural form *nuclei*, pronounced **nyook**-li-iy.

number is a grammatical term denoting the status of words as singular or plural. See AGREEMENT.

number of. The expression *a number of* + plural noun, as in *a number of people*, normally takes a plural verb in both BrE and AmE, because the plural noun is regarded as the 'head' of the noun phrase and therefore as the real subject: *A number of books by ballerinas have been published lately—New Yorker,* 1987. By contrast, the expression *the number of* + plural noun, in which the head of the phrase is *number* and not the noun, takes a singular verb: *The number of MPs has increased—Daily Telegraph,* 1987.

numeracy, a term denoting competence with basic mathematical concepts, was coined in 1959 on the analogy of *literacy* by a UK committee on education reporting in that year. The corresponding adjective is *numerate.*

numerals. In general, numerals are used in more factual or statistical contexts and words are used (especially with numbers under a hundred) in more descriptive material: *I have lived in the same house for twelve years | The survey covers a period of 12 years.* Words are used in idiomatic expressions such as *I must have told you a hundred times | Thousands of people swarmed through the gates.* Separate objects, animals, ships, persons, etc., are not units of measurement unless they are treated statistically: *The peasant had only four cows | A farm with 40 head of cattle.* With numerals consisting of four or more figures, commas should be used to divide off the thousands, e.g. *3,096 | 10,731.* In specifying

noun and verb differences

The following table lists differences of stress, pronunciation, and spelling when the same word is used as a noun and a verb, for example *compound*, *escort*, *practice/practise*, *record*, and *use*. Differences are marked by the letters s (= difference of stress, normally first syllable for the noun and second for the verb), p (= pronunciation, e.g. between yoos and yooz for the noun and verb *use*), and sp (= spelling, e.g. between *belief* and *believe*).

NOUN	VERB	DIFFERENCE
abuse	abuse	p
accent	accent	s
advice	advise	sp
bath	bathe	sp
belief	believe	sp
breath	breathe	sp
calf	calve	sp
close	close	p
cloth	clothe	sp
commune	commune	s
compound	compound	s
concert	concert	s
conduct	conduct	s
conflict	conflict	s
conscript	conscript	s
consort	consort	s
contest	contest	s
contract	contract	s
contrast	contrast	s
convert	convert	s
convict	convict	s
decrease	decrease	s
defect	defect	s
dictate	dictate	s
digest	digest	s
discord	discord	s
discount	discount	s
discourse	discourse	s
escort	escort	s
excuse	excuse	p
export	export	s
extract	extract	s
ferment	ferment	s
grief	grieve	sp
half	halve	sp
house	house	p

▶

▶ noun and verb differences
continued

NOUN	VERB	DIFFERENCE
import	import	s
imprint	imprint	s
incline	incline	s
increase	increase	s
indent	indent	s
inlay	inlay	s
insert	insert	s
insult	insult	s
licence	license	sp
life	live	sp
loss	lose	sp
misuse	misuse	p
mouth	mouth	p
practice	practise	sp
produce	produce	s
proof	prove	sp
record	record	s
reject	reject	s
relief	relieve	sp
sheath	sheathe	sp
shelf	shelve	sp
strife	strive	sp
suspect	suspect	s
teeth	teethe	sp
thief	thieve	sp
transfer	transfer	s
use	use	p
wreath	wreathe	sp

ranges of numbers, use the least number of figures possible, e.g. *13–14 | 31–4 | 1923–6*. But dates BC should be written in full: *432–431 BC* (since *432–31 BC* and *432–1 BC* represent different ranges). More detailed information will be found in *Hart's Rules for Compositors and Readers*.

nursling is the preferred spelling, not *nurseling*.

Oo

-o.
See box overleaf

O, Oh. The recommended practice is to use *O* when a name being addressed or invoked follows (*O Death, where is thy sting?*) and *Oh* as an independent exclamation (*Oh, how do you know that?*).

oaf has the plural form *oafs*.

oasis, pronounced oh-**ay**-sis, has the plural form *oases*, pronounced oh-**ay**-seez.

obeisance means 'homage, submission', and is pronounced oh-**bay**-səns.

object *verb.* The stress is on the second syllable (əb-**jekt**), and the word is often followed by *to* + noun (which can also be a verbal noun): *Would the lady object to my lighting a pair of candles?*—Dickens, 1865 | *He also objected strongly to what he called your jack-boot methods when you interviewed Mrs Hurd*—R. Simons, 1968 | *I have never smoked and I object to being poisoned by other people's indulgence*—Liverpool Echo, 1993. The same construction is used with the noun *objection*: *We have no objection at all to helping in what she calls her 'psychological warfare'*—M. Babson, 1974.

objective genitive. An example of this is *the boy's murder*, in which the genitive form *boy's* denotes not possession (as in *the boy's dog*, which is the usual function of a genitive) but the object of the noun *murder*.

object, objective *nouns.* Both words have the meaning 'something sought or aimed at' and in practice they are often interchangeable, although *object* is more common when followed by a qualifying construction, e.g. one with *in* or *of* (and is exclusively used in the expression *object of the exercise*): *Its report is a living document which . . . will gradually influence public opinion. That was the object of the exercise*—Spectator, 1958 | *His main objective was to pile up a huge personal fortune*—Saul Bellow, 1987.

objector is the preferred spelling for 'someone who objects', not *objecter*.

oblivious. The historical meaning of *oblivious* is 'forgetful, unmindful', followed by *of*: *Never before . . . has a great painter been completely oblivious of the style, or styles, of his time*—Kenneth Clark, 1949. This meaning survives, but another meaning, 'unaware of, unconscious of', which evolved during the 19c, is now more common, despite objections to it raised by the *OED* editors (who labelled it 'erroneous', changed to 'formerly regarded as erroneous' in *OED2*) and by Fowler (1926). In this meaning it is followed by *of* or (more often) *to*: *I stayed indoors all day for several days, oblivious to the damp heat of Falmouth*—C. Day Lewis, 1960.

oboe has the plural form *oboes*, and the player is an *oboist*, pronounced **oh**-boh-ist.

-o

1 Plurals of nouns ending in *-o* cause difficulty in English because there are few convenient rules for choosing between *-os* (as in *ratios*) and *-oes* (as in *heroes*). What rules there are can be briefly summarized:

▶ **a** When a vowel (usually *i* or *e*) precedes the final *-o*, the plural is normally *-os* (*trios, videos*), probably because of the bizarre look of *-ioes* etc.

▶ **b** Names of animals and plants normally form plurals in *-oes* (*buffaloes, tomatoes*).

▶ **c** Words that are shortenings of other words invariably form plurals in *-os* (*demos, hippos*).

▶ **d** Alien-looking words and comparatively recent loanwords form plurals in *-os* (*boleros, placebos*).

▶ **e** Multi-syllable words tend to form plurals in *-os* (*generalissimos, manifestos*).

▶ **f** Proper names form plurals (used allusively) in *-os* (*Neros, Romeos*).

2 In other cases, practice varies from one house style to another, and the table below gives a consensus of informed usage.

SINGULAR	PLURAL
alto	altos
banjo	banjos
buffalo	buffaloes
cargo	cargoes
casino	casinos
concerto	concertos *or* concerti
contralto	contraltos
do	dos *or* do's
dodo	dodos
domino	dominoes
dynamo	dynamos
echo	echoes
ego	egos
embargo	embargoes
fiasco	fiascos
flamingo	flamingos
fresco	frescos
gigolo	gigolos
go	goes
grotto	grottoes
hairdo	hairdos
halo	haloes
hero	heroes
hippo	hippos

▶

▶ **-o**
continued

SINGULAR	PLURAL
innuendo	innuendoes
kilo	kilos
libretto	librettos
mango	mangoes
manifesto	manifestos
memento	mementoes
memo	memos
mosquito	mosquitoes
motto	mottoes
Negro	Negroes
no	noes
peccadillo	peccadilloes
photo	photos
piano	pianos
piccolo	piccolos
potato	potatoes
proviso	provisos
radio	radios
rhino	rhinos, or (collective) rhino
salvo (= firing of guns)	salvoes
silo	silos
solo	solos
soprano	sopranos
stiletto	stilettos
tiro	tiros
tobacco	tobaccos
tomato	tomatoes
torpedo	torpedoes
verso	versos
veto	vetoes
volcano	volcanoes
zero	zeros

obscene. In a century that has tried repeatedly to define the meaning and implications of obscenity in relation to literature, the performing arts, and (above all) the cinema, the word *obscene* has gathered strength in its other main meaning, 'highly offensive or repugnant' as a moral condemnation of social circumstances such as poverty and wealth, violence, human exploitation, etc. Some examples follow: *Something in the very robustness of Germany's economy seemed to the terrorists and their sympathizers profoundly obscene—Time,* 1977 | *The idea of these old women being walled up*

and told what to do by a supersti-
tious parson was (Tibba allowed her-
self the modernism) obscene—A. N.
Wilson, 1982 | *His pay was branded*
'utterly obscene' amid calls for him to
quit and drop his name from the
company—Daily Mirror, 1992.

observance, observation.

These two words correspond to
different branches in meaning of
the verb *observe* ('to see or notice'
and 'to follow or adhere to'). *Ob-*
servance is the word normally
used in connection with respecting rules, carrying out duties and
obligations, and performing formal customs and rituals, whereas
observation is the equivalent in
the more physical senses of seeing and perceiving, has the special countable meaning 'a remark
or comment', and is used in special combinations such as *observa-*
tion car (on a train, chiefly AmE)
and (military) *observation post*. Examples: *To act on or defy a socially*
established rule has effects on all
who benefit or suffer by its
observance—A. C. Graham, 1985 |
Edinburgh can offer ethnically-based
social facilities and opportunities for
meetings for several forms of non-
Christian religious observance—
undergraduate prospectus, 1993 | *I*
didn't try to go into details on the
phone, but said that we were going
to need some police observation—
J. R. L. Anderson, 1980 | *The play-*
group leader will usually offer her ob-
servations as part of the parents'
contribution to the Statement—W.
Swann et al., 1992.

obsess has been used since the
16c as a transitive verb, often in
the passive with *obsessed* as a
quasi-adjective: *Modern society is*
obsessed with romanticizing ancient
societies—Times, 1980. In the later
part of the 20c a new intransitive
use has emerged, first in AmE

and more recently in BrE, in
which *obsess* means 'to be pre-
occupied or unduly worried
(about something)' and is usually
followed by *about* or *over*: *The only*
way to go about judging your work is
not to obsess too much over it—
Times, 1998.

obsolete, obsolescent. Both
words are derived from Latin *obso-*
lescere meaning 'to fall into disuse'. Something (either physical,
such as a piece of machinery, or
conceptual, such as a custom or
idea) is *obsolete* when it is outdated and no longer used. It is *ob-*
solescent when it is falling out of
use, i.e. is becoming obsolete but
is not yet actually so.

obtain is a formal and often pretentious word, and no one should
be afraid of using the perfectly
respectable word *get* in most contexts.

occasion. When it means 'reason, grounds', the usual construction is with *for* + noun (or verbal
noun) or with a *to*-infinitive: *Yes-*
terday was Schubert's birthday . . .
suitable occasion for a Schubertiad—
Times, 1977. When the meaning is
'opportunity', it is followed by a
to-infinitive: *I have had occasion re-*
cently to re-read Goethe's Theory of
Colours—Nature, 1971. However, it
will be seen from these examples
that the two strands of meaning
are not always distinct.

occur has inflected forms *oc-*
curred, occurring, and the noun derivative is *occurrence* (with two *r*s,
often misspelt).

octopus has the plural form *octo-*
puses. The pseudo-Latin form *oc-*
topi, except when used jocularly,
is misconceived, since the Greek
stem is *octopod-* (giving the rightly

rejected form *octopodes* in English).

-odd. The hyphen is important in uses such as *twenty-odd people* (= roughly twenty), to avoid ambiguity.

odour, a slightly genteel word for 'smell', is spelt *-our* in BrE and *odor* in AmE. The corresponding adjective is *odorous* in both varieties.

oe-, e-. There is a tendency to simplify spellings with *-oe-* in BrE to *-e-* in AmE, e.g. *estrogen* for *oestrogen* and *ameba* for *amoeba*, but both types are used.

-oes (forming plurals of nouns) see -o.

of. 1 The preposition *of* is one of the key words in structuring phrases and sentences in English, and it is sometimes possible to make a slip in usage that can give the wrong meaning. Fowler (1926) devoted a long article to this topic and gave citations from newspapers which illustrated various problems associated with its use. These usually occur in extended sentences and consist of either adding an *of* where it is not wanted (or where another preposition is called for) or leaving out an *of* where it is needed to clarify the sense. This entry deals with these topics in more summary form, with examples taken from a wide range of sources.

2 The most usual context in which *of* is wrongly inserted is at a point in a long sentence in which it is meant to refer back to an earlier part of the sentence but is in fact the wrong choice, influenced by the occurrence of another *of* close by which has nothing to do with it: *He will be in the best possible position **for** getting the most out of the land and **of** using it to the best possible advantage* (the preposition wanted is *for* not *of*) | *It could be done without unduly raising the price of coal, or **of** jeopardizing new trade* (the second *of* is redundant). In other cases, a repeated *of* is not incorrect but is unnecessary: *A series of problem contracts and **of** bad debts does not explain the situation* | *On the one hand there are the conventional rules of good manners and **of** correct behaviour.*

3 In other cases, however, *of* must be repeated to avoid misunderstanding: *He has mapped the development of the animal's nervous system and **of** its behaviour* (of repeated to establish a link with *development*). It should also be repeated in constructions with *both* when the position of *both* requires a balanced sequence: *There are teachers with low standards who think a mere pass at whatever grade is a feather in the cap both of themselves and **of** their pupils* (alternatively, one could put … *a feather in the cap of both themselves and their pupils*, but in this case the result would be awkward).

4 The other principal error lies in omitting an *of* where this is called for to clarify the meaning: *The banning of meetings and the printing and distribution of leaflets stopped the agitation* (*of* should be put in before *the printing* to show that the part after the first *and* is still governed by the word *banning*).

5 The informal type *of an evening, of a Sunday afternoon*, etc. (*All the intellect of the place assembled of an evening*—Carlyle, 1831), is beginning to sound literary or archaic, except in dialect use. In AmE, this type is often expressed in the form *evenings, Sunday afternoons*, etc., without any preposition (*She plays cards Thursdays*).

of course has a useful role as a term of insistence meaning 'as was to be expected', in which the hearer's or reader's prior knowledge or agreement can reasonably be assumed. Fowler (1926) rightly urged caution in the use of the phrase 'as the herald of an out-of-the-way fact that one has just unearthed', e.g. *Milton of course had the idea from Tacitus.* Some modern examples are: *Of course, there are a number of other phenomena, such as lightning and reflections of sunlight off tumbling satellites and orbiting debris, that can also give flashes in the sky*—Stephen Hawking, 1988 | *We were approached by Tom Lloyd, a young solicitor from Carmarthen with a passion for historic buildings—particularly, of course, those of Wales*—M. Binney et al., 1991.

offence. This is spelt *-ence* in BrE, and *offense* in AmE.

offer. The verb has inflected forms *offered, offering*.

official, officious. The main meanings of *official* are 'in the nature of an office' (*Their official duties*) and 'authorized or confirmed by someone in authority' (*The official attendance was over 10,000*). By contrast, *officious* is a judgemental word meaning 'asserting authority aggressively or intrusively', and is most commonly used of a person or the actions of a person: *Officious meter maids checking overparked cars*—L. Egan, 1977.

officialese. The term is first recorded in 1884 and was used by Sir Ernest Gowers (1965) as the heading of an article that ex-

plored the 'style of writing marked by peculiarities supposed to be characteristic of officials', i.e. pompous and opaque bureaucratic language. (Fowler had no entry on this topic in 1926.) An example given by Gowers concerned Anglo-American talks on the development of folding-wing aircraft, and was taken from a London evening newspaper: *The object of this visit is a pooling of knowledge to explore further the possibility of a joint research effort to discover the practicability of making use of this principle to meet a possible future NATO requirement, and should be viewed in the general context of interdependence.* Gowers distinguished this kind of language, characterized by verbosity and circumlocution, from *legalese*, which though sometimes equally difficult to understand is characterized by concision and is dictated by the need to ensure that what is said will stand up to challenge and scrutiny in courts of law. See further at LEGALESE; PLAIN ENGLISH

officious see OFFICIAL.

off of. This complex preposition is found in Shakespeare (*A* [= *I*] *fall off of a tree*—2 *Henry VI* II.i.98), and occurs in colloquial speech in AmE: *The night Wayne came at Randolph with a hammer to pull him off of Mary*—M. Golden, 1989. It is, however, non-standard in current British English.

offspring, meaning 'a person's or animal's child or young' has the same form in the plural: *A person is a Jew if he or she is the offspring of a Jewish mother or has been converted to the Jewish faith*—J. R. Baker, 1974 | *So these offspring shared in the eventually growing* *prosperity . . . of the region*—E. Gellner, 1983.

often. In current English this is more usually pronounced with the *t* silent. The comparative forms *oftener* and *oftenest* are permissible, although *more often* and *most often* are more commonly used.

OK. Although its origin is still the subject of much scholarly discussion, the most likely explanation is that it was derived in the 1830s from the initial letters of the American dialect form *orl korrect* (= all correct) and rapidly acquired historical associations that gave it wider currency but do not constitute its true origin (e.g. as an election slogan of 'Old Kinderhook' (Martin Van Buren), the Democratic presidential candidate in 1840). No longer regarded as an Americanism, it is possibly the only English word that is universally recognized by speakers of other languages throughout the world. The alternative form *okay* is especially useful as a verb (= to say OK to, to authorize), allowing more comfortable inflected forms (*okays, okayed, okaying*) than *OK* does.

older, oldest see ELDER, ELDEST.

Olympiad, Olympian, Olympic. An *Olympiad* is an old term for a period of four years between Olympic Games (used principally in ancient dating), and a particular celebration of the ancient Olympic Games (and is occasionally also applied in the same sense to the modern games). *Olympian* in current use refers to Mount Olympus and to the gods of Olympus. *Olympic* is used principally of the games of ancient times and their modern revival;

these are called *Olympic Games* or (for the modern games) *Olympics*.

omelette is the usual spelling in BrE, whereas *omelet* is more common in AmE.

omit has inflected forms *omitted, omitting*.

on. In AmE, *on* is idiomatic in two uses in which BrE uses a different preposition: *My father . . . had a dry-goods store on Gesia Street*—I. B. Singer, 1983 (BrE *in*) / *On weekends she would play disk jockey like that for hours*—*New Yorker*, 1987 (BrE *at*).

on account of see ACCOUNT.

-on-demand. *On demand* has been in use for many years to denote something that is available to those who want it when they want it, and in recent years has been used notably in the context of abortion (*He proved himself out of touch over the economy and by opposing abortion on demand*—*Today*, 1992). Its consolidation into a combining form has burgeoned in the context of the telecommunications industry, where we have *video-on-demand, fax-on-demand, news-on-demand*, etc.: *Clever and savvy use of telecommunications, such as toll-free 800 numbers and fax-on-demand, can give your company a cutting-edge image*—*CompuServe Magazine*, 1995.

one. 1 When the phrase *one of those who . . .* is used, it is normally preferable to follow it with a plural verb (regarding *those* rather than *one* as the antecedent), except when particular emphasis is being placed on the individuality of *one*, in which case a singular verb is called for: (plural verb) *She was one of those women who make an enchanted garden of their* *childhood memories*—Anita Brookner, 1990 | (singular verb) *'Don't you think,' said Bernard, 'that Hawaii is one of those places that was always better in the past?'*—David Lodge, 1991.

2 The use of *one* to mean 'any person', 'I', or 'me' is often regarded as an affectation, although English does not always have a ready alternative. It is probably true to say that the more *one* is associated with 'I' or 'me', the greater the affectation: *This performance commanded attention; at times . . . it brought one's blood to a boil*—*Chicago Tribune*, 1988. When it genuinely means 'any person' (including only incidentally the speaker), it seems a good deal more natural: *You must realize that there are risks that one doesn't take*—Nadine Gordimer, 1987. When *one* is used in this way there is a difference of usage between BrE and AmE when the sentence is continued with a further pronoun having the same reference. In AmE *one* is followed either by another *one* (or *one's*) or by a third-person pronoun *he* or *she* (or, to avoid gender problems, occasionally *they*), or by *his* or *her* or *their*, whereas in BrE another *one* (or *one's*) always follows: (AmE) *I like to believe one can be honest and sincere and committed in what he's doing*—*Chicago Sun-Times*, 1988 | (BrE) *If one has no base on which to formulate probing questions, can one actually give informed consent?*—*Dædalus*, 1986.

one another see EACH 3.

ongoing. First recorded in 1877, this adjective gained such widespread currency in the 1950s and later that it quickly attracted criticism as a vogue word, and, especially in the phrase *ongoing situation*, as a cliché on a par with *at the end of the day* and *in this day and age*. Other combinations, such as *ongoing operation, ongoing process,* and *ongoing relationship,* are more acceptable: *He says he wouldn't have got anywhere without Move On, who helped him secure a flat and are now giving vital, ongoing support*—*Big Issue*, 1998.

only. The position of *only* is one of the major unresolved topics of discussion in English usage. The upshot is that logical position, i.e. association with the word to which *only* most closely refers, is not always consistent with naturalness, which generally favours a position between the subject and the verb. Fowler (1926), in a long article on the subject, made a case for allowing 'illogical' positioning in a sentence such as *He only died a week ago*, which is a great deal more natural and stylistically satisfactory than *He died only a week ago*. Equally acceptable are the following examples of actual usage: *I was . . . made to attend a Catholic businessmans luncheon (where I only got wine by roaring for it)*—Evelyn Waugh, 1958 | *Those days, you only applied to one college*—*New Yorker*, 1986 | *He says he only took the job because the neon sign always cheered him up*—Julian Barnes, 1991. In written English, the logical position of *only* should be respected when serious (rather than notional or theoretical) ambiguity would otherwise result, especially in contexts such as legal language in which precision is more important than a pleasing style: *The public interest is properly served only where companies pursue the traditional goal of profit maximisation*—J. E. Parkinson, 1993. In general usage, the most natural position of *only* is where it always has been, between the subject and its verb, and invariable insistence on logical position sacrifices naturalness to pedantry.

on to, onto. *On to* is recorded in continuous use as a complex preposition from the late 16c, and the one-word form *onto* from the early 18c. In modern use both forms are found; *onto* has become more common in recent years but has still not achieved the dominance enjoyed by *into* (which goes back to Old English): *French windows opened from the breakfast-room on to the terrace and large walled garden*—Penelope Lively, 1981 | *The blue sky threw its light down onto the fields below*—L. Norfolk, 1991. Note that in some uses *on* is used as a full adverb and needs to be spelt separately: *They drove onto the beach* means 'they parked the car on the beach', whereas *They drove on to the beach* (with the sentence falling into two parts between *on* and *to*) means 'they continued their journey until they reached the beach'. Care also needs to be taken to retain the identity of *on* in phrasal verbs when these are followed by *to*: *It was some time before she **cottoned on** to what he meant.*

onward, onwards. The only form for the adjective is *onward* (*resuming their onward journey*), but *onward* and *onwards* are both used for the adverb, with a preference for *onwards* in BrE: *He'd subscribed to all sorts of causes, from the Spanish Civil War onwards*—A. Price, 1981.

op. cit. is a shortening of the Latin phrase *opere citato* meaning 'in the work already cited'. It is used in text to refer back to earlier references, normally preceded by the name of the author in the form 'Bloomfield, op. cit., pp. 54–5'.

operate has derivative forms *operable* ('able to be operated on', especially in medical contexts) and *operator*.

opportunity. The expressions *have* (or *take*, etc.) *the* (or *an*, *every*, etc.) *opportunity* are followed either by a *to*-infinitive or by *of* + verbal noun: *I was eager to snatch at every opportunity to get myself established as a writer, film-maker, what-have-you, in an effort to find a clearly defined career*—Chris Bonington, 1973 | *He takes the opportunity to castigate the creeping hypocrisy and social climbing which had always called forth his most bitter satire*—*Transactions of the Yorkshire Dialect Society*, 1978 | *The primary school kids have the opportunity of working with micros in their normal classroom activities*—*Listener*, 1983. For is normally used when an ordinary noun follows: *Happily there was no opportunity for soddishness about whom I should go with*—D. Craig, 1970.

opposite. As an adjective denoting position, *opposite* is followed by *to* (*Two people directly opposite to each other*); it is also used with the same meaning as a preposition without *to* (*Two people directly opposite each other*). As a noun, *opposite* is followed by *of* (*The effect was the opposite of what they intended*).

optimal, optimum. Both words entered the language in the late 19c and are used in the meaning 'best or most favourable (in given circumstances)' and therefore mean rather more than simply 'best': *He positioned himself so that he had optimum sight lines down the side street*—I. Melchior, 1975 | *Pursuing policies that would be optimal in a first-class world when one actually* *lives in a . . . third-best world can be highly inefficient*—Dædalus, 1979.

opus. When denoting a musical composition and in the phrase *magnum opus*, the recommended pronunciation is **oh**-pǝs, with a long ō. The plural is either *opera* (**op**-ǝ-rǝ) or *opuses* (**oh**-pǝ-siz).

or. 1 When *or* separates two singular nouns, the following verb should be in the singular: *A paint or steel company or a salt or coal mine was no place for the late Herr Baumgartner's widow*—Anita Desai, 1988. (When both nouns are plural the verb is of course also plural.) The following example is acceptable informally, but strictly *or* should be replaced by *and*, or the plural complement replaced by a singular one (. . . *is a typical method*): ⊠ *A cassette recorder or disk system are typical methods*— Choosing and using Your Home Computer, 1984. When one of the nouns is singular and the other plural, the verb normally agrees with the one nearer to it, and the same applies to mixes of person as in *she or we, you or your brother*, etc.: *The child or its parents sign the form | Were you or your brother there?*.

2 For *or* after *either* see EITHER 2B, and after *neither* see NEITHER 5.

oral see AURAL.

orator is spelt -*or*, not *orater*.

oratorio has the plural form *oratorios*.

orbit. The verb has inflected forms *orbited, orbiting*.

order see IN ORDER FOR; IN ORDER THAT; IN ORDER TO.

orderly is used only as an adjective (*They behaved in an orderly*

fashion), not as an adverb. Since the notional adverb *orderlily* is too awkward to use, *in an orderly way* is the only alternative.

ordinance, ordnance, ordonnance. An *ordinance* is 'an authoritative order', *ordnance* is 'a branch of government service dealing with military stores and materials, and *ordonnance* is 'a plan or method of literary or artistic competition' or 'an order of architecture'. *Ordnance Survey* is an official UK survey organization, originally under the Master of Ordnance, that produces large-scale detailed maps of each region of the country.

orient, oriental. Both words now sound dated and have an exotic 18c or 19c aura more associated with the world of empire and romantic adventure than with factual description. In ordinary writing it is often better to use more neutral terms such as *eastern* or (*East*) *Asian* (or terms that specify particular counties). The noun *orient* is traditionally spelt *Orient* with a capital initial letter when referring geographically or politically to countries, whereas practice varies between *orient* and *Orient* when it is used in general (often literary) reference to the east. That is the rule normally stated, but it is often difficult to be sure of the distinction: *She was a blonde. They have a great time in the Orient, scarcity value*—G. Black, 1972 | *Flaubert left Europe a Romantic, and returned from the Orient a Realist*—Julian Barnes, 1985 | *The need to give punters the opportunity to additionally sample delights from the orient hardly seems necessary*—Guardian, 1989 | *The orient has three species of tarsiers*—C. Willock, 1991. The adjective *oriental*, meaning 'eastern' with reference to a part of the world, is normally spelt with a small *o*.

orient, orientate, *verbs*. Both words are used (especially in the adjectival forms *oriented* and *orientated*) with the same meaning 'to place in a particular way in relation to the points of the compass' and 'to establish one's bearings': (orient) *Man needs relations with other people in order to orient himself*—R. May, 1953 | *In a youth-oriented society for a woman to grow old means to run the risk of being ignored*—A. Hutschnecker, 1981. | (orientate) *It was very much a London orientated magazine*—N. Sherry, 1987 | *Kant's own philosophy was undeniably orientated towards problems that lay at the heart of the philosophical enterprise*—P. Gardiner, 1988. These examples show how commonly the words are used in abstract or figurative contexts, and as the second element in combinations preceded by a noun (*youth-oriented*, *London orientated*). There is no meaningful criterion for choosing between them, except that *orient* is shorter and therefore less cumbersome in some contexts.

originator is spelt *-or*, not *originater*.

ornament. The noun is pronounced **aw**-nə-mənt, whereas the verb has a more distinct -ment sound in the third syllable.

orthopaedic, denoting the branch of medicine concerned with treating deformities of the bones and muscles, is spelt *-paedic* in BrE and *-pedic* in AmE. The corresponding noun *orthopaedics* (AmE *orthopedics*) is normally treated as singular.

-os (forming plurals of nouns) see -o.

ostensible, ostensive. *Ostensible* means 'apparent but not necessarily real' or 'professed': *Despite their ostensible commitment to revolution, they played an ambivalent and ultimately counter-revolutionary role*—E. Acton, 1992. It is often used in the adverbial form *ostensibly*: *Ostensibly the visit was designed to mark the 20th anniversary of the normalization of relations between China and Japan*—Keesings, 1990. *Ostensive*, a much rarer word, means 'directly demonstrative' and is normally used in technical contexts with words such as *definition* (meaning a definition that shows what it describes, e.g. a definition of the term *italics* printed in italics): *If one attempts to teach a dog by way of ostensive definition, it invariably responds by sniffing one's finger*—A. F. Chalmers, 1992. To complete the picture, *ostentatious*, which is less likely to be confused with the other two, means 'pretentious and showy'.

other. **1** For *each other*, see EACH 3.

2 *OTHER THAN*. When *other* is used as a pronoun or adjective, use of *other than* is straightforward and causes no comment: *I'd never known anything other than hard times*—D. Dears, 1974. Objections are raised when *other* in this phrase is forced into the role of adverb (which it does not otherwise have), and Fowler (1926) regarded it as 'ungrammatical and needless' when a genuine adverb, *otherwise*, is available; so in the following example he would have urged use of *otherwise than* in place of *other than*: *Other than at football matches or on coach journeys, people sing less spontaneously than in previous generations*—T.

Portsmouth, 1992. However, the grammar of *other than* is not always so clear-cut, as the following example shows: *I married her . . . but it never even occurred to me that our marriage would be other than a marriage in name only*—A. Roudy-bush, 1972. Is *other* here an adjective linked to *marriage* or an adverb linked to *be*? (The answer is a bit of both.) In AmE, this use goes unnoticed; in BrE it is increasingly common and generally unexceptionable, and often more idiomatic than the awkward alternative *otherwise than*, but readers should be aware of the caveat attached to it in more pedantic circles.

otherwise. *Professor Southern gave us some stimulating reflections about the aims, development, and achievements (or otherwise) of the Honour School of Modern History*—W. A. Pantin, 1972 | *It's the balance of foods you eat that is healthy or otherwise*—*Which?*, 1989. Fowler (1926) castigated this use of *or otherwise* to mean 'or the opposite (of a given noun, adjective, or adverb)' and urged rephrasing (e.g. *achievements or failures, healthy or unhealthy*), but these alternatives clearly do not convey the same sense of antithesis. In any case, the language has moved on, and the type condemned by Fowler is now in standard use.

ought. In current use the verb *ought* is followed by a *to*-infinitive: *You ought to have a cooked breakfast, these cold mornings*—David Lodge, 1988. Since it is a modal verb, it forms a negative directly with *not* and forms a question by plain inversion: *Things are being permitted that ought not to be permitted*—*Guardian*, 1972 | *If Canada should disintegrate . . . what ought the U.S. to do?*—*Wall Street Journal*, 1990. In the past, *ought* does not inflect, and the tense is expressed by the verb following it: *I remembered . . . that I ought to have put Sal out. . . . She barks rather a lot*—Edmund Crispin, 1977. See also DIDN'T OUGHT.

our, ours. 1 A difficulty arises when *our* is used in conjunction with another qualifying word as in *The Italian and our troops* or *Our and the Italian troops*. Here a better alternative is *The Italian troops and ours*, but not ✸ *Ours and the Italian troops*.

2 In clauses introduced by *which of us*, a following pronoun should normally be in the third person, relating to *which* rather than to *us*: *Which of us would wish to be ill in his kitchen, especially when it is also the family living-room?*. If gender-neutrality is required, *his or her* (or informally *their*) has to be used.

ourself. The standard reflexive form of *we* and *us* is *ourselves* (as in *We are going to enjoy ourselves*), but a form *ourself* is recorded from the 14c onwards in uses corresponding to *we* used of a single person (*I loved your father, and we love ourself*—Shakespeare, *Hamlet*, IV.vii.40) and is occasionally found in modern English in contexts in which *we* stands for people in general or a group regarded collectively: *She tells us things about ourself*—Martin Amis, 1991 | *We see ourself as the biggest club in Britain, with a stadium to match*—*Today*, 1992. However, this use is not regarded as standard. See also THEMSELF.

out. 1 In current use *out*, unlike *in*, is primarily an adverb (*We went out*), and to form a preposition it normally needs the addition of *of* (*We went out of the house*). Use of *out* as a direct preposition without *of* is nonstandard in BrE, although it is found in AmE and some other varieties: *Now he looked past Bacon, out the bay window behind him*—T. Wolfe, 1987 (US) | *I drove out the gates and left them open behind me, swinging in the wind*—S. Koea, 1994 (New Zealand).

2 As a verb, *out* goes back to Old English in various meanings, 'to drive out or expel', 'to disable', '(of news or information) to become known', 'to disclose or speak out', and others. In the 1990s, the last meaning developed a new application in the context of the gay rights movement, namely 'to reveal the homosexuality of (a prominent or famous person)': *She 'outs' dozens as bi* [= bisexual]—*instead of exclusively straight or gay*—The Face, 1996. The process is called *outing*, and a person who does it is sometimes known as an *outer* or *outist*. These uses are likely to develop meanings in other contexts to do with exposing the private circumstances of individuals when this suits those with a particular cause to promote.

outdoor, outdoors. *Outdoor* is an adjective (*outdoor games*), whereas *outdoors* is an adverb (*The concert was held outdoors*) or noun (*the great outdoors*).

outfit. The verb has inflected forms *outfitted*, *outfitting*, and a derivative form *outfitter*, in both BrE and AmE.

output. The past tense and past participle of the verb are either *output* (preferably) or *outputted* (occasionally). The present participle is *outputting*.

outside of. *Outside*, unlike *out*, functions equally well as an adverb and preposition. Nonetheless, *outside of* is used, especially in AmE, in two main meanings: (1) 'exterior to, outside': *People in show business refer to those outside of it as 'civilians'*—Shirley MacLaine, 1987, and (2) 'with the exception of': *Outside of an unfortunate sermon in which he confused the words for charity and diarrhea . . . he never put a foot wrong with his hosts*—W. Sheed, 1985.

outstanding has two primary meanings which are open to ambiguity: (1) 'remarkable or conspicuous (among others of its kind)' (*the outstanding performance of the evening*), and (2) 'not yet settled or completed' (*three outstanding matters to discuss*). In practice, however, context and (in speech) intonation are likely to render ambiguity theoretical rather than actual.

outta is a representation of a slang (especially Black AmE) use of *out of*, and is found in nonstandard language such as descriptions of rock music: *Well-formed soul—with added beats—straight outta South London*—New Musical Express, 1995.

outward, outwards. The only form for the adjective is *outward* (*the outward journey*), but *outward* and *outwards* are both used for the adverb, with a preference for *outwards* in BrE: *The small circles of desert around waterholes and settlements join up and spread outwards, until a new desert has been created*—Observer, 1977.

outwit has inflected forms *outwitted*, *outwitting*.

outwith is a Scottish preposition meaning 'outside, beyond', and along with *wee* (for 'small') is the first non-English English word that visitors to Scotland notice (and sometimes adopt): *Do you live outwith the city? | We can discuss that outwith the meeting.* It is a transposition of *without*, corresponding to its physical meanings (see WITHOUT 1).

over. *The national view is a graphic composite of local reports across the country from over 50 (Oops! Make that 'more than' 50) reporting stations—Chicago Sun-Times,* 1989. Objection to the use of *over* to mean 'more than' followed by a numeral arises only in America and mainly in newspapers, and it does not seem to apply to designations of age, so that an American can say *I am over 50* without fear of censure. In BrE all these uses go unchallenged.

overall. 1 PRONUNCIATION. When the word is a noun (singular *overall* or plural *overalls*) the stress is on the first syllable; when an adjective it normally falls on the first syllable and when an adverb on the third, but the stress is variable in context.

2 PARTS OF SPEECH. As a noun, an *overall* (in BrE) is a coat-like piece of clothing worn over ordinary clothes to protect them against stains etc., and *overalls* (plural) are protective trousers or dungarees or a combination suit worn by people doing manual work. As an adjective, *overall* is always used in attributive position (i.e. before a noun), as in *the overall effect.* As an adverb, *overall* normally qualifies a whole sentence, as in *Overall, the performance was excellent.*

3 OVERALL MAJORITY. An *overall majority* is the amount by which the largest number of votes, par-

liamentary seats, etc., exceeds all the others added together.

overflow, as a verb, has the past form and past participle *overflowed.*

overlay, overlie. 1 The addition of the prefix *over-* makes both verbs transitive (i.e. take an object) and therefore they do not entirely correspond to the grammatical functions of *lay* and *lie.* The past tense and past participle of *overlay* is *overlaid,* and of *overlie* are (past) *overlay* and (participle) *overlain.* The primary meaning of *overlay* is 'to cover (one thing) with another' as in overlaying a surface with a coating or in smothering a child by lying on top of it (*overlie* is also used in this meaning and is somewhat more common). Both words are used in geology to mean '(of a stratum) to lie over (another)'.

2 *Overlay* (with stress on the first syllable) is also a noun, whereas *overlie* is only a verb.

overly. The use of *overly* in place of the prefix *over-,* e.g. *overly confident* instead of *over-confident,* is still regarded as an Americanism although it is well established in British usage: *That same novel is now with Macmillan. I am not 'overly' hopeful*—Barbara Pym, 1977 | *Fitzpatrick's male adversary is an impassioned, overly emotional man—Times,* 1985 | *She is not overly cheerful about the future of British drama*— M. Geare, 1993. It is interesting to note how frequently *overly* is used in the context of feelings or emotions.

overseas is now the usual word for the adverb (*He was sent overseas*) and the adjective (*overseas postage rates*). *Oversea,* formerly used as an adjective, has largely fallen out of use.

oversight. Care needs to be taken to distinguish the two primary meanings, (1) 'supervision': *There must be a representative of Scotland in the United Kingdom Cabinet—with a general oversight over the economy and the framing of Scotland's budget*—Lord Home, 1976, and (2) 'a failure to notice or do something' (the more common meaning, corresponding to *overlook* rather than *oversee*): *'By a quite exceptional oversight,' said Rufus, 'I don't just happen to have any picture postcards of the Acropolis about me at present'*—Barbara Vine, 1987 | *This procedure avoids possible oversight, and is a record that the answers have been considered*—R. M. Coates, 1991. In some cases the meaning may not be so clear, e.g. *Congressional oversight has proliferated*—*Time*, 1977. Normally, however, the context will clarify which meaning is intended.

overtone, undertone. Both words denote an extra layer of meaning or significance seen in a word or statement. An *overtone*, which is also commonly used in the plural *overtones*, suggests subtle additional meaning (and corresponds roughly to the meaning it has in music, i.e. 'a tone above the lowest in a harmonic scale'): *The prevailing tone of the book is highly satirical, with strong overtones of slapstick farce*—R. L. Wolff, 1977. An *undertone* is rather an unexpressed or underlying feeling (and again roughly matches the musical meaning 'a subdued tone of sound'): *Earlier this month it was announced that Loch Morar, too, would be screened for a monster, already christened with suitably Tolkienesque undertones, as Morag*—*Nature*, 1970.

ovum, meaning 'an egg cell', is pronounced **oh**-vəm and has the plural form *ova*.

owing to see DUE TO.

ox has the plural form *oxen*.

oxymoron is a figure of speech which brings together words of opposite meaning for special effect, e.g. *a cheerful pessimist* and *harmonious discord*. The word is derived from Greek words for 'sharp' and 'dull'.

Pp

pace, from the Latin word *pax* 'peace', means 'by the leave of' and is used in more formal (especially academic) writing to refer to someone whose opinion has been considered and rejected: *Tolstoy . . . is not, pace Albert Sorrel and Vogüé in any sense a mystic—* Isaiah Berlin, 1978. It is pronounced **pah**-chay or **pay**-si , and to avoid momentary confusion with the English word *pace*, is normally printed in italics.

package. The figurative meaning 'a set of proposals or arrangements considered as a whole', common in combinations such as *package deal* and *package holiday*, is a 20c development first in AmE and more recently in BrE: *The mass audience . . . is . . . merely given packages of passive entertainment—*Marshall McLuhan, 1967 | *Reassured, the package tourists sink into their seats—*Julian Symons, 1973.

paid see PAY.

pair. 1 Used as a collective noun, *pair* is treated as a plural when it denotes two separate items and as a singular when it denotes a unit: so *a pair of gloves, scissors, scales, shoes, trousers*, etc. are singular whereas a pair of *bachelors, dogs, idiots, rock-climbers*, etc. (all taken from collocations occurring in *OED2*) would normally be plural. Examples: (singular) *On the front of the radiator grille was mounted a pair of very large Cibie spotlights that dwarfed the standard headlamps—*M. Booth, 1980 | *To draw a heavy plough through wet clay soil, a pair of oxen yoked together was used—*M. Graham-Cameron et al., 1984 | *In addition to the various gripping wrenches, a pair of general-purpose pliers is always useful—*D. Holloway, 1992 | (plural) *The next pair of readings are concerned with what has perhaps been the single most salient political issue in British education in the twentieth century* – M. Flude et al., 1989 | *A pair of Pyracantha coccinea are placed strategically, one on either side of a cottage front door—*Gardener, 1992.

2 However, the rule is not altogether rigid, and contrary examples can be found which do not seem ungrammatical: *When you've lived on subsistence for two years what do you do when your shoes wear out, when you get a £100 fuel bill, when the washing machine breaks down, when a pair of children's shoes cost you more than you'd spend on your own?—*B. Campbell, 1985 | *One pair of ruby earrings are especially important—*television news script, 1993. In referring back to a 'singular' *pair*, the plural is normally used because it refers not to *pair* but to the following (plural) noun: *She . . . handed me a pair of Japanese thongs. I slipped them on and felt the skin between my first two toes protest—*H. Engel, 1981. The standard plural form for more than one pair is (for example) *two pairs of shoes*, although *two pair of shoes* is used informally and in dialect use.

3 The phrase *pair of twins* is generally understood to mean a single *set* (the more usual word in the context of twins), not two sets: *She gave birth to a pair of male twins, one of which was a stillborn with no malformations*—Lancet, 1977.

pajamas see PYJAMAS.

palaeo-. Words of the type *palaeography, palaeolithic,* etc., are normally spelt with *-ae-* in BrE, although the AmE form *paleo-* is beginning to influence British practice.

palindrome, from a Greek word meaning 'running back again', means a word or group of words that reads the same when the letters are reversed. *Noon, level,* and *radar* are all palindromes, as is the often quoted sentence *Able was I ere I saw Elba* (fancifully attributed to Napoleon). A word palindrome is a sentence which reads the same when the words in it are reversed, e.g. *Stout and bitter porter drinks porter, bitter, and stout.*

pallor, meaning 'paleness', is spelt *-or* in both BrE and AmE.

palpable. The literal meaning, 'that can be touched or felt', is encountered in medical contexts (*a palpable swelling*), and is familiar from Shakespeare's line in the duel scene at the end of *Hamlet*: *A hit, a very palpable hit.* The figurative use, conveying the idea of something so strongly present to the mind or senses that it can almost be physically felt, is the dominant one nowadays: *The tension—friendly tension—in the room was palpable*—Atlantic, 1991. Because *palpable* has a strong literary tone and can sound affected or pretentious, in everyday language alternatives such as *clear, glaring,* and *obvious* are often better choices.

panacea, from Greek words meaning 'all-healing', denotes not just a remedy but a universal remedy and is therefore not appropriate in the context of particular illnesses, e.g. *a panacea for measles.* It is most commonly used in negative or ironic ways and in social rather than medical contexts: *Better communication is no panacea for every industrial dispute*—Times, 1974.

panel has inflected forms *panelled, panelling,* and in AmE also *paneled, paneling.*

panic has inflected forms *panicked, panicking, panicky.*

pants. In BrE *pants* (plural noun) means 'underpants', whereas in AmE it means 'trousers or slacks'. The distinction can cause problems: *I heard an American student at Cambridge University telling some English friends how he climbed over a locked gate to get into his college and tore his pants, and one of them asked in confusion, 'But how could you tear your pants without tearing your trousers?'*—N. Moss, 1973. In attributive use (i.e. before another noun), *pants* tends to be used in general contexts in both BrE and AmE, and *pant* or *pants* in fixed combinations such as *pant suit*: *I took a jackknife out of my pants pocket*—R. B. Parker, 1974 | *Then we went downtown and bought pant suits*—L. Ellmann, 1988.

paparazzo, a freelance photographer who pursues celebrities to get photographs of them, is spelt with one *p* and two *z*s. The plural (more often used) is *paparazzi.*

papier mâché, a kind of paper pulp, should be spelt with the two accents as shown, but is otherwise regarded as naturalized.

papyrus, is pronounced pǝ-**piy**-rǝs, and in the meaning 'a document written on papyrus' has the plural form *papyri*, pronounced pǝ-**piy**-riy.

paradigm. 1 is pronounced with the last syllable as in *dime*. In technical use it denotes a model or pattern of some kind; in linguistics, it means 'a representative set of inflections of a noun or verb', and so the paradigm of *come* is *come* (base form), *comes* (third person singular present), *came* (past tense), *come* (past participle), *coming* (present participle). In general use it has acquired the status of a vogue word in contexts where *example* or *pattern* might be more straightforward choices: *The television set . . . is the paradigm of consumer culture, with its disarming passivity prone to desires divorced from action*—F. Zweig, 1976.

2 The corresponding adjective *paradigmatic* is pronounced -*dig*-**mat**-ik, with the *g* fully articulated.

paradise. Of the many adjective forms that have developed from this word, the most common in current use are *paradisal* and *paradisiacal*. Not surprisingly, *paradise* itself is often found to be less awkward in this role, and is used in certain fixed compounds such as *paradise crane* and *paradise duck*.

paraffin is spelt with one *r* and two *f*s. The equivalent term in AmE is *kerosene*.

parallel has inflected and derivative forms *paralleled, paralleling, parallelism, parallelogram*. The final -*l* is not doubled.

parameter. In technical use, a *parameter* is a measurable factor that contributes to determining a system or event. In the 20c it has developed rapidly into the kind of word that Fowler (1926) described as a 'popularized technicality', many instances of which he deplored, especially when simpler alternatives are available. In popular use, a *parameter* is 'a constant element or factor, especially serving as a limit or boundary', and is best demonstrated by examples: *There are parameters to these recollections which may not be immediately apparent: the world of learning . . . and the war*—D. M. Davin, 1975 | *Lewis's refusal to accept her standards, her parameters, she regarded as threatening*—Anita Brookner, 1989. A wide choice of alternatives is available to those who feel uneasy about using *parameter* in this way: for example *criterion, factor, element, scope, boundary, limit, term, term of reference.*

paraphernalia originally denoted the personal property (Greek *parapherna* 'things set apart [from a dowry]') that a married woman was legally entitled to regard as her own. Over several centuries of use in English it has acquired the general meaning 'miscellaneous belongings'; it is still normally treated as a plural noun although occasional singular use is attested from the 18c (*a whole paraphernalia of plums*, 1845). Some modern examples follow: *Paraphernalia in his flat included Indian clubs and an adapted table to which boys were tied*—Independent, 1989 | *Painting paraphernalia . . . abound*—Observer Magazine, 1993.

parasitic, parasitical. Both forms are in use as adjectives derived from *parasite* (normally in its figurative meaning): *This parasitic castle life had left my funds comparatively intact*—Patrick Leigh

Fermor, 1986 | *These works hold a parasitical relationship to existing courses of culture*—Oxford Art Journal, 1988.

paratroops, meaning 'troops equipped to be dropped by parachute', is a plural noun. The force is called a *paratroop regiment*, and a member of this is a *paratrooper*.

parcel. The verb has inflected forms *parcelled*, *parcelling* in BrE, and in AmE usually *parceled*, *parceling*.

parenthesis. 1 *Parenthesis* is a term denoting an aside or extra remark that is added to a sentence; it is normally marked off by brackets, commas, or dashes, and the rest of the sentence is grammatically complete without it. Parentheses can be single words, phrases, or whole clauses: *In Italian, a language he had been told was the same as Rumanian, he asked to be directed to the British Legation*—Olivia Manning, 1960 | *He and Moira (then a milkman's pretty daughter) grovelled together long and effectively enough to cause the eventual birth of their son Rick*—Tim Winton, *Shallows*, 1985 | *On Thursday I come back from work to an empty house—Kate is spending the night at a girlfriend's house again—and the stillness and solitude calm me down*—Angela Lambert, 1989.

2 *Parentheses* (plural) are, in printing terminology, round brackets. See BRACKETS.

pariah, meaning 'a social outcast', is pronounced pə-**riy**-ə to rhyme with *Isaiah*.

parley, meaning 'a discussion of peace terms', has the plural form *parleys*, and as a verb has inflected forms *parleys*, *parleyed*, *parleying*.

parliament, parliamentary. Both words are spelt with an *a* in the middle, but are pronounced with the -*ia*- as a single syllable.

parlour is spelt -*our* in BrE and *parlor* in AmE.

parlous was described by Fowler (1926) as 'a word that wise men leave alone', and the current edition (1999) of the *Concise Oxford Dictionary* marks it as 'archaic or humorous'. This is a sad fate for a long-serving word, originally formed as a variant of *perilous* and for many centuries used side by side with it in the same range of meaning. It can be safely used in the expression *in a parlous state* (or *condition*) even in only moderately formal English: *He was altogether in a parlous state: the weather was bad, there was no water in the flat; he did not care to go out at nights and was seeing fewer people*—P. Ackroyd, 1988.

parricide, patricide. Both words come from the Latin word *pater* meaning 'father', but in current use *parricide* is the killing of a parent or other near relative whereas *patricide* is more specifically the killing of one's father. They are used to denote the crime or the person who commits it.

parson has a general informal meaning in current English, denoting a member of the clergy up to the level of rector. It was once a more formal term for a holder of a parochial benefice but the meaning broadened considerably from the 16c onward.

partake is followed by *in* or (especially with reference to food) *of*, and the notion of sharing should always be present. To speak of *partaking of a boiled egg* if one is eating it all is to take the word beyond its proper limits.

part and parcel. This expression, meaning 'an essential part of something', retains an older meaning of *parcel* that has otherwise not survived, namely 'a constituent or component part' (as in Swinburne's *Till the soul of man be parcel of the sunlight*).

Parthian shot. A *Parthian shot* is the same as a *parting shot*, i.e. a final remark or glance made on leaving. The allusion is to the supposed custom of the ancient Parthian horsemen of confusing their enemy by hurling spears into their ranks while in (real or feigned) flight. The earliest citation for *Parthian shot* in the *OED* is as late as 1902, although there is one for *Parthian glance* from 1875 and the allusive use is dated back to the 16c in less fixed expressions. The first example of *parting shot* is from the end of the 19c: *With this parting shot . . . Nancy flung into the house*—Hall Caine, 1894.

partially, partly. 1 The meanings of these two words overlap in ways that make it difficult to decide between them in any principled way, although certain patterns in their use can be identified. *Partially* (15c) is somewhat older than *partly* (16c) but their meanings have run in parallel except that for some of its history *partially* has meant 'in a partial or biased way', i.e. the opposite of *impartially*.

2 Fowler (1926) attempted to make a distinction in principle between *partially* and *partly* by defining *partially* as contrasted with *completely* (i.e. = to a limited degree) and *partly* as contrasted with *wholly* (i.e. = as regards a

part and not the whole). His illustrations based on this criterion were *It is partly wood | This was partly due to cowardice* and *a partially drunken sailor | his partially re-established health*, which in all cases show idiomatic uses that are not readily replaced by the alternative word. So if we say, for example, *The room is partly panelled*, we mean that only part of the room is meant to be panelled, whereas if we say *The room is partially panelled*, we mean that the panelling has still to be completed.

3 Fowler's rubric still works up to a point, but the meanings shade into each other and current usage reflects this: (partially) *I partially solved my money problems by being paid ten shillings to play regularly at the Black Horse*—Anthony Burgess, 1987 | *A partially built shopping centre, for instance, will adversely affect the tenant's business*—R. Walker, 1993 | (partly) *Her untidy blonde fringe partly covered her eyes*—J. G. Ballard, 1988 | *The door to Suzy's bedroom was wide open and her partly clothed body was spreadeagled on the bed*—T. Barnes, 1991.

4 Further observations can be made from observations of current usage:

▶ **a** *Partly* is used when it is balanced by a further *partly* or is followed by some other link phrase such as *but also*, and many instances of its occurrence fall in this category: *She was shaking all over, partly because she was so angry with Oliver and partly because she was so afraid*—Nina Bawden, 1989 | *Maria jeered caustically, driven partly by masochism but also by a need to lash out*—J. Bauling, 1993. But *partially* occurs occasionally in this role: *In practice there were* *innovations, partially because of the perceived need to reduce the influence of headmen, and partially because British officials naturally governed on the basis of their own training and inclinations*—J. D. Rogers, 1987.

▸**b** *Partly* is more often the choice when it qualifies an adjective or participial adjective that is also qualified in some other way: *Her dislike of him was of course . . . partly based upon a sense that he disliked her*—Iris Murdoch, 1980 *This is partly attributable to the increased opportunity for away travel which has increased the contact between rival groups of supporters*—D. Waddington, 1992.

▸**c** *Partially*, rather than *partly*, is normally used to qualify words describing physical deficiencies such as *blind* and *deaf*: *Any generally available additional provision for deaf or partially blind or disturbed children, and others such as dyslexic children, was not special educational provision*—S. Johnstone et al., 1992.

▸**d** Both words are used to qualify key words such as *because, due to, explain, on account of, responsible, true,* etc.

5 In sum, Fowler's rule and the other observations will serve if a rule is needed; but usage is inconsistent and the alleged distinctions in meaning do not always work in practice.

participles. **1** There are two kinds of participle in English: the present participle ending in *-ing* as in *We are going*, and the past participle ending in *-d* or *-ed* for many verbs and in *-t* or *-en* or some other form for others, as in *Have you decided? | New houses are being built | It's not broken*.

2 Participles are often used to introduce subordinate clauses that are attached to other words

in a sentence, e.g. *Her mother, opening the door quietly, came into the room | Hearing a noise I went out to look | Born in Rochdale, he spent most of his life in the area.* Participles in initial position, as in the last two examples, are acceptable grammatically but when overdone can produce a poor style, especially when the participial clause bears little relation to the main one: *Being blind from birth, she became a teacher and travelled widely.*

3 A worse stylistic flaw occurs with so-called 'unattached', 'misrelated', or 'dangling' participles, when the participle does not refer to the noun to which it is grammatically attached, normally the subject of the sentence: *Recently converted into apartments, I passed by the house where I grew up.* (No one will imagine that the speaker had been converted into apartments, but that is what the grammatical structure suggests, producing poor style.) Some examples of unattached participles follow: *Being a vegan bisexual who's into Nicaraguan coffee picking and boiler suits, you could safely assume that I vote Labour*—Private Eye, 1988 *| Driving near home recently, a thick pall of smoke turned out to be a bungalow well alight*—Oxford Times, 1990. In sum, unattached participles seldom cause real ambiguity, but they jar and can distract the reader, and are to be avoided.

4 Certain participles, such as *considering, assuming, excepting, given, provided, seeing, speaking (of)*, etc., have acquired the status of prepositions or conjunctions, and their use in a grammatically free role is well established: *'Speaking of money,' said Beryl, 'do you mind my asking what you did with yours?'*—A. Munro, 1987.

particular. In its meaning 'considered as distinct from others', *particular* plays a useful identifying or emphasizing role: *For this particular show there is an audience . . . and they arrive at 7.30 p.m.*—Guardian, 1970. In other cases, it can be superfluous: *It is entirely up to you to find these faults, if they exist, and to report them before the particular guarantee periods expire*—G. Collard, 1990.

particularly. It is particularly important to pronounce this as five syllables, and not as if it were spelt *par-tic-u-ly*.

partisan, meaning 'a zealous supporter of a cause' or 'a guerrilla in wartime', is normally pronounced in BrE with a -z- sound and with the stress on the last syllable, but in AmE a first-syllable stress is often preferred. It is also used as an adjective meaning 'loyal to a cause, biased'.

partly see PARTIALLY.

parts of speech. The traditional parts of speech (also called *word-classes*) that have been in use for English since the 16c are *noun, verb, adjective, adverb, pronoun, preposition, conjunction,* and *interjection*. Some of these are subdivided; for example pronouns can be demonstrative (*this, those,* etc.), personal (*he, she, we,* etc.), possessive (*his, theirs*), or relative (*who, which*). These categories were taken over from those used to describe Latin grammar and often barely suit the word functions and sentence structure of English. The concept of 'adverb', for example, embraces words that are far apart in both function and meaning (*ever, fast, only, safely, thankfully, well,* etc). Other words are often described in special

ways, such as *a* and *an* (indefinite article, determiner), *the* (definite article, determiner), *much* (quantifier). For general purposes, however, the traditional names remain in use despite their inadequacies, and they are used in this book rather than the more specialized terms that have been adopted in modern linguistics. The main parts of speech listed above have separate entries, to which the reader is referred for further information.

party as a synonym for 'person' occurs in informal contexts as a kind of extension of the legal use (*the injured party | the party of the first part*), but should not be used in more formal usage: *June had taken Imogen from her*—'What a stout little party'—*and settled down for the interview with Imogen on her knee*—Joanna Trollope, 1990.

passed, past. *Passed* is the past tense and past participle of the verb *pass*: *We passed a police car | The time has passed.* The related adjective, preposition, and adverb are all *past*: *for the past three hours | We drove past a police car | She hurried past.* The form *past* is also a noun: *living in the past.*

passer-by has the plural form *passers-by.*

passive. 1 The passive voice is illustrated by the sentence *Brazil were beaten by France in the final,* in which the object of the active verb becomes the subject of the passive verb and the subject is expressed as an agent introduced by the preposition *by.* Passive verbs are formed with the verb *be,* and other verbs are used to form so-called 'semi-passives' in which the past participle of the verb is at least partly adjectival (e.g. *He got changed | They seem bothered*).

2 Other forms of the passive include:

▶ **a IMPERSONAL CONSTRUCTIONS WITH IT.** *It is believed that no action should be taken | It is felt that your complaint arises from a misunderstanding.* Sir Ernest Gowers, who as a senior civil servant no doubt saw many such examples in correspondence that came his way, wrote (1965) that 'the impersonal passive . . . is a construction dear to those who write official and business letters'. 'It is reasonable enough in statements made at large,' he continued, giving the example *It is understood that the wanted man is wearing a raincoat and a cloth cap,* 'but when one person is addressing another it often amounts to a pusillanimous shrinking from responsibility' (as in the examples given at the beginning of this paragraph).

▶ **b DOUBLE PASSIVE.** This occurs with verbs such as *attempt, begin, desire, endeavour, propose, threaten,* and others involving constructions with a passive infinitive, as in *The order was attempted to be carried out | No greater thrill can be hoped to be enjoyed.* Clearly these types are often extremely awkward in not corresponding to a comparable active form (✗ *They attempted the order to be carried out | ✗ We hope no greater thrill to be enjoyed*), and a fully active construction should be used whenever possible: *They attempted to carry out the order | We can hope to enjoy no greater thrill*; in some cases the sentence can be rephrased, e.g. *There was an attempt to carry out the order.* Other verbs, such as *expect, intend,* and *order,* which are grammatically more versatile, will allow a double passive construction; we can say, for

example, *They ordered the deserters to be shot,* and therefore the double passive form *The deserters were ordered to be shot* is acceptable.

▶ **c THE TYPE *SHE WAS GIVEN A WATCH.*** This use was once questioned on the grounds that the subject of the passive verb should correspond to the object of the active verb, whereas in this case *she* corresponds to an indirect object (*They gave **her** a watch*); but it is now a part of the language and beyond such objection.

pastel, pastille. A *pastel* is an artist's crayon or a light shade of a colour, whereas a *pastille* is a small sweet or lozenge.

past master, meaning 'a person having special skill in an activity', is spelt with *past,* not (as formerly) with *passed,* although the allusion is to someone who has 'passed' the necessary training and qualification to achieve that status (originally in the context of freemasonry).

pastor is used, especially in AmE, as the term for or title of a member of the clergy in charge of a nonconformist church.

past tense. Three noteworthy special uses of the past tense of verbs are:

1 A continued action or state in indirect speech can be expressed either by the past or by the present: *Did you say you had* [or *have*] *a house to let? | How did you find out that I was* [or *am*] *the owner?*

2 A past is used in forms of enquiry about another's wish or attitude: *Did* [or *do*] *you want to come in?* (The time reference arguably differs here according to the tense: either 'Did you want to come in a moment ago, when you knocked?' or 'You knocked, so do you now want to come in?)

3 The hypothetical past tense is used in sentences of the type *It's time we left for the station*, and in unfulfilled conditions of the type *If you tried harder, you'd probably succeed.*

pâté, meaning 'a rich meat or fish paste', is pronounced **pat**-ay, and is spelt with the two accents to distinguish it from *pate* (pronounced payt, = head) and *pâte* (pronounced paht, = the paste of which porcelain is made).

patent. In the meaning 'a government authority giving a right or title', the normal pronunciation is **pat**-ənt, although **pay**-tənt is sometimes used. For the adjective meaning 'clear, obvious' (and in the corresponding adverb *patently*), and in the compound *patent leather*, **pay**-tənt is used. In AmE, **pat**-ənt is more usual in these meanings as well.

pathetic, in its modern informal meaning 'inadequate, feeble', has compromised the primary (and by no means derogatory) meaning 'arousing pity or sadness' to the extent that a statement such as *The play opens with a pathetic speech* is likely to be understood the wrong way. Regard for context needs to be borne in mind when using or encountering this word.

patio, meaning 'a paved area adjoining a house', has the plural form *patios*.

patricide see PARRICIDE.

patriot. The pronunciations **pat**-ri-ət and **pay**-tri-ət are about equally common in BrE. In the derivative words *patriotic* and *patriotism*, **pat**- is more common. In

AmE, **pay**- is the usual form for all these words.

patrol as a verb has inflected forms *patrolled*, *patrolling* in both BrE and AmE.

patron is pronounced **pay**-trən, but the derivative words *patronage* and *patronize* both have initial **pat**-. In AmE, initial **pay**- is usual for all three words.

pavement means 'a paved way for pedestrians' in BrE (corresponding to AmE *sidewalk*) and in parts of the American east coast, and the hard surface of a paved road elsewhere in America.

pay. The past tense and past participle of the verb are both *paid*.

PC, pc is now as likely to stand for *political correctness* as *police constable*, *Privy Counsellor*, or *personal computer*.

peaceable, peaceful. In general, *peaceable* means 'disposed to peace, not quarrelsome' and refers primarily to people or activities: *The visitor from beyond the planets would obtain the impression that the Earth is a very peaceable place—New Scientist*, 1991. The adverb *peaceably* occurs almost as often as the adjective: *On the whole they lived peaceably and had lots of fellowship together—*W. Green, 1988. The more common word *peaceful* means 'characterized by peace, tranquil' and the notion is more actual than potential: *The meal was peaceful, but when it was over the doors burst open and in surged a crowd of painters and models who hadn't been invited—*J. Rose, 1990. The meanings overlap rather more with the adverb *peacefully*: *The siege ended peacefully and Yacoub was later charged with taking hostages and with illegal*

possession of a firearm—Keesings,
1990.

peccadillo, meaning 'a trifling offence', has the plural form *peccadilloes* (preferred) or *peccadilloes*.

pedagogy, meaning 'the science of teaching', is pronounced **ped**-ə-gog-i (with a hard second g) or **ped**-ə-goj-i (with a soft second g). The soft sound is used in the adjective *pedagogical*. In *pedagogue*, however (now mainly used disparagingly of a pedantic or dogmatic teacher), the g is hard, **ped**-ə-gog.

pedal as a verb has inflected forms *pedalled*, *pedalling* in BrE, but usually *pedaled*, *pedaling* in AmE.

pedantry. Fowler (1926) observed that the term 'is obviously a relative one; my pedantry is your scholarship, his reasonable accuracy, her irreducible minimum of education, and someone else's ignorance'. He referred to articles in his book and left the reader to decide where on the scale of pedantry his work belonged. Fowler was rarely pedantic but his readers often were, and read into his statements things that Fowler never intended. Some examples of pedantic attitudes to usage will be found in the following entries (not an exhaustive list, and the reader may be able to add others): ALSO 2 (position of *also*), BARBARISMS (objections to mixed forms such as *television*), CIRCUM-STANCE (objection to *under the circumstances*), CURRICULUM (plural form *curricula vitarum*), DATA (*data* as invariable plural), EX- (Fowler's objection to the type *ex-Prime Minister*), FEWER, LESS (the type *12 items or fewer*), FRACTION (a *fraction* not necessarily a small quantity),

HOI POLLOI (use of *the hoi polloi*), ONLY (position of *only*), OTHER 2 (use of *other than* for *otherwise than*), PER CAPITA (use of *per caput*), TARGET (*doubled* targets are easier, not harder, to hit).

pedlar, peddler. The dominant BrE spelling has changed, along with a change in principal meaning, from *pedlar*, the traditional form for the itinerant seller of small items, to the AmE spelling *peddler*, associated especially with the selling of drugs and influenced by the verb *peddle* (itself a back-formation from *pedlar*). The development is somewhat circular but the result is that *pedlar* is falling out of use as the itinerant seller that the word used to denote disappears from the streets.

pee. Since the introduction of decimal currency in Britain in 1971 the spelling *pee* has come into use to represent the pronunciation of the initial letter of *penny*: *May I trouble you for forty-two pee?*—Ruth Rendell, 1974. Lack of precedent is the only argument available to those who condemn this pronunciation and insist on the traditional (but partly anachronistic) forms *penny* and *pence*.

peewit is the preferred spelling for the name of the bird, not *pewit*.

penchant, meaning 'an inclination or liking', is pronounced pā-shā, in a French manner with nasalized vowels.

pencil as a verb has inflected forms *pencilled*, *pencilling* in BrE, and usually *penciled*, *penciling* in AmE.

pendant, pendent, pennant. The noun *pendant* means 'a hanging jewel or ornament' or in nautical use 'a short rope hanging from the head of a mast'; the adjective *pendent* means 'hanging or overhanging' and has a few technical uses. A *pennant* is a tapering flag, especially one flown at the masthead of a ship.

pending is used (1) as an adjective meaning 'awaiting a decision or completion' (*A new edition of the book is pending*), and (2) as a preposition meaning 'during, throughout the process of' (*A final decision cannot be taken pending his trial*).

peninsula is a noun meaning 'a piece of land almost surrounded by water' (*The Spanish peninsula*) and *peninsular* is the corresponding adjective (*The Peninsular War*).

pen-name see NOM DE PLUME.

pennant see PENDANT.

penny. The plural for separate coins is *pennies* (*He had four pennies in his pocket*), and for a sum of money is *pence* (*an increase of 50 pence*). See also PEE. In North America a one-cent coin is often called a *penny* (with plural *pennies*).

pension, meaning 'a French or European boarding house', is pronounced **pä**-syã, in a French manner with nasalized vowels, and is normally printed in italic type to distinguish it from the naturalized word *pension*.

people, persons. Both words have been in use for several centuries to denote the plural of *person*, the difference usually being explained in terms of *people* referring to a group of which the exact number cannot be determined or is irrelevant and *persons* to a number of individuals who are countable or regarded separately: *A great many people feel that a hug can make their day*—Chicago Tribune, 1991 | *It is morally certain that a number of persons signed confessions to crimes of which they were innocent*—K. Lindsay, 1980. However, this distinction is not watertight, as the following examples show: *Persons may squat in buildings by reason of inability to find other accommodation*—Oxford Companion to Law, 1980 | *It now numbers some 40 people, as well as the Jersey cows, the Aberdeen Angus bull, the horse, three ponies, and a handful of fecund goats and breeding sows*—Country Living, 1991. To judge from the recent evidence, the distinction is based as much on context as on meaning, with *people* used as the general word and *persons* used in more formal contexts (e.g. law). It may not be a red herring to note that the plural *persons* also occurs in compound forms such as *barpersons* and *chairpersons*.

per. It is a sound general rule not to use this Latin word when an English equivalent exists and is idiomatic: it is better, for example, to say *The salary is £25,000 a year* rather than *The salary is £25,000 per year*, and *We will send the goods by parcel post* rather than *We will send the goods per parcel post*. *Per* is best reserved for use in official contexts, in Latin phrases such as *per annum*, and in formulaic expressions such as *miles per hour* and *kilometres per gallon*. For *as per*, see AS 9.

per capita means 'by heads' and has largely replaced the more strictly correct form *per caput* ('for each head') as the normal way of saying 'for each person or head (of population)'. Fowler (1926) regarded this use of *per capita* as 'a modern blunder, encouraged in some recent dictionaries', but its use is now standard: *During the same period, per capita consumption rose 15 percent in terms of constant prices—Dædalus*, 1990. *Per caput* is also still found, but is much less common and often has a pedantic tone: *It may be argued that per-caput cigarette consumption is not a good measure of cigarette consumption in young women—Lancet*, 1976.

per cent is normally written as two words in BrE but as one word (*percent*) in AmE. In attributive use (i.e. before a noun), it is normally written with a hyphen in BrE: *a 12 per-cent increase*. The type *—per cent of* is normally treated as singular if the noun is a collective or mass noun and as plural if the noun is an ordinary plural: *Fifteen per cent of the electorate has yet to make up its mind—Daily Telegraph*, 1987 | *Some 90% of children belong to the Pioneers in East Berlin—Encounter*, 1987. In AmE, but not in BrE, *percent* is also used as a noun, an alternative to *percentage* (*a large percent of the population*).

percentage. Since a *percentage* can be a quantity of any size, and even (unlike *part*) more than the whole, it is best to qualify it with adjectives such as *small, tiny,* or *large,* or by the adverb *only,* as appropriate: *a large percentage of books published in the USA . . .* | *all but a small percentage . . . .* See also FRACTION.

peremptory means 'admitting no denial or refusal' and not (perhaps by confusion with *perfunctory*) 'abrupt, sudden'. A *peremptory decision* is not one that has been hastily reached but one that is definitive. The word is normally pronounced with the stress on the second syllable, although an older first-syllable stress survives in legal usage.

perennial, with reference to plants, means 'lasting several years' by contrast with *annual* which means 'lasting for one growing season'.

perfect. 1 In its primary meaning 'complete, not deficient', *perfect* is an absolute and cannot logically be qualified by words such as *more, most,* and *very.* (This is a philosophical point, not a matter of grammatical correctness.) As the *OED* notes, however, *perfect* is 'often used of a near approach to such a state [of complete excellence], and hence is capable of comparison'. Such uses are found in literature from the 14c onward, including Shakespeare's *Our men more perfect in the use of arms—2 Henry IV* IV.i.153. In modern use, *perfect* is used more often than not in weakened meanings and is therefore amenable to qualification: *What figure is more perfect than the sphere—* William Golding, 1965 | *Maybe not purity but he seemed so perfect and so unreal, in a way—*Chinua Achebe, 1987.

2 *Perfect* is pronounced with the stress on the first syllable as an adjective and with the stress on the second syllable as a verb.

perfectible is spelt *-ible*, not *-able*. See -ABLE, -IBLE.

perfect infinitive. This is the type *to have been, to have said,* etc., and occurs most commonly after the verbs *appear* and *seem*: *She appeared to have encouraged him* | *That seemed to have been an isolated incident.* In each case the reported event occurred before the time of the statement itself. If the event and the reporting occur at the same time, a present (or present continuous) infinitive is used instead: *She appeared to be encouraging him* | *That seemed to be* *an isolated incident.* For the type *would have liked* (or *preferred*) *to have been*, see HAVE 2; LIKE (*verb*).

perimeter, unlike *parameter*, is rarely used in figurative meanings, but occasional uses are found, usually in the context of broader metaphors: *The perimeter of her own life was shrinking*—J. Urquhart, 1986 (Canada).

period. For the meaning with reference to time, see EPOCH. For the punctuation mark, see FULL STOP.

periodic, periodical. *Periodic* is an adjective only, and is largely restricted to technical and scientific contexts, especially in the expressions *periodic acid, periodic decimal, periodic function,* and *periodic table.* In non-technical language *periodical* is the commoner choice for the meaning 'appearing or occurring at regular intervals' (*A periodical oil change is recommended*), and is also used as a noun (= a newspaper or magazine issued at regular intervals).

permanence, permanency. The more usual choice in current use for the meaning 'a state of being permanent' is *permanence*, but *permanency* is also occasionally used in this meaning and more especially in the meaning 'something that is permanent': *A stranger is not a permanency. One can easily shed a stranger.*—Graham Greene, 1988.

permissible, permissive, permitted. *Permissible* is spelt *-ible* and means 'allowable', having potential force rather than the actual force conveyed by *permitted*. *Permissive* means 'tolerant or liberal in morals' as in the phrase *the permissive society.*

permit is pronounced with the stress on the first syllable as a noun and with the stress on the second syllable as a verb. The verb has inflected forms *permitted, permitting.*

pernickety, meaning 'fussy, fastidious', is a 19c word of Scottish origin which has spread to all English-speaking areas. In AmE, the form *persnickety* is also used.

per pro see P.P.

perquisite, prerequisite. A *perquisite* is an incidental benefit attached to a person's job or employment, and is more often used in the shortened form *perk*. A *prerequisite* is something required as a condition before something else can be done: *Sponsorship is not a prerequisite for any of our courses but we are happy for students to arrange sponsorship if they wish to do so*—university prospectus, 1993.

persistence, persistency. Both words came into English in the 16c and they remain largely interchangeable, although in current use *persistence* is commoner: *Agelessly silent, with a reptile's persistency*—D. H. Lawrence, 1921 / *By sheer persistence he'd achieved what at first seemed inaccessible*—E. North, 1987.

person. For the plural *persons*, see PEOPLE.

-person.
See box opposite

persona. In 20c usage, *persona* (in origin the Latin word for an actor's mask) has acquired two special meanings and a generalized one that draws on both: (1) a character deliberately assumed by an author in his or her writing,

-person

1 The use of *-person* as a gender-neutral suffix denoting occupations instead of *-man* began in the 1970s with *chairperson* (see CHAIRMAN), and has spread rather more slowly than might have been expected, possibly because of a reluctance to adopt forms that are more socially acceptable but are linguistically more awkward or cumbersome. The table below lists some typical formations, some having an ephemeral appearance and others likely to achieve some permanence:

WORD	DATE
anchorperson	1976
barperson	1976
chairperson	1971
craftsperson	1976
draughtsperson	1976
Englishperson	1977
everyperson	1978
henchperson	1973
newspaper person	1976
salesperson	1971
spokesperson	1972
waitperson	1980

2 The substitution of *person* for *man* in other ways, e.g. in *personhandle* and *personpower*, and in *gingerbread person*, is at present showing no sign of being taken seriously, although this may change.

(2) in Jungian psychology, the set of attitudes adopted by an individual to fit himself or herself for an appropriate social role, (3) an aspect of the personality as shown to or perceived by others: *James Spicer, his military persona now well to the fore, ignored the question and picked up the phone*—M. Hamer, 1991 | *Writer Brian Clark gave me the persona of a middle-class, middle-aged professional with a wife problem and for a time it became my trademark*—*Today*, 1991. The psychological resonance of these uses makes *persona* a more powerful word than (say) *identity*, and the development is a useful one.

personage, personality. A *personage* is 'a person of distinction or high rank', and is sometimes applied with irony or humour to someone who is self-important rather than important: *No longer was I a nondescript of the slums; now I was a personage of the theatre*—Charles Chaplin, 1964 | *Royal personages officially come of age at eighteen*—S. Weintraub, 1987. A *personality* is 'a celebrity or other person who is a focus of attention', and is used especially with reference to stars of the television and film world: *Tell us about some of the overseas personalities you have met*—J. M. Coetzee, 1990. The term *personality cult* has been used since the 1950s to mean 'the extreme adulation of an individual, especially a leader or celebrity, in terms of his or her personal characteristics': *Hollywood was devising the 'star system', the big solo buildup, the personality cult of the silent screen—Guardian, 1971.*

personally. The uses of *personally* illustrated by *The decision was made by the president personally* (= by the president and no one else) and *He took the criticism personally* (= in a personal manner) are unexceptionable. Doubts arise when *personally* is used to mean 'for myself, for my part', as in *Personally, I don't approve of such behaviour.* This use is best restricted to informal contexts. In many cases it can be simply omitted, or replaced by *for my part.*

personnel. The word is pronounced with the stress on the third syllable, and refers to the human resources of an organization or institution, originally in the armed forces and later in the business world. It is often used attributively (i.e. before a noun), e.g. *personnel carrier* (in military contexts), *personnel officer* (in business contexts), or is qualified in some way, e.g. *military personnel* and *trained personnel.* Used by itself it also means 'a personnel department' (*I'd better check with Personnel*), and it occasionally occurs with a preceding numeral to denote a number of personnel: *one copy to every 25 personnel.*

persons see PEOPLE.

perspective. The 17c meaning 'mental point of view or way of regarding something', *perspective* has developed a special use with *on* followed by the name of a subject or intellectual domain: *Per-*

spectives on Thomas Hobbes (book title, 1989).

perspicacious, perspicuous. Fowler (1926) snootily urged the use of simpler alternatives by 'those who are neither learned nor pretentious'. *Perspicacious* means 'having mental penetration or discernment, discerning', and its corresponding noun is *perspicacity. Perspicuous,* on the other hand, means 'clear to understand' (with reference to people and statements), and its noun is *perspicuity.* It is the nouns that are confused rather than the adjectives, and the following examples of correct uses may help to distinguish them in the reader's mind: *He went through the photographs. But it didn't take much perspicacity to tell that some . . . were missing*—Ruth Rendell, 1983 | *Wagner's theory had gained in complexity, but not, perhaps, in perspicuity, from its new influences*—S. M. Silk et al., 1981. Suitable alternative words are (for *perspicacity*) *perception, perceptiveness, acuteness,* and *shrewdness,* and (for *perspicuity*) *clarity, lucidity,* and *lucidness.*

persuade see CONVINCE.

persuasion. The meaning 'belief or conviction', as in *a person of no particular persuasion,* has developed into a much weaker sense 'kind or sort', as in *no one of the male persuasion.* The OED labels these uses as 'slang or burlesque', and in current use the intention is still usually humorous or jocular.

peruse is a formal word meaning 'to read thoroughly', and is often mistakenly used to mean 'to read cursorily, to glance over': *For me, it had all the wearisome unfunniness of back numbers of Punch perused in the dentist's waiting-*

room—Times Literary Supplement, 1980.

perverse, pervert, perverted.
1 *Perverse* and *perverted*, both derived from the Latin root *pervertere* 'to turn away' (from what is normal or correct), are easily confused. *Perverse* means 'stubbornly unreasonable' (usually of people but also of circumstances): *No doubt I am perverse, but I found the film sensationalist, spurious and totally unbelievable*—A. Walker, 1988 | *Amazingly, perversely, and rather to her regret (a flat battery would have been a cast-iron excuse to abort the visit) the engine fired*—David Lodge, 1988. *Perverted* means 'departing from right opinion or conduct' and is commonly used with reference to abnormal or deviant sexual behaviour: *I've seen blokes in hot countries go clean round the oojar because of the perverted practices of native women*—Brian Aldiss, 1971.
2 *Pervert* is pronounced with the stress on the first syllable as a noun (= a person who is sexually perverted) and with the stress on the second syllable as a verb (= to corrupt, lead astray).

petal has a derived form *petalled* in BrE, but *petaled* is also used in AmE.

petite, meaning 'attractively small' (usually with reference to a woman), is now usually spelt in roman type as a naturalized word.

petitio principii means 'begging of a principle' and denotes a logical fallacy in which a conclusion is taken for granted in the premiss. See BEG THE QUESTION.

petrel, petrol. The first is a bird, the second a fuel (AmE *gas*-

oline). They are both pronounced the same way, **pet**-rəl.

pewit see PEEWIT.

phantasm, phantom. In current usage *phantom* primarily means 'a ghost' or 'a mental illusion', whereas *phantasm* means 'a visual illusion' or 'a vision of an absent person'.

phantasy see FANTASY.

pharaoh, an ancient Egyptian king, is spelt -*aoh*, not -*oah*.

pharmacopoeia, meaning 'an official directory of drugs', is spelt -*poeia* in BrE and -*poeia* or -*peia* in AmE. The pronunciation in both cases is fah-mə-kə-**pee**-ə.

phenomenal. The modern generalized meaning 'extraordinary, remarkable' (*A spokeswoman . . . said the response from members yesterday was 'phenomenal'*—Guardian, 1979) is now the dominant one, although it retains little of the notion of its meaning in technical (especially philosophical) contexts, in which the meaning is 'perceived by the senses'.

phenomenon. The primary meaning now is 'an extraordinary or remarkable person or thing' rather than 'a fact or occurrence that is perceived', although this meaning runs it a close second. The plural form is *phenomena*, which is sometimes treated erroneously as a singular noun:
🗷 *Footsteps are heard all over the building causing surprise and apprehension and expectancy in those visitors who have heard about the phenomena but haven't experienced it* [correct to . . . *haven't experienced them*]—W. B. Herbert, 1992.

Philippines, the chain of islands in south-east Asia, is spelt in this way, with one *l* and two *p*s. The inhabitants are called *Filipinos*.

Philistine. A *Philistine* (with a capital initial letter) is a member of an ancient Semitic people of Palestine. A *philistine* (with a small initial letter, usually) is a person who is hostile or indifferent to culture.

-phile is more common than *-phil* in current usage in words (usually nouns and adjectives) denoting a fondness for something or someone, such as *bibliophile*, *Francophile*, etc.

phlegm, meaning 'a viscous substance discharged by coughing', is pronounced flem. The *g* is also silent in the adjective *phlegmy*, but is pronounced in *phlegmatic* (fleg-**mat**-ik), meaning 'stolidly calm and unemotional'.

phone is a well-established shortening of *telephone*, used chiefly in spoken English.

phoney, an informal word meaning 'sham, fake' (adjective and noun), is of uncertain origin and not traced in print before 1900. Its currency was greatly boosted by the use of the term *phoney war* to refer to the relative inaction in the early months of the Second World War. *Phoney* is the preferred spelling, although *phony* is also used.

phonograph is now disused in BrE as a term for a type of gramophone, but is still used in AmE for any type of gramophone or record player (before the development of the compact disc).

phosphorus, phosphorous. *Phosphorus* is the noun for the chemical element, and *phosphorous* is the adjective meaning 'containing phosphorus'.

photo is a well-established shortening of *photograph*, used chiefly in spoken English. Its plural form is *photos*, and it is commonly used in attributive position (i.e. before a noun), as in *photo call*, *photo finish*, and *photo opportunity*.

phrasal verbs. 1 A phrasal verb is a combination of verb and adverb or preposition (or both) such as *come about, draw up, put up with*, and *work out*. Phrasal verbs formed with adverbs can be either transitive (i.e. take an object, as in *He drew up a chair*) or intransitive (as in *A taxi drew up*). Phrasal verbs formed with prepositions are of course transitive (*I must go through some papers*). Phrasal verbs of all types have meanings that cannot be directly deduced from the individual words, and in some cases they have several meanings and grammatical patterns. For example, *run up* has four distinct meanings in the sentences *She ran up the road*, *She ran up to meet them*, *She ran up debts*, and *She ran up the flag*. In the first example, *up* is a preposition (governing *road*), whereas in the other three examples it is an adverb, and in the last two the objects *debts* and *flag* are governed by the verb *ran*.

2 When the object of a phrasal verb is a pronoun, it normally comes between the verb and a following adverb, e.g. *He took up my references* but *He took them up*. This separability can occur with nouns as well, though not in all cases: *I'll get down the book* can be converted to *I'll get the book down*, whereas *She heads up a team*, cannot be converted to *She heads a team up*, although *down* and *up* are both being used as adverbs in these cases. Whether or not more transparent combinations such as *They came down the stairs* or *She*

went into the house should be classed as phrasal verbs as distinct from verbs with routine complementation is still the subject of disagreement among grammarians, and this applies also to the extended type *The witch turned him into a toad*, in which both the verb and the following preposition have their distinct grammatical objects.

3 Phrasal verbs range from the informal to the neutral but are hardly ever formal in register. They form a highly productive area of current English, with recent new formations including *dumb down* (= make simpler), *factor in* (= include in an assessment or survey), *freak out* (= lose one's temper), and *scroll up* (on a computer screen). All these are informal in use.

4 Some phrasal verbs produce noun derivatives of the type *breakdown*, *copout*, *feedback*, and *tie-in*, the reversed form typified by *backdrop* and *outcome*, or both (*breakout* and *outbreak*). These also vary in register from the neutral (*breakdown*, *breakout*, *feedback*, *outbreak*) to the informal (*copout*, *tie-in*).

5 For a fuller discussion of this topic see Tom McArthur in *The Oxford Companion to the English Language* (1992), 772–6.

physician, doctor, surgeon.

The normal word for a medical practitioner in general contexts is *doctor* (abbreviated as a title to *Dr*). *Physician* is familiar from the proverb *Physician, heal thyself* (Luke 4:23) and has the same range of meaning as *doctor* but is not in general use. In current British use, a *doctor* in general practice is distinguished as a *general practitioner* (or *GP*). In AmE, *Doctor* is also used for a qualified dentist

or veterinary surgeon; and in all English-speaking countries *Doctor* and *Dr* are used (as titles only) to refer to a person who has a doctorate in a non-medical subject (e.g. *Doctor of Philosophy*). A *surgeon* is a person who is qualified to practise surgery, and in Britain (except Scotland) is addressed as *Mr*, not *Dr*.

physiognomy, physiology. *Physiognomy* (pronounced with the *g* silent) is 'the cast or form of a person's features', whereas *physiology* is 'the science of the functions of living organisms and their parts'.

pianist is normally pronounced **pee**-ə-nist with the stress on the first syllable in BrE and pi-**ah**-nist with the stress on the second syllable in AmE.

piano. The plural form of the noun is *pianos*.

piazza, meaning 'an open square or market place', is normally pronounced in the Italian manner, pi-**at**-sə, and in English contexts has the plural form *piazzas*. In AmE the pronunciation is more often pi-**az**-ə, and it has the special meaning 'the veranda of a house'.

picaresque is used to describe a type of fiction concerned with the adventures of a rogue (from Spanish *picaro* meaning 'rogue'). The type is represented in 18c English literature by Defoe's *Moll Flanders* (1722), Fielding's *Tom Jones* (1749), and other classic works, but the first record of the use of the term in English is by Sir Walter Scott in 1829.

piccolo, the smallest flute, has the plural form *piccolos*.

picket. The verb has inflected forms *picketed*, *picketing*.

picnic. The verb has inflected forms *picnicked*, *picnicking*.

pidgin. A *pidgin* is a simplified language containing vocabulary and grammatical elements from two or more languages, and is used mainly by traders who do not have a language in common. It differs from a CREOLE in being improvised for a special purpose as distinct from being the mother tongue of a speech community. The word *pidgin* is probably a Chinese corruption of the English word *business*, which is reflected also in the idiom *that's your pigeon* (= that's your affair or business).

pie. What is the difference between a *pie* and a *tart*? On both sides of the Atlantic, a *pie* can contain meat, fish, or fruit, with the filling entirely enclosed by pastry, whereas a *tart* is more likely to be open on top and with a sweet filling such as jam or custard. In Britain a mince pie is a small individual pie filled with mincemeat (a mixture of dried fruit and spices). It is worth remembering that in earlier writing pies and tarts could be much more varied in kind, e.g. *jam tart, strawberry tart, eel tart, veal tart*, etc., besides *goose pie, pigeon pie, eel pie, pumpkin pie*, etc.

piebald, skewbald. A *piebald* horse or other animal is one having irregular patches of two colours, especially black and white. A *skewbald* animal has irregular patches of white and another colour (other than black).

pièce de résistance, meaning 'the most important or remarkable item', is printed in italic type with the accents as shown. The plural form (not often needed) is *pièces de résistance*, pronounced in the same way as the singular form.

pied-à-terre, meaning 'a small house or apartment kept for occasional use', is pronounced pyay-dah-**tair** and is normally printed in italic type with the accent as shown. The plural form is *pieds-à-terre* (with the same pronunciation).

pietà, a representation of the dead Christ held by his mother, is pronounced pi-ay-**tah** and printed in italic type with an accent on the *a*.

pigmy see PYGMY.

pilau, a type of Middle Eastern or Indian spiced dish of rice, is normally spelt in this way in BrE, but *pilaf* or *pilaff* in AmE. These forms also occur, however, in BrE.

pilfer, meaning 'to steal (something trivial)', has inflected forms *pilfered*, *pilfering*.

pilot. The verb has inflected forms *piloted*, *piloting*.

pinch. The idiom *at a pinch*, meaning 'if absolutely necessary', is the BrE form; in AmE it has the form *in a pinch*.

piquant, meaning 'agreeably pungent' or 'pleasantly stimulating', is pronounced **pee**-kənt.

pis aller, meaning 'a course of action followed as a last resort', is pronounced peez **al**-ay and is printed in italic type.

pistachio, a type of nut, has the plural form *pistachios*.

piteous, pitiable, pitiful. All three words are recorded from Middle English and share the basic meaning 'arousing pity' and are to some extent interchangeable (as in *The abandoned children were a piteous sight*), although *pitiful* is the most versatile and *piteous* is the least common. *Piteous* and *pitiable* can both convey the meaning 'deserving pity', and *pitiable* and *pitiful* convey the meaning 'evoking mingled pity and contempt'. *Pitiful* alone is used in the meaning 'absurdly small or insignificant', as in *The state pension has been reduced to a pitiful sum*. Examples: *A pitiful tube squirts water to a height of a couple of feet*—J. D. R. McConnell, 1970 | *How she had suffered for him, for her poor pitiable ridiculous father*—Margaret Drabble, 1987 | *'What did I do this time?' Helen looked piteous*—Maeve Binchy, 1988 | *His blindness now struck her as utterly pitiful*—M. Forster, 1988.

pity. The type *Pity you can't come tomorrow* is an acceptable conversational shortening of *It is a pity that . . . .*

pizazz, a slang term meaning 'verve, sparkle', has many variant spellings, of which the one given seems the most common.

placebo, meaning 'a pill or medicine given for psychological effect', is pronounced pla-**see**-boh and has the plural form *placebos*.

plaid, pronounced plad, is a length of fabric worn over the shoulder as part of the ceremonial dress of members of the pipe bands of Scottish regiments. It should be distinguished from *tartan*, which is a woollen cloth with a pattern of different coloured stripes crossing at right angles, each pattern being associated with a particular clan. A *plaid* can be made from *tartan* cloth.

Plain English. 1 The expression *plain English*, meaning 'English that is clear and easy to understand', goes back to the 15c, and was the term often used in the titles of the first dictionaries that appeared during the 17c; Robert Cawdrey, for example, described the contents of his 1604 *Table Alphabeticall* as listing hard words 'with the interpretation thereof by plaine English words'. The current UK Plain English campaign was started in the 1970s and grew out of the consumer movement and the demand for fair dealing. It may be seen as belonging to the tradition of the work done by Sir Ernest Gowers in publications such as *Plain Words* (1948, later *The Complete Plain Words*, 1954 and later editions) and in the material he added to the second edition of Fowler's *Modern English Usage* (1965). A similar movement exists in the US, including the Plain English Forum set up in the 1980s.

2 Plain English insists on clarity as well as accuracy and wages war on convoluted, obfuscating language typified by the use of such words as *aforesaid, in the event of, incumbent on*, and *thereto*. It argues that inflated statements such as *Encashment of a foreign currency may incur a processing fee* may be stated more effectively as *We may charge you for changing your foreign money*. In some contexts, however, the need for precision can require the use of special terminology; this aspect is discussed in the entries for LEGALESE and OFFICIALESE. See also Martin Cutts, *The Plain English Guide* (1995).

plain sailing, meaning 'a straightforward situation or course of action', is an early 19c alteration of the original (late

17c) phrase *plane sailing*, which denoted a system of measuring short nautical distances by assuming that the earth's surface is a plane and not spherical.

plait. The noun and verb are both pronounced plat.

plan. The verb is followed either by *to* or (especially in AmE) by *on*: *The government plan to close them and redeploy their workers*—*Times*, 1986 | *Do you plan on staying with Muriel forever?*—A. Tyler, 1985.

planetarium has the plural form *planetariums*, or occasionally *planetaria*.

plaster. The verb has inflected forms *plastered, plastering*.

plastic is now normally pronounced with the first syllable as in *plan*. The adjectival form is *plasticky*.

plateau has the plural form *plateaux*, pronounced in the same way as the singular.

plateful has the plural form *platefuls*.

platonic, referring to spiritual as distinct from erotic love, is spelt with a small initial *p*. When the reference is directly to Plato (as in *Platonic dialogue*), it is spelt *Platonic* with a capital initial letter.

platypus has the plural form *platypuses*.

player has extended its meaning from being a participant in a game of sport or fun to being a participant in a different type of game, namely commercial politics. This use originated in the US and has spread rapidly into BrE, although it is largely restricted to the domain of business journalism: *Other players include the Ford Motor company, which . . . has been talking about selling its mortgages through car showrooms*—*Economist*, 1986.

plc, PLC. Both forms are used for the abbreviation of *Public Limited Company*, a status introduced in the UK in 1980.

plead. The past tense and past participle in standard BrE are both *pleaded*, but *pled* and *plead* (pronounced pled) are used as well as *pleaded* in America, Scotland, and some dialects in the UK. In legal usage, an accused person can *plead guilty* or *not guilty*, but cannot *plead innocent*, which is an informal expression only.

please. The use of *please* by itself, as in *Will you come in, please?*, is a reduced form of *may it (so) please you*. It was first recorded in the 17c, but was not used by Shakespeare, whose shortest form is *please you*.

plebiscite, referendum. *Plebiscite* is pronounced **pleb**-i-sit in BrE and usually **pleb**-i-siyt in AmE. The term is most commonly used of a direct vote of a State's electors on a fundamental matter, and is not used with reference to the UK. A *referendum* is the referral of an important specific issue to the electorate for a general vote, and is used in the UK.

plectrum has the plural form *plectrums* or (in technical use) *plectra*.

plenteous, plentiful. The normal word in current English is *plentiful*, but *plenteous* will be found especially in literary works of the 19c and earlier.

plenty is essentially a noun, and is used either by itself or with *of*

+ following noun (plural, or singular mass noun): *We have plenty | You will find plenty of books | There is plenty of time*. Use of *plenty* as an adjective without *of* is found in regional forms of English but is not standard: *Although there are plenty other ideals that I should prefer*—Robert Louis Stevenson | *Leopard Society in Sierra Leone. They kill plenty people*—Graham Greene, 1969. Use of *plenty* as an adverb meaning 'very, clearly, more than usually' is restricted to nonstandard AmE: *He seems plenty dead to me*—R. Silverberg, 1985 | *I frowned at my mother plenty*—New Yorker, 1990.

pleonasm is a term meaning 'the use of more words than are necessary to give the sense'. An example in ordinary (as distinct from literary) usage is *to see with one's eyes*.

plethora, meaning 'an oversupply, an excess', is pronounced **pleth**-ə-rə and is a singular noun.

plough is the normal BrE spelling, but *plow* is used in AmE.

plunder as a verb has inflected forms *plundered, plundering*.

plurals of nouns.
See box overleaf

plus is used primarily as the oral equivalent of the arithmetical sign + (*Three plus four is seven*). In the 20c it has gone from strength to strength as a quasi-preposition with the meaning 'with the addition of, and also' (e.g. *A cup of Epp's cocoa and a shakedown for the night plus the use of a rug and overcoat doubled into a pillow*—James Joyce, 1922). A more controversial use from the 1960s (first in Amer-

ica) makes *plus* a conjunction or adverb (with a comma following) meaning 'and furthermore, and in addition': (conjunction) *You can fly an aeroplane . . . and command a ship. Plus you ride horses*—New Yorker, 1987 | *'It's certainly a challenge. Plus it's a little overwhelming, but it's exciting,' says Nicole*—Daily Mail, 1998 | (adverb) *I'll quit romanticizing him. Plus, he never got to go on any road trips*—B. Ripley, 1987. These uses occur frequently in advertisements (e.g. *20% off everything—plus no deposit*) but should not be adopted in more formal writing.

p.m. As an abbreviation of Latin *post meridiem* 'after noon', *p.m.* is pronounced as two letters and written in the form *8.15 p.m.* (or *pm*; in AmE *8:15 p.m.*). The abbreviation is sometimes used informally as a noun: *We arrived here this p.m.* See also A.M.

pocket as a verb has inflected forms *pocketed, pocketing*.

pocketful has the plural form *pocketfuls*. See -FUL.

podium, meaning 'a raised platform or base (e.g. for a speaker or orchestral conductor)', has the plural form *podiums* or (occasionally) *podia*.

poetess is now rarely used except with historical reference, as for example to the Greek lyricist Sappho (6c BC). Occasionally it is used when the sex of the poet is in some way significant and when the noun is already qualified by an adjective, making 'woman poet' unwieldy: *He paused in his writing only to listen to a rather attractive Finnish poetess*

plurals of nouns

English nouns normally form their plurals by adding *-s*, or *-es* if the singular form ends in *-s*, *-x*, *-z*, *-sh*, or soft *-ch* (as in *church* but not *loch*). Words in *-y* form plurals in *-ies* (*policies*) unless the ending is *-ey* in which case the plural form is normally *-eys* (*monkeys*); but see MONEYS. Difficulties occur mainly when the singular form is unusual and does not allow ready application of the normal rules or when the word is of foreign origin (or both). Nouns in *-f* and *-fe* are given in the entry -FS, -VES, nouns of the type *cupful* at the entry -FUL, and nouns in *-o* in the entry -O; plurals of some Latin nouns in English are given in the entry LATIN PLURALS. For plurals of abbreviated forms (such as *MP*) see ABBREVIATIONS 3. The following table lists other plural forms that cause difficulties of various kinds.

IRREGULAR PLURALS

child	children
foot	feet
goose	geese
louse	lice
man	men
mouse	mice
tooth	teeth
woman	women

ANIMAL NAMES THE SAME IN THE PLURAL

bison	bison
cod	cod
deer	deer
grouse	grouse
salmon	salmon
sheep	sheep
squid	squid
swine	swine

NOUNS IN PLURAL FORM ONLY: TOOLS

bellows
binoculars
clippers
forceps
gallows
glasses
goggles
pincers
pliers
scissors

▶

► **plurals of nouns**
continued

---

shears
spectacles (= glasses)
tongs
tweezers

NOUNS IN PLURAL FORM ONLY: ARTICLES OF CLOTHING

braces
breeches
briefs
flannels
jeans
knickers
leggings
pants
pyjamas (US pajamas)
shorts
slacks
suspenders
tights
trousers

COMPOUND NOUNS

Attorney-General	Attorneys-General*
brother-in-law	brothers-in-law
commander-in-chief	commanders-in-chief
court martial	courts martial
daughter-in-law	daughters-in-law
father-in-law	fathers-in-law
Governor-General	Governors-General*
lay-by	lay-bys
man-of war	men-of-war
mother-in-law	mothers-in-law
passer-by	passers-by
Poet Laureate	Poets Laureate*
sister-in-law	sisters-in-law
son-in-law	sons-in-law
stand-by	stand-bys

The forms Attorney-Generals, Governor-Generals, and Poet Laureates are also used

---

reading a sequence about her marital problems—D. M. Thomas, 1990. In general, *poet* is now regularly used of both female and male writers of poetry. See -ESS.

poetic, poetical. In general, *poetic* is the more common word, but choice is often dependent on personal preference or on sentence rhythm. There are, however, a few fixed expressions, e.g. *the poetical works of, poetic justice, poetic licence.*

Poet Laureate. The plural is *Poets Laureate*, although *Poet Laureates* is often used.

pogrom, meaning 'an organized massacre', is pronounced **pog**-rəm. It is of Russian origin, first applied to the massacre of Jews and later applied more generally.

point in time. The expression *at this point* (or *moment*) *in time*, meaning 'currently, now', is a modern cliché that is more often heard in speech, or in reported speech, than seen in print. See CLICHÉS.

point of view is largely interchangeable with *standpoint* and *viewpoint*. The reference of all three is general; when the use refers to an opinion on a specific matter *view* (alone) or *opinion* is often a better choice: *Their point of view is largely traditional* but *They take a largely traditional view on this question.*

polemic, polemical. *Polemic* is a noun meaning 'a controversial discussion' or 'a verbal or written political attack'; the corresponding noun is either *polemic* or (more usually) *polemical.*

policeman, policewoman. Both terms are tending to be replaced by the gender-neutral term *police officer.* In the UK, an officer holding the rank of constable is a *police constable* (PC) or *woman police constable* (WPC).

policy. There are two separate words with this spelling: (1) meaning 'a course or principle of action' derived ultimately from the Greek word *polis* 'city', and (2) meaning 'a contract of insurance' derived ultimately from the Greek word *apodeixis* 'evidence, proof'.

political correctness. The term *political correctness* (often abbreviated to *PC*) arose in the 1980s, first in America and soon afterwards elsewhere. It deals with many areas of social interaction; in language it is concerned with avoiding or replacing words and uses that cause offence or are seen as discriminating against certain sections of society, e.g. by being racist or sexist or in other ways, and extends to the avoidance of terms that may be regarded even coincidentally as offensive, such as *black* in *black economy* and *blind* (*to*) meaning 'unwilling to recognize (a fact)', and to other words that offend various groups, e.g. deaf people, homosexuals, racial groups, women, and old people. The political correctness movement is also devoted to promoting an alternative terminology that seeks to assert a more positive aspect to negative or undesirable qualities, such as *deficiency achievement* for *failure*, *differently abled* for *disabled*, *non-waged* for *unemployed*, and many compounds formed with *-challenged* (*intellectually challenged*, *vertically challenged*, etc.: see CHALLENGED). Although the basic intentions of political correctness have attracted widespread sympathy, its more extreme forms have been met with derision or even hostility. A *Sunday Times* leader of 1991, for example, warned that 'American politics is being corrupted and diminished by the doctrine of Political Correctness which demands rigid adherence to the political attitudes and social mores of the liberal-left, and which exhibits a malevolent intolerance to anybody who dares not comply with them'. See also SEXIST LANGUAGE.

politic, political. The normal adjective in general meanings is *political*. Apart from its use in the fixed expression *body politic*, *politic* is confined to the meaning 'judicious, expedient' (with reference to an action) and 'prudent, sagacious' (with reference to a person) and is normally used after a verb (such as *be*) rather than attributively (before a noun). The corresponding adverbs are *politicly* (from *politic*, but not often needed) and *politically* (from *political*). *Politic* is also found as a verb meaning 'to engage in politics' (usually with disparaging overtones), and its inflected forms are *politicked*, *politicking*.

politics is treated as a singular noun when it means 'the art or science of government' (*Politics is a popular subject at many universities*) and normally as a plural noun when it means 'a particular set of ideas, principles, etc.'(*What are your politics?*).

polity means (1) 'a form or process of civil government or constitution', and (2) 'a society or country as a political entity'. It should not be confused with *policy*, in its meaning 'a course or principle of action'.

polytechnic, a term for an institution of further education, has largely fallen out of use in the UK since 1992, when polytechnics were legally entitled to call themselves *universities*.

pond is used jocularly to mean the sea, especially the Atlantic as separating Britain and America: *Jackie Collins, born British, wrote . . . huge, earnest tomes which even started to feature safe-sex warnings when she took up residence across the pond*—J. Burchill, 1993.

poof, a derogatory slang term for a homosexual or effeminate man, is also written *poove* (and pronounced accordingly). The plural forms are *poofs* and *pooves*.

poorly is both an adverb (*They all performed poorly*) and an adjective (= unwell, *Her husband had been poorly for months*). As in this example, the adjective is normally used after a verb (such as *be*), rather than in attributive position (before a noun).

popularized technicalities. *See box overleaf*

popular music, pop music. The two terms are not interchangeable. *Popular* music is a generic term for music of all ages that appeals to popular tastes (e.g. one can refer to nineteenth-century popular music, the popular music of Greece, etc). *Pop music* is a more specific term for the commercialized popular music of the later half of the 20c, especially the 1950s and 1960s, and has in turn largely given way to the phenomenon of *rock music* and other special forms.

pore, pour. The verb *pore* means 'to think closely about (a subject)' and is chiefly used in the phrasal verb *to pore over* (a book etc.). It is sometimes mistakenly written as *pour*, perhaps by false analogy with 'pouring attention' over something.

porpoise is pronounced **paw**-pəs, not with the second syllable as in *poise*.

portfolio has the plural form *portfolios*.

popularized technicalities

This was Fowler's term (1926) for technical terms that are adopted into general use, and the one he named as being then most in vogue was ACID TEST. Some popularizations (e.g. *leading question*) involve a change in meaning and are therefore usually more controversial. A range of examples from various domains, some known to Fowler and others more recent, are given in the table below.

WORD	TECHNICAL DOMAIN	DATE OF POPULARIZED USE
allergy	medicine	mid-20c
asset	law	17c
chain reaction	chemistry	mid-20c
chronic	medicine	19c
clone	genetics	late 20c
complex	psychology	early 20c
devil's advocate	religion	19c
feedback	physics	mid-20c
fixation	psychology	early 20c
function	mathematics	18c
leading question	law	20c
nth degree	mathematics	19c
parameter	mathematics	early 20c
persona	literary criticism	early 20c
protagonist	drama	mid-20c
quantum leap *or* jump	physics	mid-20c
syndrome	medicine	mid-20c

portico has the plural form *porticoes* (preferred) or *porticos*.

portmanteau words are words formed by merging or blending two or more other words, e.g. *brunch* (*breakfast* + *lunch*), *motel* (*motor* + *hotel*), and *smog* (*smoke* + *fog*). Modern formations of this type are often used for items of social concern or popular culture, e.g. *blaxploitation* (*black* + *exploitation*), *docudrama* (*documentary* + *drama*), *edutainment* (*education* + *entertainment*), *ginormous* (*giant* + *enormous*), *sexcapade* (*sex* + *escapade*).

Portuguese (with two *us*) is the singular and plural form for the noun meaning a native or national of Portugal, and also the corresponding adjective.

position *verb*. *Uniformed constables had been positioned to re-direct traffic*—J. Wainwright, 1979. The use of *position* as a verb, meaning 'to place in position' has met with some criticism, usually from those who object to any verb made relatively recently from a noun (in this case early 19c). But *position* has a useful role (in physical and abstract contexts) that is not fulfilled by *place*, *put*, or *pose*.

position of adverbs see ADVERB 3. Fowler's classic article on this subject in *Modern English Usage* (1926) was originally published in *SPE* [Society for Pure English] *Tract* xv (1923), and is now mainly of historical interest.

possessive see APOSTROPHE.

possessive pronouns and determiners. For various points concerning these, see GENDER-NEUTRALITY; HIS; OUR, OURS; THEY, THEM, THEIR.

possessive with gerund. For the type *She does not like my* (or *me*) *smoking in bed*, see VERBAL NOUN.

POSSLQ, a shortening of 'person of the opposite sex sharing living quarters', is a coy term for a live-in partner that is surprisingly common, and it is often heard as an acronym in the form **pos**-əlk.

postdeterminer see DETERMINER.

post hoc, ergo propter hoc means 'after it and therefore because of it', and refers to the fallacy of assuming that if event A is followed by event B, event B is caused by event A. (*On Sunday we prayed for rain, and on Monday it rained. Therefore our prayers were answered.*)

posthumous, meaning 'occurring after death', is pronounced **pos**-tyuh-məs, i.e. with the *h* silent.

postmaster general. The customary plural is *postmasters general*. The use is now often historical, the office having been abolished in the UK in 1969.

potato has the plural form *potatoes*.

potence, potency. For the meaning 'power, the quality or state of being potent', *potency* is the usual word, and this is also used in the context of the male ability to achieve sexual erection or orgasm. *Potence* is used in a number of technical applications but not in general contexts.

potter, meaning 'to occupy oneself in a desultory but pleasurable way', is normally used with *about* or *around*. Its inflected forms are *pottered, pottering*. In AmE the usual spelling is *putter*.

poverty, poorness. *Poverty* is the usual noun corresponding to *poor* in its meanings to do with lack of wealth or lack of things regarded like wealth (e.g. *poverty of inspiration*). *Poorness* is more usual in meanings to do with quality or evaluation (e.g. *the poorness of his performance*).

p.p. The formula traditionally stands for *per procurationem* meaning 'through the agency (of)', and is used in business correspondence when one person is signing on behalf of another: *A p.p. B*. In this case, A is the person writing the letter and B is the person signing it on behalf of A. However, *p.p.* is also understood to mean *per pro*, i.e. 'for and on behalf of', and in this case the formula is often used in reverse order, with A as the signatory and B the writer. American usage wisely avoids this ambiguous convention altogether, preferring a more explicit annotation such as 'signed by A in B's absence', and this practice has begun to influence British use.

-p-, -pp-. For the inflection of words such as *trap*, *gallop* and *kidnap*, see DOUBLING OF FINAL CONSONANTS IN INFLECTION.

practicable, practical. *Practical* usually has a general application, denoting what is possible in practice as distinct from theory, and can also describe a person ('inclined to action rather than speculation, able to make things work well'), whereas *practicable* means 'able to be carried out, feasible', is more usually applied to a particular instance under consideration, and occurs much less often in attributive position (before a noun): *Where it makes sense and is practicable, the pupil may be moved up or down a key stage for the subject in question*—W. Swann et al., 1992 | *I need to be practical but would like to look feminine as well*—Clothes Show, 1991 | *Woodblock has been used for a beautiful, yet practical, floor covering*—Ideal Home, 1991 | *He said that the American system, where the debtor pays the advice agency which then deducts a levy before paying the creditor, was the most practical*—Credit Management, 1992. The negative forms are discussed at the entry for IMPRACTICABLE, IMPRACTICAL.

practically. The earlier (17c) meaning 'in a practical way' (*try to deal with the problem as practically as possible*) has been overwhelmed since the 18c by the meaning that is now the dominant one, 'virtually, almost': . . . *sitting through exams with practically nothing to show for them afterwards*—Rosemary Sutcliff, 1983.

practice, practise. In standard BrE, *practice* is used for the noun and *practise* for the verb, whereas in AmE *practice* is the dominant spelling of both noun and verb.

pre-. This prefix is often joined to the word it qualifies without a hyphen, e.g. *prearrange, predetermine, preoccupy*. But when the word begins with *e* or *i*, or when the formation coincides with another word, it is usual to insert a

hyphen, e.g. *pre-eminent, pre-ignition, pre-position* (to distinguish it from *preposition*).

precede, proceed. Note that *precede*, meaning 'to go before' is spelt *-cede*, whereas *proceed*, meaning 'to go ahead', is spelt *-ceed*.

precedence, precedent. In BrE, both words are pronounced with the stress on the first syllable, but in AmE the stress is sometimes put on the second, as it is in *precede*. *Precedence* means 'priority in time, order, or importance', whereas a *precedent* (countable) is 'a decision that may be taken as a model for future action'. The use of *precedent* as an adjective meaning 'preceding in time or order' is now rare.

preciosity, preciousness. *Preciosity* is now virtually restricted to the meaning 'over-refinement in art or language, especially in the choice of words', leaving *preciousness* as the noun corresponding to the general meanings of *precious*.

precipitate, precipitous. 1 The two words overlap in meaning and were used interchangeably from the 17c to the 19c. *Precipitous* has a physical meaning 'sheer like a precipice': *There was a precipitous wooden stair to the ground floor*—A. Craig, 1990. In its abstract sense it is concerned with the over-rapid progress of an action and retains the notion of steep descent, and is therefore often found in the company of words such as *decline* (*A number of factors might be responsible for such a precipitous decline*—A. Wilentz, 1989), whereas *precipitate* is concerned rather with the inception of an action and means rather 'hasty, rash, inconsiderate' or 'headlong, violently hurried': *His precipitate action was clearly calculated to make* *life harder rather than easier for the PLO as he abandoned responsibility for civil servants in the West Bank.*—D. McDowell, 1990. It is in this second set of meanings that the two words come closest, since any action that is *precipitate* in its inception is likely to be *precipitous* in its performance or consequences.

2 Of the corresponding adverbs, *precipitously* encroaches on *precipitately*, especially in AmE: *I left precipitously because I didn't want to work there any longer*—A. Cross, 1986 (US) (*precipitately* is wanted) | *Angus had precipitately fled on learning that the king was loose and in vengeful mood*—J. Burke, 1990.

précis (= summary). The accent of the French original should be retained in the English form of the word.

preciseness, precision. Both words have the same general meaning 'the condition of being precise, accuracy', but *precision* is the more natural choice and is used in attributive position (before other nouns) as in *precision bombing, precision timing,* etc.

predeterminer see DETERMINER.

predicate. *Predicate* and *predict* are distantly related but their meanings are distinct. The primary meaning of *predict* is 'to foretell', whereas the primary use of *predicate* is followed by *on* in the meaning 'to found or base (on a principle or assumption)': *Crime predicated on sexual disorder* | *distrust*—Listener, 1977. When *base* or *found* would do as well (as in the example given) it is better to use one of them: ☒ *The emotion was predicated on one particular hope: that one day the high purposes*

would be recognized, and the actors justified—A. Wroe, 1991.

predominantly, predominately. *The huts are predominantly in valleys near rivers, and invariably the local area was swarming with mosquitoes*—R. Sale et al., 1991 | *The music was predominately '60s and '70s pop, but that didn't seem to bother the inimitable Mr Hurst*—Bookseller, 1993. Both words mean 'as the most important factor or element, mostly, largely' and both have long histories, although *predominately* was rare before the 19c and *predominantly* remains the more common of the two.

preface see FOREWORD.

prefer. **1** The inflected forms of the verb are *preferred, preferring,* but other derivatives have a single *-r-* (*preferable, preferably, preference, preferential, preferment*).

2 When the subject of *prefer* is the same as that of a following subordinate verb, the normal construction is with a *to*-infinitive or with a verbal noun: *I prefer to stand* or *I prefer standing*. When the following verb is in the negative, the *to*-infinitive is the usual option: *I prefer not to live and work in the same room*—C. K. Stead, 1986. When a second person or thing intervenes as subject of the subordinate verb, the normal construction in BrE is with noun (or pronoun) + *to*-infinitive: *I'd prefer you to stay.* An alternative is *that* + clause, which is the more usual choice in AmE: *I'd prefer that you stay.* (A further, less formal, alternative is the type *I'd prefer it if you stayed.*)

3 When *prefer* is followed by a pair of alternatives, these are separated by *to*: *I prefer whisky to* *brandy* | *I prefer swimming to jogging*. Clearly in these cases a construction with a *to*-infinitive would lead to a clash of *to*'s and is not possible: ☒ *I prefer to swim to to jog*, but an alternative is to use *rather than*: *I prefer to swim rather than to jog* (but not *I prefer to swim than to jog*).

preferable is pronounced with the stress on the first syllable. Because it is already a comparative form, it should not be preceded by *more*, although it may be followed by *far*, *greatly*, or *much*: *Since it was fed with steaks served in gold-plated bowls, the creature presumably regarded a dog's life in Romania as greatly preferable to its existence in Britain*—M. Almond, 1992.

prefix. In grammar, a *prefix* is a word or element added at the beginning of another word to adjust or qualify its meaning, such as *ex-* (*ex-husband*), *non-* (*non-smoking*), and *super-* (*supermodel*).

prejudice, in the meaning 'bias' or 'partiality', is followed by *against* or *in favour of*, but not (on the analogy of *hostility*, *objection*, etc.) to: *a prejudice against eating late*, not ☒ *a prejudice to eating late*. In its meaning 'irrational dislike', it can be followed by *towards*: *the hostility and prejudice that exists towards homosexuality*.

premature. In BrE this is pronounced **prem**-ə-tyuh-ə or prem-ə-**tyuh**-ə. In AmE the first syllable is often pronounced pree-.

premier. 1 In BrE the normal pronunciation is **prem**-i-ə, with the first syllable short. In AmE the dominant pronunciation is prə-**mee**-ə, with the stress on the *i*.

2 The main meaning of the noun is 'a prime minister or other head of government'; in Canada it denotes the chief executive officer of a provincial government (with a capital initial letter when used as a title, e.g. *Premier Robert Bourassa*.

3 As an adjective *premier* is enjoying a period of great popularity on both sides of the Atlantic in the meaning 'first in order of importance, order, or time': *Hypersonic flight has become the premier area for aerospace research in the United States*—*Mechanical Engineering*, 1991. In football, Premier Leagues have emerged in England, in Scotland, and now (conceptually) in Europe.

première is now fully established as a noun meaning 'the first performance or showing of a play or film', and as a verb meaning 'to give a première of' (*The film will be premièred next week*). The BrE pronunciation is **prem**-i-air, with the first syllable short, and in AmE it is normally prə-**mee**-ə, with the stress on the *i*.

premise, premiss. A *premiss* (usually pronounced **prem**-is) or (rarely) *premise* is a previous statement from which another is inferred; the plural is *premisses* or *premises*. In the plural, *premises* also means 'a house or building with its grounds'. As a verb, *premise* (pronounced like the noun or to rhyme with *surmise*) means either 'to say or write by way of introduction' or 'to assume from a premiss'.

prepared to. In its generalized meaning 'willing to', *prepared to* has gone the same way as *ready to*; in neither case is any element of preparedness or readiness necessarily involved, especially when it is used in the negative: *I am not prepared to wait any longer.*

Sir Ernest Gowers, in *The Complete Plain Words*, warned that 'such phrases as these are no doubt dictated by politeness, and therefore deserve respect. But they must be used with discretion', and in the second edition of *Modern English Usage* (1965) condemned such examples as *I am prepared to overlook the mistake* as 'wantonly blurring the meaning of prepare'. But his argument that the expression should be reserved for cases in which there is some element of preparation, as in *I have read the papers and am prepared to hear you state your case*, was based on an unworkable distinction which ignored the role of idiom in such matters. Whatever influence Gowers may have had in Whitehall, it has not touched the rest of the world, where *prepared to* and *not prepared to* are regularly used in the simple meanings 'willing to' and 'unwilling to': e.g. *If non-executives are to carry out their duties properly, they must be prepared to blow the whistle—Independent*, 1991.

preposition. 1 A preposition is a word such as *after*, *in*, *to*, and *with*, which usually stands before a noun or pronoun and establishes its relation to what goes before (*the man **on** the platform | came **after** dinner | What did you do it **for**?*). The superstition that a preposition should always precede the word it governs and should not end a sentence (as in the last example given) seems to have developed from an observation of the 17c poet John Dryden, although Dryden himself did not always follow the rule in his own prose. It is not based on a real appreciation of the structure of English, which regularly separates words that are grammatically related.

2 There are cases when it is either impossible or not natural to organize the sentence in a way that avoids a final preposition:

▶**a** In relative clauses and questions featuring phrasal verbs: *What did Marion think she was up to?—*Julian Barnes, 1980 | *They must be entirely reliable and convinced of the commitment they are taking on—Times Educational Supplement*, 1987 | *Budget cuts themselves are not damaging: the damage depends on where the cuts are coming from—Spectator*, 1993.

▶**b** In passive constructions: *Even the dentist was paid for—New Yorker*, 1987.

▶**c** In short sentences with a *to*-infinitive or verbal noun: *There are a couple of things I want to talk to you about—*F. Knebel, 1972 | *Hand-turned treen are a joy to look at—Daily Telegraph*, 1980.

3 **CONCLUSION**. In many cases, especially in more formal writing, it is preferable to avoid placing a preposition at the end of a sentence where it might look stranded. In many other cases, and in conversational English generally, it is impossible to contrive the sentence in such a way as to avoid a final preposition without producing awkwardness or unnaturalness, and it is inadvisable to try.

prerequisite see PERQUISITE.

presage. The noun is pronounced **pres**-ij, with the stress on the first syllable, and means 'a portent or presentiment'. The verb can be pronounced the same or as pri-**sayj**, with the stress on the second syllable, and means 'portend' or 'give a warning of'.

prescience, prescient. The usual pronunciations are **pres**-

i-əns and **pres**-i-ənt, with the first and second syllables both short.

prescribe, proscribe. A single letter distinguishes two words of very different meaning. A *prescribed* book (for example) is one that is chosen for a course of study, whereas a *proscribed* book is one that is forbidden or banned. *Prescribe* also has an important meaning used in medicine and more widely: 'to recommend or provide (a remedy or course of action)': *He prescribed a change of air and a long rest.*

prescriptive. The term is fairly recent (1930s) with reference to language, and denotes a concept of grammar as laying down (or 'prescribing') rules rather than observing and describing the language in use (this latter concept being called *descriptive*).

present is pronounced with the stress on the first syllable as a noun, and with the stress on the second syllable as a verb.

presenter see ANNOUNCER.

presently. There are two meanings which serve well to illustrate the interactions of British and American English. The older meaning 'at the present time, now' dates from the 15c, is still the dominant meaning in AmE, but has been largely overtaken in BrE by the second sense 'in a while, soon'. These two meanings are shown by the examples that follow: *Dr Otto von Habsburg abandoned claims to the monarchy in 1961 . . . and is presently a member of the European Parliament—Times*, 1989 | *Her feet hurt and she was thirsty. Presently she set off to walk back to her lodgings—Hilary Mantel*, 1986. In recent usage, the older meaning has started to reappear more sig-

nificantly in BrE, doubtless under continued American influence. Although this use is often criticized, it has excellent historical credentials and the context usually makes the choice of meaning clear. See also MOMENTARILY.

present tense. The natural and most frequent use of the present tense is in contexts of present time, whether actual (*The door is open*) or habitual (*The door is always open* | *Paris is the capital of France*). It is also used of past events in certain contexts, such as newspaper headlines (*Clinton says he is sorry*) and in narrative (see HISTORIC PRESENT).

prestige. 1 The word originally meant 'illusion, conjuring trick' and hence 'deception', and acquired its current favourable meaning 'reputation derived from status or achievements' in the 19c, the link being the element of magic common to both meanings. It is still pronounced pres-**teezh** in an only partly naturalized way; the *OED* (1909) recorded an anglicized form (**pres**-tij) but this has not survived.

2 *Prestige* occurs frequently in attributive position (i.e. before another noun) in such combinations as *prestige car*, *prestige suite* (in a hotel), *prestige location*, etc., to denote something of superior quality, especially in the jargon of advertising.

prestigious. This older meaning 'deceptive, illusory', relating to the older sense of PRESTIGE, has given way to its current meaning 'having a great reputation or influence' to the extent that the earlier use has been largely forgotten. The newer meaning is first recorded in a novel by Joseph Conrad: *'You have had all these im-*

mense sums . . . What have I had out of them?' It was perfectly true. He had had nothing out of them—nothing of the prestigious or the desirable things of the earth—Chance, 1913.

presume see ASSUME.

presumptuous. The form *presumptious*, though formerly (15c–19c) valid, is now erroneous.

pretence. The usual AmE spelling is *pretense*.

pretty. 1 *Pretty* is used as an adverb with the meaning 'fairly, moderately', as in *The performance was pretty good | He did pretty much as he liked*. The adverb corresponding to the usual meaning of *pretty* is *prettily*: *She always dresses so prettily*.

2 It is also used ironically (i.e. with a meaning opposite to the normal) as an adjective in such uses as *A pretty mess you have made of it* and *Things have come to a pretty pass*.

prevaricate, procrastinate. Because their meanings, or at least the implications of their meanings, overlap, these two words are often confused. To *prevaricate* (derived from Latin *praevaricari* meaning literally 'to walk crookedly') is 'to speak or act evasively', whereas to *procrastinate* (derived from Latin *cras* meaning 'tomorrow') is 'to put off or delay'. You might *prevaricate* in order to *procrastinate*, but the senses should be carefully distinguished. Examples: *She prevaricated, wanting the story verified or denied before sharing it with him*—L. Grant-Adamson, 1989 | *Coleridge never arrived, and early in January the now beleaguered Southey decided that his endlessly procrastinat-*

ing friend must be brought back from London—T. Mayberry, 1992.

prevent. When *prevent* is followed by an object + verbal noun, the usual construction now is (for example) *prevent him going* or *prevent him from going*, rather than *prevent his going*, which (though considered formally more correct by some) is falling out of use. Examples of each type: *Two women climb up the iron bars, which are meant to prevent people or animals falling under the tram*—J. Berger, 1972 | *Cushla was only just quick enough to grab Colin's arms to prevent him from belting Restel across the head*—N. Virtue, 1990 | *His shoes were locked up to prevent his running away*—Penelope Fitzgerald, 1986. When *prevent* is used in the passive, the construction with *from* is the normal option: *Tanks are being prevented from entering the center of the city*—New Yorker, 1989.

preventable is the preferred spelling, not *-ible*. See -ABLE, -IBLE.

preventive, preventative. Both words are in use as adjectives meaning 'serving to prevent', especially in medicine, and also as nouns denoting a substance or procedure that does this. *Preventive* is the commoner by a long way, understandably in view of its more comfortable form: *Preventive medicine may be more effective if problem-based learning programmes are established in place of the traditional methods of education*—Physiotherapy, 1990 | *Ask about . . . ivermectin—the heartworm disease preventive you give your dog once a month*—Outdoor Life, 1990 (US). When *preventative* occurs it is more usually in generalized contexts qualifying words such as *action* and *measure* rather than (for example) *medicine: When we hear talk of a 'preventative strike' we must translate that term into what it really means: a surprise attack*—V. Mollenkott, 1987 (US).

priest. In its Christian context a *priest* is an ordained minister of the Roman Catholic or Orthodox Church, or of the Anglican Church (above a deacon and below a bishop), authorized to perform certain rites and administer certain sacraments. Women who are ordained ministers of the Anglican Church are also called *priests*. The term *priestess* is used only of a female priest in non-Christian religions.

prima donna, meaning 'chief female singer' of a company or 'a temperamentally self-important person', has the plural form *prima donnas*.

prima facie, meaning 'based on a first impression' (as in *prima facie evidence*), is usually pronounced **priy**-mə **fay**-shi in BrE, although there are several alternative forms in AmE.

primarily. In BrE, under American influence, the stress is increasingly heard on the second syllable, rather than (more awkwardly) on the first.

primeval is now the dominant spelling, not *primaeval*.

principal, principle. The spellings are occasionally confused even by the wariest users of English. (The usual mistake is to use *principle* for the adjective *principal*.) *Principal* is an adjective and noun and essentially means 'chief' (*my principal objection | Meet the principal of my college*), whereas *principle* is a noun only and means 'a fundamental law or

truth' (*Is there a principle behind your argument?*) or (in the plural) 'rules of conduct' (*They seem to have no moral principles*).

prioritize, meaning 'to establish priorities for (a list of items)', is first recorded in 1968, and is often cited as an example of unwelcome verb formations in *-ize*. It is nonetheless a generally useful word, despite its associations with the world of business and management jargon: *Government resources have been constantly diminished by the need to prioritize defence*—The State of Prisons, 1991 | *Butlins offered a comfortable exoticism, prioritizing pleasure for all*—S. Ewen et al., 1991.

prior to is an alternative for *before* that is normally appropriate only in formal contexts, where it conveys the extra meaning 'as a necessary preliminary to': *Candidates must deposit security prior to the ballot*. In general use it is often pretentious and unnecessary.

prise, meaning 'to remove or open gently or with difficulty', is the normal form in BrE, but in AmE *pry* (a 19c shortening) and *prize* (probably arising from confusion with the third-person form *pries*) are more often found: *The hoard of money was prised out of Blue Rabbit and hidden at the back of his football-boot locker*—Joanna Trollope, 1990 | *The girl pried the lid from the showbox*—Tom Drury, 1992 (US).

pristine. 1 The usual pronunciation now is **pris**-teen, although the stress varies between the two syllables (and is often placed on the second in AmE).

2 The primary meaning of *pristine* is that present in Latin *pristi-*

nus which meant 'ancient, original' in a favourable sense: *The translators . . . have happily preserved for us the pristine simplicity of our Saxon-English*—Disraeli, 1841. It is a short step from the notion of 'in its original newness' to 'new as if original' and hence simply 'pure or clean as new', the meaning acquired by the word in the 20c. Although objected to by language purists, the developed meaning is well established alongside the original meaning: *Thinking of the sour blackened brick of the place (scoured clean to a pristine rust once more)*—Penelope Lively, 1991 | *The living room was as pristine as I'd ever seen it*—F. Cooper, 1993.

privacy. In BrE, the pronunciation **priv**-ə-si, with a short first syllable, has largely replaced **priy**-və-si, although the second is still heard and is the usual one in AmE and in other parts of the English-speaking world.

privation see DEPRIVATION.

privilege. Note the spelling with two *i*s, not *privelege*.

prize see PRISE.

proactive is a vogue word, formed on the analogy of *reactive*, that came into prominence in the 1970s, and is used to mean 'creating or controlling a situation by taking the initiative', usually in the context of business administration: *a new kind of management able to take risks, . . . manage change, and be more proactive*—*Financial Times*, 1984. The back-formation (or parallel formation, perhaps) *pro-act* may raise eyebrows: *This versatility is allowing us to proact rather than react to changing market conditions*—*Industry Week*, 1986.

probe *noun*. The meaning that has come to the fore in the 20c, especially in the language of newspapers, is the one given first in the 1995 edition of the *Concise Oxford Dictionary*, i.e. 'a penetrating investigation'. Its appeal to journalists lies largely in its brevity and consequent suitability for use in headlines. In older editions of the *Concise Oxford*, which listed meanings in historical or logical order rather than in order of current frequency, the first meaning given was 'a blunt-edged surgical instrument used for exploring wounds etc.', and from this developed the use with reference to devices used in space exploration.

problematic, problematical. Both forms are used in BrE and AmE with no discernible difference in meaning, but *problematic* is slightly commoner.

proceed see PRECEDE. Note that *procedure* is spelt with only one *e* in its second syllable.

process. The familiar noun and verb are both pronounced **proh**-ses. The other verb *process*, meaning 'to walk in procession', is a back-formation from the noun *procession* and is pronounced proh-**ses**.

pro-choice see PRO-LIFE.

procrastinate see PREVARICATE.

produce is pronounced with the stress on the second syllable as a verb, and with the stress on the first syllable (**prod**-yoos) as a noun (meaning 'goods produced, especially in agriculture').

proffer, meaning 'to offer (a gift or service)', has inflected forms *proffered, proffering*.

program, programme. The standard spelling in BrE, except in computer language, is *programme*, and in AmE it is *program*. In the context of computing, *program* is used in both AmE and BrE, and as a verb has inflected forms *programmed, programming* in BrE (with the variants *programed, programing* also available in AmE). Historically, the spelling *program* is better established in BrE, but it was replaced in the 19c by the French form *programme*, which however did not establish itself in the US.

progress. In BrE the noun is pronounced with the stress on the first syllable, and the verb (= make progress) with the stress on the second syllable. In the transitive meaning 'to cause (work etc.) to make progress', however, the word is usually pronounced with the stress pattern of the noun. In AmE the stresses are normally the same, but the word is pronounced with a shorter first syllable, prog- rather than prohg-.

progressive tenses see CONTINUOUS TENSES.

prohibit. In current usage, *prohibit* can be followed either by a noun or pronoun denoting the thing prohibited (*The law prohibits the export of livestock without a licence*) or by a noun or pronoun denoting the person prohibited, followed by *from* + verbal noun (*A new law will prohibit you from exporting livestock . . .*). It is no longer possible to use a *to*-infinitive (as it is with *forbid*): ☒ *A new law will prohibit you to export livestock . . . .*

project. In BrE the normal pattern is **proj**-ekt with the stress on the first syllable for the noun, and prə-**jekt** with the stress on

the second syllable for the verb. In other English-speaking countries (though not in AmE) a pronunciation with long first syllable (proh-) is also found.

pro-life, pro-choice are used as adjectives, primarily in AmE but increasingly in BrE, to denote respectively those who are opposed to the practice of abortion and those who think mothers should be left to make a choice in the matter. The terms are also applied in other areas of medical practice involving matters of life and death, such as sustaining life-support systems for those who are severely handicapped or unlikely to make a recovery.

prolific is derived from the Latin word *proles* meaning 'offspring', and is properly applied to someone or something that produces either offspring or something compared to offspring such as writings, works of art, etc. Like many adjectives in English (e.g. *generous, thoughtful*), it is often transferred from the producer to the thing produced (e.g. *a prolific output* as well as *a prolific writer*), and objections to this use that are sometimes made are hard to justify, although alternatives such as *abundant* and *numerous* are available to those who are inclined to be cautious in such matters: *McGonagall . . . had just had his prolific collection of bizarre poems translated into Russian, Chinese, Japanese and . . . Thai—Times, 1977.*

promiscuous. The sense relating to sexual behaviour is now so dominant that we need to be reminded of an older meaning 'casual, random' in more general contexts that is found in Dickens and other literary contexts: *I*

*walked in . . . just to say good mor-
nin', and went, in a promiscuous
manner, up-stairs, and into the back
room*—Pickwick Papers, 1837.

prone. 1 for *prone to* see APT.

2 In its meaning 'lying face
down', *prone* contrasts with *supine*, which means 'lying face up'.

pronounceable is spelt with an
e in the middle.

pronouns. 1 A pronoun is a
word used to refer to (and instead
of) a noun or noun phrase that
has already been mentioned or is
known, especially in order to
avoid repetition, e.g. *We invited the
Jones family to our party because we
like* **them** and *When Jane saw what
had happened* **she** *laughed*. Pronouns include the familiar forms
I, we, he, she, it, they, you (plus their
object forms *me, us, him, her, it,
them, you*); the possessive pronouns (also now called possessive
adjectives or possessive determiners) *my, your, his, her, its, our,
their* (and the group *mine, yours,
his, hers, its, ours, theirs*, which are
normally used predicatively, i.e.
after a verb as in *The responsibility
is ours*); the reflexive pronouns
myself, yourself, etc.; the demonstrative pronouns *this, that, these,
those*, the relative pronouns *that,
which, who, whom, whose*; the interrogative pronouns *what, which,
who, whom, whose*; the indefinite
pronouns *all, any, both, each, either,
none, one, everybody, everyone, nobody, no one, somebody, someone*;
and the so-called 'extended' pronouns *whatever, whichever, whoever,
whosoever, each other, one another*.

2 When a pronoun refers back
to a person or thing previously
named, it is important that the
gap is not so large that the
reader (or hearer) might have difficulty relating the two, and that

ambiguity is avoided when more
than one person might be the
antecedent, as in the following
exchange in a play (where the
ambiguity is deliberate): *Septimus:
Geometry, Hobbes assures us in the
Leviathan, is the only science God
has been pleased to bestow on mankind. Lady Croom: And what does he
mean by it? Septimus: Mr Hobbes or
God?*—Tom Stoppard, 1993.

pronunciation. 1 Note that the
correct spelling of this word is
pronunciation, not *pronounciation*,
and it is pronounced accordingly.

2 The British pronunciations
given in this book follow the
so-called 'received standard' based
on the forms used by educated
speakers in southern England, although it is recognized that
other forms of pronunciation are
equally valid. American pronunciations, when given, follow the
pattern identified as 'General
American', i.e. 'the range of
United States accents that have
neither an eastern nor a southern
colouring' (J. C. Wells, *Accents of
English* (1982) Vol. I, p.10).

3 For disputed or controversial
aspects of pronunciation (many
to do with the placing of the
main stress), see the entries at
APARTHEID, CONTRIBUTE, CENTRIFU-
GAL, CONTROVERSY, DECADE, DESPIC-
ABLE, DISTRIBUTE, FOREHEAD,
FORMIDABLE, HARASS, KILOMETRE,
MUNICIPAL, PRIVACY, SUBSIDENCE.
See also ACCENT, NOUN AND VERB
DIFFERENCES.

4 Significant systematic
changes in pronunciation that
have occurred in the 20c include
(under AmE influence) the placing of the stress in adverbs ending in *-arily* on the *-ar-* instead of
earlier in the word (as in *necessarily, primarily*, etc.), the simplification of the final syllable of nouns

in -*ein* and -*ies* (e.g. *protein, rabies, scabies*) to a single sound (-een and -eez instead of -ee-in and -i-eez as formerly), and a change from **-ee**-i-ti to **-ay**-i-ti in words of the type *deity, homogeneity, spontaneity,* etc.

propaganda, meaning 'an organized programme of information in support of a cause or political policy', is not (despite its appearance) plural in origin but a singular noun taken from the modern Latin title *Congregatio de propaganda fide* 'congregation for propagating the faith' (originally a committee of Catholic cardinals), in which *propaganda* is a form of a verbal adjective. In current use, the sense is always derogatory.

propel has inflected forms *propelled, propelling.*

propellant, propellent. The noun *propellant*, meaning 'a thing that propels' (especially a rocket fuel or the agent in aerosol sprays), is the more familiar word. *Propellent* is an adjective meaning 'capable of driving or pushing forward'.

propeller is the only spelling in BrE for the revolving set of blades on a ship or aeroplane; in AmE *propellor* is also used.

proper noun see NOUN.

proper terms.
See box opposite

prophecy, prophesy. *Prophecy*, pronounced **prof**i-si, is the noun, and *prophesy*, pronounced **prof**-i-siy, is the verb.

proportional, proportionate. Both words mean 'in due proportion, comparable', and are used almost interchangeably, except in certain fixed expressions such as *proportional parts* and *proportional representation*. Otherwise, when *proportional* occurs it tends to be in more formal and technical contexts: *By 1979 all the beds and hospital places, which were provided up to the prescribed national levels proportional to the catchment population, had been opened*—D. Tomlinson, 1991 | *Clinton needed 270 electoral votes from among the 50 states to secure victory—each state carries a number of votes proportionate to its population*—*Today*, 1992.

proposition. 1 The noun *proposition* has various well-established meanings arising from its basic sense of 'something proposed', e.g. a scheme or proposal, a statement in logic that is subject to proof or disproof, and a formal statement of a theorem or problem in mathematics. A more generalized meaning, 'an enterprise or undertaking', was regarded by Fowler (1926) as an intrusive Americanism which he wanted to see abandoned in favour of alternatives such as proposal, task, undertaking, enterprise, etc. Clearly this advice has not been heeded, and it would be difficult to sustain such an objection now in the face of the overwhelming evidence of usage. Note that *proposition* is normally used with reference to the viability or likely success of the thing in question: *'Call this a store?' he would say. 'Call this a paying proposition?'*—A. Tyler, 1980 | *Tinkering with the possibilities becomes an enticing proposition*—D. Shekerjian, 1990.

2 The use of *proposition* as a verb arose in America in the 1920s in two main meanings: (1) to present (someone) with a proposition, and (2) to request sexual favours from. The second meaning is now usually the one that comes first to mind: *In Hyde Park,*

485

proper terms

This is the technical name for terms denoting groups of animals and birds, such as *flight* (of swallows) and *pride* (of lions), and occasionally people. Some, such as *herd*, have more general application (e.g. to cows, sheep, and elephants), while others are peculiar to one context and are largely fanciful inventions that have been passed from one antiquarian writer to another without any real authority in usage (e.g. a *siege* of herons and a *knob* of waterfowl). The table below lists these in alphabetical order of the animal or bird concerned. Those marked with an asterisk (*) are recorded in special lists of proper terms that were popular in the 15c, notably the *Book of St Albans* attributed to Juliana Barnes (1486).

ITEM	TERM
apes	shrewdness
asses	herd *or* *pace
badgers	*cete
bears	*sloth *or* *sleuth
bees	hive, swarm, drift, *or* bike
birds	flock *or* flight
boar	sounder
boys	blush
buffalo	herd *or* gang
cats	*clowder *or* *glaring
cattle	herd *or* drove
chickens	brood *or* *peep
colts	*rag *or* *rake
cooks	*hastiness
coots	*covert
cranes	herd
curlew	herd
deer	herd *or* mob
dogs	pack *or* kennel
doves	flight, *dole, *or* *piteousness
ducks	(on water) raft, bunch, *or* paddling; (in flight) team
elephants	herd
elk	herd *or* (AmE) gang
ferrets	*business
finches	charm *or* *chirm
fish	shoal
flies	cloud
foresters	*stalk
foxes	*skulk
geese	gaggle *or* (in the air) skein, team, *or* wedge
giraffes	herd

▶

► proper terms
continued

ITEM	TERM
goats	flock, herd, *or* (dialect) trip
grouse	pack *or* covey
hares	*husk *or* *down
hawks	cast
hermits	*observance
herons	*siege
horses	team; (breeding) stud *or* *haras
hounds	kennel, pack, cry, *or* *mute
insects	flight *or* swarm
kangaroos	mob *or* troop
kittens	kindle
ladies	bevy
lapwing	*desert
larks	*exaltation *or* bevy
leopards	*leap
lions	pride
magpies	*tiding
mallard	*sord *or* *sute (= suit)
martens	*richesse
merchants	*faith
moles	*labour
monkeys	troop
mules	*barren
nightingales	*watch
nuns	*superfluity
partridges	covey
peacocks	*muster
pedlars	malapertness (= impertinence)
penguins	rookery
pheasants	head *or* (dialect) nye
pigeons	kit (flying together)
pigs	herd
plovers	stand, wing, *or* *congregation
porpoises	herd, pod, *or* school
prisoners	*pity
pups	litter
quail	bevy *or* drift
racehorses	string
ravens	*unkindness
roes	bevy
rooks	parliament *or* *building
seals	herd *or* rockery; pod (= small herd)

►

▶ **proper terms**
continued

ITEM	TERM
sheep	flock *or* herd; (dialect) drift *or* trip
sheldrake	*dropping
snipe	wisp *or* *walk
sparrows	*host
starlings	*murmuration
swallows	flight
swans	game *or* herd; wedge (in the air)
swine	herd; *sounder (tame), *drift (wild)
waterfowl	bunch *or* knob
whales	school, herd, *or* gam; pod (= small school)
widgeon	company *or* trip
wildfowl	bunch, trip, *or* plump; knob (less than 30)
wolves	pack *or* *rout
women	gaggle (derisive)
woodcock	*fall
wrens	herd

---

that black whore had propositioned him as he walked from work toward the Tube—New Yorker, 1975.

proprietor is the standard spelling, not *-er*.

proscribe SEE PRESCRIBE.

prosecutor, a person who prosecutes, especially in a criminal court, is spelt *-or*, not *-er*.

prospect is pronounced with the stress on the first syllable as a noun, and with the stress on the second syllable as a verb (as in *prospecting* for gold, etc.).

prospectus. The plural form is *prospectuses*. The form *prospecti* is not only pedantic but ignorantly pedantic, since in Latin *prospectus* is a fourth-declension noun with a plural form *prospectus* (which is not used in English).

prostate, prostrate. The *prostate* (or *prostate gland*) is a gland surrounding the neck of the bladder in male animals. *Prostrate* is an adjective and verb: the adjective is pronounced with the stress on the first syllable and means 'lying horizontally', especially in the figurative sense of being overcome by grief or some other strong feeling, and the verb is pronounced with the stress on the second syllable and means 'to throw (oneself) on the ground in submission'.

protagonist. 1 This is a good example of what Fowler (1926) called a 'popularized technicality', i.e. a term used in a special domain (in this case, ancient Greek drama) and extended into general use with consequent (and controversial) shifts in meaning. In its literary use, *protagonist* meant 'first actor', i.e. the chief character in a play (often also the name by which the play is known, as with Sophocles' *Oedipus*

Rex and Euripides' *Orestes*). The *protagonist* was accompanied by a *deuteragonist* and sometimes by a *tritagonist*, representing dramatic roles of second and third importance.

2 One consequence of all this for the use of *protagonist* in English is that there is strictly only one *protagonist* in any given situation. Another is that to speak of a *chief protagonist* or *leading protagonist* is tautological, since a protagonist is by definition the leading personage. The second point is cogent, but the first has little validity outside the context of ancient drama, beyond which the word had already progressed by the 19c: *If social equity is not a chimera, Marie Antoinette was the protagonist of the most . . . execrable of causes*—J. Morley, 1877. The objection sometimes heard, that only one person can truly be 'first', belongs to the realm of philosophy, not language. We may therefore refer to the *protagonists*, the chief characters in a piece of literary fiction or the leading figures in various walks of life, as well as to the *protagonist*: *The two protagonists, the cuckoo and the nightingale, present a series of antithetical statements about the power of love, in which the cuckoo finally gains the edge*—Dictionary of National Biography, 1993 | *Many commentators believe that the superpower divide has its source in ideology, thus making impossible any long-term co-operation or peace between the protagonists*—S. Smith et al., 1991.

3 A further development in meaning represents a more serious departure from the word's origins, and is illustrated by this example: *There is a tendency of protagonists of the computational theory of mind to boast that they are restoring the Aristotelian emphasis on cognition and thought*—R. Tallis et al., 1991. Here, *protagonist* (perhaps influenced by the coincidence of the word's form with the common prefix *pro-*) has come to mean 'advocate or proponent' rather than 'leading figure' (one may involve the other, but we are concerned here with meaning and not implication). In this meaning, alternatives such as *advocate*, *proponent*, or *supporter* are normally preferable, although it is true that they do not convey quite the same sense of innovation and personal involvement. Whatever warnings are uttered now, the new meaning, given its genuine overlap with the older one, will undoubtedly become dominant in the end. For now, however, the advice must be one of caution.

protean, meaning 'able to change form, versatile' (after the ancient mythical figure Proteus), is normally pronounced with the stress on the first syllable, and is spelt with a small initial *p*.

protector is spelt *-or*, not *-er*.

protégé meaning 'a person under the patronage or tutelage of another', should be printed with the two accents in place.

protest. 1 The noun is pronounced with the stress on the first syllable, and the verb with the stress on the second syllable.

2 *Anatoly Koryagin, who has been imprisoned for protesting the use of psychiatry for political purposes*—New Yorker, 1987. This transitive use of the verb, with the object of the protest as the grammatical object, is a 20c development that is widely accepted in AmE but has not yet become established in

BrE, although it is beginning to appear: *The ruin of Belfast's Black Mountain protested by the local community—Independent*, 1991.

protester is spelt -*er*, not -*or*.

protractor, the instrument used in geometry, is spelt -*or*, not -*er*.

provable is spelt without an *e* in the middle.

proved, proven. The two forms relate to two different verbs derived from Old French *prover* (ultimately from Latin *probare*). In standard BrE, *proved* is the normal past tense and past participle of the verb *prove* (*They proved their point | Their point was proved*). *Proven* survived as a past participle in dialect use and is current in the Scottish legal term *not proven* (usually pronounced **prohv**ən) and occasionally in general use in Britain generally (pronounced **proo**-vən), especially in attributive position (i.e. before a noun): *His love of precise dates and proven facts*—N. Shakespeare, 1989. In AmE, *proven* is at least as common as *proved* both as a past tense and as a past participle.

provenance, provenience. *Provenance* (pronounced with the stress on the first syllable) is the BrE word, and *provenience* (pronounced pro-**vee**-ni-əns) its AmE equivalent, meaning 'place of origin of a manuscript, work of art, etc.' and in more general applications.

provided that, providing that. The form *provided* is often preferred, and *that* may be omitted in both cases: *In summer he will show visitors around the chapel provided he likes their faces and they are not wearing shorts—Linguist*, 1992 | *It works well enough providing*

I keep my blanket around me—Jeanette Winterson, 1987.

proviso has the plural form *provisos*.

prox. is an abbreviation of Latin *proximo* (*mense*) meaning 'of the following month' and is still used occasionally in more formal commercial correspondence following a day (e.g. *the 7th prox.*) to denote a date in the month following.

prudent, prudential, prudish. While *prudent* is a judgemental word meaning 'circumspect, judicious', *prudential* is merely descriptive in identifying actions and attitudes that have to do with prudence, e.g. *prudential motives* are motives determined by considerations of prudence. To complete the picture, *prudish* is an entirely distinct word and means 'affecting extreme modesty or propriety in sexual matters'.

pry see PRISE.

PS is an abbreviation of *postscript* and is used to add an additional point at the end of a letter, after the signature. Further additions are preceded by *PPS*, *PPPS*, and so on, although no one normally writes more than two except in jest.

pseudonym see NOM DE PLUME.

psychic, psychical. Although *psychical* is the older word (attested in 1642 in the *OED*), *psychic* (1836) is now more common and has a wider range of meaning, most notably 'connected with or having occult powers'. In more neutral senses to do with the mind or the soul, *psychical* is sometimes used to avoid these occult associations, e.g. in the expression *psychical research*.

psychosis has the plural form *psychoses*.

ptomaine, denoting a kind of compound formerly associated with food poisoning, is pronounced **toh**-mayn, with the initial *p* silent.

publicly is the correct form of the adverb from *public*, not *publically*.

pucka see PUKKA.

pucker, meaning 'to gather into folds', has inflected forms *puckered*, *puckering*. See also PUKKA.

pudenda, pudendum. Both forms are used to refer to the female genitals; the first is plural and the second singular in construction.

puisne is pronounced like *puny* and is derived from French *puis né* meaning 'born afterwards', hence 'inferior'. A *puisne judge* is a judge of a superior court inferior in rank to chief justices.

pukka, meaning 'genuine', is derived from a Hindi word *pakkā* meaning 'ripe, substantial'. This spelling is preferred to *pucka*.

pulley. The noun has the plural form *pulleys*, and the verb (meaning 'to work with a pulley') has inflected forms *pulleys*, *pulleyed*, *pulleying*.

pun. Punning, 'the humorous use of words to suggest different meanings', has been a feature of language at least since the time of Aristotle, who approved of them in some kinds of writing. Some famous historical examples include the description by Pope Gregory I (6c) of English slaves as *Non Angli, sed angeli* ('not Angles, but angels') and, from a much later date (1843) the reputed message of Sir Charles Napier to the British War Office reporting his conquest of the Indian province of Sind with the single Latin word *Peccavi* ('I have sinned'). About 3,000 puns occur in the works of Shakespeare, among them Mercutio's dying words in *Romeo and Juliet* (III.i.98; modernized spelling): *Ask for me tomorrow, and you shall find me a grave man*. An intentionally dreadful pun can be found in a mock epitaph of Byron, dated 1807, for John Adams, a carrier of Southwell, who died of drunkenness: *For the liquor he drank, being too much for one, He could not carry off,—so he's now carri-on*. In modern usage, puns occur frequently in casual conversation and are much loved by writers of newspaper headlines: see JOURNALESE.

punctuation see the individual entries for APOSTROPHE, BRACKETS, COLON, COMMA, DASH, EXCLAMATION MARK, FULL STOP, HYPHEN, QUESTION MARK, QUOTATION MARKS, SEMICOLON.

pundit is a general term meaning 'a learned expert or teacher' (often slightly disparaging in tone and giving way to *guru* in more favourable contexts), but *Pandit* is the form used when prefixed to the name of a learned Hindu (e.g. *Pandit Nehru*). Both forms are derived from a Sanskrit word meaning 'a learned man'.

punter. *Our choice of venue is usually the Mermaid Restaurant, where punters can dine al fresco at white plastic tables, rain or shine, in season or out—Daily Telegraph*, 1992. This meaning of *punter*, 'a customer or client', developed in the 1960s from an older meaning 'a gambler; a backer of horses', i.e. a customer of a bookmaker, by way of several underworld slang meanings including 'an accomplice in a crime', 'a victim of a swindle', and then 'a client of a prostitute'. In the 1980s it became a more salubrious vogue word, and it is still going strong, having attained enough respectability to be used in more highbrow contexts: *For the punters, it may not be all bad: alternative bookings* [at Covent Garden] *could include leading foreign dance and opera companies—BBC Music Magazine*, 1999. The older meanings continue to be used, as do two other words having the form *punter*: 'someone who propels a punt on a river' and 'someone who punts a football'.

purchase, both as a noun and as a verb, is a formal word not normally used in general contexts (especially conversation). By contrast *buy* as a noun is somewhat informal (*a good buy*), and so English lacks a word of neutral register for the meaning 'the act of buying' or 'something bought', and has to resort either to rephrasing or to circumlocutions such as *acquisition* or *investment*.

purée, meaning 'a smooth cream of fruit or vegetables', is spelt with two *e*s and with an accent on the first *e*.

purple has a derived form *purplish*, with no *e*.

purport. 1 The word is pronounced with the stress on the first syllable as a noun and with the stress on the second syllable as a verb.

2 The verb's most common construction in current English is with a *to*-infinitive, as in *He had seen 'what purported to be a saucer phenomenon'*—R. Ferguson, 1991 | *Almost all the conditions and diseases that over-the-counter drugs of the past century were purported to relieve are still prevalent today— Addictive Diseases*, 1977 | *The Family Court of Australia held in contempt a layman who falsely purported to be a lawyer*—D. Pannick, 1992. The use of *purport* followed by a *that*-clause, though recorded in the *OED*, has been largely superseded by a construction with an intervening verb, of the type *purport to show* (or *confirm*) *that*: *She accepts without question research which purported to show that most women despised each other*—M. Whitford et al., 1989.

3 In the 1977 example above, *purport* is used in the passive, and in the 1992 example it is used with a person as the subject. Both these uses were frowned on by Fowler (1926), who regarded *suppose* (. . . *were supposed to relieve* . . .) as a more suitable choice in the first case and *claim* (. . . *falsely claimed to be* . . .) in the second; in other cases *allege* and *profess* are also possible. Despite Fowler's objections, these uses have become established and cause little adverse comment today.

purposely, purposefully. *Purposely* is the older word (15c) and means 'on purpose, intentionally' (*Lindsey straightened her shoulders, purposely avoiding his gaze—*). Evans, 1993), whereas the more recent word *purposefully* (19c) corresponds to the adjective *purposeful* and means 'with a strong purpose, resolutely': *Beatrix was carrying a wicker basket over one* *arm and as he watched she set off purposefully down the drive*—D. Simpson, 1987. A third word, *purposively* (20c), means 'for a particular purpose', and is more usual in technical contexts: *Socialism . . . would have to be built by active human beings working purposively and creatively*—J. Dignan et al., 1992. Occasionally *purposively* is used when *purposefully* is probably meant: *'Gerrart-of-it!' said the larger of the two, moving purposively towards me*—Will Self, 1993.

purveyor, meaning 'a supplier' (normally in commercial contexts), is spelt *-or*, not *purveyer*.

put, putt. *Put* (pronounced like the verb) is used in athletics (*shot-put*), whereas *putt* (pronounced like *gut*) is the term used in golf.

putrefy, meaning 'to go rotten', is spelt *-efy*, not *putrify*.

pygmy is derived from a Greek word *pygmē* meaning 'the length of the forearm' and largely for this reason the spelling with *y* is preferable to the form *pigmy*.

pyjamas is the standard spelling in BrE, but in AmE it is *pajamas*. It is a plural noun in ordinary use (*Where are my pyjamas?*), but takes a singular form when used attributively (i.e. before a noun, as in *pyjama jacket* and *pyjama suit*).

pyramidal, meaning 'having the form of a pyramid', is pronounced with the stress on the second syllable.

pyrrhic, used of a victory won at too great cost to be of use to the victor, is named after Pyrrhus, the king of Epirus who defeated a Roman army at Asculum in 279 BC but sustained heavy losses and was unable to exploit his success.

Qq

qua, pronounced kway or kwah, is a somewhat formal word, with the air of philosophy and logic about it, derived from the Latin relative pronoun *qui*, and is used in English with the meaning 'considered as' or 'in the capacity of' when a person or thing can be regarded in different ways or from different aspects, normally in the sequence 'A qua B' where B defines A more closely: *Dressed in an Armani suit . . . and espadrilles, he plays a cop qua existential hero—Literary Review,* 1989. In practice *qua* is used more flexibly, for example in the form 'A qua A' (with the same noun repeated) and in sentences lacking the first noun altogether, as the following 20c examples show: *Look at the sky . . . What is there so extraordinary about it? Qua sky*—Samuel Beckett, 1956 | *I don't think that 'Hard Times' is a particularly good novel qua novel, whatever it may be as a social document*—Broadcast, 1977.

quadrennium, meaning 'a period of four years', has the plural form *quadrenniums*. The Latin word from which it is derived is *quadriennium*, but the first *i* has been lost under the influence of other words of this type such as *decennium* and *millennium*.

qualm, meaning 'a misgiving or uneasy doubt', is pronounced kwahm, not any longer kwawm.

quantum leap, and the older form *quantum jump*, meaning 'a sudden large increase', are one of the more striking examples of 20c POPULARIZED TECHNICALITIES.

quarrel. The verb has inflected forms *quarrelled, quarrelling* in BrE, and usually *quarreled, quarreling* in AmE.

quarter. 1 Practice varies in the hyphenation of *quarter* in compounds, and the following forms are recommended: *quarter day, quarterdeck, quarter-final, quarter-hour* (but *a quarter of an hour*), *quarter-light, quartermaster, quarter sessions.*

2 The BrE designation of time as *a quarter to ten* is normally expressed in AmE as *a quarter of ten*, and BrE *a quarter past ten* in AmE as *a quarter after ten*.

3 The word *of* is optional in expressions of the type *for a quarter (of) the price*.

4 The inflected forms of the verb are *quartered, quartering*.

quarto has the plural form *quartos*.

quasi- is used in combination with a following noun to denote things that are seemingly or only partly entitled to the name, e.g. *a quasi-conjunction, quasi-independent*. The recommended pronunciation is **kway**-ziy rather than **kwah**-zi.

quatercentenary, pronounced kwat-, means 'a four-hundredth anniversary' and is derived from the Latin word *quater* meaning 'four times'. It is a common error to treat the word as if it began with *quarter-*.

quattrocento, pronounced kwat-roh-**chen**-toh, denotes the style of Italian art of the 15c, i.e. 1400–99.

queer. The word was first used as an adjective and noun meaning 'homosexual' in the 1920s. Although it is still generally regarded as derogatory or offensive when used by heterosexual people, it has been adopted in recent years by homosexuals referring to themselves, especially in terms such as *queer-bashing* and *queer rights*. See GAY.

question see BEG THE QUESTION, INDIRECT QUESTION.

question mark. 1 The principal use of the question mark (?) is to indicate a direct question: *Are they leaving tomorrow? | What time is it?* It is also used when the question is put in the form of a statement: *They told you that? | Surely it's the same one? | I wonder if you can help me?* It should not be used in indirect questions in which the question is reported rather than expressed (*He asked what time it was*), but should be used in tag questions of the kind *She's much taller now, isn't she?*.

2 A question that makes a formal or polite request does not always have a question mark: *Would passengers on platform 2 please proceed to platform 5*.

3 A question mark is conventionally placed before a word about which there is some doubt, e.g. uncertain locations on maps and uncertain dates (*Thomas Tallis, ?1505–85*).

questionnaire is spelt with two *n*s and is normally pronounced with an initial syllable kwest- rather than kest-.

queue. The verb has inflected forms *queues, queued, queuing.*

quiet, quieten. As a verb, *quiet* has been used transitively (with an object) since the 16c in the meaning 'to make (someone or something) quiet', and is still in use in this sense: *The unexpectedness of this departure from the routine at first disquieted but then quieted us all*—M. Lindvall, 1991. Since the 18c, and especially in North America, it has also been used intransitively: *When I switched to opiates at least I quieted down*—New Yorker, 1992. The alternative verb *quieten* appeared (often with *down*) in the 19c in both transitive and intransitive uses; because *quiet* was available, it was regarded by Fowler (1926) as a 'superfluous word', but in more recent usage the stigma has mostly disappeared, leaving *quieten* now the more common choice than *quiet*: *The youth . . . revved the engine, then quietened it down to the soft ticking-over*—J. Wainwright, 1973 | *Arnica also helps to calm and quieten the upset child*—Health Shopper, 1990 | *Her travelling companions had quietened, as if someone in authority had arrived*—K. Newman, 1990.

quiet, quietness, quietude. The most commonly used of these nouns is *quiet*, which denotes a state of silence or tranquillity (*the quiet that precedes a storm | a period of peace and quiet*). *Quietness* is more the condition of being quiet as applied in a particular instance (*the quietness of a congregation at prayer*), and *quietude* is a literary alternative for *quietness* (*Their two and one-half acres retain a bucolic quietude*—Angeles (US), 1991).

quincentenary see ANNIVERSARIES.

quit has the past tense and past participle *quitted* or (especially in AmE) *quit*.

quite. 1 *Quite* is a highly mobile word with a wide range of uses qualifying adjectives and adverbs (*quite heavy* | *quite often*), singular nouns (*quite a lot*), and verbs (*We quite understand* | *I'd quite like to*). It causes difficulty because it has two branches of meaning which are not always distinguishable, especially in print which lacks the support of voice intonation. In idiomatic uses, the sense intended is not always clearly one or the other but varies on a scale between them. The two meanings are (1) the older 'stronger' meaning 'completely, entirely' (*You are a humourist . . . Quite a humourist*—Jane Austen, 1816), which remains the dominant sense in AmE but tends to be restricted to set expressions in BrE (e.g. *I quite agree*), and (2) the 'weaker' meaning 'rather, fairly' which emerged in the 19c and is now the dominant meaning in BrE (*The music was at times quite loud* | *We quite like what you have done*).

2 When *quite* qualifies adjectives and adverbs, there is a broad distinction in usage in that the weaker meaning normally occurs with so-called 'gradeable' adjectives (those that can be qualified by *more, very, somewhat,* etc.) such as *cheap, good, bad, heavy, interesting, large, small* (and where appropriate the corresponding adverbs *cheaply, well, badly, interestingly,* etc.), whereas the stronger meaning occurs with non-gradeable or 'absolute' adjectives that denote all-or-nothing concepts such as *different, enough, excellent, impossible* (and the adverbs *differently, enough, excellently, impossibly*). So *quite good* will normally mean 'fairly good' whereas *quite different* will normally mean 'entirely different'. However, this distinction is not watertight, and

examples can readily be found (especially with adverbs) which either leave the choice of meaning unclear or suggest a meaning somewhere between the two extremes (as more idiomatic uses often tend to): *I can get by quite happily in Navajo*—T. Allbeury, 1973 | *The actual writing style of agony columns has changed quite noticeably over the years*—P. Makins, 1975.

3 The use of *quite* with a verb is much more common in BrE than in AmE, and can have either the stronger meaning (*I quite agree* = I agree entirely | *We quite understand* = we understand completely) or the weaker meaning (*They'd quite like to come* = they'd rather like to come). The choice of meaning is entirely dependent on the type of verb being used.

4 When preceded by a negative (*not, never,* etc.), *quite* has the stronger meaning: *Jazzed up drinks aren't quite our style*—advertisement in *Country Life*, 1972 | *A bona fide kook who is never quite able to get in gear till he finally dies paddling his canoe across the Atlantic*—*Publishers Weekly*, 1973 | *Who hadn't quite made up their minds about what should be done with Hitler and Mussolini and the Nips*—*Islander* (Victoria, B.C.), 1973 | *We should not be quite so narrow-minded, blinkered and xenophobic about the rest of the world*—*Hansard*, 1992.

5 The combination *quite a* (or *an*) followed by a noun (without an adjective between) is an Americanism that has extended into BrE and can refer to quantity or quality (or both): *The Eiffel Tower . . . is quite a piece of Mecano: there are more than 18,000 structural components in the 985 ft high tower*—*Guardian*, 1972 | *Occasionally he collects quite a crowd as*

he sits there cross-legged and expounds his philosophy—Ruth Prawer Jhabvala, 1975. When an adjective or adverb comes between *quite a* (or *an*) and the noun, *quite* tends more towards the weaker meaning: *The death of Wyatt's father in 1818 left him quite a wealthy man*— Dictionary of National Biography, 1993. But compare the following, in which the order *a quite* + adjective (or adverb) suggests a stronger, more positive meaning: *The items are programmed in a quite interesting way*—Gramophone, 1977.

6 The use of *quite* as a reply expressing agreement or confirmation is a characteristic of BrE: *'No takers,' I said. 'Quite. By the way, I'm sorry to say "quite" all the time but . . . my work lies amongst Americans and they expect Englishmen to say it.'*—K. Bonfiglioli, 1976.

7 It is clearly better to regard *quite* as operating in the realm of idiom rather than of distinct word sense, and as drawing on a range of meaning that varies subtly between the extremes of the traditionally distinguished 'stronger' and 'weaker' meanings.

quota has the plural form *quotas*.

quotation marks. 1 The main use of quotation marks (also called *inverted commas*) is to indicate direct speech and quotations. In writing it is common to use double quotation marks (" "), and in printing practice varies between the double and single style ('). Single marks are commonly associated with British practice (as in the Oxford and Cambridge styles) and double marks with American practice (as in the Chicago style), but the distinction in usage is not always so clear-cut.

2 The main rules of practice in BrE follow, with indications of any variant practice in AmE:

▸**a** In direct speech and quotations, the closing quotation mark normally comes after a final full stop: *She said, 'I have something to ask you.'* It should come after any other punctuation mark (such as an exclamation mark) which is part of the matter being quoted: *They shouted, 'Watch out!'* (the final full stop is omitted after an exclamation mark in this position) | *Did I hear you say 'Go away!'?*.

▸**b** When the quoted speech is interrupted by a reporting verb such as *say, shout*, etc., the punctuation that divides the sentence is put inside the quotation marks: *'Go away,' he said, 'and don't ever come back.'*

▸**c** If a quoted word or phrase comes at the end of a sentence or coincides with a comma, the punctuation that belongs to the sentence as a whole is placed outside the quotation marks: *What is a 'gigabyte'?* | *No one should 'follow a multitude to do evil', as the Scripture says.* In AmE, however, it is usual to place quotation marks outside the sentence punctuation (and note the more characteristic double quotation marks): *No one should "follow a multitude to do evil," as the Scripture says.*

▸**d** When a quotation occurs within a quotation, the inner quotation is put in double quotations marks if the main quotation is in single marks (or vice versa, especially in American practice): BrE *'Have you any idea,' he asked, 'what a "gigabyte" is?'* | AmE *"Have you any idea," he asked, "what a 'gigabyte' is?".*

quote has a derived form *quotable*.

Qur'an is now a frequent spelling in English of KORAN.

q.v. is an abbreviation of the Latin phrase *quod vide* (= which see) and is used to indicate a reference incorporated into running text, e.g. *Events of the following year were dominated by the General Strike (q.v.).*

Rr

rabbit. The verb (= hunt rabbits or, usually as *rabbit on* = talk excessively) has inflected forms *rabbited*, *rabbiting*.

race. In its meaning relating to divisions of humankind, *race* is used imprecisely, and should be restricted to the major divisions characterized by distinct physical features. For other groupings, more appropriate alternatives are *nation*, *people*, and *community*.

racism, racialism. These two 20c words are used interchangeably in the meaning 'belief in the superiority of a particular race'; *racialism* is somewhat older, and is closer in form to *nationalism* (on which it was modelled), but in current usage *racism* is far more common.

rack in the phrase *rack and ruin* means 'destruction' and is normally spelt in this way in BrE, although it is originally a variant of the older form *wrack* (which is still sometimes used). *Rack* is one of nine nouns and seven verbs with this spelling, and has no historical connection with the more familiar forms, e.g. 'a framework for holding things'. The verb *rack* as used in *to rack one's brains* and *racked with guilt* is also sometimes spelt *wrack*.

radiator is spelt *-or*, not *-er*.

radio. The noun has the plural form *radios*, and the verb has inflected forms *radioes*, *radioed*, *radioing*.

radius. The recommended plural is *radii* (pronounced **ray**-di-iy), not *radiuses*.

rage. The word has been in use as a noun since the 14c, but it is perhaps a sign of the times that a special use has developed in the 1980s and 1990s relating to random violent behaviour by frustrated individuals, especially on public roads and motorways. Some of the reported incidents of *road rage* have led to severe injury and even death. In a more sinister development, we find references to rage in other contexts, such as *cycle rage, golf rage, lane rage* (in swimming pools), *trolley rage* (in supermarkets), and *air rage* (in aircraft). This is certainly one to keep an eye on.

railway, railroad. The usual word in BrE is *railway*, and in AmE *railroad*. *Railroad* is used in both varieties as a verb meaning 'to coerce into a premature decision'.

raise, rise *nouns* An increase of salary is called a *rise* in BrE and a *raise* in AmE.

raison d'être means 'a purpose or reason that accounts for or justifies or originally causes a thing's existence'. As a loanword it is normally printed in italic type in English contexts. The plural form is *raisons d'être*.

rancour meaning 'malignant dislike', is spelt *-our* in BrE and *rancor* in AmE.

rapport, meaning 'harmonious relationship', is pronounced with the stress on the second syllable and the final *t* silent, despite having been fully naturalized by the beginning of the 20c.

rarefy, meaning 'to make or become less dense or solid', is spelt *-efy*, not *rarify*.

rarely, seldom. It is acceptable to say *rarely if ever* or *seldom if ever* but not (except informally) *rarely ever* or *seldom ever*: *We rarely if ever go out* | ☒ *We rarely ever go out*. In the second example, *hardly ever* or *scarcely ever* could be substituted.

rateable is the preferred spelling, not *ratable*.

rather. 1 *Rather* is common in BrE as a so-called 'downtoner', i.e. an adverb that reduces the effect of the following adjective, adverb, or noun, as in *It is rather expensive*, *You were driving rather fast*, and *He's rather a fool*. With nouns, the sequence is *rather + a +* singular noun, and the construction is not possible in the plural, so instead of ☒ *They're rather fools* you have to say *They're rather foolish*. When *rather* qualifies an adjective followed by a noun, two sequences are possible: *rather a large glass* or *a rather large glass*; the plural construction is *rather large glasses*.

2 The phrase *rather than* has two main meanings which shade into each other: (1) 'in preference to', and (2) 'instead of'. When a noun follows there is little difficulty: *I suggested beer rather than wine*. With other parts of speech certain difficulties arise:

▸ **a** With pronouns, the case of the pronoun following *rather than* is normally the same as the word preceding *rather than*: *I wanted to see her rather than him* | *She, rather than he, decided to come.*

▸ **b** With verbs, an *-ing* form is used after *rather than* when the meaning tends towards 'instead of': *When she voiced her grievances quietly and calmly, rather than screaming them, her family paid attention to her for the first time*—M. Herbert, 1989. When the balance is between individual words and not phrases or clauses, the forms used before and after *rather than* tend to match: *This is the first time during a downturn in the economy when training by companies has increased rather than decreased*—Hansard, 1992 | *In the video Jones is, in the main, observing rather than advocating the ruthless antics of the hard men*—Daily Mirror, 1992.

▸ **c** When the meaning is more to do with preference and rejection than with parallel alternatives, and so especially after the verb *prefer* itself, an infinitive (with or without *to*) is more natural after *rather than*: *Better to part with what they must now, rather than lose more later*—M. Shadbolt, 1986 | *Many Vietnamese soldiers preferred to kill themselves rather than be captured*—Independent, 1989 | *He began to realize, too, what hardship she had suffered rather than ask his family for money*—C. West, 1989. (For *prefer* see also PREFER 3.)

▸ **d** A mixed style, with an infinitive before and a verbal noun after *rather than*, is less natural in contexts based clearly on preference rather than alternatives: *What they are saying is that . . . it is better to give way and let them have what they want rather than standing up for the rule of law*—R. Muldoon, 1986.

3 After a comparative form such as *better*, *more*, etc., *than* and not *rather than* is the preferred construction, although *rather than* is sometimes more natural when the two parts of the construction

are far apart in the sentence: *It is better to give way and let them have what they want rather than standing up for the rule of law*—R. Muldoon, 1986.

4 The expression *would rather* (and its contracted form as in *I'd rather* etc.) is complemented by *than* + infinitive (without *to*): *A college would rather fall below its intake targets and lose revenue than take in sociology students*—R. Holland, 1977. For *had rather*, see HAD 3.

ratio has the plural form *ratios*.

ravel. The verb has inflected forms *ravelled*, *ravelling* in BrE and usually *raveled*, *raveling* in AmE. The usual meaning is 'to entangle or become entangled', but *ravel out* has the opposite meaning, the same as *disentangle* or *unravel*.

raze is now the standard spelling for the verb meaning 'to destroy or tear down' (as in *The building was razed to the ground*), not *rase*.

re, meaning 'with regard to, concerning', is a piece of commercialese that is best suited to business language. In everyday writing it is a convenient abbreviation that is less troubling when it stands at the beginning of a statement, especially in the rapid-turnover world of faxes and e-mails where it fits nicely: *Re your invitation, yes I'd like to come.* The strictures of Fowler (1926) and A. P. Herbert (1935) were not of the real world.

re-. Words formed with the prefix *re-* are generally unhyphened (*rearrange, regroup, reopen, reuse,* etc.) except when the second element begins with an *e* (*re-enter, re-evaluation,* etc.) or when the

combination needs to be distinguished from another word with the same spelling, e.g. *re-collect* = collect again (*recollect* = to remember) and *re-sign* = sign again (*resign* = give up one's job). Other words in this last category include *re-count, re-cover, re-creation, re-form* (and *re-formation*), *re-serve, re-soluble, re-solve, re-sort*.

reaction. In the later part of the 20c *reaction* has been used to mean little more than 'first impression' or 'initial response': *Most people's reaction to the Oz trial and sentences has been what one might call a gut-reaction*—Listener, 1971. To do the word justice, it should involve some element of *reacting* to something that affects the person having (or asked to have) the reaction, rather than simply to passive hearing or reading of information. But the weakened meaning is well established, especially in the world of radio and television interviews: *What is your reaction to the extension of VAT to domestic fuel?*

readable see LEGIBLE.

real. 1 As an intensifying adverb *real* is a characteristic Americanism and even in AmE is informal: *You look real nice today, Carla*—New Yorker, 1987. The standard adverb in most contexts is *really*.

2 As an adjective *real* tends to be overused in an intensifying role equivalent to adjectives such as 'significant, important, strong': *It may be too late to halt the brain drain and decline in morale unless the Government shows a real commitment to research*—Daily Telegraph, 1992 | *The Clinton team had no real defence plans when it took office, beyond a vague determination to cut spending*—Economist, 1993. In such contexts a more exact word, such as *strong* in the first example and *significant* in the second, can be more effective.

-re and -er. 1 One of the great dividers separating the spelling of BrE and AmE is that many nouns are spelt with a final *-re* in BrE but with a final *-er* in AmE (in many cases preserving an earlier English spelling from which BrE has since departed): *calibre | caliber, centre | center, fibre | fiber, litre | liter, louvre | louver, manoeuvre | maneuver, mitre | miter, ochre | ocher, reconnoitre | reconnoiter, spectre | specter, theatre | theater*. In BrE *metre* (= a metric measure) is distinguished from *meter* (= a measuring device) whereas in AmE both words are spelt *meter*.

2 In other cases, however, the AmE spellings are the same as the BrE, usually because an *-er* form might affect the pronunciation, e.g. *acre, lucre, massacre, mediocre, nacre*, and *ogre*.

reason. 1 The construction after *the reason is* can be with *that* or *because*: *One reason was that the Kuwaitis wouldn't give anyone a visa, except female print journalists—Photography*, 1991 | *The reason I like the Beatles is because they remind me of Chuck Berry—Q*, 1991. See the longer review of this question at BECAUSE 3.

2 The combination *reason why* followed by a clause is recorded from the 13c and is a standard construction: *Is there any good reason why we should have news bulletins, local and national, every hour on the hour, chat shows . . . and wall-to-wall discussion programmes?—Listener*, 1984. Objections occasionally heard are based on a spurious view of logic in language (i.e. *why* is already contained in *reason*) and cannot be regarded as sound. However,

when *reason, why*, and *because* all occur in succession, the borderline into redundancy is crossed and the result is patently poor style: *The reason why First Secretary Mikhail Gorbachev is the first Soviet leader to promote such close cooperation with the U.S. is because* [use *that*] *he bears the map of the U.S. on his forehead—letter in Chicago Times*, 1989.

rebel is pronounced with the stress on the first syllable as a noun and with the stress on the second syllable as a verb. The verb has inflected forms *rebelled, rebelling* in BrE and AmE.

rebound, redound. 1 *Rebound* is pronounced with the stress on the first syllable as a noun and with the stress on the second syllable as a verb.

2 The image with the verb *rebound* is of something bouncing back, and with *redound* it is of a tide or wave flooding back (from Latin *unda* 'wave'). When circumstances *rebound on* someone they have a harmful effect on the person or people responsible for them: *The allegation may rebound on the party making it—*J. Kendall, 1992. In some uses, however, the rebounding can be directed elsewhere: *The strategy of encouraging, supporting and protecting deliberate non-payers is deeply flawed, as it will rebound on the most vulnerable—Marxism Today*, 1990. When a circumstance *redounds to* someone's advantage or credit, it contributes to it: *Each piece of field research aims at achieving a 'scoop' which will redound to the anthropologist's credit, and the more interesting and exciting the raw data the better—*I. M. Lewis, 1992. Although contrary examples of *redound* occur occasionally, the distinction between the notions of harm (*rebound on*) and advantage (*redound to*) generally holds good and is worth observing.

rebut has inflected forms *rebutted, rebutting*.

receipt, recipe. In current English the meanings of these two words are distinct and cause no difficulty, but readers of Victorian or earlier literature should bear in mind that a *receipt* could then be what we now know as *recipe* ('a formula and method for preparing food'), while both a *receipt* and a *recipe* could mean what we now call a *prescription* (in the medical sense).

receive is a key word supporting the rule of spelling '*i* before *e* except after *c*'. See I BEFORE E.

received pronunciation (RP), received standard are names given to the form of speech associated with educated speakers in the southern counties of England and used as a model for teaching English to foreign learners. This system is the basis of the guidance given on pronunciation in this book, while it is recognized that other speech patterns and types exist. The American equivalent is called *General American*. See PRONUNCIATION.

recess. The dominant pronunciation of both the noun and the verb is with the stress on the second syllable, but the noun is increasingly heard with the stress on the first syllable.

recherché, meaning 'rare or exotic', is partly naturalized and is normally printed in roman type with the French accent retained.

recipe see RECEIPT.

reciprocal. The reciprocal pronouns are *each other* and *one another*. See EACH 3.

reciprocal, mutual. see MUTUAL.

reckon. 1 The inflected forms are *reckoned, reckoning*.

2 The use of *reckon* without any element of calculation or consideration as in *I reckon it's time to go now* has a tinge of the American south about it, although it was a standard use in literary English as recently as the 19c (*I reckon, said Socrates, that no one . . . could accuse me of idle talking*—Jowett translating Plato, 1875). It is noteworthy that a word considered not so long ago as satisfactory for translating the conversation of Socrates should now be regarded as unacceptably informal for normal use, and one is left wondering whether the fortunes of the word in this meaning will change again and for the better. See also CALCULATE.

recognize, recognition. Both words should be pronounced with the g fully articulated.

recommend. In addition to its familiar constructions with a direct object + *to*-infinitive (*I recommend you to control your temper*) and with a *that*-clause (*We recommend that you stay at the local hotel*), *recommend* is one of a class of verbs, once dwindling but now showing signs of recovery, that allows the subjunctive to be used, the effect being one of formality rather than archaism: *One of the observers from the International Commission of Jurists . . . had recommended she be approached*—Nadine Gordimer, 1990.

reconnaissance is now fully naturalized and is pronounced ri-**kon**-i-səns.

reconnoitre is the BrE spelling, and *reconnoiter* the spelling in AmE.

record is pronounced with the stress on the first syllable as a noun and with the stress on the second syllable as a verb.

recount, re-count. The verb *recount* (with the stress on the second syllable) means 'to tell in detail, narrate'. *Re-count* (with hyphen) is both a verb (with the stress on the second syllable) meaning 'to count again' and a noun (with the stress on the first syllable) meaning 'a fresh count'.

recourse see RESOURCE.

recrudescence means in medical use 'the breaking out again of a disease', and in generalized use should be restricted to contexts in which something harmful or unwelcome recurs. Fowler (1926) noted that the word was becoming fashionable as a simple synonym for 'revival' or 'reappearance' among journalists in his day. He called this a 'disgusting use' and we can see what he means when we come across such absurd uses as the following: *Both works, however, may be thought to share a secret, and a set of clues, which bear witness to the recrudescence of a hippy magic*—K. Miller, 1989.

recto, meaning 'the right-hand page of a book', has the plural form *rectos*. The left-hand page is called the *verso*.

rector. In the Church of England, the title is used of an incumbent of a parish where all tithes were formerly paid to the incumbent, as distinct from a parish with a *vicar* as incumbent,

where the tithes formerly passed to a chapter or religious house. The word has a different meaning in some other churches, and is also used for the head of some schools (especially in Scotland), universities, and colleges.

recur has inflected forms *recurred, recurring*.

Red Indian, redskin. These terms are now considered offensive and have fallen out of use in favour of *American Indian* and (preferably) *Native American*.

reducible is spelt *-ible*, not *-able*. See -ABLE, -IBLE.

reductio ad absurdum is a method of proving the falsity of a premise by showing that the logical consequence is absurd. An example is that if eating less makes one healthier, the logical conclusion is to eat nothing.

redundancy. *'She is lively and vital enough to be a member of a terrorist gang.' 'Lively and vital,' said Harvey, 'lively and vital—one of these words is redundant.'*—Muriel Spark, 1984. English idiom is characterized by redundancy, or apparent redundancy, and it is misguidedly pedantic to pick holes in discourse that includes it. Examples of idiomatic repetition of words or ideas include *HIV virus* (the *V* in *HIV* already means 'virus'), *the hoi polloi* (*hoi* = 'the'), *LCD display* (the *D* in *LCD* already means 'display'), *safe haven* (a *haven* is by definition safe), and *armed gunman* (a *gunman* is by definition armed).

refectory. The recommended pronunciation is with the stress on the second syllable, although in some religious houses the stress is placed on the first.

refer. The inflected forms are *referred*, *referring*. The derivative adjective is spelt either *referable* (one r; pronounced with the stress on the first syllable) or *referrable* (two rs; pronounced with the stress on the second syllable).

referendum. The recommended plural is *referendums*, although *referenda* is common.

refill is pronounced with the stress on the first syllable as a noun and with the stress on the second syllable as a verb.

reflection is now the dominant form, although *reflexion* is the older.

reflector is spelt *-or*, not *-er*.

reflexive verbs are the type constructed with *myself, herself, ourselves*, etc., in which the subject of the verb and the object are the same person or thing, as in *We enjoyed ourselves* and *Make yourself at home*.

reform. The verb *reform* (with the stress on the second syllable) means 'to improve by removing faults'. *Re-form* (with hyphen) means 'to form again'.

refrigerator is spelt *-or* and without a *d* in the middle, although the popular shortening of the word is *fridge*.

refuse. The noun, meaning 'waste material', is pronounced with the stress on the first syllable, whereas the verb, meaning 'to withhold consent for', is pronounced with the stress on the second syllable.

refutable should be pronounced with the stress on the first syllable, although a second-syllable stress is increasingly common.

refute means 'to prove (something) false by argument', and the element 'by argument' is important; it should not be used simply as an alternative for *deny* or *repudiate*, which imply straightforward rejection without argument. In the first of the following examples *refute* is used appropriately, whereas in the second it is not: *The criticisms . . . that Ruskin saw architecture only two-dimensionally, and that he never seems to have looked at a building structurally, are refuted with ample quotations*—Journal of the Royal Society of Arts, 1979 | ⊠ *I refute Mr Bodey's allegation that it is our policy not to observe publication dates*—Bookseller, 1980.

regalia, meaning 'the insignia of royalty' has become extended in use to non-royal contexts such as that of civic dignitaries. In both cases it is a plural noun.

regard. 1 *Regard* is used in a number of complex prepositions, *as regards, in regard to, with regard to*, as well as the form *regarding*; all have more or less the same meaning, although the first three are more common at the beginning of sentences.

2 In its meaning 'to consider, judge', *regard* is regularly followed by *as* + noun or adjective, with *regard* itself either active or passive: *We regard recording as an essential element in the actual teaching process*—Language for Life, 1975 | *Job security is more generally regarded as unquantifiable*—Financial Times, 1975 | *Canon Watson was regarded by many as the leader of the charismatic movement in the Church*—Daily Telegraph, 1984. This construction differs from that for *consider*, which is normally followed by a direct complement

without *as* or by the infinitive *to be*: see CONSIDER.

regime is fully naturalized in terms of spelling, but is still pronounced in a French manner.

register office is the official form in the UK of the term for a State office for conducting civil ceremonies and recording births and deaths. *Registry office* is also widely used, but it is unofficial only.

regress is pronounced with the stress on the first syllable as a noun and with the stress on the second syllable as a verb.

regret has inflected forms *regretted*, *regretting*, and a derivative form *regrettable*.

regretful, regrettable. *Regretful* means 'feeling regret' and applies to a person, whereas *regrettable* means 'causing regret' and applies to an action: *He did not crave recognition, but was understandably regretful about his lack of it*—E. Cashmore, 1982 | *Now let us come to the point: are you willing to overlook this—this regrettable incident and try again?*—M. Forster, 1990. The corresponding adverb *regretfully* (= in a regretful way) is commonly misused for *regrettably* (= as is to be regretted): ☒ *Regretfully, that is no ground for leniency towards him*— *New Statesman*, 1976.

regularly should be pronounced with all four syllables articulated, not as if it were spelt *reguly*.

reign, rein. The simple nouns are not often confused, but the idiom *give free rein to* (= allow full scope to) is sometimes used in the form *give free reign to* (as if it meant 'give free rule to'?), especially in AmE: *They say that if they are given free reign to invest and*

produce they will grow richer—*New Yorker*, 1987.

reject is pronounced with the stress on the first syllable as a noun and with the stress on the second syllable as a verb.

rejoin, re-join. The verb *rejoin* (with the stress on the second syllable) means 'to say in answer'. *Re-join* (with hyphen) means 'to join again'.

relate. The verb has a long history, being first recorded in Caxton. In the 20c it has acquired a jargon-based meaning 'to have an attitude of personal sympathy towards': *Group formation such as takes place in the classroom tends to be adult-centred and dependent upon the varying ways children relate to the teacher*—*Childhood Education*, 1950 | *Married people can still relate* [sc. to people outside the marriage]— *Guardian*, 1971.

relation, relationship, relatives. As nouns, *relation* and *relative* both mean 'a person related by blood or by marriage', and both are idiomatic in the plural. (For some reason, however, *relation* is the normal choice in the explicit context of wealth: *He resented . . . the mother who had inconsiderately died and left him a poor relation*—Julian Symons, 1978.) The state of a person's connection with relations or relatives is his or her *relationship*, which is also used in the wider context of people's dealings with one another: *How difficult and unnatural are in-law relationships!*—*Daily Telegraph*, 1970 | *You need to consider the quality of the relationship which exists between your son and the teachers, your son and his peers, and between you and the teachers*— *Where*, 1972. In modern use, *relationship* has a sexual connotation which should always be borne in mind when using this word: *She can't forgive me for leaving and I've had to accept that our relationship's finally over*—Woman, 1991. *Relation* is often preferred to denote the way things (especially concepts and ideas) relate to each other (*There seemed to be little relation between charge and geographical location, except in Scotland and Northern Ireland, where the cost of water was low*—A. H. Little, 1975), is the normal choice in meanings to do with activities and procedures, as in the expression *business relations*, and is the only choice in fixed expressions such as *in relation to* and *bear some* (or *no* etc.) *relation to*.

relative clauses. 1 A relative clause is a clause that is connected to a main clause by means of a relative pronoun such as *who, which, whose,* or *that*. In the preceding sentence, the part from *that* to the end is a relative clause with the word *clause* as its antecedent. There are two types of relative clause, called 'restrictive' and 'non-restrictive'. A restrictive clause gives essential information about the noun or noun phrase that comes before, as in *She held out the hand that was hurt*, in which 'the hand' is defined or identified as 'the one that was hurt'. By contrast, in the sentence *She held out her hand, which I clasped in both of mine*, the information in the relative clause introduced by *which* is additional information that could be left out without affecting the core structure or meaning of the sentence, and this type is called a non-restrictive clause.

2 The relative pronoun *that* or *which* can be omitted when it introduces a restrictive clause, especially when it is the object of the verb in the relative clause and occasionally (but more informally) when it is the subject: *It reminded him of the Exhibition he was going back to*—Penelope Fitzgerald, 1977 | *It was your geography caused the doubt*—Tom Stoppard, 1993. Choice between *that* and *which* in clauses of these types is discussed at the entry for THAT 3.

relatively, like COMPARATIVELY, is widely used as a 'downtoning' adverb meaning 'fairly, somewhat', without any real notion of relativity or comparison: *The natural question to pursue is whether the Chinese state has been able to maintain control in this relatively open geopolitical region*—Dædalus, 1993.

relevance, first recorded in the 18c, has almost completely ousted the alternative form *relevancy*.

reliable has, surprisingly, been in common use only since about 1850, and was once objected to on the ground that it ought to mean 'able to rely' and not, as it does, 'able to be relied on', since *rely* cannot by itself take an object, as most verbs forming passive adjectives in *-able* can (*bearable, believable, curable,* etc.; but note *dependable*, recorded from the 18c). See also UNACCOUNTABLE.

remit. The noun, meaning 'terms of reference', is pronounced with the stress on the first syllable or (less often) on the second, and the verb, meaning 'to send (money)', is pronounced with the stress on the second syllable. The inflected forms of the verb are *remitted, remitting*.

Renaissance is spelt with a capital initial letter when it refers to the period of revival in classical forms of art and literature in the 14c to 16c. In this meaning it is commonly used in attributive position (before another noun: *A whitestone Italian Renaissance mansion on Sixty-third Street*—R. Doliner, 1978). In the general context of any 'revival', it is spelt with a small initial letter: *A renaissance occurred in 1969 when Adler proved that bacteria have specific chemoreceptors*—*Nature*, 1975. The anglicized form *renascence* is an unnecessary affectation.

rendezvous. The plural is spelt the same, but is pronounced with the final syllable as -vooz.

repairable, reparable. *Repairable* is the normal choice with reference to physical repair (*There is a reasonable chance that the tyre will be repairable*—*Police Review*, 1972), whereas *reparable* (pronounced with the stress on the first syllable), refers to abstract things, especially losses, and except in the negative form *irreparable* has an archaic flavour, as intentionally in the following example: *The loss is reparable, but your lives are greater worth*—Ellis Peters, 1993.

repeat, repetition. The 20c use of *repeat* in broadcasting, meaning 'a radio or television programme that has been transmitted before', with its attributive use as in *repeat showing, repeat fee*, etc., has tended to put *repetition* in the shade even in the meaning 'the act of repeating' (as distinct from 'a thing repeated'), which is the meaning historically more closely associated with *repetition* than with *repeat*: *Members of the powerful 1922 Committee executive told Mrs Thatcher there must be no repeat of the dispute between Downing Street and Mr Lawson over the Exchange Rate Mechanism*—*Times*, 1989. *Repeat* is also common in attributive position in medical contexts, with the meaning 'further or repeated': *Strangely, it was decided that a repeat investigation was not required and I was allowed to go on caring for the patient throughout her stay*—A. Morton-Cooper, 1990.

repel has inflected forms *repelled*, *repelling*.

repellent, repulsive. *Repulsive* is the stronger of the two words, implying physical recoiling rather than just a feeling of disgust: *I was given some repulsive food which, by the end of the second day, I trained myself to eat*—Brian Aldiss, 1991 | *He had a genuine liking for Lehmann, whose exacting, aristocratic and somewhat dictatorial manner some found repellent*—F. Spalding, 1991. For *repellent* the spelling *-ent* is preferable to *-ant* for both the adjective and the noun.

repertoire, repertory. These are essentially the same word, being the French and English equivalents of Latin *repertorium* meaning 'an inventory or catalogue'. A *repertoire* is a stock of dramatic or musical pieces which a player or company regularly performs; *repertory* also has this meaning and in addition denotes a type of theatre involving regular changes in the choice of plays performed during a season. In this meaning it is often used attributively, as in *repertory theatre, repertory actor*, etc., and is common in the shortened form *rep*.

replace, substitute. **1** The typical construction is to *replace* A with B (or, in the passive, B *is replaced by* A), or B can simply *replace* A, whereas with *substitute* it is to *substitute* B *for* A or to *substitute* B without any continuation (more usually in the passive: B *is substituted*). (In all cases, A is the person or thing 'going out' and B the one 'coming in'.) Examples: (replace) *The credit card holder can be replaced with a document holder or a roll of paper tape, for other data capture purposes*—New Scientist, 1972 | *It is nice to see 'stewardess' and 'steward' gradually being replaced by the general term 'flight attendant'*—Scientific American, 1982 | *Rugby nightmares replaced nightmares about witches, which had been the basis of my bad dreams for several years*—C. Jennings, 1990 | (substitute) *Visibility on the course, however, was too poor to permit the senior relay and a three-mile race was substituted*—Liverpool Echo, 1976 | *As land becomes scarce, farmers rely more on additional fertilizer to expand output, in effect substituting energy in the form of fertilizer for land in the production process*—D. Adamson, 1990.

2 The use of *substitute* for *replace* is a more usual error than the reverse: *During this period of contraction, both passenger and freight services were withdrawn at an alarming rate, being substituted by short-lived bus services and road freight transport*—Bishop's Castle Railway Society Journal, 1990. When a football commentator reports that a player is being *substituted*, he is referring to the outgoing player and means *replaced*, but the choice is determined by the dominant influence of the noun *substitute* by which the incoming player is known.

replaceable is spelt with an *e* in the middle to preserve the soft sound of the preceding *c*.

replicate. The 20c use in the meaning 'to reproduce, imitate,

or copy exactly', originally in technical contexts but spreading into general use, is an extension of a word that has been in use since the 16c in other meanings. It is best avoided when more straightforward alternatives are available, such as *duplicate*, *be modelled on*, *imitate*, etc.

reportage, pronounced rep-aw-**tahzh** in a semi-French way, now usually means 'the reporting of events for the press or broadcasting': *His study of the Hyde Park orators might have been taken as a masterly piece of reportage*—London Review of Books, 1979. Its older meanings 'repute' and 'gossip' have fallen out of use.

reported speech, or *indirect speech*, is the reporting of what someone has said with a 'reporting' verb such as *said*, *replied*, *cried*, etc. In reported speech, the actual words spoken are usually changed with regard to the subject and tense of the verb to suit the viewpoint of the person now reporting, and quotation marks are not used, so that what appears in direct speech as (for example) *'They have a few points to add,' she remarked*, in reported or indirect speech becomes *She remarked that they had a few points to add*. See also INDIRECT QUESTION.

reprehensible, meaning 'deserving censure', is spelt *-ible*, not *-able*. See -ABLE, -IBLE.

reprieve, both verb and noun, is spelt *-ie-*, not *-ei-*.

reproducible is spelt *-ible*, not *-able*. See -ABLE, -IBLE.

reputable, meaning 'of good repute', is pronounced with the stress on the first syllable.

resource, resort, recourse

1 The three words all have to do with finding help or support and are chiefly distinguished from one another by the typical phrase patterns in which they operate. These are given in the table below.

resource	*a simple resource, at the end of one's resources, a person of many resources, to fall back on one's own resources*
resort	*as a last resort, in the last resort; (verb) to resort to, without resorting to*
recourse	*to have recourse to, without recourse to, one's usual recourse*

2 In general, *resource* denotes what one adopts for help or support whereas *recourse* denotes a process or avenue of finding support. There is an area of possible confusion in the overlap between *to resort to* (especially in the past, *to have resorted to*) and *to have recourse to*: *More than 100 governments had resorted to torture or the maltreatment of prisoners* — Keesings, 1990 | *How many times has one ever had recourse to a term like anadiplosis?* — J. Culpepper, 1992. One normally *resorts* to things in extreme circumstances and has *recourse* to them more routinely.

request. The noun is commonly followed by *for* (*a request for more time*). The verb, unlike *ask*, cannot be used in constructions of the type �='We requested them for more time*; the correct sequence is either *We requested more time from them* or *We requested them to give us more time*.

require. The construction with a *to*-infinitive, as in *I require to know your names*, is not idiomatic in BrE but is known in other varieties of English. The type *Do you require tea?* is chiefly confined to BrE.

research. In BrE the noun and verb are both traditionally pronounced with the stress on the second syllable, but first-syllable stressing of the noun (**ree**-serch), influenced by American practice, is increasingly heard, especially on radio and television.

resistible is spelt *-ible*, not *-able*. See -ABLE, -IBLE.

resoluble, resolvable. Both words are in use in the meaning 'able to be resolved', but *resolvable* is commoner.

resort, re-sort. The verb and noun *resort* (pronounced ri-**zawt**) has a wide range of meanings. *Re-sort* (with hyphen and pronounced ree-**sawt**) is a verb meaning 'to sort again or differently'.

resource, resort, recourse. *See box above*

resource is pronounced either ri-**zaws** or **ree**-saws, the first being more usual in BrE and both being used in AmE. The same patterns apply in the plural form.

respect. As well as *respecting*, there are several complex prepositions all meaning 'regarding, as concerns': *in respect of, in respect to, with respect to*. The first two are more formal in character, and are normally found in business correspondence.

respective, respectively are useful words when two or more items need to be distinguished (in the order in which they occur, when they are named separately) in relation to what follows in the sentence: *MEPs are paid the same as national MPs in their respective countries—Which?*, 1984 | *Iraq and Syria have been ruled by small minorities (Sunni Arabs and Alawite officers respectively)—International Affairs*, 1991. In the first of these examples, the presence of *respective* shows that the national MPs are paid at different levels depending on their countries, and in the second the presence of *respectively* shows that the Sunni Arabs ruled in Iraq and the Alawite officers in Syria (and not a combination of both in both countries). In other cases, *respective* (in particular) is redundant or replaceable by a simpler word such as *own* or *various*: *The parade dispersed, the Commandos returning to their respective units, and soon the village green was quiet*—B. Millin, 1991.

respite is pronounced either **res**-piyt or **res**-pit.

responsible is spelt *-ible*, not *-able*. See -ABLE, -IBLE.

restaurateur, meaning 'a restaurant owner', is spelt *-ateur* with no *n*.

restive, restless. Despite its form, *restive* is close in meaning to *restless*, but conveys a stronger implication of disruptive consequences: *The picket's mood turned restive, apprehensive—New Society*, 1977. It is also used in the special context of a horse that refuses to move forwards.

result. *They tried hard to get a result but rain stopped play and the game ended in a draw*—television news broadcast, 1993. The use of the noun to mean not just an outcome but a favourable outcome, familiar now in the language of sports commentators, seems to have its origin in plural uses going back to the 1920s: *Take some of those pamphlets with you to distribute aboard ship. They may bring results.*—Eugene O'Neill, 1922.

résumé, pronounced **rez**-yuh-may, means 'a summary' in BrE, and in AmE (often with the first accent or both accents omitted) has the additional meaning 'a curriculum vitae'.

reticent is developing the meaning 'reluctant to act', which is somewhat more developed than its standard meaning 'reserved, reluctant to speak': *Not everyone is as reticent as London's civil servants about moving to Docklands—Times*, 1992. This meaning is likely to become established, although at present it is non-standard.

retiral, meaning 'retirement from office', is largely confined to Scottish use: *Young person required for civil engineering stores to fill vacancy due to retiral*—advertisement in *Lochaber News*, 1978.

retrieve is spelt *-ie-*, not *-ei-*.

rev *verb*. The inflected forms are *revved, revving*.

reveille, pronounced ri-**val**-i, is the current spelling for the word meaning 'a morning awakening' (especially in service life).

revel. The verb has inflected forms *revelled, revelling* in BrE and in AmE also *reveled, reveling*.

revenge *verb* see AVENGE.

reverend, reverent, reverential. **1** In its general meaning, *reverend* means 'deserving reverence', and is most often found in clerical contexts even when it is not a formal title, whereas *reverent* means 'showing reverence' in wider contexts: *He also formed close links with the network of local Puritan ministers . . . whom he described in his will as 'my reverend and pious friends'—Dictionary of National Biography,* 1993 | *There was a reverent silence, broken only by the hissing of the gas-jets in the wall-brackets*—P. Ling, 1993. *Reverential* means 'characterized by reverence', and the main difference in meaning between it and *reverent* is that *reverent* describes a feeling or attitude and is judgemental whereas *reverential* denotes a connection with reverence and is informational: *When she walked into a village the Africans would often clap their hands in a reverential way*—W. Green, 1988.

2 *Reverend*, abbreviated *Revd* (no full stop) or *Rev.*, is most commonly found as a title applied to certain members of the clergy.

reversal, reversion. *Reversal* is the noun corresponding to the verb *reverse*, and means primarily 'the changing (of a decision)', whereas *reversion* corresponds to the verb *revert*, as in *The style represents a reversion to classical Japanese tradition*.

reversible is spelt *-ible*, not *-able*. See -ABLE, -IBLE.

review, revue. A *review* is 'a general survey or assessment of something' and has many special applications, including a published criticism of a book, play, etc. A *revue* is a theatrical entertainment consisting of a series of short acts or sketches. In this meaning the word is sometimes spelt *review*, but since this form coincides too closely with the meaning mentioned above and can cause confusion, this spelling is not recommended.

rhetorical question is an assertion put in the form of a question without expecting an answer, e.g. *Who do they think they are?*

rhino has the plural form *rhino* (collective) or *rhinos* (individual).

rhyming slang is a type of slang of cockney origin in which a word is replaced by words or phrases which rhyme with it, e.g. *apples and pears* (= stairs), *plates of meat* (= feet), and *trouble and strife* (= wife). The rhyming words are sometimes arbitrary (as in the first example) and sometimes significant (as in the other examples).

rhythmic, rhythmical. The two forms are virtually interchangeable, choice normally being determined by personal preference or the flow of the sentence. However, it is usually preferable to be consistent within a single piece of writing.

ribbon, riband. *Ribbon* was originally a variant of the older form *riband* (pronounced like *ribbon* with a *d* at the end) and is now overwhelmingly the dominant form. In general use *riband* is normally confined to heraldry and to sports prizes, notably the Blue Riband for the fastest sea crossing between Southampton and New York in the 1920s and 1930s.

rick, meaning 'a sprain' or (as a verb) 'to sprain', is spelt *rick* rather than *wrick*. Both forms seem to have their origin in dialect.

rickety, meaning 'insecure or shaky', is spelt *-ety*, not *-etty*.

ricochet. The inflected forms of the verb are *ricocheted* (pronounced **rik**-ə-shayd) and *ricocheting* (pronounced **rik**-ə-shay-ing).

rid. The past tense and past participle are now normally *rid* rather than *ridded*, but *ridded* occurs occasionally in active constructions such as *He ridded the stable of flies. Rid* must be used in constructions of the type *I thought myself well rid of him.*

right, rightly. 1 *Right* is used as an adverb meaning 'in the right way, in a proper manner' with a number of verbs, notably *do right, go right* (as in *Nothing went right*), *guess right, spell something right, treat someone right*. In general, however, and especially when the adverb precedes the verb or qualifies an adjective, *rightly* is the more natural choice: *One of them was rightly furious as the escaper had whipped . . . his overcoat*—A. Miller, 1976 | *Frayn has not forgotten the underdog . . . The shrinking violet (as he rightly recognizes) is the most dangerous plant in the glades of privilege*—Listener, 1976 | *Many a skate park, rightly, refuses admittance unless skaters wear protective helmets and pads*—Times, 1977. *Rightly* is commonly used with *so* to express approval for something described by a preceding word or clause: *She was angry, and rightly so.*

2 *Right* is also idiomatic in the meanings 'directly, immediately' or 'completely' in phrases such as *right away* and *right now*, and in

uses such as *I'll be right with you* and *Turn it right off.*

3 In an older use now considered archaic in BrE (but still in use in regional AmE), *right* means 'very, extremely' without any notion of rightness in the judgemental sense: *I was right glad . . . to see your writing again*—Coleridge, 1800 | *Miz Wilkes is right sensible, for a woman*—Margaret Mitchell, 1936. In BrE it remains in standard use only in certain titles and forms of address, such as *Right Honourable* and *Right Reverend.*

rightward, rightwards. The only form of the adjective is *rightward* (*a rightward glance*). For the adverb, *rightward* and *rightwards* are used both in BrE and in AmE (*turn rightward/rightwards*).

rigour is spelt *-our* in BrE and *rigor* in AmE. The corresponding adjective is *rigorous* in both varieties. Note also the spelling *rigor* in the medical sense ('a sudden feeling of cold and shivering') and in the Latin phrase *rigor mortis*, the stiffening of the body after death.

ring. There are two unrelated verbs with different inflections. The one to do with bells has a past form *rang* and past participle *rung*, whereas the one to do with circles and bands has *ringed* in both forms.

riot. The verb has inflected forms *rioted, rioting.*

rise see ARISE.

risky, risqué. *Risky* is the general word meaning 'involving risk', whereas the French loanword *risqué* means 'slightly indecent' (especially with reference to humour) and therefore risking shock.

rival. The verb has inflected forms *rivalled*, *rivalling*, and in AmE usually *rivaled*, *rivaling*.

rivet. The verb has inflected forms *riveted*, *riveting*.

road, street. **1** According to a law of Henry I of England (1100–35), a street 'was to be sufficiently broad for two loaded carts to meet and for sixteen armed knights to ride abreast' (Ekwall, *Street-Names of the City of London*, 1954). The history of *road* and *street* and of other terms such as *lane*, *avenue*, *crescent*, *gate*, *place*, *row*, *terrace*, *rise*, and *vale*, is extremely complicated, with fine distinctions between (for example) a wide lane and a narrow street. In current usage, a *street* is normally a paved way in a town or city, whereas a *road* is a way (paved or not) in a village or in open country. In certain fixed expressions there is inconsistency of choice, since *one-way street* follows the distinction just given but *no through road* does not (necessarily).

2 Names attached to particular roads and streets are established by custom, although it is possible to refer to something called 'Street' generically as a *road* and something called 'Road' as a *street*. Note also that a division of the carriageway of a major road (especially a motorway) is called a lane, as the frequent instruction on road signs to 'keep in lane' reminds us.

roast, roasted. Meats and things associated with them are normally described as *roast*: *roast beef*, *roast lamb*, *roast meat*, *roast potatoes*, etc. (but *a roasted chicken* and *a well-roasted joint* are also possible), whereas nuts are normally called *roasted*: *roasted chestnuts, roasted peanuts*, etc. (*roast chestnuts* is also possible but less often *roast peanuts*). The past participle used as a verb is always *roasted*: *They had roasted a chicken for lunch | pork roasted in a lemon sauce.*

rob is used chiefly to mean 'to steal from'; its object is either a place (*rob a bank*) or a person, optionally with *of* followed by the thing stolen (*robbed her of her jewels*). An older use with the thing stolen as the object of *rob* (*He robbed money from the till*) is no longer standard.

rodeo has the plural form *rodeos*.

roguish, meaning 'like a rogue', is spelt this way.

role, meaning 'an actor's part' and related senses, is normally spelt without an accent, although *rôle* is also valid.

romance should be pronounced with the stress on the second syllable. Pronunciation with first-syllable stress is non-standard.

Romania is the official spelling of the country name. Other forms such as *Roumania* and *Rumania* will be found in older writing.

Roman numerals.
See box overleaf

rondo, a term in music, has the plural form *rondos*.

roof. The standard plural form is *roofs*, but *rooves* is often found, causing dismay in some circles (*Almost daily now I am troubled by the sound of 'rooves'. Is there no hope of a cure?*—letter in *Times*, 1986). *Rooves*, with its softer

Roman numerals

are used less often than formerly, but still appear on older clock faces, on the preliminary pages of books, and following the copyright symbol in the credits of cinema films and television productions. In January 1990, the Oxford Dictionary department received many queries about how the new year should be written in Roman numerals, as the answer (MCMXC, as everyone now knows) needed some thought. The main principle is that a sequence of letters having the same value or decreasing in value represents positive values, whereas a smaller value preceding a larger is subtracted from the larger (i.e. M = 1,000 + CM = 900 (1,000-100) + XC = 90 (100-10) = 1990). (1999 is MCMXCIX, not MCMIC and still less MIM, as has been suggested, because a smaller value is followed by a higher value at the next available level; for those who reject the subtraction principle altogether as a late and inauthentic compromise, 1999 must be written MDCCCCLXXXVIIII.) With the turn of the millennium, things get easier (MM). The table below gives the main values for each of the letters used (lower case and capitals).

units	i, ii, iii, iv, v, vi, vii, viii, ix	I, II, III, IV, V, VI, VII, VIII, IX
tens (up to 40)	x, xx, xxx, xl (*occasionally* xxxx)	X, XX, XXX, XL (*occasionally* XXXX)
50	l	L
tens (60 to 90)	lx, lxx, lxxx, xc (*occasionally* lxxxx)	LX, LXX, LXXX, XC (*occasionally* LXXXX)
hundreds (up to 400)	c, cc, ccc, cd (*occasionally* cccc)	C, CC, CCC, CD (*occasionally* CCCC)
500	d	D
hundreds (600 to 900)	dc, dcc, dccc, cm (*occasionally* dcccc)	DC, DCC, DCCC, CM (*occasionally* DCCCC)
1,000	m	M

sound, may well win out in the end, but for now it is better to use *roofs*.

room is pronounced with either a long or a short vowel sound, but the longer is more common.

roomful has the plural form *roomfuls*. See -FUL.

root, rout. The *OED* records two verbs spelt *root* (and pronounced like *boot*), and no fewer than ten verbs spelt *rout* (and pronounced like *bout*). An overlap occurs in

the meaning 'to poke about', which can be either *root about* or *rout about*, each pronounced in its own way. Choice depends largely on regional identity. Of the many other meanings of these words, *root for* (= encourage by applause) is mainly confined to American slang but is occasionally heard in Britain.

rosary, rosery. A *rosary* is a set of prayer beads, and is also used to mean a rose-garden alongside the newer (19c) form *rosery*, although *rose-garden* is now the usual term.

rotary, rotatory. Both are 18c formations and each has a wide range of uses, but in current use *rotary* is much commoner.

rottenness is spelt with two *n*s.

rough, roughen. *Rough* is used as a verb chiefly in the expressions *to rough it* (= do without basic comforts), *to rough out* (= to make a sketch of), *to rough up* (= to attack). Otherwise the verb from *rough*, meaning 'to make or become rough' is *roughen*: '*Yes,*' *she agreed, her voice roughening*—E. Richmond, 1991 | *A faint stubble roughened his chin and just beneath his jawline was a small crescent-shaped scar*—L. Wilkinson, 1992.

round see AROUND.

rout see ROOT.

rout, route *verbs*. The *-ing* forms of these two verbs are respectively *routing* and *routeing*.

rowing boat is the normal term in BrE, and *row-boat* (or *rowboat*) in AmE.

rowlock, meaning 'a device on a boat for holding an oar', is pronounced **rol**-ək. The equivalent term in North America is *oarlock*.

royal we see WE 2B.

RP see RECEIVED PRONUNCIATION.

-r-, -rr-. Words of one syllable containing a single vowel *a, e, i, o,* or *u* double a final *r* when a suffix is added (*bar, barred, barring; fur, furry; stir, stirred, stirring;* but *pour, poured, pouring*). Words of more than one syllable double the *r* when the stress is on the final syllable (*confer, conferred, conferring; incur, incurred, incurring*)

but retain a single *r* when the stress is earlier in the word (*enter, entered, entering; offer, offered, offering*). Verbs in *-fer* form adjectives in *-ferable* (with one *r*) with the stress on the first syllable (*preferable*; but *transferable* has the stress on the first or the second syllable) or in *-ferrable* (with two *r*s) with the stress on the second syllable (*conferrable*), or both (*referable, referrable*).

rubbish is used in BrE to mean 'household refuse'. The corresponding term in AmE, and in some other non-British varieties, is *garbage* or (in some contexts) *trash*, and a *dustbin* outside Britain is a *garbage can* or *trash can*.

rucksack, a pack for carrying on the back, should be pronounced **ruk**-sak, although its use is diminishing in favour of the more home-grown form *backpack*.

rule the roost, meaning 'to have full control or authority', is first recorded in about 1400 in the unexplained form *rule the roast*, which lasted until the 19c when *roast* was replaced by *roost*, thereby at least producing a clear image.

Rumania see ROMANIA.

rumbustious, a chiefly BrE word meaning 'lively or noisy', is spelt *-ious*, not *-uous*.

rumour is spelt *-our* in BrE and *rumor* in AmE.

runner-up has the plural form *runners-up*.

Russian. In its ethnic and political reference, *Russian* (noun and adjective) has become even more complex to define since the collapse of the Soviet Union in 1991.

The 1995 edition of the *Concise Oxford Dictionary* gives the following options for the noun: (1) a native or national of Russia, the Russian Federation, or the former Soviet Union, (2) a person of Russian descent. (In the 1999 edition, the references to the Federation and the Soviet Union have been dropped.) When the term is found in print, the historical context is all-important.

Ss

's. For the possessive forms *'s* and *s'*, see 's AND s' AND 'OF' POSSESSIVES.

sabre is spelt this way in BrE, and *saber* in AmE.

sac, a French loanword, is used in English in medical and biological contexts to denote a bag-like cavity, enclosed by a membrane, in an animal or plant.

saccharin, saccharine. *Saccharin* is a noun denoting a sugar-substitute, and *saccharine* is an adjective meaning (literally) 'sugary' or (figuratively) 'unpleasantly over-polite or sentimental'.

sack. The expressions *to sack* (someone) or *to give* (someone) *the sack*, meaning 'to dismiss' and *to get the sack*, meaning 'to be dismissed', are all still informal only despite a history of use since the 19c, possibly as a loan translation of the French phrase *donner son sac*.

sacrilegious, meaning 'violating what is regarded as sacred', is formed from the noun *sacrilege* and is spelt with the first *i* and the *e* in the order shown, not (by confusion with *religious*) the other way round.

sad has developed a new meaning 'pathetically inadequate or unfashionable' and is applied to people or their actions. It is easy to see how this arose from the traditional meanings of the word, but it is informal only, and the derivative form *saddo* for 'a pathetic person' is confined to BrE.

sadly is a somewhat overused alternative to the sentence adverb *unfortunately*, and has lost some of its force: *The Headmaster of Winchester College asks: 'Is there any other ancient cathedral city in Western Europe with so much fast, heavy, long-distance traffic planned to run so near?' Sadly, the answer is 'Yes, York'*—Times, 1973 | *Sadly, his collection was sold and dispersed throughout the world after his death*—Lancashire Life, 1978.

saga. The traditional use of the term *saga* to refer to medieval Norse narrative poems, especially those written in Iceland, dates from the early 18c and continues untroubled by more recent extensions of meaning, first to long novels or series of novels that recount family histories over several generations (for example, Galsworthy's *Forsyte Saga*) and then, in the 20c, to any long or complicated sequence of events, real or imaginary: *'Found her! Where?' 'In Marseilles. Told me about it for two hours over dinner. It's a saga.'*—H. Wouk, 1978.

said. 1 *Said* is used as an adjective in legal contexts to refer to something mentioned earlier: *And you ceased to be the tenant and occupant of the said premises in the summer of 1915, did you not?*—P. Ling, 1993, 1972. Its extension into ordinary usage is normally jocular: *Marks are awarded for wiggling one's chiffon-clad bottom to the said music*—Punch, 1992.

2 Inversion of the normal order *he said, they said*, etc., is a standard stylistic device in reporting direct speech, especially when the speaker is identified by name rather than by a pronoun: *'I shall go directly,' said Judd. 'I should not like to be marked out in any way.'*—Hilary Mantel, 1989. More debatable, however, is the journalistic convention of using inversion as an eye-catching feature at the beginning of a sentence, e.g. *Said a Minister: 'American interests are not large enough in Morocco to induce us to . . . '.* See INVERSION 1.

sailor, sailer. The spelling is *sailor* when referring to a person, and *sailer* when referring to a ship in relation to its performance, e.g. *a slow sailer.*

Saint, when preceding a name, is spelt with a capital initial letter, and is shortened to *St* (no full stop in BrE though one is normal in AmE). The plural is *SS* or *Sts*, as in *SS | Sts Peter and Paul.*

sake. The standard forms are *for appearances' sake*, *for Christ's* (or *God's* etc.) *sake*, *for old times' sake*, with a singular or plural possessive form for the preceding noun. Practice varies in *for conscience'* (or *conscience's*) *sake* and *for goodness'* (or *goodness*) *sake*. In AmE, *sake* is sometimes used in the plural form *sakes*: *'Shush, for God's sakes!'* warned my mother*—L. S. Schwartz, 1989.

saleable is the recommended form, although *salable* is used by some printers and publishers.

salubrious, salutary. Both words are derived from the Latin word *salus* meaning 'health'. *Salubrious* essentially means 'giving health' and hence also 'pleasant, agreeable' (*The Prince of Wales bestowed a polite eye upon her, then turned to the rather more salubrious prospect of his favourite savoury*—A. Myers, 1992), whereas *salutary* means 'producing healthy effects' and hence 'beneficial', usually in an admonitory context in association with words such as *effect*, *lesson*, and *reminder* (*Those incidents are a salutary reminder of the dedication of police officers to protecting the public*—Hansard, 1992).

salvo. There are two words, (1) 'a firing of guns together', plural *salvoes* (preferred) or *salvos*, and (2) 'a reservation or excuse', plural *salvos.*

same. 1 *Same* (or *the same*) was once commonly used as a pronoun in literary English (*But he that shall endure unto the end, the same shall be saved*—Matthew 24:13 (Authorized Version, 1611)), but is now largely confined to legal and business contexts: *The cross motion for an order for renewal of plaintiff's motion for alimony pendente lite is denied, no sufficiently persuasive ground in support of same having been demonstrated*—New York Law Journal, 1973. In general use the effect is usually jocular or pseudolegalistic, except in uses of the type *My wife ordered lemon sole and I had the same.*

2 When *same* is connected to a following word or phrase, the usual link word is *as*: *Your car is the same make **as** mine.* When a clause follows, *as* may be replaced by *that*: *I've bought the same make of car **as** you have got* or *I've bought the same make of car **that** you have got*, and as a relative pronoun *that* may even be omitted in the normal way: *I've bought the same make of car you have got.* In more formal contexts, however, *as* should be used.

sanatorium is the customary word in BrE for an institution for treating invalids, but in AmE it alternates with *sanitarium* (but the variant *sanatarium* is erroneous).

sanction. 1 The dominant current meaning of the noun is 'a penalty for disobeying a law or rule' and is usually found in the plural, as in the phrase *economic sanctions*. This older meaning goes back to legal terminology of the 16c and 17c. A second, more recent (18c), meaning is 'approval or encouragement given to an action', and it sits happily beside the other one despite being virtually opposite in sense.

2 In the case of the verb, the historical order of senses is the other way round, with 'authorize, approve' as the earlier and 'impose sanctions on' as the later, although this second meaning is not often used: *Georgina Dufoix, the only politician so far sanctioned for allowing the Palestinian guerrilla chief . . . into France — Independent, 1992.*

's and s' and 'of' possessives. 1 The use of '*s* and *s*' to form respectively singular and plural possessive forms of nouns (*a woman's hat | their friends' house | the dog's dinner*) is a survival in an altered form of Anglo-Saxon inflections (normally *-es*) that have otherwise disappeared from English. (For rules see APOSTROPHE 1, 2.) Their use is commoner with nouns that represent humans or animals, as in the examples just given; in other cases the alternative construction with *of* is more usual: *the petals of the flower | the windows of the house*. There are, however, notable exceptions to this general rule:

▶ **a** nouns denoting time or space: *a day's journey | a stone's throw | at arm's length*.

▶ **b** in a number of fixed expressions (in which the possessive noun is often in effect personified): *at death's door | out of harm's way | in his mind's eye | for heaven's sake*.

▶ **c** nouns denoting vessels or vehicles: *the car's wheels | the ships' masts | the plane's engines*.

▶ **d** names (or common nouns) for countries and large places: *Russia's tourist industry | London's homeless | the region's wildlife*. In all these cases there is probably an element of personification, making the nouns concerned 'honorary' living things.

2 Apparent exceptions also occur in uses that are not really possessives at all but denote a looser relationship: *the soil's productivity | the painting's disappearance*. (Compare uses in relation to people, such as *Napoleon's defeat | John's concentration*.)

3 Conversely, the type of construction with *of* known as a 'partitive genitive', e.g. *a glass of water | a dose of salts*, cannot be expressed with a form in '*s* (✘ *a water's glass | ✘ a salts' dose*).

4 It should be noted that some '*s* and *s*' forms with human or animal nouns cannot be converted into *of* forms, usually because the relationship is not simply possessive: *the man's reward | the writer's criticism | the boys' explanation | Sophie's revelation*.

5 For the type *a friend of my father's*, see DOUBLE POSSESSIVE.

sanguine, sanguinary. Both words are derived from the Latin word *sanguis* (stem *sanguin-*) meaning 'blood'. *Sanguine* originally meant 'blood-coloured' but now primarily means 'optimistic, confident' from an earlier association of blood (one of the four bodily 'humours') with this type of temperament. By contrast, *sanguinary* has retained its more physical meanings 'accompanied by blood' and 'bloodthirsty'.

sari is the dominant spelling for the traditional item of dress worn by Indian women, rather than *saree*. The plural form is *saris*.

sat, used for *sitting*, is largely associated with local or dialect usage, but evidence of its use is more widespread than this might suggest: *I can't help thinking of that Tim sat there juddering his leg up and down*—Kingsley Amis, 1988 | *Now, I'm sat in a nice car, my husband at my side*—A. Duff, 1990 (New Zealand). This use remains marginally non-standard nonetheless.

Saturday see FRIDAY.

sauté, meaning 'lightly fried', is spelt in this way. The verb has inflected forms *sautéd* (one *e* only), *sautéing*.

savannah, a grazing plain in subtropical regions, is spelt in this way in BrE but more often as *savanna* in AmE.

save as a conjunction (in combination with *that*) or preposition equivalent to *except* or *but* has a more formal or literary ring to it: *There was little chance of seeing her . . . save as a sari-shrouded figure on the occasion of her marriage*—M. M. Kaye, 1978 | *He had no answer—save that British scientists had been reorganised so often in recent years that it was time for stability*—New Scientist, 1991.

saw, meaning 'to cut with a saw', has the past form *sawed* and past participle *sawn* or (occasionally) *sawed*. As an adjective referring to a shotgun, *sawn-off* is the only form used.

Saxonism is a semi-technical term for a word of Anglo-Saxon rather than Latin origin, e.g. *hundred* as distinct from *century*. Over the centuries since the Norman Conquest the Latinate stock of vocabulary has increased greatly, and recent years have seen a special recourse to words of Latin and Greek origin to give what is regarded as an appropriate importance to great new discoveries such as *television* (of mixed Latin and Greek origin) and *computers*. At various times there have been movements to encourage the use of Anglo-Saxon words, typified in the 19c by the efforts of the English poet William Barnes to promote words such as *bodeword* instead of *commandment* and *gleecraft* instead of *music*. Fowler, however, was not among these Saxonizers, noting (1926) that 'the wisdom of this nationalism in language—at least in so thoroughly composite a language as English—is very questionable'.

say. 1 In ordinary use *say* occurs as a noun only in the expression *have a say* (or variants of it such as *have a bigger say*).

2 The use of *say* as an imperative in uses such as *Let's meet soon—say next Friday* is an established idiom.

sc. is short for Latin *scilicet* (= *scire licet*, 'one may understand or know') and is used with the meaning 'that is to say' to introduce an explanation of a difficult or unclear term, e.g. *the policy of the NUT (sc. National Union of Teachers)*.

scallop, pronounced **skol**-əp, is the preferred spelling for the name of the mollusc, not *scollop*. The verb (meaning e.g. 'to decorate with scallop designs') has inflected forms *scalloped, scalloping.*

scallywag, a word of unknown origin, is normally spelt in this way in BrE, but in AmE other forms such as *scalawag* and *scallawag* are also used.

scaly, meaning 'covered in scales', is spelt in this way, not *scaley.*

scampi, meaning 'large prawns', is a plural noun (of Italian origin), but is sometimes treated as singular in the sense 'a dish of scampi'.

scant, scanty. Both words have meanings to do with smallness or insufficiency. *Scant* is of Norse origin and came into English as several parts of speech including noun and verb as well as adjective. In current use it is only an adjective and even then its use is largely confined to certain set combinations such as *scant attention* and *scant regard*. It is only used in attributive position (i.e. before a noun), whereas the related adjective *scanty* can also be used after a verb and has more general scope, although it tends to be used with reference to concrete rather than abstract nouns (e.g. *a scanty lunch | scanty clothing | property in London is scanty*).

scarcely. 1 The standard construction is *scarcely . . . when . . .* : *Scarcely had he begun when Claverhouse ordered him to rise*—A. Boyle, 1990. The construction with *than*, though increasingly common and perhaps suggested by the analogy of *no sooner . . . than . . .* , is nonstandard: ✖ *But scarcely had he*

begun to investigate these new, if somewhat less adventurous, hunting-grounds, than the entire party was 'summoned back to Hobarton by Sir John'*—I. Tree, 1991. A construction with a following comparative adjective or adverb is however acceptable: *There could scarcely be a less promising environment for an amphibian than the desert of central Australia*—David Attenborough, 1988 | *In Wilson's eyes the condition of the British seaman was scarcely better than it had been half a century earlier*—A. Marsh, 1989.

2 *Scarcely,* like *barely* and *hardly,* has a negative force without being grammatically negative, and another negative should be avoided in the same sentence unless it is in a following subordinate clause: *There is scarcely an aspect of the race that is not rife with meaning*—New Yorker, 1989.

scarf. The word for a piece of outdoor clothing has the plural form *scarves,* whereas for the unrelated word meaning 'a joint or notch in timber, metal, etc.' it is *scarfs.*

scarify, pronounced with the first syllable as in *scab,* is a semi-technical word meaning 'to scratch or make incisions in', and has nothing to do with the verb *scare.* A verb *scarify,* pronounced like *scare* and formed on the analogy of *terrify,* meaning 'to scare or frighten', has been in existence since the 18c but is regarded as colloquial or even nonstandard.

scenario. 1 The pronunciation is normally si-**nah**-ri-oh in BrE and si-**nai**-ri-oh in AmE. The plural form is *scenarios.*

2 The word came into English from Italian in the late 19c as a term for the outline plot of a play, ballet, novel, etc., and was extended to the world of film in the early 20c. From the 1960s a new meaning exploded into use, and the word now commonly refers to any supposed or imagined series of events, or even to a static situation: *How then do we decide which class to assign a couple to where he is a builder and she is a secretary (not that uncommon a scenario)?*—R. Symonds, 1988 | *But in the worst-case scenario, if the heir to the throne cannot hold his marriage together, there could be no throne left for him, or his eldest son, to inherit*—Today, 1992. This use of *scenario* is often regarded with suspicion, but it is hard to see why when so many other comparable figurative uses (such as *scene*) pass without comment. In its right place, when the imagined events or circumstances form a related sequence and are therefore comparable to the elements of a story-line, the word is a useful one.

scene, used figuratively in expressions such as *a scene of mayhem*, is part of the standard language. More informal are uses of the type *not my scene* and *the jazz scene*, originally associated with youth slang but now used more generally.

sceptic, sceptical. A *sceptic* (pronounced **skep**-tik) is someone who doubts accepted opinions or judgements and differs from a *cynic*, whose doubts concern human values and motives. *Sceptic* is also an adjective, but the more common adjectival form is *sceptical*. In AmE the words are spelt *skeptic* and *skeptical*.

sceptre is spelt *-re* in BrE and *scepter* in AmE.

schedule. The dominant pronunciation in BrE is **shed**-yool, but the American form **sked**-yool is beginning to exert an influence, especially among younger speakers.

schism, meaning 'the division of a group into opposing sections', is now commonly heard as skizm in place of the older form sizm recognized by the OED (1910).

schist, a term in geology for a type of layered rock, is pronounced shist.

scholar should be used to mean a learned person or the holder of a scholarship (at a school or university), not as a substitute term for a school pupil.

school, shoal. The two words are of the same Middle Dutch origin and are used with the same meaning of large numbers of fish and other sea animals swimming together. They are unrelated to the more familiar word *school*, which is derived from Latin *schola*.

scion, meaning 'a descendant of a (noble) family', is pronounced **siy**-ən.

scissors is treated as a plural noun in its basic meaning (*The scissors are in the drawer*), but has a singular use in certain sports, where it is usually elliptical for a longer phrase such as *scissors movement* or *scissors pass* (*The ordinary scissors is the least effective of the four styles*).

scone is mostly pronounced skon in BrE, but skohn is also heard, especially in southern England, and is the dominant pronunciation in AmE. *Scone*, a village in central Scotland which was the site of a palace where the kings of Scotland were crowned, is pronounced skoon.

score = 20. *A score of* + plural noun is normally treated as a plural, the plural noun being regarded as the 'head' of the noun phrase: *A score of customers were waiting at the door.*

Scotch, Scots, Scottish. 1 The favoured terms are *a Scot* or *Scotsman* or *Scotswoman* for a person from Scotland, *Scottish* as the general adjective relating to Scotland, and *Scots* for any of the dialect forms of English spoken in (especially Lowland) Scotland (to be distinguished from *Scottish English* which is a variety of standard English). *Scots* is also used in certain expressions such as *Scots law* and the *Scots Guards*.

2 The adjective and noun *Scotch*, though regularly used by Burns and Scott, fell out of favour in the 19c and is now confined to certain fixed expressions such as *Scotch broth, Scotch eggs, Scotch mist*, and *Scotch whisky*. Outside the UK, and especially in America, *Scotch* is likely to occur more often.

scrimmage, scrummage. *Scrimmage* is the more general word for 'a rough struggle or brawl' and is a technical term in American football, whereas *scrummage* (more usually shortened to *scrum*) is the term used in rugby football.

seance, a term for a spiritualist meeting, is now normally spelt without an acute accent on the first *e*.

seasonable, seasonal. *Seasonal* means 'occurring at or associated with a particular season' (*the seasonal migration of geese*), whereas *seasonable* is a more judgemental

word meaning 'suitable for the season or time of year' (*There was a seasonable crispness in the air*).

second. The pronunciation is with the stress on the first syllable in all uses except the verb meaning 'to transfer to another use or employment', when the stress falls on the second syllable.

second hand is normally spelt as two words in uses such as *heard at second hand*, and is hyphened when used as an adjective (*a second-hand car*) or adverbial phrase (*They always buy second-hand*).

secretary should be pronounced as four syllables with the first *r* fully articulated, not as if it were spelt *seketerry* or *sekretry*.

sect is a word of Middle English origin denoting a party or faction holding views other than those of the majority (especially in a religious body). Historically it has been applied by Anglicans to various non-conformist groups (e.g. Methodists and Quakers) and it is now used of various groups, always with unfavourable connotations.

seeing is commonly used as a kind of conjunction, often followed by *that*, with the meaning 'because, considering that': *He was the kid-brother whom I helped as far as I could, seeing that we had no mother*—B. Cobb, 1971. The forms *seeing as* and *seeing as how* occur in informal contexts.

seem. For the type *seems to have been*, see PERFECT INFINITIVE.

seldom see RARELY.

self. Except in commercial contexts (*a cheque drawn to self*), *self* is now used as a substitute for *my-self* or *oneself* only in jocular or informal contexts or in more casual styles of writing: *A.A. [sc. Alcoholics Anonymous] requires memory, the acknowledgement of actions' effects on self and others, then apology and atonement*—B. Holm, 1985.

self- is a highly productive prefix forming compounds of various types, in most of which *self-* acts as the object on which the action or attribute signified by the second element operates, e.g. *self-betrayal* (= betrayal of oneself), *self-awareness* (= awareness of oneself), *self-addressed* (= addressed to oneself), etc. In other uses *self* is an agent, e.g. *self-educated* (= educated by oneself), *self-evident* (evident in itself), and *self-service* (= service by oneself). Occasionally the second element is sufficient by itself and *self-* is arguably redundant, as in *self-assured*, *self-conceited*, and *self-confident*, but the prefix serves a reinforcing role and most of this type are idiomatic.

semi- is the most active and versatile of the prefixes meaning 'half' (the other two being *demi-* and *hemi-*) in forming compounds, often with adjectives and verbal participles as the second element (*semi-automatic*, *semi-detached*, *semi-skilled*, etc.) and occasionally nouns (*semicircle*, *semi-final*). *Semi-* and *demi-* are Latin in origin, whereas *hemi-* is Greek.

semicolon. The semicolon is the least confidently used of the regular punctuation marks in ordinary writing, and the one least in evidence to anyone riffling through the pages of a modern novel. But it is extremely useful, used in moderation. Its main role is to mark a grammatical separation that is stronger in effect than a comma but less strong than a full stop. Normally the two parts of a sentence divided by a semicolon balance or complement each other as distinct from leading from one to the other (in which case a COLON is usually more suitable): *Most of his tools are old, handed down from his father and grandfather and uncles; here they are, handle upward, in tubs of oil and sand to stop them rusting*—Blake Morrison, 1993. It is also used as a stronger division in a sentence that already contains commas: *What has crippled me? Was it my grandmother, frowning on my childish affection and turning it to formality and cold courtesy; or my timid, fearful mother, in awe of everyone including, finally, me; or was it my wife's infidelities, or my own?*—Angela Lambert, 1989.

senator is spelt *-or*, not *-er*.

senior citizen. *She is a retired person, a senior citizen, you might say*—Barbara Pym, 1977. *Senior citizen* is a modern euphemism (first recorded in the 1930s) for an elderly person or old-age pensioner, and is more politically correct because it refers positively to status rather than negatively to age. It is now widely used in official contexts.

sensational. The original meaning 'relating to sensation or the senses', first attested in the mid-19c, has been all but driven out by its extended meaning 'causing or intended to cause an exciting or startling effect' (i.e. causing a *sensation* in the corresponding sense): *Watergate was such a sensational piece of skulduggery*—*Times*, 1980.

sensible, sensitive. 1 The primary meaning of *sensible* is 'having (common) sense', i.e. the opposite of *foolish*, and of *sensitive* 'easily offended or emotionally hurt'. In these uses they hardly get in each other's way. Where they overlap is in meanings to do with reactions involving the senses or feelings: you are *sensible of* something when you apprehend it with emotional consciousness and are *sensitive to* something when you react to it with strong emotional feeling, the words 'consciousness' and 'feeling' characterizing the difference between the two. However, *sensible of* now sounds old-fashioned, and a more likely choice of words might be *conscious of* or *aware of*, although these admittedly denote intellectual rather than emotional perceptions.

2 The nouns *sensibility* and *sensitivity* are harder to keep apart. *Sensibility* corresponds to *sensible* (in its familiar meaning) much less closely than *sensitivity* does to *sensitive*, and chiefly denotes (often in the plural) a person's delicate finer feelings: *Walter was a little hurt at this since he did most of the cooking at their place, but Zimmerman was too upset to worry about Walter's sensibilities*—Ben Elton, 1992. *Sensitivity* has a wider range of meanings concerned with physical or emotional reactions of various kinds: *My reference to it was simply a tease, and all the more tempting given Victor's known sensitivity on the point*—Climber and Hill Walker, 1991 | *It is difficult to see how we can have sensitivity to plants and rivers, trees and ecosystems if we have no sensitivity to the caged animal*—Animal Welfare and the Environment, 1992.

sensitize, not the arguably more correct form *sensitivize*, is the standard word in meanings to do with making things sensitive, normally in physical senses (in photography, for example).

sensual, sensuous. 1 *Sensual* is the older word (15c) and originally described feelings that involved the senses as distinct from the intellect. As it became more closely associated with aspects of physical indulgence characterized by the expression *sensual pleasure* (principally sexual but also to do with food), *sensuous* came into use (first apparently by Milton in 1641) to take over the meanings that *sensual* had once had in relation to aesthetic rather than carnal sensations.

2 In current usage, this distinction holds good for those who want a rule: (sensual) *Modigliani appreciated Kisling for what he was, a sweet-natured, high-spirited, sensual young man*—J. Rose, 1990 | *The Hindu god of love, Kama, is the husband of Rati, the goddess of sensual desire*—P. Allardice, 1990 | (sensuous) *All the sensuous elements of the previous years have been banished; colour has been reduced to a severe combination of browns, dull greens and greys*—J. Golding, 1988 | *The passage exemplifies the distancing effect of simile, and the more sensuous effect of metaphor*—E. Black, 1993.

3 But in the hurly-burly of general usage the meanings are too close, and *sensuous* has begun to go the way of *sensual*, especially in modern popular fiction: *He looked forward to this drink, the first of the day, with a sensuous desire*—Barbara Vine, 1987 | *There was something extremely sensuous about having a man dry her hair, especially this man*—A. Murray, 1993. Although

the complex subtleties of sense perception cause meanings to merge into one another, it is prudent to remember the basic distinction when using these words, so that *sensuous* can retain its full force of meaning in uses that are primarily to do with aesthetics, for example in the context of music or poetry: *Cesti's great gift was for melody: sensuous and eminently singable*—G. Abraham, 1985.

sentence. 1 Many users of this book will have been taught that a sentence is a group of words that makes complete sense, contains a main verb, and when written begins with a capital letter and ends with a full stop (or a question mark if it is a question or an exclamation mark if it is an exclamation). This is a good working definition, and rather than pick holes in it we might more profitably add certain riders to it:

2 A sentence can contain ellipsis, i.e. a verb and other words can be understood or suppressed: *It had been a good party. An unforgettable party, actually. And still was*—A. Huth, 1992. (Ellipsis of *it had been* in the second sentence and *it* in the third.) Grammarians may argue about whether these are all true sentences, but for practical purposes it is sensible to regard them all as qualifying for the term, if only to make straightforward discussion about language structure possible.

3 There are three basic kinds of sentence. A *simple sentence* normally contains one statement: *It has been a good party*. A *compound sentence* contains more than one statement, normally joined by a conjunction such as *and* or *but*: *It has been a good party and we enjoyed it | It has been a good party but I've known better*. A *complex sentence* contains a main clause and one or more subordinate clauses, such as a relative clause introduced by *which* or *who*: *It has been a good party, which we enjoyed very much*.

sentence adverb. 1 Certain adverbs, such as *actually, basically, clearly, frankly, interestingly, normally, regrettably, strictly*, and *usually*, have the special role of qualifying entire statements rather than individual words. Some of these are adverbs of time and frequency and retain a closer connection with the verb despite being separated from it: *It is normally very difficult to get a new sport accepted for the Olympics*—New Yorker, 1984. The others have a more independent role in referring not to the content of the statement but to an external consideration, such as the opinion of the speaker, even though they may not be explicitly expressed as such: *Regrettably, most overseas hotels are not well equipped for disabled holidaymakers*—holiday brochure, 1990 (= as is to be regretted) | *Clearly therefore, we suggest, this points to a 'mole' within British Telecom Prestel headquarters*—Times, 1984 (= as is clear). This phenomenon is commonly associated with 20c usage, but examples of earlier date are recorded.

2 The examples given so far are mostly unexceptionable, but controversy arises with *thankfully, regretfully*, and, above all, *hopefully*: *Hopefully, our experience will be of use to them*—Independent, 1989. This may be because, unlike the others, there is no phrasal basis corresponding to *it is clear that* (for *clearly*) or *to be frank* (for *frankly*), since 'it is to be hoped that' is passive whereas *hopeful* is 'active' (i.e. the person so de-

scribed does the hoping). See
HOPEFULLY.

separate. Note the spelling with
two *a*s, unlike *desperate*. The verb
is pronounced **sep**-ə-rayt, and the
adjective **sep**-ə-rət.

sepulchre is spelt *-re* in BrE and
sepulcher in AmE.

sequence of tenses. This refers
to the pattern of tenses in a sequence of verbs within a sentence. If a simple statement such
as *I'm afraid I haven't finished* is put
into indirect speech by means of
a reporting verb such as *said*,
thought, etc., the tense of the reported action changes in accordance with the time perspective of
the speaker: *He said he was afraid
he hadn't finished*. However, the
tense of the reported verb can
stay the same if the time relative
to the speaker is the same as that
relative to the person reported:
She likes beans can be converted
either to *She said she liked beans*
or to *She said she likes beans*, and *I
won't be here tomorrow* can be converted either to *He said he wouldn't
be here tomorrow* or to *He said he
won't be here tomorrow*.

sergeant, serjeant. The normal
spelling in the context of the police and the army is *sergeant*; *serjeant* is usually restricted to the
titles of certain ceremonial
offices, such as the *serjeant-at-arms*
with reference to the British parliamentary or civic official.

series is spelt the same both as
a singular and as a plural noun.

serviceable is spelt with an *e* in
the middle, to preserve the soft
sound of the *c*.

serviette see NAPKIN.

sesquicentenary see ANNIVER-
SARIES.

sett is still a common variant
spelling of *set* in the meanings (1)
a badger's burrow and (2) a
paving-block.

seventies see EIGHTIES.

several is an adjective and pronoun. As an adjective, it is only
used with plural countable nouns
(*several people* but not *several furniture*) and is more positive in implication than *a few*. However,
unlike *a few*, *several* cannot be
qualified by an adverb such as
quite or *only*.

sew, sow *verbs*. *Sew* means 'to
form stitches with a needle and
thread' and has the past form
sewed and the past participle *sewn*
or *sewed*. *Sow* means 'to plant
(seed)' and has the past form
sowed and the past participle *sown*
or *sowed*.

sewage, sewerage. *Sewage* is
waste matter carried by sewers,
and *sewerage* is a system of
sewers.

sexcentenary see ANNIVERSAR-
IES.

sexist language. Roughly since
the 1970s, certain established
uses of language have come to be
regarded as discriminatory
against women, either because
they are based on male terminology or because women appear
to be given a status that is linguistically and socially subsidiary.
Specific aspects of this will be
found at the entries for -ESS,
GENDER-NEUTRALITY, -MAN, MS,
-PERSON. Since the 1980s, many
official style guides (including Ju-
dith Butcher's *Copy-editing*, third
edition, Cambridge, 1992) have included advice on how to avoid

sexist language. In 1989 the General Synod of the Church of England debated a report on the need to introduce non-sexist language into the liturgy, and in the same year a revised version of the Bible substituted *one* for *man* in such contexts as *Happy is the **man** who does not take the wicked for **his** guide*. It is in the realm of idiom that male-biased language will most likely persist, since it is difficult to reconstruct without awkwardness or affectation such compound words and phrases as *manpower, maiden voyage, every man for himself*, and *the man on the Clapham omnibus*.

shall and will. 1 The customary rule is that to express a simple future tense *shall* is used after *I* and *we* (*In addition to my duties in the House, I shall be having further meetings later today*—Hansard, 1992) and *will* in other cases, whereas to express intention or wish the reverse applies (*We will give people a new right of access to open country, create new national parks and step up protection for special sites— It's time to get Britain working again* (Labour Party), 1992); but it is unlikely that this rule has ever had any consistent basis of authority in actual usage, and many examples of English in print disregard it. In general, the rule applies more strongly to *I* than to *we*.

2 Furthermore, the distinction is often difficult to establish, especially in the first person when the speaker is also the performer of the future action and intention is therefore implied at least partially. *Will* and (occasionally) *shall* are used as auxiliary verbs to refer to future action or state, but other, more natural, ways of expressing this are commonly preferred, such as *am going to*: *I'm*

going to teach him people are more important than money—Maurice Gee, 1992.

3 When *shall* and *will* are used in conversation, they are normally contracted to *'ll*, especially after pronouns, leaving the difference between the two words irrelevant: *They'll cook and clean for a week before a party*—New York Times, 1976 | *I'll remember this sodding day until the day I die*—Dirk Bogarde, 1980.

4 *Shall* has been largely driven out by *will* in all parts of the English-speaking world other than England. It survives mostly in first-person questions or suggestions (*Shall I help you to try again?*—B. Jagger, 1986 | *'Shall we take our drinks to the bedroom?' she said softly*—J. Francome, 1990), in legal language (*The landlord shall maintain the premises*), and in the contracted negative form *shan't* (*'Have no fear . . . I shan't throw in the towel, I promise you.'*—M. Russell, 1979), but *shan't* is not used in American English. In the English of England (*not* of Britain), *shall* half survives in such (now old-fashioned and affected) uses as *Yes, you shall take some eggs back to your aunt*—C. Harvey, 1992 (a command or assurance) and *Shall you come tomorrow?* (seeking information rather than making a request), but *will* (or sometimes *can*) is just as common, especially in speech, and is more natural.

5 There is not much doubt that *will* will win, and *shall* shall lose, in the end.

shambles. The word now most commonly used to mean 'a mess or muddle' has a colourful history. It started life in Old English in the singular form *shamble* meaning 'a stool or footstool', came to refer to a table or stall for the sale of meat, and was then applied (in the plural, *shambles*) to the slaughterhouse from which the meat came. From the 16c it meant any scene of blood and carnage. The modern meaning arose as recently as the 1920s, and is still disliked by many because it debases a powerful word. In these last two senses *shambles* is normally treated as a singular noun, usually in the form *a shambles* (*The house was a shambles* or *The house was in a shambles*).

shamefaced, meaning 'showing shame', is a 16c alteration of an older word *shamefast*, meaning 'bashful', and should be spelt as one word. The adverb *shamefacedly* should be pronounced as four syllables.

shampoo. The verb has inflected forms *shampoos, shampooed, shampooing*.

shanghai, meaning 'to kidnap for naval service', inflects awkwardly in English, but the recommended forms are *shanghais, shanghaied, shanghaiing*.

shan't see SHALL AND WILL 4.

sharp is used as an adverb only in expressions such as *at 10 o'clock sharp* (= exactly) and *He pulled up sharp* (= abruptly). In other meanings of *sharp*, the correct form of the adverb is *sharply* (*Prices dropped sharply* | *She spoke to them sharply*).

shave. The verb has a past form and past participle *shaved*, but the adjectival form is normally *shaven*, as in *clean-shaven*.

she. 1 For *she* or *her* after the verb *be*, see CASES 2A.

2 For the expression *he or she*, see GENDER-NEUTRALITY.

s/he. *A child's sexual orientation is determined before s/he enters school—American Educator*, 1978. This written representation of 'he or she' as a gender-neutral pronoun is generally limited to the domain of reports and dead-pan English. Because it cannot be articulated, it is unlikely to penetrate further into the realms of standard usage. See GENDER-NEUTRALITY.

sheaf has the plural form *sheaves*. The verb meaning 'to make into sheaves' is *sheave*.

shear, sheer. *Shear* is a verb meaning 'to remove by cutting' or 'to cut the wool off (a sheep)', and has the past form *sheared* and the past participle *shorn* or (in the context of metal-cutting) *sheared*. *Sheer* is an adjective describing a steep cliff or ascent and is also used in expressions such as *sheer luck*.

sheath is pronounced sheeth (like *teeth*) in the singular and sheedhz (like *seethes*) in the plural.

sheep is the same in the singular and plural.

sheikh, pronounced shayk or sheek, is the preferred spelling of the word for an Arab chief or leader.

shelf has the plural form *shelves*, and the corresponding verb is *shelve*. The compound form *shelfful* should be written with a hyphen for clarity, and its plural is *shelf-fuls*.

show, shew. The normal spelling is *show*. *Shew* is used in Scottish law and in citations from the Bible and Prayer Book.

shibboleth. The primary meaning in current English is 'a custom or phrase that distinguishes a particular class or group of people', either one approved of or one deprecated in others (*Apparently, to wear a hat in the cafeteria was a student shibboleth*—I. Young, 1990), and is an extension of the biblical meaning of a Hebrew word used by Jephthah as a test-word by which to distinguish the fleeing Ephraimites (who could not pronounce the *sh* sound) from his own men the Gileadites.

shine. The normal past forms and past participle are *shone*, but *shined* is used in AmE and in both varieties in the meaning 'to make (something) shine': *The car is a red Mercedes, newly shined*—S. North, 1989 (UK) | *It occurred to me that this was not a reflection from his glasses or his crown, no matter how much they shined*—D. Pinckney, 1992 (US).

shingles, the disease, is normally treated as a singular noun (*Shingles sometimes follows a bad case of measles*), but it can be plural when the emphasis is on the resulting blisters rather than the illness itself (*The shingles were extremely painful*).

ship see BOAT.

shire. In England, the *shires* are traditionally the foxhunting areas of Leicestershire, Northamptonshire, and the former county of Rutland. Since the reorganization of local government in 1972 and 1986 the term *shire county* has been applied to the 39 counties outside metropolitan areas which have county councils, as distinct from London and the six metropolitan counties.

shoe. The verb has inflected forms *shoes, shoeing,* and (past tense and past participle) *shod*.

shop *verb*. In BrE the verb is used intransitively (i.e. without an object) in its meaning 'to buy things at shops', whereas in AmE it is also used transitively with the meaning 'to examine or buy goods at (a store)': *One man who had shopped the entire store complained that he hadn't found what he was looking for*—S. Marcus, 1974. The informal transitive use 'to inform on (someone)' is chiefly BrE.

short-lived is pronounced shawt-**livd** in BrE and shawt-**liyvd** in AmE.

short, shortly *adverbs*. The roles of these two words are fairly clearly separated. *Short* usually means 'before the expected time or place, abruptly' (*We cut short the celebration* | *They pulled up short*), whereas *shortly* is most often used to mean 'before long, soon' (*She is expected to arrive shortly*).

should and would. 1 As with *shall* and *will*, *should* has been largely driven out by *would* as an auxiliary verb, but there is the added consideration that *should* also (in fact more often than not) denotes obligation or likelihood (*Now I think we should bring down the curtain on this little episode, and go to bed*—A. Browning, 1992 | *The main advantage of digital mobile phones is that you should be able to have more of them*—Economist, 1993).

2 As an auxiliary verb, *would* is more usual than *should* when stating a condition or proposition and is the only choice when asking a question (*They would like to stay* | *I would think so* | *Would you*

bring the children?). Should is sometimes used in the first person
(singular and plural) for statements and propositions, especially in the English of England (*'I
should like one of these,' says
Claudia*—Penelope Lively, 1987) and
in tentative statements of opinion
(*I should say that there is not only increasing public awareness of the
problems of smoking and its long-
term consequences to the health of
smokers, but [etc.]*—Hansard, 1992),
and is always used in inverted
constructions expressing a condition: *St Bernards had placed a fee
on this transfer should he go to a
Football League club*—N. Sands, 1991.

3 *Would* has to be used when referring to unfulfilled conditions
and hypotheses (*Ordinarily, I would
have chosen an empty table*—Brian
Aldiss, 1991) and to habitual action
in the past (*These he would produce
with a flourish during our
Wednesday- and Sunday-evening
sessions*—Will Self, 1993), and to express the future in the past (*Horri-
fied, she realised she would have to
write and thank everyone*—P. Street,
1990).

4 In conversational English, the
contracted forms *I'd, you'd,* etc.,
are often used in simple statements instead of the full forms,
so that the *should/would* distinction is not an issue (*Better ask
yourself which you'd choose*—P. D.
James, 1986 | *I'd be delighted to join
you*—Kingsley Amis, 1988), but in
meanings to do with obligation
or likelihood (see paragraph 1)
the full form *should* has to be
used.

should of. This erroneous form
of *should have* arises in all English-
speaking countries because the
contracted form *should've* is indistinguishable from it in speech. It
is often associated with the

speech of children or poorly educated adults: *Well, you should of
buyed some cigarettes for yourself so
it's your own fault*—S. Mackay, 1984.

shovel. The verb has inflected
forms *shovelled, shovelling* in BrE,
and in AmE usually *shoveled, shov-
eling.*

show. The past tense is *showed* (*I
showed it to them*), and the past
participle is normally *shown* (*Have
you shown it to them?*) but occasionally *showed: Mr Marr hadn't
shown up at any of the places where
he should have been*—Nigel Williams,
1992.

shrilly, meaning 'in a shrill
manner', is pronounced **shril**-li,
with both ls fully articulated.

shrink has a past tense *shrank*
and a past participle *shrunk*, but
shrunken is the normal adjectival
form in both physical and abstract senses: *She was a thin sickly
child with a tremendous head of dark
curly hair, a tiny shrunken face and
enormous eyes*—S. Stewart, 1991 |
*Eliot discussed the shrunken sense in
which 'culture' was applied to the
arts*—R. Crawford, 1990.

shrivel has inflected forms *shrivelled, shrivelling*, and in AmE usually *shriveled, shriveling.*

shy. The adjective has comparative and superlative forms *shyer*
and *shyest*, and derivative forms
shyly, shyness.

sibling is a kind of popularized
technicality, a word reintroduced
by anthropologists in the early
20c and useful now as a gender-
neutral term for 'brother or sister': *Small groups drifted through the
classroom: mothers and fathers, large
numbers of children*—Edward's pupils
along with older and younger
siblings—Penelope Lively, 1990. The

word is also common in the expression *sibling rivalry*: *Moses . . . shows more than a hint of sibling rivalry in his attitude to his brother Aaron*—C. Raphael, 1972.

sic, the Latin word for 'so, thus', is added in round or square brackets after a quoted word or phrase about which some doubt might be expected in the reader's mind, because of a misspelling (which the quoting writer does not want to correct) or some other oddity of use: *Mr Foot . . . started work to settle the miners [sic] dispute even before kissing hands with the Queen*—OED2 citing *The Guardian*, 1974, drawing attention to rather than silently correcting a missing apostrophe. It should not be used as a supercilious comment on the quoted writer's style or supposed looseness of grammar, as in the following example: *I probably have a different sense of morality to [sic] most people*— *Chicago Tribune*, 1994, quoting Alan Clark.

sick see ILL.

sickly is an adjective meaning 'weak in health', and is not used as an adverb.

siege is spelt *-ie-*, as is *besiege*.

sienna, the pigment and its colour of yellowish-brown (*raw sienna*) or reddish-brown (*burnt sienna*) is spelt with two *n*s despite being derived from the name of *Siena* in northern Italy.

sieve, a device for separating solids from liquids, is spelt *-ie-*, and pronounced siv.

signal. The verb has inflected forms *signalled*, *signalling* in BrE, and in AmE usually *signaled*, *signaling*.

signatory is now the usual spelling (not *signatary*) for the noun meaning 'a party or state that has signed an agreement', and the corresponding adjective.

significant other is a coy term for a live-in partner and normally occurs in facetious contexts. See also POSSLQ.

silken see -EN ADJECTIVES.

sillabub see SYLLABUB.

sillily, though formally correct, is too awkward for normal use and is usually replaced by the phrase *in a silly way* or by other one-word adverbs such as *foolishly* or *stupidly*.

silo has the plural form *silos*.

similar is followed by *to*: *It seemed to me that she was acknowledging an emotion similar to my own*—C. Rumens, 1987.

simile is a figure of speech consisting of a direct comparison using a construction with *as . . . as . . .* , or with the first *as* omitted: *Soft as rain slipping through rushes, the cattle came*—Edmund Blunden. Some similes belong to a stock type, e.g. (*as*) *drunk as a lord*, (*as*) *fit as a fiddle*, etc. See also METAPHOR AND SIMILE. Others are constructed with *like*, e.g. *Her skin is like honey*.

simplistic is first recorded in its modern meaning as recently as the late 19c. It differs from *simple* in implying a simplicity that is excessive or misleading rather than direct and useful: *She's quite right . . . It is simplistic to speak of malice*—Tom Stoppard, 1976. To preserve this useful distinction, care should be taken not to use *sim-*

plistic when *simple* itself is adequate.

sincerely. For *Yours sincerely*, see
LETTER FORMS.

sinecure, meaning 'a position
that requires little or no work
but provides profit or honour', is
normally pronounced **siy**-ni-kyoo-
ə, with the first syllable like *sign*.

sine qua non is normally pronounced **see**-nay kwah nohn, although other pronunciations are
heard. It means 'an indispensable
condition or qualification'.

sing. The past form is *sang* and
the past participle is *sung*, although *sung* is found for the past
tense in literature of the 18c and
19c.

singeing, meaning 'burning
lightly', is spelt like this to distinguish it from *singing* (formed
from the verb *sing*).

Sinhalese is the recommended
form of the noun and adjective
associated with Sri Lanka, rather
than *Singalese*, *Singhalese*, and
other variants.

sink. The verb has the past tense
sank (but formerly and occasionally still *sunk*) and the past participle *sunk*. The adjectival forms
sunk and *sunken* are not readily
distinguished: *sunken* is often
used to mean 'submerged' (*a
sunken ship*), 'fallen in, hollow'
(*sunken cheeks, sunken eyes*), and
often 'below the normal level'
(*sunken garden*). *Sunk* is the form
normally chosen for technical expressions such as *sunk fence, sunk
key*, and *sunk panel*, although in
these cases too *sunken* is sometimes used. In general use *sunken*
is the more common choice for
attributive uses (i.e. before
nouns).

sinus has the plural form *sinuses*.
In Latin the plural is *sinus*, not
sini.

siphon is the recommended
form for the noun and the verb,
not *syphon*.

sister, a senior female nurse,
usually in charge of a hospital
ward. The equivalent term in
AmE is *head nurse*.

sister-in-law means (1) one's
wife's or husband's sister, (2)
one's brother's wife, (3) one's
brother-in-law's wife. The plural
is *sisters-in-law*.

sit see SAT.

sitting-room, living-room.
These are the standard terms in
current use for the main room of
a house equipped for comfort.
Lounge is 'non-U' (see U AND NON-
U) when applied to a room in a
private house, and *drawing-room* is
now old-fashioned.

situate, meaning *situated*, survives in legal language and occasionally in the language of estate
agents' descriptions, in the UK
and beyond: *The premises situate at
Lukashya turn-off, Mungwi Road—
Times of Zambia*, 1977. It has no
place in general usage.

situation is a useful noun for expressing the meaning 'a set of
circumstances, a state of affairs',
especially when preceded by a defining adjective, e.g. *the financial
situation, the political situation*, etc.
It is less useful, indeed often redundant, when a noun precedes:
crisis situation adds nothing to *crisis* and *bankruptcy situation* adds
nothing to *bankruptcy* because
both words implicitly denote situations in themselves. On the
other hand, *hostage situation* is a
convenient short way of saying 'a

situation in which hostages have been taken' because *hostage* is not already a 'situation' word.

sixties see EIGHTIES.

sizeable, with an e in the middle, is the recommended spelling.

skeptic, skeptical see SCEPTIC, SCEPTICAL.

ski. The noun has the plural form *skis*, and the verb has inflections *skis*, *skied* (pronounced skeed), *skiing* (pronounced skee-ing). Words ending in -i (in this case from Norwegian) are always awkward in English, and some people prefer to use the forms *ski'd* and *ski-ing* rather than try to force the word into an uncomfortable English pattern, but these look if anything even more ungainly.

skier, skyer. A *skier* (pronounced skee-ə) is a person who skis, whereas a *skyer* (pronounced skiy-ə) is a high hit in cricket.

skilful, skilled. 1 *Skilful* is spelt in this way in BrE, and usually *skillful* in AmE.

2 *Skilled* is the word to use when referring to types of work (also *semi-skilled*, *unskilled*), and is classificatory in function, whereas *skilful* is evaluative and can refer to people and their achievements (*a skilful painter | a skilful painting*).

skill-less should be spelt with a hyphen to avoid the awkward collision of three *l*s.

skyer see SKIER.

slack, slacken. Both words have been in use since the 16c, and remain interchangeable in many meanings. There are, however, some areas of preference: *slacken* is generally more dominant in the sense 'to make or become slack (or slacker)': a breeze, demand, one's energy, one's pace, a rope, the tide, all *slacken*, and we *slacken* our efforts, our grip, our opposition. In the meaning 'to be lazy or idle' *slack* is used, but only in progressive tenses: *She thought I was slacking* but not ☒ *She thought I had slacked*.

slander see LIBEL.

slang. 1 The term *slang* is first recorded in the 1750s, but it was not used by Dr Johnson in his *Dictionary* of 1755 nor entered in it as a headword (he used the term *low word*, with implications of disapproval). Nonetheless, the notion of highly informal words or of words associated with a particular class or occupation is very old, and this type of vocabulary has been commented on, usually with disfavour, for centuries. More recently, the development of modern linguistic science has led to a more objective assessment in which slang is seen as having a useful purpose when used in the right context.

2 Drawing the line between colloquial language and slang is not always easy; slang is at the extreme end of informality and usually has the capacity to shock. In English slang often has associations of class or occupation, so that many slang words have their origins in cant (the jargon of a particular profession, e.g. *bogus, flog, prig, rogue*), criminal slang (*broad* = female companion, *drag* = inhalation of tobacco smoke, *nick* = to steal), racing slang (*dark horse, no-hoper, hot favourite*), military slang (*bonkers* = crazy, *clobber* = beat or defeat, *ginormous* =

huge), and most recently computing slang (*hacking* = breaking into networks, *surfing* = browsing on the Internet). Other words stay largely within their original domain of usage, such as drugs slang (*flash* = pleasant sensation from a narcotic drug, *juice* = a drug or drugs) and youth slang (*blatantly* = definitely, *wicked* = excellent).

3 Slang words are formed by a variety of processes, of which the following are the main ones:
▶**a** established words used in extended or special meanings: *flash* and *juice* in the previous paragraph, *awesome* = excellent, *hooter* = nose, *take out* = kill.
▶**b** words made by abbreviation or shortening: *fab* from *fabulous*, *pro* from *professional*, *snafu* (= *situation normal: all fouled up*).
▶**c** rhyming slang: *Adam and Eve* = believe, *butcher's* (*hook*) = look.
▶**d** words formed by compounding: *airhead* = stupid person, *couch potato* = person who lazes around watching television, *snail mail* = ordinary mail as opposed to email.
▶**e** merging of two words: 'portmanteau' words such as *ditsy* = *dotty* + *dizzy*, *ginormous* = *gigantic* + *enormous*.
▶**f** backslang, in which the spelling or sound of other words are reversed: *yob* from *boy*, *slop* from *police*.
▶**g** reduplications and fanciful formations: *heebie-jeebies*, *okey-doke*.
▶**h** words based on phrases or idioms: *bad-mouth* = to abuse, *feel-good* as in *feel-good factor*, *in-your-face* = aggressive, *drop-dead* = extremely (beautiful etc.), *must-have* = essential, *one-night stand* = brief sexual encounter.
▶**i** loanwords from other languages: *gazump*, *nosh*, *shemozzle* from Yiddish, *kaput* from German, *bimbo* from Italian (= little child).
▶**j** words taken from dialect or regional varieties: *manky* = dirty, from Scottish; *dinkum* = genuine, right, Australian and New Zealand.

4 Slang uses are especially prevalent in areas in which direct language is regarded as taboo or unsocial, such as death (*to kick the bucket, to hand in one's nosebag, to snuff it*), sexual functions (*to have it off, to screw*), and excretion (*to dump, to sit on the throne*).

5 Slang is by its nature ephemeral, and relatively few words and uses pass into standard use. Examples of these include *bogus, clever, joke*, and *snob* (all classed by Dr Johnson as 'low words'). Conversely some words that were once standard have passed into slang (e.g. *arse, shit, tit*).

6 The first work to record English slang was published as B.E.'s *Dictionary of the Canting Crew* in 1699. Modern works include Eric Partridge's famous *Dictionary of Slang and Unconventional English* (edited by Paul Beale, 1984), *The Slang Thesaurus* (edited by Jonathon Green, 1986), and *The Oxford Dictionary of Modern Slang* (edited by John Ayto and John Simpson, 1992).

slate *verb*. There is an important difference between its meanings on the two sides of the Atlantic. In BrE it means 'to criticize severely', whereas in AmE it usually means 'to nominate' or 'to designate or schedule' (as in *slating* a meeting). The context will normally clarify which sense is meant, but care is needed in interpreting newspaper headlines such as *Summit meeting slated*.

slavish is spelt without an *e*.

slay, meaning 'to kill', has the past tense *slew* and the past participle *slain*. In BrE it has a literary flavour, but it is an ordinary word for violent killing in AmE, appearing in newspaper headlines such as *Serial killer slays seven*, which sometimes get carried over into British newspapers as well.

sled, sledge, sleigh. All three words are derived from Dutch and are used for vehicles that carry people or goods over snow. In BrE *sledge* is the normal word for vehicles of various sizes pulled by people or animals (*toboggan*, a native American word, is also used for the type used for sport on slopes). *Sled* is used mainly in North America for a large vehicle pulled by animals, and *sleigh* for the larger type of vehicle drawn by horses or reindeer.

sleight, as in *sleight of hand*, is pronounced like *slight*. It is the noun equivalent of the adjective *sly*, as *height* is of *high*.

slimy is spelt without an *e*.

sling has the past tense and past participle *slung*.

slink has the past tense and past participle *slunk*.

sloe-worm see SLOW-WORM.

slogan was originally a Gaelic word for a warcry, but the dominant meaning now is the less specific one 'a watchword or motto' (*ban the bomb, business as usual*) or 'a short catchy phrase used in advertising' (*Persil washes whitest*).

slough. The noun meaning 'bog or swamp' is pronounced to rhyme with *now*. The separate word (noun and verb) to do with an animal's skin is pronounced to rhyme with *stuff*. In AmE, the first noun is often written *slew* and pronounced sloo.

slovenly is used as both adjective and adverb; the form *slovenlily* would be too awkward and is not used.

slow, slowly. In current English the normal adverb for general purposes is *slowly* (*We drove slowly down the road | She slowly closed the door*). Literary uses of *slow* as an adverb died out in the 19c (*As the stately vessel glided slow beneath the shadow*—Byron, 1812), and in current usage it is confined to the expression *go slow*, to compounds such as *slow-acting* and *slow-moving*, and to occasional informal uses (*It was easy to drive slow and look into lighted uncurtained windows*—L. Ellmann, 1988). The comparative and superlative forms *slower* and *slowest* are however regularly used as well as *more slowly* and *most slowly*: *Neurotransmitters make the heart beat faster or slower*—Scientific American, 1974 | *I tried to keep one thing—the foot—in focus throughout, because it seemed to be moving slowest*—Photography (Argus), 1990.

slow-worm, a small legless lizard, is the dominant current spelling (formerly also *sloe-worm*). The word is unconnected with either *sloes* (the fruit) or the adjective *slow*.

slur. The verb has inflected forms *slurred, slurring*.

slush, sludge, slosh. *Sludge* is usually applied to something relatively thick and less liquid, e.g. to wet clinging mud or slimy deposits, whereas *slush* more typically describes thawing snow or melting ice. *Slosh* (in its related uses) is a verb meaning 'to move with a splashing sound'.

sly. The adjective has comparative and superlative forms *slyer* and *slyest*, and derivative forms *slyly*, *slyness*.

smell *verb*. The form for the past tense and past participle in BrE is *smelled* or *smelt*; in AmE *smelled* is usually preferred. When the verb is used intransitively, the quality of the smell is normally expressed either by a phrase introduced by *of* or by an adjective, and not an adverb: *His jacket smelt of horses and tobacco and general maleness*—A. Fraser, 1975 | *As she stooped lower her breath, caught in all the black veils, smelled terrible*—Molly Keane, 1988. A comparative construction with *like* is also possible: *This smells like a poncey brothel*—L. Henderson, 1970. When an adverb is used it is normally an intensifying adverb (*His jacket smelled strongly of horses . . .* | *. . . it smelled extremely putrid*), and this applies when *smell* is used absolutely with the meaning 'to smell badly, to stink': *The prison cell smelt abominably.*

smite has the past tense *smote* and a past participle *smitten*. In its physical meaning 'to hit', *smite* is falling into disuse in ordinary contexts, but *to be smitten* is still going strong in its figurative meaning 'to be infatuated or obsessed' (*He was smitten by her beauty*).

smog, formed from *smoke* + *fog* and first recorded in 1905, is one of the most enduring portmanteau words of the 20c.

smoky is spelt without an *e*.

smoulder, meaning 'to burn slowly', is spelt in this way in BrE and usually *smolder* in AmE.

snaky, meaning 'winding or sinuous', is spelt without an *e*.

sneak *verb*. Its origins are shrouded in mystery (despite earlier similar forms in Old English and other Germanic languages) as it emerges full clad in the works of English playwrights around 1600: *A poor unminded outlaw, sneaking home*—Shakespeare, *1 Henry IV*, iv.iii.58, 1596. In current use it is inflected regularly, with a past tense and past participle *sneaked*; the bizarre form *snuck*, which has no precedent in other verbs in -*eak* and -*eek* (*creak, leak, peak, peek, reek, squeak*, etc.) has insinuated itself into several varieties of English, including those of North America, but is not yet treated seriously in BrE. An odd word with an odd history, perhaps with further oddities to come.

snivel. The verb has inflected forms *snivelled, snivelling* in BrE, and in AmE usually *sniveled, sniveling*.

so. 1 *The weather is so uncertain*. Fowler's (1926) reservations about what he termed the 'appealing *so*' (i.e. the use of *so* to appeal for agreement) had more to do with group psychology than good use of language. The use is thoroughly idiomatic in conversational English, although in more didactic contexts, such as *that aesthetically so brilliant world of Greater Greece*, it sounds decidedly affected or has 'a certain air of silliness' (as Fowler expressed it).

2 *So that* is well established as an alternative to *in order that*, but it is often used to denote result as much as intention: *Police . . . confiscated hundreds of pairs of laces from 'bovver boots' so that the youngsters wearing them could not kick anyone—Daily Telegraph*, 1980. In more recent usage, *so* is often used alone with the same meaning, leaving the causal connection even more tenuous: *My father had been a minor diplomat, so as a child I had lived in France, Turkey and Paraguay—Graham Greene*, 1980 (here *so* definitely denotes result rather than purpose).

3 For *do so*, see DO 3E.

sobriquets.
See box opposite

so-called is traditionally used before a name or description to signal doubt about relevance or entitlement, as in *this so-called work of art*. In recent usage it has been applied in a way that simply calls attention to the description, or distances the user from it, without necessarily questioning it: *the so-called generation gap* (i.e. the phenomenon that people call the generation gap). In speech intonation normally makes the meaning clear, and in print the context does the same.

sociable, social. These two words relate to different meanings of *society*, and should not normally get in each other's way. *Social* is a classifying word that relates to society in the broad sense of the relation of human beings to one another (*Man is a social animal | a social occasion*). A *social worker* is one who deals with those in society who need help, and *social security* is financial assistance given to them. *Sociable* is a judgemental word relating to the quality of human relations (corresponding to *society* in the sense 'companionship, good com-

pany'). A *sociable* person is one who is friendly and able to deal well with social occasions, and a *sociable* evening is one marked by friendliness and good humour.

sociologese. The seemingly pretentious and opaque language found in some writing on sociology was an obvious target for Sir Ernest Gowers in his edition of Fowler's book (1965). Among several examples, all unattributed, the following was typical: *The technique here reported resulted from the authors' continuing interest in human variables associated with organizational effectiveness. Specifically, this technique was developed to identify and analyse several types of interpersonal activities and relations, and to provide a method for expressing the degree of congruence between two or more of these activities and relations in indices which might be associated with available criteria of organizational effectiveness*. But there is a difference between sociology written for sociologists (which this is) and sociology intended for a wider readership (if there is such a thing). For reservations about choosing linguistic targets from technical domains, see more generally GOBBLEDEGOOK, JARGON, PLAIN ENGLISH.

sojourn. '*You seem to have acquired a very utilitarian view of universities, from your sojourn in Rummidge,*' said Professor Penrose, *who was one of the very few people Robyn knew who used the word sojourn in casual conversation—David Lodge*, 1988. The word is normally pronounced **soj**-ən.

solemnness is spelt with two *ns*, if needed instead of the more usual *solemnity*.

soliloquy see MONOLOGUE.

sobriquets

A sobriquet (preferred spelling, not *soubriquet*) is a nickname that has become so firmly attached to a particular person, place, or thing, that it is understood independently of the real name and is often used in preference to it. The table below gives a selection (some have more than one).

NAME	STANDS FOR
Albion	England
alma mater	one's college or university
Athens of the North	Edinburgh
Auld Reekie	Edinburgh
Auntie	the BBC
Bard of Avon	Shakespeare
Beefeater	Yeoman of the Guard
Big Apple	New York
Black Country	the industrial west Midlands of England
Black Death	the 14c plague in England
Black Prince	the eldest son of Edward III
City of Dreaming Spires	Oxford
Emerald Isle	Ireland
Garden of England	Kent
Iron Duke	the Duke of Wellington
Jack Tar	a sailor in the Royal Navy
John Bull	an Englishman
Kiwi	a New Zealander
Left Bank	the artistic district of Paris
Maid of Orleans	Joan of Arc
Old Nick	the devil
Old Lady of Threadneedle Street	the Bank of England
The Pond	the Atlantic Ocean
sport of kings	horseracing
Stars and Stripes	the flag of the USA
Swan of Avon	Shakespeare
The Thunderer	*The Times* (newspaper)
Tinseltown	Hollywood
Tommy (Atkins)	a British soldier
Uncle Sam	USA
Union Flag (or Union Jack)	the British flag
Virgin Queen	Queen Elizabeth I of England

solo has the plural form *solos*.

soluble, solvable. Substances are *soluble*, not *solvable*, but problems and difficulties are *soluble* or *solvable*. The opposites are *insoluble* and *unsolvable*.

sombre is spelt this way in BrE, and *somber* in AmE.

sombrero, a broad-brimmed Mexican hat, has the plural form *sombreros*.

some. 1 The use of *some* to mean 'very much' or 'notably such' in sentences of the type *This is some party* is still considered suitable mainly for informal contexts, and Churchill's famous line in a speech in 1941, *Some chicken! Some neck!* (in response to a warning that England would have her neck wrung like a chicken), does not seem to have affected popular perception of it. It is also used ironically with the opposite meaning in sentences such as *Some friend he is to treat you like that!*

2 In AmE *some* is used to mean 'to some extent', as in *She thought about it some*, in the same way that *any* is used to mean 'at all' (*You haven't aged any*), and is occasionally used with the meaning 'somewhat' to qualify an adjective *He's going to be some pissed off when he finds out about this*—M. Machlin, 1976. These uses are not found in BrE.

3 When *some* is used before a number, the number should be an approximate or rounded one: *There are in Britain some two hundred and twenty known varieties of hover fly*—*Punch*, 1966.

4 The phrase *some of us* may be treated as a first-person or a third-person phrase depending on the degree of involvement by the speaker or writer: *Some of us want to change our plans* includes the speaker whereas *Some of us want to change their plans* excludes or at least distances the speaker from the intended change of plans. The choice only arises when a personal or possessive pronoun or adjective (here *our* and *their*) follows in the sentence.

somebody, someone. 1 Both words have been in use since the early 14c and are largely interchangeable. *Some one* occurs as two separate words less often than *any one* (see ANY 4), but uses of the type *Some one thousand eggs have been collected* should be borne in mind.

2 For clashes of agreement in sentences of the type *I really resent it when I call somebody who's not home and they don't have an answering machine*, see AGREEMENT 4.

someday is now commonly spelt as one word in BrE as well as AmE when it is used as an indefinite adverb: *He likes writers and wants to be one someday*—J. McInerney, 1988. When it is further qualified, and therefore more compositional in character, it is written as two words, as in *Let us meet some day soon*.

someplace is a common alternative for *somewhere* in AmE, but still sounds somewhat alien in British contexts: *She can get a good job herself someplace and they can get married*—Lee Smith, 1983.

somersault is now the dominant spelling for the acrobatic movement, rather than *summersault*.

sometime, some time. 1 *Sometime*, spelt as one word, is an indefinite adverb with two main meanings: (1) 'former', as in *their friend and sometime partner*, and (2) 'at some time in the future', as in *I'll tell you about it sometime*. When *some* and *time* both retain their separate meaning, they are spelt as two words: *Do you have some time to spare? | The job will take some time to finish*.

2 *Sometime* is also used to mean 'occasional', especially in the phrase *a sometime thing*, but this use is not standard: *The Federal bureaucracy has grown unwieldy and* *party discipline in Congress is a sometime thing*—Newsweek, 1980.

sometimes, some times. The common adverb *sometimes* is written as one word: *I sometimes like my coffee black. Some* and *times* are spelt as two words when they retain their separate meanings, normally as a noun phrase: *We used to have some times, in the old days*.

something. The practice, originally in AmE and now spreading to BrE, of adding *-something* to a multiple of ten to denote an age range (most often but not exclusively *thirty-something*) is a convenient informal device: *This comic strip collection chronicles the demands of a 'thirtysomething' career woman*—Publishers Weekly, 1989.

somewhen would be a useful word if people took it seriously, but its use has always been rare and only in the company of a better established word such as *somewhere* or *somehow*: *I shall write out my thoughts more at length somewhere, and somewhen, probably soon*—John Stuart Mill, 1833 | *I cherished the belief that somehow and somewhen I should find my way to Oxford*—J. C. Masterman, 1975.

son-in-law means one's daughter's husband. The plural is *sons-in-law*.

soon. *No sooner*, being a comparative expression, is followed by *than*, not *when*: *No sooner had a vaccine for Marek's Disease been found than Fowl Pest swept through our poultry flocks*—Country Life, 1972.

soprano has the plural form *sopranos*.

sort of see KIND OF.

soufflé is spelt with an acute accent on the *e* and is pronounced **soo**-flay.

sound. The adverb is confined to the expressions *sound asleep* and *sleep the sounder* (as in *He slept the sounder for a long walk*).

soundbite, meaning 'a short pithy extract from a recorded interview', is a media word of the 1980s that is still going strong, along with *photo opportunity* and *spin doctor*. All three terms arose first in the US, and have spread rapidly to other parts of the English-speaking world.

south, southern, southerly see EAST.

southward, southwards. The only form for the adjective is *southward* (*in an southward direction*), but *southward* and *southwards* are both used for the adverb, with a preference for *southwards* in BrE: *the longer transhumant routes from the Pyrenees southwards to Catalonia*—Times Literary Supplement, 1976.

sow *verb* see SEW.

spadeful has the plural form *spadefuls*. See -FUL.

spastic has been used since the 18c to refer to victims of cerebral palsy and other afflictions causing spasmodic movements of the limbs. Its use in the 1970s and 1980s, especially by young people, in the generalized meaning 'inadequate, incompetent', with reference to people, not only is deeply offensive but has compromised the normal use of the word to an extent that makes it too seem derogatory now. In these circumstances a phrase such as 'suffering from cerebral palsy' is preferable for the adjective and 'person suffering from cerebral palsy' for the noun.

-speak. George Orwell's term *Newspeak*, used in his novel *Nineteen Eighty-Four* to describe a sinister language used for official communications, gave the English-speaking world a new suffix that could be used to form terms for any special mode of speaking or writing. Examples of its wide use include *Britspeak, criticspeak, gutterspeak, netspeak* (the language of television networks), and *royalspeak*: *'I am most grateful and touched that you have decided to name a locomotive after me,'* it [sc. a telegram] *said in classic royalspeak*—Guardian, 1981.

speciality, specialty. In the primary meanings, 'a product, activity, or service in which a person or group specializes' and 'a special feature or skill', *speciality* is the word in BrE and *specialty* in AmE: *We had eaten nothing with the champagne except a small dish of potato crisps, a speciality from the island of Maui*—David Lodge, 1991 | *She considered dog issues her specialty*—T. Drury, 1991 (US).

special, specially see ESPECIAL, ESPECIALLY.

species is pronounced **spee**-sheez, and is unchanged in the plural. Note that *specie*, pronounced **spee**-shi, is a technical term for coin as opposed to paper money.

specious, spurious. *Specious*, like the Latin word *speciosus* from which it is derived, began its life meaning 'having a fine outward appearance' (from Latin *species* 'outward form'), but in the 17c acquired the unfavourable connotations that now characterize its meaning as 'plausible but in fact

wrong' as in *a specious argument*. *Spurious*, which is sometimes confused with *specious*, is derived from the Latin adjective *spurius* 'false', and means 'not genuine, not being what it purports to be'. A *specious* claim is one that is attractive but insubstantial whereas a *spurious* claim is one based on a false premiss.

spectator is spelt -*or*, not -*er*.

spectre is spelt this way in BrE, and *specter* in AmE.

spectrum has the plural form *spectra*.

speculator is spelt -*or*, not -*er*.

speed *verb*. The past tense and past participle are *sped* when the meaning is 'to go fast' (*The car sped past* | *By that time she had sped down the road*) and *speeded* when the meaning is 'to break a speed limit' or when the verb is followed by *up* (*He often speeded to get there in time* | *The reform process needs to be speeded up*).

spell *verb*. The form for the past tense and past participle is *spelt* or *spelled*. *Spelt* is more usual in BrE, especially in the primary meaning 'to write or name the letters of a word'; *spelled* is more common in AmE and in the phrasal verb *spell out* = to explain in detail.

spelling.
See box opposite

spill. The form for the past tense and past participle is *spilled* or *spilt*: *He nearly spilled his drink*—John Updike, 1988 | *The lounge boy . . . left too much change on the table and a puddle where he'd spilt the Coke*—Roddy Doyle, 1990 | *Other multinationals doubtless polluted waterways or spilt their toxics*—

spelling

1 Before the invention of printing in the 15c, English and other European languages lacked any regularity of spelling and usage was largely based on personal preference. Despite the development of rules, English remains notoriously beset by irregularities of spelling, and various proposals have been made over the years for reforms that would make spelling more straightforward in the interests of native speakers and foreign learners alike. These proposals have usually been based on phonetic principles, so that a reformed spelling conforms more to pronunciation, but questions of whose pronunciation forms the basis and which spellings are appropriate when more than one is available for a particular sound (e.g. *ou* as in *count* or *ow* as in *cow*) have not been resolved. Another objection is that a phonetic orthography would obscure word origins and connections, especially in groups of words in which the stress pattern changes, e.g. *adore* / *adoration* and *nation* / *national*. In any case, no machinery for reform exists, and it is unlikely that significant change can be achieved except by the weight of ordinary usage. (For a fuller discussion of this issue, see *The Oxford Companion to the English Language*, 1992, 973–6.)

2 A major cause of confusion is the exceptional tolerance English has for variant spellings. This works in unpredictable ways, so that *accessary* / *accessory* and *judgement* / *judgment* are all permitted spellings whereas *accomodation* is not a permitted variant of *accommodation* nor *millenium* of *millennium*. In this book, preferred spellings are given when legitimate alternatives exist and correct spellings are identified when other occurring forms are not legitimate.

3 There are two broad categories of spelling difficulty: (1) systematic problems that occur in words belonging to a certain type (e.g. the formation of nouns from verbs in *-dge*, such as *acknowledgement* and *judgement*) and in the inflection of words (e.g. the plural of nouns in *-o* such as *potato* and *solo*, and the *-ed* and *-ing* forms of verbs such as *benefit* and *unravel*), and (2) individual difficulties attached to particular words (e.g. *embarrass* with two *r*s but *harass* with one, and *millionaire* with one *n* but *questionnaire* with two) and sets of words that can be confused (e.g. *desert* / *dessert* and *hoard* / *horde*). The second category includes words adopted with little change from other languages, causing problems of inflection in English (e.g. *shanghai* and *ski*).

4 Guidance on the more important systematic features of spelling and inflection will be found in the following separate entries: ABBREVIATIONS, CO-, CONTRACTIONS, DE-, DIS-, DOUBLING OF FINAL

▶

▶ spelling
continued

CONSONANTS WITH SUFFIXES, -ER AND -EST FORMS, -ER AND -OR, -EY AND -Y IN ADJECTIVES, -FUL, HYBRID FORMATIONS, I BEFORE E, -IZE, -ISE IN VERBS, LATIN PLURALS, -LESS, -LIKE, -LY, MIS-, NON- , -O, PALINDROME, PRE-, -RE AND -ER, SELF-, SEMI-, -T AND -ED, -UM, UN-, -XION.

5 For differences in British and American spelling, see AMERICAN ENGLISH 3.

6 The table below lists words in common use that cause particular spelling difficulties. Some of these are also given as separate entries.

WORD	COMMENT
accommodate, accommodation, etc.	two *c*s, two *m*s
acknowledgement	*-dge-* preferred form
acquaint, acquaintance, etc.	*acq-*
acquire	*acq-*
acquit	*acq-*
aggressive, aggression, etc.	two *g*s, two *s*'s
apostasy	ends *-asy*
appalling	two *p*s, two *l*s
artefact	*arte-* preferred to *arti-*
asphalt	not *ash-*
bail / bale	see entry
baulk	see entry
biased	preferred to *biassed*
breach / breech	see entry
changeable	*-eable*
chord / cord	see entry
commemorate	two *m*s followed by one *m*
committee	two *m*s, two *t*s
complement / compliment	see entry
connoisseur	two *n*s, two *s*'s
consensus	not *concensus*
cooperate, cooperation, etc.	no hyphen
desiccated	one *s*, two *c*s
desperate	two *e*s
diphthong	not *dipthong*
dispatch	preferred to *despatch*
dissect	two *s*'s
dissipate	two *s*'s, one *p*
draft / draught	see entry
ecstasy	ends *-asy*
eighth	two *h*s

▶

▶ spelling
continued

WORD	COMMENT
embarrass, embarrassment, etc.	two *r*s, two *s*'s
enthral	one *l*
exhilarate	two *a*s
fulfil	one final *l*; AmE also *fulfill*
gauge	*-au-* not *-ua-*
guard, guardian, etc.	*-ua-* not *-au-*
harass, harassment, etc.	one *r*, two *s*'s
hoard / horde	see entry
idiosyncrasy	ends *-asy*
impostor	ends *-or*
install	two *l*s
instalment	one *l*; AmE *installment*
judgement	*-dge-* preferred form
liquefy	ends *-efy*
manoeuvre	*-oeu-*; AmE *maneuver*
mayonnaise	two *n*s, one *s*
medieval	*-e-* preferred to *-ae-*
mellifluous	two *l*s followed by *fl*
memento	*mem-* not *mom-*
millennium	two *l*s, two *n*s
millionaire	two *l*s, one *n*
minuscule	not *miniscule* (see entry)
mischievous	not *-ievious*
misspell	two *s*'s
moccasin	two *c*s, one *s*
necessary	one *c*, two *s*'s
occurrence	two *c*s, two *r*s
Portuguese	*u* before and after *g*
practice / practise	see entry
principal / principle	see entry
questionnaire	two *n*s
rarefy	ends *-efy*
recommend	one *c*, two *m*s
restaurateur	no *n*
resuscitate	*-s-* followed by *-sc-*
Romanian	*Rom-* not *Rum-*
sacrilegious	*-i-* followed by *-e-*
separate	two *a*s
stationary / stationery	see entry
supersede	not *-cede*
threshold	one *h*
unwieldy	not *-wieldly*

▶

► **spelling**
continued

WORD	COMMENT
veterinary	not *vetinary*
wholly	preferred to *wholely*
withhold	two *hs*

Guardian, 1994. Although *spilt* was the more favoured form until the end of the 19c *spilled* seems to be more common in the 20c (especially in the past form), but *spilt* is secure in the expression (*crying over*) *spilt milk*. There is no clear evidence of a distinction in the patterns between BrE and AmE.

spin *verb*. The form for the regular past tense and past participle is *spun*: *The other man spun towards the sound, gun extended, ready to fire* —A. Lejeune, 1986 | *I was spun round, and dragged back* —A. Billson, 1993. Before the 20c *span* was commonly used for the past tense but this is now a deviant form.

spinach. The recommended pronunciation is **spin**-ij, but **spin**-ich is usual in AmE and also occurs in BrE.

spin doctor, someone who speaks at a senior level for a political party and gives a favourable 'spin' (i.e. interpretation) to events, is a vogue media term of the 1980s and 1990s: see SOUND-BITE.

spinney, a BrE word for a small wood or copse, has the plural form *spinneys*.

spiral. The verb has inflected forms *spiralled*, *spiralling* in BrE, but often *spiraled*, *spiraling* in AmE.

spirit. The verb has inflected forms *spirited*, *spiriting*.

spiritual, spirituous. The two words now have distinct meanings, *spiritual* being the general word relating to the spirit or soul, and *spirituous* referring to distilled alcoholic drinks. In older writing up to the end of the 19c *spirituous* is sometimes found as a synonym of *spiritual*.

spirt see SPURT.

spit *verb*. The form for the regular past tense and past participle in BrE is *spat*, but in AmE either *spat* or *spit* is used: *I was so mad I could have spit*—New Yorker, 1989.

spitting image, meaning 'an exact double', is an established phrase, although it is in origin a misunderstanding of *spit and image* (*spit and picture* also occurred), which was itself an extension of the early 19c phrase *the* (*very*) *spit of*. A transitional form *spitten image* is first recorded in 1910. The older forms are also occasionally found: *Look at this, Father, appeared last Friday on Sister Philomena, the very spit and image of the nail marks in the palms of our Blessed Lord*—Hilary Mantel, 1989.

spiv, a 20c British colloquial expression for 'a man characterized by flashy dress, who makes a living by illicit or unscrupulous dealings', emulates the American genius for inventing short words (e.g. *blurb, stunt*) whose sound is curiously suited to their meaning. *Spiv* may be connected with the late 19c slang words *spiffed* 'smartly dressed' and *spiffy* 'smart, spruce'.

splendour is spelt *-our* in BrE and *splendor* in AmE.

split infinitive. 1 A split infinitive occurs when a word (usually an adverb) or phrase comes between the particle *to* and the verb of a so-called *to*-infinitive (*to really love | to really and truly love*). No other grammatical issue has so divided English speakers since the split infinitive was declared to be a solecism in the 19c: raise the subject of English usage in any conversation today and it is sure to be mentioned. The term itself is first recorded as recently as the 1890s, although the controversy is somewhat older and the practice very much so. Examples occur in Middle English (though only twice in Chaucer) but it went out of fashion from the 16c to the end of the 18c, and no examples have been found in Shakespeare (unless we count Sonnet 142: *Root pity in thy heart, that when it grows, Thy pity may deserve to pitied be*). During the 19c it came back into favour, with examples to be found in Fanny Burney, Thomas Hardy, and most famously in a poem of Byron: *To sit on rocks to muse o'er flood and fell, To slowly trace the forest's shady scene—Academy*, 1897.

2 Now, at the end of the 20c, the split infinitive is widely held to be an error on the grounds that the particle *to* and its verb belong together. The basis for this belief is highly questionable.

Other separations occur, for example between a verb and its auxiliary verb (*I have never said so*), but as a matter of style (rather than grammar) the objection can be valid, especially when the adverb can be placed naturally in another position or when the split is a lengthy one: *We talked about how everything was going to suddenly change*—Nigel Williams, 1985 (defensible on grounds of emphasis, perhaps, but the normal order is *We talked about how everything was suddenly going to change*) | *You two shared a curious dry ability to without actually saying anything make me feel dirty*—Philip Roth, 1987 (split here for effect).

3 On the other hand, the split infinitive avoided, usually by putting the adverb before or after the entire *to*-infinitive, can lead to results that are just as unnatural, often stylistically poor, and in some cases ambiguous or misleading: *Rhys considers it unwise to attempt radically to alter taxes on large cars, as proposed by Labour*—Autocar and Motor, 1990 | *It should be the Government's task quietly to advocate such a comprehensive strategy with our American allies*—Times, 1998. In both examples the natural position of the adverbs *radically* and *quietly* is after the word *to*, and in the first case the important connection between *radically* and the verb it qualifies (*alter*) is compromised. In some cases, the adverb becomes attached to the wrong verb: *It was in Paris that the wartime alliance began finally to break up*—television broadcast, 1998. It is arguable in these cases that the adverb, or adverb phrase, has a stronger claim to association with the verb than does the purely functional particle *to*. In writing it is often possible to rephrase so as to avoid the hazard altogether, but in speech a sentence once begun has to be finished, and sometimes an infinitive is better split either because the rhythm of the sentence demands it or because ambiguity might otherwise result.

4 When an adverb, especially an intensifying adverb such as *actually, even, ever, further, just, quite, really*, belongs with a verb that happens to be an infinitive, it is usually better (and sometimes necessary) to place it between *to* and the verb: *I want to really study, I want to be a scholar*—Iris Murdoch, 1987 | *In face of all this Patrick managed to quite like him*—Kingsley Amis, 1988. In some cases, an adverbial phrase is also inseparable from its verb: *It allowed Fernanda Herford to slightly more than double her money*—Julian Barnes, 1993.

5 RECOMMENDATION. The split infinitive, though recent as an object of disapproval in the broader context of the history of English, has sufficient weight of opinion against it to recommend avoidance when possible, and especially when it is stylistically awkward. But it is neither a major error nor a grammatical blunder, and it is acceptable and at times necessary when considerations of rhythm and clarity call for it.

spoiled, spoilt. In BrE the normal form for the past tense and past participle is *spoilt*, although *spoiled* is also used and is the dominant form in AmE. As an adjective in attributive position (i.e. before a noun, as in *a spoilt child*) *spoilt* is always used in BrE and sometimes in AmE.

spokesperson see -PERSON.

sponge has derivative forms *spongeable* and *spongeing* (both with *e*), but *spongy*.

spontaneity is traditionally pronounced spon-tə-**nee**-i-ti, but the alternative spon-tə-**nay**-i-ti is becoming increasingly common.

Spoonerism. The Revd W. A. Spooner (1844–1930), Dean and Warden of New College, Oxford, has given his name to this most endearing form of linguistic error involving the transposition of letters, although those commonly attributed to him are likely to be spurious, e.g. *a well-boiled icicle* (for *a well-oiled bicycle*) and *a half-warmed fish* (for *a half-formed wish*).

spoonful has the plural form *spoonfuls*.

spouse is a convenient gender-neutral term, less formal in tone than it once was, for a married man in relation to his wife and a married woman in relation to her husband.

spring *verb*. The past tense is *sprang* or occasionally (especially in AmE) *sprung*. The past participle is *sprung*.

spry. The inflected forms and derivatives are *spryer, spryest*; *spryly, spryness*.

spurt is the dominant spelling for the noun and verb to do with gushing and sudden increase of effort, not *spirt*.

squalor is spelt *-or* in both BrE and AmE.

squeeze *verb*. The past tense and past participle are *squeezed*. The past form *squoze* is nonstandard or dialectal, despite its use by President Ronald Reagan at a press conference in 1985 when commenting on a small skin cancer: *I picked at it and I squoze it and so forth and messed myself up a little.*

stadium. The plural forms are *stadia* (with reference to the ancient world) and *stadiums* (with modern reference).

staff. The plural in the meanings 'pole' and 'body of employees' is *staffs*. In the music meaning it is *staffs* or *staves*.

stalactite, stalagmite. A *stalactite* hangs down from the roof of a cave, and is formed from dripping water containing rich minerals. A *stalagmite* rises up from the floor and is formed from deposits also caused by dripping. Both words are derived from the Greek word *stalassō* meaning 'to drip', and are pronounced with the stress on the first syllable in BrE but with the stress on the second syllable in AmE.

stanch see STAUNCH.

stand *verb*. In BrE candidates *stand* for office, whereas in AmE they *run* for it.

standard English. The term has been variously defined and heavily politicized, but essentially it is the form of English that is most widely accepted and understood in an English-speaking country and tends to be based on the educated speech of a particular area, in England the south-east (although it can be spoken in a variety of accents). It is used in newspapers and broadcasting and is the form normally taught to learners of English. For a fuller treatment see *The Oxford Companion to the English Language* (1992), 982–3.

standpoint see POINT OF VIEW.

state. It is usual to spell it with a capital initial letter when it refers to political entities, either nations (*The State of Israel | a State visit*), or parts of a federal nation (*the State of Virginia | crossing the State border*), and when it means 'civil government' (*Church and State | the Secretary of State*). This applies both to names and to general reference when necessary to avoid possible ambiguity with the general meanings of *state* (as in *the state* [= condition] *of Israel*). In other contexts a lower-case initial is used (*a police state | the welfare state*).

stately is an adjective only (as in *a stately home*). The notional adverb *statelily* would be too awkward and is not used.

stationary, stationery. *Stationary* is an adjective and means 'not moving' whereas *stationery* is a noun and denotes paper and writing materials. Both words are derived from the Latin word *stare* 'to stand'. The relevance of this to *stationary* is obvious, and the connection with *stationery* (and *stationer*, a supplier of stationery) is through the medieval Latin word *stationarius* which meant 'a bookseller', who was a fixed (as distinct from itinerant) shopkeeper.

statistics *noun* is treated as singular as the name of the science (*Statistics is merely a form of knowledge*), and as plural when referring to items of statistical information (*The statistics of suicide are striking*). The singular form *statistic*, denoting a single piece of information, is well established: *The statistic of 22.2 unemployed to every notified vacancy in Scotland—Times*, 1973.

status is pronounced **stay**-təs and has the plural form *statuses* (the Latin plural is *statūs* and is not used in English).

staunch, stanch. *Staunch* (pronounced stawnch) is used both for the verb meaning 'to restrain the flow of blood' (with the blood or the wound as its object) and for the adjective meaning 'trustworthy, loyal'. The variant form *stanch* (pronounced stahnch) is preferred in AmE for the verb.

stave *noun.* One of its meanings is the same as that of *staff*, a set of lines on which musical notes are written. The plural of both forms is *staves*.

stave *verb.* Both *staved* and *stove* are used for the past tense and past participle. *Staved off* is more usual in the meaning 'averted or deferred (danger or misfortune)' and *stove in* is more usual in the meaning 'crushed by forcing inwards'.

stencil as a verb has inflected forms *stencilled*, *stencilling* in BrE, and usually *stenciled*, *stenciling* in AmE.

stereo as a noun has the plural form *stereos*.

stewardess denotes a female steward, especially on a ship or aircraft. *Flight attendant* is now the preferred term with English-speaking airlines. See -ESS.

sticking place, sticking point. The phrase *sticking point* is first recorded in 1826, and in its common modern meaning 'the limit reached of progress, agreement, etc.' not until the 1960s. The allusion is to a line in Shakespeare's *Macbeth* (I.vii.60), where *place* is used: *But screw your courage to the sticking place, And we'll not fail.* The reference here seems to be to screwing up the peg of a musical instrument until it becomes tightly fixed in its hole.

stigma. The plural in its special meanings (e.g. 'the marks on Christ's hands and feet on the Cross') is *stigmata*, with the stress either on the first or on the second syllable. In the figurative sense 'a mark of disgrace or discredit', the plural is *stigmas*.

stigmatize, meaning 'to describe as unworthy or disgraceful', behaves like *regard* in being followed by *as*: *Negro styles traditionally stigmatized as 'race' music—Times*, 1977.

stile, style. There are three words here, all derived from the Latin word *stilus* meaning 'a writing tool'. The two words spelt *stile* are (1) from Old English, meaning 'a set of steps for crossing a fence' and (2) probably from Dutch, meaning 'a vertical piece in the frame of a panelled door'. The word *style* in its familiar meanings is spelt with a *y* from a false association with the Greek word *stulos* meaning 'column'.

stiletto, the knife and the high-heeled shoe, has the plural form *stilettos*.

still life, the genre of painting, has the plural form *still lifes*.

stimulus has the plural form *stimuli* (pronounced **stim**-yoo-liy with the last syllable as in *lie*).

stimy, stimie see STYMIE.

sting. The verb has the past tense and past participle *stung*.

stink. The past tense of the verb is *stank* and the past participle is *stunk*. *Stunk* is occasionally used for the past tense, but is not now standard.

stoep pronounced like *stoop*, is a South African word for a terraced veranda in front of a house.

stoic, stoical. As an adjective, *stoic* is normally used attributively (i.e. before a noun, as in *stoic virtues* and *stoic indifference*), and preserves a more direct reference to the philosophy of the ancient Stoics from whom the word is derived. In predicative position (i.e. after a verb) *stoical* is more usual, and in all its uses conveys the more generalized allusive sense of personal restraint and self-control. A *stoic indifference* is the kind of indifference that the Stoics taught and practised, whereas a *stoical indifference* is indifference that is, on its own terms, concentrated and resolute. When the reference is to people rather than qualities, *stoical* has to be used: one can have *stoic* or *stoical* resolution but one can only be *stoical* oneself.

stone *adverb.* Combinations such as *stone-cold* and *stone-dead*, in which *stone* is used adverbially ('like a stone'), have been recorded for centuries. More recently, *stone* has developed a freer adverbial use as a mere intensive equivalent to *very* or *completely*. It is not easy to pinpoint the date of this development, but it is now common, especially in AmE: *People . . . got stone drunk and cruised through red lights*—Garrison Keillor, 1989.

stood is used for *standing* in non-standard uses comparable to *sat* for *sitting*, such as: *My husband was stood on the opposite side of the pits*—*Cycling Weekly*, 1993. The origins of this use are obscure and probably dialectal.

stop, stay. In 19c fiction people frequently *stopped* with friends (overnight in their house), *stopped* for dinner, or *stopped* at home. In modern English we would use *stay* instead of *stop* in all these cases. But the older use still survives: *'She's stopping with her daughter,' the woman said. 'She'll be back on Thursday.'*—Hilary Mantel, 1985. It is also to be seen in the phrasal verbs *stop off* and *stop over*, meaning 'to make a break in a journey' (especially a long journey), and in the noun equivalents *stop-off* and *stopover*.

storey, story. For *storey* and *floor* see FLOOR, STOREY. The plural form is *storeys*. In AmE *story* is the usual form and its plural is *stories*; and what in BrE is a *three-storeyed* house is in AmE a *three-storied* house.

straight away, meaning 'immediately', is first recorded in the 17c. It continued to be used as two words until the beginning of the 20c, when (probably under the influence of the fast-fading adverb *straightway*) it began to be written as one word, and uses of this form are frequent: *He couldn't decide whether to make for home straightaway*—Steven Wall, 1991. In AmE, *straightaway* is also an adjective meaning 'direct' (of a course of action) and a noun meaning 'a straight course or section'.

straight, strait. *Straight* is a Middle English past participle of the verb *stretch* and has many meanings in modern English, primarily 'extending uniformly in the same direction without a curve or bend'. *Strait*, which has the basic meaning 'tight, narrow', is used as a noun meaning 'a narrow passage of water connecting two seas', in the plural as in *dire straits*, and in combinations such as *strait-laced* and *straitjacket* (*straightjacket* is also used but the better spelling is *strait-*).

strategy, tactics. In war, as in politics and business, *strategy* is used of an overall plan of action embodying certain principles and objectives, and *tactics* is used of the detailed means adopted to achieve them. *Tactics* is normally treated as a plural, with *tactic* available as a singular form with the meaning 'a tactical manoeuvre or device'.

stratum is normally pronounced **strah**-təm, and has the plural form *strata*. The use of *strata* as a singular noun (with a plural *stratas*) is erroneous: ☒ *The earth's crust contains stratas of hot, dry rock and natural aquifers*—C. Wheater et al., 1990.

street see ROAD.

strength should be pronounced with the g fully articulated, not as if the spelling were *strenth* (to rhyme with *tenth*).

strew has a past tense *strewed* and a past participle form *strewn* (preferred) or *strewed*.

stricken, a past participle of *strike*, survives chiefly in compound adjectives such as *grief-stricken* and *panic-stricken*. In compositional uses such as *He has become stricken with remorse*, it sounds archaic.

stride. The verb has the past tense *strode* and the past participle *stridden*. The participle is not readily remembered, and *strode* is sometimes mistakenly used instead: ☒ *Great strides are being strode in the cultivation of preteen female engineers*—The Face, 1987.

strike. The verb has the past tense *struck* and the past parti-

ciple *struck* or, in certain contexts, STRICKEN (see separate entry).

string. The normal form for the past tense and the past participle is *strung*. A musical instrument with strings is called a *stringed* instrument, but if the strings need renewing it is *restrung*.

strive *verb*. The regular past tense is *strove* and the past participle *striven*, but *strived* is commonly used for both in AmE: *We've strived to lead the way in offering you the tools you need*—Money (US), 1993.

stubbornness is spelt with two *n*s.

stucco, a word of Italian origin for a type of plaster covering walls, has the plural form *stuccos*, and as a verb it has inflections *stuccoes, stuccoed, stuccoing*.

studio has the plural form *studios*.

stupefy, meaning 'to make insensible' or 'to astonish', is spelt *-efy* (like *liquefy* and *rarefy*), not *-ify* (like *dignify* and *modify*).

stupor, meaning 'a dazed state', is spelt *-or* in BrE and AmE.

sty. The word meaning 'a pen for pigs' has the plural form *sties*. The word for 'an inflamed swelling on the eyelid' should be spelt *sty*, not *stye*, and also has the plural form *sties*.

style see STILE.

stymie is now the regular spelling of the word used in golf and in the meaning 'to obstruct or thwart', rather than *stimy* or *stimie*. The verb has inflected forms *stymies, stymied, stymieing*.

subjunctive mood. 1 The subjunctive mood, one of the great shifting sands of English grammar, is a verbal form or mood expressing wish or hypothesis in contrast to fact, and usually denotes what is imagined, wished, demanded, proposed, and so on. In modern English it is distinguishable from the ordinary indicative mood only in the third person singular present tense, which omits the final *s* (*if he make* rather than *if he makes*) and in the forms *be* and *were* of the verb *to be*.

2 The subjunctive mood was common in Old English and until about 1600, then went into decline but has become remarkably prevalent again in the 20c, first in AmE and then in other forms of English including BrE: *I was going to recommend that he be terminated*—New Yorker, 1987 | *It was as if Sally were disturbed in some way and was translating this disturbance into the habit of thought*—Anita Brookner, 1986 (UK) (note the shift to indicative mood after *and*) | *She insisted Jane sit there*—Barbara Anderson (New Zealand) | *It was suggested he wait till the next morning*—Michael Ondaatje, 1992 (Canada). In many cases, an alternative construction with *should* can also be used: *It was important that he should be included in my photographs*—Dick Francis, 1980.

3 Typical subjunctive patterns are:

▶ **a** After *if* (or *as if, as though, unless*) in hypothetical conditions: *Each was required to undertake that if it were chosen it would place work here*—Times, 1986.

▶ **b** In *that*-clauses following a verb connoting suggestion, wish, etc. (e.g. *demand, insist, pray, recommend, suggest, wish*): *Fundamentalist Islam . . . decrees that men and women be strictly segregated*—Listener, 1988 | *Your situation demands that either Kooti be nobbled or Whitmore nullified*—M. Shadbolt, 1986 (New Zealand).

▶ **c** *Be* or *were* placed at the head of a clause with the subject following in an inverted construction: *Were I to get drunk, it would help me in the fight*—John Updike, 1986 | *Statistically, afterworlds—be they Christian, Greek, Pharaonic—must be populated almost entirely by children*—Penelope Lively, 1987.

▶ **d** In negative constructions, *not* (or *never* etc.) is normally placed before the subjunctive verb (and this position identifies the subjunctive status of verbs in the first and second persons as well as the third): *Again he insisted that he not be followed*—Observer, 1987 | *One essential quality for a holiday novel is that it not be too light*—Frederic Raphael, 1988.

▶ **e** In certain fixed expressions and phrases, e.g. *as it were, be that as it may, come what may, far be it from me, God save the Queen, heaven forbid, long live the King, perish the thought, so be it.*

submissible, meaning 'able to be submitted', is a better form than the alternative *submittable.*

subpeona, a writ ordering a person to appear at a lawcourt, has the plural form *subpoenas.* In AmE it is sometimes spelt *subpena,* with the plural form *subpenas.* The verb has inflections *subpoenas, subpoenaed, subpoenaing.*

subsidence. The traditional pronunciation is səb-**siy**-dəns, with the stress on the second syllable, but the form **sub**-si-dəns, with the stress on the first syllable under the influence of *residence* and *subsidy,* is also common in standard speech.

substantial | such 554

substantial, substantive. *Substantial* is pronounced with the stress on the second syllable and *substantive* with the stress on the first syllable. Both words mean 'having substance', but *substantial* is the word in general use to denote people or things of size, importance, or value (*Scotland Yard said a 'substantial amount of firearms and explosives' had been recovered from the house—East Anglian Daily Times*, 1993), whereas *substantive* refers more to what something consists of (*The dramatic political and diplomatic developments of 1988—of more importance to the achievement of a substantive peace than anything else since 1967—owed nothing to the peace process—D. McDowell, 1990*). *Substantial* discussions are lengthy and wide-ranging ones, whereas *substantive* discussions deal with important topics. *Substantive* often occurs in technical contexts such as law and parliamentary procedure; for example, a *substantive motion* is one that deals specifically with a subject in due form.

substitute see REPLACE.

subtitles, supertitles, surtitles. *Subtitles*, printed captions that translate the dialogue in a foreign-language cinema or television film, appear at the bottom of the screen. *Supertitles* or *surtitles*, a more recent invention, translate the text of a play or opera as it is being said or sung, and are usually projected above the stage.

subtle has a corresponding adverb *subtly*.

succeed. When it means 'to be successful', *succeed* is followed by *in* + an *-ing* form, not (unlike *fail*) by *to*: *Some local preservation enthu-*siasts succeeded in getting the house listed as of architectural and historic interest—*E. Lemarchand, 1972.

succour, a rather formal word meaning 'aid, assistance, especially in time of need', is spelt *-our* in BrE and *succor* in AmE.

such. 1 *SUCH* AS AN EMPHASIZER. *How can the House express its indignant rejection of football hooliganism while setting **such a persuasive** example of undignified and daily indiscipline?—Guardian Weekly, 1986.* The construction with *such a* followed by an adjective is established and idiomatic in current English, despite occasional objections that *so* and not *such* should do the work of emphasizing here (. . . *while setting so persuasive an example*). (Compare the use of *such* qualifying a noun, to which nobody objects: *For God's sake, Beryl, don't be such a nitwit—J.* Drummond, 1975.) In some cases *such* appears to qualify the combination of adjective and noun: *It is indeed hard to see how such a gigantic work . . . can be considered 'minimal' in any way—Radio Times, 1985.*

2 *SUCH AS* WITH FOLLOWING PRONOUN. When an inflecting pronoun follows, it is more natural to regard *such as* as a preposition and to follow it with *me, her, him*, etc., rather than *I, she, he*, etc. (regarding *such as* as a conjunction with the continuation understood as *such as I am*, etc.) *They were not bad, for such as her—*Rose Macaulay, 1920.

3 *SUCH AS* OR *LIKE*. *Like* is common when a single instance follows (*a poet like Tennyson | take a girl like you*), but *such as* is preferable (and more idiomatic) when a list follows (*Members of the cat family, such as the lion, the tiger, and the leopard*). See LIKE 2.

4 SUCH . . . AS . . . OR SUCH . . . THAT . . . . *We are such stuff as dreams are made on.* The relative pronoun that follows *such* in sentences of this type is *as* and not *who*, *which*, or *that*. But *such* followed by *that* is legitimate in constructions of the following types, in which *that* is a conjunction: *Midge was such a dingbat . . . that she went to Hawaii for a vacation during World War II*—J. Irving, 1978 | *The ladies who feature with her on her home-video were such that 'a man would be lucky to get out of them alive' (hysterical laughter)*—*Listener*, 1983.

suchlike. *He left the sea, having had what amounted to a nervous breakdown, 'always thinking of the other ships that went up, the bombings and suchlike'*—*Daily Telegraph*, 1971. Fowler's verdict in 1926 was that this use of *suchlike* 'is now usually left to the uneducated' and that *the like* should be used instead. In terms of current use this judgement is too severe, especially for everyday conversational usage.

suddenness is spelt with two *ns*.

suffix. In grammar, a *suffix* is a word or element added at the end of another word to adjust or qualify its meaning, such as *-ation* (*confirmation, privatization*), *-ing* (*driving, soldiering*), and *-itis* (*appendicitis*). Some suffixes are created artificially from the end part of words to form similar types of word with different reference, e.g. *-aholic* (from *alcoholic*, forming *workaholic* etc.)

suffixes added to proper names. 1 The suffix most commonly used to form nouns and adjectives relating to people's names (usually writers, artists,

composers, etc., or founders of dynasties) is *-an* or *-ian*, and one of the oldest formations of this type is *Virgilian* (first recorded in 1513). Other formations include *Aristotelian* (1607), *Ovidian* (1617), and *Ciceronian* (1661), and it will be seen from this short list alone that some have survived more strongly than others. *Shakespearian* (with an occasional variant *Shakespearean*) is not recorded before 1755. Some words made in this way have multiple reference, e.g. *Alexandrian* (normally referring to the city of Alexandria or the literature or philosophy associated with it rather than to Alexander the Great). More recent formations include *Beethovenian* and *Shavian*, the latter derived from a Latinate form of the name of G. B. Shaw for reasons of euphony. Euphony often calls for use of other suffixes, such as *-esque* (from French, e.g. *Dantesque, Schumannesque, Turneresque*) and *-ic* (*Byronic, Platonic, Pindaric, Ptolemaic*), although in some cases the reason for a particular choice of suffix is less clear.

2 When *-ian* is added to an unaccented final syllable of a name, the syllable is normally lengthened to accommodate the addition, so that *Alfred* makes *Alfredian* (pronounced al-**free**-di-ǝn).

sugar has derivative forms *sugared* and *sugary*, each with one *r*.

suggest. 1 When followed by a *that*-clause and proposing a course of action rather than hinting at a fact, *suggest* commonly generates a subjunctive verb, and the same is true of the noun *suggestion*: *Uncle doesn't suggest that she bring a lamp from the next room*—Saul Bellow, 1987 (US) | *The*

suggestion that all HIV-positive indi-
vidual be forcibly tattooed—Dædalus,
1989 (US) | *If you want to irritate D.,*
then suggest glibly that she see a
sports psychologist—Times, 1990. Alternative constructions with
should (*He suggested that they*
should find a scenic route), and
with an ordinary tense (*I suggest*
that he has another try) are more
common in BrE than in AmE, but
in general this verb is one of the
great mainstays of the subjunctive mood in modern English. See
SUBJUNCTIVE MOOD.

2 Note that when *suggest* means
'state as a fact or hypothesis' rather than 'propose' an ordinary
tense is used: *I cannot accept John*
Peel's suggestion that punk rockers
are the only truly socialist representa-
tives we have left—Sounds, 1977.

suggestible means 'open to suggestion' (used of a person) more
often than 'able to be suggested'
(used of an idea or proposal), and
is spelt *-ible*, not *-able*. See -ABLE,
-IBLE.

suitor, meaning 'a man seeking
to marry a (particular) woman', is
spelt *-or*, not *-er*.

suit, suite. The two forms are in
origin the same word, and differences of usage are the result of
historical choices since the 17c.
In modern English we speak of a
suit of clothes, armour, and playing cards, as well as a *lawsuit* and
paying *suit* to (i.e. courting) a
woman; and a *suite* of rooms, furniture, musical pieces, etc.

sulphur and its derivatives *sul-*
phurate, sulphurous, etc., are normally spelt with *-ph-* in BrE but *-f-*
(*sulfur* etc.) in AmE.

sullenness is spelt with two *ns*.

summersault see SOMERSAULT.

summon, summons. *Summon* is
a verb only, whereas *summons* is a
noun and verb. A *summons* (plural
summonses) is an order to appear
before a judge or magistrate, and
to *summons* someone is to issue
them with a summons. *Summon*
is the ordinary word meaning 'to
call formally', as in *The chairman*
summoned the members to a meet-
ing.

Sunday see FRIDAY.

super-. The prefix dates from
the 15c and has been prolific ever
since, taking on a new lease of
life in the 20c in formations such
as *superhighway* (1925 in the physical sense in America), *superman*
(1913), *supermarket* (1933), *super-*
model (1977), *superpower* (1921),
supersonic (1919), *superstar* (1925),
and *superstore* (1965).

supercede is incorrect; the correct spelling is SUPERSEDE.

superior is not a true comparative (like *better* or *greater*, for example) and is followed by *to*, not
than: *The taste of an open mushroom*
grilled with garlic, parsley and butter
is so splendid, and superior to snails
given the same treatment—Times,
1980. In the language of advertising, *superior* has the depleted
meaning 'above average in quality' (*a superior housing development*
| *made of superior leather*).

superlatives see ADJECTIVE 3, -ER
AND -EST FORMS.

supersede is the correct spelling for the verb meaning 'to take
the place of'. It is derived from
the Latin word *sedeo* 'sit', but the
influence of *accede, intercede, pre-*
cede, and others (derived from
Latin *cedo* 'go') often mistakenly
causes this word to be spelt *super-*
cede.

superstitions. A superstition in language, like any superstition, is a widely held belief with no rational basis. In English these include the beliefs that sentences should not begin with *and* or *but*, that a preposition should not end a sentence, that *none* should always take a singular verb, and that infinitives should not be split. See also FETISH 2.

supervise is spelt *-vise*, not *-vize*. See -IZE, -ISE.

supine see PRONE.

supple has the adverbial form *supply* (two syllables) rather than *supplely* (three syllables).

suppose, supposing. Both words are used as quasi-conjunctions to introduce an assumption or hypothesis: *Supposing the plan succeeded and his wife got stuck away in a nuthouse?*—H. Howard, 1973 | *Suppose the guards were more alert, security measures more effective*—R. Ludlum, 1978.

supposedly is pronounced as four syllables.

suppressible, meaning 'able to be suppressed', is spelt *-ible*, not *-able*. See -ABLE, -IBLE.

suppressor, a device for suppressing electrical interference, is spelt *-or*, not *-er*.

sure, surely. 1 In all parts of the English-speaking world, *surely* is the dominant form in the meaning 'in a sure or certain manner' (*slowly but surely*) and in the use inviting or presupposing agreement (*Surely that can't be right*). In BrE, *sure* is limited as an adverb to fixed expressions such as *sure as eggs is eggs* and *as sure as God made little apples*, and to

use as a form of assent in replying to a question or proposition, although this is better established in AmE: *'Is that a fact?' 'Sure,' murmured Archibald*—P. G. Wodehouse, 1914 | *I asked if you could finish your lunch, and they said sure, no hurry*—Rex Stout, 1975 (US). (*Surely* is also used in this way.)

2 In other adverbial uses *sure* is most closely associated with AmE: *Parts of it were pretty, sure*—Alison Lurie, 1969 | *A chemical fire. You worry about those, sure, said Clerk*—New Yorker, 1988.

surmise, meaning 'to infer doubtfully' and (as a noun) 'a conjecture or suspicion', is spelt *-ise*, not *-ize*. See -IZE, -ISE.

surprise is spelt *-ise*, not *-ize*, as a noun and a verb. See -IZE, -ISE.

surveillance is pronounced sǝ-**vay**-lǝns, with the *-ll-* articulated.

survey is pronounced with the stress on the first syllable as a noun and with the stress on the second syllable as a verb.

surveyor is spelt *-or*, not *-er*.

survivor is spelt *-or*, not *-er*.

susceptible has two principal meanings, each with its own construction. In the meaning 'likely to be affected by', it is followed by *to*: *Stinnes had reached that dangerous age when a man was only susceptible to an innocent cutie or to an experienced floozy*—Len Deighton, 1984 | *The leopard frog . . . is particularly susceptible to a kidney carcinoma*—Scientific American, 1973. When it means 'allowing, admitting of', it is followed by *of*: *In the late fourteenth century, one finds Wyclif using the word 'nation' (which was susceptible of a wide variety of* *usages), to denote men who had been bred in England*—J. A. F. Thomson, 1992. It should not be used as a synonym of *liable to* or *prone to*: *Fast aircraft with swept-back wings are susceptible to dutch rolls*—B. Jackson, 1976.

suspect, suspicious. 1 *Suspect* is pronounced with the stress on the first syllable as a noun (*the chief suspect*) and adjective (*a suspect package*), and with the stress on the second syllable as a verb (*They suspect something*).

2 As an adjective, *suspect* is close in meaning to *suspicious*; both mean essentially 'causing suspicion'. The chief differences are (1) that *suspicious* can also be used to describe a person (= feeling suspicion, as in *They were suspicious of our intentions*), and (2) that *suspect* has additional connotations regarding worth or reliability (*suspect farm produce*).

3 The adverb *suspiciously* can mean either 'in a manner expressing suspicion' or 'in a manner causing suspicion', depending on the context: *She looked at us suspiciously* is an example of the first meaning and *She was behaving suspiciously* is an example of the second. An adverb *suspectly* is recorded but is hardly ever used in current English.

suspender. In BrE a *suspender* is a clip device holding up the top of a stocking or sock, whereas in AmE *suspenders* are what in BrE are called (men's) *braces*.

suspense, suspension. The two words used to be interchangeable in several meanings, but have since gone their separate ways. *Suspense* is used primarily to denote 'a state of anxious uncertainty or expectation', and is common attributively (i.e. be-

fore a noun, as in *suspense thriller*) to refer to a form of writing or drama. *Suspension* has more physical and technical meanings (as in a car's *suspension* and a *suspension bridge*) as well as the non-physical meaning 'the state of being suspended from an office or position'.

sustain. Fowler's view in 1926 was that '*sustain* as a synonym for *suffer* or *receive* or *get* belongs to the class of formal words, and is better avoided', and its use in the contexts of injuries, losses, hardship, etc., is still widely disliked. Fowler was anxious to confine it to circumstances that involved prolonged endurance (*Scarce one* [of the cities] *was now capable of sustaining a siege*—Macaulay, 1849), but there is a thin line dividing this kind of brave resistance from more temporary kinds. In its other meanings, 'to keep in being', 'to maintain in a certain state', 'to give support to', and others, *sustain* is unexceptionable.

swap, meaning 'exchange' (noun and verb) is the preferred spelling, not *swop*.

swat, swot. *Swat* is the spelling for the verb meaning 'to hit sharply' and the corresponding noun. *Swot* (originally a dialect variant of *sweat*) is a BrE colloquialism meaning 'to study hard' and 'someone who studies hard'.

swath, swathe. The word meaning 'a ridge of grass left after mowing' and 'a strip' is spelt *swath* (pronounced swawth; preferred) or *swathe* (pronounced swaydh). The noun and verb meaning 'a bandage or wrapping' and 'to wrap in bandages' is spelt *swathe* (pronounced swaydh).

sweat see GENTEELISM.

swell. The verb has the past tense *swelled* and the past participle *swollen*, although *swelled* is sometimes used for the past participle when the reference is to a specified increase in size or numbers rather than to an unwelcome or harmful expansion or swelling: *Unlike the dailies, the number of titles was not swelled by relaunches and changes of status*—C. Seymour-Ure, 1992.

swim. The past form of the verb is *swam* (*She swam to the shore*) and the past participle is *swum* (*Have you swum recently?*), but the reverse will be found in older writing: *Who, being shipwrecked, had swam naked to land*—Dr Johnson, 1750 | *As she sprang to meet it, with an eye that swum to thanks*—Tennyson, 1847.

swine is a normal word for *pig* in AmE, but in BrE is mostly used either as a collective plural or (more often) informally as a singular or plural to refer contemptuously to a person or thing one objects to.

swing. In current use the past tense and past participle of the verb are *swung* (*He swung his leg round* | *The street names were swung from signs on corners*), but *swang* will be found for the past tense in older writing: *His arms dangled rather than swang*—Hilaire Belloc, 1912.

swinging, swingeing. *Swinging* is the ordinary present participle of the verb *swing*, whereas *swingeing* means 'forcible, severe' (as in *swingeing tax increases*), and is part of an archaic verb *swinge* meaning 'to strike hard'.

swivel. The verb has inflected forms *swivelled, swivelling* in BrE, and in AmE usually *swiveled, swiveling*.

swop see SWAP.

swot see SWAT.

syllabub, a sweet dessert made of cream, is preferably spelt *syll-*, not *sillabub*.

syllabus has the plural form *syllabuses*, not *syllabi*.

syllepsis (from a Greek root meaning 'taking together') is a figure of speech in which a word, or a particular form or inflection of a word, is made to fit two grammatical structures but is formally correct only for one, e.g. *She's a lovely, intelligent, sensitive woman who has and continues to turn around my life in a wonderfully positive way*—Woody Allen reported in *Times*, 1992 (*to turn* fits with *continues* but not with *has*). Constructions of this type are technically ungrammatical, but they occur from time to time in the more spontaneous world of conversational speech. The terms *syllepsis* and *zeugma* (from a Greek word for 'yoking') are both used for the type characterized by a meaning difference in the 'shared' word rather than a grammatical one: *Sir Geoffrey Howe, who had arrived in a limousine, the editor of the Daily Telegraph, who had arrived in a motor-boat, and Dave Nellist, who had arrived in an anorak*—Matthew Parris, 1991. There is much inconsistency in the way these two terms are applied.

sylvan is more common than silvan as the (chiefly poetic) word for 'wooded' or 'rural', despite its origin in the Latin word *silva* meaning 'wood': *amid scenes of sylvan beauty*—A. Wainwright, 1990.

symbolic, symbolical. Both words mean 'serving as a symbol' or 'involving the use of symbols', but *symbolic* is much more common: *On the day before Easter, there is a symbolic burning of a cloth-draped wooden statue of Judas—* C. Hammerschlag, 1988.

sympathetic, in the meaning 'eliciting sympathy' rather than 'feeling sympathy', dates from the beginning of the 20c. Despite Fowler's reservations (he wrote in 1926 when it was still a new meaning), it has become rapidly established in standard English: *Despite the sympathetic portrayal of his father in these anecdotes, Lawrence turned against him after the death of his mother—*J. Meyers, 1990.

sympathy see EMPATHY.

symposium meaning 'a gathering for discussion', has the plural form *symposia* (preferred) or *symposiums*.

syndrome, pronounced **sin**-drohm, is originally a medical term for 'a set of symptoms'. Its use as a vogue word in general contexts meaning 'a characteristic combination of opinions, emotions, behaviour, etc.', is as recent as the 1950s; it is generally acceptable, but not when *syndrome* is simply a synonym for *factor* or *aspect*, i.e. a single circumstance rather than a set of circumstances coming together, which lies at the heart of its meaning: ☒ *The falling roll syndrome [in schools] was a problem of the greatest magnitude and one never experienced before—West Lancashire Evening Gazette*, 1983.

synecdoche, pronounced si-**nek**-də-kee, is a figure of speech in which a more inclusive term is used for a less inclusive one or

vice versa, as in *England came out to bat* (*England* more inclusive for 'the England team') and *a fleet of fifty sail* (*sail* less inclusive for 'ships'). See also METONYMY.

synonyms are words that have the same or a near meaning, such as the pair *close* and *shut*, or the trio *begin, start,* and *commence*. Some word sets of this kind arise because words coming into English from other languages failed to drive out those already in use; for example, *close* is a Middle English (13c) word derived from Old French, and joined the existing Old English word *shut*. Other pairs of words have different levels of appropriacy; for example, *kill* is a general word whereas *slay* is literary or rhetorical, and *little* carries connotations of affection that are not present in the more neutral word *small* (compare *my little house* and *my small house*). Many words are loosely described as synonyms although their meanings are close rather than identical (e.g. *danger* and *risk, entreat* and *implore, leave* and *depart*), and few synonyms are interchangeable in all contexts.

synopsis, meaning 'a summary or outline', has the plural form *synopses* (pronounced -seez).

synthesis, meaning 'a process of bringing together or connecting', has the plural form *syntheses* (pronounced -seez).

syphon see SIPHON.

systematic, systemic. The word in general use in the meaning 'done according to a plan or system' is *systematic*, and one can equally speak of *systematic* learning (i.e. following a system or set of principles) and a *systematic* search (i.e. one done methodically); the second is only a slight extension in meaning of the first. The much less common word *systemic* is mostly confined to technical uses in medicine and linguistics, and has the underlying meaning 'relating to a system as a whole rather than to a part of it'.

Tt

table *verb*. In BrE to *table* a proposal means to place it on the agenda for discussion, whereas in AmE it means to put it aside for an indefinite period.

tableau, meaning 'a group of figures representing a scene', has the plural form *tableaux* (pronounced **tab**-lohz).

table d'hôte, meaning 'a meal consisting of a set menu at a fixed price', is printed in roman type with a circumflex accent on the *o*.

tablespoonful has the plural form *tablespoonfuls*, but in practice the type *three tablespoons of*—is more usual.

taboo is a noun, adjective, and verb, and is pronounced with the stress on the second syllable in all three. The noun has the plural form *taboos*, and the verb has inflected forms *taboos, tabooed, tabooing*.

tacky. It is a little surprising that this currently fashionable term meaning 'tawdry, in poor taste' has nothing to do with the word meaning 'slightly wet or sticky', but is of American origin and is an extension of a noun *tacky* (or *tackey*) that was used disparagingly to describe a weak horse or a poor white person from the southern States. It is first recorded in the newer meaning in the 1880s in uses that sound modern, e.g.: *Two little cards (with his name printed on them in gilt. Tackey? Ugh)*—I. M. Rittenhouse, 1883.

tactics see STRATEGY.

tactile, tactual. Both words mean 'relating to the sense of touch', but *tactile* has become the more usual choice.

tag question. This is the grammarians' name for a question added at the end of a statement and acting as a reinforcer rather than seeking an answer, as in *You will do this for me, **won't you**? | She has been to America, **hasn't she**? | I don't need an umbrella, **do I**?*. In each case the verb in the main statement has been changed into an equivalent question; if the statement is positive the tag is negative, and vice versa, although a positive tag can follow a positive statement in the type *You heard it too, did you?*. The use of tag questions is subject to regional variation; for example, in some regions (including Wales in the UK and S. Asia outside it) *isn't it* is used as an all-purpose tag irrespective of the form of the statement: *You're going home now, **isn't it**?*—A. R. Thomas, 1994.

talisman, meaning 'an object supposedly endowed with magic powers', has nothing to do with the word *man* and the plural is therefore *talismans*. Its ultimate origin is an Arabic word connected with the Greek word *telesma* meaning 'consecrated object'.

talkative. This word is surprisingly early (15c). Fowler (1926) forbore to attack it despite its being a 'hybrid', i.e. the Latinate suffix *-ative* has been added to the Eng-

-t and -ed

A number of irregular verbs have competing past forms and past participles in -t and -ed (e.g. *leapt* and *leaped*); the most common of these are given in the table below. In some cases the length of the vowel is shortened in the -t forms (e.g. lept instead of leept for *leapt*). It is difficult to establish distinctions based on region or meaning, but two tendencies are discernible: (1) the form in -ed is more often preferred in AmE, and (2) in BrE there is a stronger preference for the -t form when it is used as a participial adjective, as in *The cakes are burnt* as distinct from *We burned the cakes*

VERB	-T FORM	-ED FORM
bereave	bereft	bereaved
beseech	besought	beseeched
burn	burnt	burned
cleave	cleft	cleaved
dream	dreamt	dreamed
dwell	dwelt	dwelled
earn	earnt*	earned
kneel	knelt	kneeled
lean	leant	leaned
leap	leapt	leaped
learn	learnt	learned
smell	smelt	smelled
spell	spelt	spelled
spill	spilt	spilled
spoil	spoilt	spoiled

earnt is not standard, but is increasingly found

lish word *talk*. But he pointed out that this was the only example of its kind relating to this suffix, and did so 'with a view to discouraging imitation'. So far he has largely succeeded; imitation hybrids such as *writative*, *babblative*, and *scribblative* are recorded in the *OED*, and Shakespeare used *forgetive* (= inclined to forge, not really a hybrid), but these have not lasted.

-t and -ed.
See box above

tangible. The primary meaning is 'perceptible by touch', but in practice figurative uses tend to be more common, in which the

meaning becomes 'clearly intelligible, not imaginary or hypothetical', as in *tangible evidence* and *tangible proof*.

tantalize means more than just tease or torment, as is shown by the word's origins in the treatment meted out to the legendary Phrygian king Tantalus, who was forced to stand in water which receded when he tried to drink and under branches that drew back when he tried to pick the fruit. The word is therefore best used when it retains an element of torment caused by something offered and then withdrawn, although this cannot always be as explicit or obvious as it was for Tantalus: *Foremost among their key sources was a man whom the authors still tantalizingly refuse to name—Time*, 1974.

Taoiseach, the title of the Prime Minister of the Irish Republic, is pronounced **tee**-shək.

target. 1 The figurative use of *target* meaning 'an amount or objective to be achieved' arose during the Second World War and is now more common than the primary meaning. Sir Ernest Gowers, the senior Whitehall civil servant and writer on language, grew rapidly tired of the word: *We were offered a great variety of things that we might meritoriously do to our targets. We might reach them, achieve them, attain them or obtain them; we were to feel greatly encouraged if we came in sight of the target to which we were trying to do whatever we were trying to do, and correspondingly depressed if we found ourselves either a long way behind it or (what apparently amounts to the same thing) a long way short of it—ABC of Plain Words*, 1951. While care should be taken to avoid contexts that are jarringly incongruous (such as *keeping abreast* of targets, perhaps), the physical image is less strong than it is (for example) with *ceiling*, and Gowers' strictures now seem somewhat obsessive. To complain, as some do, that a *doubled target* is larger, and therefore necessarily easier to hit rather than harder, smacks strongly of pedantry. Used with care, *target* has a useful role alongside alternatives such as *aim, goal, object,* and *objective*.

2 The verb, meaning 'to single out as an object of attack', has inflected forms *targeted, targeting*.

tarmac. The verb has inflected forms *tarmacked, tarmacking*.

tart see PIE.

tartan. 1 see PLAID.

2 *Tartan* is used allusively in informal and normally affectionate compounds to denote people or things connected with Scotland; the *tartan army* is the body of Scottish supporters at football games abroad, and the *tartan tax* is an increment on income tax that might well fund Scottish devolution.

tassel. The inflected forms are *tasselled, tasselling* in BrE and in AmE usually *tasseled, tasseling*.

tasty, tasteful. *Tasty* is now restricted to the context of food (and some transferred uses) and is not used in the context of *good taste* (= aesthetic judgement), for which *tasteful* is the appropriate adjective. The opposite word *tasteless*, however, is used in all meanings, physical and abstract.

tattoo. The verb has inflected form *tattoos, tattooed, tattooing*. It can have as its grammatical object either the design that forms the tattoo (*A heart was tattooed on her left arm*) or the part of the body on which the design is put (*Tattooed his cheek with a winged fist*).

tautology is the repetition of the same idea or meaning in a phrase or sentence, as in a *free gift* (all gifts are free), a *new innovation*, and to *return again*. Some tautologies are contained within a small group of words such as a noun phrase (e.g. *future prospects, past history, no other alternative, the general consensus*). Others occur in the way sentences are put together (the tautologous words are printed in bold): *The activities of the club are not limited **only** to golf | There is no need for **undue** haste |*

*The Cold War came to a **final** close in Germany yesterday.* Except when used as a literary or rhythmic device in which the effect is intentional, this kind of tautology is normally regarded as an error and should be avoided.

taxi. The noun has the plural form *taxis*, and the verb has inflected forms *taxis, taxied, taxiing.*

teaspoonful has the plural form *teaspoonfuls*. The phrase *three teaspoons of* — is also available.

techno-. The word *technology* and its main derivatives, *technological* etc., date from the 17c, but it was not until the 20c that the first element *techno-* became a formative element in such compounds as *technocracy* and *technocrat* (both first recorded in 1919), *technophobia* (1965, interestingly somewhat earlier than *technomania* of 1969), *technofreak* (1973), and *technobabble* (1987), all associated with computing and other areas of advanced technology. Other formations refer to types of synthesized electronic music, e.g. *technopop* (1980) and *technorock* (1983), and have led to the independent word *techno*, used as an adjective and a noun: . . . *the energized electrobeats and keyboard surges of dance-floor techno—Rolling Stone*, 1994.

teem. It sometimes causes surprise that the two apparently close meanings involved here are of two distinct verbs. One, from an Old English word meaning 'to give birth to', means 'to be full of or swarming with' (as in *a sea teeming with fish*), and the other, from an Old Norse word meaning 'to empty', means 'to pour or flow copiously' (as in *teeming with rain*). Neither should be confused

with the verb *team*, as used in the phrasal verb *team up with*.

teenager, meaning a person aged from 13 to 19, or sometimes loosely any adolescent person, is first recorded as recently as the 1940s (first in America), although *teenage* is somewhat older (1920s) and *teens* (as in *a person in his teens*) is much older (17c).

teetotaller is spelt with two *l*s in BrE, but in AmE often *teetotaler*.

tele-, derived from the Greek word *tēle* meaning 'at a distance', is one of the great formative elements of modern English and a genuine mirror of technological advance over several centuries. It occurred earliest in words such as *telescope* (first recorded in 1648), *telegraph* (1794), *telegram* (1852), *telephone* (1876 in its modern sense), *telepathy* (1882), and *television* (1907, a hybrid formed on the Latin element *vision*). In more recent formations *tele-* has been even freer of etymological constraints: *telecommunication* was formed first in French in 1937 at a conference in Madrid, *telecast* was modelled on *broadcast* and *telegenic* (meaning 'visually attractive on television') on *photogenic*, and words such as *teleprinter, teleprompter*, and *teletext* were formed simply by lumping *tele-* with an existing word of whatever origin.

televise is a back-formation from *television*, and is spelt *-ise*, not *-ize*, in both BrE and AmE.

temperature, meaning 'a high or abnormal temperature' (as in *Have you got a temperature?*) is idiomatic in modern English but mostly confined to spoken forms.

tempo, a term in music, has the plural form *tempi* (preferred) or *tempos*.

temporary, temporarily. *Temporary* is pronounced **tem**-pə-rə-ri, as four syllables, with an additional stress on the *-ar-* in AmE. *Temporarily* has five syllables and until recently was pronounced in BrE with the stress on the first syllable, but the AmE pronunciation with the stress on the *-ar-* is now almost as common in BrE.

tend. There are two verbs here. One is a shortened form of *attend* and is used either with an object or intransitively with *to* in the meaning 'to take care of, look after' (*Shepherds tending their flocks | The thief was watching as she tended to her father*). The other is derived from Latin *tendere* 'to stretch' and is used with a *to*-infinitive to mean 'be inclined to' (*He tended to do what his parents advised*).

tenet, meaning 'a dogma or doctrine', is now normally pronounced **ten**-it.

tenor. The word has a strange range of meanings (a singing voice, a prevailing course or direction, a legal term, the subject of a metaphor), all relating in some way to the Latin word *tenēre* 'to hold'. The spelling is *-or* in all meanings in both BrE and AmE.

tense is the location in time of the state or action expressed by a verb. English verbs properly have only two tenses, the present (*I am*) and past (*I was*). The future is formed with *shall* or *will* (*I shall| will be*: see SHALL AND WILL), other forms of the past are formed with auxiliary verbs (*I have been | I was being*), and the past perfect is formed with the past tense of

have (*I had been*). Choice of tense mostly corresponds to actual time, but there are conventional uses of tenses other than this, e.g. the HISTORIC PRESENT in narratives (see the separate entry) and the use of the future for present as in polite requests such as *Will that be all for now?*. Choice of tense becomes more complex in reported speech (*He said it is|was a nuisance*): for this see SEQUENCE OF TENSES.

terminal, terminus. 1 In BrE these words are largely interchangeable in meanings associated with the end of routes in different forms of transport, but a *terminus* is more likely to be a road or railway station at the end of a line and a *terminal* is more likely to be a complex of buildings at an airport (or in a city for connection with an airport). *Terminus* is not used in the airport sense but *terminal* is increasingly used in the road and rail senses. In AmE *terminal* is used in all three senses, whereas *terminus* tends to refer to the location (town, city, etc.) at the end of a route.

2 The plural of *terminus* is *termini* (pronounced **ter**-mi-niy).

terminate is a formal word for 'stop or bring to an end', as in *terminating* a pregnancy, an agreement being *terminated*, and a train that *terminates* at Paris. In general contexts, a simpler word such as *stop* or *end* should normally be used.

terminus see TERMINAL.

terrain is best reserved for contexts in which a geographical or military assessment is being made (*an uneven terrain | the peculiarities of the terrain*) rather than as a simple synonym for *area, ground, region,* or *tract.*

terrible, terribly have gone the way of other words of this type, such as *awful | awfully, dreadful | dreadfully, frightful | frightfully;* that is, *terrible* intensifies something by definition bad (*a terrible mistake*) and *terribly* intensifies adjectives and other adverbs generally (*terribly important | not terribly good*). Colloquially, *terrible* is used disparagingly with neutral nouns (*a terrible speaker | What a terrible name to give a baby!*). However, the adjective and adverb retain their literal meanings 'horrifying, horrifyingly' in contexts such as *a terrible cry, terrible consequences,* and *terribly disfigured.* By contrast, *terrific* when used with neutral nouns is not disparaging but approving (*a terrific meal | a terrific speaker*).

tetchy, touchy. *Tetchy* means 'irritable, peevish', and is a near synonym of *testy,* whereas *touchy* means 'over-sensitive, likely to take offence'.

tête-à-tête, meaning 'an intimate conversation between two people', is printed in roman type with the accents and hyphens as shown. The same spelling is used as an adjective or adverb (*dined tête-à-tête*), and the plural of the noun is *tête-à-têtes.*

textual, textural. The contexts normally prevent these two words getting in each other's way: *textual* means 'relating to text' (*textual criticism*), whereas *textural* means 'relating to texture', often in figurative contexts such as music (*textural features | textural variation*).

than. 1 *Than* is normally used to introduce the second element in a comparison, and acts either as a conjunction (*He is older than I am*) or as a preposition (*He is older than me*). In uses such as *He is older than I, than* is normally regarded as a conjunction with the verb following *I* understood, but in spoken English at least the more usual choice is the type *He is older than me.* For this choice, see further at CASES 2B.

2 Other aspects of the use of *than* will be found at the following entries: BARELY, DIFFERENT 3, HARD 2, INFERIOR, OTHER 2, PREFER 3, RATHER 2, SCARCELY 1, SUPERIOR.

thankfully has been used as an ordinary adverb of manner since Anglo-Saxon times, and is still current in this meaning: *'Until Friday,' said Mrs Marsh, and shut the door thankfully behind her*—Anita Brookner, 1992. Since the 1960s, it has developed the additional role of sentence adverb, in which it qualifies a whole statement and reflects the opinion of the speaker rather than modifying anything contained within the statement: *Thankfully, however, the old style has not entirely disappeared*—Daily Telegraph, 1982. Though frowned on from time to time, *thankfully* has not attracted the venom that *hopefully* has; this may well be to do with the meanings of the two words and the associations each has (*thankfully* expresses relief whereas *hopefully* raises doubts). For more on this issue in its context, see HOPEFULLY, SENTENCE ADVERBS.

thanks to. *Thanks to the rank stupidity of Steve Gillery's bride-to-be, he had to hold his stag night on Saturday morning and rush off to the ceremony during half-time in the afternoon*—M. Gist, 1993. This ironic use, in which *thanks to* is an equivalent of *because of* or *due to*, occurs in contexts where thanks are hardly appropriate, but it is attested from the 18c (and earlier in the form *no thanks to*), and its credentials are therefore sound. Meanwhile the straightforward use of *thanks to* continues in use: *Thanks to the national radio paging system, a doctor can be alerted to an emergency by a 'bleep', carried about his person—Scientific American*, 1982.

thank you. The standard written form of the expression of thanks is *thank you* (two words), although *thank-you* (with hyphen) and *thankyou* (one word) are sometimes found, especially in ephemera such as junk mail and restaurant bills, and *thank-you* is the correct from in attributive use (before a noun, e.g. *a thank-you letter*). *Thanks* is more informal and conversational than *thank you*, as are *many thanks* and *thanks a lot*.

that is a word with many roles, and plays a major part in English sentence structure. The following are its main grammatical functions:

DEMONSTRATIVE PRONOUN: *That was what I meant*

DEMONSTRATIVE ADJECTIVE: *Why did you take that picture of me?*

DEMONSTRATIVE ADVERB: *I was that angry | It didn't hurt that much*

RELATIVE PRONOUN: *It was not the drug that had done it*

CONJUNCTION: *He had assumed that we would want to see him*

1 As a demonstrative pronoun and adjective, *that* normally refers to something already mentioned or known: (pronoun) *She had not meant it so, but it could have been read like that | How the hell did you manage that? | The witnesses, if they could be called that,* continued to repeat that they knew nothing | (adjective) *If I were you, I would keep an eye on that young man | It wasn't a nature reserve, that Ark of yours*. There are also a number of familiar idiomatic or formulaic uses: *Something worth a lot of money, that's for sure | She had a small, pretty face, I'll give you that | She cleared her throat to speak but left it at that | I just wanted to see her, that's all*.

2 Its use as a demonstrative adverb equivalent to *so* or *very* (or *so very*) dates from the 15c and has been slipping in and out of standard usage ever since. In current English it is regarded as informal in both positive and negative contexts: *'Shut up,' says Claudia . . . 'It's not that funny'—*David Lodge, 1988 | *You and your brother, you're not really that alike, are you?—Encounter*, 1989. In other contexts, however, it verges on the formal or at least neutral: *The questioning attitude that comes naturally at student age is not that easily abolished—Listener*, 1987.

3 As a relative pronoun, *that* becomes an alternative to *which* (and occasionally *who*). Although they are often interchangeable, there are some uses that are peculiar to each:

▸**a** When *that* is used it normally introduces a so-called 'restrictive' clause, which defines or gives essential (rather than additional) information about the noun or noun phrase that comes before: *the pen that my father bought for me | the pen that is over on the table* | (in each case the *that*-clause defines which pen is meant). (See further at RELATIVE CLAUSES). In these cases the *that*-clause normally follows on without a comma. *Which* can also be used in these examples, but in conversational English *that* is more usual, and in some cases it is possible to omit the relative pronoun altogether and say *the pen my father bought for me. That* can also replace *who* (or *whom*), especially when the reference is non-specific, as in *The person that I saw was definitely a woman*, and when there are two antecedents, one inanimate and the other human: *It was the drug and not her brother that had upset her*.

▶ **b** *That* is also more idiomatic than *which* in a number of cases: (1) when *which* already occurs earlier in the sentence in another role (*Which is the house that you bought?*), (2) after indefinite pronouns such as *anything, everything, nothing*, and *something* (*There is something that I forgot to mention*), and (3) after a construction with the impersonal *it* (*It is the new one that we want*). When *that* is the object of the verb in its clause, it is regularly omitted, especially in speech (*There is something I forgot to mention*).

▶ **c** *Which*, not *that*, has to be used in so-called non-restrictive clauses which give additional rather than essential information: *A new edition of the book, which has taken ten years to write, will be published this week. Which* is also used when a preposition precedes it (*Is this the book to which you are referring?*); in a corresponding construction with *that*, the preposition has to come at the end (*Is this the book that you are referring to?* or *Is this the book you are referring to?*).

4 *That* is used as a conjunction to introduce a subordinate clause, principally after verbs of saying, feeling, believing, knowing, learning, etc.: *The President admitted that he had lied | We would hate to think that they were corrupt-*

ing you | I understand that you wanted to see me. A *that*-clause of this type can also occur after the impersonal *it*: *It was natural that they should think so*. Normally the conjunction *that* can be omitted, especially in speech: *I understand you wanted to see me | It was natural they should think so*. In inverted constructions, however, in which the *that*-clause comes before the main clause, *that* is obligatory: *That they are guilty is assumed by everybody*.

the. **1** *The*, called the definite article, is the commonest word in English, occurring about once in every seven words of everyday language. It can therefore come as a surprise to know that it is pronounced in three ways, depending on its role and position. In normal use it is pronounced dhə before a word beginning with a consonant (*the table | the green house*) and dhi before a word beginning with a vowel or a softly aspirated h sound (*the apples | the other leg | the hotel*). When emphasized, it is pronounced dhee (*You mean the Sharon Stone?*). These distinctions come naturally to most native speakers, but occasional divergences are heard, especially over-emphasis of *the* in cases where the weak form is called for.

2 When two nouns are joined by *and*, a second *the* is normally omitted: *the distortion and innuendo to which several of your correspondents have resorted*. But *the* must be repeated to avoid ambiguity: *the black and the white penguins | the London and the Southampton trains*. When two nouns joined by *and* form the subject of a sentence, they are sometimes regarded as a single concept and treated as grammatically singular: *The innocence and* *purity of their singing comes entirely from their identification with the character*—Bernard Levin, 1985. See AGREEMENT 3.

3 In titles of books, plays, films, etc., *The* should be retained when it forms part of the recognized title, but can be omitted when it does not fit the structure of the sentence: *Look in The Times | a new edition of The Chicago Manual of Style* but *John is a Times reporter | J. R. R. Tolkien's Lord of the Rings*.

4 In BrE it is usual to add *the* when referring to a person by a title, as in *The Prime Minister, Tony Blair, attended the meeting*. The style *Prime Minister Tony Blair attended the meeting* is characteristic of AmE. After verbs such as *become, be appointed*, etc., the definite article can be omitted before titles or names of office that refer to a single person: *He became Prime Minister in 1997*.

theatre is spelt *-re* in BrE but usually *theater* in AmE.

their see THEY.

theirs. This possessive pronoun, as used in *The house is not mine but theirs*, is written without an apostrophe. In compound subjects connected by *and*, the correct form is (e.g.) *Our children and theirs went on holiday together*, not ⊠ *Theirs and our children went on holiday together*.

theirselves is non-standard for *themselves*, and arises from the tendency to regard *self* as a noun needing a possessive pronoun to qualify it; this is legitimate only when an adjective intervenes, e.g. *their very selves*.

them. 1 see THEY.

2 Use of *them* as a demonstrative pronoun and adjective is non-standard or dialectal in current English: *Them's my sentiments*—E. M. Forster, 1924 | *I didn't know much about planes in them days*—P. McCabe, 1992.

themself. The standard reflexive form of *they* and *them* is *themselves* (as in *The children have hurt themselves*), but a form *themself* is recorded (with plural reference) from the 14c to the 16c, when it fell out of use. In the 1980s it was rediscovered in the search for gender-neutral pronouns, and occurs from time to time with reference to common-gender singular noun or pronouns, without yet being generally accepted: *I think somebody should immediately address themself to this problem*—A. T. Ellis, 1987. The plural form *themselves* is also used in this way, but the effect is if anything more awkward: *It may be best, however, to confess to someone who will never meet her boyfriend, . . . just in case that third party got tremendously drunk at a party themselves, and blurted it out to someone else*—Independent, 1998. The final battle for a set of gender-free pronouns will probably be fought over *themself*, but for now beware of it.

then. Use of *then* as an adjective as in *the then President*, to mean 'at that time', has been continuous since the 16c and is acceptable despite occasional objections to it. Less acceptable, however, is the type with an adjective following *then*, especially when joined by a hyphen: *Four years ago great things were expected of Japan's then-embryonic biotechnology industry*. In many cases of this type, *then* can be omitted without any significant loss of meaning.

thence is a formal and literary word meaning 'from there' or 'from then': *It is very logical to feed wind-powered energy in the form of either electricity or direct heat directly into a buffer system and thence to direct use—Journal of the Royal Society of Arts*, 1976. It is no longer used in everyday English.

thereabouts meaning 'near that place' or 'near that amount' (*a hundred pounds or thereabouts*), is along with *thereby, therefore*, and *thereupon* one of the few medieval compounds formed with *there-* to survive in modern English without any hint of archaism. The variant form *thereabout* is now less common.

therefore. 1 This is the most resilient of the adverbs in *there-* and has been part of the core language since the 12c. It is always pronounced with the stress on the first syllable, and can be placed in various positions in a sentence, including the beginning. In short sentences and in constructions in which *therefore* is associated with a particular word or phrase, it is not necessary to separate it with commas: *Would I please therefore oblige her by using the musical notation provided— Guardian*, 1986 | *The relationship of patronage was therefore complex*—R. Greene, 1993. When commas are used, they have the effect of emphasizing the previous word: *Washington, therefore, can see distinct advantages in a one-way upward crawling peg—Times*, 1970.

2 When *therefore* comes at the beginning of a sentence, a following comma is optional and depends on the flow of the sentence: *You're not here as a solicitor . . . Therefore, you're entitled to call some other solicitor*—J. Wainwright, 1972 | *Therefore I wear my 'power suit', I call it, if I have to go to a board in the conference room on* the top floor with senior officials—G. Kirkup et al., 1990. When it is immediately followed by a subordinate clause, it is more likely to be separated by a comma: *Therefore, when a battery shows signs of diminishing power and range effectiveness it makes sense to replace it*—B. Smithson, 1988.

there is, there are. This impersonal formula is used to indicate the existence of something or someone in a way that avoids the need to identify them more closely grammatically. *There is* (or *was*) is used when the following noun is singular, and *there are* (or *were*) when it is plural: *There is a spider in the bath | There were three biscuits a moment ago*. When the number of the following noun is more complex, choice is normally determined by what follows immediately; for example, *There **is** a pen and three sheets of paper on the desk* sounds more natural than *There **are** a pen and three sheets of paper on the desk*. Amounts regarded as a unit are also treated as singular: *There is £500 in my account* (equivalent to 'the sum of £500'). Use of *there is*, or more often *there's*, as an invariable formula regardless of number is often found but is only acceptable informally: *There's 35 branches throughout the country*.

there you are, there you go. *There you are* is used colloquially as a dismissive expression of regret: *I felt ridiculous of course, but there you are*—S. Wall, 1991. *There you go* is sometimes used in the same way, and is also a conversational formula used to draw a person's attention to something offered: *Evan handed over her change. 'There you go then.'*—Barbara Anderson, 1993.

thesaurus. A *thesaurus* (pronounced thə-**saw**-rəs) is a dictionary organized to supply alternative words rather than to offer analytical explanations of what words mean. Because synonymy is such a complex phenomenon, most thesauruses can be, in their nature, as dangerous as they are useful. The plural is *thesauri* or *thesauruses*.

these kind of, these sort of see KIND OF.

thesis, meaning 'a dissertation', has the plural form *theses*, pronounced **thee**-seez.

they, them, their. These three pronouns have all been used since the 16c to refer back to a singular pronoun, especially an indefinite pronoun such as *anyone, everyone, nobody, someone*, etc.: *One other type of sensor . . . sets up an invisible light beam . . . If someone walks across it, they interrupt the beam*—P. Niesewand, 1979 | *The delicious aroma drifting across a neighbour's fence of food cooking over charcoal is enough to make anyone yearn for a barbecue of their own*—Practical Householder, 1986. The value of this device has been enhanced in recent years by its validity as a gender-neutral option in place of more awkward conventions such as *he or she, his or her*, etc. For a fuller discussion of this issue see GENDER-NEUTRALITY.

they're is a contraction of *they are*, and should be distinguished from the like-sounding forms *their* and *there*.

thief has the plural form *thieves*.

thimbleful has the plural form *thimblefuls*. See -FUL.

thinness, meaning 'the quality of being thin', has two *n*s.

think. 1 After *think, that* is usually omitted when a clause follows: *I think you are right*. See THAT 4.

2 *Think* can be followed by a *to*-infinitive with the meaning 'to remember': *Did you think to lock the door?*.

3 As a noun, *think* is relatively recent (early 19c) and is normally regarded as informal: *I'll have a think about it*.

thinkable, meaning 'imaginable, able to be grasped by the mind', is not recorded before the early 19c, some 450 years after its more common antonym *unthinkable*: *A crash is a moment of panic when events are out of control and outlandish predictions become thinkable*—Economist, 1991.

thirties see EIGHTIES.

this. 1 Though a less complex word than *that* (it is not a conjunction or a relative pronoun, to begin with), *this* has three distinct roles:

DEMONSTRATIVE PRONOUN: *This is what I mean*

DEMONSTRATIVE ADJECTIVE: *Would you like a glass of **this** wine?*

DEMONSTRATIVE ADVERB: *The show is not usually **this** good*

2 As a demonstrative pronoun and adjective, *this* normally refers to something or someone either present or being thought of at the time of speaking: *What had I done to deserve **this**? | Did you leave **this** book behind?* It can also refer back to an immediately preceding statement when no single word can be identified as the antecedent: *Should governments do more, or ought this to be left to the private sector?* When contrasted with *that*, *this* refers to the one immediately in mind, whereas *that* refers to the one mentioned before or known previously.

3 When used informally as a demonstrative adverb, *this* has a more specific reference to immediate experience than does the corresponding use of *that*: *Keep in mind, however, that no existing property is this typical—Real Estate Review*, 1972.

thither see HITHER.

though see ALTHOUGH. For *as though*, see AS 8.

thrash, thresh. These words were once variants of the same word, but now have different spellings and pronunciations. To *thrash* is to beat (physically and metaphorically as in *beating* one's opponents), whereas to *thresh* is to separate grain.

three-quarter, three-quarters. The noun expressing a fraction is *three-quarters* (with hyphen). The adjectival form is *three-quarter* (e.g. *a three-quarter-length coat*), and this is also the form for the players in a rugby team.

threshold is spelt with one *h* (contrast *withhold*), and the *h* is optionally silent or aspirated in speech.

thrice, an adverb meaning 'three times', was formerly in general use but is now limited to archaic or literary contexts.

thrive. The past and past participle of the verb are normally both *thrived*, although *throve* (past) and *thriven* (past participle) are occasionally used.

throes, as in *to be in the throes of*, is spelt in this way, and should be distinguished from *throws* as a part of the verb *throw*.

through. There are two important uses which are still regarded as Americanisms but are beginning to make an impression on BrE:

1 As a preposition meaning 'up to and including', as in *Monday through Friday*. British speakers are aware of this use but still regard it as non-British, useful though it is: *An eight-week summer program for disadvantaged children ages three through five—Dædalus*, 1993.

2 As an adverb meaning 'finished', as in *Are you through yet?*. AmE might well say *Are you through with the phone?*, where BrE would prefer *Have you finished with the phone?* (Note that in BrE, in the context of telephones, *Are you through yet?* would normally be taken to mean 'have you got a connection yet?') In AmE this use of *through* is often followed by a verbal noun: *'I'm through eating,* said my father, pushing his plate away—L. S. Schwartz, 1989.

thru is an informal variant of *through* in AmE: *When she was little, and had stuttered thru a sentence—Black World*, 1971. It is used more formally in the term *thruway*, meaning 'an expressway'.

Thursday see FRIDAY.

thus, thusly. *Thus* is a word with an awkward role in modern English. Used sparingly and appropriately, it is highly effective, whereas when over-used it can seem stilted and affected. It has two basic meanings, (1) 'in this way', and (2) 'accordingly, therefore'. In the first meaning, it is placed in the same position as 'in this way' would be, but sits more comfortably before a verb or participle: *He persistently declines to extend to the Press that assistance (such as circulating in advance scripts* *of major speeches, or sticking to the text of speeches thus pre-released) which so greatly facilitates newspaper production—Church Times,* 1976. In the second meaning, it can follow the word order used with *therefore,* except that initial position in a sentence often seems clumsy: *Thus the parents, in conversation at home, are able to identify themselves with the place and people under discussion—Where,* 1972. In some uses, *thus* combines the two meanings: *He attempts to defamiliarize and deconstruct the text and thus account for its persuasive power—Review of English Studies,* 1984. *Thusly* seems an unnecessary form, since *thus* is already an adverb, but it is used in AmE in jocular contexts: *On his way home George mused thusly—Boston Journal,* 1889.

tiara'd, meaning 'wearing a tiara', is preferable to the alternative form *tiaraed.*

tidal, along with *coastal,* belongs to the list of Fowler's LOST CAUSES. His objection was that a Latinate suffix (*-al* corresponding to Latin *-alis*) is attached to a word of English origin (*tide*). Such objections seem absurdly puristic today.

tidbit see TITBIT.

tight, tightly. *Tight* is used as an adverb in combination with a number of verbs, primarily in commands or instructions: *hold tight, sit tight, sleep tight.* It also occurs as the first element in a few compound adjectives, e.g. *tight-fisted, tight-fitting, tight-lipped.* In general use, *tightly* is the normal adverb.

tilde is a mark (~) put over a letter to modify its pronunciation; e.g. ñ in Spanish (as in the second *n* in *niño*) is pronounced -ny-.

till see UNTIL.

time. For words denoting lengths of time, see EPOCH.

times. When followed by an adjective or adverb in the comparative degree, *times* normally denotes an increase and not a decrease, e.g. *five times bigger,* not *five times smaller.* There are occasional exceptions for special effect, but the rule should be followed in everyday language.

timpani, tympanum. *Timpani* is a plural noun meaning 'orchestral kettledrums' (informally shortened to *timps*). *Tympanum* is the technical term for 'eardrum', and has the plural form *tympana.*

tin see CAN.

tinker, meaning 'to play about', is now normally followed by *with* rather than (as formerly) by *at: Whatever moral doubts there may be about tinkering with nature, the biotechnology revolution will not be stopped in its tracks—Oxfam News,* 1990.

tiptoe. The verb has inflected forms *tiptoes, tiptoed, tiptoeing.*

tirade is normally pronounced tiy-**rayd,** with the stress on the second syllable, in BrE, and **tiy-**rayd, with the stress on the first syllable, in AmE.

tire (of a wheel) see TYRE.

tiro, meaning 'a novice', is spelt in this way in BrE but more often *tyro* in AmE. The plural form is *-os.*

tissue should be pronounced **tish**-oo rather than **tis**-yoo.

titbit, tidbit. *Titbit* is the usual spelling in BrE and *tidbit* in AmE. The first element is probably derived from an English dialect word *tid* meaning 'tender, nice, special'.

titillate, titivate. *Titillate* means 'to excite' (as in *It titillated his fancy*), and often has sexual overtones (especially in the noun derivative *titillation*), whereas *titivate* means 'to adorn or smarten' (as in *She titivated herself up for the party*). *Titivate* is often mistakenly used for *titillate* (though the reverse mistake does not occur):
⊠ *Even now twelve heartfelt pages are titivating the senses of a Dead Letter superintendent*—Dylan Thomas, 1933.

titles see CAPITALS 2A, THE 3.

to. 1 For the type *to really love*, see SPLIT INFINITIVE.

2 In AmE, *to* is beginning to be used as an alternative for *of* to denote possession or relation: *He's married and the father to a son*— Chicago Tribune, 1989.

tobacco has the plural form *tobaccos*.

toboggan. The verb has inflected forms *tobogganed, tobogganing*, and derivative forms *tobogganer, tobogganist*.

today, tomorrow, tonight are still occasionally seen in their hyphened forms *to-day, to-night*, and *to-morrow*, but the regular spellings are now as whole words.

together see ALL TOGETHER.

toilet. *Toilet* is the commonest word in BrE for what used to be called *water closet* (or *WC*) and is still sometimes called *lavatory*. It is the word normally used on signs and notices when more specific reference to *ladies* and *gentlemen* (or *gents*) is not given. In middle-class British conversation *loo* (of uncertain origin) has become a regularly used alternative; *toilet* is regarded as non-U, and *lavatory* is now disfavoured almost as much. In AmE, the regular terms are *restroom, bathroom*, and *washroom*, with *john* as a more informal alternative. Many slang terms and euphemisms exist in both varieties (in BrE, *bog, karzy*, etc., and in AmE *can, comfort station, powder room*).

token. The phrase *by the same token* is used to connect a statement to something said previously, and means roughly 'for the same reason' or 'in the same way'. Although it is used less precisely than these definitions imply, there should always be some causal or consequential connection of this kind: *I've dined out on a few stories about her. But not ones that matter. By the same token, she could have made quite a good thing about telling how she saw you . . . that night*—D. Halliday, 1970.

tomato has the plural form *tomatoes*.

tome. A *tome* is a large heavy book, not a synonym for a book of any size.

tomorrow see TODAY.

ton. A *ton* is a unit of weight, and a *tun* is a cask or wine-measure. Both are pronounced *tun* and were once the same word, but they became differentiated in the 17c. A *tonne*, also pronounced *tun*, is a metric ton equivalent to 1,000 kilograms.

tonight see TODAY.

tonsil. The derivative forms are *tonsillectomy*, *tonsillitis*, and *tonsillotomy*, all with two *l*s.

tonsorial has nothing to do with tonsils, but is an adjective derived from the Latin word *tonsor* meaning 'barber' and is used facetiously to refer to a hairdresser or hairdressing.

too. 1 *Too* is the normal word used to qualify an adjective or adverb to denote excess: *The house is too large | I spoke too soon*. It should not be used to qualify a participial adjective when this could not idiomatically be qualified by *very*: *She was too tired* is acceptable because *tired* has acquired the role of an ordinary adjective, but *She was too affected by their criticisms* is less satisfactory because *affected* is still regarded as part of a verb. In this case a better alternative is *She was too much affected by their criticisms* or *She was excessively affected by their criticisms*.

2 When *too* qualifies an adjective followed by a noun, the usual order is (for example) *too large a house* rather than *a too large house*. In more complex sentences it is often preferable to rephrase in order to avoid a clumsy sequence of words with *too*; for example, *The incident arose from a too sudden reaction to the danger* would be better expressed as *The incident arose because they reacted too suddenly to the danger*.

toothcomb. The expression *toothcomb* or (*fine toothcomb*) arose from a misreading of the compound noun *fine-tooth comb* (i.e. a comb with fine teeth). Purists will insist on the original form, but the altered form follows the familiar pattern of idioms that lose direct association with their origins,

and is acceptable: *A novel which has been picked over with toothcombs, in search of clues to 'The Mystery'*—Times Literary Supplement, 1972.

tormentor is spelt *-or*, not *-er*.

tornado has the plural form *tornadoes*.

torpedo has the plural form *torpedoes*, and the verb has inflected forms *torpedoes, torpedoed, torpedoing*.

torpor is spelt *-or* in both BrE and AmE.

torso has the plural form *torsoes*.

tortoise should be pronounced **taw**-təs. The form **taw**-toyz, with the second syllable like *poise*, is non-standard.

tortuous, torturous. Both words are derived from Latin *torquēre* meaning 'to twist', but their literal meanings are different. The (less common) word *torturous* is a derivative of the English word *torture*, whereas *tortuous* has no such intermediary noun. A *tortuous* route is one that is twisting and winding, and a *torturous* illness or anxiety is one that is extremely painful. It is in their figurative uses, in which both words mean 'difficult or complex', that the overlap is most noticeable. A *tortuous* judgement is one that has many complicating features, and a *torturous* judgement is one that is painfully difficult to make; these are two aspects of a similar outcome. *Tortuous* is more common in this range of meanings and is usually the better choice.

total. The verb has inflected forms *totalled, totalling* in BrE, and usually *totaled, totaling* in AmE.

The derivative words are *totally* (adverb) and *totality* (noun).

tother, originally a Middle English form (*the tother*) derived from wrong division of *that other*, is still used in humorous contexts in BrE, especially in the phrase *tell tother from which* (= tell one from the other).

toupee, a kind of wig covering a bald spot, is spelt in this way without any accents.

toward, towards. In BrE *towards* is much the more common form for the preposition, whereas in AmE *toward* is more usual: *We walked toward | towards the house.*

towel has inflected forms *towelled*, *towelling* in BrE, and usually *toweled*, *toweling* in AmE.

trade marks, also called proprietary terms, such as *Bovril*, *Hoover*, *Walkman*, and *Xerox*, should normally be spelt with a capital initial in writing or print, but when they are used as verbs it is customary to use a small initial letter since the term has then become fully lexicalized (*I'll xerox the documents*). When trade marks are entered as headwords in dictionaries they normally appear with a capital initial and an explicit statement of their status; nonetheless, the trade mark owners are often hostile to their inclusion, since this can be taken to imply (although linguistically it does not) that the term has become generic and can accordingly threaten the status of the trade mark. It is an interesting area, difficult to resolve, in which actual things, the names for them, and their legal status all demand different priorities from those who use them.

trade union is the correct form, not *trades union*. The plural form is *trade unions*. But *TUC* is short for *Trades Union Congress*.

trade wind is written as two words.

traffic. The verb has inflected forms *traffics*, *trafficked*, *trafficking*. The derivative noun meaning 'someone who traffics' is *trafficker*.

tragedy, originally a term for a kind of drama in which the principal character or characters suffer death or other misfortune, has been extended in use to refer to major misfortunes in real life (*The government . . . had been captured by the extreme right and its budget measures were 'a tragedy for many good New Zealanders'—Keesings*, 1990), and then further to refer to more trivial or ephemeral setbacks, such as defeat in a sports event. The word is best reserved for uses in which serious misfortune is involved.

train station, first recorded in the *OED* as recently as 1955, seems to be taking over from *railway station* in contexts where something more specific is needed than just *station*: *A 24 year old man was later arrested as he arrived at Oxford train station*—television news broadcast, 1993.

trait, meaning 'a person's distinguishing characteristic', is usually pronounced tray in BrE, or sometimes trayt, as it is regularly in AmE.

trammel has inflected forms *tramelled*, *tramelling* in BrE, and usually *trameled*, *trameling* in AmE.

tranquillity, tranquillize, tranquillizer are spelt with two *l*s in BrE, but usually with one *l* in

AmE. The adverb is *tranquilly* in both varieties.

transcendent, transcendental. The word used in general contexts to mean 'excelling, surpassing' is *transcendent*. *Transcendental* has the basic meaning 'outside experience' and is used mainly in technical contexts: (1) in theology, to refer to God as being outside the universe, the opposite of *immanent* (see at IMMINENT), (2) in philosophy to denote the teaching of the 19c American philosopher Ralph Waldo Emerson, and (3) in the term *transcendental meditation*, a form of meditation derived from Hinduism.

transexual see TRANSSEXUAL.

transfer is pronounced with the stress on the first syllable as a noun, and with the stress on the second syllable as a verb. The verb has inflected forms *transferred*, *transferring*, but the derivative words are *transferable*, *transference*, *transferor*, and *transferee* (all with one *r*).

transgressor, meaning 'someone who violates a rule or law', is spelt *-or*, not *-er*.

tranship, transhipment see TRANSSHIP, TRANSSHIPMENT.

transient, transitory. Both words mean 'brief, fleeting', with *transient* conveying rather more strongly the notion of people or things 'passing through' while *transitory* denotes temporary situations that are more static: *The highly transient nature of the casual labour force in hotels and catering, and the low attachment to work of many casuals . . . mean that the unions' task will scarcely be an easy one*—B. Casey, 1988 | *In traditional critical study, questions about politics were rarely felt important since politics engaged with transitory activities*—T. Healy, 1992. *Transient* has special meanings in music, philosophy, electricity, and nuclear physics, and *transitory* has a special meaning in law. The noun *transience* is generally preferable to the more cumbersome word *transitoriness*.

transistor is spelt *-or*, not *-er*.

transitive verbs see INTRANSITIVE AND TRANSITIVE VERBS.

translator is spelt *-or*, not *-er*.

transliterate means 'to replace the letters or characters of a word with the corresponding letters in another alphabet'. Words may be transliterated into the Roman alphabet from their originals in Greek, Chinese, Japanese, and so on. The result is a *transliteration*, which preserves the form of the original, as distinct from a *translation*, which gives the equivalent word (often unrelated in form) in another language. For example, *pteron* is a transliteration from Greek, and *wing* is its translation.

translucent see TRANSPARENT.

transmit has inflected forms *transmitted*, *transmitting*, and derivative forms *transmitter*, *transmittal* (but more commonly *transmission*). The adjectival forms *transmittable* and *transmissible* are both in use.

transparency is more usual than *transparence* in the general meaning 'the quality or state of being transparent', and is the only form available in the concrete meaning 'a photographic slide'.

transparent is the general word used to describe anything through which light can pass, so that what is on the other side is visible, as distinct from *translucent*, which denotes passage of light but not necessarily visibility (as with frosted glass, for example). *Transparent* also has figurative senses relating to mental comprehension rather than physical vision (e.g. *Their intentions were transparent*) and to political openness and accessibility to public scrutiny.

transpire. The origin of the word is in the Latin verb *spirare* 'to breathe', and in its primary physical sense meant 'to give off vapour' or 'to perspire' (a meaning still used in the physical sciences). In the 18c it developed two abstract meanings, both looked on with suspicion: (1) 'to leak out, to become known', usually with an impersonal *it* as subject (*The two girls, it transpired, did not work in a cabaret but assisted at a gambling salon*—M. Pearce, 1992 | *It transpired later that the social workers were all under instruction to have identification*—R. Black, 1992), and (2) in the late 18c, 'to happen, to occur' (*What actually transpired upon the outbreak of the Civil War is lost in the mists of time*—E. G. Holland, 1986), a sense that probably arose from a misunderstanding of the previous one. In the course of time the first of these meanings has become accepted, but the second, despite its closeness in some contexts, is still widely disfavoured (in the 19c the American writer Richard Grant White went so far as to describe it as a 'monstrous perversion')

and it should not be used except informally.

transport, transportation. *Transport* is used both for the conveying of passengers and goods and for the vehicles used in this. *Transportation*, which is primarily an American word, is also used in BrE in first of these meanings: *Its chief original purpose was to facilitate transportation by road of the products of the Coalbrookdale iron works, which had previously been conveyed by river and canal transport*—B. Bailey, 1985. The word is also used historically with reference to prisoners sent to penal colonies overseas.

transsexual is the preferred form, not *transexual*.

transship, transshipment are the preferred forms, not *tranship*, *transhipment*.

trauma. The preferred pronunciation is **traw**-mə, but **trou**-mə is more common in AmE.

travel. The verb has inflected forms *travelled, travelling, traveller* in BrE, and usually *traveled, traveling* in AmE.

treble see TRIPLE.

trek. The verb has inflected forms *trekked, trekking*. The word implies a strong element of difficulty or arduousness, and as a synonym of *go* is used in hyperbole or for jocular effect.

trellis has inflected forms *trellised, trellising*.

tremor is spelt *-or* in BrE and AmE.

tribe. 1 *Tribe* is used without difficulty when the reference is historical (*Balbindor was a coastal Malay of the Iban tribe*—Brian Aldiss,

1993), and some ancient societies had constitutional divisions normally translated by the term *tribe* (e.g. Athens and Rome). In modern contexts, however, the associations of empire and implications of cultural superiority make it a controversial term when applied to communities living within traditional societies. When these are not technically or traditionally known by the term *tribe*, alternative terms such as *community* and *people* are usually preferable.

2 For several centuries, *tribe* has been used disparagingly to mean 'social circle' or 'set of associates', but in recent usage this meaning has become more neutral in tone: *Nick and she, they were proportioned to each other, they seemed to belong to the same tribe*—Ruth Rendell, 1988. On the whole, since its boundaries are clear, this use is unexceptionable.

tricolour, meaning 'a flag of three colours', especially the French flag of blue, white, and red, is spelt *-our* in BrE and pronounced **trik**-ə-lə. In AmE it is spelt *tricolor* and pronounced **triy**-kul-ə

trigger. The verb has inflected forms *triggered*, *triggering*.

trillion. Now that BILLION means predominantly 'a thousand million' in both BrE and AmE, *trillion* has taken over the earlier BrE meaning of *billion*, i.e. 'a million million', in place of its own former (and more rarely needed) meaning 'a million million million'.

trio has the plural form *trios*.

triple, treble. In general contexts (outside music, betting, etc.) the two words are largely interchangeable as noun, verb, and ad-

jective, but *treble* is somewhat more common for the verb (*Either way, it's bound to treble his life insurance payments*—Daily Telegraph, 1992) and *triple* for the adjective (*I was starting to get triple vision and wondering how you did that with only two eyes*—Iain Banks, 1990). Both words are used in the meaning 'three times as many', as in *treble | triple the number* and *treble | triple the size*.

triptych, meaning 'a painting or carving on three panels', is pronounced **trip**-tik. The second element is derived from the Greek word *ptukhē* meaning 'fold'.

triumphal, triumphant. *Triumphal* is a classifying word denoting things connected with victory, such as a *triumphal arch* or a *triumphal procession*. *Triumphant* is more descriptive and means 'exulting in a victory or success' with a wide range of applications: *'I thought so,' said Gray, with a small triumphant laugh*—Sebastian Faulks, 1993 | *The triumphant British team at the world microlight competition in Dunakeszi, Hungary, deserve to be congratulated*—Flyer, 1991. The two words can occasionally overlap in context: a *triumphal* entry and a *triumphant* entry can refer to the same thing, although one that is *triumphal* in fact may not necessarily be *triumphant* in tone.

trivia, like *trivial*, has an interesting history. Both words are derived in roundabout ways from the Latin word *trivium* meaning 'a place where three roads meet', and come via the medieval sense of a three-part education in grammar, rhetoric, and logic as a division of the liberal arts. *Trivia* is treated as both a plural noun and a singular mass noun: *Besides,* *trivia has its importance, too. Or, to put it another way, trivia have their importance too* — Sunday Times, 1978.

trolley is spelt *-ey* and has the plural form *trolleys*.

troop, troupe. A *troop* is an armoured unit of soldiers or a group of Scouts, whereas a *troupe* is a company of actors or performers. Correspondingly, a *trooper* is a soldier in an armoured unit (and, in America and Australia, a mounted police officer) and a *trouper* is a member of a group of actors or performers and (figuratively) 'a staunch colleague' (usually with a favourable qualifying word: *I don't think you're selfish at all. In fact, Maisie, I think you're a proper trouper* — Dick Francis, 1976).

trouble. *As a comedian he had trouble finding a persona* — New York Times, 1974. This use, in which *trouble* is followed immediately by a verbal noun, is acceptable informally, but in more formal contexts it should include the preposition *in*: *Once you have spoken to the potential recipients you should have no trouble in getting addresses* — J. Ridgway, 1984.

trousers is a plural noun in ordinary use (*Where are my trousers?*), but takes the form *trouser* when used attributively (i.e. before a noun, as in *trouser leg* and *trouser suit*).

trousseau, meaning 'clothes collected by a bride in preparation for her marriage', has the plural form *trousseaus* (preferred) or *trousseaux*, both pronounced **troo**-sohz.

trout is the same in the plural, except that *old trout* (a depreciatory slang term for an old woman) has the plural form *old trouts*.

truly. For *Yours truly*, see LETTER FORMS.

trumpet. The verb has inflected forms *trumpeted, trumpeting*.

trunkful has the plural form *trunkfuls*. See -FUL.

truths. The recommended pronunciation for the plural form is troodhz, although troothz is also heard.

try and, try to. 1 *Try*, like *come* and *go*, can be followed by *and* + verb instead of by a *to*-infinitive: *Try and survive, try and live with the system* — Gerald Seymour, 1983. This use is somewhat more informal than the construction with *to*, and also has the effect of placing the weight of meaning less on *try* and more on the following verb (compare the balance of meaning in *Try to survive . . .*). There are occasions when *and* has a somewhat larger share of the usage: (1) when *try* is already preceded by *to* (*Jack didn't stop to try and work it out* — A. Masters, 1991), (2) in casual or formulaic commands and invitations (*Turn yer light out and try and get some sleep* — Hammond Innes, 1991 | *If he'd said, let's all get together on this, let's try and solve the problem, the problem's been going on indefinitely . . .* , *he might have gained more credibility* — council meeting recorded in British National Corpus, 1994), and (3) in expressions of challenge or defiance (*Just you try and stop me* — Julian Barnes, 1992). But these are tendencies only, and contrary examples are not hard to find: *That girl was going to try to put the blame on her, she could tell* — S. Shepherd, 1988.

2 When *try* is in the negative, *to* and *and* occur more interchangeably in the same types of construction (for example, in commands), but *and* is noticeably more informal: *Don't try and change the subject!*—M. Dibdin, 1989 | *Don't try to deny it*—S. Howard, 1993 | *So Herbie didn't try and jump in the car before I could lift him*—conversation recorded in British National Corpus, 1991 | *They should not try to be fair to other countries*—New Scientist, 1991.

3 The construction with *and* is not available after any other form of *try*, i.e. not after *tries*, *tried*, or *trying* (*They tried to warn us* | *What were you trying to tell me?* | *What if she tries to ring you?* | *I . . . paced around and tried to absorb all the details*—Anita Brookner, 1986), but it is available to tenses formed by auxiliary verbs + the simple form of *try* (*So let's not try and be too funny, eh?*—T. Lewis, 1992 | *I might try and do that, I'll do it tomorrow*—conversation recorded in British National Corpus, 1992). A construction with *to* is also obligatory when *try* is followed by a negative proposition: *Try not to hang things too close, too high, or too far apart*—M. Gilliatt, 1992.

4 CONCLUSION. From all this evidence we must conclude that choice between *try to* and *try and* is largely a matter of spontaneity, rhythm, and emphasis, especially in spoken forms. Generally speaking, *try and* is somewhat more casual in effect, and is especially idiomatic in speech, whereas there are often good reasons for preferring *try to* in more formal contexts. But usage is unstable, and is likely to remain so.

tsar, czar. Both spellings are in use for the title of the former Russian emperors, but *tsar* is more common in BrE and *czar* in AmE.

-t-, -tt-. For the inflection of words such as *ballot* and *target*, see DOUBLING OF FINAL CONSONANTS IN INFLECTION.

Tuesday see FRIDAY.

tumour is spelt *-our* in BrE and *tumor* in AmE.

tun see TON.

tunnel. The verb has inflected forms *tunnelled*, *tunnelling* in BrE and *tunneled*, *tunneling* in AmE.

turban has an adjectival form *turbaned* (one *n*).

turbid, turgid. The two words are unrelated but both can describe the flowing of water in their literal meanings (*turbid* means 'opaque and cloudy' and *turgid* means 'swollen and overflowing'), and both refer to styles of writing in their figurative meanings. *Turgid*, meaning 'inflated, bombastic' (as in *turgid prose*), is the more commonly used, whereas *turbid* means 'confused, muddled'.

Turco- is the normal combining form of *Turkish* (as in *Turcocentric*, *Turco-Russian*, etc.), not *Turko-*.

turf. The noun in its countable meaning ('a single piece of turf') has the plural form *turves* (preferred) or *turfs*.

turkey has the plural form *turkeys*.

turquoise. The recommended pronunciation in BrE is **tur**-kwoiz, but a more French-like form **tur**-kwahz is sometimes heard.

turret has an adjectival form *turreted* (one *t*).

twenties see EIGHTIES.

-ty and -ness. Most English adjectives can form nouns by adding the active (originally Old
English) suffix *-ness*, and these
nouns denote either a state or
quality (*cleverness, happiness*) or an
instance of a state or quality (*a
kindness*). The suffix *-ty* (often in
the form *-ity*) represents via Old
French a Latin noun ending *-tas*
or *-itas*, and is very common in
English (e.g. *honesty, notoriety, pros-
perity, sanity, stupidity*); some forms
also denote an instance of the
quality in the way that some *-ness*
nouns do (*an ability, an ambiguity,
a curiosity, a fatality, a subtlety, a
variety*). In most cases parallel
nouns in *-ness* (*ableness, curiousness,
honestness*, etc.) are not normally
used, but in other cases a form in
-ty has developed a special meaning or a sense of remoteness
from the adjective that leaves
room for an alternative in *-ness*,
e.g. *casualty | casualness, clarity |
clearness, crudity | crudeness, enor-
mity | enormousness, ingenuity* (from
ingenious) *| ingenuousness* (from *in-
genuous*), *nicety | niceness, purity*
(with sexual overtones) *| pureness,
preciosity* (used of literary or artis-
tic style) *| preciousness, speciality |
specialness*. Some adjectives of Latinate origin that might have been
expected to have forms in *-ty* in
fact do not, and *-ness* forms are
used instead, e.g. *facetiousness,
massiveness, naturalness, seriousness,
tediousness*. Conversely there are
nouns in *-ty* for which no corresponding adjectives exist in English, e.g. *celerity, fidelity, integrity,*
utility. For other noun forms see
-ION, -MENT, -NESS.

tympanum see TIMPANI.

type of see KIND OF.

typo, meaning a typographical
error, has the plural form *typos*.

tyrannize, meaning 'to behave
like a tyrant (towards)' is used
both transitively (i.e. with an object) and intransitively followed
by *over*. Fowler (1926) rejected the
transitive use but it is now the
more common pattern: (transitive) *We can use it to tyrannize ourselves, to live in the future instead of
the present*—M. Williamson, 1992 |
(intransitive) *The priests know nothing, but pretend to know much and
tyrannize over the common people*—
New Scientist, 1992.

tyrant. In modern use the word
denotes the manner in which authority is exercised, i.e. oppres-
sively and cruelly. In its ancient
Greek context, it refers to the
manner in which authority was
achieved, i.e. by unconstitutional
means. Once in power, a Greek
tyrant might be a benevolent
ruler.

tyre, tire. The standard spelling
for a wheel's rubber covering is
tyre in BrE and *tire* in AmE. *Tire* is
the older spelling, and may be related to the word *attire*, a tyre
being regarded as a form of
'clothing' for the wheel.

tyro (a novice) see TIRO.

Uu

U and non-U.
See box opposite

uglily, though formally correct, is too awkward for normal use and is usually replaced by the phrase *in an ugly way*.

ultimatum has the plural form *ultimatums*.

ult. is an abbreviation of Latin *ultimo (mense)* meaning 'of the previous month' and is still used occasionally in more formal commercial correspondence following a day (e.g. *the 7th ult.*) to denote a date in the month preceding.

ultra vires, meaning 'beyond one's legal power or authority', is pronounced **ult**-rə **viy**-reez.

-um. For plural forms of Latin nouns ending in *-um* that have been adopted into English (e.g. *addendum, compendium*) see LATIN PLURALS.

umbilical is pronounced um-**bil**-i-kəl (preferred) or um-bi-**liy**-kəl.

un-. The prefix *un-* is used to form negatives of words with two types of meaning: (1) denoting the opposite of an adjective or its derivative (*uneducated, unhappiness*), and (2) denoting a reversal of the action implied by a verb (*undress, unlock*). Some adjectival forms in *un-* have a special and usually unfavourable sense (*unprofessional, unscientific*) and when a neutral classificatory form is needed *non-* is used instead (*nonprofessional, non-scientific*; see NON-).

For the choice between *in-* and *un-* forms, see IN- AND UN-.

unaccountable. *We are here neither in the world of sheer unaccountable miracle nor in that of repeatable experiment* — Theology, 1977. *Unaccountable* means 'that cannot be accounted *for*', and like *reliable* and a few other adjectives in *-able* is formed somewhat controversially from an intransitive verb (one that does not take an object), the linking prepositions *for* and *on* (*account + for, rely + on*) being suppressed in the *-able* forms. See also RELIABLE.

unartistic is sometimes used as a more neutral classificatory term instead of the more usual (and more judgemental) *inartistic*.

unashamedly is pronounced as five syllables.

unattached participles see PARTICIPLES 3.

unaware, unawares. 1 The adjective *unaware* is used predicatively (i.e. after a verb) and is followed either by *of* or by a *that*-clause: *She still seemed unaware of the peril that she was in* — M. Lide, 1991 | *Quite unaware that he had a month's redundancy money coming, Cornelius finished his breakfast* — R. Rankin, 1993. It is occasionally used without any further complementation: *Once having looked, he could never again be unaware* — Edith Pargeter, 1989.

2 *Unawares* is an adverb, used especially in the phrase *to catch someone* (or *be caught*) *unawares*:

585

U and non-U

The term was not known to Fowler (1926) but the idea of language use as a distinguishing feature of class most certainly was, as his article on 'genteelisms' (*paying guest* for *lodger*, *serviette* for *napkin*, etc.) shows. The term *U*, denoting the language of the upper class, was coined by the linguist A. S. C. Ross in 1954, and was turned into a kind of cult by Nancy Mitford in her book of essays entitled *Noblesse Oblige*, which explored a theme already present in her earlier writing, notably in her largely autobiographical novel *The Pursuit of Love* (1945) where Uncle Matthew (representing her father) explodes with indignation at words such as *handbag* and *notepaper*. The table below lists words considered U and non-U taken from Nancy Mitford's book, plus some pairs that have come to be distinguished in the same way since she wrote. (See also the entry GENTEELISM.)

U	NON-U
bag	handbag
bike	cycle
drawing-room	lounge
enough	ample, sufficient
false teeth	dentures
house	home
lavatory	toilet
looking-glass	mirror
luncheon	dinner
napkin	serviette
pudding	sweet, dessert
rich	wealthy
scent	perfume
be sick	be ill
sofa	settee
sorry	pardon
vegetables	greens
writing-paper	notepaper

Forms of pronunciation as well as choice of words are also a feature of U and non-U; for example, the pronunciation of *scone* to rhyme with *stone* is often regarded as non-U, as distinct from the U (originally northern) form that rhymes with *gone*, and for *either* **iy**-dhə is U and **ee**-dhə is non-U.

Social exclusiveness of a potentially sinister kind lies behind what can easily be taken for a language game. Nonetheless, the spirit of fun is hard to resist, as the poet John Betjeman found in his gently satirical poem 'How to Get on in Society' (1954):

▶

> ▶ **U and non-U**
>   continued
>
> *Phone for the fish-knives, Norman,*
>   *As cook is a little unnerved;*
> *You kiddies have crumpled the serviettes*
>   *And I must have things daintily served.*
>
> (four more verses follow)

However, everyone comes unstuck once in a while, especially when caught unawares—S. Romain, 1989.

unbeknown, unbeknownst. These alternatives for the more usual word *unknown* entered the language in the 17c and 19c respectively. They are typically used in asides in the form *unbeknown to* or *unbeknownst to* (someone), and in current use *unbeknownst* is more common: . . . *whose real father, unbeknownst to her, is her mother's one-time Jewish lover*—New York Review of Books, 1990. Both forms have a rhetorical tone but cannot now be said to be 'out of use except in dialect or uneducated speech or in imitations of these' (Fowler, 1926).

unbiased, unbiassed. The preferred form is *unbiased*, although -*ss*- is also found.

uncontrollable is now the dominant form, rather than *incontrollable*.

uncooperative, uncoordinated. Both words are now spelt as shown, without a hyphen and without a diaeresis over the second *o*.

uncountable nouns see COUNTABLE NOUNS.

under see BELOW.

underlay, underlie. 1 The addition of the prefix *under*- makes both verbs transitive (i.e. take an object) and therefore they do not entirely correspond to the grammatical functions of *lay* and *lie*. The form of the past tense and past participle of *underlay* is *underlaid*, and the forms of *underlie* are (past tense) *underlay* and (past participle) *underlain*. The primary meaning of *underlay* is 'to lay one thing under (another) to support it' as in underlaying a floor covering with another layer of material, whereas the more common verb *underlie* means 'to lie under (something)', especially in figurative senses (as in *These motives underlie all they do*).

2 *Underlay* (with stress on the first syllable) is also a noun, meaning 'material laid under a carpet', whereas *underlie* is only a verb.

underneath has from earliest times been in competition with *below*, *beneath*, and *under*, and in current use tends to be used mainly in a physical sense, e.g. (adverb) *a building with a garage underneath*, and (preposition) *underneath the arches of the bridge*. Unlike the other words, *underneath* is also a noun (*the underneath of the vehicle*).

undertone see OVERTONE.

under way. There is a choice between *under way* and *underway*, with the two-word form still marginally preferable: *I started up the bagpipes and was soon under way, marching up and down the church hall*—B. Millin, 1991 | *Don't forget that once work is underway, you should increase your building and contents insurances*—*Do It Yourself*, 1992. The reworking of the phrase as *under weigh*, which arose from associations of ships weighing anchor and setting sail, was common in 19c writers (including Byron, Marryat, and Thackeray) but has largely disappeared since the nautical connection is irrelevant to most contexts.

underwhelm. *He was . . . fluent in speech and crashingly dull. If there was an opportunity to be underwhelming, he unfailingly seized it*—*Observer*, 1984 This fanciful variation on *overwhelming* means 'unimpressive' (*underwhelmed* and occasionally the simple verb *underwhelm* are also used); it dates from the 1950s but seems much more recent. The tone is generally jocular and this should be remembered in more formal contexts.

undeservedly is pronounced as five syllables.

undoubtedly see DOUBTLESS.

uneatable see INEDIBLE.

uneconomic, uneconomical. These two words correspond to the meanings of the positive forms *economic* and *economical*. *Uneconomic* means 'not economic, not capable of being operated profitably', whereas *uneconomical* means 'not economical, wasteful'.

unequal. In its meaning 'inadequate in ability or resources', *unequal* is used with *to* followed by a noun or verbal noun (*They were*

unequal to the task | *They were unequal to completing the task*).

unequalled is spelt in this way in BrE and usually *unequaled* in AmE.

unexceptionable, unexceptional. These two words correspond to the meanings of the positive forms *exceptionable* and *exceptional*. *Unexceptionable* means 'with which no fault can be found, entirely satisfactory', whereas *unexceptional* means 'not out of the ordinary, usual, normal'. *Unexceptionable* is much more common than the positive form *exceptionable*, whereas *exceptional* and *unexceptional* are both well recorded.

unget-at-able, meaning 'inaccessible', is informal. It is spelt with two hyphens as shown.

uninterest see DISINTEREST.

uninterested see DISINTERESTED.

unique. **1** This is one of a handful of words that give rise to strong feelings. Its primary meaning is 'having no like or equal, peculiar to an individual': *Throughout these fluctuations of fortune, Edith's unique teaching style was getting more finely honed*—*Medau News*, 1986. In this meaning it is regarded (like *perfect*) as absolute in sense, i.e. something or someone is either unique or not unique; they cannot be described as *very* unique or *more* unique or *rather* unique. (On the other hand, it is possible to be *nearly* or *almost* or *perhaps* unique just as it is to be *nearly* or *almost* or *perhaps* perfect.) This objection is philosophical rather than linguistic, and grammar caters for the logically impossible as readily as it does for the patently true. And is it not at least arguable that a person with three heads is *more* unique than a person with only two? Or than a person with twelve fingers?

2 The word is derived via French from the Latin word *unicus* meaning 'single, sole' and retained close links with its roots down to the 19c, when it broke loose and became conceptually an English word, marking its independence with a developed meaning that is now the controversial one, i.e 'unusual, remarkable'. This sense is regarded as 'gradable' and is regularly qualified by *very* and other intensifying adverbs: *Your own slide guitar style is pretty unique; do you use glass or metal slides—Guitarist*, 1992. *| Some design choices become so unique that they border on the eccentric and make a property difficult to sell—Chicago Tribune*, 1995.

3 Its adoption in unconvincing contexts by the world of advertising and marketing in slogans such as *Hollywood's unique night life* and *a unique blend of Scottish heather honey and rare old malt whisky* have done much to discredit this meaning, which is a natural one. Indeed, as so often with this type of sense development, meanings that are conventionally distinguished often shade into one another, and it is difficult to apply rules in the border areas of usage: *All these diverse atmospheres merge together beautifully to create a most delightful and unique East Lindsey market town—P. Furlong*, 1989 *| Gavrilov was the outright winner of Moscow's Tchaikovsky Competition where jury and audience alike were bowled over by his flame-throwing technique, by the unique drive and physicality of his playing—Gramophone*, 1992.

4 Meanwhile *unique* continues to be used in its primary meaning, often followed by the preposition *to* which identifies the object of uniqueness; an achievement or feat can be unique, so can an identifying number (which often has to be), and so can a method or technique: *Lorne and I had often visited this particular cave in an attempt to film the Celebes Macaque, a baboon-sized monkey unique to the island—L. Blair, 1988 | Tuck stitch is one of those fabrics that almost all machine knitters recognise at once, it is so unique in its formation—Machine Knitting Monthly*, 1992.

5 Because *unique* is itself 'unique' in its primary meaning this will continue to be used, and it is more common than the strength of opposition to the weakened meaning might lead us to believe. But precise meanings are always vulnerable to drift, and in this case we are seeing a weakening of strength (as has happened to analogous words such as *peculiar* and *similar*), rather than the emergence of a distinct new meaning. If a rule is needed, prudence suggests that the weakened meaning should be used sparingly. In informal and conversational language, however, a broader range of meaning is permissible.

United Kingdom see BRITAIN.

unlawful see ILLEGAL.

unless and until is an established expression which, like *as and when*, serves to intensify doubt about the outcome. It occurs in alternative forms such as *unless or until*, *until or unless*, and so on: *Until and unless he discovered who he was, everything was without meaning—D. Potter, 1986 | Membership of the House of Commons is still the only legitimate qualification for* *real power in Great Britain and likely to remain so unless or until our national identity is totally submerged in Europe*—Spectator, 1991.

unlike is an adjective (*animals as unlike as the bear and the lion*), and a preposition meaning 'dissimilar to' (*a journey unlike any other*). Informally it is used as a quasi-adverb in constructions involving a following preposition: *Unlike with fax messages you can edit and re-use the text of e-mails once they arrive on your computer*—Times, 1998. In more formal contexts, combinations such as this can usually be replaced by alternatives such as *in contrast to* or *as distinct from*, or *unlike* without *in*.

unparalleled is spelt in this way in BrE and AmE.

unpractical means 'not practical', whereas *impractical* has a wider range of meaning: see IM-PRACTICABLE, IMPRACTICAL.

unprecedented is pronounced with its second syllable **-pres-** not **-prees-**.

unravel has inflected forms *unravelled, unravelling* in BrE and usually *unraveled, unraveling* in AmE.

unreadable see ILLEGIBLE.

unrepairable see IRREPARABLE.

unreservedly is pronounced as five syllables.

unrivalled is spelt with two *l*s in BrE and usually as *unrivaled* in AmE.

unsanitary see INSANITARY.

unseasonable, unseasonal. Any difference in meaning corresponding to that of the positive forms (see SEASONABLE, SEASONAL)

has become irreparably eroded, and the two words are both used to describe circumstances (especially weather conditions) that are not appropriate to the season in which they occur: *Younger people, because of the unseasonal heat, were wearing sweaters tied round the hips*—James Kirkup, 1991 | *The weather looked heavy and thundery, as if the unseasonable warmth would soon break*—K. McCallum, 1993. *Unseasonable* can also mean 'not opportune, untimely' more generally, although it rarely does.

unsociable, unsocial. Like the positive forms (see SOCIABLE, SO-CIAL), *unsocial* is a classifying word that essentially means 'not suitable for society' (and has the special sense denoting hours outside the normal working day), whereas *unsociable* is a more judgemental word referring to people (primarily) who dislike the company of others. To complete the picture, *antisocial* is sometimes used in the same way as *unsociable*, but properly means 'contrary to or harmful to the social order' (with reference to people and activities) and is therefore a much stronger word with more sinister implications.

unsolvable see INSOLUBLE.

unstable is the standard negative form of *stable*, but the corresponding noun is *instability*, not *un-*. See IN- AND UN-.

unthinkable is still used in its original meaning 'unable to be imagined or grasped in the mind': *You wander . . . in cool glades of unthinkable beauty*—Westminster Gazette, 1897. But far more common now is the extended and more evaluative meaning 'too unlikely or unpleasant to be considered', comparable to similar shifts that have occurred with *unimaginable* and *inconceivable*: *In these circumstances the removal of British troops was unthinkable*—C. Allen, 1990 | *Margaret Thatcher give up? Unthinkable.*—N. Wyn Ellis, 1991. Despite Fowler's objections to this use (as an expletive without the necessary 'aroma of brimstone') in a lengthy and ultimately futile tirade (1926), it is a natural development that retains the essence of the original meaning and applies it in a more realistic way, since nothing that is postulated can be literally 'unthinkable'. Fowler knew this and saw in it the word's appeal, but common usage has taken a more practical course.

until, till. 1 *Till* is not a shortened form of *until* but is the older word; the *un-* of *until* adds the element 'up to, as far as'. The two words are often interchangeable, except that *until* is more usual at the beginning of a sentence and can sound somewhat more formal, especially in speech: *Until he got Jackson's note he had been convinced that the man was suffering from some sort of regular illness*—C. Horrie et al., 1988 | *I am 22, but I will not be able to earn my first salary until I reach 24*— *Independent*, 1989 | *He didn't ask any more questions but he kept himself awake till Noreen came home*— Ann Pilling, 1987.

2 *Up until* (but not *up till*) is a needless variant, with the word *up* usually redundant and awkward: *Up until the late 1970s, 98 per cent of children raised in Northern Ireland experienced schooling only on their own side of the divide*—J. Fulton, 1991.

3 See also UNLESS AND UNTIL.

4 *Until such time as* can be effective in emphasizing uncertainty about the outcome, but it should not be made to serve as a more verbose alternative to the simple word *until*: *Such noisy groups of youngsters . . . need to be broken down into smaller groups each controlled by a responsible competent leader or instructor until such time as they become mature canoeists*—*Canoeist*, 1991.

unto is generally archaic as an alternative for *to*, and in current use it is normally restricted to fixed expressions such as *do unto others* and *faithful unto death*.

up. As well as its familiar uses as an adverb and preposition denoting a high place or position (*jump up in the air* | *walk up the hill*), *up* has an extraordinarily prolific existence in a role that can go unnoticed: as a particle forming a host of phrasal verbs such as *come up, eat up, get up, look up, sit up, start up, take up*, etc. In some of these, *up* is merely an intensifier that does not affect the basic meaning of the verb it is attached to: there is little difference in reality between *eating* your greens and *eating up* your greens except that the second is more positive. In other cases, the presence of *up* determines or affects the meaning in important ways: something *comes up* when it happens or occurs but the ordinary senses of *come* have no such connection; you can only *look at* something (i.e. *look* is intransitive) but you can *look* something *up* (i.e. *look* is transitive); and *sitting up* is almost but not quite the opposite action to *sitting down*. Most of these uses are based on native English words, and many of them have Latinate equivalents that sound more formal and often less idiomatic (*arise* or *occur* for *come up*, *consult* or *refer to* for *look up*, *initiate* or *inaugurate* for *start up*, *accept* or *assume* for *take up*, etc.). These uses of *up* cause amusement or amazement when people stop to think about them, but they lie at the heart of idiom and help define the Englishness of English. We should not be afraid to use them.

upcoming, as an alternative to *forthcoming*, is recorded in AmE from the 1950s and is beginning to appear in British usage: *He told last week of the spectator who telephoned Selhurst Park to enquire about Wimbledon's upcoming game—* Spectator, 1996.

up, down. In geographical terms, *down* means south and *up* means north, and so you go *up* to Scotland from London and *down* to Atlanta (Georgia) from Chicago. A conventional exception to this straightforward logic arises with capital or major cities; for example it is customary to speak of going *up* to London from whatever direction. In the context of railways, the *up* line (or *up* train) is the one that goes into London, and the *down* line (or *down* train) is the one that goes out of London. This rule is not, however, absolute; from Edinburgh, for example, it would be more usual to talk of going (or driving or flying) *down* to London than *up* to it because Edinburgh is also a capital city and because distance makes the geographical orientation again the primary consideration. As can be seen, usage is unstable, and there are political implications in the relative importance of places that regional sensitivities and movements for devolution are likely to intensify.

upgradable, 'capable of being upgraded or improved', is a word embodying all the resonance of an age of changing technology. It is spelt preferably without an *e* in the middle, and the corresponding noun is *upgradability*.

upon tends to sound more formal and emphatic than *on* when the two are used interchangeably: to look *upon* someone as a friend is a somewhat more imposing proposition than to look *on* them as a friend. *Upon* is the only choice in certain fixed expressions, such as *once upon a time* and *upon my word*, and in uses such as *row upon row of seats* and *Christmas is nearly upon us*.

upstairs, upstair. *Upstairs* is the normal form for both the adjective (*the upstairs rooms*) and the adverb (*go upstairs*). *Upstair* is occasionally found as an adjective, but not as an adverb.

up to see DOWN TO.

upward, upwards. 1 The only form for the adjective is *upward* (*in an upward direction*), but *upward* and *upwards* are both used for the adverb, with a preference for *upwards* in BrE: *The launcher consists of a small nozzle that directs a jet of water upward at an angle of approximately 45 degrees—Scientific American*, 1973 | *James had rounded off sums downwards rather than upwards—writing £900 for an actual £975 for example—*K. M. E. Murray, 1977.

2 *Upwards of* (or occasionally *upward of*) is first recorded in the early 18c in the meaning 'rather more than' and remains in standard use: *A goblet with coloured* twists would be worth upwards of £500—*Guardian*, 1973.

3 The adverb *upwardly* occurs mainly in the expression *upwardly mobile*, meaning 'aspiring to social and professional advancement'.

us. **1** *Us* is used informally to mean 'me' in invitations such as *Give us a kiss* and *Let's have a look.*

2 *Us* should not be used as the subject of a clause in standard English, although the use is found in some regional and dialect usage: *Us country boys should stick together.*

-us. For plural forms of Latin nouns ending in *-us* that have been adopted into English (e.g. *focus, nucleus*) see LATIN PLURALS.

usable is spelt without an *e* in the middle.

use. **1** The transitive verb meaning 'to make use of' is pronounced yooz and the past form is *used* (yoozd). The corresponding noun *use* is pronounced yoos.

2 *Used* is pronounced yoost and followed by *to* in a number of special constructions:

▶ **a** *Be* or *become* or *get used to* + noun or verbal noun means 'be (etc.) accustomed to or familiar with': *She had got used to the sissy . . . thin-blooded climate of Auckland*—D. M. Davin, 1986 | *He still isn't used to her being old enough to drive*—*New Yorker*, 1987.

▶ **b** *Use to* (usually in the form *used to* or *had used to*) + infinitive refers to what happened or existed in the past but does no longer at the time referred to: *I know what you're thinking, Patrick, and I used to think it too*—Kingsley Amis, 1988 | *She had used to squat with old Mataka on the ground*—Muriel Spark, 1969. Negatives and questions are formed with *do* + the *use* form (*What time did she use to return?*—L. Thomas, 1972 | *I didn't use to curse or swear at them*—M. Brogden, 1991) or, with somewhat more formal effect, directly with *not* or by inversion in the manner of the semi-modal verbs *dare* and *need* (*I used not to dream*—Nina Bawden, 1987 | *She used not to be so censorious of others' behaviour*—T. Barnes, 1991). The form *usedn't* (or *usen't*) is also found in casual English but is less suitable in more formal contexts.

utilize. This 19c loanword has led a precarious life for a century and a half beside the much older word *use* (13c). In many contexts *use* is adequate and preferable, but a case can be made out for *utilize* when the emphasis is on practicality and effective exploitation: *Fewer victims meant fewer death sentences and so executioners in the provinces retired and, utilizing their professionally acquired anatomical skills, became surgeons' assistants or animal doctors*—G. Abbott, 1991.

Vv

vacation is in North America the ordinary word for BrE *holiday*. In Britain it is only used in the context of universities and the law courts. The corresponding word for Parliament is *recess*.

vaccinate, though technically the same as *inoculate*, in practice tends to be restricted to smallpox (possibly because its original association with cows, from Latin *vacca* 'cow', is still strong), whereas *inoculate* is used with reference to other diseases.

vacuum has the plural form *vacuums* in general use, but *vacua* is sometimes used in scientific contexts.

vade-mecum, meaning 'a handbook or guidebook' (from modern Latin meaning 'go with me'), is pronounced **vah**-di **may**-kəm and has the plural form *vade-mecums*.

vagary, meaning 'an eccentric idea or action', is pronounced **vay**-gə-ri.

vainness is spelt with two *n*s.

valance, valence, valency. A *valance*, pronounced **val**-əns, is a short curtain round the edge of a canopy or bed. *Valence* and *valency* (both pronounced **vayl**-, the first more common in AmE and the second in BrE) are terms in chemistry relating to the power of atoms.

valet. The noun is pronounced **val**-ay or **val**-it in BrE, and also və-**lay**, with second-syllable stress, in AmE. The verb meaning 'to clean the inside of (a motor vehicle)' has inflected forms *valeted*, *valeting*, pronounced **val**-ayd and **val**-ay-ing in BrE, və-**layd** and və-**lay**-ing in AmE.

valley has the plural form *valleys*.

valour is spelt *-our* in BrE and as *valor* in AmE. The corresponding adjective is spelt *valorous* in both varieties.

vapour is spelt *-our* in BrE and *vapor* in AmE. Derivatives such as *vapourless* and *vapourish* follow the spellings of the root forms, but *vaporous* (adjective) and *vaporize* (verb) are spelt *-or-* in both BrE and AmE.

variance. The phrase *at variance* should be followed by *with*, not *from*: *Michael Hamburger . . . writes of the poet's 'moral purpose at variance with his personal needs and perceptions'* — New Yorker, 1976.

variant. In language, a variant is a legitimate form or spelling of a word that differs from the main one. For example, *judgment* is a variant of *judgement*.

variegated, meaning 'marked by irregular patches of colour', is pronounced **vair**-i-gay-tid as four syllables in BrE but in AmE more often as five syllables (with the middle *e* articulated).

various, unlike *certain*, is not normally used as a noun (followed by *of*) in BrE, although it is occasionally used in this way in AmE: *Various of his colleagues . . . offer to go with him if he is dismissed* — American Spectator, 1994.

vase. The standard pronunciation in BrE is vahz, and in AmE vays or vayz.

've. This contraction of the verb *have* is normally added to pronouns or to modal verbs such as *might* and *would*: *I've had my eye on both of you*—D. Raymond, 1985 | *You would've thought at least she could've cut the bubbles off*—Margaret Foster, 1986. Double or multiple contraction is a feature of some writing that seeks to reproduce conversational language: *Can't've been a nightmare then, can it?*—Pat Barker, 1991.

velvet has derivative forms *velveted, velvety*.

venal, venial. These two unrelated words are sometimes confused, chiefly because they are close in form but perhaps also because their meanings both have to do with forms of transgression. *Venal* means 'able to be bribed, corrupt' (from Latin *venum* 'thing for sale') and is used of people and their actions; *venial* means 'pardonable' (from Latin *venia* 'pardon') and refers in Roman Catholic teaching to minor or pardonable sins as distinct from mortal sins which bring eternal damnation.

vendor, vender. The usual spelling for this formal and legal word meaning 'seller' is *vendor*. In AmE, *vender* is also used.

venery. This represents two distinct words of Latin origin, both archaic but still of interest and likely to be confused. One is from *Venus*, goddess of love and hence 'sexual love' and means 'sexual indulgence' and the other is from *venari* 'to hunt' and means 'hunting'. Both words are pronounced **ven**-ə-ri.

venue is derived from a French word meaning 'a coming', which underlies all its English uses. It has several obsolete meanings to do with coming forward in attack (e.g. in fencing) and from the 16c referred to the place where a jury was appointed to come together for a law trial. Its primary modern sense relates to coming together more generally, denoting the place where a meeting, sports event, concert, or other organized occasion takes place. A miniature social history can be made to unfold from this interesting little word.

veranda is now the usual spelling, not *verandah*.

verbal has four meanings, all close enough to cause possible confusion: (1) 'having the nature of a verb' (*verbal noun*), (2) involving words rather than actual things (*Opposition between these two modes of speaking is rather verbal than real*—B. Jowett, 1875), (3) consisting of words (*verbal wit*), and (4) involving speech as distinct from writing (*a verbal agreement*). The most likely confusion is between the third and fourth of these meanings, and it is often advisable to use *oral* instead of *verbal* to preclude any doubt when the intended meaning is the 'involving speech' one (as in *oral examination*), restricting *verbal* to a few fixed phrases such as *verbal agreement, verbal contract*, and *verbal evidence* in which the meaning is established. Note also that *oral* occurs in several fixed expressions, such as *oral tradition* (the transmission of ancient poetry and stories by word of mouth before they were written down).

verbal noun. 1 A verbal noun (also called a *gerund*) is a form of a verb ending in *-ing* that acts as a noun, for example *smoking* in the phrase *no **smoking*** and in the sentence ***Smoking*** *damages your health*. It should be distinguished from (identically formed) participial adjectives (*a **smoking** chimney*) and participles used to form continuous tenses (*The chimney is **smoking***).

2 Because a verbal noun is a part of a verb as well as being a noun, it can retain some of the characteristics of verbs in its grammatical behaviour; for example the forms *She does not like **me** smoking in bed* (non-possessive) and *She does not like **my** smoking in bed* (possessive) are both established in ordinary usage, although the second, in which *smoking* is treated as a full noun, is often preferred in more formal writing. Fowler (1906, 1926) rejected the first type as 'grammatically indefensible', since the words defy grammatical analysis (an example he gave was *We need fear nothing from China* [change to *China's*] *developing her resources*), but the basis of his argument lay in Latin rather than English grammar and has rightly been questioned since (notably by the Danish linguist Otto Jespersen, 1860–1943). In current use, certain patterns are discernible:

▶ a The possessive is the more normal choice when the word preceding the *-ing* form is a personal name or a noun denoting a person: *One cannot say that Kafka's marvelling at mundane accomplishments was not genuine*—*London Review of Books*, 1987 | *I was now counting on my father's being able to make some provision somehow*—Ved Mehta, 1987.

▶ b When the noun is non-personal, is part of a phrase, or is in the plural, the possessive is not normally used: *They turned a blind eye to toffee apples going missing*—Jeanette Winterson, 1985 | *Then we had our old conversation about the house being haunted*—C. Rumens, 1987 | *Mrs Thatcher herself is not averse to this elegant bone being cast before her longstanding tormentor*—*Daily Telegraph*, 1987.

▶ c With personal pronouns, usage varies between the possessive and non-possessive, the possessive being more usual at the start of a sentence: *Fancy his minding that you went to the Summer Exhibition*—A. N. Wilson, 1978 | *His being so capable was the only pleasant thing about the whole dreadful day*—E. Jolley, 1985 (Australia) | *There can be no question of you disturbing the clerks*—Peter Carey, 1988 (Australia).

▶ d With indefinite pronouns the non-possessive form is more usual, the possessive sounding less natural: *He didn't think for a time of anyone clawing at his back*—D. A. Richards, 1981 (Canada) | *There are many sound reasons, then, for everyone's wanting to join in this new Gold Rush*—*Encounter*, 1988.

▶ e In sum, the possessive is on the retreat, but its use with proper names and personal pronouns and pronouns persists.

3 The *to*-infinitive also acts as a verbal noun (***To err*** *is human,* ***to forgive*** *divine*), and choice between this and an *-ing* form is largely a matter of idiom. For example, one *hopes to do* something but one *thinks of doing* something, has a *fondness for doing* something, and has *an aversion to doing* something. Care needs to be taken not to confuse these patterns, especially when more than one is used in the same sentence.

verbatim, meaning 'word for word', is pronounced ver-**bay**-tim.

verbs. **1** A verb is traditionally regarded as a word that describes the action or state which the sentence seeks to convey and is normally an essential element in a clause or sentence: *She **locked** the door* | *She **was** angry.* Verbs are either transitive (i.e. take an object, as in *She **locked** the door*) or intransitive (as in *She **smiled**);* these functions are described more fully at the entry INTRANSITIVE AND TRANSITIVE VERBS.

2 Verbs are occasionally omitted from sentences, for example in radio and television announcements (*This report from our Washington correspondent.*) or as stylistic devices, afterthoughts, ways of avoiding repetition, etc.: *Friday morning. By tube to a lecture at the London School of Economics—Encounter,* 1981 (in diary style) | *That way, they can work out their aggressions. Once a year.—New Yorker,* 1987.

3 For other aspects of verbs and their behaviour, see AUXILIARY VERBS, MODAL VERBS, PHRASAL VERBS, REFLEXIVE VERBS, VERBS FROM NOUNS.

verbs ending in vowels and -ay etc.
See box opposite

verbs from nouns. By a process called 'conversion', verbs have for several centuries been formed from nouns (and occasionally adjectives), by using the same word (e.g. *to question, to knife, to quiz, to service*), by adding a suffix such as *-ize* (*prioritize, randomize*), or by back-formation in which the noun form is shortened (*to diagnose, to televise*). Although objections are raised to some of these formations (especially the longer ones in *-ize*, such as *hospitalize* and *privatize*), it is an established

process and generally a useful one.

verger. The name for the church official is spelt as shown, except that the spelling *virger* is used of St Paul's Cathedral in London and Winchester Cathedral.

veritable featured prominently in English from the 15c to the 17c, and then fell out of use until it was revived as a Gallicism in the 19c with an intensive meaning 'deserving its name' (*a veritable feast*). In modern use it has a somewhat rhetorical or affected tone: *So tough, you'd like us all to think, but inside you're a veritable marshmallow*—M. Yorke, 1973.

vermin is normally treated as a plural in both its meanings ('mammals and birds that are harmful to other life' and 'vile or despicable people'), although it can refer to a single person or animal: *Suddenly the older of the two little girls said, 'Why is a squirrel called vermin, Dad?'*—M. Bowring, 1993. There is no plural form *vermins.*

vermouth, the drink, is normally pronounced with the stress on the first syllable in BrE, and with the stress on the second syllable (to rhyme with *tooth*) in AmE.

verse can mean (1) poetical composition in general (*She writes verse as well as prose*), (2) a line of poetry, (3) a section of a poem also called a *stanza*, and (4) each of the short numbered divisions of a chapter in the Bible.

verso, meaning 'the left-hand page of a book', has the plural form *versos.* The right-hand page is called the *recto.*

vertebra means 'a segment of the backbone'; in the plural *verte-*

verbs ending in vowels and -ay etc.

The following table lists routine inflections of representative verbs having certain awkward vowel endings in their base forms, and shows any exceptions:

VERBS IN -AY

allay	allays	allayed	allaying	
play	plays	played	playing	playable
exceptions				
lay	lays	laid	laying	layable
pay	pays	paid	paying	payable
say	says	said	saying	sayable

VERBS IN -EY

convey	conveys	conveyed	conveying	conveyable

VERBS IN -I

ski	skis	skied	skiing
taxi	taxis	taxied	taxiing

VERBS IN -IE

die	dies	died	dying

VERBS IN -O

veto	vetoes	vetoed	vetoing
video	videoes	videoed	videoing

VERBS IN -OY

enjoy	enjoys	enjoyed	enjoying	enjoyable
cloy	cloys	cloyed	cloying	

VERBS IN -UY

buy	buys	bought	buying	buyable
guy	guys	guyed	guying	

VERBS IN -Y AFTER A CONSONANT

copy	copies	copied	copying	copiable
deny	denies	denied	denying	deniable
specify	specifies	specified	specifying	specifiable
try	tries	tried	trying	triable

VERBS IN -YE

dye	dyes	dyed	dyeing*	dyable

*to avoid confusion with dying *from* die

brae (pronounced **ver**-ti-bree) it refers to the backbone as a whole.

vertex, meaning 'the highest point', has the plural form *vertices* (pronounced **ver**-ti-seez) or *vertexes*.

very, much. 1 The uses of *very* and *much* as intensifying adverbs are for the most part complementary. *Very* qualifies adjectives and adverbs (*very large* | *very slowly*), whereas *much* qualifies past participles that are used as adjectives (*a much enlarged edition* | *They were much criticized*). There is a grey area including words that are strictly speaking past participles but have come to be treated as full adjectives, notably words of feeling such as *annoyed, pleased, tired, worried*, etc., and words with a strong adjectival element such as *sheltered* (*a very sheltered upbringing*) and *involved* (*He is very involved in charitable work*). These are now more naturally qualified by *very* than by *much*. When the verb element is uppermost, *much* is preferred; we would for example speak of a *much honoured* dignitary rather than a *very honoured* one, and we would say that alternatives are *not much differentiated* in preference to *not very differentiated*. At the heart of this grey area lie words such as *respected*, in which the adjective and verb emphasis is infinitely variable: if we say *a much respected politician* we stress the process, whereas if we say *a very respected politician* we assess the effect.

2 It is worth adding that *much* can itself be qualified by *very*; consequently any of the words we have been reviewing that can be intensified by *much* can be more strongly intensified by *very much* (e.g. *very much criticized* | *very much enlarged*).

3 Some types of participial adjective are conventionally qualified by intensifying words other than *much* and *very*, e.g. *injured* (and similar words such as *burnt, scarred*, etc.) is qualified by *badly* or *seriously, bungled* by *badly* or *severely*, and *outnumbered, outvoted*, etc. by *heavily*.

4 In a 20c development, *very* is used to qualify nouns that have assumed the role of adjectives: for example, a song might be called *very sixties* (characteristic of the 1960s), and a building might be called *very art deco* (built in that style).

-ves. For plurals such as *calves*, see -FS, -VES.

vest. In BrE, a *vest* is an undergarment for the top part of the body and also a garment worn by athletes. In AmE the first of these is called an *undershirt*, and *vest* is a term for what in BrE is a man's *waistcoat* and also for a short sleeveless jacket worn by women.

vet is an accepted shortening of *veterinary surgeon* and the normal word in BrE. In AmE *vet* and *veterinarian* are used in this sense, and *vet* also means 'a veteran'. The verb, meaning (1) to treat (a sick animal) and (2) to examine or check critically, has inflected forms *vetted, vetting*.

veto. The noun has the plural form *vetoes*, and the verb has inflected forms *vetoes, vetoed, vetoing*.

via, meaning 'by way of' (*Paris to Athens via Venice*) is originally the ablative of Latin *via* meaning 'way, road', and is now fully naturalized in English. It is increasingly used to denote a form of transport rather than the route, in place of the more obvious preposition *by* (*via airmail* | *via satellite*).

viable is a 19c loanword from French, and was first used to describe a foetus or new-born child that was capable of maintaining life. Metaphorical uses developed in the 19c, but it was not until the 1940s that it became a vogue word applied to a whole range of ideas, plans, propositions, etc., regarded in terms of their practicability. Sometimes the metaphor is justified, but often alternatives such as *feasible, practicable, sustainable, tenable, valid, workable* will do just as well.

vibrator is spelt *-or*, not *-er*.

vice, a formal term meaning 'in place of' (*appointed Secretary vice Mr Jones deceased*), is pronounced **viy**-si and is originally a form of a Latin word meaning 'in place of, in the stead of'. It is the same word as *vice-* in *vice-chancellor, vice-president*, etc.

vicegerent. A *vicegerent* (pronounced viys-**jer**-ənt) is a person appointed to carry out the office of another, for example the Pope regarded as God's representative on earth.

vice versa, meaning 'the other way round', is pronounced **viy**-si **ver**-sə. It is derived from a Latin phrase meaning 'the position being reversed', and is fully naturalized in English.

victuals, pronounced **vit**-əlz, is a rather old-fashioned or rustic (plural) noun meaning 'food or provisions', and like all such words is sometimes used in humorous or affected contexts.

vie, meaning 'to compete for superiority', has inflected forms *vies, vied, vying*.

view is used in two common idioms, *in view of* and *with a view to*. *In view of* is used as an equiva-

lent of *because of* or *considering* followed by a noun (or verbal noun) to introduce a known or expected circumstance: *He was especially anxious to court the Kremlin in view of the rapid cooling of the U.S.'s interest in Ethiopia—Time*, 1977. *With a view to* is a more formal expression, is usually followed by a verbal noun, and means 'in order to achieve': *We recommend that there should be a peer review of all the departments at Chelsea . . . with a view to phasing out those which do not come up to the standard of the rest of the university—Times Higher Education Supplement*, 1981. In ordinary language a construction with *in order to* (+ infinitive) is often preferable.

viewpoint see POINT OF VIEW.

vigour is spelt *-our* in BrE and *vigor* in AmE. The adjective *vigorous* is spelt *-or-* in both varieties.

villain, villein. The two spellings are forms of a single word with two branches, originally meaning either 'a low-born rustic' or 'a serf in the feudal system' and derived from the Latin word *villa* meaning 'country house or farm'. The spelling *villain* was associated from the 17c with the worsened meaning 'an unprincipled scoundrel', while the other form *villein* slipped into historical use as the feudal system was replaced by capitalism. The distinction is preserved in current usage.

viola. The musical instrument is pronounced vi-**oh**-lə, and the flower **viy**-ə-lə. The plural form in both cases is *violas*.

violable, not *violatable*, is the derivative form of *violate*.

violoncello is the correct spelling, not *violin-*. It is an Italian word, a diminutive of *violone* which is a double-bass viol. The plural form is *violoncellos*. Normally, however, the shortened form *cello* is used.

virago, meaning 'a fierce or abusive woman', is pronounced vi-**rah**-goh and has the plural form *viragos*.

virement, meaning 'a process of transferring public funds from one account to another', was taken from French in the early 20c. An anglicized pronunciation with the first syllable as in *fire* is now usual.

Virgil is the preferred spelling of the name of the Roman poet, not *Vergil* (despite the Latin form *Publius Vergilius Maro*).

virile is pronounced **vi**-riyl in BrE, and also **vi**-rəl in AmE.

virtual has taken on a brand new meaning in the computer age. By itself it is defined somewhat obscurely as 'not physically existing as such but made by software to appear to exist', and it only begins to make sense in its most common context of *virtual reality*, a computer-generated simulation of a three-dimensional image or environment in which the user can participate by means of special electronic equipment such as a helmet with a screen inside or gloves fitted with sensors. Anything presented to the user in this form can be described as *virtual*: a *virtual hand*, a *virtual flower*, a *virtual person*, etc.

virtuoso, meaning 'a person highly skilled in musical technique', has the plural form *virtuosi*, pronounced -si or -zi.

virus has the plural form *viruses*. In computing, a virus is a self-replicating program that harms other systems. It is malicious in intention, unlike a *bug*, which is an unintentional flaw in a program.

visage, a literary word meaning 'face, countenance', is pronounced **viz**-ij.

vis-à-vis (also printed without the accent) is pronounced vee-zah-**vee** and is now mostly used as a preposition meaning 'in relation to': *The state has a duty to protect its citizens from external enemies, and this can best be achieved by maximizing its power vis-a-vis other states*—P. Gill et al., 1984.

viscount is a British nobleman ranking between an earl and a baron. The rank is called a *viscountcy*.

visible, visual. *Visible* means 'able to be seen', whereas *visual* is a classifying adjective denoting anything to do with sight or vision. The *visual arts* are those forms of art that are appreciated by the eye, and a *visual display unit* (*VDU*) is a computer screen.

vision. *'How do you find Weedin?' 'Totally,' Dougal said, 'lacking in vision. It is his fatal flaw. Otherwise quite sane.'*—Muriel Spark, 1960. This meaning, 'statesmanlike foresight', grew out of a much older set of meanings to do with intellectual perception as a metaphor based on physical seeing. Fowler dubbed it a 'vogue word', a status that to some extent it still has.

visit. To *visit with* someone, i.e. pay them a brief call, is now regarded as an Americanism although it was current in Britain in the 19c, occurring for example in writings of Ruskin and George Eliot (*Middlemarch*, 1872).

visitation, once a formal word for *visit*, is now largely confined to special meanings such as official visits of inspection and an affliction attributed to some supernatural agency or other. In AmE *visitation* also refers to the right granted by a court to a divorced parent to visit a child that is in the custody of the other parent. It should not be used as a simple synonym for *visit*.

visitor is spelt *-or*, not *-er*.

visor is the preferred spelling for the various kinds of covering for the face, not *vizor*.

vitamin is pronounced vit-ə-min in BrE and viy-tə-min in AmE and in some other parts of the English-speaking world.

viva voce, meaning 'an oral examination', is pronounced viy-və voh-chi. It is usually shortened to *viva* (plural *vivas*) and this is also used as a verb (with inflected forms *vivaes, vivaed, vivaing*).

viz. is a shortened form of *videlicet*, a Middle English word based on Latin words meaning 'it is permissible to see'; the final *z* is explained as a medieval symbol standing for the ending *-et*. The abbreviation is used to mean 'namely' in introducing a specific mention of what has been only vaguely or indirectly referred to (*my only means of income, viz. my fiddle*), and is often articulated as 'namely', although informally the more direct pronunciation viz is also used. Note that it differs

from *i.e.* (= *id est*) in identifying rather than explaining.

vogue words. In its meaning 'popular use or currency', *vogue* dates from the 17c, but the expression *vogue word* (or *term*) did not come into general use until the 20c. Fowler, who was one of the first to use the term, defined it as a word that 'emerges from obscurity . . . into sudden popularity'; he was generally open-minded about their usefulness, and it has been later critics who have tended to pour scorn on the practice of words coming into and going out of fashion. Some vogue uses arise because they are associated with events of particular public interest (such as *yomping* = marching over heavy terrain, used by Royal Marines in the Falklands war of 1982). Others fall in the category of 'popularized technicalities' (such as *chain reaction, parameter*, and *persona*). When Fowler wrote (1926), the vogue words to which he drew attention included *acid test, asset, distinctly* (as in *distinctly colder*), *far-flung* (which he liked, in the right place), *frock* (= woman's dress), *intensive, mentality, unthinkable*, and *vision* (= political foresight). Gowers, writing in 1965, retained *acid test* and *unthinkable* (!) and added, among others, *coexistence, overtones, psychological moment*, and *target*. More recent vogue uses include *designer* (as in *designer clothes*), *interface, ongoing, paradigm, parameter, spin doctor*, and *syndrome*. See also POPULARIZED TECHNICALITIES. The term *buzz-word*, meaning much the same as *vogue word*, is first recorded in the 1940s in America.

voicemail, an electronic system of storing messages from telephone callers, has achieved such rapid familiarity that it is normally spelt as one word.

volcano has the plural form *volcanoes*.

volley. The noun has the plural form *volleys*, and the verb has inflected forms *volleys*, *volleyed*, *volleying*.

volte-face, meaning 'a sudden change of opinion or reversal of policy', is pronounced volt-**fahs** and is printed in roman type as a naturalized word.

voluntarily is traditionally pronounced in BrE with the stress on the first syllable, but the awkwardness of this pattern has led, under American influence, to the stress being placed often on the third syllable (-*ar*-).

vomit. The verb has inflected forms *vomited*, *vomiting*.

vortex has the plural form *vortexes* in general use, but *vortices* (pronounced **vaw**-ti-seez) in technical contexts.

Ww

wadi is the recommended spelling for the dry bed of a watercourse in North Africa, not *wady*. The plural form is *wadis*.

wage, wages. *Wages* is normally used in the plural (*Their wages are still too low*); an older singular construction survives only in the biblical line *For the wages of sinne is death* (Romans 6:23). But *wage* is also used (*What sort of wage are you paid?*), and is the obligatory form in certain fixed expressions (*wage-earner, minimum wage*).

wagon, waggon. The form with one *g* is recommended, although the house style of some printing houses in Britain is the *-gg-* form.

wainscot, meaning 'panelling on the lower part of a wall near the floor', has derivative forms *wainscoted, wainscoting* (one *t* in each).

wait see AWAIT.

waitperson, a gender-neutral term for a male or female waiter, dates from the 1980s, first in America. The feminine form *waitress* is sometimes disfavoured as a sexist term but is still in wide use.

waive means 'to give up (a right or claim) voluntarily', as in *waiving* an immunity or *waiving* formalities. It is not formally confused with the more familiar verb *wave* except in phrasal verbs such as *waive aside* and *waive away* (= to put aside as if with the wave of the hand), which are incorrect (✖ *I cannot waive away all the teaching of history*).

wake, waken see AWAKE, AWAKEN.

wallop. The verb has inflected forms *walloped, walloping*.

want *verb.* **1** *Want* is of Norse origin and came into English in the 13c. The dominant meaning in current usage is 'to desire or wish for' (*Tom wants a computer for Christmas | What do you want to do now?*), and a range of earlier meanings equivalent to 'to lack or need' has been reduced to a few uses as in *The house wants painting* and *The standard is sadly wanting* (= inadequate), in the expression *to want for nothing* (or *not want for anything*), in advertisements (*bar staff wanted*), and in the non-standard types *You want to pull yourself together* and *You want to go straight on and turn right at the lights* (= need to, should). Occasionally the two branches of meaning merge (*The organization badly wants better leadership*), and it is easy to see how the 'needing' branch led to the 'wishing' branch.

2 Some special and modern uses of *want* are:

▶ **a** Forms in *-ed* and *-ing* in constructions of the type *We want our car washed* and *The roof wants mending* are sometimes reversed as *We want our car washing* and *The roof wants mended*. These uses are mostly regional in BrE and are non-standard.

▶ **b** *Want* is followed by a *that*-clause: *You want that I should lose*

both my lieutenants together?—A. Le-
jeune, 1986.

▶**c** *Want* is followed by *for* + object + *to*-infinitive, most often in
cases in which *want* is followed
by an intensifying word or phrase
such as *very much* or *so much*: *My
mother wanted so much for my sister
to have the best animals*—New
Yorker, 1989.

▶**d** *Want* is used for *want to*, especially in the form *if you* (etc.)
want: *It means he will be able to
come in whenever he wants*—Nigel
Williams, 1985 | *Stay home if you
want*—Fay Weldon, 1988.

▶**e** There is ellipsis of a following verb (*come, go,* etc.) in the expressions *to want in* (= to be
included) and *to want out* (= to be
excluded): *The Federal Reserve chairman Mr Paul Volcker has reportedly
told friends that he wants out*—
Guardian, 1984.

wantonness is spelt with two
*n*s.

warder, wardress. These terms
for male and female prison
guards respectively have now
been largely replaced by the
gender-neutral term *prison officer.*

warn *verb* is traditionally a transitive verb with a grammatical
object corresponding to the person or people receiving the warning: *She warned them of the danger
| She warned them that it was un-
safe.* In the 20c an intransitive
use with a following *that*-clause
has come into common use, with
the object of the warning left un-
specified: *Arafat also warned that
any Palestinian group that rejected
the idea . . . must read itself out of
the P.L.O.*—Time, 1976.

wash up in BrE means 'to wash
crockery and cutlery after use',
whereas in AmE it means 'to
wash one's hands and face'.

wastage should not be used as a
synonym of the noun *waste*, but
has special (often technical and
always non-judgemental) meanings: (1) loss by natural means,
e.g. wear or erosion, (2) an
amount wasted, (3) in the phrase
natural wastage, reduction in staff-
ing by resignations and retirement rather than enforced
redundancies. *Waste* has connotations of disapproval in its meaning 'a bad use of resources or
assets' (as in *go to waste, a waste of
time,* etc.), but is neutral when it
means 'refuse, unwanted material or food'.

waste-paper basket is the BrE
term; in AmE it is *waste-basket.*

-watch. The noun *watch*, meaning 'a state of alert', first produced a suffix (or combining
form) in the 1950s, and is known
earlier in verbs such as *firewatch*
(a term from the Second World
War), but it is essentially a creation of the 70s (*doomwatch*) and
80s in combinations to do with
animal welfare such as *badger-
watch, birdwatch,* and *whale-watch,*
and in other uses such as *crime-
watch* (the name of a UK television programme), *hacker-watch*
(precaution against computer
hackers) and *stormwatch.* Other ad
hoc uses occur, establishing
-watch as a productive element
within fairly narrow limits:
*Family-sized platters contain an entire
chicken or spaghetti for eight. . . . No
reservations, so prepare to people-
watch while you wait*—Minnesota
Monthly, 1994.

Watergate see -GATE.

watershed, originally a term in
geology referring to the flow and
division of river currents, has
been used since the late 19c in

the figurative meaning 'a turning-point in affairs': *In the social history of twentieth-century Britain the Second World War stands out as a watershed*—H. Smith, 1986. It is often used attributively (i.e. before a noun: *Ade became one of the more astute chroniclers of the daily preoccupations of ordinary people who were living through the 'watershed period'*—T. Tobin, 1973). In the UK *watershed* has a special meaning in broadcasting, denoting the time in the evening after which programmes are no longer guaranteed as suitable for viewing by children.

wave see WAIVE.

wax *verb*. In the meaning 'to assume a specified tone or state', *wax* is followed by an adjective, not an adverb: *to wax lyrical, to wax enthusiastic*, etc.: *When the Roman soldiers were asked to take part in the Claudian invasion of 43, they waxed indignant*—Antonia Fraser, 1988. This use is primarily rhetorical.

way see NO WAY, UNDER WAY.

waylay has inflected forms *waylays, waylaid, waylaying*.

ways. In March 1994 the American Secretary of State Warren Christopher said that an overall peace agreement in Bosnia was *a ways down the road*; and Tom Wolf in his *Bonfire of the Vanities* (1987) wrote *I was standing out in the street a little ways*. This use of the plural *ways*, meaning 'at some indeterminate distance (in time or place)' is related to a use (with a qualifying word) that was once standard in BrE (*Falmouth . . . is no great ways from the sea*—Byron, 1809) but is now confined to dialect use.

we. 1 The personal pronoun *we* has a wide range of reference, so that care is often needed to avoid misunderstanding. In its primary meanings it can denote any of the following: (1) you (singular or plural) and I, (2) you and I and some others, or (3) I and some others (but not you: *We are going now, but don't you hurry*). Informally, it can also mean just 'you', as in the condescending form of enquiry *How are we today?*

2 *We* is also used with indefinite reference in the following conventional uses:

▶ **a** When a writer or speaker includes his or her readers or hearers and other unnamed people in a statement or proposition: *As we saw in the last chapter . . . | What do we, as a nation, care about books? | We have to tackle the problem of inflation.*

▶ **b** When a monarch is using the first person (the so-called *royal we*). This practice is dying out, however. Queen Victoria is credited with the remark *We are not amused*, but Queen Elizabeth II is noted for *My husband and I* and generally uses the singular form when referring to herself. (Margaret Thatcher's pronouncement *We have become a grandmother*, quoted in *The Times* of 4 March 1989, was blatant affectation.)

3 *We* is sometimes used mistakenly for *us*, possibly as a kind of hypercorrection, in sentences such as: *Perhaps this product is best suited to we cloth-capped northerners*. For the wrong use of *us* for *we*, see US 2.

wear, gear. *Wear* is normally used as the second element in compounds denoting forms of clothing, such as *footwear* and *underwear*, but *gear* is used in *headgear.* Used by itself, *gear* (= clothing, attire) is now considered informal, although it was once used as a regular word in this meaning.

weave *verb.* It is worth pointing out that there are two words involved here, although their meanings overlap in figurative applications. The one meaning 'to form fabric by interlacing threads' is from Old English, and the other, meaning 'to take a winding course', is a form of a later (13c) word taken from Old Norse. The two verbs have different sets of inflection: the older word has a past form *wove* and a past participle *woven*, and the later word has *weaved* for both. Care needs to be taken to distinguish these in figurative uses; both words can be used but the image is different in each case: *Then they got on to the little scooter and weaved down the lane*—Jeanette Winterson, 1987 | *She wove her way among the crowd, bumping into people, being bumped into*—M. Ramgobin, 1986 (South Africa). (In the second example, *wove* may just be a slip for *weaved*.)

Web is normally spelt with a capital *W* when it refers to the *World Wide Web*, an information access system for the Internet. In combinations such as *web page* and *web site*, however, it tends to be spelt with a small initial letter. *World Wide Web* is often abbreviated to *WWW*.

wed (= marry). The form of the past tense and past participle is either *wedded* or *wed*. Its shortness makes it a popular word with headline-writers and journalists (*Supermodel Claudia Schiffer has ditched her boyfriend to wed Prince Albert of Monaco, it was claimed last*

night—*Sun*, 1992), but otherwise its use has become increasingly restricted to special contexts (e.g. *in a state of wedded bliss* | *With this ring I thee wed*) and to figurative uses (*This power plant is wed to a double-pivot spring strut suspension*—*Transpacific* (US), 1992).

Wednesday see FRIDAY.

week see DAY.

weir is the standard spelling for a dam built across a river. The older variant *wear* is now obsolete.

weird, meaning 'strange, unnatural', is spelt *-ei-*, not *-ie*.

well see AS WELL AS.

well, well-. There is much uncertainty about whether forms such as *well(-)made* and *well(-)received* should contain a hyphen or be spelt as two words. The normal rule is that the combination is hyphened when it occurs in attributive position (i.e. before a noun, as in *a well-made cupboard* and *a well-received suggestion*), but not when it occurs after a verb (as in *The cupboard looks well made* and *The suggestion was well received*).

well-nigh, meaning 'nearly, almost wholly or entirely', has been in continuous use since the Old English period but is now usually regarded as literary or archaic in tone: *If your country is the size of a postage stamp, your population is unsophisticated and your borders are well-nigh indefensible, you need luck*—*Economist*, 1992.

welsh. The expression *welsh on*, meaning 'to evade (an obligation)' or 'to fail to carry out (a promise)', dates from the 1930s, although the verb (of unknown origin) was used transitively (with a person as object) in the 19c. To avoid a direct and possibly offensive association with the Welsh people, it is often spelt *welch*.

Welsh rabbit, the dish of cheese on toast, has no obvious connection with the Welsh or with rabbits, but has been known in this form since the early 18c (and is the name used in Mrs Glasse's *The Art of Cookery* in 1747). Its origin is obscure, as is the emergence of the alternative form with *rarebit*, a word otherwise unrecorded.

werewolf should be spelt in this way rather than as *werwolf* and the recommended pronunciation is with the first syllable as in *ware*.

west, western, westerly see EAST.

westward, westwards. The only form for the adjective is *westward* (*in a westward direction*), but *westward* and *westwards* are both used for the adverb, with a preference for *westwards* in BrE: *He climbed the lower slopes of Big Allen and stood, looking westwards*—Ruth Rendell, 1988.

wet *verb*. The form of the past tense and past participle is *wet* or *wetted*. *Wet* is used in certain familiar contexts (*He wet the bed | After they had wet their whistles* [= had a drink]), but in general use *wetted* seems now to be more common: *Two weeks ago a heavy rain had leaked through the ceiling and wetted the box*—New York Review of Books, 1987 | *With her clothes wetted and her pockets full of big round stones*—A. S. Byatt, 1990.

wh-. Words beginning with *wh-* (*what, where, wherever, white*, etc.) are normally pronounced with the *h* unaspirated in Received Pronunciation in England and Wales. In general American, in Canadian, and in Scottish and Irish English they are commonly aspirated as hw-. Variation occurs in all these varieties.

wharf has the plural form *wharves* (preferred) or *wharfs*.

what. 1 GENERAL. As a relative pronoun, *what* is an especially complex word because it can be either singular or plural and can refer both to words that have gone before and to words that come later in the sentence. In general it stands for a group of two or more words such as *that which, those which, the thing* (or *things*) *that, anything* (or *everything*) *that*, etc.: *What you need . . . is some outside interest*—Ruth Rendell, 1974 | *Some of those who take jobs in department stores or markets steal what they can*—Time, 1970. It must not be used as equivalent to the simple relative pronouns *that, which*, or *who*, a use characteristic of highly informal or uneducated speech: *I was the only boy in our school what had asthma*—William Golding, 1954.

2 SINGULAR *WHAT*. A problem of singular or plural verb agreement arises when *what* is singular but looks forward to a plural noun or pronoun later in the sentence: *What we need is/are clear guidelines*. Fowler had a useful rule that if the sentence begins in the singular (i.e. the initial what is singular), the continuation should also be singular; so the example just given would be expressed in the form *What we need is clear guidelines*. In current use this rule is often respected, as the following examples show: *What really worries me is the numbers*—Nina Bawden,

1987 | *What bothered him was drivers who switched lanes without signalling*—New Yorker, 1989. In these cases, it is arguable that a noun phrase such as *the circumstance of* or *the fact of* should be understood after the main verb; it is not the numbers or the drivers as such that cause the worry in the first example or the bother in the second, but the fact of what they represented or were doing.

3 PLURAL *WHAT*. A different situation arises when *what* is plural: *I have few books, and what there are do not help me.* In this sentence, *what* refers back to *books*, and so its plural status is clear. When *what* refers forward, the choice is less obvious: *We seem to have abandoned what seem/seems to us to be the most valuable parts of our Constitution.* Fowler (whose example this is) had another useful rule in these cases: if *what* can be resolved into *the —s that*, with *—s* standing for a plural noun that comes later in the sentence, the construction should be plural. In the example just given, *what . . .* can be resolved into *the parts of our Constitution that . . .* , and the continuation should therefore be *seem* (plural), not *seems*. If the relative clause introduced by *what* comes at the head of the sentence, the same rule can be followed if *what* can be resolved into *that which*: *What [= that which] is required is faith and confidence, and willingness to work.* This principle is much less secure, however, since *what* in the example given (Fowler's again) can as easily be resolved as *the things which* (plural): *What [= the things which] are required are faith and confidence, and willingness to work.* Here there is clearly a choice, and naturalness and rhythm will often be de-

cisive; the important point is that the choice between singular and plural should be consistent throughout the sentence, and that a singular *what* should not be followed by a plural continuation: ✖ *What is required are faith and confidence, and willingness to work.*

4 THE TYPE *WHAT . . . AND WHICH* . . . When a relative clause introduced by *what* is followed by further relative clauses joined by a conjunction such as *and* or *but*, the *what* should be repeated when it refers to something other than at its first occurrence: *There is a definite mis-match between what universities are producing and what industry is wanting*—Daily Telegraph, 1971. In this example, the first *what* refers to one thing and the second *what* to another, and both are needed. But the temptation to use a further *what* (or worse, a relative *which*) should be resisted when this would have the same grammatical status (as subject or object in its clause) and reference, since the first *what* is adequate to sustain the sense: ✖ *Nobody is going to object to what is a popular measure and which will help those most in need* should be rewritten as *Nobody is going to object to what is a popular measure and will help those most in need* (or as *Nobody is going to object to what is a popular measure which will help those most in need*, where *a popular measure* becomes the antecedent of the second *which*).

5 *WHAT* AFTER *AS* AND *THAN*. *What* should not be used after the conjunctions *as* and *than* in comparative constructions of the following type: ✖ *People who have difficulty in 'hearing' intonation patterns are generally only having difficulty in relating what they hear (which is the same as what everyone*

else hears) to this *'pseudo-spatial'
representation*—P. Roach, 1983 (read:
the same as everyone else hears) |
⊠ *She sometimes comes out with
more than what she went in with*—R.
Hamilton, 1993 (read: *more than she
went in with*). But *what* should be
used when it is essential to the
structure of the sentence: *It was
always easier to say what such a
school should not be, rather than
what it should be*—H. Judge, 1984.

whatever, what ever. 1 *Whatever* is written as one word when
it is an indefinite relative pronoun or adjective used in statements or commands: *Fiction, in
whatever form, about real people is
more often than not a pain*—*New
Yorker*, 1975 | *Whatever you're up to
during the snowy season, a wonderful warm woolly makes the perfect
winter wear*—*Hair Flair*, 1992. It is
also used with concessive force
equivalent to 'regardless of what'
(*Whatever Ned Kelly was really like
. . . he can scarcely have been like Mr
Jagger*—*New Statesman*, 1970), and
elliptically (with the continuation
omitted) in informal uses such
as: *Her lunch-break dash to Selfrid-
ges for pantie-tights, or whatever*—
G. F. Newman, 1970.

2 A comma is sometimes
needed to clarify the meaning
when a sentence begins with a
whatever-clause, especially when
the verb of the main clause can
be understood either intransitively or as referring back to *whatever*: *Whatever they have done, they
are now leaving* means 'they are
leaving (intransitive), regardless
of what they have done', whereas
*Whatever they have done they are
now leaving* means 'they are leaving (transitive) whatever it is they
have done'.

3 *Whatever* is also the correct
form when used as an adverb to

strengthen negative statements:
*There is no sexual element
whatever*—*Daily Telegraph*, 1972.

4 *What ever* is written as two
words when *ever* is used as an intensifying word and the expression as a whole is equivalent to
what on earth, usually in direct
questions: *'Pardon me asking, sir,
but what ever happened to your pilot's licence?'*—J. Neale, 1993. See
EVER 1.

whence, whither. Both words
have centuries of history behind
them and were once routine in
their respective meanings 'from
which place' and 'to which place',
but in current use they are regarded as archaic or at least
highly formal, although they
occur occasionally in modern literature: *He has also, of course, a
passport which nails him for who he
is and whence he comes*—Penelope
Lively, 1987 | *I write, now, from my
bed, whither Dr Felton has banished
me*—M. Roberts, 1990.

whenever, when ever. *Whenever*
is written as one word when it is
a conjunction (*Whenever possible
he liked to make a point of talking to
drug users on their own ground*—
Times, 1970) or a quasi-adverb
used informally (*I'll do it at the
weekend or whenever*). *When ever* is
written as two words when *ever* is
used as an intensifying word,
usually in direct questions: *When
ever did they arrive?* See EVER 1.

where-. Words still in general
currency that are formed with
the prefix *where-* include, in addition to those listed here as separate entries, *whereas* (used in
contrasts), *wherefore* (only in *the
whys and wherefores*), *wherein* (supposedly formal but common), and
whereupon (in narration). Many
others have fallen out of use or

are regarded as archaic, but will be met in older writing, e.g. *whereat, wherefrom, wheresoever, wherethrough, whereto, wherewith.*

whereabouts *noun.* The plural form ousted the singular form *whereabout* in the 19c; when a verb follows it is more often in the plural than in the singular, but both constructions occur regardless of the number of people or things in question: (plural) *His current whereabouts were not disclosed* | *By early Friday the whereabouts of the raiders still were unknown* | (singular) *The whereabouts of the remaining two paintings is unknown.*

whereby, meaning 'by what or which means', is one of a dwindling number of *where-* forms still in common use: *It was Sir Keith Joseph who drew attention to the 'ratchet effect' in politics, whereby the right seems to have acquiesced in the changes the left brings about—* Listener, 1977.

wherever, where ever. *Wherever* is written as one word when it is a conjunction (*One knows the type . . . They're complete poison, wherever they go—* R. Barnard, 1977) or a quasi-adverb used informally (*A holiday in France or wherever*). *Where ever* is written as two words when *ever* is used as an intensifying word, usually in direct questions: *Where ever have they gone?.* See EVER 1.

wherewithal, meaning 'the means or resources for something', is always used with *the*: *You don't need the intellectual wherewithal to function in society—* Steven Pinker, 1994.

whether. 1 For the choice between *if* and *whether*, see IF 2.

2 When the alternative to the *whether* clause is a simple negative, this can take several forms, but *whether or not* is now more usual than *whether or no*: *I brooded all the way whether or not I had hit the right note—* Jane Gardam, 1985 | *'Whether the report is true or not,' said Bush, 'I know I speak for all here* [etc.]*'—* Chicago Tribune, 1989. For *whether or no,* see NO 3.

3 *Whether* is often repeated as a clearer marker than a bare *or* of an alternative that forms a separate sentence, especially when the gap between *whether* and *or* is a long one: *You must decide yourself whether each new Beaver* [= junior Scout] *should be asked to pay for his scarf and woggle, or whether these should be provided by the Colony—* J. Deft, 1983.

4 When a clause introduced by *whether* relates to a preceding word such as *matter, issue, problem,* or *question, whether* can follow directly or be separated by *of*: *Senator Ervin said the issue of whether the subpoenas were continuing was 'a difference in a teapot'—* Times, 1973 | *And as for the matter of whether the gent's armed with the sort of foresight Phillip K. Dick grants his 'precogs', you can just make up your own mind—* Sounds, 1977 | *The whole question whether women actually are more pacific by nature is not the subject of the present book—* Antonia Fraser, 1988.

which. 1 For the choice between *that* and *which,* see THAT 3. It is especially important that *which,* not *that,* should be used in so-called non-restrictive clauses giving additional rather than essential information: *A new edition of the book, which has taken ten years to write, will be published this week.* (Note that in this role, *which* is usually preceded by a comma.)

611

while | while

2 The use of *which* to introduce a clause that is grammatically a relative one but in fact adds new information or leads on to a new point has been recorded for several centuries but has become especially common in the 20c: *He does Mr Rabinowitz's teeth which is super*—Nigel Williams, 1985 | (starting a new sentence) *It was as though Hungary was not another place but another time, and therefore inaccessible. Which of course was not so*—Penelope Lively, 1987.

3 Use of *which* with a personal antecedent is now archaic only, and is familiar mainly from the Prayer Book: *O God, which art author of peace, and lover of concord*—Book of Common Prayer, 1548–9 (modern spelling).

4 When a *which*-clause is followed by another *which*-clause joined by *and* or *but*, the second *which* must have the same grammatical status as the first. In the following example the first *which* is the subject of its clause, whereas the second is the object of the verb (*found*): *In contrast Peake's use of elevated language has a childlike quality, which is appropriate given that the protagonist, Titus, is a boy, and which I found endearing.*

while, whilst. 1 Both forms are used in BrE, but *whilst* is not much used in AmE.

2 The word is a conjunction, and its primary sense is temporal, meaning 'during the time that' (*They had begun drinking while he prepared to cook*) or 'at the same time as' (*She enjoyed drawing while she was being read to*). Since the time of Shakespeare, however, other uses have emerged in which *while* (or *whilst*) means 'although' or 'whereas', with concessive or contrastive rather than temporal force (*While I enjoy his company, I couldn't live with him | I live in London, while my sister lives in New York*). The concessive use (in particular) has been disapproved of by some (including Eric Partridge in *Usage and Abusage*, 1942 and later), but it is so well established that criticism is futile. Instances of possible ambiguity between the temporal and concessive-contrastive types of meaning are sometimes adduced, but they are usually contrived and unlikely to arise in practice (such as the old chestnut *The Curate read the First Lesson while the Rector read the Second*). Examples: (temporal) *Here father and daughter sat side by side on the window seat while he coached her each evening in the school holidays*—C. Brayfield, 1990 | (concessive) *While domestic happiness is an admirable ideal, it is not easy to come by*—T. Tanner, 1986 | (contrastive) *Whilst Mackenzie carried on and ended up editing the Sun, Sutton began to question what he was doing*—C. Horrie et al., 1988.

3 *While* and *whilst* are used elliptically, with the omission of a subject and main verb such as *they were* (in the first example following) or *he was* (in the second): *Dinner ladies helping with playground supervision have been jostled and abused while trying to tackle unruly pupils*—Daily Telegraph, 1983 | *While still working for the restaurant in 1956, he began his franchising career*—Money, 1985. In this type of construction *while* (or *whilst*) is usually temporal (as in both of these examples) or concessive (as in the following example), and when concessive it tends to come before the main clause: *More recent evidence, whilst not addressing this issue directly, tends to suggest that this desired relationship is still important*—J. Finch, 1989.

4 A sentence such as the following is incorrect: ⊠ *While being in agreement on most issues, I would like to challenge one in particular.* The omission is misconceived since the full form is *while I am* and not *while I am being*; correct *while being* to *while I am in agreement* or *while in agreement*.

whinge, meaning 'to grumble peevishly', is BrE. Its *-ing* form is *whingeing*, with an *e* to preserve the soft sound of the *g*.

whirr, meaning 'to make a continuous buzzing sound', is spelt with two *r*s in BrE and usually with one *r* in AmE, and the corresponding noun follows suit. The verb has inflected forms *whirred, whirring* in both varieties.

whisky, whiskey. *Whisky* is the usual spelling in BrE (especially with reference to *Scotch whisky*) and Canada, and *whiskey* is used of the spirit made in Ireland and the USA and is the usual spelling generally in AmE.

whit, a 16c word derived ultimately from an Old English form meaning 'a thing or creature of unknown origin', is commonly used in both BrE and AmE in the phrase *not a whit* or *no whit* (= not at all, by no means): *This much ballyhooed Andrew Lloyd Webber musical is fun—if you're not bothered by theatre that cares not a whit for words and contains not one ghost of an idea*—New Yorker, 1991 | *Ashdown's latest repositioning changes Major's position not a whit*—Sunday Times, 1995. Fowler (1926) and Gowers (1965) classed it among the so-called 'Wardour Street words' (i.e. old-sounding words affectedly adopted like old-looking furniture), but it has lost most of these associations in the meantime.

Whit. *Whit Sunday* (or *Pentecost*) is the seventh Sunday after Easter, and *Whit Monday* is the day following Whit Sunday. *Whitsun* and *Whit* are regularly used as informal shortenings of *Whitsuntide*, the weekend including Whit Sunday. *Whit* is related in form to *white*, and the name is probably derived from the white robes of those newly baptized at Whitsuntide.

white. For a time it was thought appropriate to spell *white* with a capital initial when it was used as a racial term with reference to light-skinned people, but the normal preference now is for a small initial. Unlike BLACK, *white* in this sense does not have any derogatory overtones.

whiten is the usual form of the verb in current usage in the meanings 'to make white' and 'to become white', but *white* is used in the expression *whited sepulchre* (meaning 'a hypocrite', in allusion to Matthew 23:27) and in the phrasal verb *white out* meaning 'to correct (a mistake) with white correction fluid'.

whither see WHENCE.

whitish, meaning 'somewhat white', is spelt without an *e* in the middle.

whizz is the recommended spelling for the noun and verb (and also in *whizz-kid*), not *whiz*, although this too occurs.

who and whom. **1** *Who* is used as a relative pronoun (*The woman who saw you*) and as an interrogative (*Who is there?*), and *whom* is, formally, its objective form (*The woman whom you saw* | *Whom did you see?*). In all these uses *who* (or *whom*) refers to a person or to several people, but as a relative pronoun *who* can informally refer to an animal or to an organization regarded in terms of its members (*The committee, who meet on Friday, . . .*).

2 In practice, *whom* is in decline and is increasingly replaced by *who* (or *that*), especially in conversational English. (This is not a new development; examples can be found from Shakespeare onward.) In the examples given in the preceding paragraph, it would be more natural to say *Who did you see?*, and in the one before it *The woman who you saw* or *The woman that you saw* or *The woman you saw* (for the omission of the pronoun, see RELATIVE CLAUSES 2).

3 When the relative pronoun is governed by a preposition, a construction with *whom* now seems formal, or even over-formal, and an alternative construction with *who* and the preposition at the end is the usual option in everyday language: (formal) *They . . . argue about a man called Simpkins of whom the poet is jealous*—Encounter, 1987 | *Lord Jenkins likened this stance to countries . . . 'who in the two world wars have waited to see which side was winning before deciding with whom to ally themselves'*—Times, 1999 | (informal) *What did she know of his life, who he went to bed with?*—Iris Murdoch, 1993. (A mixed style sometimes occurs: *There were other people whom I would have liked to speak to*—G. Butler, 1983.)

4 The same distinction of formality applies in the choice between *who* and *whom* used as an interrogative pronoun in questions: (formal) *Whom should we support in the present fluid situation?*—Bulletin of the American Academy, 1990 | *To whom have you*

complained?—V. Finkelstein et al., 1993 | (informal) *Who do you think you're speaking to?*—W. McIlvanney, 1985.

5 Opinions about the diminishing use of *whom* vary widely from complete tolerance ('We have got rid of *ye* as the subjective form of *you*, so why not *whom* as the objective form of *who*?') to strong regret or outright disapproval. Most severely criticized now are uses in which *who* replaces *whom* in grammatically straightforward contexts which traditionally call for *whom*: *Christ, who went for who first?*—V. O'Sullivan, 1985 | *The stuff which was kept under wraps most of the time came flooding out in elections: who had fought on what side, who had killed who, who had really represented the will of the Irish people*—Independent, 1999. Then there are those who regard the use of *whom* as a sign of education and reliability: *'I don't know whom else to ask.' The elder of the two policemen, Butterworth, noticed that she had said 'whom' and decided that she was a credible witness*—Anita Brookner, 1992.

6 There are occasions when *whom* is used incorrectly (or hypercorrectly) when *who* is needed: ☒ *The baronet whom Golitsin claimed had been the target for homosexual blackmail*—P. Wright, 1987. In this sentence, *whom* should be *who*, because it is the subject of *had been* (. . . *who had been the target* . . .) and not the object of *claimed*. This type, with the insertion of a word such as *claim, say, think*, etc., is extremely common: *He is demanding £5,000 from the elderly woman whom* [read: *who*] *he says ruined his life*—Sunday Times, 1990. Note also constructions in which a whole clause introduced by *who* is the object of a verb or preposition; in these cases also, *who* is correct: *The staff have noisy arguments about who should siesta on the cold stone floor*—Len Deighton, 1976.

whoever, who ever. 1 The same distinction applies here as to *whatever* and *what ever*, *whoever* being written as one word when it is an indefinite relative pronoun equivalent to 'whatever person' used in statements or commands (*Whoever wants it can have it*) and when the meaning is 'regardless of whom' (*Whoever it is, I don't want to see them*). *Who ever* is written as two words when *ever* is used as an intensifying word and the expression as a whole is equivalent to *who on earth*, usually in direct questions: *Who ever are those people?*. See EVER 1.

2 The objective form *whomever* still occurs but it can sound formal or affected in general contexts: *To impose his will on whomever he sees comfortably settled*—Max Beerbohm, 1920. In some cases it is wrongly used: ⊠ *. . . ready at once to relax with whomever came to hand*—Anita Brookner, 1992 (*with* governs the whole following clause; the pronoun is the subject of the clause and should therefore be *whoever*).

wholly, meaning 'entirely, completely', is spelt this way, not *wholely*.

whom see WHO AND WHOM.

who's is a contracted form of *who is* (*Who's going to the party?*) or *who has* (*The person who's got my pen*). It is occasionally used in error for *whose*: ⊠ *'Conor,' called Vaun, humping a churn of milk. 'Who's turn to deliver?'*—J. Leland, 1987.

whose. 1 Despite a long-established folk-belief (which Fowler deplored) that *whose*, when used as a relative, should only mean *of whom* and not *of which*, usage over several centuries from the time of Shakespeare and Milton supports its use with reference to inanimate things as well as to people. Fowler, quoting the opening lines of *Paradise Lost* (*Of man's first disobedience, and the fruit Of that forbidden tree, whose mortal taste Brought death into the world*), insisted that 'good writing is surely difficult enough without the forbidding of things that have historical grammar, and present intelligibility, and obvious convenience, on their side', a verdict that still has the ring of good sense. The following modern examples show how awkward it can be to replace *whose* with a construction involving *of which*, especially when an adjective comes between *whose* and the following noun (as in the 1986 example): *There were pictures whose context she understood immediately*—Ian McEwan, 1981 | *He looked up again at the tank whose huge cannon seemed to be pointing at him*—P. P. Read, 1986.

2 This does not mean that *of which* cannot be used; when it fits comfortably in the sentence structure, it is a legitimate and often preferable alternative: *What seemed to be at risk was Mr. Gorbachev's 'glasnost' policy, the essence of which is more openness*—Scotsman, 1986. It has to be used, of course, in non-possessive contexts: *Important towns had their own theatres, most of which had been built in Hellenistic times.*

why. 1 For *reason why*, see REASON 2.

2 The plural form of the noun is *whys* (used in *whys and wherefores*).

wide rather than *widely* is used in a number of fixed expressions such as *wide apart, wide awake*, and *wide open*, as an element in the word *widespread*, and in the phrases *hit* (or *shoot*) *wide* and *open one's eyes wide*.

wife has the plural form *wives*.

wilful is spelt in this way in BrE, but *willful* is also used in AmE.

will see SHALL AND WILL.

wimmin, a phonetic spelling of *women*, is recorded in facetious contexts from the early part of the 20c. It was adopted by feminists in the 1980s because it dispensed with the element *-men*: *Why are these (ignorant) gay men (and sadly sometimes wimmin) stereotyping gayness?—Pink Paper*, 1990. The form has not achieved any neutral usage and must be regarded as ephemeral.

wind *verbs*. There are two verbs here. The verb meaning 'to twist, coil, etc.' is pronounced wiynd and has the past tense and past participle *wound* (pronounced wownd). The unconnected verb meaning 'to exhaust the breath' is pronounced wind and has the past tense and past participle *winded*.

windward, referring to the side from which the wind is blowing, is spelt *-ward* as adjective, adverb, and noun. The form *windwards* is no longer used.

-wise, -ways. Both suffixes were active in forming adverbs (*always, sideways | crosswise, edgewise*) up to the 19c, and tended to overlap (e.g. *edgeways | edgewise, crossways |*

crosswise), but in current use only *-wise* is now productive in the special meaning 'in the manner of —' in ad hoc formations: *Her mass of chestnut hair parted Rossetti-wise in the middle—*Rose Macaulay, 1923 | *. . . dangling his arms beside his hips and rolling his head idiotwise—*J. McInerney, 1985. From the 1940s, the suffix developed a further meaning 'as regards —'; 'in respect of —': *Plotwise, it offers little more or less* [etc.]*—Saturday Review*, 1948 | *They all keep up with me, drinkingwise—New Yorker*, 1993.

wish *verb*. The use with a simple direct object (*Would you wish a little more hot water, ma'am—*Dickens, 1854) has been replaced in BrE by *like*, but is still said to be current in AmE.

wisteria is the usual form for the climbing plant, not *wistaria*. It is named after the 18c American anatomist Casper Wistar (or Wister).

wit *verb*. This old native word for *know* barely survives in the phrase *to wit* (= that is to say, namely), in the derived forms *wittingly* and *unwittingly*, and in the first and third person singular archaic form *wot* (especially in T. E. Brown's often quoted remark (1892), *A garden is a lovesome thing, God wot!*).

withhold is spelt with two *h*s.

without. 1 Unlike the corresponding physical meaning of *within* (= inside), the original meaning of *without*, 'outside' (preposition and adverb), is no longer much used, although it will be familiar from literary contexts (*There is a green hill far away, Without a city wall—*Cecil Frances Alexander, 1848 | *The throng without was . . . becoming more numerous and* *more savage*—Macaulay, 1849). The primary current uses are in the sense 'lacking, not having' (*I came without an umbrella*) and governing verbal nouns (*She left without saying anything*).

2 Also defunct is the use of *without* as a conjunction meaning 'unless', 'except when', although it still occurs in regional or dialect use and will be found occasionally in modern fiction: *I can truthfully say he never sat an exam without he was bad with his asthma*—Pat Barker, 1991.

3 *How'd you like to make yourself a passel* [= parcel] *of money without hardly havin' to do any work?*—D. Westheimer, 1973. The use of *without* + *hardly*, which is a combination of a negative and an implied negative, is non-standard. The standard expression is *almost without* (or in some contexts, *with hardly*: *His eyes flickered to left and right, with hardly a turn of the head*—T. Barnes, 1991).

wizened, meaning 'thin and shrivelled', is a Scottish word derived from Old English that has now become a general English word.

woman see LADY, WOMAN.

-woman. This suffix denoting female occupations is in decline as the search for GENDER-NEUTRALITY gathers pace. *Policewoman* has been largely replaced by *police officer* (or *woman police constable*, *WPC*), *chairwoman*, *spokeswoman*, and others by forms in *-person*, and so on. Other compounds that remain in use generally have a cultural or historical reference, e.g. *needlewoman*, *servicewoman*. See FEMININE DESIGNATIONS.

womanly, womanish. *Womanly* is a complimentary word applied

to women and meaning 'having the good qualities of women', whereas *womanish* is applied to men and is usually derogatory in the sense 'effeminate, unmanly'. See also FEMALE, FEMININE.

womyn is a word coined by feminists to replace *-men* as a sequence of letters in the word *women*. It is unlikely to achieve general currency.

wonder is followed by *whether* or *if*, and in more formal writing can take a subjunctive verb in the past: *Hilliard wondered whether Barton were not right after all*—Susan Hill, 1971 | *They had never had a serious conversation, and she wondered if that were wrong*—Anita Brookner, 1992. In general contexts, however, an ordinary verb is normal: *She wondered if I was free to have dinner at her house*—C. McCarry, 1977. For the type *I shouldn't wonder if . . .* see NOT 5.

wont, the surviving past participle of an obsolete verb *won* meaning 'to accustom oneself to', is pronounced *wohnt* and should be distinguished from *won't*, the contracted form of *will not*. It is used in two principal ways: followed by a *to*-infinitive as in *They were wont to say*, and as a noun in the type *as is their wont*. The form *wonted*, meaning 'accustomed, habitual', is used before a noun, as in *He showed his wonted skill*.

won't, the contracted form of *will not*, is the only survivor of several forms derived from *woll* (= *will*) *not*.

woodenness is spelt with two *ns* in the middle.

woollen, woolly are the spellings in BrE, and in AmE *woolen*, *wooly*.

word order see INVERSION.

workaday, workday. *Workaday* is now used only as an adjective in the meaning 'ordinary, everyday'. The usual nouns for a day on which work is done are *workday* and *working day*. In AmE, *workday* also means 'the part of the day used for work' (as in *an 8-hour workday*).

worldly, meaning 'temporal or earthly', has two *l*s.

World Wide Web see WEB.

worsen see -EN VERBS FROM ADJECTIVES.

worser. *Changed to a worser shape thou canst not be*—Shakespeare, *1 Henry VI* v.iv, 1591. This so-called 'double comparative' has good literary credentials, but is not standard in current English.

worship has inflected forms *worshipped*, *worshipping*, and a derivative form *worshipper* in BrE, and often *worshiped*, *worshiping*, *worshiper* in AmE.

worst. The idiom *if the worst comes to the worst* has been standard in BrE since the late 16c. In AmE it usually occurs in the form *if worst comes to worst*.

worth while, worthwhile. The traditional distinction is to use the two-word form predicatively (i.e. after a verb, as in *The experiment was worth while*) and the one-word form attributively (i.e. before a noun, as in *a worthwhile experiment*). However, the one-word form is increasingly used in all contexts. Note that the correct use with a following verbal noun is *worth*, not *worth while* (*It was worth doing* | ☒ *It was worth while doing*).

would see SHOULD AND WOULD.

wrack see RACK.

wrath, wrathful, wroth. *Wrath* is an archaic or literary noun meaning 'anger', and is pronounced rawth or roth, or in AmE rath. *Wrathful* is the corresponding adjective meaning 'angry'. *Wroth* is also an adjective, and is always used predicatively, i.e. after a verb, especially in the expression *wax wroth* meaning 'to become angry'. As these words move further back into the remoteness of archaism, their distinctions are becoming blurred, with *wroth* in particular being used where *wrath* is needed.

wreak is used in the expression *wreak havoc (on)*. It is derived from an Old English verb meaning 'to avenge'. The unrelated verb *work* is also used in this connection, with its archaic participial form *wrought* occasionally coming into service: *Moko, the banana disease, has already wreaked havoc on the trade*—Times, 1983 | *A decade of inflation had wrought havoc with its portfolio of fixed interest mortgages*—Financial Times, 1984.

wreath has the plural form *wreaths*, pronounced reedhz or reeths. The verb, meaning 'to encircle with a wreath', is spelt *wreathe* and is pronounced reedh.

write. *I had written my mother about all this*—New Yorker, 1987. The transitive use with the recipient as the object is well known in AmE, but has disappeared in BrE, except occasionally in old-fashioned commercial correspondence (*Please write us at your convenience*).

writ large. *Every project has success writ large over it*—Author, 1994.

This still-popular phrase is first recorded in the 17c, and is based on a participial form of *write* that is otherwise obsolete.

wrong, like *right*, exists as an adverb alongside the regularly formed word *wrongly*. It is mostly used with a limited number of words and means roughly 'incorrectly', or 'astray', as in *We guessed wrong* and *I said it wrong*. In these cases *wrongly* can also be used, but the effect can be somewhat ponderous, and *wrongly* comes into its own in the more general meaning 'in the wrong way', especially when coming before rather than after an adjective or participle: *It arrived at Heathrow as mishandled luggage, having been wrongly off-loaded in Rome from a flight from Australia to London—Daily Telegraph*, 1972. Note that in the expression *go wrong*, *wrong* is probably not an adverb but still an adjective (agreeing with the subject as with *become* and other verbs).

wroth see WRATH.

wrought is an old past form and past participle of the verb *work*, surviving only in the term *wrought iron*, in the occasional variant *wrought up* (= worked up, i.e. agitated, nervous), and as a form of the expression *work havoc* (see WREAK).

wry has inflected forms *wryer*, *wryest*, and derivative forms *wryly*, *wryness*.

wych is the usual spelling in the name of the tree *wych elm*. It is apparently derived from a Germanic form meaning 'to bend'.

Xx

-x is used to form the plural of a number of loanwords from French that are not fully naturalized, for example *chateau* (= a castle or large house) and *plateau*. Other words tend to be treated in a more native way and form plurals in *-s*, for example *gateau*. Usage is unstable in this regard.

Xerox, a proprietary term for a make of photocopier, should be spelt with a capital *X*. As a verb, however, it is spelt *xerox*.

-xion. A small number of nouns derived from Latin words ending in *-io, -ionis* have been spelt either *-ction* or *-xion* in English. Where there is a choice, current usage tends to prefer *-ction* (e.g. *deflection, inflection*), but in other cases *-xion* is the only ending in use (the main cases are *complexion, crucifixion, transfixion*).

Xmas. In this abbreviated form of the name *Christmas*, first recorded in the 18c, the initial *X* represents a Greek *chi* (= ch), the first letter of the name *Christ*. It is a convenient shortening commonly used in newspaper headlines, on cards, and in personal letters, but it is better to pronounce it as 'Christmas' than as 'ex-mass' which some people consider tasteless.

X-ray is spelt in this way as a noun and verb.

Yy

y and i. For problems of spelling involving *y* and *i* in words, see CIPHER, GYPSY, LICH-GATE, PYGMY, SIPHON, SIREN, STYMIE, TIRO, TYRE, WYCH.

Yankee. A *Yankee* is properly an inhabitant of New England or of the northern states of the USA, and the name was used with this meaning during the American Civil War. On the other hand the shortened form *Yank* is commonly applied to Americans generally. Both words are informal only, and their origin, though widely discussed, remains unclear.

ye, a pseudo-archaic form of the definite article *the*, is used commercially in names such as *ye olde tea-shoppe*. Though pronounced yee, its first letter represents an old runic letter called 'thorn' (pronounced dh as in modern *this*), which in written form had come to resemble the letter *y*.

yeah is the conventional spelling of the informal shortened form of *yes*. In print it is used only to represent a spoken form, commonly used in the phrase *Oh yeah?* expressing doubt or disbelief.

year see DAY. A possessive apostrophe is needed in expressions of the type (singular) *a year's imprisonment* and (plural) *two years' imprisonment*.

yes, used as a noun (*refused to give a definite yes*), has the plural form *yeses*.

yet and still. 1 These two adverbs used to be more interchangeable than they are now. A sentence such as *Mrs. Throckmorton was shot in her apartment last night, and the bullet is in her yet*, in which *yet* denotes continuity of action up to the time in question, would be acceptable, especially informally, in America (the source of this extract) and Scotland, but in the English of England *still* would be used instead of *yet* and the word order would usually be different: *. . . and the bullet is still in her*. In England, *yet* is used to mean 'up to this time' or 'up to then' (1) in a question or after a negative (*Is she 21 yet?* | *She wasn't yet 18* | *Have they arrived yet?* | *They haven't arrived yet* [or *haven't yet arrived*] | *I hadn't yet decided what to do*). Note the position of *yet* in these examples, and note that with action verbs the perfect tense (formed with *have*) or past perfect tense (formed with *had*) is used, but in AmE a past tense formed with *do* is also used informally: *Did they arrive yet?* In the negative examples, *still* can also be sometimes used, e.g. *They still haven't arrived.*

2 It is worth pointing out that in Scottish English a question such as *Is it raining yet?* would be ambiguous, equivalent to the English English questions 'Has it started to rain yet?' and 'Is it still raining?'. In conversation, intonation would normally clarify, but this might need to be accentuated south of the border.

Yiddish words in English

Yiddish is a vernacular language used by European Jews, based chiefly on High German with Hebrew and Slavonic borrowings, and written in Hebrew characters. English, especially AmE, has adopted many words and phrases from Yiddish in the 19c and 20c, and some of these are given in the table below.

ITEM	MEANING
bagel	hard ring-shaped ring of bread
chutzpah	shameless audacity
klutz	clumsy or inept person
kvell	to boast or gloat
mazuma	money
need it like a hole in the head	can well do without it
nosh	food
schlemiel	clumsy person, fool
schlep	to haul or drag
schmuck	abusive term for a person
shtoom	silent
What's with you?	What's the matter?

3 In positive contexts, *yet* is used as a more formal alternative to *still* in the following types, normally with *be*, *have to*, or a modal verb such as *can*: *We'd better do it while there is yet time* | *I have yet to receive a reply* | *I can hear her yet.*

4 See also ALREADY 2.

Yiddish words in English.
See box above

yodel. The verb has inflected forms *yodelled*, *yodelling* in BrE, and usually *yodeled*, *yodeling* in AmE.

yogurt is the preferred spelling, although *yoghurt* (with an *h*) is also common. It is pronounced **yog**-ət in BrE, and **yoh**-gət in AmE and in Australia and New Zealand.

yoke, yolk. A *yoke* is a wooden crosspiece of the kind fixed over

the necks of work animals. A *yolk* is the yellow part of an egg (and is related to the word *yellow*).

you and I. For *between you and I*, see BETWEEN 5.

you know see MEANINGLESS FILLERS.

you name it is a cliché of the 1960s, still much in vogue. It means 'and so on, and other familiar things of the same kind': *'I've picked up rocks, glass, parts of beer cans—you name it,' she said—New Yorker*, 1988.

you're is an informal contracted form of *you are* (*You're sure, are you?*). It needs to be distinguished from the identical-sounding possessive word *your*.

yours. This possessive pronoun, as used in *The blame is not mine but yours*, is written without an apostrophe. In compound subjects connected by *and*, the correct form is (e.g.) *Our children and yours should have a joint party*, not ⊠ *Yours and our children should have a joint party*.

yourself, yourselves. *Yourself* (singular) and *yourselves* (plural) have two primary roles, (1) as reflexives (*Are you talking about yourself?* | *Help yourselves to biscuits*), and (2) as emphatic words in apposition to the pronoun *you* (*You yourself told me so*).

yous, youse are regional and dialectal forms of *you* (plural). In Britain they are associated especially with the speech of Glasgow and Liverpool, and they occur in American, Australian, and New Zealand literature reproducing non-standard speech: *It's the least I can do for youse*—E. Jolley, 1985 (Australia).

youth has the plural form *youths*, pronounced yoodhz. As well as meaning 'a young person' (in BrE usually a boy but in other varieties a boy or girl) and 'a young time of life' (*in their youth*), it has a collective sense 'young people', normally preceded by *the*: *The youth of Australia have been saved once more from the dreaded lurgy, marijuana*—*It*, 1971. In this meaning it is commonly used in attributive position (i.e. before a noun, e.g. *youth centre, youth movement*).

-yse, -yze. The BrE English form of the suffix is *-yse* (*analyse, catalyse, dialyse, paralyse*). In AmE the normal forms are *analyze* etc.

Zz

zap *verb* is a vogue word of the 80s and 90s meaning 'to liven or revitalize', and commonly occurs as a phrasal verb with *up*: *A whole head of garlic is olive-oiled, oven-baked, blobbed with brie, then zapped up with a sprig of fresh thyme on top*—Western Living, 1991. An earlier meaning, 'to kill', familiar from comic strips and the world of electronic games, is still in use, as is a more recent meaning, 'to switch casually from one television channel to another'. The inflected forms are *zapped*, *zapping*.

zenith is pronounced **zen**-ith in BrE and **zee**-nith in AmE.

zero. The noun has the plural form *zeros*, and the verb (normally used in the form *zero in*) has inflected forms *zeroes*, *zeroed*, *zeroing*.

zeugma see SYLLEPSIS.

zigzag. The verb has inflected forms *zigzagged*, *zigzagging*.

zinc. The adjectival form meaning 'coated in zinc' is *zinced*.

zoology. The older pronunciation zoh-**ol**-ə-ji, favoured by *OED* editors and supposedly by zoologists themselves, has largely given way in general use to zoo-**ol**-ə-ji (influenced by the common shortening *zoo*). But beware of rearguard actions.

Oxford Paperback Reference

The Concise Oxford Dictionary of English Etymology
T. F. Hoad

A wealth of information about our language and its history, this
reference source provides over 17,000 entries on word origins.

'A model of its kind'

Daily Telegraph

A Dictionary of Euphemisms
R. W. Holder

This hugely entertaining collection draws together euphemisms from all
aspects of life: work, sexuality, age, money, and politics.

Review of the previous edition
'This ingenious collection is not only very funny but extremely
instructive too'

Iris Murdoch

The Oxford Dictionary of Slang
John Ayto

Containing over 10,000 words and phrases, this is the ideal reference for
those interested in the more quirky and unofficial words used in the
English language.

'hours of happy browsing for language lovers'

Observer

AskOxford.⸱com
Oxford Dictionaries Passionate about language

For more information about the background to Oxford Quotations and
Language Reference Dictionaries, and much more about Oxford's
commitment to language exploration, why not visit the world's largest
language learning site, www.AskOxford.com

Passionate about English?

What were the original 'brass monkeys'? **Ask**Oxford.⸱com

How do new words enter the dictionary? **Ask**Oxford.⸱com

How is 'whom' used? **Ask**Oxford.⸱com

Who said, 'For also knowledge itself is power?' **Ask**Oxford.⸱com

How can I improve my writing? **Ask**Oxford.⸱com

If you have a query about the English language, want to look up a word,
need some help with your writing skills, are curious about how
dictionaries are made, or simply have some time to learn about the
language, bypass the rest and ask the experts at www.AskOxford.com.

Passionate about language?

If you want to find out about writing in French, German, Spanish, or
Italian, improve your listening and speaking skills, learn about other
cultures, access resources for language
students, or gain insider travel tips from those **Ask**Oxford.⸱com
in the know, ask the experts at

OXFORD

Oxford Paperback Reference

The Concise Oxford Companion to English Literature
Margaret Drabble and Jenny Stringer

Based on the best-selling *Oxford Companion to English Literature*, this is
an indispensable guide to all aspects of English literature.

Review of the parent volume
'a magisterial and monumental achievement'

Literary Review

The Concise Oxford Companion to Irish Literature
Robert Welch

From the ogam alphabet developed in the 4th century to Roddy Doyle,
this is a comprehensive guide to writers, works, topics, folklore, and
historical and cultural events.

Review of the parent volume
'Heroic volume ... It surpasses previous exercises of similar nature in the
richness of its detail and the ecumenism of its approach.'

Times Literary Supplement

A Dictionary of Shakespeare
Stanley Wells

Compiled by one of the best-known international authorities on the
playwright's works, this dictionary offers up-to-date information on all
aspects of Shakespeare, both in his own time and in later ages.

OXFORD

Oxford Paperback Reference

The Kings of Queens of Britain
John Cannon and Anne Hargreaves

A detailed, fully-illustrated history ranging from mythical and pre-conquest rulers to the present House of Windsor, featuring regional maps and genealogies.

A Dictionary of Dates
Cyril Leslie Beeching

Births and deaths of the famous, significant and unusual dates in history – this is an entertaining guide to each day of the year.

'a dipper's blissful paradise ... Every single day of the year, plus an index of birthdays and chronologies of scientific developments and world events.'

Observer

A Dictionary of British History
Edited by John Cannon

An invaluable source of information covering the history of Britain over the past two millennia. Over 3,600 entries written by more than 100 specialist contributors.

Review of the parent volume
'the range is impressive ... truly (almost) all of human life is here'
Kenneth Morgan, *Observer*

OXFORD

Great value ebooks from Oxford!

An ever-increasing number of Oxford subject reference dictionaries, English and bilingual dictionaries, and English language reference titles are available as ebooks.

All Oxford ebooks are available in the award-winning Mobipocket Reader format, compatible with most current handheld systems, including Palm, Pocket PC/Windows CE, Psion, Nokia, SymbianOS, Franklin eBookMan, and Windows. Some are also available in MS Reader and Palm Reader formats.

Priced on a par with the print editions, Oxford ebooks offer dictionary-specific search options making information retrieval quick and easy.

For further information and a full list of Oxford ebooks please visit: www.askoxford.com/shoponline/ebooks/

Oxford Paperback Reference

The Concise Oxford Dictionary of Quotations
Edited by Elizabeth Knowles

Based on the highly acclaimed *Oxford Dictionary of Quotations*, this
paperback edition maintains its extensive coverage of literary and
historical quotations, and contains completely up-to-date material. A
fascinating read and an essential reference tool.

The Oxford Dictionary of Humorous Quotations
Edited by Ned Sherrin

From the sharply witty to the downright hilarious, this sparkling
collection will appeal to all senses of humour.

Quotations by Subject
Edited by Susan Ratcliffe

A collection of over 7,000 quotations, arranged thematically for easy
look-up. Covers an enormous range of nearly 600 themes from 'The
Internet' to 'Parliament'.

The Concise Oxford Dictionary of Phrase and Fable
Edited by Elizabeth Knowles

Provides a wealth of fascinating and informative detail for over 10,000
phrases and allusions used in English today. Find out about anything
from the 'Trojan horse' to 'ground zero'.

OXFORD

Oxford Companions

'Opening such books is like sitting down with a knowledgeable friend. Not a bore or a know-all, but a genuinely well-informed chum ... So far so splendid.'

Sunday Times [of *The Oxford Companion to Shakespeare*]

For well over 60 years Oxford University Press has been publishing Companions that are of lasting value and interest, each one not only a comprehensive source of reference, but also a stimulating guide, mentor, and friend. There are between 40 and 60 Oxford Companions available at any one time, ranging from music, art, and literature to history, warfare, religion, and wine.

Titles include:

The Oxford Companion to English Literature
Edited by Margaret Drabble
'No guide could come more classic.'

Malcolm Bradbury, *The Times*

The Oxford Companion to Music
Edited by Alison Latham
'probably the best one-volume music reference book going'

Times Educational Supplement

The Oxford Companion to Western Art
Edited by Hugh Brigstocke
'more than meets the high standard set by the growing number of Oxford Companions'

Contemporary Review

The Oxford Companion to Food
Alan Davidson
'the best food reference work ever to appear in the English language'

New Statesman

The Oxford Companion to Wine
Edited by Jancis Robinson
'the greatest wine book ever published'

Washington Post

OXFORD